www.wadsworth.com

www.wadsworth.com is the World Wide Web site
for Thomson Wadsworth and is your direct source
to dozens of online resources.

At www.wadsworth.com you can find out about
supplements, demonstration software, and student resources. You can also send e-mail to many
of our authors and preview new publications and
exciting new technologies.

www.wadsworth.com
Changing the way the world learns®

GENERAL MASS COMMUNICATION

Anokwa/Lin/Salwen, *International Communication: Issues and Controversies*

Biagi, *Media/Impact: An Introduction to Mass Media,* Seventh Edition

Bucy, *Living in the Information Age: A New Media Reader,* Second Edition

Craft/Leigh/Godfrey, *Electronic Media*

Day, *Ethics in Media Communications: Cases and Controversies,* Fifth Edition

Dennis/Merrill, *Media Debates: Great Issues for the Digital Age,* Fourth Edition

Fellow, *American Media History*

Gillmor/Barron/Simon, *Mass Communication Law: Cases and Comment,* Sixth Edition

Gillmor/Barron/Simon/Terry, *Fundamentals of Mass Communication Law*

Hilmes, *Connections: A Broadcast History Reader*

Hilmes, *Only Connect: A Cultural History of Broadcasting in the United States*

Jamieson/Campbell, *The Interplay of Influence: News, Advertising, Politics, and the Mass Media,* Sixth Edition

Kamalipour, *Global Communication*

Lester, *Visual Communication: Images with Messages,* Fourth Edition

Overbeck, *Major Principles of Media Law,* 2006 Edition

Straubhaar/LaRose, *Media Now: Understanding Media, Culture, and Technology,* Fifth Edition

Zelezny, *Communications Law: Liberties, Restraints, and the Modern Media,* Fourth Edition

Zelezny, *Cases in Communications Law,* Fourth Edition

JOURNALISM

Bowles/Borden, *Creative Editing,* Fourth Edition

Chance/McKeen, *Literary Journalism: A Reader*

Craig, *Online Journalism*

Hilliard, *Writing for Television, Radio, and New Media,* Eighth Edition

Kessler/McDonald, *When Words Collide: A Media Writer's Guide to Grammar and Style,* Sixth Edition

Poulter/Tidwell, *News Scene: Interactive Writing Exercises*

Rich, *Writing and Reporting News: A Coaching Method,* Media Enhanced Fourth Edition

Rich, *Writing and Reporting News: A Coaching Method, Student Exercise Workbook,* Media Enhanced Fourth Edition

Stephens, *Broadcast News,* Fourth Edition

Wilber/Miller, *Modern Media Writing*

PHOTOJOURNALISM AND PHOTOGRAPHY

Parrish, *Photojournalism: An Introduction*

PUBLIC RELATIONS AND ADVERTISING

Diggs-Brown/Glou, *The PR Styleguide: Formats for Public Relations Practice*

Hendrix, *Public Relations Cases,* Sixth Edition

Jewler/Drewniany, *Creative Strategy in Advertising,* Eighth Edition

Newsom/Haynes, *Public Relations Writing: Form and Style,* Seventh Edition

Newsom/Turk/Kruckeberg, *This Is PR: The Realities of Public Relations,* Eighth Edition

RESEARCH AND THEORY

Baxter/Babbie, *The Basics of Communication Research*

Baran/Davis, *Mass Communication Theory: Foundations, Ferment, and Future,* Fourth Edition

Littlejohn, *Theories of Human Communication,* Seventh Edition

Merrigan/Huston, *Communication Research Methods*

Rubin/Rubin/Piele, *Communication Research: Strategies and Sources,* Sixth Edition

Sparks, *Media Effects Research: A Basic Overview,* Second Edition

Wimmer/Dominick, *Mass Media Research: An Introduction,* Eighth Edition

Media Now

FIFTH EDITION

UNDERSTANDING MEDIA, CULTURE, AND TECHNOLOGY

JOSEPH STRAUBHAAR
University of Texas, Austin

ROBERT LaROSE
Michigan State University

THOMSON

WADSWORTH

Australia • Canada • Mexico • Singapore • Spain
United Kingdom • United States

THOMSON

WADSWORTH

Publisher: Holly J. Allen
Senior Development Editor: Renée Deljon
Assistant Editor: Darlene Amidon-Brent
Editorial Assistant: Sarah Allen
Senior Technology Project Manager: Jeanette Wiseman
Associate Technology Project Manager: Inna Fedoseyeva
Marketing Manager: Mark D. Orr
Marketing Assistant: Alexandra Tran
Marketing Communications Manager: Shemika Britt
Project Manager, Editorial Production: Mary Noel
Creative Director: Rob Hugel
Executive Art Director: Maria Epes

Print Buyer: Rebecca Cross
Permissions Editor: Joohee Lee
Production Service: Thompson Steele, Inc.
Text Designers: Preston Thomas, Sally Steele
Photo Researchers: Laurie Frankenthaler, Abby Reip
Copy Editor: Thompson Steele, Inc.
Cover Designer: Joan Greenfield
Cover Images (top to bottom): Image Source; Corbis; Getty Images/Brand X Pictures; PhotoAlto; Getty Images
Cover Printer: Phoenix Color Corp
Compositor: Thompson Steele, Inc.
Printer: Courier Corporation/Kendallville

Printed in the United States of America
1   2   3   4   5   6   7   09   08   07   06   05

For more information about our products, contact us at:
Thomson Learning Academic Resource Center
1-800-423-0563
For permission to use material from this text or product, submit a request online at http://www.thomsonrights.com.
Any additional questions about permissions can be submitted by email to thomsonrights@thomson.com.

Library of Congress Control Number: 2004117345

Student Edition: ISBN 0-534-64708-1

Instructor's Edition: ISBN 0-534-60643-1

Thomson Higher Education
10 Davis Drive
Belmont, CA 94002-3098
USA

Asia (including India)
Thomson Learning
5 Shenton Way
#01-01 UIC Building
Singapore 068808

Australia/New Zealand
Thomson Learning Australia
102 Dodds Street
Southbank, Victoria 3006
Australia

Canada
Thomson Nelson
1120 Birchmount Road
Toronto, Ontario M1K 5G4
Canada

UK/Europe/Middle East/Africa
Thomson Learning
High Holborn House
50/51 Bedford Row
London WC1R 4LR
United Kingdom

Latin America
Thomson Learning
Seneca, 53
Colonia Polanco
11560 Mexico
D.F. Mexico

Spain (including Portugal)
Thomson Paraninfo
Calle Magallanes, 25
28015 Madrid, Spain

Chapter Opening Photos: Chapter 1, © Dex Images/CORBIS; Chapter 2, © David McNew/Getty Images; Chapter 3, Courtesy of VIBE Magazine; Chapter 4, © Getty Images; Chapter 5, © John Van Hasselt/Corbis Sygma; Chapter 6, © Mario Tama/Getty Images; Chapter 7, © Columbia/courtesy of Everett Collection; Chapter 8, © ABC/Courtesy of Everett Collection; Chapter 9, © Getty Images; Chapter 10, © AP/Wide World Photos; Chapter 11, © Duomo/CORBIS; Chapter 12, Courtesy of AT&T; Chapter 13, © Ted Horowitz/CORBIS; Chapter 14, © Paul Conklin/Photo Edit; Chapter 15, © CBS/Landov; Chapter 16, © AP/Wide World Photos

Brief Contents

Contents ■■■■■■■■

Part One Media and the Information Age
■■■■■■■■

Preface ■■■■■■■

New media and technology continue to rapidly change our conceptions of "mass media"—and are now even blurring the meaning of that term. Our theme in this text is that the convergence of these technologies and the media industries is creating a new communications environment and impacting the culture we all share. Our goal throughout the book is to prepare students to thrive in that environment as participants or media professionals or both. We maintain our theme and aim to achieve our goal by providing an approach to mass media that integrates traditional media (magazines, books, newspapers, radio, film, and television) and new media (cable, satellite, computer media, interactive television, the Internet, and digital telecommunications), emphasizing the technologies of each as well as the intersection of technology, media, and culture.

The Telecommunications Act of 1996 changed media rules to further encourage convergence and competition across media industries. Increased concentration has resulted even as the Copyright Act of 1998 changed the balance of power between the media and their audiences. We have witnessed astounding changes in the structure of the radio and telecommunications industries and rapid evolution in the newspaper, movie, and television industries, changes that directly affect the life prospects of our students and the nature of the material we present to them in introductory courses. The web seemingly pervades all aspects of the daily lives of our students, from how they research their course papers to how they listen to music, and to how they experience their own cultures, but a host of other technologies, from DVDs to MP3s and satellite radio to cell phones, are also transforming their lives.

This book shows where today's communications industries came from and how they got to where they are. But more importantly, it also seriously assesses their trajectories into the future. It helps students understand how mass media are being transformed as they converge with technologies such as the computer, the Internet, and the digital telecommunications infrastructure that underlies all the media. It helps them create a vision of their future in the information society and information economy. Our purpose, however, is not to be cheerleaders for communication technology. In fact, we raise critical and ethical issues about the implications of information technologies, parallel to our discussion of the implications of mass media. Because we have seen the lights turn on behind our students' eyes when we begin a class discussion with a headline from the morning paper, we know that students realize that the convergence of technologies we are talking about is not dry history or mere speculation, but is happening right now and affects them directly. It is important to expose them to—and to demystify—communications technologies and the economic and social forces that shape technology. This book is designed to help both professor and student do that.

NEW TO THIS EDITION

In addition to updating both coverage and examples throughout the book, we wanted, for the fifth edition of *Media Now,* to expand the book's innovative presentation of technology and the social and cultural implications of convergence to fully span the globe. As a result, we highlight global examples and issues throughout the book, not just in its final chapter. We have continued our in-depth coverage of traditional media, with full chapters for magazine and book publishing, newspapers, audio and radio, film, and TV. Readers familiar with the text will find a new chapter devoted to the recording industry. Additional major changes to this edition include the following:

■ *Updated coverage and research base*   The fifth edition provides the most current coverage possible and reflects the field's latest research. Topics with new or expanded coverage include wi-fi, third-generation (or 3G) phones, Internet 2, iTunes, Movielink, TiVo, Netflix, and media coverage of major events such as the 2004 presidential campaign, the Iraq war, and the Indian Ocean tsunami. The latest developments in media policy, including efforts to curb indecency, crack down on Internet "file sharing," and prevent further concentration of power in media industries, are examined in depth.

■ *Media around the globe*   What were they watching in South Africa while we were watching *American Idol?* New "World View" boxes highlight global perspectives on this and additional topics such as interactive television, cross-border public relations, wireless technology, the offshoring of information sector jobs, and the Internet and terrorism.

- **Expanded coverage of the recording and radio industries** Previously presented in a single chapter, these industries are now presented separately, offering more thorough coverage of each and better illustrating their key differences as well as their unique issues.

- **New visuals** This edition's revised art program includes more than 100 new figures and photos. New figures represent processes such as television program development. New photos include stills from shows such as *Desperate Housewives,* celebrities such as Leonardo DiCaprio, the break-out band Los Lonely Boys, and embedded reporters during the Iraq war.

- **Streamlined organization** Coverage of media theory focused on groups, systems, and analytical tools is now consolidated in Chapter 2, Media and Society, and coverage of media theory focused on individuals is now concentrated in Chapter 13, Media Uses and Effects. Finally, coverage of the communications infrastructure now appears in Chapter 12 to serve as a bridge to the book's third part, Media Issues.

- **WIRED** *magazine subscription* A one-year subscription to *Wired* magazine, which is included in the price of the book, helps students gain both professional knowledge and critical appreciation of the changing communication media.

Updated Proven Features

This book comes with a rich set of features to aid in learning, all of which have been updated as necessary:

- **Glossary** Key terms are defined in the margins of each chapter, and a complete glossary is included in the back of the book.

- **Time lines** Major events in each media industry are highlighted near the beginning of each chapter in Media Then/Media Now lists.

- **Box program** In addition to the new World View boxes (see page XVII), three other types of boxes appear in the text. Each is designed to target specific issues and further pique students' interest:
  - **MEDIA AND CULTURE** boxes highlight cultural issues in the media.
  - **PROFILES** focus on key media figures.
  - **TECHNOLOGY DEMYSTIFIED** boxes explain technological information in a clear and accessible way.

- **Stop & Review** Appearing periodically throughout each chapter, and available in electronic format on the Media Now Premium Website, these questions help

students incrementally assess their understanding of key material.

- **Summary and Review** Each chapter concludes with the authors' highly praised, engaging summary and review sections, which are presented as questions with brief narrative answers.

- **Integrated video and other electronic resources** Links to websites and other sources referenced in the chapter can be easily accessed through the book's Student Companion Website or InfoTrac College Edition. Also, the text's Premium Website presents more than 25 audio-video clips that are relevant to and referenced in chapters. More information about electronic resources appears below.

Teaching and Learning Resources

For this edition, important resources have been expanded and improved:

- **Media Now Student Companion Website:** http://communication.wadsworth.com/ straubhaar5 The **Media Now Student Companion Website** brings helpful learning materials to your students' computers, including web links, quizzes, and key term flash cards. Available to all students.

- **1pass** **Resources** With **1pass,** students have unlimited easy access to online study, support, and research tools. Using the unique access code printed on the **1pass** passcode card (packaged FREE with each new copy of this text), students log on to http://1pass .thomson.com for access to these additional and exclusive resources.

1pass Resources Include

Media Now Premium Website: In addition to the web links, quizzes, and key-term flash cards available on the Student Companion Website, the **Media Now Premium Website** offers *Career Profile* videos, *Critical View* video news clips, and *Media in Motion* concept animations. Students will also find Stop & Review tutorial questions, a sample final exam, and much more.

InfoTrac College Edition® *with InfoMarks*® A four-month subscription to this world-class online university library offers you and your students anytime, anywhere access to more than 20 years' worth of full-text articles from almost 5000 scholarly and popular publications, including *Advertising Age, American Journalism Review, Broadcasting and Cable, Communication World, Digital Media, New Media Age,* and *Telecommunications.* This resource now also includes access to a virtual reader drawn from the InfoTrac College Edition library, comprising articles hand-selected to work with this text. For more information about InfoTrac College Edition and InfoMarks, a linking tool, visit http://www.infotrac-college.com and click on "User Demo."

vMentor FREE live, one-on-one online tutoring! With **vMentor** your students can connect to experts who will assist them in understanding the concepts covered in your course. In vMentor's virtual setting, students interact with the tutor and other students using two-way audio, an interactive whiteboard for illustrating the problem, and instant messaging. To ask a question, they simply click to raise a "hand."

Also Available Separately for Your Students

- *Media Literacy Workbook, Second Edition* The *Media Literacy Workbook,* by Kimb Massey of San Jose State University, is an invaluable resource for students in an introductory course as it helps them explore and develop the skills necessary for active participation and critical consumption of media communication. Using this workbook, students are asked to reflect on and evaluate their own media consumption, to try new models of interpretation, and to investigate issues regarding the impact of the media on culture and society. The workbook addresses 15 core mass communication topics on a chapter-by-chapter basis, offering three activities per chapter. This workbook is a free bundled item for qualified adopters.

- *Podcasts for Media Now: Audio Chapter Reviews* Created by Kimb Massey of San Jose State University, the **Podcasts for Media Now** are structured around the chapter outlines and summaries from the text to give students a means of reviewing chapter materials and concepts in audio format. A PIN code bundled with the text provides access to digital files that can be downloaded to a student's computer or MP3 player.

Class Preparation, Assessment, and Course Management Resources

- *Instructor's Resource Manual* The instructor's manual for *Media Now* includes lecture outlines, suggested student assignments, InfoTrac College Edition exercises, sample syllabi, a television news clip correlation guide for classroom use, and a comprehensive test bank with answer key. This essential tool was written by Jeffrey C. South of Virginia Commonwealth University.

- *Multimedia Manager with Instructor Resources: A Microsoft PowerPoint® Tool* Prepared by Kyle Nicholas of Old Dominion University, this CD-ROM includes the full text of the *Instructor's Resource Manual,* ExamView, and predesigned Microsoft PowerPoint presentations that contain not only text and images from the book but also Media in Motion concept animations from the Media Now Premium Website. This all-in-one lecture tool makes it easy for you to assemble, edit, publish, and present custom lectures for your course.

- ExamView® *Computerized Testing* Create, deliver and customize tests and study guides (both print and online) in minutes with this easy-to-use assessment and tutorial system. ExamView offers both a Quick Test Wizard and an Online Test Wizard that guide you step-by-step through the process of creating tests.

- JoinIn *on Turning Point* Thomson Wadsworth is pleased to offer you JoinIn content for Audience Response Systems specifically designed for *Media Now,* allowing you to transform your classroom and assess your students' progress with instant in-class quizzes and polls. Our exclusive agreement to offer TurningPoint® software lets you pose book-specific questions and display students' answers seamlessly within the Microsoft PowerPoint® slides of your own lecture in conjunction with the "clicker" hardware of your choice.

- *MediaTutor Advantage on WebCT and Blackboard* With the text-specific, preformatted content and total flexibility of MediaTutor™ Advantage, you can easily create and manage your own custom course website. The course management tool gives you the ability to provide virtual office hours, post syllabi, set up threaded discussions, track student progress with quizzing materials, and much more. For students, MediaTutor Advantage offers real-time access to a full array of study tools, including animations and videos that bring the book's topics to life, plus chapter outlines, summaries, learning objectives, glossary flash cards (with audio), practice quizzes, web links, and InfoTrac College Edition exercises. Instructors can access password-protected Instructor Resources for lectures and class preparation. MediaTutor Advantage also provides robust communication tools, such as a course calendar, asynchronous discussion, real-time chat, a whiteboard, and an integrated e-mail system. And MediaTutor Advantage now comes with a daily news feed from *NewsEdge,* an authoritative source for late-breaking news of interest to you and your students. Jeffrey C. South of Virginia Commonwealth University prepared this comprehensive multimedia resource.

These resources are available to qualified adopters, and ordering options are flexible. Please consult your local representative for more information, user names and passwords, examination copies, or product demonstrations. You may also contact the Wadsworth Academic Resource Center at 1-800-423-0563.

ACKNOWLEDGMENTS

We wish to thank our spouses, Sandy Straubhaar and Betty Digesie-LaRose, for both their patience and valuable ideas. We also want to thank a number of our undergraduate students, as well as Julia Rolf and Chris Straubhaar, for insights into their culture and concerns.

We would also like to thank our team at Wadsworth Publishing: Holly Allen, publisher; Renée Deljon, senior development editor; Mary Noel, production project manager; Mark Orr, marketing manager; Maria Epes, executive art director; Jeanette Wiseman, senior technology project manager; Darlene Amidon-Brent, assistant editor; Sarah Allen, editorial assistant; Nan Lewis-Schulz, our production editor at Thompson Steele; and photo researchers Laurie Frankenthaler and Abigail Reip.

We wish to thank the following reviewers for their thoughtful suggestions and guidance in the preparation of this fifth edition: Michael Brown, University of Wyoming; Gene Costain, University of Central Florida; Donald Godfrey, Arizona State University; Judith Marlane, California State University, Northridge; Jonathan Millen, Rider College; Jennifer Nelson, Ohio University; Cristina Pieraccini, State University of New York, Oswego; Michael Porter, University of Missouri; Jeffrey C. South, Virginia Commonwealth University. We also wish to thank our survey respondents Robert Abelman, Cleveland State University; Jerry G. Chandler, Jackson State University; and Peter K. Pringle, University of Tennessee at Chattanooga.

We also thank the following individuals for their reviews of the previous editions: Thomas Berner, Pennsylvania State University; Elena Bertozzi, Indiana University; Larry Bohlender, Glendale Community College; Sandra Braman, University of Wisconsin, Milwaukee; Erik Bucy, Indiana University; Larry Campbell, University of Alaska, Anchorage; Richard Caplan, University of Akron; Meta Carstarphen-Delgado, University of Oklahoma; Tsan-Kuo Chang, University of Minnesota, Twin Cities; John Chapin, Rutgers University; Joseph Chuk, Kutztown University of Pennsylvania; Dan Close, Wichita State University; David Donnelly, University of Houston; Michael Doyle, Arkansas State University; Lyombe Eko, University of Maine; Linda Fuller, Worcester State College; Tom Grimes, Kansas State University; Larry Haapanen, Lewis and Clark State College; Ken Hadwiger, Eastern Illinois University; Kevin Howley, Northeastern University; Jack Hodgson, Oklahoma State University; Rick Houlberg, San Francisco State University; James Hoyt, University of Wisconsin, Green Bay; Harvey Jassem, University of Hartford; Howard Keim, Tabor College; Randall King, Point Loma Nazarene University; Seong H. Lee, Appalachian State University; William Lingle, Linfield College; Linda Lumsden, Western Kentucky University; Robert Main, California State University, Chico; Reed Markham, Salt Lake Community College; Judith Marlane, California State University, Northridge; Stephen McDowell, Florida State University; Timothy P. Meyer, University of Wisconsin, Green Bay; Kyle Nicholas, Old Dominion University; Daniel Panici, University of Southern Maine; Norma Pecora, Ohio University; Peter Pringle, University of Tennessee, Chattanooga; Hoyt Purvis, University of Arkansas; Arthur Raney, Indiana University; Humphrey Regis, University of South Florida; Ronald Rice, Rutgers University; Shelly Rodgers, University of Minnesota, Twin Cities; Marshall Rossow, Mankato State University; Gay Russell, Grossmont College; Joseph Russomanno, Arizona State University; Marc Ryan, Marist College; Tom Shaker, Northeastern University; Roger Soenksen, James Madison University; Don Stacks, University of Miami; Michelle J. Stanton, California State University, Northridge; Jill D. Swenson, Ithaca College; Michael Ray Taylor, Henderson State University; Don Tomlinson, Texas A&M University; Max Utsler, University of Kansas; Hazel Warlaumont, California State University, Fullerton; Clifford Wexler, Columbia-Greene Community College; Glynn R. Wilson, Loyola University, New Orleans; Alan Winegarden, Concordia University; J. Emmett Winn, Auburn University; and Phyllis Zagano, Boston University.

We also gratefully acknowledge the assistance of the guest writers of our advertising and public relations chapters. Dr. Daniel Stout, associate professor of advertising and public relations at the University of South Carolina, has taught advertising and mass communication courses for over 15 years. Don Bates is managing director of marketing and new media for Media Distribution Services (MDS), which is headquartered in New York, N.Y. Mr. Bates also teaches graduate and undergraduate courses in public relations for nonprofit organizations and in the use of new technology in public relations at the New School University and at the New York Institute of Technology.

About the Authors ■■■■■■■■

DR. JOSEPH D. STRAUBHAAR is the Amon G. Carter Centennial Professor of Communications in the Radio-TV-Film Department of the University of Texas at Austin. He is the Director of the Center for Brazilian Studies within the Lozano Long Institute for Latin American Studies. He is also Associate Director for International Programs of the Telecommunication and Information Policy Institute at the University of Texas. He has published books, articles, and essays on international communications, international telecommunications, Brazilian television, Latin American media, comparative analyses of new television technologies, media flow and culture, and other topics appearing in a number of journals, edited books, and elsewhere. His primary teaching, research and writing interests are in international communication and cultural theory, the digital divide in the U.S. and other countries, and comparative analysis of new technologies. He does research in Latin America, Asia and Africa, and has taken student groups to Latin America and Asia. He has done seminars abroad on media research, television programming strategies, and telecommunications privatization. He is on the editorial board for the *Howard Journal of Communications, Studies in Latin American Popular Culture,* and *Revista Intercom.*

Visit Joe Straubhaar on the Web at
http://www.utexas.edu/ftp/coc/rtf/faculty/Straubhaar.html

DR. ROBERT LAROSE is currently a Full Professor and Director of MA Studies in the Department of Telecommunication at Michigan State University. He conducts research on the uses and effects of the Internet. He has published and presented numerous articles, essays and books on computer-mediated communication, social cognitive explanations of the Internet and its effects on behavior, understanding Internet usage, privacy, and much more. In addition to his teaching and research he is an avid watercolor painter and traveler.

Visit Robert LaRose on the Web at
http://www.mov.edu/~larose

Media Now

THE CHANGING MEDIA

Communication media are on the move, constantly evolving and changing the world we live in. It's no longer enough to learn about the conventional print, radio, television, and film mass media. This chapter examines how traditional mass media, computers, and telecommunications are converging to create exciting new media forms.

THE MEDIA IN OUR LIVES

The average person spends 2700 hours per year watching TV or listening to the radio. That's 337 eight-hour days, a full-time job! We spend another 900 hours with other media, including newspapers, books, magazines, music, film, home video, video games, and the Internet (Table 1.1). That's about 3600 hours of media use—more time than we spend on anything else, including working or sleeping.

At the same time, the consumption of information sustains our economy. Most of the economic activity in the United States now involves producing, processing, or distributing information, including the output of the **mass media,** Internet, telecommunications, and computer industries. Information workers dominate the workforce, and the proportion of workers engaged in information work has doubled over the last century. Information workers include journalists, editors, computer programmers, movie actors, television producers, advertising account executives, web page designers, singers, and public-relations specialists. College students are information workers, too, though unpaid ones. Even in manufacturing industries like the auto industry, which dominated the world of work through the 1950s, information workers in managerial, technical, clerical, sales, and

Mass media is one-to-many communication delivered through an electronic or mechanical channel.

4000 B.C.E. Written language invented

1455 Gutenberg's Bible is published

1960 U.S. transitions to information society

1975 First personal computer introduced

1982 The CD, the first digital music recording medium, introduced

1991 World Wide Web begins

1995 First digital hit movie

1996 Telecommunications Act of 1996 reforms U.S. media policy

1998 First U.S. HDTV broadcasts, new Copyright Act

2004 Internet reaches 75 percent of American homes

2007–2009 U.S. transition to digital television

Table 1.1 Annual Media Consumption

Medium	Hours per person*
Television	1701
Radio*	994
Recorded music*	201
Daily newspapers	176
Internet*	154
Books	109
Magazines	125
Video games*	67
Home video	58
Movies in theaters*	14
Total	3599

*For all persons aged 12 and older, all others for persons 18+. Available at http://www.tvb.org/

Source: Veronis, Suhler & Assoc., 2002

In an **information society,** the exchange of information is the predominant economic activity.

Convergence is the integration of mass media, computers, and telecommunications.

service occupations make up a third of the work force (Aoyama & Castells, 2002). It is fair to say that we now live and work in an **information society.**

The transition to an information society is driven in part by rapid changes in technology such as the computer and digital TV. We should no longer think about the various media of communication—books, newspapers, magazines, radio, television, film, telephones, and computers—as completely distinct entities. Advances in computers and telecommunications networks have led to the merging, or **convergence,** of conventional mass media with new ones so that now we have, for example, the morning newspaper delivered to us through our Internet connections.

MEDIA IN A CHANGING WORLD

The media inform us of continual change in a global society. In the process, American media have lost their grip on the news of the world, as they now contend with regional news sources such as *al Jazeera* for hearts and minds in the Middle East and elsewhere. Meanwhile, the imperatives of world trade agreements and globalized entertainment industries are changing what we see and hear in our homes.

Today the media are changing our world in many ways, in the rise of the Internet, the integration of communications technologies, shifting media empires, new lifestyles, challenging careers, changing regulations, shifting social issues, and a new dynamic of power in society—we even see these changes in the way we study the media (see Figure 1.1, page 5).

The changing media have important implications for media industries, individual lifestyles, careers, national policy, social issues, and the balance of power in society. Later we will discuss how the new media even challenge our basic ways of conceptualizing the relationship between media and society.

Merging Technologies

Events on the world stage are not the only forces that are changing the media in our lives, however. Recently, the Internet has become almost synonymous with the concept of new media. We, members of the Internet Generation, download songs and videos, buy books

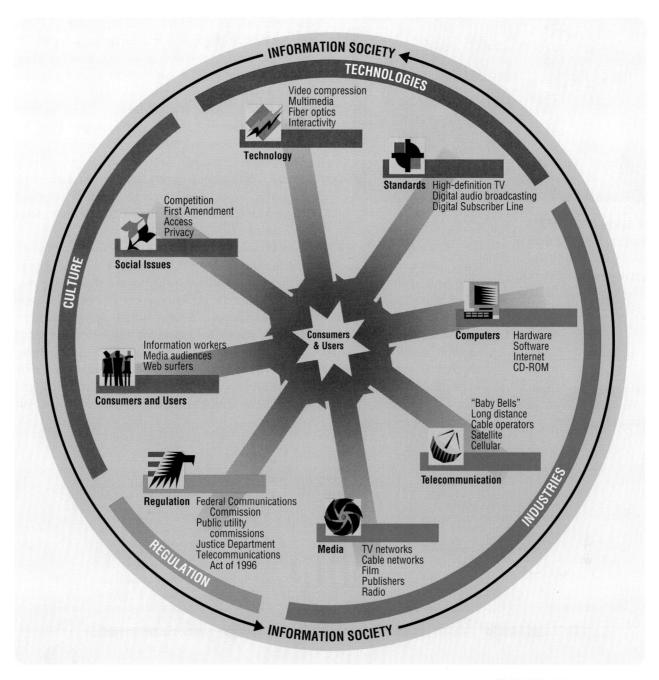

INFORMATION SOCIETY

TECHNOLOGIES

Video compression
Multimedia
Fiber optics
Interactivity

Technology

Standards High-definition TV
Digital audio broadcasting
Digital Subscriber Line

Competition
First Amendment
Access
Privacy

Social Issues

CULTURE

Consumers & Users

Computers Hardware
Software
Internet
CD-ROM

Information workers
Media audiences
Web surfers

Consumers and Users

"Baby Bells"
Long distance
Cable operators
Satellite
Cellular

Telecommunication

Regulation Federal Communications
Commission
Public utility
commissions
Justice Department
Telecommunications
Act of 1996

INDUSTRIES

Media TV networks
Cable networks
Film
Publishers
Radio

REGULATION

INFORMATION SOCIETY

and movie tickets, view news stories, participate in politics, and converse with our family and friends through a single shared medium, daily living examples of the convergence phenomenon. Everything seems to be online, from e-commerce, to virtual universities, to cybersex. With over 75 percent of the U.S. population now on the web, the Internet is coming within the reach of most Americans, although a persisting **digital divide** still leaves a number of poor, minority, and elderly people without access.

The convergence of media mentioned earlier has been made possible by digital technologies, which have moved communications media into what's often referred to as a new "digital era," in which formerly distinct forms of communication are merged together in digital communication networks like the Internet. **Digital** communication technology

■ **FIGURE 1.1**
Media Convergence
Information technology and media are converging in the information society.

The **digital divide** is the gap in Internet usage between rich and poor, Anglos and minorities.

Digital means computer-readable, formatted in 1s and 0s.

■ BEHIND THE SCENES

Sky Captain and The World of Tomorrow used digital effects to "fill in" scenes shot on an empty sound stage.

Analog communication uses continuously varying signals corresponding to the light or sounds originated by the source.

converts sound, pictures, and text into computer-readable formats by changing them into strings of electronic 1s and 0s that carry information in encoded form (see Technology Demystified: A Digital Media Primer, page 8). In contrast, **analog** communication relays all the information present in the original message in the form of continuously varying signals that correspond to the fluctuations of sound or light energy originated by the source of communication. As computers can process only digitized information, whereas humans can understand only analog "input," media messages have to be converted to digital form for transmission and back to analog form for reception.

Technological change is increasingly shaking up conventional media, and now the "old" mass media are responding with innovations of their own. The original Napster website that allowed users to share digital music files over the Internet was used by over 50 million people at its peak. It threatened the existence of the recording industry, before it was shut down by the courts for helping its users "steal" copyrighted music owned by the industry. Now the music industry has responded with online pay music services, transforming the ways that we buy and consume our music, even reinventing Napster as a subscription music business selling songs over the Internet. Now it's the movie industry's turn, as DVDs—digital video discs—broadband Internet service, and ever-faster computers are making possible not only the illegal duplication of movies but also their distribution.

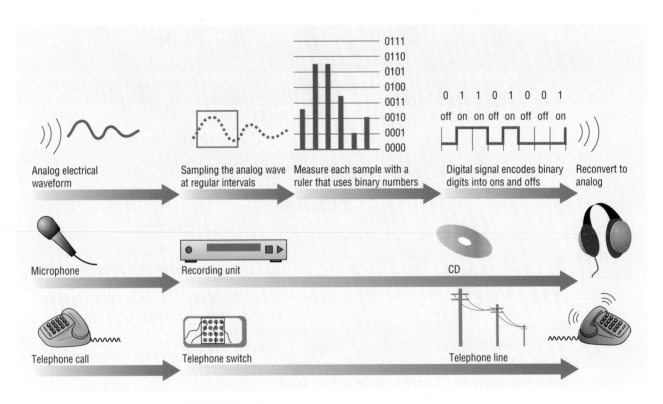

■ FIGURE 1.2
Converting Analog to Digital   The analog-to-digital conversion process occurs in a variety of media.

Merging Industries

Computer, Internet, cable television, and media firms are merging, forming partnerships, entering new businesses—and sometimes going out of business—at a dizzying rate in an effort to get the upper hand in the race to control the future of the media and to fight off challenges from upstart competitors that threaten their dominance (see Figure 1.1 on page 5).

Some examples:

- Cable TV giant Comcast now offers high speed Internet connections and telephone service to its subscribers.
- Apple Computer helped rescue the music industry by introducing its portable digital music player, the iPod.
- Former Warner Brothers chairman Terry Semel crossed over to lead, and revitalize, the Yahoo! Internet portal.
- Computer software giant Microsoft Corporation has invested in the video game, broadcasting, cable television, satellite, publishing, and Internet industries. Its software powers Movielink, a film downloading venture involving the major movie studios.
- Newspaper publisher Tribune Company is transforming itself into a multimedia news company by combining newspaper, television, cable, and Internet operations in major cities.

It makes sense for these organizations to forge alliances across once-rigid industry boundaries, because formerly distinct channels of communication, such as telephone and television, can now be integrated into a single digital network. Meanwhile, regulatory barriers that separated many industries, such as film and television, have been lowered. So large businesses and public institutions are reinventing themselves to take advantage of new ways of doing business made possible by the resulting industry and technological changes.

However, not all of these new combinations are proving successful. AOL Time Warner went back to calling itself Time Warner after a merger between the two firms failed to yield the hoped-for synergies between new media and old. Telecommunications giant AT&T was acquired by Southwestern Bell Communications in 2005 when profits from innovative services were slow to materialize. The bursting of the stock market "bubble" that fueled the growth of the Internet and the telecommunications industries in the 1990s, along with an advertising slump in the post-9/11 economy, left communications companies with mountains of debt and failed business plans that are only now starting to rebound.

© Justin Pumfrey/Getty Images

■ FUTURE TV
Digital TV promises wider and better pictures, improved sound, more channels, and interactivity.

STOP & REVIEW

1. List four examples of the convergence phenomenon.
2. What is meant by the term *information society*?
3. What are three traditional electronic mass media?
4. What are three advantages of "going digital"?
5. Explain how far each of the following has progressed in making the transition to digital media: radio, recorded music, cable television.

TECHNOLOGY DEMYSTIFIED ■■■■■■

A Digital Media Primer

All digital transmissions are composed of only two digits, 1 and 0. These are actually a series of on-off events.

Consider a simple telephone call. The digital conversion occurs on a computer card that connects your line to the telephone company's switch. First, brief excerpts, or samples, of the electrical waveform corresponding to your voice are taken from the telephone line at a rate of 8000 samples per second. The size, or voltage level, of each sample is measured and "rounded off" to the closest of 256 different possible readings. Then a corresponding eight-digit binary number is transmitted by turning an electrical current on for a moment to indicate a 1 and turning it off for a 0.

The process is reversed at the receiving end. At 8000 samples per second and eight digits per sample, the on-off signals are very numerous: 64,000 each second! Thus, when two lovers are talking on the phone and there is complete (if meaningful) silence on the line, the voltage reading is 0. The corresponding binary number is 00000000. If the lovers begin to quarrel loudly, the voltage reading might jump to the maximum: 11111111. To the couple, it seems that they are talking to each other, but in reality they are listening to computer emulations of their voices. Digital recordings use the same methods, but they employ more numerous samples and allow more volume levels to improve sound quality.

To make computer graphics, a computer stores digital information about the brightness and color of every single point on the computer screen. On many computer screens, there are 640 points of light (or picture elements, *pixels* for short) going across and 480 down. Up to 24 bits of information may be required for each point so that millions of colors can each be assigned their own unique digital code.

Similarly, when we type text into a computer each key corresponds to a unique sequence of seven computer bits (such as 1000001 for A). These sequences are what is stored inside the computer or transmitted through the Internet, in the form of tiny surges of electricity, short beeps of sound, flashes of light, or pulses of magnetism. The human senses are purely analog systems, so for humans to receive the message, we must convert back from digital to analog.

Changing Lifestyles

When new media enter our homes, media consumption patterns tend to change. In one survey, a quarter of Internet users said they watched television less since going online (Pew Research Center, 2002). Young people aged 18 to 29 now are as likely to rely on the Internet for news about political campaigns as they are network TV news or newspapers (Pew Research Center, 2004). A third of Internet visitors download music (Pew Research Center, 2003), often forgoing visits to the local record store.

Conventional mass media are learning to take advantage of these changing patterns by using new media to build larger audiences for themselves. For example, they run websites that sustain interest in popular reality shows such as *Survivor*, create "buzz" on the Internet for new movies, or add audio, video, and live discussion forums to supplement printed stories. Adding web tie-ins to conventional media benefits advertisers who can complete sales transactions at their websites and gather valuable information about consumer habits from web visits.

In addition to changing media consumption patterns, the changing media introduce us to new ways to live, as millions now work, shop, bank, and seek spiritual guidance online (Pew Research Center, 2003). Others forge new identities (Turkle, 1995) and develop new cultures (Lévy, 2001) on the Net. The changing media could mean more life choices, lower prices for goods and services, and a better quality of life for the average family. But new media might also degrade human relationships by replacing them with impersonal computer transactions, or it might lower the quality of public discourse by substituting Internet rumors for professional journalism.

The information sector of the economy includes broadcasting, publishing, telecommunications, Internet, and computer software industries.

Ladies and gentleman, now entering, your hero, your undisputed champion, a great athlete who knows no fear in the bullfight ring... El Diablo en Negro con Rojo Hankie! LET'S GET READY TO RUMBLE!
Cooky, Washington, DC

■ ONLINE BUZZ
Websites that generate "buzz" for TV shows are examples of the changing relationships between old media and new.

Challenging Careers

Convergence has and will continue to make jobs and careers highly volatile as companies continually re-engineer themselves and compete on a global scale. Most people entering the workforce today will have four or five different careers—not just jobs, but *careers*—in their future. That means that the student considering a professional career in journalism, radio, film, television, or the Internet will eventually have to acquire new skills for several very different professions. Conversely, students entering the humanities or sciences, or professions in fields such as law and medicine, may find that their second (or third, or fourth) career is in the **information sector.** Blue-collar jobs, such as prepress technicians who set type and compose pages for print newspapers and magazines, will shrink most owing to improvements in information systems and automation (Table 1.2). Most job growth will occur in occupations that require a college degree, and new technologies will keep the demand for technical graduates at especially high levels.

■ MEDIA EFFECT?
High school shootings like the ones at Columbine High raise concerns about the effects of violent movies, television programs, and video games.

Table 1.2 Occupational Outlook in Communications

Occupation	Current Employment (2002)	Median Annual Pay	Growth	Explanation
Actors, producers, directors	139,000	$23,470 (actors) $46,240 (Producers/directors)	Average	New channels, interactive media offset decline in local broadcast entertainment openings
Announcers	76,000	$19,820	Decline	Industry consolidation eliminates jobs
Advertising, marketing, promotions, public relations, and sales managers	700,000	$57,130 (advertising) $60,640 (public relations)	Faster than average	Global competition for products and services sparks growth
Broadcast and sound technicians	93,000	$27,760	Average	Industry consolidation limits growth
News analysts, reporters, correspondents	66,000	$30,510	Slower than average	Old media consolidation and decline offsets new media growth
Prepress technicians	148,000	$29,960	Decline	Automation eliminates jobs
Writers and editors	319,000	$42,790	Average	Growth in specialized magazines and technical publications

Note: Median means the midpoint of the range of salaries in the occupation.

Source: http://bls.gov/search/ooh.asp?ct=OOH

Overall, jobs in the information sector of the economy—the sector that includes broadcasting, cable TV, publishing, telecommunications, computer software, and Internet companies—are expected to grow about 20 percent over the next decade, about the same level as the overall economy. However, much of the growth will be in computer software and online media (BLS, 2004). Prospects in conventional mass media fields, however, can look a little bleak at first glance. Slower than average growth is expected because of industry mergers and a growing reliance on labor-saving computerized production techniques that could eliminate many of today's media jobs. **Offshoring,** the export of jobs to other countries, is also a growing trend in the information sector (see World View: *Will Your Job Go Offshore?,* page 12). Substantial job growth is expected for scriptwriters and editors, actors, multimedia artists, and video editors needed to fill the new "channels" on cable and the Internet, although the new jobs may no longer carry the same pay and prestige that their old "old media" counterparts did. Faster than average growth is also expected in advertising public relations management. However, all mass media occupations typically have high turnover rates, still providing many openings at the entry level for aspiring reporters, producers, announcers, and account execs. Computer skills may hold the key to finding a second career for those who don't become media stars—as many as one in 50 of all jobs are now dependent upon the Internet (University of Texas, 2000).

Offshoring is the export of jobs to other countries.

PROFILE

Yahoo! from the Old Media

TERRY SEMEL

Name: Terry Semel

Born: Brooklyn, New York, 1944

Education: B.S., Long Island University, MBA from City University of New York

Current Position: Chairman and Chief Executive Officer, Yahoo!, Inc.

Style: Born deal maker. Hands-off manager that people like working for.

Greatest Achievements: During his stint at Warner Brothers, annual revenues climbed from $1 billion to $11 billion. He oversaw big movies, including *The Unforgiven, The Matrix,* and the *Lethal Weapon* series. He was an early backer of movie distribution on DVDs.

Entry Level: He broke into the movie business selling movies to movie chain owners.

How He Got to the Top: Before Yahoo! he was chairman of Warner Brothers and before that served as president of the film distribution divisions at Disney and CBS.

Most Dubious Achievement: He was a backer of DEN (Digital Entertainment Network), an attempt to bring television-style programming to the Internet that ended in bankruptcy. He was a virtual computer illiterate when he took over Yahoo! in 2001.

Where Does He Go from Here? Now that he has turned around Yahoo!'s once-faltering advertising business, the challenge is to find new revenue opportunities in new broadband pay services. And, to make Yahoo! a Fortune 500 company.

Source: Vogelstein, F. (2004). Bringing up Yahoo. *Fortune,* 149(7), 221–225.

Shifting Regulations

The convergence of mass media with telephone and computer technologies is now also written into the official policy of the U.S. government. In the **Telecommunications Act of 1996** (discussed in Chapter 15), Congress stripped away the regulations that had protected publishing, broadcasting, cable television, telephone, and other media companies from competition with one another. With the new law, lawmakers hoped to spark competition, improve service, and lower prices in all communications media. But so far, the main impact has been a flurry of corporate mergers, buyouts, and bankruptcies, whereas the consumer benefits appear slowly. Another piece of Information Age legislation, the Copyright Term Extension Act of 1998, has perhaps had a more immediate impact on media consumers. This legislation broadens the **copyright** protection enjoyed by writers, performers, and songwriters—and the giant media corporations that own the rights to such valued properties as Bugs Bunny. However, the same legislation weakens the rights of students and professors to reproduce copyrighted printed works for their own educational use. This is also the law that backs efforts to crack down on students and other individuals who "share" music and videos online.

With the growing importance of the Internet and the spread of multinational media corporations, regulation is no longer just a national issue. International organizations such as the International Telecommunications Union (ITU), the World Trade Organization (WTO), and the United Nations are beginning to grapple with the issues of global media. For example, how can we regulate content (for example, Janet Jackson's exposed breast)

The Telecommunications Act of 1996 is federal legislation that deregulated the communications media.

Copyright is the legal right to control intellectual property.

World View

Will Your Job Go Offshore?

Offshoring is a long-term trend, perhaps most visible in the movement of automobile manufacturing jobs to countries in the Far East. But now information sector jobs are following. Global data networks and online collaboration tools make it possible for work teams to be assembled across continents and time zones. And that is not only possible but desirable: By having editing of, say, a Hollywood film continue around the clock, global media corporations can shave months off their release dates. Web developers and film crews living in developing countries are paid generous salaries by local standards, but still a small fraction of what they could command in the United States or other advanced economies. Low turnover and minimal employee benefits are further sources of cost savings for the employer. In recent years high capacity fiber-optic networks have been extended around the world, providing access to computer networks in locations that were previously beyond the reach of the information society. And, the cost of the high-speed connections has been falling dramatically so that now communication costs are only a small fraction of the labor costs, making offshoring more economically attractive.

In 2003, IBM caused a stir when it was revealed that it planned to "export" a significant number of programming jobs to India. However, in a global economy just about any job is exportable, even in creative fields. For example, *The Simpsons* is animated in South Korea, even though the animators employed there reportedly do not "get" the jokes. India is also turning into a global production center for film and video, capitalizing on the production facilities and staff who make movies for India's vibrant national film industry.

How can you be sure that your career won't be one going offshore? The best bets are occupations that require

■ **OFFSHORE INFORMATION WORKERS**
International call centers like this one in India supply skilled workers at bargain rates for U.S. employers.

close human contact. Those might include radio station managers and television directors (and, we hope, college professors), but also janitors and nursing home aides. High-level jobs that require original thinking, recognition of complex patterns, or an intimate knowledge of a culture, such as advertising executives, journalists, and television producers, may also be good bets. However, any job that can be reduced to repetitive tasks or a set of rules is sure to be either sent offshore or taken over by a computer. So, while the marketing director for an online store may be sitting in San Francisco, the people writing the HTML code, tending the web servers, and delivering customer service may all be in Bombay.

that is acceptable in one country but not another? How can nations such as France preserve their cultures against the onslaught of American-dominated film? How can developing countries expand Internet access, not to mention basic literacy, to their citizens?

Rising Social Issues

When Janet Jackson's breast was bared during the halftime performance at the 2004 Super Bowl, what effect did the exposure have on children in the audience? That event and the question it prompted remind us that the mass media themselves have long been social issues. They are criticized for their impacts on violence, sexual promiscuity, racial and ethnic stereotypes, economic exploitation, mindless consumption, and irresponsible government. Now new media content such as Internet pornography and violent video games also cause concern. Media critics and consumers are also raising questions such as, Does the Internet isolate people from real social interaction? and Does it shift power in society? (See Media and Culture: A New Balance of Power? on page 13.) Despite our

A New Balance of Power?

Just how powerful are the media? Do they affect the very underpinnings of the social order: who holds power in society and how do they keep it?

The new media can put us all at the mercy of "digital robber barons" who rule them to enrich themselves at our expense. Their dominance reduces the diversity of content and raises the cost of information. The courts ruled that Microsoft unfairly competed in the market for Internet browsers, and the company now stands accused of trying to corner the market for music and video player software as well. That increases Microsoft's power in the market for computer operating system software and lets it raise the price for Windows. Meanwhile, innovative upstarts like Napster are crushed by entrenched old media interests like Disney and Time Warner. We might well ask, is the information society just a new way for the rich to get richer?

Or, do the new media consign the poor to continuing poverty? The digital divide describes the gap in Internet access between whites and minorities, rich and poor (NTIA, 2004). As the Internet grows into an important source of employment, education, and political participation, that digital divide could translate into widening class division and social upheaval. Equal opportunity in the information economy already lags for both minorities and women, who are underrepresented in both the most visible (that is, on-camera) and most powerful (that is, senior executive) positions in the media. And although the gap in Internet *access* for women has closed, women are still excluded from a male-dominated computer culture, denying them access to the most powerful and rewarding careers in the information society (AAUW, 2000). The issue is global. The nations of the world divide between those with access to advanced communication technology and those without it.

Or, could the new media be a catalyst for a shift away from traditional ruling classes? An alliance of social movements against the excesses of global corporations orchestrates demonstrations via the Internet. Online news sites raise issues that are ignored by the mainstream press. The diverse and lively communities of the Internet may contribute to the fragmentation of culture—and power—for many, identity is defined as much by the Internet communities in which we participate as by the countries we live in or the color of our skin, characteristics that are invisible on the Internet.

questions, we acknowledge that the melding of computers and conventional mass media holds out hope for new ways to correct old media ills. For example, the V-chip allows parents to shield children from offensive TV programs. Similarly, the Internet offers access to diverse political viewpoints and active information seeking instead of passive media consumption—qualities that many critics have found lacking in the old media.

CHANGING MEDIA THROUGHOUT HISTORY

Although the changes in the media, and the changes in society that accompany them, may sometimes seem to be something radically new and different, the media and society have always evolved together. In this section we will examine how the role of the media has evolved as society developed from the dawn of human civilization (see Figure 1.3 on page 14) through agricultural, industrial, and information societies (Bell, 1973; Dizard, 1997).

Preagricultural Society

Before agricultural societies developed, most people lived in small groups as hunters and gatherers. These cultures depended on the spoken word, rather than writing, to transmit ideas among themselves and between generations. The *oral tradition,* what the historical

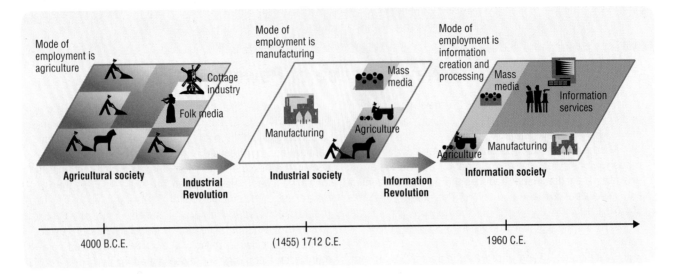

Mode of employment is agriculture

Cottage industry

Folk media

Agricultural society

Industrial Revolution

Mode of employment is manufacturing

Mass media

Manufacturing

Agriculture

Industrial society

Information Revolution

Mode of employment is information creation and processing

Mass media

Information services

Agriculture

Manufacturing

Information society

4000 B.C.E.   (1455) 1712 C.E.   1960 C.E.

■ **FIGURE 1.3**

Stages of Economic Development The three basic stages of economic development, from agricultural to industrial to informational.

reliance on the spoken word is known as, is an extremely rich one, bringing to us Homer's *Iliad* and the epic stories, folktales, ritual chants, and songs of many other cultures. These works that originated in oral forms live on today in popular culture productions like the movie *Troy* and the fairy tales and campfire stories that we still tell our children. In a sense, all culture is still oral culture as we converse with our family and friends to share our experiences with the media today.

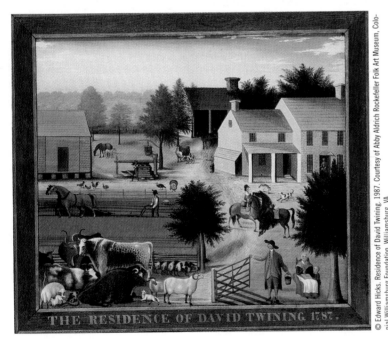

THE RESIDENCE OF DAVID TWINING 1787.

■ **DOWN ON THE FARM**

Agricultural societies are characterized by resource extraction. Written communication evolves as a specialized function.

Agricultural Society

Once agricultural society developed, most work was found on farms or in resource extraction, such as mining, fishing, and logging. Agricultural societies were more settled and more complex than preagricultural societies, and it was the ancient Sumerian culture, located in modern-day Iraq, that is commonly credited with the invention of writing in 4000 B.C.E. However, in agricultural societies, communication was primarily a specialized function—like medicine or candle making—because most people, whether peasants or nobles, were unable to read or write. The first people to specialize in correspondence, record keeping, and the copying of manuscripts were usually members of religious orders and merchant classes. With much of the rest of the populace still illiterate, couriers skilled at memorizing long oral messages were valuable communications specialists.

The primary mass medium that evolved in early agricultural societies was the hand-copied book, but circulation was limited. Hand copying was very laborious, and the ruling classes often did not want the masses exposed to new ideas through reading. Thus, most books were produced for a literate elite class of scholars and priests. We examine the evolution of the printed word further in Chapters 3 and 4.

While agricultural societies and written communication date back to ancient Sumer, the United States was still an agricultural economy, with agricultural employment the most prevalent, as recently as 1900 C.E. Today, agriculturalists comprise only about 2 percent of the U.S. population. However, many developing countries are still primarily agricultural economies.

Industrial Society

Although the beginning of the Industrial Revolution is often dated to correspond with Thomas Newcomen's invention of the steam engine in 1712, an important precursor of industrialism is found in the field of communication: the publication of the Gutenberg Bible in 1455. Johannes Gutenberg was the first in Europe to use movable metal type, dramatically improving the speed of book production and eliminating the need for time-consuming duplication through hand-copying. Eventually, thousands of identical copies of a book could be printed relatively cheaply, and mass production led to larger audiences as new types of books were printed.

© The Granger Collection, New York

■ **START THE PRESSES!**
The advent of the printing press in the late fifteenth century was a precursor to mass literacy and the Industrial Revolution.

In a sense, the Industrial Revolution extended Gutenberg's methods to the manufacture of virtually all types of goods. Industrial production was centered in large cities, triggering a mass migration from country to city and from agricultural jobs to manufacturing. By 1910, the United States had become an industrial society: Manufacturing had outstripped agricultural employment for the first time. Industrialization also encouraged the spread of literacy to cope with more complex job requirements and the demands of urban life. In the 1830s, urbanization, literacy, and the need to advertise new manufactured goods on a mass scale gave rise to the first truly mass medium, the urban newspaper (see Chapter 4). Soon, industrial methods of mass production were applied to speed up the printing process and to invent newer amusements for the urban populations, including film, radio, and television, which, along with newspapers and magazines, are the characteristic media of industrial societies.

Information Society

As we said at the beginning of this chapter, the society we currently live in is an information society, because our economy primarily depends on the production and consumption of information. Information workers were found even in preagricultural societies, in the persons of storytellers and shamans. As late as 1900, when the United States was still an agricultural society, though, only about 10 percent of the population were employed as information workers. At the pinnacle of the U.S. industrial society in 1950, this proportion had grown to about 30 percent. The point at which information work started to dominate the workforce marked the transition to an information society. This transition happened in the United States in 1960, but relatively few other nations have yet made the transition. Today, the proportion of information workers has leveled off at just about half the workforce. Since the media reflect the societies that spawn them, it comes as no surprise that the dominant medium in an information society is one that helps to create, store, and process information: the computer.

■ WIRELESS WEB
Cell phones that provide wireless Internet access and video could be the next phase of media convergence.

With respect to the media themselves, we might trace their evolution in the information society by examining the points at which various media channels made the transition to digital communication. Some of these changes predate the advent of the World Wide Web in 1991, and even the invention of the personal computer, in 1975.

Telephone   The first consumer communications medium to be digitized was the telephone, beginning in 1962. Today, most telephone conversations are converted to digital form before they leave your neighborhood and travel as computer data throughout the long-distance telephone networks (Figure 1.2), and digital subscriber lines (DSL) make the telephone line a practical medium for high-speed Internet access. Along with the latest digital mobile phones, DSL converts your voice to digits inside the handset and provides high speed Internet connections as well.

Print Media   Digitization first hit the production rooms of print media in the late 1960s. Now it is only in the final printing process that the words and images are converted from computer code to analog print image. Thousands of newspapers and magazines are also available electronically on the Internet, and many of these exist only digitally. While e-books, which display the text of books in electronic format on handheld screens have yet to catch on, other digital print products are growing in popularity. High-speed printing technologies make it feasible to print books "on demand" and to include customized content.

Film   In Hollywood the computer movement started with the special effects for *Star Wars* in 1974. Now most film editing is done on computer, and computer-generated hit films, beginning with *Toy Story* in 1995, are becoming commonplace. Movie theater sound systems are digital, and the latest Digital Light Projection (DLP) systems use digital technology to project the images as well. On the home front, the digital video disc (DVD) is fast replacing the analog videotape.

Recordings   The first digital compact disc (CD) recordings reached consumers in 1982. Now the online portability of MP3 files and subscriptions to pay music services on the Internet are revolutionizing music distribution as well as listening.

Cable and Satellite Television   In 1998 cable companies began to convert content to digital form as a way to increase the number of channel offerings on their systems. Cable went digital in part to meet competition from direct broadcast satellites (DBS) that began beaming hundreds of channels of digital programming directly to home dishes in 1995. And now many cable subscribers enjoy high-speed Internet access by installing cable modems.

Broadcasting   High-definition television (HDTV), which uses digital formats to transmit wider and clearer pictures, went on the air in the United States in 1998 and is slated to replace conventional television eventually. The next generation of radio, digital audio broadcasting (DAB, also known as high-definition radio), reached the air in 2004, to compete with new digital satellite radio services and with streaming audio on the Internet. Meanwhile, digital video recorders like TiVo threaten broadcasters with their ability to automatically skip commercials and to make personalized viewing schedules.

Thus, we can see that all of the media are becoming an integral part of our information society. Indeed, employees of newspapers, television stations, and film and recording studios are now grouped together with telecommunications workers and computer programmers as part of the Information Sector of the economy (BLS, 2004). This classification is consistent with an emerging, broader view of the media that encompasses telecommunications as well the mass media (Starr, 2004).

CHANGING CONCEPTIONS OF THE MEDIA

Reading highly encapsulated accounts of the evolution of the media, such as the above, you might get the mistaken impression that society has always followed a logical, linear progression driven by changes in communication technology. However, many aspects of society—such as economics and politics—must come together for technologies like movable type or computers to develop. This reality raises the fundamental question that we noted earlier and will consider at length in the next chapter: Do the media determine culture, or does culture determine the media?

Here we will begin by reviewing a basic model of human communication and then examining conventional views that developed when the old media seemed all-powerful. Next we will consider critical views of the media and how the new media challenge basic assumptions about the media in our lives.

The SMCR Model

The classic model that stresses the dominance of the media was developed by Wilbur Schramm (1982), often credited as the founder of mass communication studies. He created what is known as the **Source-Message-Channel-Receiver (SMCR)** model.

The *source* is the originator of the communication.

The *message* is the content of the communication, the information that is to be exchanged.

An *encoder* translates the message into a form that can be communicated—often a form that is not directly interpretable by human senses.

A *channel* is the medium or transmission system used to convey the message from one place to another.

A *decoder* reverses the encoding process.

The *receiver* is the destination of the communication.

A *feedback* mechanism between the source and the receiver regulates the flow of communication.

Noise is any distortion or errors that may be introduced during the information exchange.

This model can be applied to all forms of human communication, but here we will just illustrate it with a mass communication example, that of television viewing (see Figure 1.4, page 18). According to Schramm's model, when you are at home watching a television program, the television network (a corporate source) originates the message, which is encoded by the microphones and television cameras in the television studio.

© Courtesy of DLP Image Library

■ **COMING SOON TO YOUR LOCAL THEATER**
Digital Light Projectors (DLP) using CD-like digital storage media instead of film represent the digital revolution at your local movie theater.

The **Source-Message-Channel-Receiver (SMCR)** model of mass communication describes the exchange of information as the message passes from the source to the channel to the receiver, with feedback to the source.

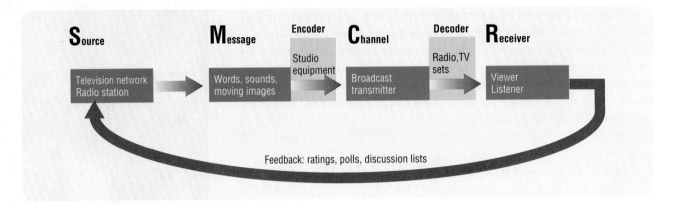

| **S**ource | **M**essage | Encoder | **C**hannel | Decoder | **R**eceiver |
| Television network
Radio station | Words, sounds,
moving images | Studio
equipment | Broadcast
transmitter | Radio,TV
sets | Viewer
Listener |

Feedback: ratings, polls, discussion lists

■ **FIGURE 1.4**
SMCR Model The SMCR model is one way of describing the communication process applied to broadcast media.

The **channel** is not literally the number on the television dial to which you are tuned, but rather the entire chain of transmitters, satellite links, and cable television equipment required to convey the message to your home. Although we sometimes call a TV set a "receiver," it is really the decoder and the viewer that is the receiver. Feedback from viewers is via television rating services. Electronic interference with the broadcast and the distractions of the neighbor's barking dogs are possible noise components in this situation.

In this classic view, mass communication is one-to-many communication, and the mass media are the various channels through which mass communication is delivered. That is, through newspapers, radio, TV, or film, the message is communicated from a single source to many receivers at about the same time, with limited opportunities for the audience to communicate back to the source.

In Wilbur Schramm's time, from the late 1940s to the early 1980s, mass media were produced by large media corporations. There an elite corps of media commentators and professional producers acted as **gatekeepers,** deciding what the audience should receive. These editors and producers, recognizing their own power, were aware of themselves as shapers of public opinion and popular tastes (Schramm, 1982).

Mass media messages were addressed to the widest possible audience. The underlying motive was to homogenize tastes and opinions to further the goals of a mass market industrial economy. Feedback was largely limited to reports from audience research bureaus, which took days or weeks to compile. The audience was an undifferentiated mass, anonymous to the source and a passive receptacle for the message. Social critics like Adorno and Horkheimer (1972) called this the industrialization of culture.

Types of Communication

Communication is simply the exchange of meaning. That definition covers a lot of ground. It obviously includes talking to your friends, reading a newspaper, watching television, and surfing the Internet. Less obvious examples of communication might include the graphic design on a T-shirt, a fit of laughter, or the wink of an eye. And, the

STOP & REVIEW

1. What are some of the ways that new media are changing society?
2. In what ways are new media affecting careers?
3. What is the significance of the Telecom Act of 1996?
4. Give examples of convergence in media industries.
5. How does the role of the media differ between industrial and information societies?

A **channel** is an electronic or mechanical system that links the source to the receiver.

Gatekeepers decide what will appear in the media.

Communication is an exchange of meaning.

meaning exchanged does not have to be profound: a sonnet by Shakespeare and a verse scratched on a bathroom wall both qualify as communication. In terms of the SMCR model, the exchange is between the source of the message and the receiver.

Mass communication is a major focus of this book but is only one of the possible modes of communication. Another hallmark of the classical approach is to classify communication according to the number of people communicating and to examine processes that are unique to each mode. The basic categories include intrapersonal, interpersonal, small group, and large group, as well as mass communication, shown in Figure 1.5. In this figure, the number of people involved grows from top to bottom with the width of the pyramids, with mass communication forms at the bottom. When a mechanical or electronic medium is used to transmit information we say that the communication is **mediated.** Now we can also distinguish between analog (on the left) and digital forms of communication (on the right) in each category. As we move from top to bottom we move between types of communication, from intrapersonal, to interpersonal, small group, large group, and mass communication. An example of each type is found in the corresponding layer of the pyramid, one for analog and one for digital:

© Francisco Cruz/SuperStock

■ **A BIG MASS**
In the conventional mass media, the audience was an undifferentiated mass anonymous to both the sources of the media and to each other.

Intrapersonal communication is an exchange of information we have with ourselves, such as when we think over our next move in a video game or sing to ourselves in the shower. Typing into a computer or Palm Pilot is electronically mediated intrapersonal communication.

Interpersonal communication includes exchanges in which two or more people take part, but the term is usually reserved for situations in which just two people are communicating. Sometimes we call that one-to-one communication. Having a face-to-face conversation over lunch and writing a letter to a friend are everyday examples. When interpersonal communication is electronically mediated, as in a telephone conversation, the term *point-to-point* communication is sometimes used.

Group communication is a situation in which three or more people communicate with one another. Not all communication that takes place in a group setting is included, however. When pairs of students talk to each other in a classroom before the start of a lecture, for example, they are engaged in *interpersonal* communication (see above).

Small-group communication, usually involving fewer than a dozen people, extends interpersonal communication into situations where group dynamics become important. For example, when students get together to "scope out" an exam, their interaction is likely to follow one of several well-known patterns of small-group interaction as they define a study plan. For example, one person in the group may dominate it. Or, they may take turns speaking and let everyone have their say; we could call that many-to-many communication.

Large-group communication involves anywhere from a dozen to several hundred participants, and the communication situation restricts active involvement to only a few of the parties. However, large-group communication still involves immediate feedback from the receivers of the message, which is not the case with mass communication. Examples are lectures, concerts, and live theatrical performances.

Of course, many communication situations do not fit neatly into these categories. Are talk-radio shows, in which audience members provide instant communication back

Mass communication is one-to-many, with limited audience feedback.

Mediated is communication transmitted through an electronic or mechanical channel.

Types of Communication

Types of communication may be distinguished according to the number of participants and the nature of the communication process.

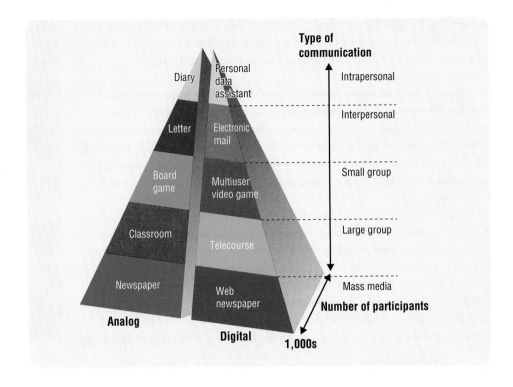

to the source—and even, in a sense, become sources themselves—still true mass media forms? What about TV shows like *American Idol* that invite viewers to direct the content? We could perhaps call that many-to-one communication. The number of participants is not always a reliable indicator, therefore. A college lecture delivered on the last day before spring break to only six students would still be a large-group communication (because of the style of presentation), even though the audience is a small group. Thus, both the nature of the communication setting and the size of the gathering must be considered.

Other classifications do stress the setting for the communication or the nature of the communication process. *Organizational communication* takes place in formally structured organizations, spans the entire spectrum of communication types as classified by size, and is affected by a person's position and function within the organization. For example, in certain highly structured organizations, most communication travels in one direction, from the bosses to the workers, with little flowing either back up the chain of command or laterally, to workers in other departments. Communication can also be distinguished between one-way communication, in which the flow of information goes exclusively from source to receiver, or two-way, in which both participants take an active role. Finally, *intercultural communication* takes places across international or cultural boundaries.

What Are the Media *Now?*

"The Media" was once commonly understood to mean the media of mass communication: radio, television, newspapers, and film came to mind when the SMCR model was first conceived. Today, some refer to these as the "old media." When standing alone, "the media" more specifically denoted major print and broadcast news organizations such as the *New York Times* and *CBS Television,* as opposed to "the entertainment media" like MGM studios and Capitol Records. However, the changes in the media environment

■ **JUST A COUPLE OF INFORMATION WORKERS**
Movie stars and their directors create and process information, so they are information workers just like the rest of us.

Asynchronous Communication   *Simultaneity,* the notion that everyone in the audience receives the message at about the same time (or "synchronously"), was once another defining characteristic of the mass media. That view made sense before consumer recording technology became commonplace in the 1960s and 1970s. Before then, you had to catch a program the first time it aired or else wait for the reruns. However, the notion never applied very well to film, not without stretching "the same time" to cover a period of several weeks.

© Courtesy of TiVo

Consumers' ability to "time shift" programs using VCRs and digital video recorders renders the notion of simultaneity obsolete, as they can choose when to watch a program regardless of the time and day it originally airs. The television networks are now time shifting themselves by retransmitting their own programs on cable channels within days of the time of their original broadcast. Situations like these that lack simultaneity are examples of **asynchronous** communication, those communication acts that are distributed across time, freeing participants from having to attend an event at a particular time. Postal mail and answering machines are two common examples of asynchronous interpersonal communication, as your mail may be delivered, and voice messages may accumulate, while you're not home.

■ **TIME SHIFTER**
Personal video recorders allow viewers to rearrange the TV schedule to their liking.

Narrowcasting   Another sign of the growing power of the audience in the new media is the practice of targeting content toward smaller and smaller audiences, sometimes called *narrow-* (as opposed to "broad-") *casting.* Advanced audience research methods have helped the media cater to smaller audiences by enhancing the richness and speed of audience feedback. The result is that **narrowcasting**—dedicating communication channels to specific audience subgroups, or market segments—is now practical. Demographic characteristics such as sex, age, and income, once the sole means of defining audiences, are being replaced by a focus on lifestyles and user needs and even on individual preferences, including purchasing behavior. Rather than homogenize audiences, the new communications media cater to specialized groups and define new niches.

Asynchronous media are not consumed simultaneously by all members of the audience.

Narrowcasting targets media to specific segments of the audience.

Multimedia Forms   Converging technologies also break down conventional distinctions between channels of communication so that we can select between modes of presentation. Consider online newspapers that show us the text of the latest story about scandal in high places but also include links to additional resources such as animated graphics that "follow the money trail" and live video of the Congressional hearings on the matter, as well as to instant polls and a discussion group where we can express our outrage. This multitude of news components means we can choose to experience the same story in five different ways, including as a conversation with other audience members. More and more media are gaining interactive features such as these that offer the information consumer new options for selecting and personalizing content and participating in a larger conversation. The change means that, increasingly, the mass media of radio, television, newspapers, and film as we once knew them are no longer quite the same.

So what are the media now? Old media forms such as newspapers, television, and film and old media institutions like the *New York Times,* CBS Television, and MGM Studios are still with us and will continue to be for a long time to come. But throughout the media environment numerous changes in the media, both big and small, are being driven by the continuing evolution of technology, regulation, media ownership, our economy, our culture, our world, and ourselves. As this evolution continues, the old media of generations past are gradually taking on new media forms such as those we've discussed here.

STOP & REVIEW

1. What do the letters SMCR stand for?
2. Use the SMCR model to describe what happens when you watch TV.
3. Is an automated teller machine interactive? Explain.
4. How do the "new media" differ from the "old media"?

SUMMARY AND REVIEW

WHAT IS THE INFORMATION SOCIETY?

The information society is one in which the production, processing, distribution, and consumption of information are the primary economic and social activities. In an information society, an ever-increasing amount of time is spent with communications media and in using information technologies such as the telephone and the computer. More and more people are employed as information workers, people who produce, process, or distribute information as their primary work activity. The information society is a further step in the evolution of society from its former bases in agriculture and manufacturing.

HOW ARE MASS MEDIA AND INFORMATION TECHNOLOGIES CONVERGING?

More and more communication is created and distributed in computer-readable digital form. This change means that the same basic technologies can be used to transmit all forms of communication—text, audio, or video—in an integrated communication system such as the Internet. Thus, separate channels of communication are no longer needed for each medium. The mass media, telecommunications, Internet, and computer software industries are all part of the same information sector of the economy—they are, in other words, converging. Laws and public policies governing the media, career opportunities in communications industries, social and personal issues arising from media consumption, and even theories of the media and their role in society are all changing.

WHAT ARE THE COMPONENTS OF THE COMMUNICATION PROCESS?

All communication processes can be described in terms of a simple model in which a corporate or individual source encodes a message and transmits it through a physical channel to the person for whom the message is intended, the receiver. We call this the SMCR model. In most communication situations, feedback is also provided between the receiver and the source. Contemporary views of the process stress that it takes place in the context of a culture shared by the source and the receiver, and that both source and receiver contribute to the creation of meaning.

WHAT IS MASS COMMUNICATION?

The conventional view is that mass communication involves large professional organizations, hundreds or thousands of people, and no immediate feedback between source and receiver. Newspapers, magazines, radio, television, and film are all examples of mass media.

WHAT ARE SOME OTHER TYPES OF COMMUNICATION?

When the communication channel is an electronic or mechanical device—such as a radio station or a movie projector—we call it mediated communication. Mediated communication may be point-to-point, one-to-many, or multipoint-to-multipoint. Communication can be characterized according to the number of people involved. Intrapersonal communication involves one person, interpersonal communication usually includes only two people, and small-group communication usually encompasses more than two but fewer than a dozen participants. Large-group communication involves dozens or hundreds of people, but feedback is still immediate. Communication can also be characterized according to the setting in which it takes place. For example, organizational communication happens inside a formally structured organization.

WHERE DID THE MASS MEDIA COME FROM?

While mass media had forerunners in agricultural and preagricultural societies, they are generally regarded as creations of the Industrial Age. Mass production methods coupled with the rise of large urban audiences for media during the Industrial Age led to the rise of print and later mass media.

WHAT IS INTERACTIVITY?

A variety of meanings have been attached to the term *interactive,* ranging from the simple ability to select content from a large number of options to devices that could pass the Turing test by faithfully mimicking human interaction. The term should be reserved for communication situations in which the user modifies the content by providing feedback to the source in real time.

WHAT ARE THE NEW MEDIA?

The long-term trend is to integrate the many specialized channels of communication into all-purpose digital networks that will provide access at the convenience of the audience. Familiar mass media forms such as newspapers, radio, and television are evolving into, or learning to coexist with, new forms that are all-digital, such as high-definition television (HDTV) and the World Wide Web. New interactive capabilities give users a new measure of control over the media channels they consume, where and when they consume the media, and even the content of those channels. Mass media sources are becoming more numerous and also less authoritative and professional. Messages are customized for smaller and smaller specialized audience segments, sometimes even using personal forms of address, and are narrowcast to these segments rather than broadcast to a homogeneous audience. Audiences are likewise becoming smaller and less anonymous than they were formerly, and they have improved and more expeditious means of providing feedback to the source of the media content—and even of participating in the creation of that content. In the process, the power of audiences increases as we move away from passive mass media to interactive new media.

MEDIA CONNECTION

For web links, quizzes, and key term flash cards, visit the **Student Companion Website** at http://communication.wadsworth.com/straubhaar5.

 For unlimited easy access to additional and exclusive online study, support, and research tools, log on to **1pass** at http://1pass.thomson.com using the unique access code found on your 1pass passcode card.

 The **Media Now Premium Website** offers *Career Profile* videos, *Critical View* video news clips, and *Media in Motion* concept animations. You'll also find Stop & Review tutorial questions, a sample final exam, and much more.

InfoTrac College Edition is a fully searchable online database offering anytime, anywhere access to more than 20 years' worth of articles from nearly 5,000 diverse and reliable sources.

 vMentor provides live, one-on-one online tutoring to connect you to experts who will assist you in understanding the concepts covered in your course.

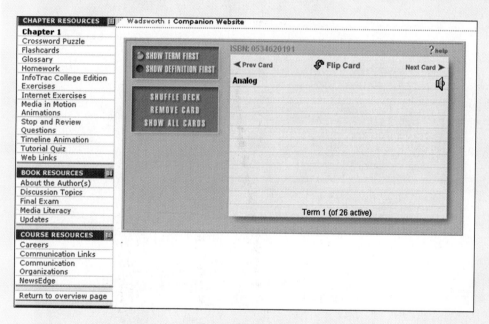

To reinforce your understanding of this chapter's Key Terms, work with its corresponding interactive Key Term Flash Cards on the Student Companion Website. You'll find them under Chapter Resources.

MEDIA AND SOCIETY

Why are there video games? Who benefits from their existence? To answer questions like these, there is nothing as practical as a good theory, or so our wise professor said. In this chapter we will begin with broad explanations of media in society. Later, in Chapter 13, we examine the media effects and social impacts that flow from the media usage and the operation of media industries that we will study here.

UNDERSTANDING THE MEDIA

Why do the media exist? Do the media shape culture or does culture shape the media? Who decides what's in the newspaper and what's important enough for a headline? What criteria do they use? There are many different answers to these questions, reflecting a wide range of assumptions about how society functions and the role of the media. When we analyze these assumptions and formulate them into models of social action or human behavior, we call them media **theories.** Here we will examine media and society: how the media help form culture, the factors that explain the existence of media institutions, the social functions that media fulfill, and how new media spread in society. In Chapter 13, we will consider why individuals use the media, and what effects the media have on us.

This chapter is organized around one of the most fundamental debates about media and society. Do the media alter the societies in which they are located or merely reflect those societies? We will begin with theories of economics and culture that strongly assert the latter and end the chapter with the opposing position, that media content and media technologies drive culture. In between, we will consider theories that occupy the middle ground, emphasizing the mutual relationship between media and culture.

Theories are general principles that explain and predict behavior.

1867	Political economy originates with the publication of Marx's *Das Kapital*	**1998**	Microsoft found guilty of anticompetitive behavior
1949	Gatekeeping is first described by White	**2000**	The Internet Bubble bursts
1962	Rogers' *Diffusion of Innovations* is published	**2004**	FCC indecency fines increase to $7.7 million (from $48,000 in 2000)
1964	McLuhan's *Understanding Media* proposes that the medium is the message	**2004**	Online political fundraising soars

MEDIA ECONOMICS

If you were to ask people who work in the media in the United States why their companies exist, probably the most frequent answer would be "to make money." Notwithstanding some important nonprofit exceptions such as Public Broadcasting, America is a capitalist society and its media institutions reflect that fact. Accordingly, the first set theories we will examine explain the media in economic terms.

Economics is a set of theories that studies the forces that allocate resources to satisfy competing needs (Picard, 2002). Economics seems to act like a force of nature. Classical economists speak of the "invisible hand" that makes societies, businesses, and individuals conform to the laws of economics. In their view, social structure, culture, and individual psychology merely reflect these economic forces. For economists, our purchase of *Rolling Stone* magazine results from a cold and calculating economic comparison of its price to the prices of competing entertainment alternatives, rather than from our passion for music. However, another group of economists, who call themselves political economists, view economic forces as the reflection of class struggle. In that view, our favorite performers and the *Rolling Stone* reporters who cover them serve major recording companies and enhance the wealth and power of their owners, who profit from the CDs we buy. We will begin with the classical economic view.

Mass Production, Mass Distribution

Throughout the history of the mass media, mass production and mass distribution have been the keys to economic success. Recalling our discussion of the historical development of the media in Chapter 1, the transition from the folk media that characterized agricultural society to the mass media associated with industrial society came about as standardized media products were distributed to ever-expanding mass markets (Figure 2.1, page 31). In this respect, the media follow an industrial economic model in which profits are reaped by producing many copies of a product at the lowest possible cost to the producer. As media companies get larger, expand their scope, and find larger audiences, they can spread the first-copy costs over more and more consumers. They reap immense profits if the production costs go down while audiences expand even if the prices charged to consumers remain stable.

Thus, all media companies constantly strive to produce media products more efficiently to reduce their costs, but large firms enjoy some natural—sometimes unfair—advantages in doing so. For example, CBS Television can better afford investments in

Economics studies the forces that allocate resources to satisfy competing needs.

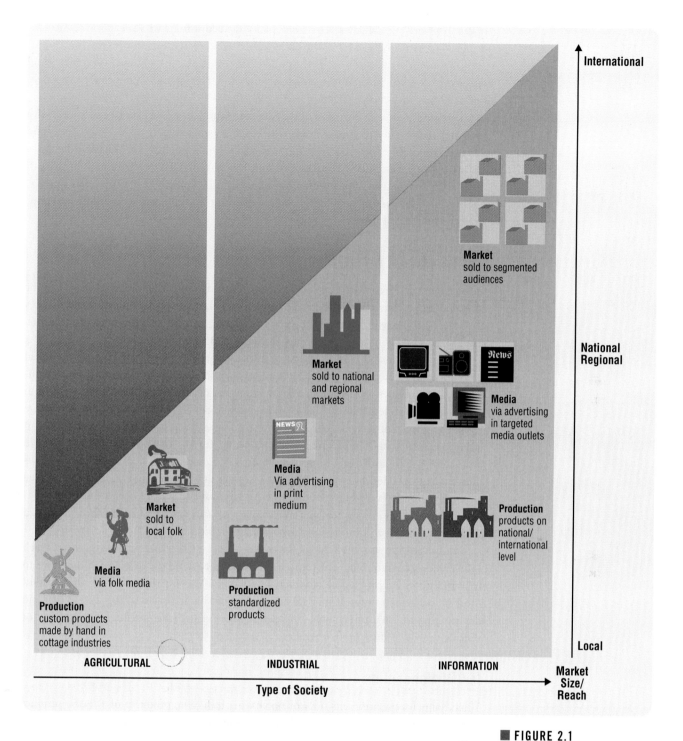

International

National Regional

Market
sold to segmented
audiences

Market
sold to national
and regional
markets

NEWS

Media
via advertising
in targeted
media outlets

Market
sold to
local folk

Media
Via advertising
in print
medium

Production
products on
national/
international
level

Media
via folk media

Production
standardized
products

Local

Production
custom products
made by hand in
cottage industries

AGRICULTURAL   INDUSTRIAL   INFORMATION   **Market Size/ Reach**

Type of Society

labor-saving technologies like computer editing for the big market television stations it owns than can family-owned, small-town television stations. That is because the large stations produce more programs and can more quickly recover the cost of the equipment from what they save on labor. Large media companies can also make bulk purchases of such mundane items as lightbulbs and copy paper to obtain substantial discounts that are not offered to smaller operations. Or media outlets may combine and slash redundant staff. In the newspaper industry, many formerly independent local papers were reorganized under common management so that a single advertising sales staff served two papers

■ **FIGURE 2.1**
Development of Mass Media
Mass media develop by building on economies of scale to reap increasing profits from larger mass markets.

instead of one. We call these efficiency measures **economies of scale.** Production efficiencies are hard to come by in the electronic media because each movie, television program, or home page is an original product. But in the electronic media the **marginal costs** are low. That is, the incremental, or marginal, cost of each additional copy is very low after that first copy is made.

Economies of scale also give big media companies an advantage when dealing with the firms that supply their operations with products and services. When CBS Television places an order for editing equipment it can make a bulk purchase on behalf of the many stations it owns, and CBS's corporate parent, Viacom, may further fatten the order with equipment for its television production units. To achieve their own economies of scale, equipment suppliers will negotiate a volume discount for CBS, while the "mom and pop" station pays the full price.

The Benefits of Competition

In the presence of competition, cost savings resulting from economies of scale may be passed along to consumers. When this happens, the **law of supply and demand** dictates that more people will consume the product, leading to further economies of scale, further improvements in production and products, and so on.

It is perhaps easiest to grasp the benefits of competition in relation to mass-produced consumer products such as color television sets. Improvements in electronics and manufacturing techniques yielded economies of scale that cut the price of a color TV set from $6000 in 1953 to less than $200 today (in today's dollars). As the price decreased, more people bought color sets, and the most efficient manufacturers earned profits to invest in larger plants and new production techniques that further lowered the costs relative to their competition and created improved products. Lower prices and improved products meant still more sales, and so on. What was a luxury item for an elite few in 1953 became a fixture in nearly every home as lower prices increased consumer demand for the product. Media such as newspapers and magazines with substantial marginal costs associated with printing each additional copy follow a similar formula.

However, competition benefits the consumer even when marginal costs are low, such as television programming distribution. For example, cable television operators have to be mindful of the prices and offerings of satellite TV companies and, to some extent, those of local video stores. If they set cable prices too high, the law of supply and demand dictates that their customers will consider signing up with the satellite TV company or visiting the video store more often.

Media Monopolies

What happens when there is little or no competition? The producer of a media product can pocket the cost savings in the form of higher profits—especially if there is no competition around to undercut the price or introduce attractive new products. In fact, why bother to become more efficient? Sometimes producers can make more money by simply raising prices, provided they are not so steep that consumers forgo making the purchase. For example, when there are two newspapers in town, they compete for subscribers by undercutting each other's prices and adding features to win new readers. But if one drives the other out of business, or if they merge, the newsstand price may rise higher than ever.

Thus, the economics of media industries can lead to ownership patterns that are not in the best interest of consumers. (Analyzing such patterns is also one of the chief con-

Economies of scale are when unit costs go down as production quantities increase.

Marginal costs are the incremental costs of each additional copy.

The law of supply and demand describes the relationship among the supply of products, prices, and consumer demand.

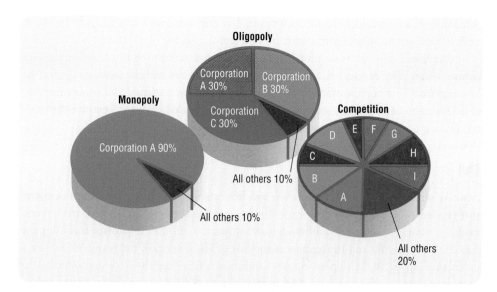

cerns of political economy, described below.) These patterns include **monopoly,** in which one company dominates an industry, and **oligopoly,** in which a few companies dominate (Figure 2.2). For example, one newspaper in town has a newspaper monopoly. New York City has three major daily newspapers—that is an oligopoly. And when there are two independent newspapers, that is a **duopoly.**

Big is not invariably bad. The greatest economies of scale should result when there is only a single provider, because the initial costs are spread among the greatest possible number of consumers (Noam, 1983). Unfortunately, big companies can behave badly when they dominate a market. They may abuse their market power to get away with underhanded tactics, such as holding back innovations like digital television because they profit from the status quo. Or they'll take profits from a business in which they enjoy monopoly dominance, such as personal computer operating system software, and use those profits to take over other competitive businesses, such as the market for Internet browser software. (Microsoft was found guilty of this.) Another abuse is to slash prices below costs to ruin smaller competitors. For example, a group owner with many radio stations in a single market may sell advertising spots for less than the local mom-and-pop radio station can afford to charge. After the giant has bankrupted (or bought up) its smaller competitor, it can raise advertising rates again to boost profits.

Similarly, monopolies and oligopolies can afford high entry costs that pose **barriers to entry** to new competitors. For example, if a mom-and-pop radio station wanted to retaliate against the big media groups by buying dozens of stations of its own, chances are they could not raise the money necessary. Large media companies can find the financing, even if they are already deeply in debt, because they have a track record with bankers and valuable assets that banks could seize. Newer, smaller entrants have few assets and inspire less confidence in investors. So, the big get bigger and the small are forced out of business, resulting in greater concentration of ownership.

When companies dominate a market, they can raise their prices—and their profits—with impunity. Some communications media are regarded as such necessities that many consumers grudgingly pay far more than the companies' actual costs. Cable television rates have consistently risen well above inflation, for example. And sometimes oligopolies forge "gentleman's agreements" to fix prices among themselves, with nearly the same effects on the consumer as a monopoly. Compact discs are an example. Discs cost record

A **monopoly** exists when one company dominates a market.

Oligopoly is when a few firms dominate.

A **duopoly** exists when two companies dominate.

Barriers to entry are obstacles companies must overcome to enter a market.

■ BUSINESSMAN OR MONOPOLIST?

The dominance of the computer industry by Microsoft Corporation, led by its chairman, William Gates, led the U.S. Justice Department to investigate him for monopoly practices.

companies less to produce than cassette tapes but cost the consumer more in the music store because a few large record companies dictate the prices.

Monopolies in communications media are especially troubling because they can also reduce the diversity of content. What if the same company owned the local newspaper, the leading local TV and radio stations, and the local cable TV franchise and commanded all of its outlets to back the same candidate for mayor? It would be very difficult for the other candidates to present their position to the people.

The Profit Motive

Now we will change our unit of analysis and examine more closely how economic forces that operate at the industry level affect individual media organizations. For privately owned media companies, everything is ultimately subordinate to the flow of **profits,** including the content of the media and the audiences they seek. The owners of the media must turn a profit after paying all their operating costs and their taxes. They also have to pay back their entry costs, the money they borrowed from banks or their investors to put their production and distribution apparatus in place, with interest. These capital costs for, say, a local newspaper include the printing presses, the newspaper building and all of the equipment and furniture in it, and a fleet of trucks to distribute the papers. Moreover, the rate of profit must match or exceed that which investors could realize if they invested in other types of businesses or just left their money in the bank (Picard, 2002). This economic pressure is so great that media sometimes compromise their public service obligations. For example, TV networks continually try to cut their news staffs to be more profitable (Auletta, 1991).

All media firms have to recoup their costs somehow. But why is there such a wide disparity in their cost to the consumer? Some media are seemingly free, such as broadcast radio and television, while newspapers charge for subscriptions by the month, and movies charge hefty admissions for a single viewing. The answer lies in the different methods the media use to recoup their first-copy costs.

First consider moviemaking, where costs are largely recovered from direct payments from the consumer. For a major film production like *Harry Potter and the Prisoner of Azkaban* the first-copy costs included the salaries for the actors and the production staff, rental of the studios and cameras, travel to the locations where the film was shot, the special effects, and all of the management overhead associated with getting the film made and shown for the public. In other words, first-copy costs include everything that goes into making the master print of the film. For this *Harry Potter* movie, these first-copy costs ran about $125 million.

All of these costs are incurred before the movie is shown in a single theater. The incremental cost for showing the movie in a second theater is minimal, about $1500 to duplicate and deliver it to each additional theater. But *Harry Potter* "opened wide" on over 3600 screens, adding another $5.5 million, and it cost another $40 million in advertising to fill the theaters.

Thus, the success of the film was not assured until all of the first-copy, marketing, and distribution costs were recovered, some $170 million in all. In the case of *Harry Potter*, box office receipts amounted to "only" $318 million in its initial theatrical run in U.S. movie theaters. That placed the film among the top 10 films of all time. However, those box office proceeds have to be split with the theater owners. So, after its United States run, *Harry Potter* was actually a flop from the studio's point of view—it lost about $10 million! But *Harry Potter* pulled in over $650 million in theaters outside the United States and promises to be one of the most popular home videos of all time—that adds another $300 million. TV networks paid another $70 million for the broadcast rights.

Profits are what is left after operating costs, taxes, and paybacks to investors.

Coca-Cola chipped in $150 million just for the right to use the film in its own advertising, and royalties from toys, video games, and other merchandising tie-ins to the film add hundreds of millions more. So, the film should net over a billion dollars for its media conglomerate parent, Time Warner.

In advertising-supported electronic media such as television, radio, and commercial websites, the cost of each additional copy is virtually zero. That is, whether one person or 20 million people view *ER,* the cost to the network is the same. So, advertising media realize profits by distributing the same product to wider and wider audiences, which generates more advertising dollars. The cost of broadcasting a program to 1000 homes is the same as broadcasting it to 2000 homes, but the value to the advertiser doubles. And so, the broadcaster can recoup the first-copy costs exclusively from advertising sales, and offer the program "free" to the viewer.

However, in the case of *ER,* each episode costs NBC $13 million. In good times, NBC can charge over $600,000 for each 30 second advertising spot, so figuring 24 spots per hour, it could realize a profit of about $1.5 million per episode. But when advertising rates fall NBC loses several million dollars per episode, although it won't reveal the actual figures. How does NBC stay in business if its top show loses money? It still might profit from the ads that the stations NBC owns in major media markets sell during *ER,* from the elevated ratings of NBC network shows that lead into *ER* on Thursday nights, or from the audiences that flow from *ER* to local newscasts on the NBC-owned local stations and to the network's late-night programs. However, NBC is also unable to profit from another very lucrative practice, selling the reruns of *ER* to local stations. That is because the show is produced by a division of another big media company, Time Warner. NBC pays a license fee to Time Warner to show *ER* episodes the first time around and for one summer of reruns. After that, the rights revert to Time Warner and it reaps the profits from the reruns. In terms of media economics, the reruns present further opportunities to offset the first-copy costs. In television, production companies sometimes take a loss on the first-run license fees, expecting to profit from the reruns.

In publishing, the first-copy costs include the salaries of all the writers and editors who prepare the stories and the preproduction workers who get them ready for the printing press. In addition, newspapers and magazines incur substantial per-unit marginal costs when they print and distribute each copy to their readers—the amount of paper and the ink consumed and the payments to delivery people rise with each copy. To offset these marginal costs, most newspapers and magazines have three revenue streams: advertising sales, subscriptions, and newsstand purchases. Advertising is usually the most important of the three, typically contributing three-fourths of newspaper revenues.

When revenues from advertisers and consumers exceed production costs, profits result. The media reinvest some of their profits to make improved products that even more consumers will want. For example, television networks invest their profits in new programs that they hope will be hits; newspaper publishers invest in color printing presses.

But profits are not always paramount. Public service media systems carry education, cultural arts, or government information. The Public Broadcasting Service (PBS) is the prime example of a not-for-profit organization in the United States. Government funds and voluntary charitable contributions cover its operating costs so it can be independent of advertisers. No profits are expected. Still, these not-for-profit media are also money-minded, they must continually raise money from grants—and from viewers like you—to cover their capital costs and operating budgets.

© Warner Bros. Courtesy Everett Collection.

■ **A FIRST-COPY COST**
The movie contract for Daniel Radcliffe, the young star of *Harry Potter and the Chamber of Secrets,* is part of the cost of making the first copy of the film.

YOUR SANDBOX

SUV

CARGO SPACE
GROUND CLEARANCE
FUEL EFFICIENCY
OFF-ROAD CAPABILITY
ON-ROAD HANDLING
AUTOMOTIVE CATEGORY
WORLD

HIGHER THAN
BMW X5
LEXUS RX330
TOYOTA HIGHLANDER
ACURA MDX
HONDA PILOT

BETTER THAN ANY
MIDSIZE SUV

INVENTED

MORE THAN A
RANGE ROVER HSE

CAR

The all-new 2005 Subaru Outback. The outstanding traction, balance and control of the Subaru Symmetrical All-Wheel Drive System, standard. Higher ground clearance. A lower center of gravity. A new suspension. The nimble handling and smooth ride of a car. The rugged off-road capabilities of an SUV. We set the bar by creating The World's First Sport-Utility Wagon. We have now raised it. The Subaru Outback. For more information on the best-selling wagon in America, see a dealer for a test-drive, visit subaru.com or call 1-800-WANT-AWD.

© 2004, Subaru of America, Inc.

SELLING THE AUDIENCE
Advertising is the major revenue source for mass media. The media sell advertising space on the basis of the size of the audience.

Syndication is rental or licensing of media products.

A copyright royalty fee is a payment for use of a creative work.

How Media Make Money

The formula for staying profitable is really quite simple. The payments received from consumers and advertisers are a company's economic base (Figure 2.3). The money from these payments must exceed the total spent on content, distribution, daily operations, taxes, and investment. Payments are made in the following forms:

- *Direct sales* occur whenever consumers pay lump sums to purchase tangible products that they can take home with them, such as compact discs. Payments are usually made to a retailer, who passes the money along to the manufacturer through intermediate distributors who restock the products in the retail stores.

- *Rentals* also involve direct payment for a tangible product, except that the consumer only borrows the product: videocassette rentals, for example. A retail outlet buys the media product from a manufacturer and recoups the purchase price by renting it.

- *Subscriptions* are payments for a continuing service rather than a single product. Newspapers, magazines, and cable companies make money this way.

- *Usage fees* include admission fees to movies or theaters and per-minute long-distance phone charges. What you "take home" is not a tangible product that you can touch, only memories of what you saw or heard.

- *Advertising* is the main economic base for most newspapers and magazines and all commercial television and radio stations. Advertisers buy commercial time or page space from the media, and the rates are set in relation to the number of people who are likely to be exposed to the ad.

- **Syndication** is the rental or licensing of content to media outlets, rather than the consumer. Newspaper cartoons and reruns of old television series are syndicated to the media outlets that distribute them locally.

- *License fees* compensate the creators of media content for the use of their original ideas. For example, songwriters receive **royalty fees** collected from radio stations that play their songs, as well as from live performances of their music, and retail sales of their recordings. The fees paid by the TV networks to the producers of the programs that are shown in prime time are another example.

- *Subsidies* are provided for communications media that society considers desirable but that commercial interests do not find profitable. PBS is subsidized by federal, state, and local taxes; contributions from corporations, private foundations and public institutions; and charitable contributions from individual viewers like you.

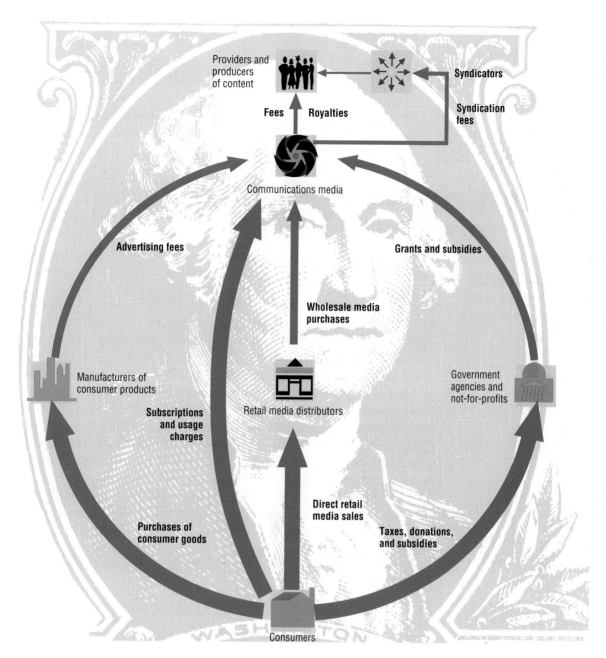

FIGURE 2.3

Media Revenue Sources There are four main ways of paying for media: advertising, direct sales, subscriptions, and public subsidies. Media organizations in turn pay the producers of the content either directly or through syndication agreements and royalty fees.

From Mass Markets to Market Segments

Economic factors also dictate the relationships between media and their audiences. From our discussion so far, it seems natural that communications media would strive for products that had the broadest possible appeal. Indeed, until recently this was the case. Now, however, technological changes and receptivity by audiences and advertisers are all encouraging media to engage in narrowcasting, to target smaller, more specific audience segments with more specialized content (Owen & Wildman, 1992). Improvements in the information available about media audiences and markets for consumer products and in the efficiency of media production and distribution brought about by information technologies have converged to make this approach profitable. Revisiting Figure 2.1 (page 31), this development marks the transition from the mass media of industrial society to the targeted media of the information society.

■ SYNDICATION
First-run syndicated programs such as *Wheel of Fortune* are sold directly to individual TV stations.

The same trend is found across the media. In television, the 1970s were a time when CBS, NBC, and ABC ruled the screen. Together, they accounted for over 90 percent of the prime-time audience, and top shows like *All in the Family* reached up to half the people watching television. Their sponsors sold mass-market products like Lay's potato chips that appealed to a broad spectrum of viewers. For the sponsors, this was a good deal—a relatively inexpensive way to present a mass-market item to a mass audience.

Now, with competition from specialized cable and satellite channels, top-rated network television shows reach only half the audience they once did, and advertisers offer a dizzying array of variations on their products. Several factors contribute to such finely grained audience segmentation. First, information technologies, such as desktop publishing, have lowered media production costs. That makes it possible to profit from smaller audiences. Second, advertisers value smaller audiences if they contain high proportions of their target market. For example, a computer software ad that appears in *Personal Computing* magazine might reach more potential computer software buyers than one that appears in *People* magazine and so *PC* is more worthwhile to the software advertiser, even though the cost of reaching each individual *People* reader (many of whom are not in the market for software) is lower. Third, sophisticated research techniques and databases of electronic consumer information make it practical to aggregate a large audience of potential customers across multiple narrowcasted media more efficiently than by making a single mass media buy (see Chapter 10). And, audiences and creative developers are gravitating toward more specialized media and consumer products. New media forms, such as music video channels, reflect new trends that excite the profit motive of media developers, advertisers, and consumers alike. Finally, media forms like the broadcast TV networks that have lost audiences to narrowcasters have had to respond with more narrowly targeted programs of their own.

New Media Economics

Popular sites on the World Wide Web and electronic commerce have pushed segmentation to a new extreme: personalization. The logic behind personalized content, customized for individuals, is similar to that of narrowcasting except the market segments shrink to specific individuals. Personalization works to the advertisers' benefit, giving them the ability to target ads very precisely to specific people who are actually in the market for their products. For example, if someone checks out a site carrying information about new computers, the next ad to pop up on their screen might be from a computer manufacturer. The conventional media can't customize to any significant degree simply because with an audience of one, the first-copy costs could never be recovered through economies of scale. Yahoo! can greet its users by name and personalize their color schemes, news topics, featured sports teams, and advertisements. A TV station attempting the same thing would have to do a separate "take" of the evening news for each audience member; change the sets, the anchors, and the stories for each one; and operate a separate transmitter and studio for each viewer! However, the print media can also personalize media to a limited degree. For example, they can print personal greetings in advertisements ("Dear Mr. LaRose, Isn't it time you bought a new computer?") and by assembling customized versions of college textbooks for individual classes.

Manufacturing has also become personalized so that products can be produced, as well as marketed, at an individual level. From a website, a consumer can select hardware and software options for her new computer from thousands of possible combinations, for immediate delivery. Machines aren't assembled until after the orders come in, yielding immense savings in parts inventories and unsold computers. A new term, mass customization, describes this process.

And when information is itself the product, the Internet challenges the basic assumptions of media economics, since reproduction and distribution costs all but disappear (Kahin & Varian, 2000). That means, in the long run, it may no longer make sense to charge for exclusive access to content as the old media do, but rather to charge only for the timeliness or convenience of information (Gilder, 2000; Odlyzko, 2001). Indeed, that would seem to be the crux of the battle between the "free downloading" style of the Internet and the pay music service approach of the music industry.

Many websites make money in proven "old media" ways—through advertising, subscriptions, direct sales of content, and usage fees—but others thrive on unique financial models. Many web pages make a living off referral fees, small payments for sending visitors to other sites as they click on ads or web links. Endorsements are fees that companies pay to be the "featured" provider of a particular product for a website's subscribers—these made AOL profitable. Other sites provide "shopping guide" information for products such as automobiles, and make money from listing fees paid by the manufacturers. Electronic commerce sites like Amazon.com are the most obvious departure (although cable shopping channels are a parallel), integrating retailing and media consumption. Auction sites like eBay return commissions on sales transactions between visitors (TV commercials that sell products through toll-free numbers also do this). And, there are interesting variations on well-established economic models; for example, Google requires advertisers to bid for prime space on the right-hand margins of their search pages whereas conventional media charge fixed rates for ads.

During the "dot-com" boom of the late 1990s, when stock market speculation drove up the value of Internet stocks, all you needed to go into business on the web was a good idea that would attract investors. Following the dot-com bust of 2000, *staying* in business once the investors' money ran out was the problem. Most online companies that remain do turn a profit, however. Some, like eBay, thrive on unique business models, whereas others target specialty products that are not readily available in all parts of the country. Retailers like JCPenney find that the combination of real-world stores (made of bricks) and online marketing (via mouse clicks) provides new revenues. We call this hybrid clicks and bricks.

Similarly, websites run by established media companies such as the *New York Times* also have an edge over those run by Internet companies such as Salon.com. The old media companies have deeper pockets to subsidize unprofitable websites, and they can recycle content that is supported by conventional media cash flows. The incremental advertising dollars from web ads help cover the cost of running the website, and the site builds audiences for a day when the Internet may be the dominant news medium. That's why the online *New York Times* is free, although the paper version costs a dollar.

What does this mean for the consumer? A look at the airline industry starts to answer that question. Airline tickets bought online can be offered at a discount because they cost a quarter as much to process as a ticket bought through a travel agent. The airline example

© David McNew/Getty Images

■ WHICH MODEL?
Arcade video games are a new media version of an old media way of making money, the usage fee.

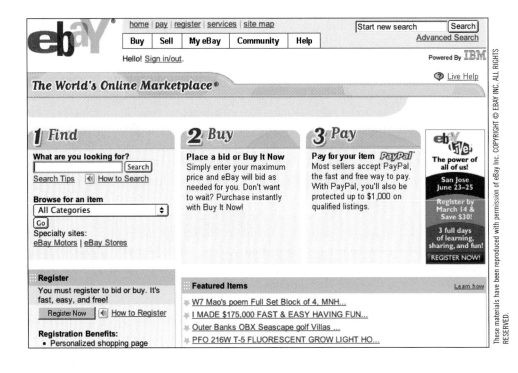

also illustrates a theory of how **electronic markets** operate on the Internet (Steinfield & Whitten, 2000). In this view, consumers gravitate to the Internet when they find that they can reduce their transaction costs, such as by avoiding the travel agent's commission and saving the time it takes to call the agent. Consumers also save on search costs. The Internet can save the hassle of driving around to car dealerships and wrangling prices out of salespeople. Instead, a single site presents all the comparative information, complete with detailed price quotes for just the options that the consumer most desires. The theory of electronic markets also predicts that intermediaries, such as car dealerships, that do nothing more than distribute products for manufacturers may eventually disappear, an effect called *disintermediation.* However, intermediaries that provide information in a way that reduces transaction and search costs should thrive, like the comparison auto shopping sites.

STOP & REVIEW

1. What are economies of scale?

2. Why is the first copy of a mass media production the most expensive?

3. What are the basic types of media ownership patterns?

4. How do the mass media make profits? Why are profits necessary?

5. What are some of the new ways that websites make money?

CRITICAL STUDIES

Electronic markets theory explains that people use e-commerce to minimize their search and transaction costs.

Critical studies examines the overall impact of media.

The economics of media in a capitalist society is only one of many theories that stress the dominance of social forces over the media. One competing theory, postmodernism (see Media and Culture: Postmodernism) argues that economic determinism is being replaced by cultural determinism. Another emphasizes the active role audiences play in interpreting content (see Chapter 13). We turn now to **critical studies,** which examines the relationship between the media and society from Marxist, feminist, ethnic, and media criticism perspectives. Generally, critical scholars believe that the media reflect culture but do not create it, or that the media merely present us with the symbols that we use to con-

Postmodernism

Modern society began with the Enlightenment in the eighteenth century. Modernity is a way of viewing the world in which reason is the source of progress and science has universal explanations for all natural phenomena. Modernity is characterized by innovation, dynamism, and seeing change as positive. It is also reflected in social institutions, such as representative forms of government, large companies, and banks. The dawn of the modern era also coincided with the Industrial Revolution, so we can think of it in terms of industrialization, the growth of science and technology, urbanization, and the evolution of mass media and culture.

Many scholars agree that in art, culture, and society we are now in a postmodern era. What is taking place is a break with modernity, both in modes of thinking and in economic and political institutions. We have moved from an era of economic determinism, in which economic phenomena determine all others, to a time of cultural determinism (Baudrillard, 1983). Now messages carried by communications technologies take on new meanings, different from or even opposed to what was originally intended. We have moved from an era of universal laws and truths based in rational science to one in which local, particularistic, subjective understandings are more important and more valid. The postmodern view is that there is no universal truth, that what you think depends on your own experience, which depends on what groups you

belong to, what media you pay attention to, what your family taught you. And what you think is equally as valid as what anyone else thinks, even if they belong to a privileged elite and carry titles like "president" or "college professor."

A corollary of this view is that developments in the information society encourage cultural fragmentation. Groups and individuals customize their own information and cultural experience so that people share very few experiences in common. According to Jean Lyotard (1984), the new media permit many new forms of expression, creating new forms of knowledge and new social formations. As more and more groups express their own ideas through proliferating multimedia channels—and even define their identities in terms of those channels—society becomes more focused on these groups and less concerned with nation states and other vestiges of the modern era.

But what comes after postmodernism, and are we already there? One can look at recent developments and conclude that instead of fragmenting into minicultures, the world is reorganizing itself for a titanic "clash of civilizations," pitting the United States and its allies against Islam. In the media realm, giant media corporations are beginning to assert themselves on the Internet in ways that may further homogenize popular culture.

struct culture. That notion originated with nineteenth-century writers, such as Ralph Waldo Emerson and Walt Whitman, who celebrated the rise of popular media that were a genuine reflection of the people. Contemporary critical scholars, such as Fernand Braudel (1994), interpret history in terms of deeper economic, psychological, and cultural factors in which great leaders, epic battles, and new media are but superficial manifestations. These perspectives focus on the need for **media literacy,** a critical understanding of media. That means that we should not just accept the media at face value, almost as if it were a natural phenomenon like the weather. We should try instead to understand the causes underlying media changes—to be literate about media. Critical studies scholars therefore call on us to be active rather than passive consumers of the media and to be skeptical about the motives and actions of the media industry. In contrast to the SMCR model introduced in Chapter 1, the critical studies approach emphasizes the feedback link and an active process in which the human receiver "decodes" the messages that the human source encodes.

Media literacy means learning to think critically about the role of media in society.

Political Economy

Political economy draws inspiration from *Das Kapital,* the classic critique of capitalist society penned by nineteenth-century political economist Karl Marx. Marx wrote that society is based on the relations between those who own the means of production (for

Political economy analyzes patterns of class domination and economic power.

© AP/Wide World Photos

■ **WHAT'S YOUR POINT?**
Do cable talk show hosts like Bill O'Reilly offer fresh perspectives or do they merely reinforce a hegemony of ideas?

example, factories and printing presses) and those who work for them. In this view, it is the owners' interests that are reflected by media and culture, because the dominant groups in a society—usually those that own the major corporations—want to create an underlying consensus, or **hegemony,** of ideology favoring their continued domination. Although consumer needs and the law of supply and demand still affect the media, they are secondary in an economic system devoted to preserving the interests of the ruling classes. In this critique, changes in technology often further the domination of a ruling class made up of those who own the industries. Today, the ruling class are media and computer entrepreneurs like Bill Gates and old media barons like Rupert Murdoch, owner of News Corp.

This analysis suggests that media reflect the interests of media owners, advertisers, and, through the advertisers' corporations, the general nature of what the people in power want said (Altschul, 1995). Thus, although we may see news reports that criticize major corporations, we seldom see anything in the media that questions the basic premise of an economy in which a few large companies maintain social dominance. Consider the recent round of bankruptcies and accounting scandals that rocked some of America's largest corporations. You may remember the many critical news stories, and well-publicized arrests of the wrongdoers. Can you recall stories that asked why a few large corporations control the economy, or that called for the overthrow of an economic system that values profits over human values? The media are unlikely to carry those stories because they depend on large corporations for advertising sales. (It is safe to criticize the evil corporations, though, because they are going out of business and won't be buying any more ads!) In addition, the same groups of people who sit on the boards of directors of major media companies also sit on the boards of other major corporations, and the banks that support them. Now the same economic class that dominates the old media is asserting control over the Internet as well (McChesney, 1996).

Even noncommercial media, such as public television, are influenced by economic interests. Public service media are supported, in part, by businesses through direct donations. Large charitable foundations, such as the Ford Foundation, that donate money to public television are controlled by the same class of people who control the large corporations. So, programs critical of large corporations or the interests of the ruling classes are largely left unmade. For example, who would fund a hard-hitting expose of corporate pollution of the environment?

Of course, media owners are not the only groups who influence what the public sees and thinks. These moguls must compete with various other interests, such as stockholder groups that demand tighter controls on corporate bookkeeping. Thus, any hegemony, or consensus of opinion, reflected in media is a potential source of group conflict (Gramsci, 1971), but usually the conflicts are resolved in favor of those who hold economic power—unless other groups organize to make their views heard and contest power. In the Enron case, the public was assured that Congress would investigate and the courts would act if there was corporate wrongdoing—and so the people in power headed off any open rebellion, or even meaningful changes in the policies that allowed the abuses to take place.

Communications media support the political and economic status quo in other ways as well. Citizens who can afford the price of a computer or even just a newspaper subscription can participate more fully in politics by reading coverage of Congress and local

Hegemony is an underlying consensus of ideology that serves the dominant groups in society.

public meetings. Unequal access remains important in the Information Age. African-Americans and Hispanics are less likely than Anglos to have phone service (Mueller & Schement, 1995) or Internet access (NTIA, 2004), making access to technology a new dimension of social stratification. The tensions arising from such inequalities do not usually undermine the underlying social order, though. Gramsci (1971) argued that the media (and educational institutions) convince the poor to accept the hegemony of ideas that keeps factory and television station owners on top of society. For example, media owners are very reluctant to air any critical coverage of policies that benefit them. During a growing public debate about limiting concentration of ownership by media corporations in 2002, major media played down the issue and only a campaign over the Internet by public interest groups forced Congress to act to pressure the FCC to not permit greater concentration.

Political economy has cultural implications as well. As commercial media reach into more societies, everyone in the world becomes aware of Coca-Cola and Nike shoes. That may affect their consumer desires and undermine ties to their traditional cultures. The growth of consumer culture is thus a key aspect of critical media theories (Featherstone, 1990). The danger is that commercial messages may impact our innermost desires and conceptions of ourselves, making us feel dependent upon the consumer products for our happiness, all the while fattening the profits of their manufacturers.

The conversion of what was once public information, such as census data, into a commodity that can be bought and sold by private companies, such as market research databases, furthers the dominance of the capitalist ruling classes (Schiller, 1996). The modification of copyright and patent laws to favor their owners is another example (Schement & Curtis, 1997). Now, the personal information that we provide to websites has also become a commodity (Campbell & Carlson, 2002). Political economists believe that such actions further reinforce a hegemony of power that acts against the interests of common citizens.

Feminist Studies

Feminist critics of the media have concerns that parallel those of political economists to some degree, but focus on the oppression of women by men rather than the oppression of the working class by the ruling class. Thus, communication media serve the purposes of the patriarchy that runs society. The oppression also has economic dimensions. Women typically earn only about two-thirds of what men make in comparable jobs, so the perpetuation of sexism in the images we see in the media benefits the owners of media organizations and fellow members of the ruling class who run corporate America.

Over the years, feminist media scholars have focused on the fact that too few women appear in the media and are limited to a few stereotypical roles (for example, housewife, nurse, secretary). We will examine those patterns of content and their impact in greater depth in Chapter 13 when we examine media effects. Here we are concerned more with the reasons why such portrayals exist. These include the underrepresentation of women as media producers and in the corporate decision structure, as well as social norms that prescribe only certain roles for women. For example, women are bombarded by advertising messages that stress their role as consumers of mass-produced goods and unrealistic ideals of feminine beauty that in turn drive sales of products targeted to women. These critiques link feminism with political economy in looking at underlying reasons for the structure and content of the media.

Feminists also take issue with the way media are targeted by gender. They argue that media for women, such as romance novels or soap operas, have been denigrated as less

■ FEMINISM ON THE LINE
Women reinvented the telephone,
converting it to an instrument of
social interaction.

serious than male-oriented spy novels. They see the pleasure women take in such media as a form of resistance to male dictates about what is enjoyable (Radway, 1984). Meanwhile, video games (Cassell & Jenkins, 1998) seem designed to alienate and exclude women and, in so doing, exclude them from the inner world of computer knowledge reserved for men. Other studies examine women's particular subjectivity or sense of interpretation of what media mean (Livingstone, 1998).

Looking at information technology, feminist scholar Lana Rakow sees the telephone as a "gendered technology" (Rakow, 1992) through which women sustain themselves as women (Moyal, 1988) but also through which they complete gendered work—work that is culturally assigned to women. According to this view, the phone is deeply embedded in a social hierarchy that relegates women to certain narrowly defined roles, such as the household "communications specialist" who maintains social relationships over the telephone. Rakow (1992) observes that the stereotype that women talk too much on the phone is a consequence of traditional female family roles. The telephone may have given women new freedom to communicate with the world beyond the home, but at the same time, the communication took place inside the home, diminishing opportunities to make new social contacts. Thus, communication technology serves the purposes of the patriarchy that runs society.

Women influence the development of technology, nonetheless. The telephone was intended as an instrument of communication for the (male-dominated) business world, and telephone companies discouraged "trivial" social use of the telephone (mostly by women) to keep the lines clear for important (that is, male-originated) business calls. However, women staged a quiet rebellion against these restrictions, forcing the redesign of the telephone system, by expanding its capacity to handle the social and other uses women made (Fischer, 1992).

Ethnic Studies

Many of the same issues apply to minority racial and ethnic groups, including African-Americans, Latinos, and Asians. Many scholars (and political groups like La Raza) have criticized media for disproportionately showing African-Americans, Latinos, and Arabs in such stereotypical roles as maids, criminals, or even terrorists. We will examine the extent of ethnic stereotyping and its consequences in Chapter 13 when we examine media effects.

Scholars like Herman Gray (1995) also critique a deeper level of structural problems with race and media. They argue that racial depictions are a form of ideology, designed to keep whiteness associated with dominance and power, while black and brown minorities are pointed toward inferior social roles. Racial disparities are also reflected in the economics of the media. Advertisers undervalue minority audiences, for example, even after correcting for income levels (Napoli, 2002). That benefits advertisers of products targeted to minorities by reducing their advertising costs. Minorities have a difficult time obtaining financing, a barrier to minority ownership in broadcasting (Braunstein, 2000). That reduces competition for white-owned media outlets serving minority communities.

Media Criticism

Another critical studies approach looks at the media as a kind of literature and applies traditions of literary criticism (Newcomb, 1992). Here, long-standing cultural conventions dictate the content of the media rather than capitalist economics or power relationships in

© Richard Sheinwald/Bloomberg News/Landov

■ **FLASH: IT'S RAINING!**
The news media perform their surveillance function by alerting us to important things going on around us, such as the approach of a hurricane.

society. This approach focuses on *genres,* categories of creative works that have a distinctive style and format, such as horror or science fiction. Over time, genres become storytelling formulas that evolve out of the interaction between producers and audiences (Allen, 1992). They transfer from one medium to another. For example, romance and adventure genres were transported from print novels to film, radio, television, and now to computer games like "Everquest" and "The Simms."

Media criticism scholars also probe for verbal and visual symbols in media (Seiter, 1992; Berger, 1992b). In this **semiotic analysis,** words, sounds, and images are interpreted individually as signs, or symbols of something other than the literal action. The sign has two components: a *concept,* or the thing signified, and a sound-image, or signifier. For example, in a *Star Trek* episode a musical theme (signifier) functions as a sign to announce that the starship *Enterprise* is about to come to the rescue (concept).

Where do symbols come from, and what makes some more powerful than others? A related approach is to look for archetypes and symbols taken from psychological theories. Analysis of media content is often seen as analogous to Freud's interpretation of dreams, since both media creators and audiences are relying on images created through psychological processes like condensation (fusing symbols together) and displacement (replacement of one symbol by another) (Freud, 1949). Other scholars draw upon the work of Carl Jung (1970), who interpreted recurring cultural themes as the expression of underlying *archetypes,* unconscious symbols of concepts like motherhood that all cultures share.

We see that the audience has a role to play in the selection of content. Media creators have to follow certain conventions and produce media that fit the expectations of their audiences. Otherwise, they risk alienating those audiences. So, the audience wields a great deal of power in the creative process.

STOP & REVIEW

1. What is a political economist?

2. How can the evening TV news create a hegemony of ideas?

3. What is the essence of the feminist critique of the media?

4. How do genres develop?

SOCIAL FUNCTIONS OF THE MEDIA

Next we turn to sociological theories that emphasize the mutual dependence of media and society. These theories represent a middle ground between cultural determinism and technological determinism. The first such theory, **functionalism,** states that society cannot function without the media, but also the media exist to serve the needs of our society and our cultures.

Semiotic analysis describes how meaning is generated through the "signs" used in media "texts."

Functionalism examines the social functions media fulfill.

What Are the Media's Functions?

We have to keep track of what is going on around us—sociologists call this surveillance. We have to correlate and interpret those events and what they mean—this is the process of interpretation. We have to transmit values from one generation to another in order to maintain society. And we need and want to be entertained and amused (Wright, 1974).

Surveillance   Certain media specialize in providing information to help people with their surveillance of the environment, alerting them to important events that affect them directly, from stock market dives to approaching storms—newspapers and CNN, for example. We also use the telephone and electronic mail to keep up with what is going on in our personal lives. The World Wide Web is a powerful surveillance tool, because its users can seek out information on topics of interest rather than passively waiting for the media to bring it to them.

Interpretation   Information is not of much use until it is processed, interpreted, and correlated with what we already know. We ourselves, the groups we belong to, and the media all contribute to this process. The newspaper editorial page helps us interpret the headlines, *60 Minutes* tells us why a crisis developed, and Internet newsgroups comment upon and interpret current events and social trends.

Values Transmission/Socialization   One of the most important functions of culture is to pass ideas from one generation to another. Anthropologists observe that as soon as human beings had language, they were using it to pass on ideas to their children. Today the media have assumed the roles of storytellers, teachers, and even parents. For example, textbooks like this one pass along concepts about the media to a new generation of students. But this function is not limited to media with an obvious educational or informational purpose, such as *Sesame Street*. The newest *Star Wars* movie series teaches the values of loyalty and friendship to young moviegoers, lessons that their parents may have learned from the first *Star Wars*.

Entertainment   The media also entertain. With the exception of magazine-style information programs such as *60 Minutes,* the top 10 programs on network television have always been entertainment oriented. Newspapers complement their news and commentary with entertaining diversions on the sports and lifestyle pages. Americans spend enormous amounts of time and money going to feature films, listening to music, watching television comedies, and, now, "surfing" the Internet just for fun.

New Media Functions

Do new media have new functions? In particular, the Internet has attracted attention for its function in building and maintaining new "virtual" communities, even cultures. And now information is interpreted and correlated *by* us through the Internet instead of *for* us by the conventional mass media. For example, political discussion groups like alt.politics often come up with their own interpretations of the day's events, which are not found in any mainstream electronic media. The Internet has become an all-purpose medium through which virtually any societal function can be performed: completing commercial transactions, providing social support, treating the ill, and delivering government services.

Shaping the News

Another theory grounded in sociology is *agenda setting*. It examines the relationship between the events of the day, the decisions of media professionals, and media content, with a special emphasis on the content of the news. It analyzes the important role played by media editors and so may be placed a little further along the continuum of cultural determinism versus technological determinism than the theories that preceded it.

Agenda Setting

In an election year, who sets the public agenda: the candidates or the media? Some figures, like the president, can routinely command media attention. The media tend to focus on those countries and those issues that the president is talking about, visiting, negotiating with, or fighting (Gandy, 1982). Other public figures and interest groups try to set the agenda by harping on an issue in their public statements, but they succeed only if their words are picked up in the news. Other times, the media set the agenda for the candidates. For example, extensive coverage of human rights abuses by American soldiers put the Iraqi prison scandal on the agenda in 2004. Thus, agenda setting bestows political power on the media. Agenda setting theory also describes how media coverage affects public opinion. We will consider that aspect when we examine media effects in Chapter 13. However, the media are not all-powerful. For example, the media's constant harping on the Clinton-Lewinsky scandal had no effect on the president's approval ratings, perhaps because adultery was not a highly relevant issue for the public (Yioutas & Segvic, 2003). Or, the new media environment, with its many competing (and sometimes unprofessional) voices may be undermining the power of the "old media" to set the public agenda (Williams & Carpini, 2004).

■ **SETTING THE AGENDA**
Presidents command so much attention from the press that they can define the important issues of the day, setting the agenda of public debate.

Gatekeeping

How do the media set the agenda? The gatekeeping theory (White, 1949; Shoemaker, 1991) emphasizes the crucial role of the so-called gatekeepers, the media executives who can either open or close "the gate" on a story. For example, in 1998, ABC Television developed a story about lax personnel procedures at Disneyland, alleging that child molesters were being hired into the Magic Kingdom. The president of ABC News acted as a gatekeeper when he pulled the story, perhaps fearing that his corporate masters (Disney Corporation also owns ABC) would object.

Gatekeepers can squelch new ideas and suppress the news of events that others might find important. For example, if an editor decides not to send a camera crew to a public protest against environmental policy, she excludes the views of the "green" activists from the public debate. However, media outlets compete with each other for audiences, so the gatekeeping actions of any one news editor are unlikely to have much impact. Gatekeepers get fired if they leave out too many stories that their viewers want to see and that the competition is willing to show them. So, the consensus that forms among editors to keep certain stories in the news while excluding others may bias the public agenda and reinforce a hegemony over ideas.

Framing

A related theory examines how writers *frame* a story (Atheide, 1974; Gitlin, 1983). Reporters decide what to include within the view, or frame, of a story and what to leave out, much as a painter chooses what to put in the frame of a painting. They must decide not only what facts to put in but also what conceptual framework to put them in, what context to include, and how to interpret the facts. For example, instead of killing the Disneyland story, ABC might have omitted the child molester issue and framed the story as a critique of the theme park's hiring practices. In colloquial terms, all these decisions affect the "spin," or bias, of the story.

Where do frames come from? French media critic Pierre Bourdieu (1998) contends that even in countries where there is supposedly freedom of expression, there is invisible self-censorship. Journalists realize what is permissible and pre-edit their own work to be consistent with those perceived norms—if they wish to remain employed. For example, news producers at ABC "just know" they should avoid stories about animated movies that are not produced by their corporate parent, Disney.

Are the Media Biased?

Interestingly, both conservative and liberal critics of the U.S. media accuse them of having a biased frame of reference. For example, conservative critics complain that most reporters are Democrats, that Hollywood films tend to make military figures and businesspeople look bad, and that popular records undermine the morals of our youth. Liberals insist that media ignore underlying social problems such as poverty and ignorance in favor of safer human interest and crime stories that bolster ratings. For their part, most journalists would deny that they are biased in either direction. Instead, they would insist that they are objective observers who adhere to the ethical precepts and standards of their profession (see Chapter 15).

DIFFUSION OF INNOVATIONS

Another theory with its roots in sociology helps us understand why people adopt new communication behaviors (Rogers, 1995). **Diffusion** is a process by which an innovation—a new way of doing things—is communicated through media and interpersonal channels over time among the members of a community.

For example, researcher Everett Rogers (1986) (see Profile of Everett Rogers, page 49) observed that VCRs diffused very quickly in the United States, going from 1 percent of American households in 1980, to 20 percent in 1985 (to 85 percent in 2000). Prices are important in diffusion. VCR prices declined rapidly, from $2200 in 1975 to under $100 in 2004, which made VCRs more accessible. Now DVDs are rapidly replacing VCRs, following a similar pattern. As a general rule, all new technologies follow a similar price pattern: the first few units sold cost 10 or more times as much as the last units sold, a direct consequence of the economies of scale discussed earlier in this chapter.

Why Do Innovations Succeed?

How quickly an innovation diffuses depends on several other factors besides their cost. What are the relative advantages of the new idea compared to existing ways of doing things? How compatible is it with existing ways of doing things? How complex is a new technology to operate? How easy is it to try out the new way before committing a lot of time or money to it? Can people observe others using the innovation successfully? Information that we acquire from the media and from observing others form our expectations of how it will perform for us, persuading us to adopt it or not.

Diffusion is the spread of innovations.

■ EVERETT ROGERS

The Most Widely Cited Social Scientist

Name: Everett Rogers

Education: Ph.D., Iowa State University, 1957

Position: Professor, University of New Mexico, Department of Communication and Journalism

Style: Casually collegiate; sports jacket, no tie

Most Notable Achievement: His work on the diffusion of innovations is widely recognized both within and outside the field of communications studies; it is the most widely cited work in social science.

Most Dubious Achievement: His early work on diffusion in developing countries was criticized for promoting the interests of developed nations and ruling elites at the expense of the peasants, a position that he has since modified in favor of a "grassroots-up" approach to development of communication.

Entry Level: After getting his Ph.D., Dr. Rogers first taught at Iowa State, then Ohio State, and then at Michigan State University's Department of Communication.

His Inspiration: During his time in Iowa, he learned of 1940s studies of how new varieties of seed corn spread from farm to farm. He realized that the same principles might apply to innovations of all types.

How He Got to the Top: Success came through the two things that major universities value most: numerous scholarly publications and lucrative grants. The number of times other scholars cite one's work is another way of "keeping score" in academia. Citations indicate how influential one's work is, and it is here that Ev, as he is known, reigns supreme. And, oh yes, teaching counts too. Additionally, he is a world-renowned lecturer, and he has also advanced his career through a series of appointments at prestigious universities, including Michigan State University, Stanford, and the Annenberg School for Communication at the University of Southern California.

In Memoriam: Everett Rogers passed away in October, 2004.

VCRs scored very high on all these counts. The VCR offered a clear expansion of viewing options, was compatible with both television hardware and home video "software," was similar in concept to older tape recorder technology, and was easy to use (except perhaps for time-delayed recording). And by the mid-1980s most people had a chance to watch family and friends using them.

Factors other than the attributes of the innovation affect diffusion of innovations. One is the amount of previous experience people have had with similar technologies. For example, among the first people to use portable cellular telephones in their cars were those who had already used mobile radios. Some people are naturally more innovative than others and may be more inclined than others to try out new gadgets. Social norms play a role. Cellular phones went from being associated with blue-collar delivery truck drivers, to being chic for executives, to being a fashion accessory for teens.

How Do Innovations Spread?

Diffusion of new communication technology goes through a predictable sequence of stages. First, we gain knowledge about the new idea from the media and from people we know. For example, we may read about new e-books in an electronics magazine or see our

■ **FAILURE**
Not all innovations succeed. Apple's early personal data assistant product, *Newton,* failed to catch on because of a faulty handwriting-recognition program.

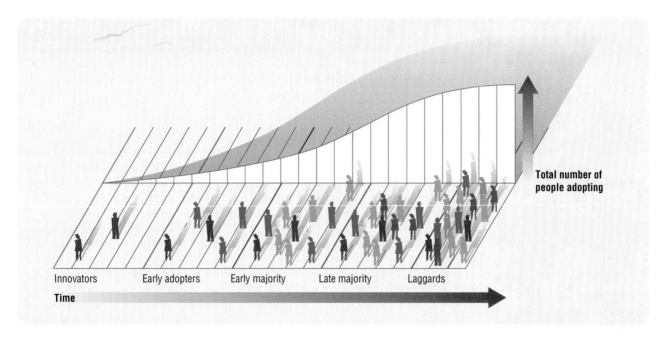

Total number of
people adopting

Innovators   Early adopters   Early majority   Late majority   Laggards

Time

■ FIGURE 2.4

Diffusion Some people adopt new ideas earlier than others. The majority of people tend to adopt only after innovators and early adopters have forged the way.

classmate use one. Then we weigh the merits. Does it cost too much? How much do we need the lecture notes that are available only in the e-book version? Finally, we decide to try it and make our purchase. Afterward, we continue to reassess our experience with the innovation and either confirm, reject, or modify our use of it. We may find that our own handwritten lecture notes are more useful than the e-book's and regret our purchase. In other words, we decide which innovations to pursue according to the expected outcomes of our adoption decision, and we then continually monitor the fulfillment of those expectations.

People do not adopt new ideas at the same rates (Figure 2.4). Those who first use an innovation are called *innovators.* People who follow up on innovative ideas through specialized media such as trade journals or interpersonal contacts are early *adopters.* Those who join the trend as it begins to go mainstream make up the early majority. Those who wait to see what most people are going to do constitute the late majority. Those who wait until the very end are called laggards. If your family's first VCR was purchased in the mid-1970s, you were innovators. If you still don't have one, you are lagging behind the majority of the population, at least when it comes to consumer electronics innovations. That's nothing against you—you may be an innovator when it comes to music or fashion.

Interactive communication technologies diffuse in a characteristic way. First, a certain minimum number, or critical mass, of adopters is necessary for it to be useful enough for most people to go along with the trend (Lin, 2003). E-mail is a good example. What good was e-mail to the first two Internet users in 1969? They couldn't send messages to their family or friends. E-mail spread very slowly at first. Now over two-thirds the population has e-mail, so it is very useful.

Since information technologies are relatively flexible tools, they tend to be used in new, unanticipated ways by their adopters. Rogers (1986) called this reinvention. For instance, early adopters of home computers were attracted by educational software for children. Once the children had them, they used them to play computer games instead. Now the personal computer is being reinvented again, as a tool to send electronic mail and access information on the Internet. Thus, in its emphasis on the attributes of innovations, the diffusion of innovations approach may initially seem technologically deterministic, but it also stresses the ability of people and their cultures to act as counter influences in the spread of innovations.

TECHNOLOGICAL DETERMINISM

Now we arrive at the opposite end of the continuum from cultural determinism. Some social critics maintain that communications media change everything else in society. In this view, technology drives social change, so it is sometimes called **technological determinism.** Variations on this theme stress the social effects of media messages and the technological culture that gives rise to them.

The Medium Is the Message

The most famous media technological determinist, Marshall McLuhan, argued that print (*The Gutenberg Galaxy,* 1962) and electronic media (*Understanding Media,* 1964) were truly revolutionary, an idea captured in his famous aphorism "The medium is the message." He proposed that new communication technologies determine culture and that it is the form of the media rather than their content that matters. For example, in McLuhan's view, the invention of the printing press led to the rise of the scientific method, and later to our technological society, by forcing thinkers to put their words in linear order and their arguments in a logical progression—just like the words on a printed page. This led to thinking about the natural world in the same linear fashion, instilling the notion that it, too, had a beginning and an end, causes and effects.

McLuhan did not live to witness the Internet, but he coined a phrase that perhaps describes it well. The *global village* draws the entire world together into an electronically mediated small town. "By electricity we everywhere resume person-to-person relations as if on the smallest village scale" (McLuhan, 1964, p. 255). When he wrote that in the 1960s, he was thinking of broadcast television and the telephone, long before the Internet—or CNN—was a reality.

© Bernard Gottfryd/Getty Images

■ THE MEDIUM IS THE MESSAGE
Marshall McLuhan, the late communication scholar, argued that the way we think is determined by the nature of the media we consume.

Technology as Dominant Social Force

Others focus on social systems and worldviews that promote technology and dominate culture. Neil Postman (1992) argued that computers foster *technopoly,* in which technology is deified and extends its control to all aspects of life. Technopoly compounds the excesses of *technocracy,* in which the scientific method is applied by experts to technology for the improvement of life, but also to the destruction of culture.

Similarly, French sociologist Jacques Ellul (1990) argued that the pursuit of technological improvement led to the social dominance of an elite of scientists, engineers, and managers for whom technology became an end in itself, devoid of moral foundation. But for Ellul, the technologists' efforts were ultimately ineffective. Technology is a bluff in his words. Technologists promise a great deal to ensure their status in a society conditioned to welcome technological progress. But, they deliver very little, not even a truly satisfying evening's entertainment on TV, an effective magazine ad, or a true relationship on the Internet.

Media Drive Culture

Other views emphasize media content over technology. In the early nineteenth century, the so-called English School, led by Matthew Arnold, held that people moving from the countryside into the cities would become refined by coming in contact with "high culture" media such as the ballet and the opera. Implicit was the idea that media should

Technological determinism explains that the media cause changes in society and culture.

exist to educate, not entertain, a point echoed by some present-day critics, such as Neil Postman (1992).

Instead, Theodore Adorno (Horkheimer & Adorno, 1972) argued that mass-produced cultural goods of low quality replaced high culture and traditional folk culture. If people were easily entertained by pop music, would they ever attend a classical opera? As mass audiences consumed popular culture, would everyone begin to think and act alike? For example, they might believe that the antiseptic 1950s family portrayed in *Leave It to Beaver* was a realistic model for their own family (Real, 1989). Another view is that mass media overwhelm the "true" culture of the people in the interest of perpetuating class hegemony (Carey, 1972). Neil Postman argued that literacy and reasoning skills decline as a result of overexposure to popular culture. In his words, we are "amusing ourselves to death" (Postman, 1986).

In Chapter 13 we examine media effects research in some depth, another perspective associated with technological determinism. Does the violence on TV cause violence in society? Do the stereotyped portrayals of women and minorities found throughout the media reinforce sexism and racism? Do ads for commercial products and political candidates influence our behavior as consumers and citizens? These are all questions of the effects that the media have on us as individuals that, collectively, affect our culture.

As we learn more about the relationship between media and society, scholars continue to debate which perspective is most valid. Throughout *Media Now* we try to present both sides of the debate so that you, the reader, can decide for yourself which is the best explanation.

STOP & REVIEW

1. Give examples of gatekeepers.
2. What are the main social functions of the mass media?
3. Using the "diffusion of innovations" paradigm, explain how the use of VCRs spread through society.
4. How does technological determinism differ from cultural determinism?

SUMMARY AND REVIEW

HOW DO ECONOMICS INFLUENCE THE MEDIA?

First-copy costs in mass media entail virtually all the investment in the production of a work. Examples are the master print of a film or the printing plates from which newspapers are printed. Economies of scale occur when manufacturers make so many copies of something that they learn how to make each of those copies more cheaply. By the law of supply and demand, cheaper copies can reach far more people, creating a broader audience. Producers want to spread production costs and also their entry costs—the initial costs of establishing a media enterprise—across a broad audience in order to increase profits and satisfy their investors.

WHY IS MEDIA OWNERSHIP IMPORTANT?

Media can be structured as monopolies, where one company dominates the industry; as oligopolies, where a few companies dominate; or in competition, where a number of companies vie for dominance. The patterns of ownership have a great deal to do with the diversity and nature of the media's content, their availability and accessibility to people, and their role in society. Generally speaking, the more the ownership of media is concentrated in the hands of a few, the less diverse and more expensive the media are.

WHAT ARE THE SOURCES OF MEDIA REVENUE?

Most revenues come directly from the end user of media products. Direct sales of media products occur when consumers pay out a lump sum and take a tangible media product home with them, such as a CD. Rentals also involve a payment for a tangible product, except that the consumer pays only to borrow it, as in a videotape rental. Subscriptions permit newspapers and magazines to be sold on a continuing basis over time for a standard fee. Usage fees are charged for access to intangible media products, such as movie theater admissions and telephone calls, that consumers can't literally take home. The media collect advertising revenues by selling access to their audiences to advertisers, who in turn pay for advertising by charging higher prices to consumers.

WHAT IS THE ROLE OF PUBLIC SUBSIDIES?

Public subsidies, from either voluntary contributions or taxes, are provided for socially desirable content that commercial interests do not find it profitable to provide. The educational and cultural programs on the Public Broadcasting Service (PBS) are prime examples.

WHAT IS SEGMENTATION?

Technological changes, industry changes, and receptivity by audiences and advertisers are all encouraging media to segment their audiences, that is, to focus on smaller, more specific audiences with more specialized programs or contents. The targeting of media content to appeal to the tastes of a particular narrow audience segment is called narrowcasting.

WHAT ARE THE NEW MEDIA ECONOMICS?

The Internet takes segmentation to its logical conclusion by personalizing content and ads for individual users and by facilitating a new form of industrial production known as mass customization. Sites on the Internet make money in new ways through referral and listing fees and endorsements. New forms of economic support come from electronic commerce and auctions. Internet companies have extremely low barriers to entry compared to conventional electronic media. Electronic commerce sites succeed by reducing search and transaction costs for their users.

HOW DO POLITICAL ECONOMISTS EXPLAIN MEDIA?

Social structure is determined by efforts of dominant classes to maintain their wealth and power. The dominant class in society uses its ownership of the media to influence their content. This class creates a consensus, or hegemony, of ideas that reinforces its position of dominance. In this view, maintaining class dominance is furthered by the profitability of media enterprises. This tends to keep media content within the bounds of this hegemonic set of ideas.

WHAT DO FEMINIST AND ETHNIC STUDIES CONTRIBUTE?

The sex-role and ethnic stereotypes that appear in the media may be there for a reason: to perpetuate the dominance of white males in society.

WHAT IS SEMIOTICS?

Semiotics is a systematic way of looking at media content to examine the symbols and signs contained in it. The signs in media communicate something of symbolic value to the audience; they include visual images, music, camera angles, words, and so on. The producer creates or encodes a meaning into the sign, but the audience may decode or interpret a different meaning.

WHAT ARE GENRES?

In media content, formulas, or genres, evolve over time. These formulas are things like soap operas, mystery novels, and action cartoons. They represent an agreement between producer and audience on what kinds of stories ought to be told and how, or on how a music video ought to look, or on how a talk show host ought to act.

WHAT ARE AGENDA SETTERS AND GATEKEEPERS?

Agenda setters from government, businesses, and political interest groups try to influence what the media cover and what "spin" media give to that coverage. Within the media themselves, a variety of media professionals make decisions about what goes into and what stays out of news and entertainment media. They are the gatekeepers.

WHAT SOCIAL FUNCTIONS DO MEDIA SERVE?

Among the functions sociologists have identified for communications media are surveillance (keeping track of our world or environment), interpretation (making sense of what we learn), value transmission (passing values on from one generation to the next), and entertainment.

HOW DO NEW MEDIA SPREAD?

New technologies spread like a disease, from person to person, slowly at first but gradually picking up speed. People consider an innovation's relative advantages, its compatibility with existing practices, its complexity, and any opportunities they have to observe the innovation in action before they try it out themselves. Some people are innovators, some are early adopters, followed by the majority of adopters, late adopters, and laggards. Interactive technologies seem to require a critical mass of users before large numbers will adopt it.

WHAT IS TECHNOLOGICAL DETERMINISM?

Technological determinists argue that changes in society and culture are driven by advances in media technology and by the content of the media to a large extent. They oppose the view of cultural determinists, who maintain that culture determines the nature of the media and their content.

MEDIA CONNECTION

For web links, quizzes, and key term flash cards, visit the **Student Companion Website** at http://communication.wadsworth.com/straubhaar5.

 For unlimited easy access to additional and exclusive online study, support, and research tools, log on to **1pass** at http://1pass.thomson.com using the unique access code found on your 1pass passcode card.

 The **Media Now Premium Website** offers *Career Profile* videos, *Critical View* video news clips, and *Media in Motion* concept animations. You'll also find Stop & Review tutorial questions, a sample final exam, and much more.

 InfoTrac College Edition is a fully searchable online database offering anytime, anywhere access to more than 20 years' worth of articles from nearly 5,000 diverse and reliable sources.

vMentor provides live, one-on-one online tutoring to connect you to experts who will assist you in understanding the concepts covered in your course.

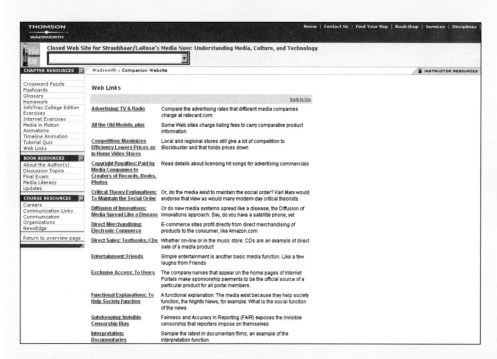

The Student Companion Website provides live, maintained and updated links for all web resources mentioned in the chapter. You'll find them under Chapter Resources.

What is the latest vibe? This chapter examines the development of books and magazines, from manuscripts hand-copied by medieval monks to the current proliferation of custom printed books, and from early mass market magazines to online publications that exist for only a few readers in cyberspace.

HISTORY: BEFORE AND AFTER GUTENBERG

The history of the print media is a continual cycle of technological innovation, followed by competition between new forms and uses of media, increased consumer demand, growing literacy, and changes in society wrought by media. (See Media Then/Media Now, page 58.)

Early Print Media

Technology facilitates publishing and influences what formats are possible in media, but it does not define their contents. For example, **novels,** book-length fictional works, flourished with printing because mechanical reproduction allowed quantities of books to be produced less expensively. However, the concepts and forms that characterize the novel originated much earlier: Greek poets produced epic works such as the *Odyssey* (Homer, 800 B.C.E.). And the Japanese *Tale of Genji,* recognizable as a novel by current standards, was written by Lady Murasaki Shikibu in the eleventh century. Thus, the antecedents of novels about daily life, romances, mysteries, and horror or terror existed well before the advent of printing.

Novels are extended fictional works usually of book length.

700 Arab traders introduce paper to the West

1234 Movable metal type invented in Korea

1455 Gutenberg Bible published

1641 First book published in the American colonies

1731 First magazine published

1846 Rotary press (type on cylinder) invented in the United States

1860 Heyday of the dime novel begins (through 1880)

1900 Magazine muckraking reporting popularized

1923 *Time* magazine introduced

1950s Advertising shifts from magazines to television

1980s Desktop publishing begins

1998 Digital Millennium Copyright Term Extension Act enacted

2004 Google and others put book contents on line

The early development of writing, paper, and printing took place in the Middle East and China. In 105 C.E. the Chinese began making paper from rags, but it was not until 700 C.E. that Arab traders brought this new technology to the West. Earlier, during the T'ang Dynasty in China (618—906 C.E.), Chinese printers used wooden blocks to print characters, and then developed movable clay type in 1000 C.E. The Koreans further refined the printing process by developing *movable metal type* in 1234. However, these inventions did not spawn a large printing industry. Printing did not evolve further until 1455 C.E. when Johannes Gutenberg of Germany (re)discovered movable type (Carter, 1991).

Until Gutenberg's press, books were a limited medium throughout the world because they had to be hand-copied. For thousands of years, printed materials were available only to the few best-educated people in society, such as the Mandarin bureaucratic elite of China. Few people in the early civilizations of Greece, Egypt, China, Islam, and Rome were literate or had access to libraries.

Reading and writing were initially the job of clerks and priests. For instance, in Europe, monks often devoted their lives to copying text and creating beautiful illustrations by hand. Some surviving examples, among them the Irish *Book of Kells,* (800 C.E.), are considered major works of art today. Books tended to build on earlier *oral traditions;* for instance, early Greek epics such as the *Iliad* (800 B.C.E.), medieval European literature such as Icelandic sagas, and the folk stories and fairy tales collected by the brothers Grimm.

A key development in print media was the growth of **literacy** in Europe, fueled by the distribution of books in the everyday language spoken by most people in a particular region, such as Italian or Swedish. Prior to 1100, written communication was nearly always in Latin, the language of the Roman Catholic Church. Thus, to be literate, people had to learn a second language. By the 1200s, written versions of daily languages were more common, and as a result literacy became more commonplace in the 1300s and 1400s among the political elite, the commercial and trading class, and such professionals as the sea captain Christopher Columbus. Outside this group, though, most people remained illiterate.

Throughout the Middle Ages in Europe, few books other than the Bible and religious or philosophical commentaries were available for people to read. This began to change by the 1300s and 1400s. Universities were established to train more people as clergy and clerks. A number of the most important books that were printed and circu-

Literacy is the ability to read and understand a variety of information.

lated in Europe came from the Hebrew Middle East (the Bible, the Torah) or the Arab Middle East (books on science, math, astronomy, and navigation). Many came from ancient Greece also: classic works of science, literature, and philosophy, such as Plato's *Republic,* which influenced European ideas of government. Reproducing these classic works gave a greater number of people access to ideas from books that had survived in hand-copied form for centuries. For instance, in the late 1400s, Christopher Columbus learned from an Arab book on geography that he might be able to reach India and Southeast Asia by sailing west across the Atlantic Ocean. People such as Columbus probably would not have had access to such books one hundred years earlier. Clearly, the European explosion of print technology and printed contents built on a much larger world context.

The Gutenberg Revolution

The Gutenberg Bible was published in 1455, the result of Johannes Gutenberg's development of movable type and mechanical printing five years earlier. These presses were technology breakthroughs that made new forms of mass production possible—they could print many more books, handbills, and newsletters at a much lower cost. For example, by 1470 a French printed Bible cost one-fifth of what a hand-copied manuscript had cost. As the new technology gained momentum, printing and reading became a cyclical process that reinforced itself. As more people had sufficient money and interest to buy books, book production increased and benefited from **economies of scale,** which made individual books cheaper (see Chapter 2). That permitted even more people to buy books. (See Media and Culture: Goodbye, Gutenberg, page 60.)

The Bible, prayer books, and hymn books were among the earliest publications. Beyond the Bible and religious pamphlets, new products were often more entertainment oriented and aimed at broader groups of people with less education. *Broadside ballads* were single sheets of words for popular songs, whereas *chapbooks* were cheaply bound books or pamphlets of poetry, ballads, or prose that were aimed at a broader audience, much like current small-format paperbacks. Libraries provided one means of popularizing books and making them more accessible to the public. Sir Thomas Bodley started the first modern lending library of printed books in 1602 in Oxford, England. Years later, as printing and binding costs continued to decline and thus make books more affordable, publishers began to distribute books directly to the public by selling them through bookstalls in railway stations. Thus, book publishing accelerated rapidly: two million titles were issued worldwide in the 1700s and eight million in the 1800s. By 1900, a best-selling novel could sell 600,000 copies in the English-speaking world (Dessauer, 1981).

The First American Print Media

In America, also, print media began with copies of religious books. The *Bay Psalm Book* was the first book published in America, printed in 1640 by the Puritans in Massachusetts on the first press that the English brought to the colonies. Soon thereafter came newspapers in Boston, New York, and Philadelphia (see Chapter 4), magazines, and nonreligious books such as **almanacs.**

One of the more influential publishing figures in the American colonies was Benjamin Franklin, a major innovator in printing, science, politics, and practical inventions. As a

■ **HANDMADE**
Among the earliest books were illuminated manuscripts, carefully created by hand.

Economies of scale are when unit costs go down as production quantities increase.

Almanacs are book-length collections of useful facts, calendars and advice.

Goodbye, Gutenberg

Did reading change the way our brains work? Marshall McLuhan thought so. In *The Gutenberg Galaxy: The Making of Typographic Man* (1962), he argued that reading led to a new "typographic man," to a more linear way of thinking, more about cause and effect, more freed from the constraints of our immediate environment. For example, life before widespread literacy was dominated by a cyclical relationship to the environment, the immediate cycle of daylight that dictated when you worked and when you slept, and the longer pattern of what you did on a farm in a certain season. After reading became widespread, people were more likely to be interested in things outside their local community, more likely to look for larger patterns of cause and effect, and more likely to see the environment as something they could control, not something they obeyed. At a more social level, readers were more likely to identify with people and issues beyond their immediate communities. In another book, *The Imagined Community,* Benedict Anderson argued that reading was largely responsible for the development of nationalism, the intense individual identification with their nations that enables those countries to command such loyalty that people are willing, even excited to go to war. Anderson traced such individual passion for the nation to the experience of reading the same novels and newspapers across the breadth of the national territory, so that people began to imagine themselves as part of a larger community defined by all the people reading the same things.

In a later 1967 book, *The Medium Is the Message,* McLuhan observed that electronic media had further changed most people to a new sort of orientation, not based on the typographical logic, but focused instead on decoding and understanding television. Some studies of learning in the United States and Germany among young people seem to show new patterns in which many children who are not good

© Bettmann/Corbis

■ **GUTENBERG'S PRESS**
Printed books helped people identify with nations.

at reading are in fact sophisticated at learning from computer games and television screens with complex arrays of numbers and images (Bachmair, 2003). However, typographical man still has many advantages in our society. People who are good at deep involvement and comprehension in reading still tend to do better in school, particularly college, which is still the main avenue to the best paying jobs in our society. It may be some time before people can really function well as adults in an information society without still being competently typographic.

printer, Franklin constantly experimented to see what kinds of print media would find an audience. In 1732 he published one of America's first successful nonreligious books, *Poor Richard's Almanack,* which contained moral advice, farming tips, and a variety of other information. Franklin's almanac urged American colonists to work hard to get ahead, so much so that when Max Weber looked for classic texts of how Protestant values promoted capitalist industry when writing his own classic, *The Protestant Ethic and the Spirit of Capitalism,* he often quoted Franklin. Almanacs, along with educational primers, religious books, and law books, were among the most popular books in the colonies. Franklin and other book printers also produced political pamphlets. Thomas Paine's *Common Sense* (1776), which urged readers to support independence from Great Britain, sold 100,000 copies in 10 weeks.

In 1731 Franklin also started the first **subscription library** in the future United States, beginning an American tradition in which lending libraries greatly helped popularize book reading. Still, the high cost of books and the difficulty of gaining access to them aided the rise of less expensive newspapers and magazines.

Early Magazines   *Magazines* began to develop in Great Britain in the 1700s. They carried fiction and nonfiction in varying degrees, depending on the readership. The first was the British *Gentleman's Magazine* of 1731, whose editors deliberately left news to the papers and focused on elegant and amusing writing about literature, politics, biography, and criticism (Riley, 1993). This formula still characterizes much of magazine content: a periodical weekly or monthly selection of humor, fiction, and essays about politics, literature, music, theater, and famous people.

The first American magazines debuted in 1741 in Philadelphia, the nation's first center for magazines. William Bradford's *American Magazine* lasted for three months, and Ben Franklin's *General Magazine and Historical Chronicle* for six months. Publishers tried to popularize several other short-lived magazines prior to the American Revolution, but all were limited by too few readers and writers and by the high costs of publishing and distribution.

During the American Revolution, from 1775 to 1789, many magazines took a more political tone. For example, Thomas Paine edited *Pennsylvania Magazine,* which urged revolution. Despite the emphasis on politics, many magazines in the 1700s were called **miscellanies** because they carried such a variety of contents and tried to appeal to a small, far-flung, and diverse audience. After the American Revolution, magazines took a while to succeed economically. Magazines were given no cost break in postal rates until 1879 (Riley, 1993), so few magazines were widely read or long-lived until the 1800s (Tebbel, 1969).

The fledgling American publishing industry was given a significant economic boost by the first U.S. Congress with the passage of the Copyright Act of 1790. This legislation gave authors and their publishers exclusive rights to their publications for a period of 14 years (renewable for an additional 14 years). During that time, anyone who wished to reproduce the work would have to make a payment, called a royalty fee, to the copyright holder for the use of the work. This was intended to promote new creative works by guaranteeing a financial return to their originators.

As the 1700s drew to a close, American magazines were aimed at the better-educated and wealthy elite and a small but growing middle class. Many were still political, including *Port Folio,* the first magazine to achieve substantial national circulation. Politics then centered on whether to have a strong central government, a federal system, or a more state-oriented, decentralized one. The political organ of the Federalist movement, *Port Folio* advocated a strong central government and contained essays such as Alexander Hamilton's "Federalist Papers." It was opposed by anti-Federalist magazines, such as the *National Magazine of Richmond,* which was also notable for being one of the few magazines published outside the dominant publishing centers of Philadelphia, Boston, and New York.

In the early 1800s there was a new trend toward somewhat more specialized "literary miscellanies," such as the *Saturday Evening Post* (1821–1969), whose editors wanted to popularize the emerging American literature. They covered weekly events, politics, and art and included reviews, travelogues, short stories, serialized fiction, and so on. "Special miscellanies" focused on more specific topics and audiences. Sarah Josepha Hale's *Ladies' Magazine* of Boston was the first successful American magazine targeted toward women, and it was soon followed by *Godey's Lady's Book.* By the 1840s, magazines began to shift their attention toward broader and more sustainable mass audiences.

Subscription libraries lent books to the public for a fee.

Miscellanies were magazines with a wide variety of contents.

HARPER'S WEEKLY.
JOURNAL OF CIVILIZATION.

Vol. V.—No. 219.] NEW YORK, SATURDAY, MARCH 9, 1861. [Price Five Cents.

PRESIDENT LINCOLN HOISTING THE AMERICAN FLAG WITH THIRTY-FOUR STARS UPON INDEPENDENCE HALL, PHILADELPHIA, FEBRUARY 22, 1861.
From Photographs by F. D. Richards, Philadelphia.—[See Next Page.

© Hulton Archive/Getty Images

■ THE CIVIL WAR, ILLUSTRATED

The vivid illustrations of Civil War action in *Harper's Weekly* attracted large audiences in the 1860s.

Dime novels were inexpensive paperback novels of the nineteenth century.

Genres are types or formats of media content.

During the Civil War era, magazines began to have a much broader impact on public life. Several magazines grew to fame during the Civil War for their coverage and illustrations dramatizing scenes of the war. Magazines such as *Harper's Weekly* created an important new form of publication, the illustrated newsweekly, the predecessors of today's *Newsweek* and *Time.* While daily newspapers focused on a short time frame (today's headline news), the weekly magazines had something different to offer: illustrations, more in-depth coverage, longer pieces, more investigative reporting, and a focus on trends rather than on daily events.

America Reads   In the mid-1800s, improving social conditions fostered a mass audience for books and magazines. An expanding public education system taught more people to read. Wages increased, more people moved to the cities to work in the burgeoning industrial economy, and an urban middle class grew. Prices fell with economies of scale, improved printing technology, and more demand for print media. Access to books increased as the number of public libraries tripled between 1825 and 1850.

Perhaps most important, however, was the *popularization* of book content. Many American novelists earned loyal fans by addressing the uniquely American national experience and interests. James Fenimore Cooper wrote compelling novels about the struggles of both white settlers and indigenous people on the frontier. In novels such as *The Last of the Mohicans* (1826), Cooper dramatized the attraction of the West. Immigrants sometimes cited his novels as part of what they knew about America, part of what drew them.

Novels had political effects. A prime example is Harriet Beecher Stowe's *Uncle Tom's Cabin* (1852), which sold 300,000 copies in its first year and did much to inspire popular opposition to slavery (Davis, 1985).

From 1860 to 1880, even more popular material appeared in cheaper formats. The **dime novels** addressed a broader audience of middle-class and even working-class people. For instance, some 250 million Horatio Alger books were sold. This popular hero managed to rise out of poverty by hard work, thrift, planning, and other popular virtues. In fact, the term *Horatio Alger story* eventually became a popular synonym for a tale of hard work and social mobility.

Magazines, along with newspapers, grew into a major mass medium in the 1800s. Magazines kept expanding their readership by moving beyond general-interest magazines, such as the *Saturday Evening Post,* to more specialized **genres.** One genre with mass appeal was women's magazines, such as *Good Housekeeping* and *McCall's.* By 1910, both the *Saturday Evening Post* and *Ladies' Home Journal* circulated to over a million readers (Tebbel, 1969).

Magazines benefited particularly from a major change in their delivery system. The Postal Act of 1879 gave magazines special rates. This de facto subsidy to magazine distribution continues today: publishers pay lower third-class rates for mailing, yet the magazines are treated as full-cost first-class mail. As a result, by 1900 there were 1800 magazines in the United States, a large increase from the 260 that existed in 1860 (Riley, 1993).

Twentieth-century Americans were now mostly literate, and many of them had enough income to afford magazines. They had more leisure time to read, as both the agricultural and industrial economies developed, and their interest in civic affairs, the arts, professional matters, and politics boomed. Many new kinds of magazines—investigative magazines, digests, newsmagazines, and pictorial magazines—competed with newspapers for position as the dominant mass medium for these readers. An increasing sense of openness and freedom in the press expanded the range of what topics were acceptable for magazines. By the early twentieth century, "pulp" fiction magazines, named for the cheap, pulpy paper they used, began to push the bounds of social acceptability with police stories, romance, crime mysteries, scandals, science fiction, and fantasy. For example, Conan the Barbarian started well before Arnold Schwarzenegger in the 1930s pulp fiction stories of Robert E. Howard.

135,000 SETS, 270,000 VOLUMES SOLD.

UNCLE TOM'S CABIN

FOR SALE HERE.

AN EDITION FOR THE MILLION, COMPLETE IN 1 Vol., PRICE 37 1-2 CENTS.
" " IN GERMAN, IN 1 Vol., PRICE 50 CENTS.
" " IN 2 Vols., CLOTH, 6 PLATES, PRICE $1.50.
SUPERB ILLUSTRATED EDITION, IN 1 Vol., WITH 153 ENGRAVINGS,
PRICES FROM $2.50 TO $5.00.

The Greatest Book of the Age.

© The Granger Collection, New York

■ **AGAINST SLAVERY**
Harriet Beecher Stowe's *Uncle Tom's Cabin* was a best-seller in its day and also helped set the agenda for opposition to slavery.

Muckraking   In the late 1800s and early 1900s, magazines began to overtake newspapers in investigative reporting and crusades for reform. Much of this investigative reporting, known as **muckraking,** was done for magazines such as *McClure's* and *Collier's,* nationally circulated, inexpensive magazines that reached millions of readers and had a great impact on public opinion. The term *muckraking* refers to reporters being willing to stir up and sift through the unpleasant aspects of public life that most people ignore, looking for misdeeds by public figures without worrying about offending sensibilities or insulting the people under investigation. Magazine journalism attracted crusading reporters, looking for controversial, striking content that would draw in a mass audience.

During the Progressive Era, from 1890 to 1920, many reform politicians, unions, rural associations, and magazine and newspaper reporters protested the power of big business and the conservative politics of the parties and politicians in power. Reformers pushed for more liberal social, economic, and political reforms, like the regulation of food and drug purity, a shorter workday, a minimum wage, job safety rules, reduced political patronage and corruption, and government regulation of big-business excess. For example, in 1902 Ida Tarbell wrote a classic muckraking exposé of Standard Oil Company under John D. Rockefeller for the magazine *McClure's.* The article, with its vivid descriptions of the abuses committed by the company, was very popular.

Muckraking often led to landmark reform legislation. The Pure Food and Drug Act (1907) resulted from an article in *Collier's,* "The Great American Fraud" by Samuel Hopkins Adams. The Mann Act (1909), which prohibited transportation of women across states lines for immoral purposes, resulted from an article in *McClure's* by Burton J. Hendrick on "Daughters of the Poor." And Upton Sinclair's *The Jungle,* a book about Chicago slaughterhouses, was published in 1905 and led to the Meat Inspection Act (1906).

STOP & REVIEW

1. What key elements of print media developed first outside Europe?
2. What were the first subjects of printed books?
3. What were the first magazines concerned with?
4. What was the role of the print media in the Civil War?
5. How did muckraking affect magazine development?

Muckraking is journalism that "rakes up the muck" of corruption and scandal.

© Bettmann/Corbis

■ MUCKRAKER

Ida Tarbell gained prominence as one of the leading turn-of-the-last-century magazine writers by exposing the abuses of Standard Oil Company.

The term *muckraking* has now lost its crusading political sense and today refers more to the investigation of sexual scandals and other "dirt" on public figures. However, contemporary journalists continue to target corruption and abuses of power with a crusading spirit that sometimes results in positive change. Some current magazines—*The Nation* and *Washington Monthly* come to mind—still specialize in muckraking journalism. Many web magazines and *blogs* have also continued this tradition, as they made especially clear during the 2004 presidential election, when some online mega-size sites, like TomPain.com served as significant sources of commentary and opinion.

Modern Magazines

After the 1920s, magazines had to compete with radio and film, which increasingly dominated as new mass media. Some magazines did not adjust to the new mass media market and disappeared. Some "quality" magazines like *Harper's Monthly* and *Atlantic Monthly* kept a loyal audience but barely survived. The new competitors refocused their content on topics of mass appeal, such as "modern life," current issues, and success stories (Payne, 1993). They sold many more copies, were less expensive to produce, and cost less to readers.

Some were truly major mass media for a time. The *Saturday Evening Post* refocused on the accomplishments of American business, inspirational success stories, action stories, romance, and some factual reports. It reached a circulation of 3 million in 1937, with a profitable advertising base. However, its formula for appealing to a middle-class audience never adjusted to subsequent competition from television. As advertising shifted to television in the 1950s and 1960s, the *Post* lost money and went out of business in 1969, despite an enthusiastic readership and a circulation of 6.8 million.

The *Ladies' Home Journal* did much better with its more narrowly targeted audience. It ranked eleventh in circulation among magazines in 2003. But it had a great deal of competition from other women's magazines and had a much less important position relative to other American national media now than it had in 1900 (MRI Research, 2004).

One of the first successful modern *targeted magazines* from 1925 was the *New Yorker*, which emphasized an audience that was "upper-class, highly educated, literate and sophisticated" but had only a modest circulation (Payne, 1993). The *New Yorker* continues to be successful and paved the way for more recent magazines focused on a number of American cities.

One of the most successful magazine formulas, or genres, was the **newsmagazine.** These publications competed with the newspapers very directly, providing extensive news coverage and commentary. In 1923, Henry Luce and Briton Hadden started *Time* magazine. They felt that people were being bombarded with information but were still uninformed. *Time* would sift through the clutter, summarize what was important, and offer a point of view on it, according to Walter Isaacson, managing editor of *Time* (March 9, 1998).

Time's success as a newsmagazine led Time Inc. to introduce *Life,* an illustrated *photojournalism* magazine in 1936. *Life* met the public's desire for a photographic report of world events with photos of the week's events, with captions and a fairly short news analysis, creating a visual style of journalism that later fed into television news approaches. In fact, competition from television led to the 1972 failure of *Life,* which was primarily focused on images, while *Time* and *Newsweek,* which balanced photo images with extensive text and reporting, continued to do well even after television became popular. Many

Newsmagazine is a weekly magazine focused on news and analysis.

LIFE

COLONEL JIMMY STEWART

WELCOME
JIM

SEPTEMBER 24, 1945 **10** CENTS
BY SUBSCRIPTION: TWO YEARS $8.50

■ **GET A LIFE**
The colorful photojournalism of *Life* magazine pioneered a visual approach to the news that was later copied by television.

Queen of All Media

■ OPRAH WINFREY

© UPI Photo/Laura Cavanaugh/Landov

Name: Oprah Winfrey

Born: January 29, 1954, in Kosciusko, Mississippi

Education: Tennessee State University; earned a B.A. in 1973

Recent Position: Talk-show host

New Position: Magazine publisher, *O, The Oprah Magazine*

First Job: Worked part-time as a radio announcer for WVOL in Nashville in 1971, and then as a full-time reporter at WTVF-TV.

Original Claim to Fame: She took over an ailing morning show, *A.M. Chicago* in 1984. By the next year, her show was so successful that it was expanded to an hour format and renamed *The Oprah Winfrey Show.* Now it is in syndication across the country.

Most Notable Achievement: An abused child herself, she worked hard to bring the issue into the open and lobbied hard for legislation to protect children. In 1994 President Clinton signed the "Oprah Bill," a law designed to protect children from abuse.

Latest Achievement: She wants people not only to watch television but also to read. To that end, she discussed books and authors on her show for many years, catapulting a number of generally deserving books into greater public awareness and readership. Now she is trying to create a new alternative among women's magazines to draw her fans toward that as well.

---

magazines still depend on high-quality photography and illustration. In fact *Life* was revived for a while but as an irregular periodical.

Magazines as a mass medium peaked in the 1940s and 1950s. Magazines such as *Look* and *Life* were losing money because much of their audience and their advertisers shifted their focus to television. However, the magazines that continued to target specific audiences prospered. As a result, in 1950 there were 250 magazines with total sales of 147 million (Alsop, 1997, p. 929). In 2003 there were 6234 consumer magazines with total sales of 352 million (Audit Bureau of Circulation, 2004). The last four decades have seen a proliferation of even more specialized magazines for even more specific audiences. Traditional women's magazines, for example, have been joined by a host of magazines aimed at younger girls (*Teen*), young women (*Mademoiselle*), working women (*Working Woman*), young working women (*Cosmopolitan*), and feminists (*Ms*).

This trend has only accelerated—today there's a magazine to cover almost every hobby, occupation, and interest, from canoeing to dairy farming. For example, *Oprah* magazine (see Profile: Queen of All Media) became profitable quickly—a remarkable success in the magazine world. If a new magazine targets the right niche and audience segment, and succeeds over time, it opens the door for a wide variety of similar new magazines.

By the late 1990s, with **desktop publishing,** cheap photocopying, and the publication of magazines in virtual form on the World Wide Web, there were much lower barriers to entry into the magazine business. Ambitious twenty-somethings aimed to make it big on a shoestring by publishing on the web. However, as with print magazines, there is a constant shakeout among Internet-based magazines and most of them fail.

Desktop publishing is editing, laying out, and inserting photos on a desktop computer.

Book Publishing Giants

Many publishing houses have been around since the early 1800s, such as Harper & Row. However, many of the most active American hardback publishers, such as McGraw-Hill and Prentice-Hall, set up shop in the early twentieth century. As printing costs declined during this time, more Americans could afford hardback books, and the publishing industry grew. Thus, many major publishers increased the number of books available to the general public. The strongest segments of the pre–World War II publishing industry were educational, professional, and reference books—a book selling 50,000 copies, particularly a nonfiction book, could be judged a best-seller (Dessauer, 1981).

For both books and *pulp magazines* that specialized in short stories, the first half of the twentieth century was a boom era for detective stories, science fiction, and westerns (Folkerts & Teeter, 1994). Behind this publishing boom was the low "book rate" for mailing books, which made both mail-order sales and marketing via book clubs much cheaper. Mail-order book clubs, such as the Book-of-the-Month Club and the Literary Guild, scared publishers at first but ultimately benefited them by popularizing book reading and buying.

World War II also helped popularize reading by ushering in the *paperback* era. Most of the publishing houses established during this time, such as Pocket Books and Bantam Books, grew up around paperback books. Young people away from home at war read more, and as they returned home and entered college (assisted by educational benefits for veterans), they began reading textbooks and continued to read even more mass market paperbacks. As educational institutions and the public began demanding more textbooks, serious literature, and nonfiction, publishers introduced larger-format trade paperbacks to complement "pocket-size" paperbacks. *Chain bookstores* in suburban shopping malls that sprang up in the 1950s began to promote book purchases and now account for more than half of all bookstore sales.

New York gradually became the main publishing center in the United States, but in the late 1900s, publishers proliferated on both coasts, along with some in the Midwest and the South. A number of niche publishing companies were established, such as West, for specific industries, like the legal system. Tor Books and DAW Books publish large numbers of science fiction paperbacks.

Small new publishers are constantly entering the field, despite the frequent consolidations of publishing houses (one major wave of mergers occurred in the 1960s and another in the 1990s–2000s). Today, there are more than 75,000 American book publishers, if you count the small publishers that rely on desktop publishing technology and publish only a few titles per year, often in very specialized areas.

Today, several trends cause a sense of unease in book publishing. Sales of the classic 4¼-by-7-inch mass market paperback, the mainstay of the industry since the 1940s, fell briefly but are rising again. Sales of discounted hardbacks and trade paperbacks have grown, but their readers are aging. This change in the profile of readers has industry people worried. Another threat to publishers comes from their own distributors. Large book chains like Barnes and Noble are beginning to publish their own books, threatening such lucrative niches as how-to home improvement titles. In retaliation publishers like Random House are considering distributing to the public themselves. (NEA, 2004.)

A number of companies hope to take advantage of what the Internet has to offer them and are edging slowly toward digital publishing. Some, like Random House, entered e-publishing in a fairly big way but pulled back. However, e-publishing by nonprofit organizations has proceeded quickly. One can easily download entire books, such as the annual reports of the World Bank, or extensive reports by nonprofit groups like the

Children's Alliance, as PDF files (Portable Document Format by Adobe). Another form of electronic publishing, making books on demand, is already having an impact, especially in areas like customized versions of textbooks. Both Amazon.com and Google.com are making the contents of many books available electronically. Google plans to make books in several top academic libraries available online.

TECHNOLOGY TRENDS: FROM CHAPBOOK TO E-BOOK

For 500 years since Gutenberg, most improvements in publishing technology revolved around finding faster ways to press ink on paper, although progress was slow for around 400 years.

After Gutenberg

The invention of the first *rotary press* in 1846 was a significant advancement in printing. Unlike previous presses that printed on single sheets of paper one sheet at a time, rotary presses used rotating cylinders of type to print on both sides of large, continuous rolls of paper. Thus, by the end of the nineteenth century, a single press could print tens of thousands of copies per hour, a thousandfold increase from the early 1800s.

Typesetting, however, remained a slow manual process requiring typesetters to locate and put in place individual letters of type to form each word, just as Gutenberg had done. This process was made vastly more efficient in the 1890s when *linotype* machines were introduced. Linotype machines cast entire lines of type from molten lead instantly so that one typesetter could do the work of five (Sloan, Stovall, & Startt, 1993).

It was also in the late 1800s that printing processes for illustrations enjoyed great improvement. Printed illustrations had been a staple of magazines dating back to the Civil War period (1861–1865), but only a few publications could afford them because they required the painstaking hand engraving of wood or metal master plates. In the 1860s a new printing process invented by the French, *lithography,* speeded the printing of illustrated pages by replacing engraving with a type of chemical etching. Soon, even this process was improved upon. *Photoengraving* transformed illustrated publications by chemically etching images onto the surface of metal plates through a photographic process, a vast improvement over handmade lithographs. So, by the 1890s, photographs were routinely reproduced in a wide range of print publications.

After World War II, *offset printing* was introduced and produced further advances in the quality, speed, and economy of printing. Now an entire page of print, complete with illustrations, could be photographed and the photographic image transferred to a smooth metal plate. The plate was treated so that only the desired areas attracted the ink and transferred them to a rubber roller, and then to paper.

Courtesy of VIBE Magazine

■ **A MAGAZINE FOR EVERY VIBE**
Music magazines have specialized to cover music from a wide variety of genres.

Publishing in the Information Age

By the 1960s, computerization began to lead to many other changes in the print media. At first, computers were put to work assisting typesetters, automatically hyphenating and spacing the type on each line. In the 1970s, computers replaced typesetting machines—and many typesetting people as well—by transferring text directly to photographic film that in turn was transferred to metal printing plates. The computerization of the layout and pasteup process further simplified printing, as did the *digitizing* of photographs so that they could be edited and placed on a page electronically. In other words, all the work that goes into creating a page to be printed—setting type, adding headings, putting text into columns, making text "wrap around" photos or illustrations, and cropping and placing photos—could now be done faster and less expensively with *pagination* software rather than by hand. Now most magazine titles are produced with **computer-to-plate** technology that transfers the page images composed inside the computer directly to printing plates, eliminating the intermediate step of transferring the page to film. In the 1980s, more power and speed were packed into desktop computers. *Scanners* for digitizing photos became cheaper. Software products like PageMaker enabled users to lay out pages on a personal computer.

Photocopying technology made offset printing unnecessary, at least in low-volume applications. That is, to make offset or other high-quality printing worthwhile, you must print a certain minimum number of copies because the cost of producing the original copy—in this case the metal printing plate—has to be spread over a large number of reproductions to be economical. (See discussion of first copy costs in Chapter 2.) However, photocopying relies on a fundamentally different process, using an inexpensive piece of paper as the original copy. Similarly, high-speed *laser printing*, which allows users to print computer-readable information onto paper, uses the same basic approach as photocopying and yields high-quality print and images. As a result, desktop publishing has done much to decentralize print media. Now, almost anyone with a personal computer can produce his or her own books, magazines, "fanzines," flyers, and posters. Although computers are no substitute for writing talent, visual design ability, or editorial skills, the layout templates and spelling and grammar checkers that come with desktop publishing products have given many an amateur effort a professional appearance.

Another Information Age innovation, *custom publishing*, takes advantage of the flexibility of computer-based publishing to print selected parts of books for special purposes. For example, publishers of college texts—including the publishers of this text—have long fought local copy shops over the legality of photocopying college course packets by prosecuting them in the courts for copyright violations. By printing selections from popular textbooks themselves, publishers hope to get the sales that formerly went to the copy shops. Custom publishing has now been extended to **print-on-demand** technology that prints entire books only as they are ordered by customers.

And, perhaps surprisingly, the advent of the electronic cash register has transformed the publishing industry. For book publishers, electronic scanners are transforming how best-seller lists are compiled. The conventional method for compiling such lists was to poll bookstore clerks by phone, a method that neglected some important book outlets (such as airports and grocery stores) and that also may have been influenced by the clerks' own tastes in literature. The new method gathers data directly from cash register scanners at a wide range of retail book outlets, including the supermarkets and drugstores that tend to cater to less refined tastes than bookstores do.

E-Publishing

The effects of computer technology on book publishing go beyond the time and labor saved with the latest software. For example, the Internet is having a major impact on

Computer-to-plate technology transfers page images composed inside a computer directly to printing plates.

Print-on-demand technology prints books only when they are ordered by customers.

publishing, particularly one of the most widely ballyhooed capabilities of the Internet, *electronic commerce,* or the ability to buy and sell online. With such "virtual bookstores" as Amazon.com, shoppers enjoy the convenience of searching for titles online with powerful search engines rather than waiting while harried bookstore clerks search through *Books in Print.* Amazon now offers the opportunity to browse inside selected books, a pleasure formerly available only to bookshop patrons. And virtual bookstores take note of your purchases and recommend other books that you might like to read—it's almost like having a personal librarian. In addition, the vast inventories and searchable databases of the Internet give new life to **backlist,** or older books, and to obscure titles from small publishers that cannot find shelf space in the "real" bookstore down the street. Similarly, a growing number of authors are bypassing conventional publishers altogether and selling their desktop-produced books directly through the web.

One innovation that is gaining momentum is the conversion of already published books to online formats. This movement was given an enormous boost in 2004 when online search engine Google contracted with leading libraries to scan their collections, and make them available online (see below). *Encryption* technologies help solve the problem of unauthorized duplication, printing, and use of copyrighted works by restricting access to paying customers. And publishers are trying to develop ways to avoid rampant swapping of copyrighted works online—the problem that the music industry initially encountered with Napster.com (see Chapter 5). A lingering problem with online books seems to be the hardship of reading text on a computer screen (Frost, 1996). Computer text is harder—and about 60 percent slower—to read than ink on paper, and even the most portable laptop computer is not really welcome in bed or on a beach chair. Help may be on the way, though—in the form of ubiquitous wireless connections to the Internet and new computer display technologies that users might feel comfortable curling up with in front of a fire. Some call this concept "electronic ink," a thin, flexible plastic display that will change the text and graphics you see, an improvement over today's flat-screen computer screens.

One of the current stumbling blocks to e-publishing is the battle over *standards,* the technical characteristics that must be agreed on for a technology to be widely manufactured and used. For example, Adobe is leading now with PDF (Portable Document Format), which has been used for several years to download reports and books over the web. There is also the question of which type of hardware for reading will dominate the new business: PCs, handheld computers like Palm Pilots or the Blackberry, or new specialized e-book readers. (See Technology Demystified: Cuddling Up with a Nice Electronic Book? page 71.)

The magazine industry has also jumped on the Internet bandwagon. Thousands of titles have planted their mastheads on the World Wide Web, although few have yet to see profits. Many of these publications offer electronic versions of their current print issues, articles from past issues, or special features (pitched to web surfers) that are not found in the print versions. There are also a growing number of periodicals that are available on the web. For example, *Slate,* originally published by Microsoft Corporation, features commentary on public affairs. And for academics, there is the *Journal of Computer Mediated Communication* (JCMC).

No discussion of trends in publishing technology would be complete without considering what the library of tomorrow might be like. Libraries have been computerizing their card catalogs for decades, and many catalogs are now accessible through the World Wide Web—some even let researchers order books for convenient pickup or delivery. Increasingly, researchers can search on keywords from their computers and have access to abstracts of articles and even the full text of scholarly publications. Additionally, some services, like Lexis-Nexis and InfoTrac, offer extensive full texts of newspaper, magazine, and specialized publication content. However, these services are restricted to those who buy access directly by subscribing or indirectly by enrolling at a university whose library

Backlist books are not actively promoted but are still in print.

Cuddling Up with a Nice Electronic Book?

There is something very sensuous to many people about a printed book. Even small paperbacks have their advantages: cheap, portable, no batteries required, durable. Nicely bound books with large type intrigue the romantic and the collector. Both entice us to curl up by a nice fire, in a warm bath, or in bed—and relax.

Can a high-tech plastic device weighing one to three pounds, with a limited battery life but a brighter screen, ever offer serious competition to print books, the oldest medium around? Several new electronic book readers, including NuvoMedia's RocketBook and the Softbook, appeared in 1998 to test the idea. Electronic books have their appeal. No night-light is required, although a battery is. You can mark passages electronically, search for key words, or get constant updates for timely material, like tax laws. You can carry a pile of titles around with you a lot more easily. You can download titles from the Internet, as well as buy them at shops or by mail. And, with the cost of both reader and "books" dropping fast, they are becoming a viable alternative to paper books.

By 2000, most publishers were getting interested, although few e-books were sold. By 2004, e-books were rebounding but were being read on laptops and computer servers, not separate readers. Many students get e-books through their library sites or "e-reserve reading." College students with limited budgets are turning to online books that sell for half the price of the hardback version.

The advent of electronic books may well be one of the ultimate tests of just how well computers can interface with

■ SUPER BOOK?

Futuristic technology has spawned the electronic book, a device that can hold the equivalent of hundreds of books in a compact package weighing only a few ounces.

people. Can the advantages of electronic scanning, searching, and a built-in light compete with a book's simple interface, low cost, portability, and traditional charm?

pays for the access. But increasingly, as more and more local libraries offer Internet access as one of their services available to the public, the *search engines* of the web are also becoming a staple of library research. Additionally, many local libraries provide access to numerous database services like those just mentioned. The impact of Google's bold plan to digitize major library collections remains to be seen. They face an enormous task.

So, what to do with those old stacks of books and journals that haven't been converted to electronic formats yet? Making images of the pages is relatively simple. But digitizing printed texts, so that they can be searched or cut and pasted into a term paper, for example, requires *optical character recognition* (OCR) software that converts printed words to computer-readable characters. But OCR software is not foolproof, so the resulting text still has to be carefully proofread by a human. In addition, the texts' copyright holders, or their heirs, must be tracked down and compensated so for now the copies will be limited to out of copyright works (70 years old in the U.S.). Only selected printing of new books will be available. In the long run, though, old texts will have to be scanned or they will be lost as they yellow and crumble into dust. Already we can see some publishers taking the initiative to put old issues on CD-ROM or the web. For example, the *Complete National Geographic* is available in a collection of 30 CD-ROMs for about $200 and contains a digitized version of every page of the magazine from the first issue in 1888.

INDUSTRY: GOING GLOBAL

As we've discussed, a range of smaller trends can be seen in both book and magazine publishing. Major industry trends have been identified, too, including corporate consolidation, improvements in magazine circulation and advertising, book and magazine specialization, audience segmentation, and convergence with other digital media.

Magazine Economics

Magazines are a targeted medium. But to be profitable, they strive for the largest possible audience they can reach within their potential target group, and they still follow such economic rules as *economies of scale.*

Magazines make money from single copy sales, from subscriptions, and from advertising. The mix of revenue from these sources varies greatly among different kinds of magazines. But overall, half comes form advertising, a third from subscriptions, and the rest from single copy sales (MPA, 2004, p. 14). Many consumer magazines make most of their money from subscriptions. In 2003, subscriptions accounted for almost 86 percent of total magazine circulation. Single copy, or newsstand, sales accounted for 14 percent (MPA, 2004). However, single copy sales are important: They bring in more revenue per magazine, because subscription prices are typically at least 50 percent less than the price of buying single issues. Further, potential readers explore a new magazine by buying a single issue; all those insert cards with subscription offers are included in magazines to encourage potential readers to subscribe. Some magazines are distributed only by subscription. Most are highly specific or technical magazines, such as *Broadcast Educator,* which are often published by professional associations. Some of these may feature a small amount of highly targeted advertising. A few magazines, like *Consumer Reports,* contain no advertising to avoid being tainted by the interests of advertisers.

For most magazines, advertising is a crucial source of revenue. The easiest way for a magazine to improve its profitability is to increase the number of its ad pages, but the magazine must reach the right audience for the advertiser. Overall, advertising pages have gone down in the last several years, so competition by magazines for ads is very intense. Nonetheless, magazine ad revenues are climbing again after a decline in the post-9/11 period (Magazine Publishers Association, 2004).

For some consumer magazines, ads are a far more important source of revenue than circulation, and for many nonconsumer magazines, like trade magazines for professions or industries, advertising is generally more important than circulation. For example, in the computer and telecommunications industries, many magazines, like *Network World,* are sent free to professionals who make decisions about purchasing equipment or services that the magazine might advertise. A magazine's decision to cater to such subscribers convinces advertisers with high-tech equipment to sell to place their ads in that magazine.

STOP & REVIEW

1. What were some of the first general-public, nonelite magazines?

2. What were some of the first targeted magazines?

3. What are the main recent trends in print media production technologies?

4. What are the main recent trends in print media delivery technologies?

5. Which are the main publishing groups? To what conglomerates do they belong?

6. How are computers and the Internet affecting book publishing and selling?

Table 3.1 Holdings of Top Five Publishing Groups

Group	2003 Total Revenue	Magazines	Books
Time Warner	$38.2 billion	*Time, People, Sports Illustrated,* etc.	Warner Books; Little Brown, etc.
Walt Disney	25.4 billion	*Walt Disney Comics*	Disney Press, Hyperion
Viacom	23.2 billion		Simon & Schuster, Scribner, Pocket Books
Bertelsmann	17.8 billion	*Family Circle, McCalls*	Random House
News Corporation	15.2 billion	*Weekly Standard*	HarperCollins, Avon Books

Source: *Variety's Global 50* (http://www.Variety.com)

Magazine Industry Proliferation and Consolidation

The magazine industry has both proliferated and *consolidated.* New magazines, both conventional and Internet-based, spring up constantly. Most of them die rather quickly or are acquired by larger groups, which can provide them with publicity, advertising contacts, and better circulation prospects. However, the magazine industry is also one of the media areas where a new entrant or competitor can best break in by appealing to a new segment of the market that is not yet served by other magazines. For instance, *Rolling Stone* magazine went quickly from a small counterculture or "hippie" magazine in 1969 to a widely read rock music and counterculture lifestyle magazine by the 1970s. It has since become the most popular mainstream music magazine.

In the 1990s, a number of start-up efforts were focused on World Wide Web-based magazines, but new print magazines continued to appear too. During that decade, Ziff-Davis capitalized on the rapidly growing interest in personal computers to build a very profitable magazine empire by publishing magazines such as *PC Week, PC Magazine,* and *MacWeek* before being bought out by its main competitor, CNET, in 2000. Still, there were 440 new magazines in 2003, with the most popular new titles being hobbies, regional publications, and sports (Magazine Publishers Association, 2004).

Table 3.1 shows the magazine and book publishing holdings of the five major publishing groups. It shows that major **conglomerates,** like Time Warner, now have significant divisions in almost all print media. So the magazine and book publishing operations of these corporations were to be operated not only to be profitable in and of themselves, but also to create synergies (such as cross-promotion or multiple usage of content) with other operations within the same group (such as Internet or television). However, the difficulty of achieving such synergies led to a major shake-up within Time Warner in 2002, in which television, magazines, and other individual units reclaimed much more business autonomy.

Magazine Circulation and Advertising

Magazines remain competitive with other media. In fact, as magazines proliferate within new niches or segments, they can draw in audiences that have been interested primarily in other media. For example, men have often been considered much more likely to watch TV than to read magazines. However, a number of new men's magazines have emerged, from *Maxim* and *FHM* to *Gear and Stuff, Cigar Aficionado, Dads,* and *Maximum Golf.* Many of these did very well in both circulation and advertising.

Conglomerates are made up of diverse parts from across several media industries.

Table 3.2 Top Magazines for Men and Women

Men's Titles	Men's Readership in millions	Women's Titles	Women's Readership in millions
Parade magazine in newspaper	38	Parade Magazine in newspaper	40.6
USA Weekend magazine in newspaper	23.2	Better Homes and Gardens	29.8
Reader's Digest	17.8	USA Weekend magazine in newspaper	26.1
National Geographic	18.1	Reader's Digest	25.9
Sports Illustrated	16.3	People	22.7
Field & Stream	14	Good Housekeeping	22
People	12.6	Family Circle	20.5
TV Guide	12.4	Woman's Day	19.8
Time	12.8	TV Guide	15.6
Newsweek	11.4	National Geographic	14.4

Source: MRI Research, Magazine Pocketpiece, http://www.mriplus.com. (2002)

Table 3.2 shows the most popular magazines for men and women, based on the numbers who say they read each title. However, these figures also show that the age of the mass market magazine is still with us. *Reader's Digest, People,* and *TV Guide* are among the leading magazines distributed through the conventional magazine channels of yearly subscriptions and newsstand sales. But note that the most popular magazines have been newspaper supplements: *Parade,* and *USA Weekend* rank near the top for both men and women. On average, people now read magazines about as often as books but quite a bit less than newspapers. With over 17,000 magazines and related periodicals being published, magazine readership is quite fragmented. There are sizable subgroups, particularly among younger people, who typically read magazines but not newspapers or books. Magazine readership is highest among those aged 18 to 24 and 35 to 44; it is much lower among those over age 55 (Veronis, Suhler and Associates, 2004).

Compared to other media, magazines are maintaining about the same share of advertising revenues that they have had in the past. Because readers of specific magazines look at ads targeted quite directly to them, advertising research shows that these consumers are more likely to trust magazine ads, see them as complementary to the content, and use them to decide between products than are viewers of network TV, cable TV, or the Internet (Publisher's Information Bureau, 2004). However, the number of magazines has grown rapidly in recent years so that advertising revenue is being split among more competitors, which threatens the viability of both new and established magazines. Even among consumer magazines, hundreds of new titles appear every year to share the total "pie" of advertising revenue.

Magazine Distribution and Marketing

Magazines are distributed directly by retailers, such as supermarkets and newsstands, and by subscription. Magazine mailing lists are commodities of great value to other magazines, catalogs, and direct-mail marketers. A crucial link between publishers and retailers

Courtesy of PC Gamer

Courtesy of Official Xbox Magazine

are magazine wholesalers and distributors. Many retailers simply take what the wholesaler delivers, because the wholesalers have the capability of doing their own market research or the staff to do selective ordering. So the distributors have a great influence on whether a new magazine gets delivered to newsstands and thereby reaches the public. One exception is Wal-Mart, which is selective in what it takes, bypassing distributors. In fact, Wal-Mart has become a major power in magazine retailing, as it is in retailing other forms of media, as well. Wal-Mart decided not to carry several magazines, like *Maxim, FHM,* and *Stuff,* whose covers were considered too sexually provocative. That worried their publishers, since Wal-Mart sells such a large proportion of magazines.

The Economics of Book Publishing

Some books are read by millions. Book publishing has been transformed by the search for best-sellers just as Hollywood has been transformed by the search for the box office smash. Every publisher would like to have millions of readers trying to buy the latest *Harry Potter* book. Just as with other media, when large publishing houses are bought up by larger conglomerates, they tend to become more oriented toward the bottom-line profit. Corporate managers then tend to feel more responsibility to stockholders than to readers.

However, there are still some publishers more motivated by the urge to publish a certain kind of book that they feel is important to the world. There are hundreds of small publishers, like academic presses, political groups, and religious organizations, that concede the best-sellers to Random House but still hope to reach many people with their message in book form.

Like movies and recordings, most books are sold directly to consumers primarily through a variety of intermediaries, like stores, book clubs and, increasingly, online operations like Amazon.com or megaretail stores like Wal-Mart. For more specialized books, like those published by academic or technical presses, most sales are to libraries rather than to individuals, although falling library budgets threatens to change that. But even these presses dream of selling a larger number of books to individual buyers, both to increase their revenue and so that their books are more widely read.

■ BOOK READING WIZARD
Millions of children who had not read full-length novels before were motivated by the tales of Harry Potter and his wizard school friends.

■ YOU'VE GOT BOOKS
Large bookstore owners, like the one portrayed by Tom Hanks in *You've Got Mail,* often drive out small bookstores like the one managed by Meg Ryan's character in the film.

Book Publishing Houses

Publishing houses are the organizations that supervise the overall production of books, including the development of new books, editing, printing, and marketing. Book publishers in the United States include commercial publishers, universities, religious groups, trade associations, and vanity presses that will publish anything as long as the author provides the money. Even though the computerized publishing technologies discussed earlier in this chapter make the publication of smaller, more specialized projects possible, major mass market books continue to become more expensive to produce because marketing and other costs have increased. As a result, many publishers feel that they have to concentrate on selling more copies of fewer books.

Bookstores

Bookstores buy books directly from publishers to stock their shelves. Booksellers range in size from national chains to small, independent bookstores. While national chains seem increasingly to dominate sales, some independent stores hang on. In Austin, Texas, in 2003, for example, a number of people joined a campaign called, "Keep Austin Weird"; one of its principal points was to keep people patronizing local book and record stores, instead of chain stores.

Large chains of medium-size stores, like Waldenbooks, are typically located in malls and sell great quantities of books. There are also growing chains of book and magazine superstores, such as Barnes & Noble and Borders. These are typically large, stand-alone stores located near malls or other major commercial areas. They have expanded quickly in the 1990s, selling an increasing number of books and magazines but

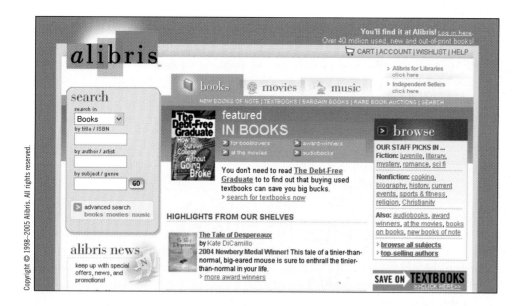

■ **BEYOND AMAZON**
Alibris's business model has enabled it to partner with Amazon, not just compete against it. Selling new, used, rare, and out-of-print titles to individuals, businesses, and libraries either directly or by connecting buyers and independent professional booksellers, Alibris helps to support independent publishers and booksellers.

are stumbling now as some stores are closed. One of the effects of this expansion is a growing tension between superstores and the smaller bookstores they often push out of business, a very real phenomenon reflected in the movie *You've Got Mail* (1998).

Book Purchasers

Although over 175,000 new book titles were published in 2003, the readership is uneven. Book sales are up five percent since 2002 (American Association of Publishers, 2004). Americans buy an average of four books a year, but that is deceptive. Many people do not read literary works. Some read the Bible or other religious works but few others. Many read reference titles for work purposes. And do cookbooks count? The United States tends to lag behind most other industrialized nations in books read per year. A 2002 study commissioned by the National Endowment for the Arts showed that readers of literature are disproportionately female, white, college educated, and middle aged (NEA, 2004).

Selling Books Online

"Virtual bookstores" like Amazon.com rival major bookstore chains as the largest book retailers and currently account for about 10 percent of all book sales in the United States. Amazon.com operates only via the Internet and has no physical retail stores at all. It claims an inventory of over 1.1 million titles, although many of the books are not physically available in its own warehouse. Amazon.com often plays middleman, taking orders over the Internet and arranging to have books shipped to customers from publishers or even used book sellers. Amazon.com's success has crushed competition.

Internet book sales may mitigate the current publishing industry trend of pushing *blockbuster* best-sellers rather than a wide variety of titles. Many electronic customers prefer older *backlist* titles to current best-sellers. Aided by electronic search engines, Amazon.com customers buy many books off publishers' backlists, which are often devoted to older editions of classic fiction, plays, and nonfiction. Internet sales of books benefit customers looking for more diverse or even obscure titles. And that may be a boon to authors and publishers of books other than best-sellers.

WHAT'S TO READ? MAGAZINE AND BOOK GENRES

In the following sections, we examine some of the principal genres and forms in books and magazines.

Magazines for Every Taste

There are currently at least 17,000 different magazine titles in the U.S., including 6000 for consumers and approximately 440 new titles every year, with over half of those targeted to consumers (Magazine Publishers of America, 2004). There are closer to 75,000 if you define magazines broadly.

Generally, magazines have several advantages as segmented media. Although magazines are somewhat constrained by limited newsstand space they can continue expanding into more specialized topics and treatments until they can no longer find audiences large enough to be worthwhile. And their formats and economic base are more flexible. A small-circulation magazine can still be profitable if those it reaches are interested enough in its contents to support it or if that audience is important to specific advertisers.

Additionally, magazines (and books) perform an important set of communications functions for elite audiences. Political activists are served by a variety of magazines ranging from the liberal, such as *The Nation,* to the conservative, such as the *National Review.* Intellectual magazines, such as the *New York Review of Books,* try to set the stage and agenda for academic and political debates on various issues, often by reviewing and summarizing books that they hope will help shape those debates. Some government policy-oriented magazines, such as *Foreign Affairs,* pride themselves on having an influential readership and on the fact that their articles sometimes affect policy debates.

Similarly, the crucial needs of business audiences—information about professional development, specific business areas, and current economic trends—are met by magazines, trade journals, newsletters, and newspapers. Some business magazines are fairly general, such as *Business Week* and *Fortune,* whereas others, such as *Advertising Age* and *Broadcasting and Cable* cover specific industries. Some trade publications, such as *Variety,* blur the distinction between newspapers and magazines by publishing both daily and weekly editions. Newsletters often serve only a few hundred readers who are willing to pay hundreds of dollars a year for the information offered. An example is *Telecom AM,* an Internet-based daily newsletter by Warren Publishing on the telecommunications industry.

Several magazine niches, such as entertainment, women's health, Internet, and fashion, have experienced shakeouts, primarily because audience circulation and economic support by advertisers were divided among too many magazines, or the subject area in question suffered an economic setback. For example, financial magazines folded in response to an economic recession in the early 2000s (Wall Street Journal, 2003). Still, a number of new magazines have survived their first few years and have established stable or growing audiences, and new magazines still spring up all the time. Some magazines, like *Oprah,* become successful quickly.

Reader studies show that photos in both articles and advertisements hold much attraction for magazine readers. However, visual magazines now tend to serve much more specific, segmented audiences. For example, bridal magazines, fashion magazines, sports magazines, and even rock-music magazines depend a great deal on visual appeal. *Rolling Stone* (1968–present) magazine made photographer Annie Leibowitz famous,

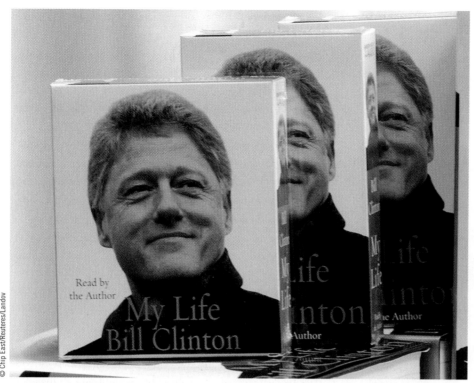

■ DOWNLOAD THIS

The audiobook market is expected to exceed $1.1 billion by 2008 with a significant portion of the growth coming from audiobook downloads.

and Richard Avedon gained fame from his photos in fashion magazines. Magazine readers cite high-quality photos and images as one reason why they still prefer reading print magazines to looking at the same content on the Internet (Publishers Information Bureau, 2004).

Book Publishing

Books are diverse and hard to characterize in general terms. Some books are sacred, some are sensational; some are eagerly read for pleasure, some are assigned reading in college courses. According to the Association of American Publishers, the major categories of book genres, are as follows:

Trade books. Hard- or softcover, including "serious" fiction (like Dan Brown's *The DaVinci Code*) and most nonfiction, such as cookbooks (like the softcover version of *The Joy of Cooking*), biographies, how-to books, and art books.

Professional books. Reference or professional education books aimed at doctors, lawyers, scientists, researchers, managers, and engineers (such as *The Programmer's Guide to Windows® NT*).

Elementary, high school, and college textbooks. Such as *Media Now: Communications Media in the Information Age, Fifth Edition.*

Mass market paperbacks. Softbound books, generally smaller in format and less expensive than trade paperbacks (such as *Teeth of the Tiger* by Tom Clancy).

© Vince Bucci/Getty Images

Religious books. Bibles, other sacred texts, hymnals, prayer books, and commentaries.

Book club editions. Clubs that publish, sell, and distribute their own editions of mass market books, professional books, and other specialized books. The Quality Paperback Book Club, for instance, issues trade paperback versions of current hardcover best-sellers.

Mail-order publications. Books largely created by publishers to be sold by mail. These are usually classic novels or specialized series on such subjects as cooking, western history, wars, cars, and aviation (such as the Time-Life series on cowboys).

Subscription reference books. Books sold as a package or series, including encyclopedias, atlases, dictionaries, glossaries, and thesauruses (such as *Encyclopaedia Britannica*). (Many of these "books" are now often sold to computer owners as periodically updated CD-ROMs. In fact, print encyclopedias have almost gone out of business in the United States.)

Audiovisual and multimedia. Videotapes, CD-ROMs, computer discs, slides, and audiotapes marketed primarily to schools, companies, and training groups, but also to individuals, by both regular publishing houses and new multimedia publishing companies (such as Microsoft's *Encarta* encyclopedia series).

University and scholarly presses. Scholarly or artistic books of primary appeal to scholars and libraries (such as Jan Nederveen Pieter's *Globalization and Culture*).

■ **ONCE AND FUTURE BEST-SELLERS**

Sometimes a film version can bring back novelists such as J.R.R. Tolkien to the best-seller charts for fiction books. Actor Sean Astin signs autographs in books including the "Lord of the Rings" Visual Companion. Astin plays "Sam Gamgee" in the film, the first of three movies based on the classic trilogy by author J.R.R. Tolkien.

MEDIA LITERACY: THE CULTURE OF PRINT

U.S. media policy has always assumed that competition among ideas in various media outlets is crucial. Print media, especially magazines and books, have traditionally been among the most competitive, so there has never been any great concern about regulating them in the United States.

Books as Ideas, Books as Commodities

Of course, before the Internet, relatively few people really had the freedom to speak to others via the media, but it has been assumed that competition would bring out diverse points of view and approximate a fairly free discussion among knowledgeable people. Now most of the readership of books is concentrated on the output of a few publishers. To make the best profit, those publishers tend to push a handful of potential best-sellers, rather than a broad catalog of fiction and nonfiction. People are beginning to wonder whether the trend toward maximizing sales of a few books in the U.S. book publishing industry means a reduction in the ability of a diversity of authors to find publishers for their ideas. Given that books are very important in national intellectual and political life, some writers and publishers fear that it will be hard for manuscripts other than probable blockbuster best-sellers to find a publisher if the number of houses continues to decline.

This concern is partially met by a steady rise of new, small publishing houses and by the number of people who are self-publishing their own manuscripts on the World Wide Web. That is, while book publishers consolidate and treat books largely as one media commodity among many, new publishing houses continue to spring up, signaling growth and diversity in the print industry. Although these new publishers tend to be small and to reach far fewer people than the largest book publishers, collectively they are a significant force. New electronic publishers, online sources of news and information, and the very fact that a growing portion of the U.S. population has effective access to the Internet certainly increase the potential for competition and a greater diversity of viewpoints. Electronic publishing is still finding its way, but online sources of information have been exploding, including computer network access to wire services, magazine sites, magazines that publish only online (such as *Slate*), newspaper copy, and an increasing number of alternative Internet information sources, such as discussion groups focused on various issues and events. However, low-income households have limited access to the Internet so although diverse points of view are available, not everyone can access them.

Redefining the Role of Magazines

As magazines compete with an ever broader array of media that provide many options for readers, they are constantly required to think about what they do best in comparison to other media. They can offer high-quality imagery for artwork, photos, and advertisements, which remains crucial for industries and readers in areas such as fashion. And they can offer greater depth than radio, TV, or even newspapers, so people interested in an analysis of news and events still depend on magazines such as *Newsweek* for general news, *People* for celebrity gossip, and *Rolling Stone* for music news.

Yet, to remain competitive, they must change to accommodate the needs of audiences and the times. For example, *Time* magazine has been successful over the years in redefining the role of the newsweekly in an era when people do not really need it for news. Norman Pearlstine, the editor in chief of Time Inc., sees "the role of the newsmagazine in providing synthesis and analysis" and "in the notion of storytelling through personality, which had been so much the *Time* hallmark" (Pogrebin, 1998). However, even a highly successful magazine like *Time* must change to suit its readership. For example, a study by the Project for Excellence in Journalism found that the number of pages leading news magazines devoted to national affairs has declined over the last two decades while entertainment and celebrity coverage has increased (and international coverage has remained about the same (http://www.stateofthenewsmedia.org/).

Intellectual Property and Copyright

Copyright issues have become crucial points of contention for print media. In recent years, both book publishers and academic journals have cracked down on students and professors who photocopy material that has been copyrighted by publishers. The enforcement of copyright rules can be seen in the fees that most legitimate photocopy shops now add to university course packets. Similarly, publishers are becoming increasingly concerned about the many informal newsletters, websites, and new electronic publications that "borrow" or sample images, photos, sections of text, and headlines from newspapers, magazines, and books. Because publishers and authors are determined to collect royalties from such reproduction and use, new **intellectual property** rules have changed as electronic distribution increases. If you do copy a photo of your favorite star

Intellectual property is a creative work.

onto your website from a magazine, by law, whoever holds the copyright—the photographer, her photo agency, or the magazine itself—would like you to pay for the use of the photo.

Individual authors and photographers have rights to their intellectual property during their lifetimes, and their heirs have rights for 70 years after the author's or photographer's death, so any publication less than 125 years old has to be checked for its copyright status. The duration of copyright protection has increased steadily over the years; the life-plus-70-year standard was set by the Copyright Term Extension Act of 1998, which increased the 50-year limit established by the 1976 Copyright Act. Supporters of such legislation like to defend these increases with tales of starving writers and their impoverished descendants, but in reality the beneficiaries are more likely to be transnational publishing conglomerates. And note that copyright laws serve a dual purpose. In addition to protecting the rights of authors so as to encourage the publication of new creative works, copyright is also supposed to place reasonable time limits on those rights so that outdated works may be incorporated into new creative efforts. Therefore, the extended copyright protection frustrates new creative endeavors such as including poetry and song lyrics on Internet sites.

And what about starving students who have to pay high fees for course packets and textbooks—who feels sorry for them? One of the basic precepts of copyright law is *fair use,* the notion that some copyright infringements serve a higher social purpose, such as education, and should be permitted. These "infringements" include making single copies for personal use, citing short passages in scholarly works, and making multiple copies for classroom use. So, if a student makes his own copy of a course packet, that's fair use and no copyright royalty is owed. Now, what if the student is short on time and asks a copy shop to make the copies for him? That is a copyright violation, at least according to a landmark decision that the publishing industry won against Kinko's print shops in 1991—a decision that sharply boosted course packet prices, since Kinko's got out of the business and other copy shops that still do course packets now have to pay a copyright fee on materials in them. Thus, the continual bolstering of copyright protection and the associated hardball legal tactics of transnational publishing giants has had a chilling effect on the exercise of fair use rights.

And once a copyrighted text is available online, how do we control copying in a medium where multiple perfect copies can be made with a tap on a keyboard? Various technological fixes, including digital "watermarks," pay-as-you-go access to copyrighted works, and the encoding of copyrighted material are some of the possibilities.

Censorship, Freedom of Speech, and the First Amendment

First Amendment issues are also crucial to the publishing industry. Freedom of speech and of expression in print media is well established in the United States, but over the years a number of community and religious groups have objected to the contents of various books, magazines, and new Internet publications. Usually such groups have objected to published contents that they see as being overtly sexual or likely to incite violence or the sexual abuse of women. Since the turn of the twentieth century, most books in the United States have been exempt from overt **censorship,** although novels like *Lady Chatterley's Lover* (1928), by D. H. Lawrence, went through periods of being censored. By today's standards, many readers would consider Lawrence's sexually explicit passages fairly tame, but the book challenged the understood limits of its time.

Censorship is the prohibition of certain media contents by government, religious or other societal authorities.

Even today, books get pulled from library shelves for various reasons. For example, *The Catcher in the Rye* (1951), by J. D. Salinger, has been challenged for rough language and *The Adventures of Huckleberry Finn* (1885), by Mark Twain, for racial stereotypes and epithets.

The focal point for discussions about censorship of books is usually the local library or school system, because campaigns to ban books usually focus on what is available through libraries or assigned in schools. Librarians have evolved a number of strategies for reconciling freedom of access with the desire to protect children or other vulnerable audiences from adult content. Some books are not shelved but have to be requested; access to others is restricted by age. For example, a number of libraries in 1992 restricted access by those under 18 to Madonna's book *Sex*.

The Internet poses similar challenges for libraries, because local libraries now offer Internet access as one of their services to the public (in fact, many see libraries as the preferred way to give disadvantaged groups access to the web). Additionally, the search engines of the web are becoming a staple of library research, but those search engines can be used to seek out a wide variety of controversial material that may contain sex, violence, or hate speech. (See Chapter 14 for discussions of laws to require libraries to use *filtering* programs to screen out controversial material.)

Magazine sales have also been challenged in some communities and by various legal decisions. Most stores that distribute sexually explicit magazines now shelve them in a section that is off-limits to those under age 18. Some stores, such as convenience store chains, have gone further, blocking off the covers of such magazines from open view or removing them altogether.

Need to Promote Education and Literacy?

Readership of both magazines and books is limited by the growing problem of adult illiteracy in the United States. Although the official literacy rate is 98 percent, many adults have low-level literacy skills. In 1992, the National Adult Literacy Survey found that upwards of 20 percent of the adult population lacks the literacy skills required to function effectively in society. For example, people with the lowest levels of literacy are unable to locate an item of information in a paragraph of a simple newspaper article. (Similar results were anticipated from a 2003 update of the survey.) And international surveys show that there are more functionally illiterate adults in the United States than in most other industrialized nations.

Reading is also at risk among those who know how to read. The percent who read literature when they are not "forced to" by school or work is declining in America. Only 47% of adults 18 or older read literature, in a 2002 survey, down 10 points over 20 years (NEA, 2004). The decline in reading among young adults is especially alarming. According to the NEA study, literary readership has declined nearly 30% among young adults 18–34 in the last 20 years.

Who is illiterate? Recent immigrants who are not literate in English account for about a quarter of the total. Poverty is also a determining factor; two-fifths of those with the lowest level of literacy skills live below the poverty line. However, people with poor reading skills are found throughout the population. Most of them are in a state of denial; only about a third of those at the lowest literacy level admit they have difficulty reading (Bowen, 1999). Here's a simple test for you gentle reader: Can you read and understand the front page of the *New York Times*?

SUMMARY AND REVIEW

WHAT KEY ELEMENTS OF THE PRINT MEDIA WERE DEVELOPED FIRST OUTSIDE EUROPE?

A number of essential ideas were brought to Europe; for example, using rags to make paper was imported from China. Other printing techniques, such as movable metal type, developed in parallel form outside Europe but were probably not a direct influence on the development of European print media.

WHAT WAS THE IMPACT OF PRINTING IN EUROPE?

The advent of printing by Gutenberg greatly accelerated the growth of literacy by making books cheaper and more widely available. Education became more widespread because texts were easier to get. Printing affected religion by making the Bible widely available, politics by boosting news circulation, and economics by increasing knowledge and skills.

WHY AND HOW DID MAGAZINES DEVELOP?

In 1741 the first U.S. magazines, Bradford's *American Magazine* and Ben Franklin's *General Magazine,* appeared. During the American Revolution, many magazines took a more political tone. Few magazines were popular or long-lived during this time. They covered weekly events, politics, and art and contained reviews, travelogues, short stories, and serialized fiction; they were aimed at an educated elite. By the 1820s, magazines of more general interest, such as the *Saturday Evening Post,* began to appear. The number of magazines increased during the Civil War, and they began to reach wider audiences. The Postal Act of 1879 made distribution cheaper.

WHAT WAS THE ROLE OF PRINT MEDIA IN THE CIVIL WAR? HOW DID THE WAR AFFECT THE MEDIA?

Books and magazines affected the issues debate that led up to the Civil War. *Uncle Tom's Cabin,* for example, is a book widely credited with helping influence northern U.S. opinion against slavery. Several magazines, such as *Harper's Weekly,* grew to fame during the Civil War as a result of their print coverage and their illustrations, which dramatized scenes of the war. Illustration became prominent tools of magazine journalism. Circulations grew.

WHAT WAS "MUCKRAKING"?

Muckraking characterized the period around 1900, when crusading magazines turned their attention to scandals and corruption in government and among industry cartels.

WHEN DID MAGAZINES PEAK AS MASS AUDIENCE MEDIA?

After 1900, many new kinds of magazines sprang up. News photo magazines, such as *Life,* and general-interest magazines, such as the *Saturday Evening Post* and *Collier's,* continued to serve a broad audience up through the 1950s, when both their photojournalism roles and entertainment functions were undercut by television.

WHAT FORM HAVE MAGAZINES TAKEN AS MODERN MASS MEDIA?

They have become more targeted to more segmented audiences. Instead of addressing a broad mass audience, magazines now tend to focus on very specific audiences for politics, hobbies, interest groups, and demographic groups.

WHAT ARE THE TRENDS IN PRINT MEDIA DELIVERY?

The mail was crucial for enabling magazines to reach a broad audience in an affordable manner. After the 1990s, electronic delivery by the World Wide Web was becoming an alternative for magazine delivery.

WHAT IS DESKTOP PUBLISHING?

Desktop publishing is the creation of publication-quality documents using the increased power and speed of desktop computers, laser printers, and scanners that digitize photos or illustrations into computer-readable form. Desktop publishing has done much to decentralize print media. Laypeople can now produce local or specialized media, and professional media also use desktop publishing for their products. This advance in technology has led to the proliferation of magazines and small book-publishing houses.

WHAT ARE THE MAIN TRENDS IN BOOK PUBLISHING?

Increasing numbers of books are being published and purchased by consumers, students, and businesses. Large publishing houses are consolidating even as smaller ones proliferate.

WHAT ARE THE TRENDS IN MAGAZINES?

General-interest magazines have declined as specialized, targeted magazines have grown in numbers and diversity.

WHO READS MAGAZINES?

The average adult spends about as much time on books as on magazines, but younger people read magazines more.

WHAT IS THE TREND AMONG PRINT MEDIA READERS RELATED TO OVERALL LITERACY?

There seems to be an overall trend toward less reading, in part because overall functional literacy seems to be declining.

IS THERE A TREND TOWARD CONSOLIDATION IN PRINT MEDIA?

Book publishing has become more concentrated and internationalized. Magazine publishing has concentrated in a similar way, but more new magazine companies have continued to enter the field.

WHAT ARE CONCERNS ABOUT COMMODIFICATION IN THE PUBLISHING INDUSTRY?

Treating books simply as another media commodity tends to lead publishers to focus on blockbusters and publish fewer other books, thus reducing the diversity of their contents.

However, this trend is offset by an explosion of small publishing houses and Internet sites.

WHAT CURRENT THREATS ARE THERE TO FREEDOM OF SPEECH AND OF THE PRESS?

Freedom of speech and of expression in publishing is well established, although a number of groups object to the contents of various print media, usually because those contents are seen as overtly sexual. Several freedom of speech issues are controversial now for new media.

WHAT ARE THE MAIN COPYRIGHT ISSUES FOR PRINT MEDIA?

A major issue in print media is the photocopying of copyrighted material. The Copyright Term Extension Act of 1998 extends the period of protection to the life of the author plus 70 years. Many newsletters and new electronic publications borrow images, sections of text, and headlines from newspapers, magazines, and books. Publishers and authors want to collect royalties in return for such use. As electronic distribution increases, new intellectual property rules have been developed.

MEDIA CONNECTION

For web links, quizzes, and key term flash cards, visit the **Student Companion Website** at http://communication.wadsworth.com/straubhaar5.

 For unlimited easy access to additional and exclusive online study, support, and research tools, log on to **1pass** at http://1pass.thomson.com using the unique access code found on your 1pass passcode card.

 The **Media Now Premium Website** offers *Career Profile* videos, *Critical View* video news clips, and *Media in Motion* concept animations. You'll also find Stop & Review tutorial questions, a sample final exam, and much more.

 InfoTrac College Edition is a fully searchable online database offering anytime, anywhere access to more than 20 years' worth of articles from nearly 5,000 diverse and reliable sources.

vMentor provides live, one-on-one online tutoring to connect you to experts who will assist you in understanding the concepts covered in your course.

Interested in a career in publishing? Watch Elisa Freeling describe her job as a copy editor in the Career Profile video for this chapter.

The war correspondent is one of the many romantic images of journalism to come down through the years. The number of newspapers has decreased, but they still attract a profitable and influential readership. Online newspapers, along with mergers and consolidation, the rise of blogs, ethical issues, and how to treat the privacy of public figures and private citizens, give print journalists a great deal to think about.

NEWSPAPER HISTORY: JOURNALISM IN THE MAKING

The history of newspapers is also the history of our ideas about what journalism should be. Mainstream newspapers have always had to make compromises with commercial interests and political powers, but their history reflects the evolution of a free press from European origins and the American Revolution. Many editors and writers have worked hard to face down government censorship and commercialism over the years, and their stories are crucial to understanding the role and function of journalism today. In the history of newspapers, we can see the evolution of a social responsibility model, developing better journalistic practices and ethics.

Newspapers Emerge

Before there were newspapers, there were newsletters. Medieval banks published financial and trade-oriented newsletters. Irregular news sheets in Holland, Great Britain, and France during the Thirty Years' War carried news about foreign events after 1618, as well

1640s	Diurnos, first daily newspapers, published	**1878**	New Journalism movement originated by Joseph Pulitzer
1690	First American newspaper, *Publick Occurrences Both Foreign and Domestick,* published	**1895**	William Randolph Hearst pushed yellow journalism
1733	Peter Zenger trial establishes truth as a defense for press against libel charges	**1972**	Watergate scandal inspires new era of investigative reporting
1783	First daily newspaper published in America, *Pennsylvania Evening Post and Daily Advertiser*	**1982**	*USA Today* national daily launched
1789	First Amendment to Constitution enshrines freedom of press	**1989**	First news blog
1833	The *New York Sun,* first Penny Press daily, begins publication	**2004**	Political blogs rival newspaper columns in readership
1848	Associated Press wire news service begins operation		

as commercial or economic issues. These news sheets, called **corantos,** were gradually replaced by daily reports, or **diurnos,** that focused more on domestic events, such as the civil war in Great Britain between king and Parliament between 1640 and 1650 (Stephens, 1989).

During this time, there was no freedom of the press. In the early days of newspapers in Europe, authorities granted licenses to print newspapers and other materials so that they could control the content. More open societies began to recognize the importance of *freedom of speech,* and criticism of this form of censorship grew. At about the same time, marketplace competition for goods began in Europe, and the idea developed of a **marketplace of ideas** in which different voices could compete for attention. John Stuart Mill was a political thinker who influenced American ideas about democracy. He and other early advocates of democracy promoted the idea of an active, informed citizenry and a *free press* to assist in the wide circulation of ideas (Altschull, 1995).

The Colonial and Revolutionary Freedom Struggles

Early American newspapers struggled with the question of control by colonial authorities, and that struggle gave birth to freedom of the press. The first U.S. newspaper, *Publick Occurrences Both Foreign and Domestick,* in 1690 contained stories that scandalized the British Crown and Puritan authorities; it was shut down after one issue. In 1704, Boston postmaster John Campbell started the *Boston News-Letter,* published "by authority" of the royal governor.

In 1721, James Franklin started an independent newspaper, the *New England Courant,* with no "by authority" approval. As a result, he was jailed and forbidden to publish. So, James made his brother, Benjamin, the new editor. Ben Franklin was very successful as a newspaper editor, and he soon moved to Philadelphia to start the *Pennsylvania Gazette.*

The question of editorial *independence* and criticism of authority was raised again in 1733 when Peter Zenger published a newspaper openly critical of the British governor of

Corantos were irregular news sheets that appeared around 1600.

Diurnos were seventeenth-century ancestors of the daily newspaper.

Marketplace of ideas is the concept that the best ideas will win out in competition.

New York and was jailed for criminal **libel.** Despite British legal precedent to the contrary, Zenger's lawyer argued that the truth of a published piece was itself a defense against libel. Appealing to the American jury not to rely on British law and precedent, Zenger won the libel case, which established the important principle that true statements are not libelous.

In the Zenger case and other events that followed, the British colonial authorities were still trying to control the fledgling American press, particularly as calls for revolution grew. British domination left colonists, particularly journalists and printers, convinced that freedom of speech and of press were essential. They insisted that even radical statements, such as calling for the overthrow of an unjust government, be permitted. The first American editorial cartoon in 1754 showed a snake chopped into eight pieces, and its caption, "Join or Die," urged the colonies to unite against the British. The political press that emerged was very important in building support for the American Revolution and in defining the role of the American free press. Partisan newspapers proliferated. Newspapers published key documents including the Declaration of Independence (1776) and the debates over the Constitution in 1787.

The First Amendment

Freedom of the press was formally established in the United States at the Constitutional Convention in 1787. The desire to protect freedom of speech and of the press resulted in the *First Amendment* to the Constitution. It says

> Congress shall make no law respecting an establishment of religion, or prohibiting the free exercise thereof, or abridging the freedom of speech, or of the press; or the right of the people peaceably to assemble, and to petition the Government for a redress of grievances.

Despite this strong stand for freedom of the press, there was soon an attempt to limit **seditious** speech under the 1798 Alien and Sedition Acts, and several newspaper writers and editors were charged with sedition in 1798–1800. However, when the acts expired in 1800, they were not renewed because a consensus had grown for freedom of the press.

Diversity in the Press

Diverse viewpoints are essential to the functioning of the press in a free society. After the American Revolution, the politicization of newspapers continued, representing a wide diversity of political views. These publications took on more partisan leanings and were often openly involved in political campaigns such as the abolition of slavery.

Advertising and commercial interests began to be important as well. Benjamin Franklin was successful in part because he was a clever writer of advertising copy. In 1783 the first daily newspaper in the United States, the *Pennsylvania Evening Post and Daily Advertiser,* was begun. By 1800 most large cities had at least one daily, but circulations were limited because printing presses were slow, and readers had to be literate and relatively wealthy: one copy cost as much as a pint of whiskey, around five cents. Newspapers were one of the forces that drew people into thinking about themselves as Americans, forming an "imagined community" of people who had access to the same information and identified with each other (Anderson, 1983). However, real differences existed among Americans, and not all were allowed to belong to the larger community. Thus, newspapers also began to reflect the voices of diverse, excluded audiences, such as African-Americans and Native Americans.

Libel is a harmful and untruthful criticism that damages someone.

Seditious speech undermines the government.

■ LEADING STAR
Frederick Douglass used the
North Star to push for abolition
of slavery.

Native American Press   The first Native American newspaper, the *Cherokee Phoenix,* was established by the Cherokee nation. In 1829 the Georgia legislature took away all the legal rights of Native Americans, including freedom of speech. In 1832 the editor of the *Cherokee Phoenix* resigned in protest, and its publication became erratic. It was not until 10 years later that a new Cherokee nation newspaper was firmly established. Several other Native American groups published newspapers, and some of them suffered similar discrimination, such as suppression by state authorities to limit sympathy for Native American claims to retain their lands.

African-American Press   The first African-American newspaper, *Freedom's Journal,* was established in 1827 in New York City. The newspaper had strong ties to the abolitionist press, and its goal was to encourage racial unity and the progress of African-Americans in the North.

Another important African-American paper, the *North Star,* was founded in 1847 and edited by Frederick Douglass, an escaped slave. It had the following prospectus:

> Frederick Douglass proposes to publish in Rochester, New York, a weekly antislavery paper with the above title. The objective of the *North Star* will be to attack slavery in all its forms and aspects; advocate universal emancipation; exact the standard of public morality; promote the moral and intellectual improvement of the colored people; and . . . hasten the day of freedom to our three million enslaved fellow-countrymen.

He called it the *North Star* because that star was how slaves escaping at night guided themselves. Douglass attacked slavery and other laws restricting people of color. Along with others, he helped push what abolitionists called "the War to Free the Slaves," the U.S. Civil War, in 1861.

The Penny Press

For democracy to function, ideas must be widely circulated as well as diverse. The early 1800s saw technological innovations in the field of printing (see Chapter 3), which in turn permitted lower-cost papers aimed at a broader audience. At the same time, social conditions favorable for the creation of the mass audience and mass newspapers were building. More people were learning to read via the expanding public education system, wages were increasing, more people were moving to the cities, and an urban middle class was growing. Newspaper publishers responded to this market by creating and selling cheaper newspapers. Thus, in both the United States and Britain, the 1800s brought forth the **Penny Press.** However, there were certainly many people who still could not read or afford newspapers, particularly among the waves of immigrants who arrived in the United States from the 1840s on.

In 1833 Benjamin Day launched the first low-cost daily mass newspaper. Called the *New York Sun,* the paper sold for a penny—hence the Penny Press nickname. To offer his paper at that price, Day not only had to rely on advertising as well as sales, but also had to reach out further to the urban audience, using newsboys to sell papers in greater volume. This kind of daily was one of the first media to create a truly mass audience, big enough to attract advertisers and justify their investment. And with the advent of the *rotary press* in

Penny Press were daily newspapers that sold for one cent.

the early nineteenth century (see Chapter 3), costs decreased even further. As newspapers began to address larger, more diverse and less clearly partisan audiences, modern journalism also began to evolve. Stories were less overt in their political tone, trying to reach across party lines. Stories were aimed at the common man, the rising force behind Andrew Jackson and other politicians. This combination of factors spawned the modern daily newspaper.

Another boon to the mass newspaper was the deployment of the telegraph in 1844, which led to a marked improvement in speed and reach in news gathering. By the time of the Mexican-American War from 1846 to 1848, telegraph technology enabled newspapers to get news of the war almost instantly—right after it arrived by ship from the front in Mexico City.

Additionally, in 1848 several New York newspapers started the New York Associated Press news service to share the cost of covering stories: Reporters employed by the service covered events and sold their stories to all the papers, so each newspaper saved money by hiring fewer of its own reporters. The service expanded with the ability to send stories over the telegraph, thus becoming the first **wire service.** This and other regional wire services joined in 1892 to become what is now called the Associated Press (AP). Wire services helped newspapers lower their costs, add more general-interest material, and appeal to a wider audience.

Journalism continued to develop toward today's style of the inverted pyramid (tight summaries followed by the main news). A focus on local and daily events of wide popular interest, current daily news, and a more objective perspective, was fostered by the sharp coverage of the AP.

© The Granger Collection, New York

■ **ONLY A PENNY**
The *New York Sun* was the first low-cost daily mass newspaper, first published in 1833.

Following the Frontier

Newspapers expanded westward with the American population in the years before the Civil War. During this period, several writers who later became famous for their books and short stories, including Mark Twain, made their names as newspaper journalists.

As cheaper presses also moved west, newspapers proliferated and diversified. For example, the second half of the 1800s saw over 130 Spanish-language newspapers started in the Southwest (Huntzicker, 1993). Frontier newspapers were often blunt and antagonistic, and their editors were opinionated. Many chastised eastern liberals for sympathizing with the "Indians." Jane Grey Swisshelm, founder of the *St. Cloud Visiter,* criticized the politicians of St. Cloud, Minnesota. They retaliated by destroying her press, but they made her reputation, as she rebuilt her press and exposed the mob who had destroyed it (Huntzicker, 1993).

War Coverage

Although newspapers helped Americans build a nation, they also played a catalytic role in the conflict that tore it apart. The debate over slavery and the events leading up to the Civil War were well covered by the Penny Press. The Civil War (1861–1865) expanded newspaper readership because people wanted immediate news of the conflict. That interest,

Wire services supply news to multiple publications; they were named originally for their use of telegraph wires.

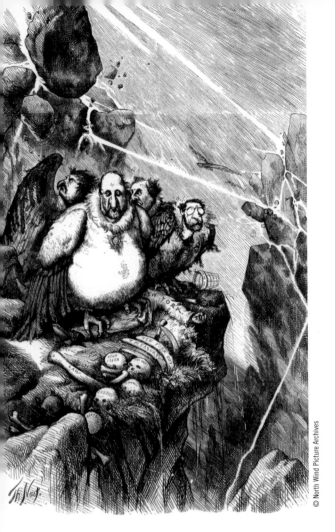

■ **NASTY WIT**

Harper's Weekly magazine editorial cartoonist Thomas Nast was famous for cartoons denouncing corrupt politicians.

New journalism was the investigative reporting of the nineteenth century.

fueled by reports telegraphed directly from the front, reinforced newspapers' focus on yesterday's events and headlines. Not surprisingly, northern and southern papers often saw things very differently, and several northern papers had a major influence on the positions and strategy of the northern states. The *New York Tribune* under Horace Greeley championed the abolition of slavery.

The New Journalism

Newspapers plunged into the post–Civil War industrial expansion, flourishing in the cities where industries grew and people flocked to get jobs. Along with other industries, newspapers saw a chance to grow, and they more aggressively pursued advertising and newspaper sales.

A focus on investigative journalism led to the era of the **new journalism,** in which several newspapers crusaded for various causes, building on the antislavery crusade. The new journalism was lively, brash, self-conscious, impetuous, and sensational. It concentrated more on news, increasingly defined as the latest events of the day, and less on editorials and essay columns. *Scoops* were more important, as were gossip, big headlines, and action pictures (Everett, 1993).

This period was characterized by muckraking, as crusading newspapers turned their attention to the "muck" of scandals and corruption in government and industry across the country. (For more on muckraking, see Chapter 3.) City bosses tried to corrupt the press by paying for favorable coverage. Although some newspapers were bought off by political bosses like the Tweed Ring in New York, others doggedly pursued anticorruption stories. The *New York Times* rose to prominence partly as the result of its successful campaign against the Tweed Ring. *Harper's Weekly* magazine editorial cartoonist Thomas Nast made strong visual statements against the Tweed Ring. After the campaign eventually brought down the Ring, subsequent investigations showed that a significant number of papers had received the Ring's patronage, and many of them died when this source of money was cut off (Smythe, 1993).

Furthering their appeal, newspapers of this era added a new visual element, the news photograph. During the Civil War, photographer Matthew Brady had popularized photographic images, but they could not be reproduced in newspapers or magazines. However, in 1880 a process for integrating photos and text on the same page was developed, and the first bona fide newspaper photos appeared.

Toward the end of the 1800s, newspapers began reaching even broader audiences. In the largest cities of the day, large-circulation papers pursued a mass audience directly with sensational stories on sex, murder, scandal, popularized science and medicine, and other human-interest events. As European immigration increased, many immigrants published foreign-language newspapers.

Yellow Journalism

The next chapter in the history of the American newspaper was not so illustrious. It grew from the rivalry of two nineteenth-century media moguls, Joseph Pulitzer and William Randolph Hearst, and from changing newspaper economics.

Hungarian immigrant Joseph Pulitzer came to the United States in 1858 to join the army and turned to journalism after the war. In 1878 he managed to pull together enough money to merge two struggling St. Louis newspapers into one, the *St. Louis Post-Dispatch,* and established himself as a nonpartisan social critic by conducting a series of popular crusades against the corruption and complacency noted above. In 1883 Pulitzer bought the *New York World,* with the intention of publishing a newspaper for the underdogs in New York City. For example, he hired Elizabeth Cochrane, known as Nelly Bly, who became famous by feigning insanity to investigate the notorious Blackwell Island insane asylum. Her stories on poor conditions and abuse of patients prompted official investigations and improvements (Everett, 1993). The *World* became the paper that others imitated.

One of the imitators was William Randolph Hearst. In 1895, Hearst inherited his family's fortune and came to New York City to buy the ailing *New York Journal.* There followed a dramatic war between Hearst's *Morning Journal* and Pulitzer's *World.* One of Hearst's chief weapons was a journalistic style that came to be called **yellow journalism.** This style emphasized sensational photos and story selections, large headlines, an abundance of personality and human-interest stories, and sometimes even hoaxes and fake interviews. A famous example of Hearst's yellow journalism was his spectacular coverage of the 1898 explosion of the U.S. battleship *Maine* in the Havana harbor, which Hearst blamed on the Spanish, although the cause of the explosion is unknown to this day. Many historians credit Hearst's coverage with helping to push the United States into war with Spain over Cuba and the Philippines (Sloan, Stovall, & Startt, 1993). Yellow journalism was thus an extension of the new journalism phenomenon but lacked its sense of social responsibility.

Yellow journalism was more than just a result of the competition between two men. During the 1880s and 1890s, papers were no longer read only by the elite but also by the general population. With this shift in the marketplace came a shift in the sources of income from circulation to advertising. The newspaper that survived sold its ads and subscriptions at the greatest profit, and these sales depended on the size of the paper's audience. In other words, the lowering of journalistic quality was a result of change in the marketplace; Hearst and Pulitzer were simply responding to the change. But in the process commercialism grew as a threat to the ideal of the press in a free society.

© Hulton Archive/Getty Images

■ **PRESS HERO**
Joseph Pulitzer pioneered the new journalism, which was sensational but news-oriented, and focused on scoops, headlines, and pictures.

Responsible Journalism

Although yellow journalism may have gotten out of hand, both Hearst and Pulitzer contributed substantially to the development of the profession. Pulitzer created a new journalism that defined social responsibility for newspaper coverage. Hearst encouraged higher salaries, bylines, and other recognition for journalists. These innovations were important milestones in the evolution of journalism as a valued and respectable profession. Both Pulitzer and Hearst helped mentor and create a number of good journalists.

Publishers shifted formats to keep pace with changing social conditions. **Tabloids** such as the *New York World* exaggerated the sensationalist trend that characterized many dailies around 1900. They focused on things that often preoccupied city dwellers trying to make sense of their rapidly changing world, such as divorce, murder, and other crime. African-American papers also shifted to a more urban focus as their audiences migrated north. On the other hand, the immigrant ethnic press declined as readers assimilated into American society and as their children learned to read in English.

Yellow journalism was the sensationalistic reporting of the nineteenth century.

Tabloids are newspapers focused on popular, sensational events.

■ SMILE!

Photojournalists can capture images that drive stories home and make people buy newspapers.

The **social responsibility model** calls on journalists to monitor the ethics of their own writing.

Responsible journalism advanced in 1896 when Adolph Ochs bought the *New York Times.* Ochs turned the nearly dead paper into an exceptional twentieth-century newspaper of record. He resisted sensationalism in photos, extravagant typefaces, fake stories, and stunts, which many readers had tired of. He stressed impartiality and independence. He made sure that advertising was clearly distinguishable from stories, unlike other papers that made money by allowing ads to masquerade as legitimate stories.

Newspapers Reach Their Peak

Newspapers peaked as a mass medium between 1890 and 1920. The U.S. population tripled between 1850 and 1900 to almost 76 million people. In contrast, newspaper circulation increased twenty-fold to 15.1 million in 1900 (McKearns, 1993). In 1900, there were 1967 English-language dailies, and 562 American cities had competing dailies. New York City alone had 29 dailies.

By 1910 the newspaper industry had grown larger than its resources—advertising and circulation—could support. Inevitably, merger and consolidation began to trim the numbers back. Usually, stronger papers acquired weaker ones to get their circulation and advertising base. The new group owners were businessmen who bought, sold, killed, and consolidated daily papers in medium-size cities to maximize profits. The largest owners were Hearst and the Scripps-Howard chain, which closed over 15 papers each. The chain phenomenon continued into the 1930s, as Harry Chandler (the Times-Mirror group), Frank Gannett (the Gannett group), John Knight (Knight-Ridder Publications), and others joined the chain ownership trend. By the end of the 1930s, six chains controlled about a quarter of newspaper circulation (Folkerts & Teeter, 1994). Increasingly, businessmen rather than journalists ran newspapers, and commercial values intruded further into the newsroom.

Thus, concentration of ownership and newspaper closings began to erode the diversity that marked the late nineteenth-century press. During this time, antitrust regulators became concerned about *monopolies* or *oligopolies* emerging, particularly among the news services that completely controlled the market and supplied the newspapers with much of their material: Associated Press, United Press, and the International News Service.

Professional Journalism

The excesses of yellow journalism and the rising tide of commercialism in newspaper operations sparked the further evolution of the journalistic profession from a free press to a **social responsibility model.** One of the key points was the evolution of journalists from ink-stained wretches, as they were known in the 19th century, to the college-educated professionals of the 20th century. That depended on professional education, with the rise of accredited journalism schools. Another key development was the rise of professional associations with well-structured codes of ethics (see more about journalistic codes of ethics in chapter 15).

Daily newspapers helped shape the events of the late nineteenth and early twentieth centuries, so much so that attempts were made to make the press behave more responsibly in times of national crises. During the first half of the 1900s, newspapers crusaded both for and against government policies, such as entering World War I (1914–1918). For example, sensational newspaper coverage of the 1915 German sinking of the British ocean liner *Lusitania,* which killed over a hundred U.S. citizens, aroused public sentiment in favor of entering World War I against Germany.

The government created the Office of War Information to ensure that official government positions would be covered. They also closed German-language newspapers and censored news during WWI to make sure that no military secrets leaked out through the newspapers. U.S. government propaganda was more restrained during World War II, but controls were still placed on newspaper coverage to avoid divulging military secrets. Censorship was abolished with the end of hostilities in 1945, but the give-and-take between the government and the press over the preceding decades of crisis helped to entrench the social responsibility model—so much so that the press assumed a rather uncritical stance toward national policy.

Competing for the News

Newspaper content was affected by competition from radio, which had exploded in the late 1920s and could offer much more current headlines. To set themselves apart, newspapers pursued deeper news analysis and interpretation. Newspapers could deal with complex government programs and economic crises, reporting various points of view in and out of government, with in-depth investigative reporting, a technique not well suited to radio. And, they were able to display pictures of products on sale; radio couldn't do that.

But television could. In the early 1950s, television also ate into the national advertising base that newspapers had once dominated. However, local dailies continued to be important social and political institutions, so although newspapers continued to consolidate, at least one daily survived in nearly all towns large and small. The number of competing newspapers in major cities declined sharply. By 2004, fewer than 30 cities boasted two newspapers. Newspaper chains steadily grew in dominance, as the number of dailies declined. Gannett, Knight-Ridder, and Scripps-Howard often owned the only daily newspaper in town. By 2004, Gannett owned 101 newspapers in the United States.

However, some new journalistic voices also emerged. As printing costs decreased with technological change, new print competitors emerged. Suburban newspapers, often owned by chains, followed the middle class away from city centers into the suburbs. City and regional magazines competed for news and advertising. Weekly shopping newspapers popped up almost everywhere and cut into a major staple of newspaper income, the classified ad (Marsh, 1993).

Newspaper owners worried that younger readers were not acquiring the newspaper habit as they relied more on the electronic media for their news. One response was to focus on community news, issues, and services, whereas larger newspapers often accentuated the trend toward investigative reporting and critical analysis.

The Watchdogs

Through their coverage of the civil rights movement, the Vietnam War, and the emergence of advocacy movements championing the rights of other ethnic minorities, women, and gays, some crusading papers adopted a critical stance toward the status quo.

■ VIETNAM WATCHDOG
The *New York Times* was accused of violating national security for publishing the classified *Pentagon Papers.*

Since World War I, most media had supported the government out of a sense of patriotic duty. But with the Vietnam War (1966–1976) and the Watergate scandal (1972–1974), journalists began to see themselves as "watchdogs," outside critics with a primary responsibility to keep an eye on government mistakes.

In a crucial test of press freedom, the *New York Times* leaked secret government documents, known as the Pentagon Papers, that proved the United States had been illegally bombing neutral Cambodia during the Vietnam War. Such coverage set the news media in conflict with government authorities (Braestrup, 1977).

In 1972, still during the Vietnam conflict, Carl Bernstein and Bob Woodward, two investigative reporters working for the *Washington Post,* broke the story of the Watergate scandal. In 1972 Republican Party operatives had burglarized Democratic Party headquarters in the Washington, D.C., Watergate complex, looking for documents that might damage Democratic Party candidates. With the help of a confidential informant in the Nixon administration, Bernstein and Woodward uncovered the foul play and cover-up that followed. These revelations ultimately led to Richard Nixon's resignation from the presidency. Many observers of the press regard that era as something of a golden age of investigative reporting and as a paradigm for the role the press should play in public debates in a free society. Unfortunately, readers were less impressed. The critical coverage placed newspapers in conflict with the values of some of the older, middle-class readers who were a crucial part of their circulation base. Since Watergate, many agree that the role of watchdog has devolved into one of attack dog as newspapers search for sensational "gotcha" stories that sell newspapers. Investigative reporting has given way to scandal-mongering and public voyeurism in the massive attention given the insider stock trading case of Martha Stewart in 2002 or the Michael Jackson trial (for more on investigative reporting, see "Media Literacy: Responsible Reporting" later in this chapter).

The *civic journalism* approach, followed by one-fifth of U.S. papers (Pew, 2004) uses a more explanatory, less conflict-oriented approach and tries to involve citizens more in organizing civic events. *Public journalism* is similar, often getting media outlets to cooperate in civic information projects. *Participatory journalism* tries to get even noncitizens involved in news reporting and photography.

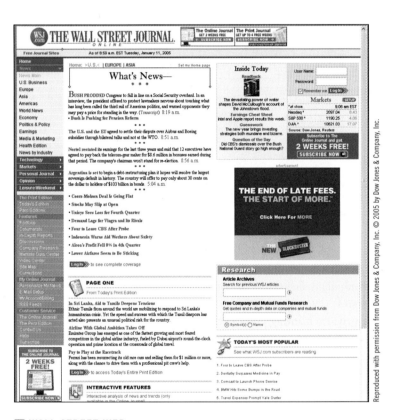

■ **WALL STREET WEB**

Even traditional newspapers like the *Wall Street Journal* have moved their contents on to the World Wide Web. The *Journal* was one of the first of a growing number of newspapers that charges for access to online content.

Newspapers in the Information Age

Now local newspapers and the diversity of opinion they represent are increasingly under attack by competition from new technology. In the late twentieth century, newspaper coverage resembled television news more and more, emphasizing color photography, eye-catching graphics, and shorter stories with less "serious news." The introduction of *USA*

Today in 1982 set the stage for this change, and now all major newspapers have adopted elements of its colorful style. *USA Today* was created by the Gannett chain to fill a perceived niche for a national newspaper that could contend for the attention of the average newspaper reader, in contrast to the *New York Times* and the *Wall Street Journal,* which appeal primarily to elite audiences across the country. *USA Today,* as well as other national papers, took advantage of new systems of newspaper distribution via satellite and computerized news production. That makes it possible to deliver national newspapers to doorsteps everywhere in the country, further eroding local newspaper sales. (For more about these technologies, see the section "Technology: Roll the Presses!")

National and local newspapers are now accessible over the World Wide Web, a new source of competition for local dailies. Electronic media sites like cnn.com and msnbc.com and their cable television counterparts are adding to the competitive landscape for news. Most local newspapers have responded with their own online editions. However, the online efforts mostly are not moneymakers as yet and the Internet poses serious threats both to newspaper economics and journalistic standards. The many e-commerce, auction, and portal sites on the web threaten the economic lifeblood of the local newspaper—its classified advertising. Both national and local newspapers are increasingly in competition with the constant flood of news and rumor from Internet-only news sites, a torrent that is too often unfiltered by journalistic standards. Meanwhile, Internet blogs routinely "scoop" conventional newspapers. Sometimes they undermine journalistic standards, but other times provide a check on lax reporting by the mainstream press.

Industry consolidation has continued, with the net loss of over 250 daily newspapers since the Watergate era. The latest trend is to consolidate operations geographically, by acquiring suburban and metropolitan newspapers in the same market, for example. Led by the Tribune Company, there was also a push to eliminate rules against owning newspaper and electronic media outlets in the same market so that consolidation can take place across media as well as across geographic boundaries. Those non-chain papers that are left often struggle to maintain a semblance of editorial independence. Newspaper readership began to decline until 2000, with the biggest losses suffered in small markets where independents abound, but has been slowly increasing since (Newspaper Association of America, 2004). Still, the proceeds from advertising are showing impressive growth. Ad sales by daily newspapers now top $45 billion a year, five times what they were in the journalistic halcyon days of Watergate (Newspaper Association of America, 2004). Print newspapers continue to dominate advertising for local supermarkets and for local automobile and home electronics dealers. In 2003, newspapers brought in more ad revenue than any medium except direct mail advertising.

STOP & REVIEW

1. What case established the precedent for freedom of the press in colonial America?

2. What was the Penny Press? What led to it?

3. What was the new journalism?

4. What was yellow journalism?

5. What roles did Pulitzer and Hearst play in newspaper development?

6. Why did newspapers begin to consolidate and newspaper chains form?

7. What was the impact of Watergate on American journalism?

TECHNOLOGY: ROLL THE PRESSES!

Advances in publishing technology were reviewed in Chapter 3. Here we will consider innovations that made a unique contribution to the newspaper industry where speed is of the essence in all phases of gathering, publishing, and disseminating the news.

Newsgathering Trends

Before the telegraph, the speed of news was the speed of transportation systems, from the clipper ship to the pony express. In 1848, the telegraph revolutionized news gathering with the first *newswire,* the earliest of "online" services. A generation later, the telephone also improved the speed of newspaper writing, even though some late-nineteenth-century reporters disdained it as a "lazy" way to avoid honest footwork (Sloan, Stovall, & Startt, 1993).

Until 1922 only the words traveled by wire, not the pictures. In that year the first wire photo was transmitted, on the occasion of the election of a new pope in Rome. By breaking Pope Pius XI's picture down into a fine grid of black and white dots, it was possible to transmit it by wire from the Vatican, one picture dot at a time.

Today, all the modern means of electronic communication are found in the newsroom. Reporters scan radio, TV, and cable channels, once again prompting grumbles about "laziness" from the old-timers. The high-tech reporter can also monitor police communication frequencies and can get tips and confirm stories via e-mail. By monitoring Internet news sites, blogs, chat rooms, listservs, and newsgroups (see Chapter 9), reporters can turn up leads and track down rumors.

Reporters also use computers to access search engines and sift through mountains of raw data, a technique known as computer-assisted reporting (CAR). For example, by taking advantage of public and commercially available databases, reporters can write stories about trends in crime and poverty and objectively compare areas or groups of people with one another without relying on self-serving handouts from politicians or lobbying groups. CAR can also "dig out the dirt" by rummaging through computerized files of personal information. Reporters can find financial connections between Hollywood stars and political candidates, ferret out criminal records of people who hold positions of public trust, and find the names of dead people who "voted" in recent elections. More sophisticated approaches replicate the functions of social scientists (see Chapter 13) by analyzing trends in voter behavior in depth, finding correlations between crime and poverty rates and their possible causes, and producing detailed maps of pockets of poverty or crime in a region (Tankard & Lasorsa, 2000).

Led by Tribune Company, news organizations are combining multiple media in the same newsroom. They can cut costs by sharing raw video, audio, and still photographs and edit them for several different media using digital workstations linked to high-speed computer networks. However, the various media have differing traditions of how to cover a story, so the reporters as well as the newsroom technologies may have to change before that effort succeeds. Some of the efforts to get different kinds of reporters to work together in combined newsrooms have led to considerable conflict.

The convergence trend has led to a new form of journalism, *backpack journalism,* also known as multimedia reporting. In addition to a notepad, the multimedia journalist totes a miniature digital video camera (a mini DV, see Chapter 7) and a tape recorder in a backpack. Instead of writing the story in the old-fashioned linear text way, the reporter combines text, interactive graphics, video, and sound to make a story with multiple versions. By "posting" the story in multiple media, including conventional newspapers and TV news shows, as well as on the web, the journalist can let readers of the story obtain additional details in nonlinear sequences and even interact with the reporter in newsgroups, online chats, or the reporter's own blog. In the process, stories may become more reporter-driven and less editor-driven, a significant challenge to the traditional newsroom power structure (Stevens, 2002).

Production Trends

In Chapter 3 we saw how innovations such as the rotary press, linotype, and phototypesetting greatly increased the number of pages that could be printed in an hour's time. Newspaper editions grew from a few pages to hundreds of pages, and circulation mounted into the hundreds of thousands as a result.

Teletypesetting was a significant improvement in the 1950s. Stories could be typeset once by a highly skilled typesetter employed by a wire service, then punched out onto paper tape by the local newspaper, and then automatically fed into the newspaper's own typesetting machines to produce a near-perfect copy. Later, in the late 1960s and the early 1970s, data contained on the paper tapes were stored in computer memory, paving the way for the computerization of print production. Now, reporters compose and edit their stories on a computer, compositors lay out the pages of newspapers on the computer, and original pages are mastered inside the computer system. The latest *computer-to-plate* processes generate the printing plates directly from computer images, using sophisticated cousins of the ink-jet and laser printers found in the home. That eliminates the expensive step of photographing the layouts and chemically processing them for the press run. When high-speed computer printers come into use, the newspaper may be analog only at the point that the ink meets the paper. Further down the road, the high-speed printers may make personalization of newspapers possible, creating multiple custom editions and even personalizing content for individual readers, just like an Internet news site.

Satellite delivery of copy to remote printing plants also speeds the news to your door. Newspaper copy, complete with photo layouts, is sent by satellite from central editorial offices to remote printing plants in distant cities. Today, the *New York Times,* the *Wall Street Journal,* and *USA Today* are printed in several different locations to make local same-day delivery possible almost anywhere in the country.

Online Newspapers

Improvements in transportation technology are a part of the story here, as the horse-drawn trolley gave way to the train and later to the automobile and the airplane. Why not just distribute the paper electronically? That idea is nothing new. Nineteenth-century financial barons had stock tickers in their homes. In the 1930s, newspapers experimented with "faxing" newspapers to special home radio receivers (Shefrin, 1993). In the 1980s newspapers invested millions in *videotex* services that sent digitized news to the home over phone lines and crude computer terminals. Early consumer online services such as CompuServe and America Online followed suit.

Online newspapers currently balance the web presence of major national newspapers, like the *New York Times,* and the wild growth of new types of Internet-only "newspapers" that range from blogs to neighborhood newsletters. A huge diversity of forms is growing to meet a staggering number of would-be writers and readers. As in many aspects of the Internet, it helps a newspaper online to have a long reputation based in a successful existing newspaper. In addition to a large and fairly stable print readership, for example, the *New York Times* had 18.5 million unique monthly visits—enough that it was reconsidering whether it could get away with charging for online access (Reuters, Jan. 7, 2005), something which only the *Wall Street Journal* had previously been able to do. Many online readers are drawn by the brand name and credibility of existing media, particularly the elite national newspapers. A smaller number of other readers use online

editions of regional or local daily or weekly newspapers to keep up on the news of former hometowns, former schools (for readers of their university newspapers) or other places that interest them.

Online versions of existing papers can add a number of features. Several major newspapers now send out an email to readers who have registered for the service with daily highlights. Those usually have headlines and sometimes a sentence or two of the lead paragraph from main sections of the paper. Most major papers also permit researchers to do archival searches through past issues, although many also now charge for those.

There are now thousands of newspapers on the web worldwide, many with complete versions of their daily editions. The news services have also moved online and many online newspapers double as their own news services, making local breaking stories available to other papers over the web. The new electronic papers have many features that their print ancestors lack. These include continuous updates of breaking news, sports scores and stock prices; computer-searchable classified ads; interactive forums where readers exchange views; and audio and video clips from major stories.

In an effort to improve on the conventional newspaper, so-called *portal* websites like Yahoo! are building on the concept of the "daily me" first advanced by the former director of MIT's Media Lab, Nicholas Negroponte (1995). Registered visitors can select the type of coverage, topics, and formats to fit their personal lifestyles. Potentially, this concept could be expanded to include intelligent agents, software programs that will develop a profile of what you like to read, listen to, or watch

STOP & REVIEW

1. What are the main recent trends in newspaper production technologies?

2. What are the main recent trends in newspaper delivery technologies?

3. How are newspapers using the Internet?

4. How will computers and telecommunications affect the newspaper of the future?

5. How will the Internet affect newspaper advertising?

and then interact with information providers on the Internet to find things that you might like. The new digital video recorders (DVRs) (see Chapter 8) provide a model for that mode of personalization. Another concept might be dubbed "the daily us," since it enlists the search habits of friends, colleagues, and subject matter experts to help the reader locate relevant information. Or the online paper of the future could add locally meaningful annotations to national news stories ("hurricane hits land, drops 12 inches of rain in your backyard").

Another booming online "news" service is a series of websites that merge news sites and press releases. If you don't change your homepage after buying a new computer, you will probably see the manufacturer's constantly updated set of news and product release information. Your alma mater may use your e-mail address to send a weekly or daily e-mail containing news items hyperlinks. Less commercial information sources are also trying to attract you to their websites. Sierra Club or TomPaine.com would love to inform you about the environment or politics. Even alternative news organizations like InterPress News Service (http://www.ipsnews.net/) offer alternatives to Reuters, which is featured prominently on Yahoo! and others. Several of these services will also send a daily or weekly e-mail with links to new stories, making the user more likely to come back regularly.

A lower-tech approach is also catching on, the web log, or blog, for short. These online diaries are personal interpretations of the events of the day, many written by newspaper reporters in their off-hours. Several reporters have been fired or furloughed for writing things on their blogs that conflicted with newspaper editorial policy. There are now over 4 million blogs on the web, covering everything from elections to music.

The barriers to reading electronic newspapers while at the breakfast table or hanging on a commuter train strap may eventually be removed by the development of so-called "electronic ink." That's a flexible plastic computer display that can be seen even in bright sunlight and that changes the words and images it displays as you turn the virtual "pages." A wireless Internet connection (see Chapter 8) would connect you to the news of the day.

INDUSTRY: KEEPING THE NEWS IN CHAINS?

Although newspapers continue to consolidate into the hands of large chains owning dozens of papers, there are new options for the newspaper reader. Although competing dailies are largely a thing of the past, readers have improved access to national publications, both in print and on the web, and to small-scale local publications and blogs on the web that fill specialized niches in the media landscape.

The Newspaper Landscape

Many types of newspapers are published in the United States. Although the overall number of daily newspapers has been steadily declining, there are actually more newspapers with national reach now, utilizing satellite delivery and local printing, as well as increasing numbers of local and specialized weeklies published via desktop technologies. A mass audience still exists for major metropolitan, national, and regional dailies. There is also a considerable audience for weekly newspapers, such as local weeklies oriented toward entertainment or shopping.

Dailies Newspapers published at least five days a week are termed *dailies*. As described below, dailies can be national, metropolitan, or suburban. Their numbers have steadily declined, from a high of 2200 in 1910 to 1456 in 2003 (Newspaper Association of America, 2005). Daily newspaper circulation dropped slightly to about 58 and a half million in

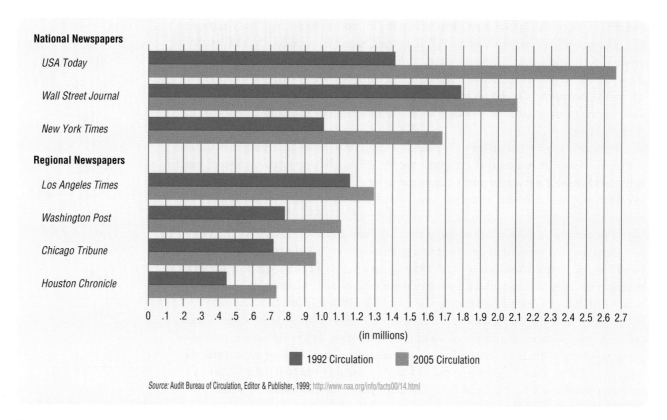

National Newspapers

USA Today

Wall Street Journal

New York Times

Regional Newspapers

Los Angeles Times

Washington Post

Chicago Tribune

Houston Chronicle

0 .1 .2 .3 .4 .5 .6 .7 .8 .9 1.0 1.1 1.2 1.3 1.4 1.5 1.6 1.7 1.8 1.9 2.0 2.1 2.2 2.3 2.4 2.5 2.6 2.7

(in millions)

■ 1992 Circulation   ■ 2005 Circulation

Source: Audit Bureau of Circulation, Editor & Publisher, 1999; http://www.naa.org/info/facts00/14.html

■ **FIGURE 4.1**
Circulation Changes
Circulation of national newspapers 1992 and 2004.

2003. Over half of adult males (57 percent) and females (52 percent) still read a newspaper daily, but readership is lower among younger adults and teenagers (40 percent). (NAA, 2005) Many readers look only at certain sections that are of particular interest to them. Even among newspaper readers, most consider television to be their main news source, although better-educated audiences tend to rely more on newspapers and less on television. Among better-educated readers, Internet news sources are also beginning to compete with newspapers, although many people now use the Internet to read newspaper sites.

National Dailies   The circulation of national newspapers is actually growing. Since the 1980s, several metropolitan newspapers have created national daily editions, distributing via satellite to multiple locations. For example, the *Wall Street Journal,* with the largest circulation, is considered a specialized business paper but has a broad general readership as well. As Figure 4.1 shows, the national dailies roughly maintained their positions from 1992 to 2004, whereas most of the regional dailies declined slightly. Overall, daily newspapers with circulation over half a million grew slightly. Medium-size dailies (circulation of 100,000 to 499,999) declined slightly, and smaller papers declined substantially.

Metropolitan and Suburban Dailies   Compared with the national dailies, such as the *New York Times,* some of the larger metropolitan daily newspapers, such as the *Chicago Tribune,* have shown significant declines in circulation, and many closures and consolidations have resulted. Others, like the *Houston Chronicle,* have grown.

A typical scenario in two-newspaper towns is that one gains most of the circulation, advertising revenues, and classified ad business, sending the other paper into a downward spiral, ending in closure or merger with its competitor. However, once a single newspaper dominates a city, it tends to be sustainably profitable. Even local monopoly newspapers are more profitable, however, when they share content and management costs with other

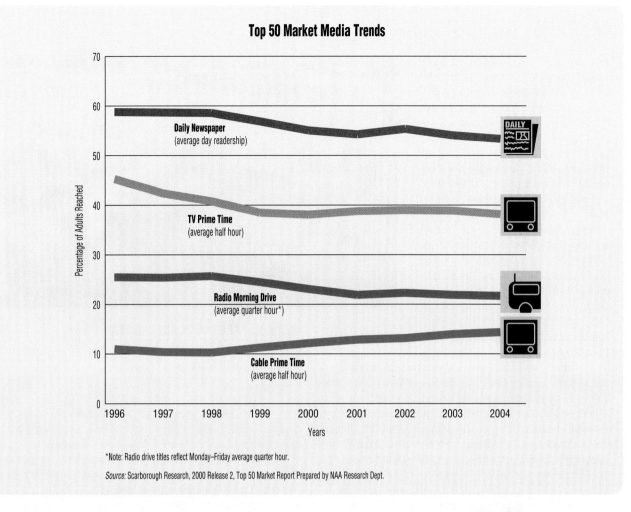

Top 50 Market Media Trends

Percentage of Adults Reached

Daily Newspaper
(average day readership)

TV Prime Time
(average half hour)

Radio Morning Drive
(average quarter hour*)

Cable Prime Time
(average half hour)

70
60
50
40
30
20
10
0

1996 1997 1998 1999 2000 2001 2002 2003 2004

Years

*Note: Radio drive titles reflect Monday–Friday average quarter hour.

Source: Scarborough Research, 2000 Release 2, Top 50 Market Report Prepared by NAA Research Dept.

■ FIGURE 4.2
Market Trends Traditional media survive but their audiences are declining.

newspapers belonging to an ownership chain, which is one reason chain ownership will continue to grow unless it is limited by regulation.

The circulation of local daily newspapers has declined over time in part because many readers have shifted to national dailies, newsweeklies, or newsmagazines, or to television, radio, or the Internet (Figure 4.2). Additionally, many large cities, such as Detroit, have declined as centers of population. Instead, suburban areas have increasingly become centers of industry, business, and entertainment, not just "bedroom" communities. Many people no longer commute downtown or even go there to shop, to eat, or for entertainment. Consequently, suburban newspapers have risen in importance and circulation. The numbers of these newspapers have grown by over 50 percent since 1985. One such paper, *Newsday,* of Long Island, New York, is now among the top 10 American newspapers in circulation.

Small-town dailies are also gaining in numbers and circulation as many small towns continue to grow in economic importance. In response, many traditional metropolitan dailies have added suburban sections and may even publish regional editions, such as the San Fernando Valley and Orange County editions of the *Los Angeles Times.* Spanish language dailies are growing in the U.S.A. Their circulation has tripled since 1990 to 1.7 million.

Weeklies Most weeklies used to cover small-town or rural areas that were too small to support a daily. Many still do, but now about a third of weekly papers cover the suburbs, and that number is growing rapidly. In 2003, there were 6704 weekly newspapers with a combined circulation of over 50 million.

© EPA/Gill Allen/Landov

McPaper Goes Global

Newspapers around the world have had to change to compete as television seduces audiences for entertainment and news. *USA Today*, the Gannett Group's national newspaper, was designed to compete with television. It is more visual, with color photos, color weather maps, and icon-oriented charts. It has more human-interest and feature stories, and generally runs much shorter stories than other national newspapers. Some critics accuse *USA Today* of losing what is distinctive about newspapers: greater depth, more analysis and news, less entertainment. Some call it "McPaper"—the newspaper equivalent of fast food, attractively packaged and seemingly tasty, but not necessarily as nourishing as some of the alternatives.

However, *USA Today's* use of graphics and concise stories to communicate news and information essentials quickly gained a broad audience in the United States and a number of imitators around the world. A surprising number of elite newspapers, from the *Times of London* in Great Britain to the *Folha de São Paulo* in Brazil have borrowed visual design, bigger headlines or other elements for more downscale but popular papers like *USA Today* in order to increase or maintain their own circulations. The management team at the *Folha de São Paulo* in Brazil modeled *USA Today* quite consciously (Silva, 1990), somewhat surprising for a paper that had prided itself on long analyses by famous writers. However, the managers felt that they were able to incorporate the

■ THE MCPAPER LOOK GOES GLOBAL
Even the *Times of London* moves to bigger headlines and photos to maintain its audience.

best of the new model—more visuals, an eye-catching design, clearer section organization—without losing their critical edge or depth. Many of their critics disagree.

Overall, this kind of planned incorporation of global models into national media has been termed glocalization by Robertson (1995). Others (Canclini, 1995) might call it hybridization, a sort of blending over time of global and local, particularly when it is more gradual and less planned than the way *Folha de São Paulo* did it. (For more on this idea, see Chapter 16.)

Other forms of weekly papers are appearing in many areas, including entertainment-oriented alternative weeklies like the *Boston Phoenix* or the *Austin Chronicle* that are given away at music stores, bookstores, and other locations. These weeklies cover dining out, movies, live concerts, and local events. Some areas also have political weeklies, and yet others have ethnic, or minority group-oriented weeklies that focus on news and events within their particular community and add a great deal of diversity to news coverage. These alternative weeklies doubled in circulation since 1990 to 7.6 million. For example, the *Earth Times* is a national environmental newspaper (http://www.earthtimes.org) focusing much more than general newspapers on the environment, social issues, and international issues. There are hundreds of ethnic newspapers published in the United States, along with newspapers for sexual minorities, military personnel, or religious groups, as well as over a thousand college newspapers. The number of papers for environmental groups, unions, and political interest groups is smaller but still significant. Most of these papers are weekly, but many, particularly college newspapers and some of the ethnic newspapers, are daily.

Wire Services and Other Newspaper Sources Many news service organizations contribute to newspaper content. With the exception of the largest metropolitan dailies, surprisingly few of the words that appear in the local newspaper are actually written locally. Most national and international stories are taken directly from the newswires, with at most the first few paragraphs rewritten to put a unique local angle on the news. Most stories farther back in the front section are lifted whole from wire-service accounts.

Earlier we discussed that the Associated Press was the first wire service in America; today it is still the leading national newswire, although Reuters is widely used, both in newspapers and in web pages. For international news, the AP competes with Agence France Presse, Reuters, and the Interfax News Agency, which covers Russia and other countries formerly part of the Soviet Union. However, there are dozens of other news services, including those run by major newspaper chains, such as Gannett, or major metropolitan newspapers, such as the Los Angeles Times–Washington Post News Service, through which stories written by their own reporters are distributed to other newspapers that subscribe to the service. There are myriad other news services not directly affiliated with newspapers that gather news and write stories about specialized topics such as finance (the Bloomberg News Service). And, if we count all the newspapers that distribute stories to other publications via their web pages, there are literally thousands of news services today. News services once relied on dedicated networks of wires and clanking electromechanical printers. Now just about anyone with a web page can be a news service—if he can write good copy or if he writes in an entertaining way that draws readership. Many blogs comment on everything from what's new in indie rock to commentary on the 2004 presidential race from every possible point of view. Several of the main political bloggers in 2004 became media celebrities, like Ana Marie Cox, better known online as wonkette.com (see Media and Culture: Blogging the Elections, page 106).

With the Internet, wire services are not only a source of news but are also coming into direct competition with newspapers. Readers can get the latest national news directly from a wire service's own website without waiting for tomorrow's newspaper. Additionally, information portals like Yahoo! prominently feature wire-service reports

■ **REUTERS EVERYWHERE**
The Reuters news service now supplies newspapers like the *New York Times* and also competes with them as a news source for information sources like Yahoo.com.

Blogging the Elections 2004

Weblogs are a striking new cultural, political and journalistic phenomenon. By 2004, the Pew Internet and American Life Project found that more than four million Americans have their own blogs. All but a few are read only by personal friends, if that. However, a number of specialized blogs are beginning to have impact. For example, music blogs let you read about your passion for Cantonese pop (or whatever) and even download MP3s. Some are important enough that music labels have begun to lobby them to get songs listed.

Most visibly, the 2004 Presidential elections emerged as the year of the political web log. Political blogs often hover between being clearinghouses for activism and outlets for information. On both right and left, blogs were one of the hottest new instruments for fanning the flames of passion among activists. Before the race settled down to the final party nominees George Bush (Republican) and John Kerry (Democrat), the Democratic primaries were greatly affected by blogs. The initially wildly successful Democratic primary campaign of Howard Dean was driven in part by passionate young bloggers who created a buzz of political excitement, raised millions of dollars, and organized a grassroots campaign of house-parties, street canvassers, and phone callers. People with a minimum of technical know-how (see Tech Demystified: Blogging Made Easy on page 108) could reinforce each other's enthusiasm over the web.

As the race went on, several blogs emerged as the must-reads. Ana Marie Cox of Wonkette.com, covering her first presidential election, was getting over 900,000 views in September, larger than the daily readerships for well-known political pundits, like R.W. Apple of The New York Times, who have covered presidential elections for decades. As the election got closer, blog reading got more partisan. On the left, Markos Moulitsas, who ran the blog Daily Kos, at dailykos.com, was getting close to a million page views a day toward the end, which forced him to add new servers and shut down many features just to avoid crashing. He ended up leading a left blog alliance as he cited and linked to many other major Democrat-leaning blogs. On the right, major bloggers became a part of an inter-linked series of media. For example, several conservative bloggers critiqued Dan Rather, CBS News and its news based on memos claiming that President Bush got special treatment in the Air National Guard. Within 24 hours, the bloggers' critical scrutiny of the typefaces in the 1970's memos as evidence against their authenticity were on the Drudge Report, then Fox News, the other networks, and the front pages of the country's leading newspapers. So blogs are now a major national news source, too, as well as a personal means to say just how much you like/dislike Cleveland's indie rock scene.

Fred R. Conrad/The New York Times

■ COLUMNISTS STILL COUNT
Some columnists like the *New York Times* Thomas Friedman are read by leaders in a number of countries.

from Reuters and Associated Press that enable readers to bypass newspaper editors' judgments about what stories might be of interest to their audience. To compete, newspaper websites now offer access to wire-service reports, extra coverage by their own writers, and specialized editions such as the *New York Times* Knowledge Network (www.nytimes.com/college/).

Newspaper syndicators supply newspapers with comics, the crossword puzzles, and editorials by national columnists, all staples of the back sections of newspapers. The King Features Syndicate, a subsidiary of the Hearst Corporation, is the largest. Syndicators employ the cartoonists and the editorial writers or make distribution arrangements with the writers' "home" newspaper organizations. They then resell the funnies and commentaries to other newspapers on a contractual basis.

Chain Ownership

There is a new trend: consolidating newspapers with other types of media outlets, including radio, television, cable, and Internet. For example, in 2000, the Tribune Company (Chicago) acquired the Times-Mirror Company, the parent of the *Los Angeles Times* and *Newsday* (New York). This merger puts major newspapers from the three largest urban centers into a vertically integrated group that will have newspapers working directly with radio, television, cable channels, and Internet sites to

© Rick McKay/Cox Newspapers

■ BLOGGER WONKETTE RIVALS NEWSPAPER PUNDITS

Newspaper political pundits like R.W. Apple of the *New York Times* or David Broder of the *Washington Post* have covered national politics and presidential elections for decades. Ana Marie Cox of Wonkette.com was covering her first, along with several other newly famous bloggers, like Markos Moulitsas of DailyKos.com. Toward the end of the 2004 campaign, they were getting over 1,000,000 views sometimes, much larger than the newspaper pundits' daily readerships.

Blogging Made Easy

Do you have something to contribute to public discourse? Are you brimming with witty ideas and passionate opinions that you are sure millions want to hear? Do you want to be the next Wonkette (see Media and Culture: Blogging the Elections, page 106)? These are some of the reasons for joining about five million other people who already have their own blogs.

Every college student has the basic means to blog. You can make a web page by simply typing your witticisms and rants into Word and selecting the "save as web page" option from the Edit menu. Every time you come out with a new "issue" of your blog, you just make a new web page. Your university has web server space (see Chapter 9) set aside for you and technical support advice if you are unsure how to upload your material. Your Internet service provider can also help you; most include a small amount of free server space in your basic subscription fee. If you are really serious, there are also blog hosting services that will help you out for a modest monthly fee. Hosting services will also provide you with industrial-strength server technology to support advanced interactive features and high traffic loads and also give you reports on your visitors.

But first you need some visitors. To encourage them you list your blog with any, or all, of the many blog directories on the web. You can find those by typing "blog directory" into Google. Blogarama, Blogwise, and Yahoo! are among the most easily found, and the listings are free. They have simple online registration forms that will index your site by location, language, and keywords.

Do you want to include personal photos, eye-catching graphics, animations, and custom navigation bars? Would you like to update your blog on the web without uploading your page over and over and let visitors post their comments, too? Those are very easily done, as well. A wide variety of free templates is available; just look in Google under "blog templates."

If you are a constantly spouting font of online opinion, or if you want continually changing information to attract visitors to your blog, you may want Really Simple Syndication (RSS) for your blog. RSS helps you post continually updated information to or from other websites and distribute your latest headlines and rants to the browser screens of your most faithful readers (Flash! I just finished lunch!). For advanced features like these you might wish to opt (for a modest fee) for a web log "platform" program that will help you manage your site. Wonkette uses one called movable type.

What else, besides a "potty mouth," international fame, and a staff of six, does Wonkette have that you haven't got? Advertising revenues, that's what. First, you need an audience. But then there are services that will help you sell ads on your blog, too. Advertisers prize the highly involved opinion leaders that frequent blog sites.

---

share content. In contrast, large chains such as Gannett tend to buy newspapers that already have a **local market monopoly,** pursuing national horizontal integration of newspapers across the United States. Table 4.1 shows the media holdings of the five largest newspaper groups. As of 2003, 10 companies owned newspapers that distribute more than 53 percent of the nation's weekday circulation, up from 46 percent in 1999. Anti-trust action was threatened against Gannett in 2005.

Local market monopoly is domination of one or more local markets by a firm.

Table 4.1 Top Five Newspaper Ownership Groups 2004

Company	Circulation	Number of Holdings	Other Major Daily Newspapers Media
Gannett Co.	8,335,000	101	22 television stations, 100 plus websites
Knight-Ridder	788,000	32	Real Cities network, 36 regional websites
Tribune Co.	3,650,000	11	Shares in WB Network, AOL, Excite@Home
Advance Publications, Inc.	2,903,000	27, plus 40 business weeklies	Condé Nast magazines, Fairchild Publications, stakes in AOL, Time Warner and Discover
The New York Times Co.	2,403,000	18	New York Times Digital, NYTimes.com, GolfDigest.com, Boston.com

Source: http://www.thestandard.com/companies; corporate websites, Yahoo Financial Reports

CONTENT: TURNING THE PAGES

Newspaper Sections

Most newspapers contain several distinct sections that serve different audiences: national news, international news, editorial and commentary, local news, sports, business, lifestyles, entertainment, comics, and classified advertising. Sections make it easier for newspaper readers to navigate to these specific interests. *USA Today* is widely credited with accelerating this trend with its sections: *News, Sports, Money,* and *Life.* Most newspapers also have Sunday supplements that are technically magazines. As we noted in Chapter 3, some of those magazines, like *Parade,* have among the highest circulations of national magazines.

Newspapers vary a great deal in the sections they emphasize. National newspapers focus on international news, national news, editorials and commentaries, and business news, with some lifestyle and entertainment news of a general nature. Metropolitan dailies usually lighten the news sections, focus more on local and regional news, and add more about lifestyles, entertainment, sports, and comics, with more localized ads for such businesses as supermarkets and auto dealers. Weekly newspapers go even further toward local news, shopping news, and ads. Observers of newspaper content sometimes fear that an emphasis on journalism and "hard news" is being diluted as newspapers try to compete with television, cable, and, recently, the Internet. In fact, studies have shown a trend toward less "hard" news about politics and economics, and more news on lifestyles, entertainment, and sports, particularly in metropolitan and regional dailies (Barnhurst and Merone, 2001).

Some daily and weekly newspapers highlight crime and other sensational stories. Notable specialized weeklies include sensationalist tabloids, such as the *National Enquirer,* but also include the *Sporting News* and numerous local shopping papers that contain nothing but classified ads.

Newspapers focus sections on specific audience segments so that ads can be targeted and to build overall circulation by providing something for everybody. For example, men and women both read the main news, comics, classifieds, and television listings, but men read the financial and sports sections more often, while women turn more to the entertainment and food/cooking sections.

MEDIA LITERACY: RESPONSIBLE REPORTING

Political Economy: Local Monopolies on the News

Most U.S. cities are served by only one newspaper. The result is a local market monopoly that has both political and economic effects. Politically, the one newspaper is likely to reflect a single editorial perspective, although other local media may reflect alternate viewpoints. Economically, the choices available to both advertisers and readers are reduced, which can lead to higher subscription and advertising rates.

In the 1980s, the Reagan administration relaxed restrictions on horizontal integration in the belief that the role of government should be reduced so that competition could thrive. As a result, major newspaper group owners have steadily acquired more newspapers. In 2000, Gannett added 21 newspapers to the 74 it already owned, and by 2004, it owned 101. Furthermore, in 1992 rules against *cross ownership,* owning newspapers and other types of media outlets (for example, radio and TV) in the same markets, were relaxed. In 2002, the FCC under Michael Powell proposed to further relax rules against cross-ownership of newspapers and other media, despite a great deal of opposition from many members of Congress. Courts intervened, returning the rules to the FCC for further study. The Court found that the FCC's analysis of local market competition, in which a college newspaper could own as much as a daily metro newspaper, was flawed. Major media are pressing hard for cross ownership as the next logical step in deregulation of ownership, but the issue was dropped in 2004.

Joint operation agreements are one solution to the problem of excessive concentration. When competing newspapers cannot survive economically, they can negotiate an agreement with each other to share facilities, production costs, administrative structure, and advertising while attempting to maintain editorial independence. That negotiated limit on competition was permitted by the Newspaper Preservation Act of 1970. Only about 40 cities now have competing daily newspapers, and 12 of those maintain two newspapers only through joint operation agreements.

In Detroit, for example, the liberal *Detroit Free Press* and the more conservative *Detroit News* now have a joint operation agreement. They share facilities, although they try to keep their writers separate, sometimes physically but more often just organizationally. The two newspapers produce separate editions on weekdays and combined editions on weekends. During elections the separate editorial pages in the combined Sunday edition sometimes endorse different candidates with opposite editorial rationales. Still, some readers fear that the overall diversity of opinion between the two may well have decreased.

Freedom of Speech and the First Amendment

Newspapers have been far more protected in freedom of speech than have electronic media such as radio and television. There have been few attempts in the United States to limit freedom of speech or of the press, especially in political as opposed to "moral" terms (pornography or obscene language).

For example, during the 1950s, the anticommunist campaign of Senator Joseph McCarthy resulted in several authors being blacklisted, which prevented them from publishing books or writing for Hollywood films and television. However, McCarthy steered away from directly attacking the print press, especially newspapers, over issues such as how they covered communism.

Freedom of the press has made it possible for journalists to take unpopular stands. It tends to protect journalists in the United States from being pressured to avoid certain stories, although subtle pressures exist within many newsrooms to not cover certain things. In many other countries, the pressures are not subtle. Many journalists around the world face perils running from censorship of stories, to being fired for making powerful enemies, to being threatened or even killed. The Committee to Protect Journalists has confirmed that 389 journalists have been killed because of their work around the world in the last 10 years. That does not include far more numerous cases in which it is likely that a journalist was killed because of his or her work but the circumstances of the case are not absolutely clear.

One of the most famous cases for Americans in 2002 was Daniel Pearl, a correspondent for the *Wall Street Journal* in Pakistan, covering the war in Afghanistan. He was invited by an informant to meet militants connected with the Taliban, kidnapped, held in exchange for the release of other militants, and ultimately murdered and mutilated on camera. His kidnap and murder made it clear to American readers what many journalists face when they pursue stories that put them in conflict or even contact with desperate and dangerous people. A Brazilian journalist, Tim Lopes, was tortured and murdered by drug dealers in even more gruesome fashion in June 2002 after going to a street party in a Rio slum looking for evidence of drug sales to young people at dances.

Joint operation agreements allow competing newspapers to share resources while maintaining editorial independence.

Sometimes new developments in technology and media raise new issues about freedom of the press, in the United States and elsewhere. The Internet brings a variety of new ways for people to express themselves. Nonjournalists try to compete with journalists in providing news-style information on websites and elsewhere. Journalists see the Internet as an outlet for things they want to say that don't fit in the news formats they write at work. This raises questions about the consequences of how journalists express themselves outside their newspapers on the Internet. For example, Steve Olafson was fired from the *Houston Chronicle* for anonymously (using the pseudonym "Banjo Jones") criticizing that newspaper on his web log, offering opinions on news that he covered for the paper.

First Tell the Truth!

Do newspapers tell truth or lies? The accuracy of the information they report has long been the primary concern of most journalists and of their newspapers. Accuracy means getting the right information, avoiding bias, and condensing or presenting the news in such a way that it remains truthful. It usually implies trying to be objective, reporting without favoritism or self-interest. It means avoiding stereotypes and unsubstantiated allegations. Accuracy is a professional obligation, a question of ethics that is treated in more detail in Chapter 15. But accuracy is also a question of credibility for media organizations that can affect their success at all levels, from economic survival to perceived prestige.

Sometimes newspapers err in accuracy. When they make a relatively minor front-page error, they often acknowledge it with a small correction hidden on the bottom of page 2. However, it is important that substantial errors, particularly those that may have damaged the reputations or careers of the persons covered, be acknowledged more openly. For example, in 2004 both the *New York Times* and the *Washington Post* admitted that they had not been critical enough of the rationale given by the Bush Administration for going to war against Iraq. Both newspapers said that their stories about issues like the existence of weapons of mass destruction in Iraq had relied too much on official sources and had not dug deeply enough in checking the facts. This acknowledgment was widely considered an unusual and commendable instance of candor by major newspapers about their role in possibly accelerating a movement of public opinion toward supporting the beginning of the war.

Another key aspect of accuracy in journalism is truthfulness in the use of sources. When a quote is presented in a newspaper, it is assumed to be a literal quote from a real person. This is again a question of individual ethics, but it is so important for organizational success that most news media also have very strict rules about it. Most major media fire reporters for making up quotes or fabricating sources. For example, the *New York Times* in 2003 fired Jayson Blair for making up many stories. A top editor was also let go for faulty editorial and personnel supervision, and fact-checking.

A thornier problem is material attributed to a source that turns out to be a composite of several real people. When sources prefer (or even demand) to remain anonymous, one controversial solution is to combine the quotes of several real people into a composite source, or "person," that is not recognizable and won't get the real sources into trouble with their employers or institutions. For example, during the Watergate scandal, Bob Woodward and Carl Bernstein often quoted a source inside the Nixon administration called Deep Throat. They insisted that "he" was a real, though anonymous, person, but others suspected he was a composite of several different sources.

Material in both news reports and columns that is not attributed to someone specific is assumed to be the original writing of the author. Using someone else's material, either verbatim or closely paraphrased, without giving credit is **plagiarism.**

Plagiarism is using the ideas of another without citation.

Finally, with both quoted remarks and facts or events, journalistic ethics has been assumed to require very careful checking for accuracy. The usual practice is to verify quotes with the sources and to double-check all facts by requiring that two independent sources confirm them. Many newspapers also employ fact-checkers. Major newspapers honor these practices more consistently than do tabloids. Accuracy is even more of a question with some news sites on the web. One of the reasons that websites for well-known newspapers are important news and information sources for Internet users is that they continue to offer a relatively good level of accuracy, compared with many other sites that are not so careful (see Chapter 15). But increasingly blogs provide an important check on the accuracy of mainstream journalism.

Libel

Press freedom is not absolute, even in the United States. Neither the publication of material that constitutes libel, nor defamation, nor the invasion of privacy is protected by the First Amendment. Libel and slander refer, respectively, to printing and to saying untrue things about private citizens that might damage their reputations. Saying true things about someone is not libel. For example, bloggers who go online to say nasty things about their private personal relationships may find themselves facing a libel suit, even while the same nasty comments (for example "coward," "spendthrift") can be made about public figures like George Bush.

Laws against libel are supposed to protect the reputations, welfare, and dignity of private citizens. Public figures, such as media professionals, celebrities, and public officials, are not generally protected against libel, on the theory that they have chosen to act in the public sphere, not to remain "private" citizens. This is because U.S. legal policy balances libel concerns against the watchdog role of the press, which is to expose corruption or incompetence on the part of officials or public figures. When people take a public position and seek publicity for their views, then libel against them is also harder to prove. They have become public figures who, like George Bush, can be said to have deliberately entered into public debate, where controversy can be expected.

Paparazzi Journalism

Privacy issues revolve around a conflict between the public's right to know something and the right of private citizens to keep it to themselves. Journalists often have to make ethical decisions about how far to pursue a story and how to treat the subjects of their stories.

In many ways, the media treats public figures differently than they do private citizens, including in regard to the right to privacy. For example, political figures and entertainers are widely considered to have given up a claim to privacy. However, many questions remain about just how closely public figures can be scrutinized before the boundary of ethical behavior is crossed. Perhaps the most drastic example for many is the way that press photographers, particularly the celebrity-chasing paparazzi, pursue celebrities. This phenomenon of hyperaggressive paparazzi photographers was fictionally reflected in the 2004 film, *Paparazzi,* produced by Mel Gibson, who is apparently quite angry about paparazzi.

Being a Good Watchdog

Investigative reporting became a hallmark of the newspaper profession in the 1960s and 1970s with Vietnam and Watergate. Today, however, true investigative reporting is a novelty rather than the norm. Critics contend that too few journalists search out stories but rather wait for the stories to come to them. Famed Watergate reporter Carl Bernstein criticized American journalists on this point in a book about the Bush administration's promotion of the Iraq war through the media. He felt that, unlike reporting of the Watergate scandal, the press was doing an inadequate job of actually investigating the story. In fact, both the *New York Times* and the *Washington Post* later apologized to readers for not covering the build up to the war critically enough. Instead, they were waiting to report what was given to them. Many in journalism agree and believe that investigative reporting, an offshoot of muckraking, is no longer fulfilling its "watchdog" role for the American public. Or it may be that cutting-edge investigative journalism is migrating to the web.

■ **PAPPARAZZI**
Photographers often hound celebrities as depicted in the film Papparazzi (2004).

The watchdog role has spread from major national newspapers to smaller, more local newspapers, and to web logs. Although many local and metropolitan papers do not do much real investigative reporting, quite a few do, about both local and national issues. Investigative reporting by local newspapers in Texas helped turn up material about illegal fund-raising in the state by House Majority Leader Tom DeLay that turned into a local legal investigation covered by the national press. Online sensational journalism entered the national press watchdog scene first with Matt Drudge's online revelations about Monica Lewinsky's affair with President Clinton. Web-based blogs expanded that role during and after the 2004 presidential election. Conservative bloggers closely scrutinized the memos obtained by Dan Rather of CBS News for a critical story about President Bush's service in the Air National Guard and showed that some of them seemed to have been falsified. This forced an embarrassing retraction by CBS News. That episode showed two things about blogs as watchdogs; many of them are very partisan (see Media and Culture: Blogging the Elections, p. 106), and they are run by people driven by political passion. In fact, blogs are becoming part of a more partisan media system that serves as both watchdog and agenda-setter for the less partisan press. Conservative bloggers often turn up material that then appears on conservative talk radio shows, then in cable talk shows, then Fox news, then perhaps the national press. Similar patterns can be seen emerging on the liberal side, particularly among bloggers.

Another danger is that the watchdog role will devolve into scandal-mongering. Newspapers have to decide in how much detail to report sexual affairs and other sensational or scandalous issues. Do those covered in the news have a right to keep the intimate details of their lives private? The issue remains very current: sex "sells" now as much as ever (see Chapter 15 on media ethics).

Journalism Education

Do journalists need to be specifically trained or educated in journalism? Newspapers vary somewhat in their opinions on this issue, but most newspapers, particularly in medium-size

PROFILE

Newspaper Columnist and Gadfly

MAUREEN DOWD

Name: Maureen Dowd

Current Job: Op-ed columnist for the *New York Times*. Writes "Liberties" twice a week.

Previous Job: *Time* magazine and Metro section of the *New York Times*

Style: Known for remarkable insight into the character of those she writes about, but also for a slash-and-burn, "take no prisoners" style.

Most Notable Achievements: Pulitzer Prize for coverage of the first (George H.) Bush White House. Is considered the first thing to read in the Wednesday and Sunday *Times* by many, particularly political insiders. Has done famous profiles of President Bill Clinton, Vice President Al Gore, House Speaker Newt Gingrich, and filmmakers Oliver Stone and Woody Allen, among others.

Most Dubious Achievements: To some critics, she seems obsessed with personality, atti-

tude, one-liners, zingers, and the worlds of Washington, Hollywood, and New York, perhaps to the exclusion of more substantive issues. A sample from a 1994 column from Oxford, England: "President Clinton returned today for a sentimental journey to the university where he didn't inhale, didn't get drafted, and didn't get a degree."

Education: Immaculata High School and Catholic University in Washington, D.C.

First Job: Washington Hilton's Pool and Tennis Club. Sold tennis balls to Morley Safer and Paul Anka.

First Media Job: Taking reporters' stories in dictation and cleaning them up at the *Washington Star*.

Inspiration: Her Irish-Catholic family, particularly her mother and her father, a Washington, D.C., cop.

and small markets, seek the benefits of a journalism education when hiring reporters, editors, and copywriters.

Journalism education does teach skills that are highly useful: how to write various kinds of stories, edit, copyedit, compose a page, write editorials, and write features. Furthermore, most journalism programs provide laboratory newspapers, internships, or other experiences with which student journalists can practice what they have learned in class. However, students need to work very hard on two key things: learning to write very well and gaining some in-depth expertise in an area important for journalistic coverage. If a journalism graduate doesn't know as much or write as well as applicants who hold some other kind of liberal arts degree, the journalism degree itself will not guarantee him or her a job.

Besides teaching writing and technical skills, journalism programs make student journalists think about ethics in the media. There is not always an obvious "right answer" to ethical dilemmas, and it helps a great deal to have thought about possible ethical issues before they arise on the job (see Chapter 15 for extended coverage of journalism ethics).

Newspapers, Gatekeeping, and "Information Glut"

Newspapers perform important political functions for audiences. Some newspapers that focus on government policy, such as the *New York Times,* pride themselves on having an influential readership and on sometimes shaping policy debates with their articles (see Profile: Maureen Dowd, page 114). The *Wall Street Journal* focuses on reaching the business elite but aims at government policy makers, too. The *Christian Science Monitor* offers internationally oriented news. The *Los Angeles Times,* especially its Calendar section, serves the film, music, and television industries. Readers look to these newspapers in part to tell them what is important in these areas.

Some news readers are responding positively to the way the Internet permits them to radically expand the information available to them, as well as focus and personalize their news. However, many others continue to prize and pay for the classic editing and **gatekeeping** functions that a good newspaper provides. As the *New Yorker* magazine has noted, "Newspapers are not just yesterday's news; the good ones are carefully prepared buffets, cooked up by skilled editors who sift the news and present it in a way that makes each edition unique. Computers, for all their strengths, are very poor at replicating human judgment and intuition, and those qualities are what editing newspapers is all about." Mark Willes, former chairman of the Times Mirror Company and publisher of the *Los Angeles Times,* said, "As we have this continued proliferation of news and information sources, we all need editors, and that is one of the things that newspapers provide. . . . The Internet is the epitome of an unedited information glut" (quoted in "Demolition Man," the *New Yorker,* Nov. 17, 1997, page 89).

Google has developed a popular news search program, but promising as it seems, this sort of automated profiling and selection from Internet information still does not duplicate the editing function of a good newspaper. Editors do several things that really require human intuition and creativity. First, they perform a gatekeeping function: they tell you what various experts think you ought to know. Thus, you avoid the frustration of reading only more of what you already know. Second, newspapers and magazines can make intelligent suggestions about new things that you may be interested in *beyond* what you already know. This helps you avoid the claustrophobic narrowness of interests implied by Negroponte's idea of a "daily me," that is, a newspaper customized exactly to our own specific interests.

By definition, however, gatekeepers do in fact keep things out—things that sometimes the reader may want to know. This may be due to a simple lack of space, or the editor or other gatekeeper may have a political or economic agenda for keeping information out of readers' hands. Can newspapers be trusted to report truthfully on or even investigate wrongdoing by their own corporate parents? Since newspapers are now scrutinized by blogs, talk radio, cable news and other news commentary media, who is keeping watch over the press watchdogs?

> ## STOP & REVIEW
>
> 1. What are the main national daily newspapers, and why are they growing?
> 2. How and why do local market monopolies in daily newspapers develop?
> 3. What are the policy implications of concentration of newspaper ownership?
> 4. What role can newspapers play in relieving the "information glut"?
> 5. What First Amendment issues affect print media?
> 6. What are the current issues in privacy and accuracy for the press?

Gatekeeping is deciding what will appear in the media.

SUMMARY AND REVIEW

WHAT ESTABLISHED THE PRECEDENTS FOR PRESS FREEDOM IN COLONIAL AMERICA?

The colonial press was often critical of British governors. In a key case in 1733, Peter Zenger published a newspaper critical of the British governor of New York. Zenger was jailed for criminal libel. Despite British legal precedent to the contrary, Zenger's lawyer successfully argued that the truth of a published piece was a defense against libel.

WHO DEVELOPED THE POLITICAL PRESS THAT SUPPORTED THE AMERICAN REVOLUTION?

Zenger was instrumental. James Franklin of the independent *New England Courant* was jailed and forbidden to publish without prior approval. Benjamin Franklin moved to Philadelphia and started the successful and independent *Pennsylvania Gazette*. Most newspapers at the time were partisan, supporting either the independence movement or the British Crown. A number of key documents and ideas were published in the newspapers, including the Declaration of Independence.

WHAT WAS THE PENNY PRESS? WHAT LED TO IT?

By 1800 most large cities had at least one daily, but circulation was limited to the literate and relatively wealthy. By 1830 new technological inventions made possible lower-cost papers aimed at a broader audience. More people were learning to read, public education was expanding, wages were increasing, and more people were gathering in cities. Benjamin Day launched the first low-cost daily, the *New York Sun,* in 1833. It sold for only a penny.

WHAT WAS THE ROLE OF PRINT MEDIA IN THE CIVIL WAR? HOW DID THE WAR AFFECT THE MEDIA?

Newspapers affected the issues debate that led up to the Civil War. African-American leader Frederick Douglass pushed hard for the abolition of slavery with the *North Star.* The newspapers covered the Civil War, with great disagreement apparent between northern and southern papers. Several northern papers had a major influence on the positions and strategy of the northern states. Illustration became a prominent tool of journalism during the war. Circulation grew.

WHAT WAS MUCKRAKING?

Muckraking characterized the post–Civil War period, when crusading newspapers turned their attention to exposing scandals and corruption in government and among industry cartels. Muckraking contributed to several acts of legislation designed to reform various industries.

WHAT ROLE DID SENSATIONALISM PLAY IN NEWSPAPERS?

After the Civil War, the new journalism used sensational coverage of crime, police news, scandals, disasters, and celebrities and included features about prominent personalities and social events such as weddings, deaths, and parties. Sensationalism initially peaked in the yellow journalism of William Randolph Hearst and others at the end of the 1800s, although many would argue that it is just as strong today.

WHEN DID NEWSPAPERS PEAK AS MASS AUDIENCE MEDIA?

The efficiency of newspaper printing increased rapidly and probably peaked between 1890 and 1920, which coincided with the peak of the newspapers' impact as mass media. The newspaper industry had grown larger than its advertising and circulation could support. In addition, motion pictures and the phonograph also began to vie for people's attention and money. By 1927, radio would be a competitor as well, followed by television in the 1950s.

WHAT ARE THE MAIN RECENT TRENDS IN NEWSPAPER DELIVERY TECHNOLOGIES?

Newspapers were often delivered directly in cities and in bulk along railroads and shipping lines. In the 1990s, delivery by the World Wide Web was becoming an alternative for "newspaper" delivery.

WHAT IS THE IMPACT OF THE INTERNET ON NEWSPAPERS?

Newspapers can now reach audiences through the World Wide Web, particularly nationally known newspapers like the *New York Times*. Newspapers must now also compete for readers with a rapidly increasing variety of websites. Additionally, newspapers must compete with some of their own sources as wire services like Reuters become directly available through sites like Yahoo! as well as other sources of news and commentary like blogs.

WHAT ARE THE MAIN NATIONAL DAILY NEWSPAPERS? WHY ARE THEY GROWING?

The *Wall Street Journal* is a specialized business paper with a broad general readership. The *New York Times* specializes in interpretation of the news and focuses on media and business. *USA Today* carries shorter news items and more entertainment. National dailies have responded to a public interest in national and international news and have been able to reach national audiences at an affordable price by using new technology for satellite delivery to primary plants.

WHAT ARE THE MAIN SECTIONS AND CONTENTS OF NEWSPAPERS?

The national newspapers stress international news, national news, editorials and commentaries, and business, with some lifestyle and entertainment news. Metropolitan dailies usually focus more on local and regional news, and add more local lifestyles, entertainment, sports, and comics. Many weeklies focus almost exclusively on local events, shopping, and entertainment.

IS THERE STILL A MASS AUDIENCE FOR NEWSPAPERS?

Almost three-fifths of all American adults still read newspapers daily, but compared with older readers, audiences are smaller among younger people.

IS THERE A TREND TOWARD CONSOLIDATION AND CONCENTRATION OF OWNERSHIP IN NEWSPAPERS?

The number of daily newspapers has been steadily declining as ownership becomes more heavily concentrated in several large chains, such as Gannett and Scripps-Howard.

WHY ARE THERE CONCERNS ABOUT CONSOLIDATION IN THE NEWSPAPER INDUSTRY?

A number of formerly competitive newspapers have entered into joint operation agreements to share facilities, costs, administrative structure, and advertising while attempting to maintain editorial independence. However, the lack of competition and the nature of the joint operation may well reduce independence and diversity in editorial points of view. Chain ownership may similarly reduce local independence and standardize editorial and reporting approaches across the country. Cross-ownership at the local level between newspapers, radio, television, and cable is also a concern, particularly when newspapers owned by chains are also part of media cross-ownership.

WHAT ARE THE MAIN POLICY ISSUES FOR NEWSPAPERS?

Freedom of press for newspapers has been limited at times by concerns about libel, pornography, and obscene speech, but within the media and courts, freedom of speech has usually been the dominant principle.

WHAT ARE THE MAIN ETHICAL ISSUES FOR NEWSPAPERS?

The main ethical issue for newspapers currently revolves around how to treat subjects of stories and, to some degree, sources for stories. Although newspapers usually respect the privacy of people who are not public figures, the issue is a subject of some discussion today. Accuracy and truthfulness in reporting and independence from commercial pressures are also key ethical principles.

MEDIA CONNECTION

For web links, quizzes, and key term flash cards, visit the **Student Companion Website** at http://communication.wadsworth.com/straubhaar5.

 For unlimited easy access to additional and exclusive online study, support, and research tools, log on to **1pass** at http://1pass.thomson.com using the unique access code found on your 1pass passcode card.

 The **Media Now Premium Website** offers *Career Profile* videos, *Critical View* video news clips, and *Media in Motion* concept animations. You'll also find Stop & Review tutorial questions, a sample final exam, and much more.

 InfoTrac College Edition is a fully searchable online database offering anytime, anywhere access to more than 20 years' worth of articles from nearly 5,000 diverse and reliable sources.

vMentor provides live, one-on-one online tutoring to connect you to experts who will assist you in understanding the concepts covered in your course.

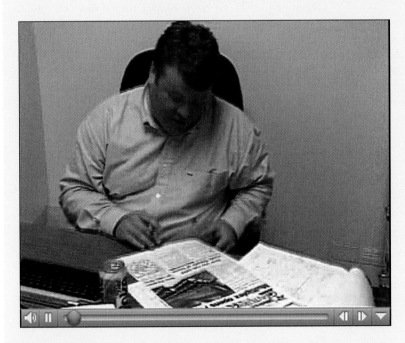

Newspaper publisher Dave Price discusses the various career paths you can take in newspaper editorial and sales in the Career Profile video for this chapter.

5

Recorded music on CDs and MP3s provides much of the soundtrack of our lives, both new sounds like 50 cent and classic sounds like Ray Charles. This chapter discusses how the organization of the recording industry, its changing content, and its impact on American culture have changed over the years. Now the music industry faces a challenging future, as it reorganizes in response to technological change.

HISTORY: HOW THE SOUND BEGAN

Well before there was a written language, people sang songs and told stories to share knowledge and to entertain. Modern recorded music and radio (see Chapter 6) stand on the shoulders of shamans, village storytellers, poets, wandering minstrels, and court jesters.

Before There Was Recorded Music

The roots of today's popular music can be traced to earlier musical traditions. Rock rhythms have roots in drumming in African religious ceremonies (Hart, 1990). African-American gospel music took root in the nineteenth century and is still performed today by groups like Sweet Honey in the Rock. White gospel spread from churches to country-and-western recordings with such songs as "Rock of Ages." Appalachian folk songs, such as "I'll Fly Away" on the "O Brother Where Art Thou?" soundtrack, are still often recorded. Delta blues songs, like Robert Johnson's "Crossroads," have been recorded by the 1960s blues band Cream and its former guitarist, Eric Clapton, in 2004. Cajun music

1877	Edison introduces the speaking phonograph	**1956**	Stereo recordings introduced
1924	Radio play of music leads to decline by half in record sales	**1981**	MTV music channel appears on cable TV
1934	First magnetic tape recorder	**1982**	CDs revolutionize "record" sales
1940	Frank Sinatra becomes the first modern teen music and radio idol	**1996**	U.S. Patent issued for MP3
		1999	Napster introduces Internet file-sharing
1948	two new record formats, 45 rpm and 33⅓ rpm, introduced	**2000**	Napster Internet site ordered to end unauthorized file sharing
1951	*Rocket 88* is the first rock song.	**2003**	Apple introduces iTunes and legal Internet sales of music take off

is performed by the contemporary group Buckwheat Zydeco. Mexican border *rancheras* (love songs) are recorded by pop artists such as Linda Ronstadt on her album *Canciones de mi Padre*. Ballads and hymns from the British Isles have directly influenced the Irish dance music of The Chieftains and the New Age sound of Enya.

After the advent of printing, and the development of musical notation, music began to travel easily as *sheet music*. Some of the earliest printed materials were lyrics and musical notations. In America, the sheet music industry dates back to the late nineteenth century. Tin Pan Alley originated with New York-based musicians who wrote sheet music for the popular songs of the day. Back then, songwriters, not performers, had a more central role and were more widely recognized. Thus, people flocked to buy the latest sheet music of well-known composers or lyricists, such as *ragtime* great Scott Joplin, and march composer John Philip Sousa, rather than waiting until a performer made the music popular.

The Victrola

During the late 1800s and early 1900s, attempting to reproduce music for the public, inventors created mechanical devices such as music boxes and **nickelodeons.** The first **acoustic** recording technology was developed in 1877 by Thomas Edison. He produced a prototype of a "phono-graph," which played back the nursery rhyme "Mary Had a Little Lamb." Edison imagined using the device to record dictation or to act as a telephone answering machine, but musical entertainment quickly became its main use. Several years later, in 1882, Emile Berliner created the gramophone, which played flat disks known as 78 rpm "records."

The *phonograph,* or record player, was a major breakthrough. In 1890 an entrepreneur named Lippincott started putting coin-operated phonographs in penny arcades, and in 1906 the Victor Talking Machine Company introduced the home **Victrola.** As people became accustomed to listening to recorded music in their homes, the phonograph quickly became a widely used medium. By the end of World War I (1914–1918), over two million players were being made and sold annually. Record sales soared from 23 million in 1914 to 107 million in 1919.

Nickelodeon is a phonograph or player piano operated by inserting a coin, originally a nickel.

Acoustic is a sound that is not electronically amplified.

Victrola was the trade name for an early phonograph.

Early Recorded Music

The penny arcade and home Victrola introduced more people to new kinds of music and helped increase the availability of music more rapidly than ever before. The notion of *popular music* caught on, as writers and composers began to discover what kinds of music most appealed to a mass audience. Jazz, such as New Orleans Dixieland, became popular in the 1920s and 1930s. Show tunes from then-new talking movies, such as Al Jolson's songs from *The Jazz Singer* (see Chapter 7), were also popular. Blues was popular among African-American audiences but did not cross over to other audiences much at that time (Romanowski & George-Warren, 1995).

Big Band and the Radio Days

Radio had an immediate impact on recorded music. When people could first hear music at no cost on the radio, they bought fewer records. In 1924, as radio was taking off, record and phonograph sales dropped by almost half. That produced a panic in the record industry similar to the current reaction to Internet music downloads. Later, however, listeners bought their own recordings of music they had heard. In fact, the recording industry began to rely on radio to make people aware of recording artists, and the performers they heard on the radio began to establish preeminence over the composers of the music in the popular mind.

Because early recording technology had not achieved very **high fidelity,** and because radio fees for recording artists had not yet been worked out, music was primarily broadcast live. Networks introduced the most popular groups and orchestras to the entire country. Radio stimulated a demand for a variety of musical genres, ranging from classical to country and western, making big stars out of singers like Bing Crosby.

Big Band Music and the World War II Generation

The most popular music in the 1930s and 1940s was the "big band" sound. Developed from jazz, it was the pop—short for "popular"—music of its day. Band leaders such as Glenn Miller and Tommy Dorsey put together orchestras that introduced a number of singers, such as Frank Sinatra, who continued to lead pop music into the 1950s.

Record sales had dipped to under six million in 1932, and some predicted the death of the phonograph. One event that helped revive record sales was the appearance of teen idol Frank Sinatra in 1940. Wherever Sinatra went, he was pursued by hordes of screaming teenage girls. Mass production had kept record prices down around a dollar, making records fairly affordable, and the fans began asking stores for the latest Sinatra record.

New Musical Genres

National radio networks featured the pop music and live music of the day: big bands, light classical music, and movie and show tunes. However, some important developments in musical *genres* were happening in regional recording companies and radio networks. For example, a network of southern stations carried the Grand Ole Opry and bluegrass acts, such as the Carter Family, who were featured on recording labels that served largely southern audiences. These new music genres built on the main regional musical traditions of American music such as southern *gospel, blues,* and *bluegrass.*

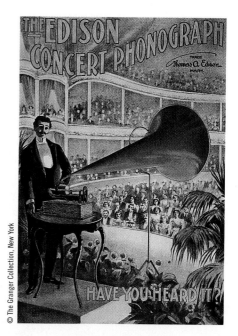

© The Granger Collection, New York

■ **NOW HEAR THIS**
The phonograph, pioneered in 1877 by Thomas Edison, was already gaining popularity in the 1890s. (The big horn was the loudspeaker.)

High fidelity is accurate reproduction of natural sound.

They also reflected the popularity of *western* music and singing cowboys in the movies, like Gene Autry, who began to sell enough records to interest major recording labels. Genres blended, too. Artists like Bob Wills and His Texas Playboys blended big band "swing" and western tunes to create "western swing." The combination of bluegrass, gospel, western, and western swing eventually became known as country and western, or country, led by singers like Jimmy Rogers and Hank Williams. It followed southern migrants north as they looked for jobs in the industrial Midwest and East. A recording industry focused on this music grew up in Nashville, where the Grand Ole Opry was broadcast. Nashville musicians were eventually to play on "country" format stations from San Francisco to Boston. National music labels like Capitol and RCA began to pick up country stars and project their music far beyond the South and Southwest.

The *blues* followed African-American migrants from the South to Chicago and New York, where a harder, electric blues developed in the 1940s and 1950s that greatly influenced rock and roll. For example, rock bands of the 1960s, such as the Rolling Stones, did versions of Chicago blues songs by Muddy Waters and Howlin' Wolf. Gradually, blues and gospel songs were blended with elements of pop music into new genres such as rhythm and blues (R&B). Black music was originally considered "race" music by the recording industry, which did not target it to white audiences for most of the 1930s–1950s. However, although R&B initially served a largely African-American audience, in the early 1950s, some of its artists, like Chuck Berry or Little Richard, were playing music that white audiences saw as part of the rock and roll they liked.

Rock History

People like to debate the origins of rock and roll in the early 1950s, and what was the first real rock song. Rock built on a variety of roots, hybridizing them together into a blend that gradually took on an identity that people could call a new genre. It was explored and developed by a lot of people, not unlike the development of television sets where a number of people worked in parallel on a similar idea.

Rock's deepest roots were in blues, like Big Mama Thornton's original *Hound Dog* (1953) that Elvis later covered. Jump-blues shouter Wynonie Harris, with *Good Rockin' Tonight* (1948) linked blues and small-combo R&B to the rock and roll of the 1950s. Country-western and boogie-woogie roots combined in Arthur Smith's *Guitar Boogie* (1948), which was the first national hit with an electric guitar.

Rock's nearest roots were in rhythm and blues music, which produced a song that some claim was the first rock and roll song, *Rocket '88* (1951) by Jackie Brentson and His Delta Cats, later known as the Ike Turner Band (circa 1951). A slower paced, harmony-oriented branch of rhythm and blues called doo-wop produced another contender, the Penguins' *Earth Angel* (1954). A blend of jump-blues and western swing produced *Rock Around The Clock* (1954) by Bill Haley And The Comets. It was the first rock record to become a hit and register loudly in the national consciousness. Elvis covered a song *That's All Right, Mama* (1954) by blues singer Arthur 'Big Boy' Crudup, that some critics think was the most important in getting widespread acceptance of rock. Elvis, Carl Perkins, Jerry Lee Lewis and Roy Orbison, future rock greats, first emerged on Sun Records, one of the labels that first produced rock records, along with blues by Howlin' Wolf and country music by Johnny Cash.

Some white audiences also tuned in to listen to R&B singers themselves, listening to black stations and buying race records, which the industry finally began to market to the mainstream audience. Ray Charles helped turn R&B into soul music which crossed even further into the pop charts. The majority of the radio-listening and record-buying

Ripping Off Black Music?

What happens to cultures when one group "borrows" music from another? For some, like African-Americans, it seems that other people have ripped off their musical traditions and ideas, even ridiculing them in the process. For example, many white Americans in the 1920s and 1930s enjoyed seeing Al Jolson, who performed in blackface, doing his versions of African-American jazz and blues music, but they would have not watched or listened to black singers doing their own songs. However, many African-Americans felt insulted by the whole idea of a white man doing their music in blackface, and black musicians felt excluded from performing their own music outside of media and performance venues aimed at African-Americans. Thus, white musicians appropriated the music and ideas of another group. Some black musicians did eventually benefit from the exposure given their music, but many died in poverty and obscurity.

The tradition of white covers of black music continued in the 1950s and 1960s with Elvis, the Beach Boys, the Beatles, and the Rolling Stones doing covers of blues, rhythm and blues, or soul songs, often selling far more records than the original artists. Now black hip-hop and rap musicians are often very popular. However, it still seems that white artists like Eminem, "borrowing" their genres, often make more money on a given album. Another critical question is whether such musical mingling loses its authenticity, its faithfulness to its roots. Critics like Herman Gray have argued that black music performed by white people lacks authenticity, a sense of the context in which it was created. Certainly a critical issue for an artist like Eminem, performing in a genre that came from and is still predominantly performed by African-Americans, is whether both black and white audiences consider his music and performance authentic enough to be worth listening to.

A largely positive interpretation of such trends would be that such musical "borrowing" is a natural part of an ongo-

■ **RIPPED OFF?**
Blues legend Robert Johnson originated many of the great hits of the 1960s performed by Eric Clapton, Led Zeppelin, and others.

ing process of cultural hybridization. That refers to the combination of cultural traditions in a way that creates new forms that are distinct blends going beyond the original elements to become something new. A current example might be Eminem himself, who is produced by an African-American rap artist, or a black *fusion* musician like Jamaican reggae singer Shaggy, who can blend rap elements, reggae and white pop ("Angel of the Morning") into a song like "Angel." In this view, African-American and white American music have been mingling, to the long-run benefit of both, for hundreds of years.

audience turned to R&B and soul music as it gave rise to the Motown sound of the Supremes and the Temptations, which was a major part of the pop music of the 1960s.

However, many white audiences heard black music only when a white artist **covered** it. A number of early white rockers, like Elvis, copied R&B styles, carrying R&B to audiences who would not have listened to black singers. By the 1960s, other rockers, particularly in England, were digging deeper in black music and turning blues songs into rock songs (see Media and Culture: Ripping Off Black Music?, above), again taking songs by people like Robert Johnson to people who would not have listened to the originals. Radio stations and new recording labels began to create new genres of music and radio formats that featured them, including rhythm and blues, and rock and roll. Small, independent labels developed new artists and new audiences who had not been served by major record

Covers are artists' performances of others' songs.

labels or network radio. Chess Records in Chicago, for example, carried a number of blues and rhythm-and-blues artists who were played only on what were called "black" stations back then.

The recording industry began to rely on radio more than ever as a promotional device to make the public aware of new music and to help the recording industry sell records. The relationship got a little too close when record labels bribed **disc jockeys (DJs)** to play their records, a practice known as **payola.**

In the late 1950s and early 1960s, most of the young audience was listening to the same overall mix of rock and roll, pop, and some R&B, such as the Isley Brothers. Rock was still somewhat unified as a genre until the late 1960s, with Motown, English groups including the Beatles and the Rolling Stones, and heavy rockers such as Led Zeppelin and Jimi Hendrix all popular as "rock" (Limmer, 1981).

The Record Boom and Pop Music

The recording industry had slumped somewhat during World War II due to shortages of some components like shellac, and a musicians strike that lasted two years. Technological innovations revitalized the recording industry and had an impact on radio as well. In 1947, the Minnesota Mining and Manufacturing company (3M) introduced magnetic tape, which improved sound fidelity, reduced costs, and made editing easier. This enabled the recorded music industry to produce the music of more artists less expensively and with better quality. In 1948 and 1949, Columbia introduced the large 33⅓ rpm long-playing record and RCA introduced the smaller 45 rpm record (rpm stands for revolutions per minute). The 33⅓ rpm long-playing (LP) albums prevailed for albums, while the faster-spinning 45 rpm records dominated releases of single songs (Sterling & Kittross, 1990).

These record standards affected radio (Chapter 6). The 45 rpm singles were well suited for DJ-oriented radio that focused on hit singles. They cost much less than albums and they appealed to young music fans. However, the 33⅓ long-playing (LP) albums held more music and appealed to the high-fidelity enthusiasts of the 1950s who were into longer classical jazz pieces. Both sold well in the 1960s, but LPs began to outstrip 45s in sales in the 1970s and 1980s.

For a while, the limits of the 45 rpm single had limited pop songs to a length of a little over two minutes. Some producers, like Phil Spector, managed to pour entire symphonies of densely layered production into a 2–3 minute single, like "River Deep, Mountain High" by Ike and Tina Turner, but by the mid- to late 1960s, some groups were beginning to find the format very constraining. The Beatles, together with their producer, George Martin, were creating increasingly elaborate arrangements with multiple segments and layers of instruments, as on songs like "Penny Lane." Others, from the Rolling Stones ("Their Satanic Majesties Request") to the Beach Boys ("Smiley Smile"), followed the trend to longer songs and complex themes. One solution was the concept album, like "Sergeant Pepper's Lonely Hearts Club Band," which strung together a number of cuts that were still mostly short enough to fit standard 2–3 minute song radio formats. However, the Beatles and others steadily pushed toward longer songs that allowed more complex ideas and arrangements. Both long cuts and concept albums pushed record buyers toward 33⅓ long-playing (LP) albums. Many new FM radio stations moved toward a format of "album-oriented rock," stressing longer songs that no longer fit on 45 rpm singles, so their listeners also moved toward albums to get the latest music. Both rock groups, like Pink Floyd, and soul/funk groups, like Parliament and Funkadelic, began to explore the new possibilities. Another strong new direction that expanded rock's horizons came from singer–songwriters like Bob Dylan, who scandalized folk purists by

A **disc jockey (DJ)** is a radio station announcer who plays records and often emphasizes delivery and personality.

Payola occurs when record companies give bribes to DJs to get their records played.

strapping on an electric guitar and doing rock albums like "Highway 61 Revisited" (1965).

Another format option, the eight-track cartridge tape, was introduced in 1965 as a means of playing recorded music. Audiocassette tapes were introduced in 1963, triumphing by the 1970s. Cassette tapes were smaller and offered recording as well as playback, while the eight-track systems were for playback only.

The Rock Revolution Will Be Segmented

After 1970, both recording companies and FM radio stations began to diversify into distinct rock formats, such as album-oriented rock (Bruce Springsteen), Top 40 (Michael Jackson), rock oldies (Chuck Berry), heavy metal (Led Zeppelin), and adult contemporary (Linda Ronstadt). Other music genres also showed up in their own FM radio formats: R&B/urban (Funkadelic), disco (KC & the Sunshine Band), and country and western (Tammy Wynette).

Rock's diverse roots fed further diversification into a number of branches or subgenres, which produced new radio formats. In the 1970s, "rock" added new genres like punk (the Sex Pistols), country rock (the Eagles), folk rock (Richard Thompson), new wave (Elvis Costello), heavy metal (Kiss), and glam rock (David Bowie). Fusions of rock, R&B, and soul with Jamaican rhythms added ska (the Specials) and reggae (Bob Marley). The 1980s and 1990s added blues rock (George Thoroughgood), grunge rock (Nirvana), techno (the Information Society), alternative (R.E.M.), industrial (Nine Inch Nails), new age (Enya), rap (Dr. Dre), gangsta rap (Ice T), and hip-hop (Usher). By the 1990s, dozens of subgenres had descended from 1960s rock, pop, and soul roots. Rap and hip-hop have become a favored genre for political and social commentary. Several early rap groups, like Public Enemy, did a number of songs clearly designed as political commentary to challenge ideas about the relations between black youth and the police, for example. In a current example, a 26-year-old Palestinian American, Will Youmans, raps under the name of the Iron Sheik about the plight of Palestinians. His lyrics talk about United Nations resolutions and other material far from what is considered typical for commercial rap. Consequently, his channels for distributing his music are usually not commercial radio but community festivals, political rallies, and the Internet. He doesn't release CDs through major labels or get much radio play. Still, some radio shows on some noncommercial stations will play music like his or radical Latino and African-American rappers; more common is play on Internet radio stations and music-streaming or download websites. The continuing formation of smaller recording labels gave expression to musical subgenres and the subcultures that enjoyed them. This was the result of technological developments that lowered the price of recording tapes, records, and CDs.

In 1982, a new round in the recording format wars began with the introduction of compact disc recording. **Audiophiles** were not very impressed with the shiny new discs at first, finding their sound rather harsh and brittle. But the recordings were more compact and relatively immune to dust and scratches compared to LP phonograph records.

By the late 1990s, CDs had pushed vinyl 33⅓ record albums and cassettes off the record store racks (although some listeners persisted in their love of vinyl, spawning a comeback of sorts for LP records). Retail CD distribution also moved to the Internet, in online music stores and catalog sellers that sold recordings on websites for delivery through the mail. Radio stations joined the digital trend with hundreds of radio stations broadcasting on the Internet, using technologies such as RealAudio and MP3, although in 2002 **copyright** fees for music were imposed on Internet radio stations, cutting back the number of such stations.

■ **WHAT I SAY**
Ray Charles blended gospel and R&B to create soul music and cross over into pop stardom.

Audiophiles are those who seek the highest audio reproduction quality.

A **copyright** is a legal privilege to use, sell, or license creative works.

Digital Recording

Increasingly, both musicians and music consumers are recording music in new digital forms. For musicians, recording costs have plummeted and their ability to create special effects cheaply on their own computers has soared. As a result, the music industry role as gatekeepers over who gets to record has diminished and lots of bands have made their own CDs, even if they can't get anyone to buy or distribute them. Consumers have also been given a number of new options about how they obtain, buy, record, store, and mix music, which millions of people are exploring. Furthermore, the line between producers and consumers is blurring. People at home can now take elements or tracks of various pieces of music and remix them to create their own versions, even if they don't see themselves as musicians. For example DJ Dangermouse remixed Joy-Z's *The Black Album* and the Beatles' *White Album* into a new mix he called *The Gray Album,* which he received a court order not to distribute.

Both in the United States and worldwide, the number of people recording music is skyrocketing as music recording equipment costs go down. Digital equipment is lowering the costs of music recording. Furthermore, what used to require specialized mixing and effects equipment can increasingly be done on home computers. By the 1990s, some artists, like Fat Boy Slim, were essentially doing professional recording on their own computers. Like Moore's Law, which says that computing power will steadily double in power while its cost drops by half (see Chapter 19), it seems that digital recording software similarly precipitously drops in price and grows in power.

These rapid decreases in cost permitted artists in many locales around the world to record their own local music. As a result, both in the United States and around the world, truly local music industries are now possible. Austin (Texas), Salvador (Brazil), Shanghai (China), and many other places have local music markets in which a local artist can record, sell CDs, get on the radio, and promote their own concerts. Although musicians based locally would clearly like national or global success as well, increasingly musicians can get a good start and sometimes even survive economically with a local base, working with local labels, local concert venues, and local radio stations. This is easier in Brazil where living costs are lower, than in the U.S. For example, one Austin guitarist, while famous locally, had to work for 20 years to afford to buy a house.

■ MP3 TO GO

Digital music players like the Apple iPod permit users to play MP3 recordings.

Music on the Internet

The true potential of digital recording was unleashed as users began playing and recording music on CD drives built into personal computers, as well as sending and receiving music over the Internet. In 1999, Shawn Fanning accelerated this change with Napster, a fileserver that let people exchange songs as digital music files via the Internet.

To the consternation of the recording industry, computer owners have increasingly been downloading digital music files from the Internet where they could be copied for free. In 2000, when recording companies used lawsuits to force some "free" music exchanges like Napster to shut down over copyright violations. Today, tens of millions are still downloading music, using exchange programs like Morpheus and KaZaA. Most music downloads were copyright violations, and some groups like Metallica joined music industry groups in suing to stop what they considered piracy. However, some musicians began to see the Internet as a new way to reach their fans and to circumvent the stranglehold of

■ LONELY NO MORE
Los Lonely Boys moved quickly from the Austin, Texas local scene to national stardom with music blending blues roots, harmony vocals, and Spanglish lyrics.

Resisting the March of (Recorded) Progress

The music industry establishment has a hard time adjusting to new technologies. Even though the industry usually ends up making a great deal of money from new ways of recording and distributing music, it has resisted everything from the Victrola to the iPod. March composer and band leader John Philip Sousa hated the Victrola. He thought it made music sound canned and tinny. Worse for him (and very typical of industry leaders), he feared the economic changes technology would bring. He wondered who would pay to come to his concerts if they could listen to records at home. To be fair, it was not at all clear to him that he would make money selling records, which was a completely new idea. When he first heard one of Thomas Edison's recordings, he could not envision the economics of selling recordings, which would make trillions of dollars over the course of the twentieth century.

Adaptations were required. New legislation extended copyright protection to recordings, so that illegal copies could be prohibited and royalties from sales guaranteed. That enabled a profitable recording and sales industry to blossom. Musicians and people in the recording industry panicked again when radio came along. They thought, we can't have this stuff going out over the air." They saw broadcast music as a complete loss of revenue. So Sousa and others helped found the American Society of Composers, Authors and Producers (ASCAP) to license the use of its members' music to radio stations, elevators and stores playing background music, and concerts where local bands played others' music. As a result, radio promoted the sale of recordings, and musicians, producers, agents, and music industry executives made more money than ever.

Magnetic tape recording seemed like a real threat, so the industry persuaded Congress to tax each blank tape a few cents, which went to the industry to compensate its losses. Needless to say, music on cassette tapes and eight-track cartridge tapes also sold hundreds of millions of dollars of music shortly thereafter. The industry has struggled even harder with digital technologies because they offer cleaner, more accurate copies, which could lead to more widespread illegal copying. So the industry fought digital audio tape (DAT) and managed to keep the technology away from consumers. The industry really liked CDs because they didn't initially seem to lend themselves to copying. However, with advances in computer-based technologies, copying CDs eventually became pretty easy, making even higher fidelity copies than magnetic tape copies. People in the music industry were initially horrified and angry over Apple Computer's advertising slogan "Rip, Mix, Burn," which urged users to copy ("rip") CDs into their computers, mix songs using new software, and burn a new CD in their computer drives, so they could then create their own mixes to play in various media. Suddenly the deathfight over DAT in retrospect seemed particularly short sighted, since lots of people already had computers. Soon, however, the very same company that had urged people to "Rip, Mix, Burn," was helping the industry sell tens of millions of dollars worth of legally downloaded songs to mix and burn with.

Future industry leaders, like our readers, would do well to remember that technology does tend to change the existing economic arrangements, but that simply fighting it seldom works. It is better to work with the new industry leaders, like Apple, to come up with new ways to sell music and make money.

major record labels. The record industry very slowly moved to create a system for letting people get music online for a charge (see Media and Culture: Resisting the March of (Recorded) Progress, above).

In 2003, Apple broke ground by creating a download service, the iTunes Music Store, that included music from almost all labels. Resistance by major labels was an extreme limit on earlier attempts at legal download services. Steve Jobs of Apple was the first to present a convincing package of technology and price and persuaded the music industry to go along. Copyright on songs was protected because a downloaded song could be copied only onto a limited number of computers, portable players, or music CDs. Apple's copy-protection software is called FairPlay, and other competing companies are creating their own. Apple's unwillingness to cooperate on standards may well cause real problems for Apple, other companies and users. However, Apple sold 10 million songs in the first six months, and a number of other services followed.

Although MP3 music players have been available for several years, 2003 and 2004 saw an explosion. Apple's iPod led, but others, from Sony to Dell Computer, perceived an attractive market and rushed in quickly. A number of companies now are offering similar download stores, with comparable features and cooperation from the music industry. Wal-Mart competes on price. Others offer services and software with different features. Unfortunately, no single standard for compressing or copy protecting such legal music purchases and downloads has emerged, even though the MP3 standard is what most people use for extralegal downloads and copying of music. Users are consequently a bit perplexed about which standard to invest in.

Curiously, CD sales rebounded following the introduction of pay music services. This called into question the music industry's contention that downloading cut into recorded music sales. Instead, it now appears that downloading and in-store record purchases complement one another.

STOP & REVIEW

1. How did music genres evolve from earlier music traditions?
2. What are the major genres and traditions that fed into rock and roll?
3. How did record/CD sales and radio effect each other over time?
4. How have music recording formats changed since World War II?
5. What has led the segmentation of rock into sub-genres since the 1960s?
6. What has been the impact of MP3s and Internet music downloads on the recording industry?

TECHNOLOGY: LET'S MAKE MUSIC

The first music recordings were purely *analog*. With Thomas Edison's phonograph of 1877, sound waves were recorded as indentations on a spinning cylinder covered with malleable tinfoil. In the first phonographs, the sound was amplified mechanically through the Victrola's trumpet-shaped horn. Listeners turned the cylinders by a hand crank or a hand-wound clockwork mechanism.

From the Victrola to the CD

The cylinders were replaced by more durable flat gramophone disks first invented in 1882 by Emile Berliner (Brinkley, 1997). In the early twentieth century the hand cranks gave way to electric motors. In later electronic equipment, movements of the stylus, or "needle," generated an electric current that was amplified and sent to the speakers. There, the current activated an electromagnet attached to a vibrating membrane inside the speakers that reproduced the original sound waves (see Technology Demystified: Experiments with Electromagnetism, Part I, page 133).

In the recording studio, the mechanical system used by Edison was replaced with electric microphones. Modern microphones all employ a thin membrane that catches the sound waves, but have differing methods for converting the mechanical energy of sound waves to electrical current. The "condenser mics" found in recording studios have a pair of thin, electrically charged flexible metallic plates inside. As the sound waves press against one of the plates, its vibrations push electrical charges back and forth between the plates, creating an electrical current that matches the sound.

Early records spun at a rate of 78 rpm and had one or two songs per side of a ten-inch disc. The high rpms gave reasonable sound quality but limited the length of the material. Beethoven's Ninth Symphony was sold on several 78 rpm disks inserted in paper sleeves and bound together in a cardboard-covered album.

In 1948 two new recording formats were introduced. The 33⅓ rpm long-playing (LP) records held 23 minutes of music per side, enough to squeeze the Ninth into a

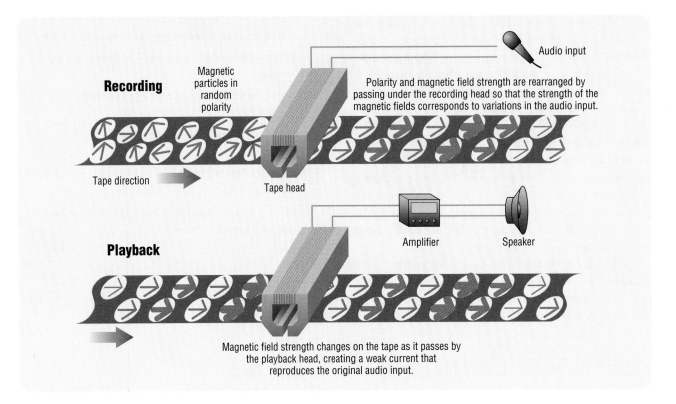

Recording

Magnetic particles in random polarity

Polarity and magnetic field strength are rearranged by passing under the recording head so that the strength of the magnetic fields corresponds to variations in the audio input.

Audio input

Tape direction

Tape head

Playback

Amplifier

Speaker

Magnetic field strength changes on the tape as it passes by the playback head, creating a weak current that reproduces the original audio input.

■ FIGURE 5.1
Audio Recording Music is stored in tiny magnetic particles on the surface of audio tapes.

Electromagnetic recording is a method of storing information as magnetized areas on a tape or disk.

Stereo is splitting recorded sound into two separate channels.

two-record set. The 45 rpm records held one three-minute song to a side. Both new formats used better needles and amplification to achieve improved sound that was thought of in the 1950s as high fidelity.

Magnetic tape came along at about the same time. In **electromagnetic recording,** flexible plastic tape passes over a recording head, an electromagnet that imparts a residual magnetic field to tiny magnetic particles stuck to the surface of the tape (Figure 5.1). The strength of the magnetic field varies with the intensity of the sound waves that hit the microphone at a particular moment. When played back, the tape runs over another electromagnet, the read head, which responds to the magnetic patterns stored on the tape by sending an electric current to the speakers. (See Technology Demystified: Experiments with Electromagnetism, Part I, page 133.)

Tape recording permitted a series of gradually improved recordings to be put on to record. Initially, recordings were only a single *monaural* track, but recording equipment in studios gradually increased the number of tracks recorded to two (stereo), four, then eight, then 32, even before the process was ultimately digitized. The listening experience improved dramatically in 1956 with the first **stereo** recordings. Stereo tricks us into hearing the musicians as though they were sitting in different chairs in front of us, whereas the previous monaural recordings made it seem that all the sounds were coming from the same point. Stereo adds the illusion of depth to the music. To accomplish the illusion, we divide the music into two separate sources, or tracks, and replay them so that they are heard over different speakers. Modern multispeaker systems extend the illusion by positioning additional speakers behind the listener to give the sensation of "surround sound." In fact, the new standard for sound, both for stereo music listening and for home-theater-style movie viewing, is multispeaker systems that position one bass speaker and at least four others strategically in the room.

Compact discs (CDs) arrived in 1982. As we note in Chapter 1, CD recorders convert sound waves into the 1s and 0s of computer data. During playback, another laser

TECHNOLOGY DEMYSTIFIED ■■■■■■

Experiments with Electromagnetism, Part I

Many people remember the day in grade school when the teacher came in with a battery, a length of wire, iron filings, and some rusty nails and said, "Class, today we are going to learn about electromagnetism." That memory is the key to understanding many modern communication systems, so let's refresh it for you.

Your teacher—let's call her Ms. Kotter—wound the wire tightly around one of the iron nails and connected the ends of the wire to the battery. Then she was able to pick up the other nails with the one wrapped in wire. This demonstrated the basic principle of electromagnetism: a flowing electric current generates a magnetic field. This is what happens inside your stereo speakers, where an electromagnet tugs back and forth at an iron disc attached to a flexible membrane that beats the air in time to your music.

Next, Ms. Kotter disconnected the wire and showed you that the magnetized nail could no longer pick up other nails.

That proved that the electric current flowing through the wire made the nail into a magnet.

Although that nail could no longer pick up other nails, it could still pick up the iron filings, something it could not do before. This demonstrated that the nail had a weak residual magnetic field, just like the tiny metallic particles on the surface of an audiotape have after they pass under the recording head.

For an animation that shows how magnetic tape records audio, go to "Media in Motion: Magnetic Tape" on your Media Connection CD-ROM. To learn more, go to InfoTrac College Edition and search for "tape recorders."

Note: For more on electromagnetism, see Part II of this box, "Why Is Radio Spectrum Scarce?," on page 164 in Chapter 6.

---

shines on the surface of the disc, but the light is scattered when it hits the pits, turning the laser's reflection off for a brief moment. This pattern of "lights on" and "lights off" regenerates the computer data and, eventually, the original sound (Benson & Whitaker, 1990). CDs faithfully reproduce the entire range of sound frequencies audible to the human ear and are less vulnerable to dust and scratches than earlier recording media. They also provided more capacity than the recording media that came before it. Now Beethoven's 9th fits on one side of a CD. In fact, the size of the CD was set so that it could fit the 74 minute playing time of Beethoven's "greatest hit."

However, today's CDs are not the last word in high quality musical recording. From the start, audiophiles complained that compact discs had a tinny, cold sound to them. In devising the standards for CDs, certain compromises had to be made to limit the amount of digital information required to record a song, such as limiting the number of computer bits per sound sample and providing only two audio channels. Super Audio CDs (SACD) carry 8 times the information of conventional discs so that a richer sound results and multichannel stereo is possible. Audio DVDs (DVD-A) offer a competing high-end option, especially now that recordable DVDs are becoming available.

New Digital Formats

Music recording technology and computer media are now converging rapidly. The latest recordable CDs (CD-R and CD-RW) and digital video discs (DVDs; see Chapter 9) are equally at home in the CD bays of personal computers and in conventional stereo systems. But files of music data can also be stored on a computer's hard drive. New DVDs pack 7.1 channels of surround sound (the ".1" designates a separate channel for bass) and are compatible with both stereo systems and amplifiers.

Another option is the personal digital stereo player, first introduced in 1998. They store "near" CD-quality music downloaded from the Internet or "ripped" (copied) from CDs, using the digital recording and storage format known as **MP3**. We say "near" CD quality because this format uses digital compression (see Chapter 12) that does not make perfect reproductions but

MP3 is a sound digitization and compression standard, short for MPEG-2 Layer 3.

sounds just as good to the listener and takes up only a tenth of the space to store. The players originally appeared as personal portable playback devices, like the Apple iPod, but some, including the iPod, have evolved into "jukeboxes" capable of storing thousands of songs on a computer disc. Other listeners prefer to store the files on their computers and connect them to their stereo systems. Some software now uses the .WAV format, which *compresses* the music less than does MP3, resulting in greater fidelity but larger size files.

Multichannel surround sound is also growing online and off. Windows Media Audio 9 has 7.1 surround sound built in, but comes with rights management features that prevent ripping. Multi-channel sound is also coming to two new reading technologies, Super Audio CDs and DVDs. But these also have built-in piracy protection, and a new MP3 version that also supports multi-channel sound may not prove popular for lack of source material that can be readily ripped.

Widespread "sharing" (the recording industry prefers the term "piracy") of MP3s online led to the development of the music industry's secure digital music initiative. This makes it possible to encrypt (or scramble) the music so that it can be downloaded only by paying customers of industry-backed online music services. Much to the dismay of users, the technology also makes it possible to put an "expiration date" on the music if the subscriber doesn't keep paying and also to prevent users from ripping their own CDs from the songs they download. That's at the core of the business strategy for the industry's pay music services including Real One Rhapsody and Napster. Another element of the music industry's strategy is to add copy prevention to popular CDs so that they cannot be easily copied onto the Internet. However, too much copy protection meets consumer resistance. The Data Play format, introduced in the spring of 2002, held five CDs on a single disk the size of a half-dollar and retailed for less than a conventional CD. But consumers balked at the copy restriction technology built into the format, which prevented "file sharing." Data Play died by winter.

For example, Apple's FairPlay digital rights management system lets users make a certain limited number of copies of a song downloaded from its iTunes Music Store. The format permits sharing among a reasonable, but small, number of digital music players, computers, and burns to CD. To limit piracy, the software makes it hard to share music online. Apple combines this copy protection using the compression standard called **AAC.**

AAC is based on an international standard called MPEG4 that covers video and interactive applications as well as audio. Apple has made AAC its own unique implementation of the standard. Microsoft has developed Windows Media Audio (WMA), used by Wal-Mart, BuyMusic and Yahoo!'s Musicmatch for their online music stores. As a result, an Apple iPod cannot play WMA format songs downloaded from Wal-Mart, and a Dell or Samsung player cannot play music from the iTunes store. One way around these conflicts is to record the songs on a music CD then "rip" them back into your computer. Or, you can wait for more players that play both standards, such as the PC-based iPod from HP, to appear. Or, wait for either Apple or Windows to win the battle for supremacy.

New "format wars" rage in cyberspace instead of on record store racks. Users report no discernible differences in sound quality between WMA and AAC, the choice hinges more on whether you wish to support Apple over Microsoft in the battle for your ears. WMA is preferred by the music industry because it can prevent further copying and can also be streamed (played in real time) instead of just downloaded. The latest version, WM9 has been superior to Apple's in that it supports 8 channel stereo. Another option is MP3PRO which cuts the size of MP3 files in half and also offers multichannel and streaming capabilities. However, music purists (at least those with high speed Internet connections and spacious disc drives) prefer to "share" their music in the .WAV or .APE formats because they exactly reproduce the original sound without compression.

AAC Advanced Audio Coding

■ **WHAT'S NEW NAPSTER CAT?**
Napster started out as the main source of illegal music downloads, was bankrupted by music industry lawsuits, and is back as a legal, for-pay service.

However, your next portable music player could be your cell phone. Already millions download ring tones of their favorite songs to "play" on their cells. Advanced high speed wireless networks that are already being deployed in Europe and East Asia (see Chapter 12) will offer the capacity for speedy downloads and cell phones with digital storage and stereo headphones on board are in the making.

Technology is also aiding the music industry trade association RIAA as it tracks music piracy online. The RIAA uses a library of digital fingerprints, that it says can uniquely identify MP3 music files that have been traded on the Napster service as far back as May 2000. Such fingerprints can separate those who copied their own CD into MP3s on their computer form those who downloaded a fingerprinted version of a file that has been identified as in circulation on file sharing Internet services. The RIAA uses the information to persecute, er, prosecute copyright infringers, so file sharers beware!

Now the downloaders are again gaining the upper hand. They use newer file sharing software like Bit-Torrent that stores fragments of files on many different computers and reassembles them for downloading so they cannot be traced so readily. Others have "hacked" Apple's iTunes to make it a platform for most formats.

INDUSTRY: THE SUITS

Our music exists in a contradictory time of countervailing trends. New digital technologies seem to allow many more new entrants in music recording, music production, and distribution. However, economic and regulatory changes have also encouraged unprecedented concentration of the ownership of most of the major players (in terms of hits, sales, and profits) all across the music industries. So the music that is such a part of our culture is controlled by "the suits," the men and women in business suits who run the record industry.

PROFILE

The Very Model of a Modern Music Mogul

Name: David Geffen

Born: Brooklyn, 1943

Education: A few semesters at the University of Texas, UCLA, and Brooklyn College

Position: One of three codirectors of Dreamworks Film Studio; also promotes theater and music productions

Most Notable Achievement: One of the first agents representing music groups, like the Eagles, to also run his own label, Asylum. One of the first to really turn rock music into a big business. One of the first to cross over from the music industry to film business to theater.

Most Dubious Achievement: One of the first to turn rock into such a big business that the business part began to overwhelm the music part.

How He Got Started: He went from the mailroom to the trainee program at the William Morris Agency, where he was one of the first to see rock as a potentially really big business.

His Inspiration: His mother, who ran her own small garment business. He liked the way she always controlled a transaction to make the most money possible from it.

How He Got to the Top: He also saw where the next big chance was. He went from music agent at William Morris to having his own company, Asylum, in cooperation with Warner Brothers. After a false start in film there, he got Warner to finance his new company, Geffen Records, which he parlayed into building a companion, Geffen Film Company, and then into Broadway musicals, like "Cats."

Where Does He Go from Here?: Like earlier industry magnates, he has begun to think like a philanthropist, financing the rebuilding of theaters in Los Angeles, such as the Geffen Theater in Westwood, and funding the David Geffen School of Medicine at UCLA.

■ DAVID GEFFEN

The Recording Industry

The key elements of the recording industry are the talent (the singers and musicians), the recording studios, the recording companies and their various labels, the distributors, independent promoters, and the retailers. Also important to musicians' success are their songwriters, managers, and arrangers. Most hope to get a contract from a record company to make money.

The Talent Groups form at a local level. There are tens of thousands of aspiring local groups and singers throughout the United States. For example, the college club scene in Austin, Texas, produced Fastball, among other groups, and Burlington, Vermont, spawned Phish and Dispatch. Such acts perform locally, try to get concert or dance bookings out of town, become better known, and make a recording to circulate to record companies. Many move to larger, more competitive locales, more frequented by record company scouts, such as Los Angeles, Nashville, and New York. A number achieve regional status as traveling acts that circulate in a state or region. A few are discovered and make it big, but most break up, whereupon the more talented musicians form new groups and move on. Talent scouts from record companies are always looking around college towns, festivals, and concert circuits for new acts, but competition is fierce.

Recording Studios and Record Companies   It used to be that recording companies would bring promising acts into the recording studio, where engineers and arrangers could capture their music on tape for an album or single. Recording studios are now relatively cheap to create and can be found in most cities of even a few hundred thousand people. Aspiring groups can increasingly cut or record a tape or CD locally for $500–$600. That CD or tape won't be of top quality or reflect professional assistance with arrangements, but with it a group can look for more club dates and promote its recordings on the Internet as CDs or MP3 music files. They can also promote their music to talent scouts from record companies.

However, recording companies are still the main gatekeepers of the music business; they decide who gets recorded in a professional way. Professional studios, arrangers, and supporting musicians or sidemen are still costly and still concentrated in Los Angeles, Nashville, and a few other hubs of the music industry. Even more important, the recording companies still decide who gets distributed and promoted nationally on the radio, in concerts, and in record stores.

Some of the major recording companies have a number of separate labels, each with a separate image and intended market segment. Sony Records has the Columbia and Epic labels; Warner Brothers Music (now owned by Bromfman) has Rhino, Elektra, Warner, Sire, and Atlantic. Recorded music is very much an international industry. Sony is a Japanese company, and BMG, Arista, and RCA are owned by the German firm Bertelsmann. Foreign owners have not pursued different kinds of musical content from domestic owners. (See Table 5.1.) Rumors of further mergers among the top companies abound. At the end of 2003, Sony and Bertelsmann merged their music operations, and the Canadian former owner of Universal, Edgar Bromfman, Jr., had bought Warner Brothers Music. Universal-Vivendi was considering the sale of Universal Music Group.

Recording companies decide which albums and songs to promote via radio, billboards, newspaper ads, and magazine ads. Recently, major labels, like the movie industry, rely on first-week sales to determine whether a new release will be a hit. The labels' cost of bringing a CD to the public is very high, starting with recording, mixing, and producers' costs. Labels also often have to pay an independent promoter to get a song on the radio. They also have to pay producers, directors, and crews to do a music video that will make it onto MTV. All that can cost millions, so the labels are often tempted to slow or

Table 5.1 Top Five Music Industry Ownership Groups

Group	Global Market Share	U.S. Market Share	Record Labels/Sales Groups
Universal Music Group	26%	30%	Decca, Geffen, MCA, Def Jam, Deustsche Grammophon, Universal
Sony-Bertelsmann (BMG)	26	32	RCA, Arista, Jive, BMG, Columbia, Epic
Warner Brothers Records*	12	17	Warner, Reprise, Atlantic, Elektra, Rhino, Sire, Warner, Chappell
EMI	12	10	Blue Note, Virgin, Capitol
Others	25	11	

* Now owned by Edgar Bromfman Jr.

Source: "Lowering the volume," *LA Times,* December 29, 2003; "Music labels are merging," *Austin American-Statesman,* Nov. 7, 2003. *2004 is music to diskeries' ears,* http://Variety.com, Jan. 5, 2005.

RAP EMPIRE
Dr. Dre has moved beyond his own music to produce others like Snoop Dog, and found labels like Death Row.

even stop promoting a group that is not an immediate big hit, maybe even cancel the group's contract.

Many groups increasingly tend to go with independent labels, rather than majors. An independent label is one owned by someone outside of the five majors, and can vary in size from tiny (three or four employees) to medium size (50 or so employees). Some independent labels work on very low promotion and profit margins so that they and a group can make money after selling as few as 25,000 copies, compared to the millions required for a major label hit. So most tend to see the promotion of a band as a long-term project. And some see file sharing as an ally, a way for people to hear about new groups on their labels, who often then buy the CD. As in the movie industry, there is an increasing synergy between indie labels and music producers. If a new group on an independent label does well, it may be picked up for distribution by one of the big five, either by striking a deal with the indie label or buying out its contract. A few groups, like Boston-based Dispatch, have formed their own labels, although they still use majors like Universal for distribution. Dispatch saw Napster and similar download services as ways to make their music known. Dispatch testified for Napster at legal hearings.

An important part of the promotion of the most promising groups with national potential is making a music video for MTV. Since MTV came on the scene in 1981, it has had great influence on which records become popular and even what gets played on radio stations. MTV was originally focused on heavy metal but diversified to offer rap, alternative, and other genres, and then moved to nonmusic shows. MTV2 focuses increasingly on top hits. MTV has over 65 million subscribers and reaches the whole country. It is now difficult to have a radio hit without having a music video.

Another controversial and expensive part of music promotion to radio stations is independent promoters. These promoters are hired by record companies to convince radio stations to play new records. There have been several scandals involving payola, or bribes from promoters to station managers or program directors to play records, which led to calls for reform of the business of promoting music to radio stations. One example was paying stations substantial "fees" for access to their play lists. By the end of 2004, all four music groups (EMI, Warner, Universal and Sony-BMG) were being investigated over payola.

Music Distribution   The record companies distribute recordings in a variety of ways. Rack jobbers supply the recordings seen in sale racks at many large retail stores, although some stores, like Wal-Mart, deal directly with record companies. Other kinds of distributors sell to retail music stores that specialize in recordings and related videos. This retail business was dominated by big chain record stores, including Sam Goody, Musicland, and Tower, but increasingly those stores are in trouble, like Tower, which went bankrupt. Huge general retailers such as Wal-Mart now dominate. The power of such retailers was apparent when, starting in 1997, Wal-Mart refused to carry certain recordings that it considered offensive; its action had major effects on sales by artists such as Marilyn Manson. Some artists now change lyrics in order to ensure that major chains, like Wal-Mart, will carry them. Specialized retailers like Tower had a hard time competing with big discount stores like Wal-Mart, online CD sales by Amazon and clubs like BMG, and the new online digital purchase services, like the iTunes Music Store (or Wal-Mart, too).

Record clubs such as Columbia and BMG sell CDs and cassettes directly through the mail and Internet on a large scale. These clubs are all big enough to deal directly with the record companies. Specific recordings are also pitched via TV commercials for direct-mail ordering. And a growing number of people buy albums through Internet stores, such as Amazon.com.

The other quickly rising form of distribution by sale is the purchase and download of music over the Internet from online stores: the iTunes Music Store, Wal-Mart, Music-match, Napster, Sony, and RealNetworks. Despite the visibility and popularity of these new services, they have not yet approached the profitability of older forms of distribution, like the sale of CDs. For example, Apple charges 99 cents per song but has to pay the label 65–70 cents for licensing rights to the song, plus credit-card fees of up to 25 cents a transaction, so Apple nets only around 10 cents. In fact, so far iTunes barely breaks even and Apple primarily makes money selling iPods to play the downloaded tunes on. But the economics are likely to improve as more people use these services, creating better economies of scale.

The combined effect of all these competing forms of distribution, plus the continued growth of illegal file sharing, has been decreases in CD sales. From a peak of almost 800 million albums (CDs, plus records and tapes) sold in 2000, the sales declined to 655 million albums at the end of 2002. Sales declined another 10 percent in 2003 but still represented $28 billion in sales worldwide (*LA Times,* Dec. 29, 2003). Sales of music rebounded in 2004. CD sales were up 2.4% higher and almost 150 million paid digital downloads added to sales' improvements.

Music Industry Associations   The Recording Industry Artists Association (RIAA) and other trade associations function as the industry's lobbying and legal arm. The American Society of Composers, Authors and Producers (ASCAP) represents more than 170,000 songwriters, lyricists, and music publishers. Broadcast Music Incorporated (B.M.I.) has close to double that number of creative artists and publishers, with 300,000 affiliates. Both help artists collect royalties from live performances by others, radio plays of recorded music, Internet radio, elevator music, use in commercial sound channels for stores, and other ways in which music gets played. ASCAP and BMI both monitor play on media, collect royalties from media, and distribute them to artists. For songs covered by others, on every album with at least 10 tracks, the music publishers representing the authors of the songs earn 7.5 cents per track, which they distribute to the writers with whom they have agreements.

A number of alternative ways of looking at artists' rights to, and benefits from their music are developing. Some artists, like Phish or the Grateful Dead, are very accepting of fans' recording and sharing concerts, assuming that people will buy tickets and CDs anyway. Others, like Dispatch, see record companies as something to avoid and see Internet file sharing and music blogs with MP3 downloads as good ways to market and sell their music. Perhaps the most revolutionary new idea is the Creative Commons, in which artists make their music available, not only for simple download and listening, but for taking

STOP & REVIEW

1. How has the digitization of recording formats affected the industry?

2. What is the relationship between recordings, labels and major music companies?

3. What is the impact of record clubs and major retailers like Wal-Mart on the music industry?

4. What copyright challenges are raised by Internet music technologies?

apart and rebuilding. A number of artists, from the Beastie Boys and David Byrne to Gilberto Gil (now the Minister of Culture in Brazil), made a CD published in Wired Magazine's November 2004 edition that allowed sharing, sampling, and rebuilding (also available at http://creativecommons.org/wired/). These artists' idea is that music is to be shared, sampled and reworked to spur creativity, and they seem to assume that people will still buy their CDs or pay to go to their concerts and download their music, anyway. However, other artists are unwilling to risk that and have lined up behind the Recording Industry Association of America (RIAA)'s efforts to legally restrain file sharing. (See "Sharing or Stealing?" at the end of the chapter.)

WHAT ARE WE LISTENING TO? GENRES OF MUSIC

As we have seen, music industry executives, "the suits," increasingly look for targeted genres that cater to specialized audiences. Increased competition for audience segments has increased the importance of music research and targeted marketing.

Music Genres and Audience Segments

One of the best ways the music industry is able to effectively market its products is through first researching the demographics of who is buying what genres and then targeting its marketing of that music primarily to those specific groups.

For example, *Billboard Magazine* has a number of separate hit lists for different categories or genres of music, such as Contemporary hits, Country hits, Alternative country, Adult contemporary, Alternative, Modern rock, New adult contemporary, Urban/R&B, Spanish (broken down into Mexican-American and Tropical/Caribbean), and Christian. These music genres correspond to many of the radio formats that are discussed in Chapter 6. However, one of the main differences you'll see there is that whereas the music industry is mostly concerned with marketing current artists in the above categories, a number of radio formats now cover classics and oldies, such as Country classics, Rock/pop oldies (now including '70s and '80s music formats), Classic rock, and Urban/R&B oldies. Although the music industry still maintains many of the oldies artists in its album catalogs, its promotion budgets focus on the new artists. Still, until recently, many people were still acquiring CD versions of albums that they might have earlier owned in 33⅓ rpm record versions but back catalog sales have been tapering off.

Genres often subdivide. Country split into hit/contemporary, classic/traditional, alternative country, bluegrass, and *ranchera* (Mexican-American country music) branches. Rock has grown and subdivided into many subcategories, such as soft rock, hit pop (Top 40), modern rock, alternative, heavy metal, industrial, techno, trance/rave, punk, ska, and jam bands. Christian genres grew quickly and then subdivided into traditional Gospel and Contemporary divisions, with the latter varying to include country, rock, and even rap-related Christian music.

Music is also one of the few instances in which American audiences are exposed to cultural products from outside the United States. English rock and pop have had a strong presence since the 1960s, so much that many American listeners take it for granted, along with music from Canada and Australia. Musicians from other English-speaking countries

Rappin' The World

Rap and hip-hop have flowed quickly and widely out into the rest of the world; where many people are listening to U.S. hip-hop and rap artists like 50 Cent and Dr. Dre. This type of music is popular in a wide variety of countries, from China to Mozambique, so much so that some people are worried about musical homogenization, as hip hop and rap replace earlier imports, like U.S. rock, and local music. Clearly, this wave is sinking in. The authors have heard people singing or humming along to hip hop in Brazil, France, Mexico, Mozambique and Taiwan. U.S. hip-hop dominates among imported music in many countries.

For many, however, the big story is not Chinese kids listening to Eminem, but Chinese kids and others doing their own hip-hop and rap. A remarkable number of countries are producing their own rap, and local rap tends to do much better on the local charts than the imports. Many musicians also see rap as an appropriate music of protest to use in their own circumstances. Moroccans living in France listen to rap from home to feel less culturally isolated, or to protest their living conditions in France. A Brazilian documentary, *Little Prince's Rap Against the Wicked Souls* (2000) shows a local rap group cheering on a vigilante who takes on drug gangs when the police don't act.

Some critics insist that hip-hop and rap reflect a specific urban African-American culture and history, so other cultures' appropriations of them would be a new form of cultural imperialism, homogenization, or Americanization. For example, the original film *Black Orpheus* (1959) introduced Brazilian samba and bossa nova to the rest of the world, so many Brazilians were shocked when a remake, *Orfeu,* (1999) featured as much Brazilian hip-hop as samba. Many others see hip-hop and rap as just another global musical genre to be appropriated and localized. For example, well-known Brazilian samba and pop musician Caetano Veloso defended the use of hip-hop in *Orfeu* as highly appropriate for dramatizing issues in Brazilian slums and a good fit for the adaptability of Brazilian culture (2000). Analyzing this as musical hybridity, it seems that cultures have never been static, that they always take in new forms and ideas (Pietersee, 2004). Rap itself is a hybrid of many roots, particularly from Africa. So it fits well with the ongoing diaspora of African musical traditions across the globe, that previously nourished rock and samba, among many others.

have had an easier time breaking into the U.S. market, even when they sing in a notably different dialect, like that of Jamaica (calypso, reggae, ska, dance hall). A number of other musicians have also learned to sing in English to break into both U.S. and global markets. Scandinavian groups like Abba or Bjork have become familiar this way. Even some unlikely ones like the speed metal band Sepultura from Brazil have broken into the U.S. market by recording and performing in English. The broad genre of World Music represents a relatively serious music industry effort to market singers and groups that are often extremely popular in their home markets into the United States. Some examples have included bossa nova and samba from Brazil, Celtic music from Great Britain and France, various African genres, and other Latin American and Caribbean music, along with Balkan, Greek, and others.

MEDIA LITERACY: WHO CONTROLS THE MUSIC?

One of the most important issues to understand, in order to be media savvy or literate, is who makes the decisions on music: who to record, distribute, and promote. The music industry seems large and diverse, with dozens of recording labels. However, how large and diverse is the group of people making content decisions?

Recorded Music in the Age of the New Media Giants

Recording studios, record companies, and radio stations were once owned by many kinds of individuals and small groups. However, by 2004, the largest group, Clear Channel, had a network of over 1220 stations, over one-tenth of *all* American radio stations. Clear Channel now owns most of the stations in many cities and towns. The company also has substantial control over concert bookings via its entertainment division. It wants to achieve economies of scale and synergy among different forms of music distribution. (For more on Clear Channel radio operations, see Chapter 6.)

The music business has never been regulated in the same way that broadcasting traditionally was. Most of the major film studios—Warner Bros., Disney, Columbia, and Universal—have traditionally been involved in the music recording and distribution business. However, the music business is now seen as less profitable than some other media businesses, so a number of sales and mergers have taken place. As in the film industry, many of these mergers involved international companies like Sony, Bertelsmanm and Seagrams of Canada.

Some had hoped that the Internet would provide a meaningful counterforce to the music industry giants but the success of the industry in shutting down file sharing sites and intimidating their users makes that prospect increasingly dim. Instead, music lovers are left with the choice between the dominance of two other global corporations—Apple or Microsoft—over their online music choices. The European Union cast Microsoft in the role of bad guy, finding its media player strategy to be anticompetitive and ordering it to distribute a version of Windows without the media player built in. Apple always likes the role of lovable underdog to Microsoft's heavy, but in this case Apple enjoys a level of market dominance that often attracts the attentions of antitrust authorities. And, although Apple's digital encoder is based on an "open" standard, the ironically named "FairPlay" software that goes with it is owned by Apple. So you see, Apple is playing the monopolist's game to win. If you would like to opt out of the battle for market dominance, there is Ogg Vorbis, a free encoder that some claim is better than either of the commercial offerings and which was developed by a group dedicated to the overthrow of Big Media.

Is MTV Too Powerful?

Ever since its first appearance on the nation's cable systems in 1981, MTV has had a tremendous impact on music and the recording industry. Groups that got their videos in the MTV rotation were virtually assured of success as radio stations began to orient their playlists to the acts with the most popular music videos, with record and CD sales rising accordingly for those groups featured on MTV. And good music was no longer enough: performers had to look as good as (or better than) they sounded, and be willing to adorn their on-screen personae with images of sex and violence. Through its musical selections, MTV was initially accused of favoring (predominantly white) heavy metal bands over (predominantly African-American) rap groups, although by the 1990s, some people began to accuse MTV of the reverse, favoring rap and hip-hop over alternative, modern rock and other alternatives.

MTV has since diversified its style with a richer mix of music and a departure from the music video format that characterized its early years. But concerns about its dominance remain. It has expanded into subchannels like MTV2, which extends its dominance over music-related channels. Together with its sister channel, VH-1, MTV also stands accused of using its clout to demand exclusive rights to new hit videos and also of leveraging record companies for extremely favorable copyright licensing fee arrange-

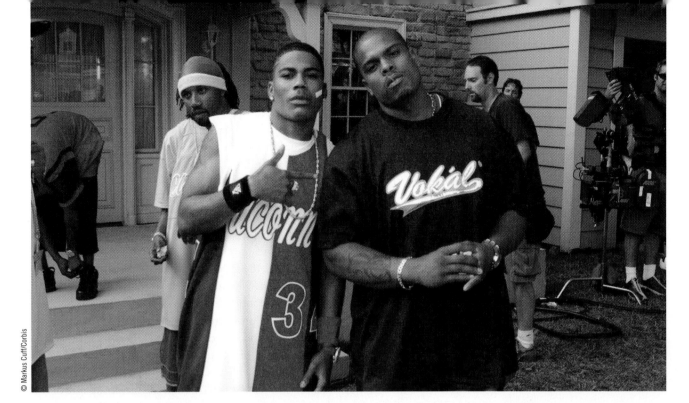

■ **MTV**
Getting a good video on MTV is crucial to the success of musicians like rapper Nelly.

ments. If true, these would be anticompetitive practices that limit the ability of competing music video services to turn a profit.

MTV's influence grew further as its parent corporation, Viacom, completed its acquisition of CBS television in 1999. Through that deal, Viacom added Country Music Television to its stable of music video channels and also acquired Infinity Broadcasting, one of the largest group station owners in the radio industry. MTV is also extending its influence globally, cloning local versions of itself in Brazil, India, Australia, Latin America, Asia, and Europe. In these countries, it is also very difficult to have a hit record without a heavily played video on MTV, which makes MTV a global gatekeeper over music.

Sharing or Stealing?

Reuse of copyrighted music has been a major issue for the recording industry. When artists record a piece of music written by someone else, whether for direct sale or for broadcast, they have to obtain permission and usually pay a *royalty*, a fee charged for use of the writer's intellectual property. Some well-known court cases have been fought over whether an artist used another's basic melody. This problem has been accentuated with the rise of sampling in rap music and multimedia, where artists record and reuse bits, or samples, of existing works. Courts decided in 2004 that any sampling requires getting permission and paying royalties.

Distribution of music over the Internet raises another copyright and intellectual property problem. Virtually flawless digital recordings can be transmitted over the Internet for recording on a hard drive, digital tape, disc, or recordable CD. Technical solutions are being sought to prevent illegal copying and transmission, while permitting the legal sale of music over the Internet. Internet sites, such as KaZaA or Gnutella, had allowed users to swap high-quality digital files that contain music. This practice spread quickly, with 22 million people using Napster by February 2001. Much of the music being swapped between computers is copyrighted, and swapping those songs can be considered piracy—violation of the copyright of the artists or recording companies who own it. So as a listener, you have a legal dilemma when you turn to the Internet and MP3s to look for diversity of music. By looking for new talent on the Internet, you can help new bands get around the gatekeeping of the music and radio industries, but if you only listen to their MP3s and don't buy their CDs, they won't survive. Students may also face administrative and legal pressure from their universities to stop downloading music. The major music companies are beginning to pressure universities to stop students from using university technology to download music illegally.

Individual groups like Metallica, recording companies like EMI, and representatives of the entire industry, like the Radio Industry Association of America, sued Napster and other services to stop them from allowing people to trade copyrighted music. The rulings eventually killed Napster, although it later reappeared as a pay music service, and other services sprang up almost immediately, since the industry had not yet provided an attractive alternative for Napster or Gnutella users. The music companies were all being very cautious about online distribution, because both legal and technological means that would allow them to continue to control and profit from copyrighted music distribution were still unclear. A series of new legal download services, such as iTunes Music Store and Wal-Mart, were beginning to generate very significant sales.

According to some surveys of users, legal download sales began to cut into illegal downloads, as lawsuits against individual file-sharers by the RIAA and the increasing ease of use of legal services made legal downloads more attractive. In 2004, Forrester Research surveyed 12-to-22-year-olds and adults 23 and older. They found that about half the kids had downloaded songs in the past month, compared with 12 percent of the adults. The good news for the industry was that nearly half of the young downloaders said that they were buying as many CDs as ever: 3.6 every 90 days for one group Forester called "Young Samplers."

Pity the Poor, Starving Artists

In their struggle against file sharing a favorite tactic of the RIAA has been to call attention to the plight of poor, starving artists whose livelihoods have been ruined by illegal downloading. Some artists, notably Metallica, agree, and have filed suits of their own. Other, less established artists see downloading as a way to break through the creative stranglehold that the industry has on new acts and reach the public on their own terms.

And, it is comical that the industry should accuse music fans of starving the musicians when the industry itself has been bleeding artists dry for years. Rock 'n Roll bad girl Courtney Love "did the math" for the suits a few years back at an RIAA gathering: She pointed out that in the end, a band with a hit record gets only a modest middle class income, not the riches that aspiring musicians imagine.

What's more, you don't even own your own songs. Standard industry practice is to have the artist sign over the rights in their first recording contract. The Copyright Term Extension Act further empowers the media giants at the expense of the artist. Would your garage band like to record its own rendition of some song that would now be public domain under the old act, a hit from 1932? You can't under the new copyright laws.

Artists disagree on how to deal with record companies. Most just sign on and hope for the best. However some are exploring their options. Many groups go to independent labels because no big label wanted to sign them. But some groups create their own label, or go to a smaller one to keep more control or get a better deal in terms of revenue sharing. Independent labels, those that are not owned by the big conglomerates, are growing with roughly 3700 in the USA in 2004. Many of these independent labels are actually distributed by major recording companies, but not all. Some are getting creative about how to distribute themselves.

Getting Distributed Means Getting Creative

Both recording artists and record companies are grappling with the Internet, which has toppled established techniques for promoting talent and marketing music sales. Downloads on the Internet have meant declining CD sales, at least up until 2004. Paid download services, like iTunes from Apple, Rhapsody from RealNetworks, MSN Music from Microsoft or Wal-Mart have produced some increasing numbers of music sales, but people tend to buy one or two preferred songs by an artist, rather than a whole album. Both artists and record companies have struggled to figure out how to use the Internet positively, to make people aware of their music and then to actually sell it.

So far recording artists and computer/Internet companies have been more creative than the recording industry, which was largely on the defensive until 2004. A number of artists have been using the Internet to promote their music. The Grateful Dead, Phish, Jack Johnson and a few other groups that were famed by fans as performance oriented jam bands, had long encouraged fans to tape and trade copies of concerts. It became a lot easier to share music using the Internet, and had the effect of promoting these bands' music to generations of younger fans. Both some newer groups like Dispatch and well known recording artists like Dr. Dre have promoted music exchanges through programs like Napster, or more currently KaZaA and Lime Wire, in order to make their music more widely known and available. Some, like the Beastie Boys, in the Creative Commons group let certain songs be copied freely online, remixed or sampled by other artists for use in their own new recordings. Creative Commons is a new approach to licensing intellectual property rights: declaring that the recordings come with "some rights reserved," as opposed to the traditional "all rights reserved." The new license form was developed by Stanford Law School professor Lawrence Lessig, who opposes traditional licensing for restricting creative use of existing material too much. This new approach fits well with some artists who want to make their music widely available to promote it, while still maintaining some control over it. In a similar vein, many musicians post free music online on their own sites, such as www.bobdylan.com.

Another new means to promote music to very specialized interests is Internet radio. Latino and Lebanese-American rappers, among others, use Internet radio to reach people who aren't necessarily concentrated into large, easily identified geographic areas for conventional radio coverage. As Internet radio slowly takes off, recording companies have demanded that webcasters pay royalties for recorded music they play. Two industry groups, the Digital Media Association (DMA) and the Recording Industry Association of America (RIAA), agreed in 2003 to a proposal for royalty fees that Internet radio services must pay record companies for webcasting their songs.

Recording companies are finally beginning to get a bit more creative about distribution over the Internet. Universal Music will experiment with Group Shazam and some other relatively unknown acts by signing them to a digital-only label. It will release their songs through services like iTunes and Rhapsody. They hope signing acts with small, but established audiences will earn the company a profit on digital sales alone. This also lets them avoid the costs of the conventional distribution model: making a music video, paying music promoters to push the songs to radio stations, and advertising.

Some new distribution groups are arising. EMusic started an online music service that will give independent musicians a new option. The site will sell music from over 3,000 independent labels, a total of a half-million tracks. It may help fans locate small, obscure and eccentric music; help musicians find their fans; and grab a chunk of the more than $2 billion in revenues generated annually by independent music labels. Another kind of alternative is a company called ArtistShare. Bypassing labels, distributors and retailers, ArtistShare sells discs over the web and turns over all the proceeds (minus a small fee) to the artist.

Music Censorship?

The record industry had some self-censorship up through the 1960s. To get on the Ed Sullivan Show in 1964, the Rolling Stones changed the lyric "let's spend the night together" to "let's spend some time together." Even in the 1960s, FCC rules against obscenity and indecency restrained many radio stations from playing songs with lyrics like the Jefferson Airplane's "up against the wall, mother fxxxer." But many major rock groups carried by big labels began to use graphic language and explicit themes. This spread from rock to rap and hip hop, so that quite a bit of the most popular music by the 1980s had some explicit lyrics.

Congressional hearings in 1989 resulted in warning labels on record and CD covers, but their effectiveness had been questionable. In fact, many music sellers noted that warning stickers on labeled music sells faster, and sells at a higher volume, to both children and adults. In part, lyrics that might be considered problematic were very pervasive. Studies by George Gerbner found that among the top hits of 1995 and 1996, only 12% of the songs had no tobacco, alcohol, illicit drugs, crime, violence, or sexual lyrics, which has not changed much since. In fact, even more challenging artists, like Eminem, are now widely distributed and played on radio.

However, the times may be changing. Wal-Mart, the largest single retailer of recorded music, has refused to carry a number of recordings in both rock and hip-hop whose lyrics they consider to be offensive to the values of their customers. Changes seem to be coming at the FCC, too. After the 2004 presidential election highlighted moral concerns among a substantial part of the electorate, the FCC has become more aggressive about punishing obscenity or indecency on the airwaves. The FCC has pursued indecent speech by people like Howard Stern, but the music industry is watching to see if it extends to music too.

SUMMARY AND REVIEW

WHAT KIND OF MUSIC INDUSTRY EXISTED BEFORE THE PHONOGRAPH?

Music was performed live for audiences. It was also printed as sheet music and sold for home performance. The phonograph made casual listening easier and increased the sizes of audiences for music.

WHAT WERE THE MAIN ORIGINAL TRADITIONS IN POPULAR MUSIC?

Blues is an African-American musical tradition based primarily on guitar and distinctive plaintive lyrics. Gospel originated as southern Protestant religious music. Country music developed from English, Scottish, and Irish roots with similar instrumentation and ballad forms.

HOW DID RADIO CHANGE THE MUSIC INDUSTRY?

It further increased the reach of musical performances. It also increased the size of the audience to a truly mass audience and emphasized performers over composers. It created national audiences for music but also permitted regional genres—such as country and western and blues—to evolve.

HOW DID RADIO BROADCASTING AFFECT THE RECORDING INDUSTRY?

At first, the recording industry's sales fell off, as people moved to purchase radios instead. Over the long run, the recording industry came to rely on radio to make people aware of artists, and recordings that they could purchase.

WHAT WERE THE MAIN MUSIC GENRES IN THE 1920S AND 1930S?

The most popular, particularly on the national radio networks, were probably big band music and jazz. Country, blues, classical, Broadway tunes, and gospel were also popular.

HOW DID PHONOGRAPH FORMATS CHANGE, FROM VICTROLA TO LONG PLAY?

The first recordings played music off wax cylinders. The music was not electronically amplified. The next phonographs used flat records. Later ones added electronic amplification of the sound. Speeds were reduced from 78 rpm to 45 or 33⅓ rpm, and records were made larger so that they could play more music, longer. Finally, stereo sound was introduced.

HOW DO COMPACT DISCS WORK?

Whereas phonographs reproduce analog sound from grooves in records, CDs reproduce sound digitally, from 1s and 0s recorded as pits on the CD surface. The digital signal is then reconverted to analog form and sent as electrical impulses to the amplifier and then to the speakers.

HOW DOES MAGNETIC RECORDING ON TAPE WORK?

The tape passes over a recording head, an electromagnet, that rearranges the magnetic fields on the tape according to an electric current produced by a microphone. When playing back, the tape runs over another electromagnetic head, which responds to the patterns stored on the tape and generates another modulated current that is sent to a loudspeaker.

HOW IS THE INTERNET AFFECTING MUSIC DISTRIBUTION?

Some artists are now releasing music over the Internet to increase their audience. Internet users are also exchanging copyrighted music files over services like Gnutella, leading record companies to fear that they are losing control over the business. Record companies and recording artists have sued both MP3 exchange services and Internet radio stations to get better compensation.

WHAT ARE THE KEY COMPONENTS OF RECORDING INDUSTRY ORGANIZATION?

They include the talent (the singers and musicians), the recording studios and technical producers, the recording company, the distributors, and retailers. Recording studios are diversifying as cheap digital systems based in computers let small studios and even individuals record music, too.

WHAT ARE RECORD LABELS?

Labels of record companies are particular names for a group of recordings, which usually represent a consistent type of music. One company may own several diverse labels.

HOW ARE RECORDS DISTRIBUTED AND SOLD?

Record companies decide which albums and songs to promote through radio, billboards, newspaper ads, magazine ads, and music videos. The record companies distribute recordings in a variety of ways, including rack jobbers, retail music stores, big chain stores, Internet stores or catalogs, and record clubs.

WHAT ARE THE LIMITS ON FREEDOM OF SPEECH IN RECORDINGS?

The record industry practiced some self-censorship up through the 1960s. But major rock groups carried by major labels began to use more graphic language and explicit themes. Congressional hearings in 1989 resulted in warning labels on record and CD covers, but their effectiveness has been questionable, since even more challenging artists, like Eminem, are now widely distributed and played on the radio.

WHAT ARE THE MUSIC COPYRIGHT ISSUES?

Issues include making sure that artists get reimbursed for radio and Internet play and trying to forestall piracy of digital recordings over the Internet.

MEDIA CONNECTION

For web links, quizzes, and key term flash cards, visit the **Student Companion Website** at http://communication.wadsworth.com/straubhaar5.

 For unlimited easy access to additional and exclusive online study, support, and research tools, log on to **1pass** at http://1pass.thomson.com using the unique access code found on your 1pass passcode card.

 The **Media Now Premium Website** offers *Career Profile* videos, *Critical View* video news clips, and *Media in Motion* concept animations. You'll also find Stop & Review tutorial questions, a sample final exam, and much more.

InfoTrac College Edition is a fully searchable online database offering anytime, anywhere access to more than 20 years' worth of articles from nearly 5,000 diverse and reliable sources.

 vMentor provides live, one-on-one online tutoring to connect you to experts who will assist you in understanding the concepts covered in your course.

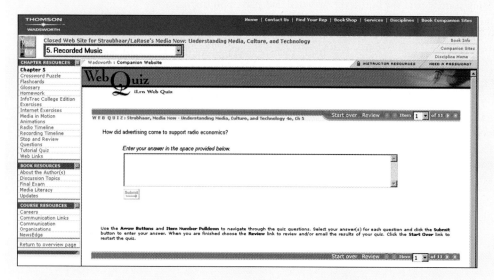

To improve your understanding of this chapter, work with its corresponding interactive Stop & Review tutorial questions.

6

HOWARD STERN ONLY ON
SIRIUS SATELLITE RADIO
HOWARD STERN ONLY ON
SIRIUS SATELLITE RADIO
SIRIUS BOOMBOX
SIRIUS
AUDIOVOX
SIRIUS SATELLITE RADIO

Will Howard Stern, the king of all media, be the death of all broadcast radio? Since the 1920s, radio has evolved in response to changes in available programming, popular music styles, and recording technology. This chapter discusses how the organization of the radio industry, its content, its impact on American culture, and related social issues have changed over the years. Now radio reorganizes in response to deregulation and technological change.

HISTORY: HOW RADIO BEGAN

Save the *Titanic:* Wireless Telegraphy

In 1896 Italian inventor Guglielmo Marconi created a "wireless telegraph" that used **radio waves** to carry messages in Morse code. This was the first practical use of radio. Marconi employed his business flair to establish the Marconi Wireless Telegraph Company, in Italy, then Britain and the USA, setting up a series of shore-based radio stations to receive and retransmit telegraph signals to oceangoing ships, where telegraph wires could not reach. His company also manufactured and operated the radio equipment. By 1913 Marconi dominated radio in Europe and the United States.

In 1912 the wireless telegraph played a pivotal role in the *Titanic* disaster. The British ocean liner struck an iceberg and sank suddenly in the North Atlantic. It sent radio distress calls, tapped out in Morse code over the Marconi wireless system, which was relayed to the Marconi radio operators in New York. Not only was radio crucial to saving many passengers, but it became central to reporting news about the disaster, which riveted people on both sides of the Atlantic. This incident attracted public attention to the fledgling technology—so much so, that the U.S. Congress took note and placed radio licensing

---

Radio waves are composed of electromagnetic energy and rise and fall in regular cycles.

1896	Marconi develops radio transmitter, goes into business	**1949**	DJ era of radio begins
1906	De Forest invents vacuum tube	**1970**	FM stations increase, go stereo, target segmented audience
1920	Frank Conrad starts KDKA in Pittsburgh	**1996**	Telecommunications Act sets off radio station merger frenzy
1926	RCA starts NBC Radio Network; AT&T pulls out of broadcasting	**2006**	Howard Stern's show moves to satellite radio
1934	Federal Communications Commission started		

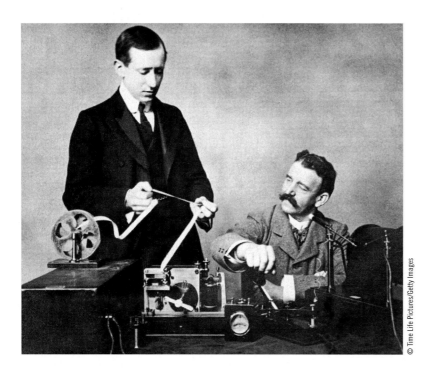

© Time Life Pictures/Getty Images

■ **BEFORE CDS**
Early radio broadcast Morse code not music. Here Marconi receives the first transatlantic signal.

Radio Act of 1912 first licensed radio transmitters.

Patents give an inventor the exclusive rights to an invention.

Vacuum tubes amplify and modulate signals by controlling the flow of electrical charges inside a glass tube.

under the supervision of the Department of Commerce in the **Radio Act of 1912.** Thus began regulation of the airwaves.

During World War I, the U.S. Navy accelerated radio technology by intervening in **patent** disputes between Marconi and other early inventors, standardizing the technologies. After the war, Marconi tried to buy U.S. patents to consolidate a U.S.–European communications monopoly, but the U.S. government opposed foreign control of a technology that clearly was crucial for military purposes. The Navy still held temporary control over radio technology and assets. It proposed making radio a government operation. A negotiated settlement forced Marconi, an Italian citizen, to sell its American assets to General Electric (GE). In turn, it set up a new company with American Telephone & Telegraph (AT&T) and Westinghouse called Radio Corporation of America (RCA) to develop the radio business in the United States. GE, RCA, and AT&T also set up a patent pool in 1920 so that they could all manufacture radio equipment. Without a pool, none of them owned the patents to make completely functioning radio transmitters or receivers (Streeter, 1996).

Broadcasting Begins

New technological developments before World War I made it clear that radio could be used for varied purposes. In 1906, Lee De Forest invented the **vacuum tube,** which permitted radio transmission and reception of sound, voice, and music. In 1906, Canadian inventor and physicist Reginald Fessenden made experimental broadcasts of voices and music over radio waves. Lee De Forest broadcast the presidential election returns in 1916 (Sterling & Kittross, 1990). However, few at that time saw broadcasting to individual home receivers as a viable potential business.

Attitudes began to change after the Navy returned radio to civilian hands by 1920 (see World View: BBC, License Fees, and the Road Not Taken, next page). Frank Conrad, a Westinghouse engineer, began the first regularly scheduled radio broadcasts in the United States in 1920, attracting interest and newspaper coverage. A Pittsburgh department store decided to sell radios to pick up Conrad's broadcasts. Then Westinghouse realized that regular radio broadcasts could help sell radios, so it opened station KDKA in Pittsburgh in 1920. Just as Westinghouse had hoped, the availability of the station encouraged people to start buying radio receivers—100,000 in 1922 and over 500,000 in 1923 (Sterling & Kittross, 1990).

■ **SOS**
Distress signals from the *Titanic* called public attention to radio communication.

It did not take people long to think of other things to do with radio. For example, retail stores started radio stations just to promote their goods. Electronics companies, such as the RCA Radio Group, set up more broadcast stations to make more people want to buy radios. Newspapers saw news potential; schools and churches saw educational potential. With so many rushing into the new medium, the Commerce Department was asked to combat **frequency** interference by supervising radio broadcasting. As a result, the department issued hundreds of **licenses** in 1923.

Two visions of radio probably determined its future. One came in 1916. David Sarnoff, then commercial manager of American Marconi, wrote a prophetic memo to his boss. He proposed "a plan of development which would make radio a 'household utility' in the same sense as the piano or phonograph. The idea is to bring music into the house by wireless. . . . The Receiver can be designed in the form of a simple 'Radio Music Box' and arranged for several different wavelengths, which should be changeable with the throwing of a single switch or pressing of a single button." Sarnoff's memo was ignored, but he anticipated perfectly the physical form that radio would take within 10 years, and later, as head of RCA, he had a chance to help make this vision of radio and a similar vision of television a reality.

At first, Sarnoff opposed the idea of commercial radio and proposed that listeners pay a tax on new radios that would help pay for programming, an arrangement not unlike the system later used by the BBC (British Broadcasting Corporation) in Great Britain. Later Sarnoff made his peace with commercial radio and television, and helped propel RCA's main network, NBC, into a leadership role for a number of years in both radio and television.

The second key vision for radio—entertainment supported by advertising—came from AT&T's station WEAF, started in 1922 in New Jersey. Following the model of the telephone industry, AT&T charged content providers a fee for the use of its radio stations. The fee was based on how much airtime they used. This evolved into letting manufacturers sponsor programs to advertise their goods, then into advertisers paying to have their ads carried on programs. WEAF broadcast the first "commercial" in 1922. Advertisers immediately responded to the opportunity, and commercial broadcasting grew quickly. By 1927, radio had attained a distinct shape. Privately owned stations, linked into networks that determined most of the program choices, focused on popular entertainment, heavily tilted toward music, supported by commercial advertising, a model it retains today. Furthermore, the quick shaping of radio by commercial interests laid down a pattern that other media followed, both in the United States and abroad. Looking ahead, one could argue that the global shape of broadcasting today reflects this then-unique arrangement of radio in the United States.

A number of strong economic interests came together to set this pattern. RCA and other radio manufacturers wanted to sell radio sets. They wanted the most broadly appealing content broadcast to sell more radios. Radio stations and, soon, radio networks came to see a way to make a great deal of money selling advertising. Networks arose to supply

Frequency is the number of cycles that radio waves complete in a second.

Licenses grant legal permission to operate a radio transmitter.

BBC, License Fees, and the Road Not Taken

In 1922–1923, the British sent a commission to the United States to study radio development. They observed a rush toward a radio industry dominated by musical entertainment and paid for by advertising. The British commission saw that as an enormous waste of the medium's cultural and educational potential. On returning home, they recommended a very different formula: a public radio monopoly oriented toward education and culture, financed by a license fee paid by listeners, and overseen by a board intended to keep it independent of both government and private interests, such as advertisers. This system, which became known as the British Broadcasting Corporation (BBC), is still highly regarded for cultural and educational broadcasting, although many find some of the programming elitist, dry and stuffy. It represents an alternative considered, but not chosen, by the United States in the 1920s.

The BBC has trouble coping with the increase in commercial competition in the U.K. Some who no longer listen resent paying the license fee. It has also struggled, like many news operations, to continue extensive world coverage on a limited budget. However for many, it also represents a more cultural and educational form of radio.

stations with the most popular entertainment in a way that spread costs across a number of stations. Advertisers saw a way to help create and then reach a mass consumer public, turning people first and foremost into consumers by promoting their goods on the airwaves.

Radio offered advertisers direct access to the home. To increase the size of the audience for their ads, advertisers steered stations toward entertainment programs, which were more lucrative than news or education (Streeter, 1996). In the 1920s regulators and the radio industry worried that audiences would reject radio if it carried too much advertising. However, people were so enthusiastic about the new medium that they accepted the ads without much objection, and a commercial advertising-based model was firmly entrenched by 1927 (Barnouw, 1966).

AT&T became the first broadcast network, as it used its phone lines to link several of its stations. It began to dream of having a monopoly in this new medium with WEAF as the flagship station for its network. However, the U.S. government and major electronics companies opposed AT&T's domination of both broadcasting and telephony (Sterling & Kittross, 1990). Thus, to keep its telephone monopoly, AT&T sold out to RCA in 1926 and agreed to act as a transmission medium for all radio networks on an equal basis. This solution reinforced a policy, the **common carrier** principle, that held that telephone companies were not to be involved in creating the content of communication, only transmitting it. That policy lasted until 1996.

The initial government regulation, the Radio Act of 1912, called for licensing of transmitters by the Secretary of Commerce but was not very specific in granting powers. Self-regulation did not work either, resulting in substantial frequency interference between stations. The **Radio Act of 1927** created the Federal Radio Commission (FRC). It defined the broadcast band, standardized frequency designations, and limited the number of stations operating at night, when AM signals carry farther than during the day and are more likely to interfere with other stations.

Common carriers must carry any signal and cannot own the content.

Radio Act of 1927 created a Federal Radio Commission.

The Rise of Radio Networks

RCA set up its radio network, the National Broadcasting Corporation (NBC), in 1926. Networking, linking stations together to share programming costs, made each station cheaper to operate by realizing *economies of scale* (see Chapter 2). RCA eventually had

■ **AND NOW, LIVE FROM NEW YORK!**
Early network radio was all live, but also very popular and eagerly supported by advertisers like Tums.

enough stations for two separate networks—NBC Red and NBC Blue. NBC "Red" was the main NBC network. Competition soon came from the Columbia Broadcasting System (CBS), which moved quickly to put together a network to rival NBC. NBC and CBS networks had their own stations, called owned-and-operated stations, or **O&Os,** but both began to attract a number of **affiliated** stations, which they did not own but which carried network programs as well. By 1937, NBC had 111 affiliates and CBS had 105 (Sterling & Kittross, 1990).

Early network radio programming in the late 1920s and 1930s was focused on music but also included news, comedy, variety shows, soap operas, detective dramas, sports, suspense, and action adventures. Thus, many of the kinds of programming that we now see on television were developed on radio. Many radio performers came in from vaudeville-style theater, particularly comics Fred Allen, George Burns, and Gracie Allen. Comic books lent heroes such as Superman and Green Lantern to radio adventure shows. Pulp-fiction westerns like *Riders of the Purple Sage* fed into radio westerns such as *Gunsmoke.*

Because recording technology had not achieved very high *fidelity,* music was primarily broadcast live. Recording artists were also initially unwilling to let radio play their recorded and copyrighted, music until a royalty system was devised to compensate them. Networks introduced the most popular groups and orchestras to the entire country. National radio networks featured the major pop music of the day: big bands, light classical music, and movie and show tunes. Eventually, however, radio also stimulated a demand for a variety of musical genres, ranging from classical to country and western.

Radio Network Power

There was concern that the radio networks were abusing their power in one-sided dealings with their affiliated stations and with the on-air talent. The FCC's 1941 **Chain Broadcasting** ruling prohibited the networks from forcing programming on affiliates and put the networks out of the talent-booking business. The FCC also forced NBC to sell off its second network in 1943, which became the American Broadcasting Corporation (ABC).

Network radio remained strong through World War II. Money spent on radio ads doubled from 1939 to 1945, surpassing expenditures on newspaper ads in 1943. Radio was

O&Os are stations owned and operated by networks.

Affiliates are stations that contract to use the programming of a network.

Chain broadcasting is synonymous with a broadcasting network.

the paramount information medium of the war, both domestically and internationally. Internationally, the use of radio for propaganda purposes frightened many people and stimulated research into the power of mass media over their audiences (see Chapter 13).

Edward R. Murrow broadcast memorable live reports from London during World War II, dramatically covering the German bombing of London and other battlefields. His reports conveyed vivid, realistic, and often highly moving word pictures. He emerged as one of the most credible and admired newsmen in the well-respected CBS news organization (Whetmore, 1981) and helped network radio achieve pre-eminence as a source of news as well as entertainment.

Competition from Television

From 1948 on, television exploded across the United States (see Chapter 8), picking up steam in the 1950s until most people in the United States not only had a television but were watching it at least several hours a night. Radio was quickly and adversely affected. Many nonmusical broadcast programming genres, from news to soap operas, moved to television. Radio networks saw their own parent corporations, such as RCA and CBS, refocus their energy on new television networks that promised to be a major new source of profit. Audience attention and listening, especially during the prime evening hours, also moved to the new medium. People who did not have a television imposed themselves on neighbors who did. Advertising followed popular programs and audiences to television.

Westerns such as *Gunsmoke,* soap operas like *As the World Turns,* and comics like Red Skelton discovered that adding pictures to the sounds added a great deal to what their original radio genres could do. Dramas, in particular, offered much higher impact with visuals, but so did news, soaps, westerns, comedies, science fiction, game shows, quiz shows, and variety shows.

The same networks that dominated radio moved to television: NBC and CBS. They were entranced with both the audience and advertiser response to television, seeing it as an even more profitable medium than radio. So their radio networks were left to struggle, to try to find new niches and functions.

Networks Fall, Disc Jockeys Rule

As television's popularity skyrocketed, and it became the main source of mass entertainment nationwide, network radio began to slip. The number of network affiliates dropped from 97 percent of all AM stations in 1947 to 50 percent in 1955, while network revenue dropped even more. When much of the prime-time radio entertainment audience shifted to television, stations began to leave the networks and radio station management explored new ways to attract a more local audience.

Radio advertising shifted from a national to a local focus and began to rely on cheaper, more localized **formats,** such as recorded music, news, and talk. Radio's success began to depend on the talent of each station's own announcers and on their ability to find the right music mix for their local market: programming strategies organized around a **playlist** of music and focused on a particular genre or audience.

Radio stations began to create new radio formats that featured rhythm and blues, and rock and roll. Disc jockeys (DJs) played records aimed at local audiences, so although many records became national hits, local music such as bluegrass in the South, blues in Chicago, and country and western in rural areas all saw stations grow up to serve those who wanted that music (see Media and Culture: DJs Rock Around the Clock on page 157).

Formats for radio labels content aimed at a specific audience.

Playlists are the songs picked for air play.

DJs Rock Around the Clock

Top 40 radio, or formula radio, was born in 1949 and was the most popular format through the 1960s. It focused on the top-selling records, on gimmicks to attract attention, and on the delivery and personality of the disc jockey, or DJ, who picked and announced the records. DJs became popular public figures in their own right. Alan Freed, a Cleveland DJ, was mixing rhythm and blues (R&B) with Sinatra. He popularized the term *rock and roll* to help get white audiences to listen to R&B and helped promote "Rock Around the Clock," by Bill Haley and the Comets, the first rock and roll single to become number one on the charts. Freed and other DJs became famous.

Stations competed on the basis of their DJs. The record companies, who wanted their records promoted, also tar-geted the DJs. This led to abuse, known as payola, where record companies gave gifts or even bribes to key DJs. Some major-market DJs were making up to $100,000 a year from payola; this led to a public scandal, congressional hearings, and amendments to the Communications Act. However, the DJs did help the music industry grow rapidly; in particular, they helped turn rock music into an enormous success. Rock and pop music became closely linked with the baby boomers, who had enormous numbers and great purchasing power. Today's radio personalities or DJs are not so much the focus of payola, which has become more corporate, with independent music promoters paying music directors or radio corporation executives top place songs on the radio (see "The Recording Industry," Chapter 5).

What we know now as Contemporary Hit Radio (CHR), or **Top 40,** was probably invented by Todd Storz in 1949. He wondered why radio could not be more like a jukebox, playing the hit songs that people really wanted to hear the most, over and over. Top 40 was the dominant radio format from the 1950s until the early 1970s. Until radio became more segmented in the 1970s, stations, particularly Top 40 formats, played roughly the same overall mix of rock and roll, pop, Motown, and some R&B. Rock was still somewhat unified by Top 40 stations until the late 1960s, when Motown, surf music, English groups including the Beatles and the Rolling Stones, and heavy rockers such as Led Zeppelin and Jimi Hendrix were all being played on the same "rock" stations (Limmer, 1981).

© AP/Wide World Photos

The FM Revolution

The growth of FM radio revived radio in the 1960s. FM has high-fidelity sound but a short range—within the line of sight of the radio transmitter. That also allows for more stations in each market by reducing interference with stations in nearby markets that use the same frequency. Both FM and 33⅓ rpm records moved into stereo sound (two separate, coordinated channels of music) which had started in 1956. By the late 1960s, many popular groups were recording songs much longer than the two- to three-minute cuts typical of Top 40 AM radio, which were fine for new formats on FM. Sometimes those songs were squeezed onto a 45 rpm record, but most fans just began to buy the 33⅓ rpm album (LP) that the hit song was on.

■ **THIS IS THE WOLFMAN HOWLIN' ATCHA!**
DJs like Wolfman Jack characterized radio from the 1950s to the 1980s.

Top 40 is a radio format that replays the top 40 songs heavily.

Radio continued to grow, along with the boom in pop music. AM licenses were becoming difficult and expensive to obtain, whereas licenses for FM stations were much easier to get. Since each market could have at least 15 FM stations, there was a tendency to focus on *segmented* audiences with more specific formulas and formats.

Rock's diverse roots fed further diversification into a number of branches or *subgenres,* which produced new radio formats. In the 1970s, "rock" split into Top 40, new wave, heavy metal, punk, soul, and disco. The 1980s and 1990s added formats for alternative, industrial/techno, new age, ska, reggae, rap, and hip-hop. And as they had first done the 1960s, radio stations began to adopt the new musical genres (discussed in Chapter 5) as distinctive formats. These stations gave expression to musical subgenres and the subcultures that enjoyed them and the advertisers that coveted those subcultures. Subcultures like punks, skaters or hip-hop tended to not only listen to different music but consume very different clothes and shoes which opened an opportunity to let marketers target them via specific radio formats. This development was enabled by technological developments that lowered the price of recordings and also the cost of starting radio stations.

Some targeted FM radio formats, such as classical, jazz, or album-oriented rock, took advantage of the musical quality of FM's higher fidelity and new stereo capability. Much of the audience was also interested in improved sound quality, because high-fidelity stereo systems were becoming much more popular, and that had a decisive appeal for discerning listeners (Jones, 1992). FM came to dominate the radio industry. By 1993, FM stations drew 77 percent of the audience.

A New Generation of Network Radio

Though radio was characterized almost completely by local operations in the 1970s and 1980s, some new forms of network radio began to emerge in the 1990s. In some cases, this resulted from stations buying into centrally produced program formats distributed via satellite. In other cases, large radio ownership groups began to act like the radio networks of old, looking for economies of scale from centralized program production.

To meet the demand for interesting music, news, and talk programs on dozens of FM and AM stations in each market, a number of outlets began to produce programs for **syndication.** One example is "shock jock" Howard Stern, whose controversial talk-radio show started in New York. Because the show attracted a large audience, Stern's parent station group began to offer it over satellite to other stations. Conservative pundit Rush Limbaugh also developed a network of stations that carried his syndicated program. Other companies began to offer complete radio formats, such as "The Arrow's" classic rock format on syndicated distribution. In a related trend, advertising, the DJ's patter, traffic, and weather are increasingly broadcast from a distant location using local information.

The early 1980s saw a boom in financial speculation in radio stations because their values had been rising rapidly. Then several years of meager earnings drove most speculators out. Changes in ownership limits established in the **1996 Telecommunications Act** permitted radio station groups to acquire many more stations and grow much larger. The new regulations lifted national caps on how many stations a group could own but limited ownership within a specific radio market, depending on the size of the market.

Over 4400 stations changed hands in 1996 and 1997. Over 700 individual local owners sold their stations to groups. Even large ownership groups began to merge. Large groups like Capstar were acquired by other groups like Clear Channel. By 2004, Clear Channel Communications emerged as the largest, with over 1200 stations (http://www.clearchannel.com). In a number of towns, 80 to 90 percent of radio ad revenues are now controlled by stations belonging to only two or three groups. That fact raises strong

■ STERN DISPOSITION
Shock jock Howard Stern led talk radio for years but has jumped to satellite radio to avoid FCC indecency rules.

Syndication is rental or licensing of media products.

1996 Telecommunications Act deregulated radio ownership rules.

questions of whether content diversity is now being limited by having only a few companies making almost all content decisions. (See Issues section: "Who Controls the Airwaves?".)

As a result of the huge merger wave that began in 1996, merged and reorganized stations initially lost money as competition among large groups shook out. Clear Channel, for example, lost $16.9 billion in the first three months of 2002, mostly writing off losses on stations that were overvalued when purchased. For the long term, it is not clear whether bigger groups will be more profitable or not. Radio ads have been priced very low for years, so radio has become attractive to advertisers. Radio is no longer limited to narrow audience segments. By taking advantage of consolidated advertising sales across all the group-owned stations in a market, advertisers can easily reach a broad audience, picking up teens from Top 40 (now known as Contemporary Hit Radio, or CHR), middle-aged listeners from country, or adult contemporary (see Table 6.1). That rationale for consolidation seems to be playing out as very large ownership groups like Clear Channel have begun to profit from offering national-level advertising placement.

© Neal Preston/CORBIS

■ ONLY ROCK 'N' ROLL
The Rolling Stones are one of the bands that launched album-oriented FM radio in the 1960s.

Alternative, Rap, and Hip-Hop Radio

Radio stations, particularly in FM, have continued to change formats to follow the evolution of both music genres and audience interests. The industry tries hard to target specific audience segments with unique, nonoverlapping formats, but the musical development of artists draws the audience across a changing pattern of formats. For example, Sheryl Crow first appeared in "alternative" format stations. Later, though, she appeared on the air in a number of different FM radio formats: hot adult contemporary, adult alternative, rock, and contemporary hits.

Rap and hip-hop have become dominant genres in both CD sales and radio formats. Rap emerged from New York street disc jockeys who used turntables as instruments to set up a beat to rap, talk in improvised rhymes, over. Both African-Americans and Latinos have been involved in the development of rap since the early days, but black artists have been promoted more heavily by the music industry, so much so that rap and hip-hop are perceived by many as black genres. As such, rap and hip-hop have given black artists perhaps their highest visibility in pop music and Top 40 radio since Motown in the 1960s.

Latino artists have created a strong rap and hip-hop tradition of their own, as well as cross-feeding in the overall hip-hop tradition with black artists, like Puffy, who has done raps in Spanish. An increasing number of Spanish-language rap format radio stations are a good example of how music genres, like rap or hip-hop, grow and subdivide, closely followed by radio formats. Some artists start in a smaller subformat, then move to more widespread formats, as Latino artist Cypress Hill did when he moved from Latino to hip-hop stations and gained overall hip-hop radio popularity. Some white artists like Eminem have also become both popular on the radio and accepted within the hip-hop community. Rap and hip-hop have also spread internationally, so raperos in Mexico now create music that flows back into the United States, as well as vice versa.

Table 6.1 Radio Formats and Audiences

Format*	Number of Stations	Audience Share (AQH)**	Typical Content	Target Audience — Sex	Target Audience — Age
News/talk/sports	2179	15.9	Dr. Phil	Mostly male	25–55
Country, classic, new	2066	13.2	Alan Jackson	Male/female	25–44, 55+
Religious/gospel/Christian	2014	5.5	Dr. Dobson	Mostly female	35+
Adult contemporary	1556	12.8	Eric Clapton	Mostly female	35–44
Adult standards	1196	3.0	Frank Sinatra	Male/female	65+
Oldies, 70s–80s, rhythmic oldies	1060	7.1	Earth, Wind and Fire	Male/female	35-65
Rock, classic rock, AOR	869	9.0	Led Zeppelin	Mostly male	18-44
Spanish (all including news talk)	750	6.4	Los Tigres del Norte	Male/female	18–45
Contemporary Hit (CHR), rhythmic	569	10.3	Dr. Dre	Male/female	12–34
Alternative, adult alternative	454	4.0	Patty Griffin	Mostly male	18–44
Urban, urban oldies, urban AC	52	7.6	Black Eyed Peas	Male/female	12–45
Classical, fine arts	291	2.2	Pavarotti	Male/female	55+
New adult contemporary, smooth jazz	141	2.3	Kenny G.	Male/female	25+

* These general formats combine specific format variations that might compete with each in a market.
** AQH is the average number of persons listening to a particular station for at least five minutes during a 15-minute period. The format share is the percentage of all those listening in an area who are listening to a particular format.

Source: Arbitron, 2004 (http://www.arbitron.com/); *Broadcasting and Cable, Billboard;* Radio Guide, SA/Format Guide (http://www.radioguide.com/formats.html)

Satellite Radio

Satellite radio now competes with conventional terrestrial radio broadcasts. The signal comes directly from a satellite down to small dishes or antennas and specialized receivers. Like satellite television, satellite radio offers the potential of far more channels than can be offered by terrestrial broadcasters, which are limited to at most 20–30 FM channels and a dozen or so AM channels in most American cities and towns (See the "Technology" section). That would permit far more segmentation of radio than currently exists, offering more potential variety of channels than currently exists.

Currently, two companies dominate satellite radio: XM Satellite Radio and Sirius Satellite Radio. Both charge a monthly fee for music services. Some XM and Sirius music channels have limited commercials, but being largely commercial-free seems to be a major part of their attraction for some customers. Both services are available either via portable receivers in automobiles or home receivers. In 2004, XM started the year with 1.3 million subscribers and finished in December 2004 with 3.1 million and Sirius finished with almost 1 million.

■ **YOU'RE ALL WE NEED**
Despite changes in technology to play and deliver music, singers like Mary J. Blige are still what draw people.

As of 2004, both had 100 music channels. That challenges the offerings of local radio in terms of specificity and audience segmentation. However, what really brought both protests and lawsuits in 2004 from regular broadcast stations was when both satellite services also began traffic and weather reports for major cities. That challenges the local advantage of broadcast radio in a very direct way. Since much of radio listening takes place during drive-time commuting hours, the ability of local radio stations to offer local news, traffic, and weather has been a crucial comparative advantage that they do not want to lose to satellite radio services. Satellite radio was almost moving into another radio staple, talk. Sirium signed Howard Stern to a satellite radio-only deal beginning in 2006 after he felt hassled by FCC rules on broadcast radio. Both stations and critics fear that satellite radio could lead to a decline in both number and variety of local radio stations, plus a concentration of programming decisions in the hand of fewer companies, as well as fewer jobs in the radio industry.

Internet Radio

Internet radio is another growing option. Web radio networks plus web radio servers list thousands of Internet radio stations. Web radio stations cover an ever-expanding variety of genres. They cover mainstream pop artists and include many of the familiar formats of commercial radio, like country and western, or adult contemporary. Local commercial and PBS stations find webcasting a convenient way to reach both local and nonlocal listeners. However, much of the current excitement in Internet-based radio lies in the extraordinary diversity of interests, formats, and genres that are represented. A listener in rural Iowa who wants gospel flavored Latino hip-hop probably won't find it on the local airwaves but can easily do so on web-based stations.

According to Arbitron, the radio ratings company, over 4 million people a week tune in to the three leading online networks: AOL Radio Network, Yahoo's Launchcast, and Microsoft's MSN radio.

Radio continues as an enjoyable and even crucial medium for millions of listeners, from those who want the hits to those who want the news from NPR. However, as an industry, radio is challenged by shakeouts in ownership, by competition from Internet and satellite radio, and changes in formats as genres and listener interests constantly change.

TECHNOLOGY: INSIDE YOUR RADIO

How the New Radio Technologies Work

Like the waves that we make in our bathtubs when we drop the soap, radio waves rise and fall in regular patterns, called cycles. The number of cycles that the waves complete in a second is their frequency and is measured in **Hertz (Hz).** Radio waves have much higher frequencies than waves in a bathtub and do not require a transmission medium, such as water, to propagate. Radio waves can travel much farther than bathtub waves because the electromagnetic energy they use can be detected at a distance. They are propagated primarily by "line of sight" to distant receiving antennas that are within direct

Hertz (Hz) is a measure of the frequency of a radio wave in cycles per second.

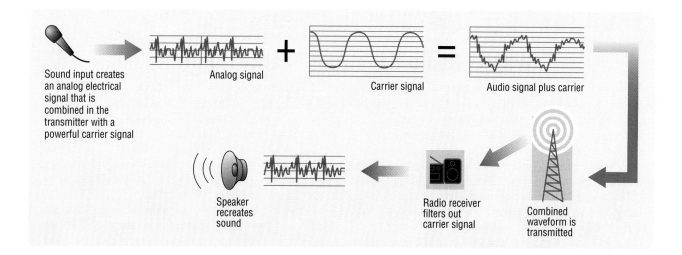

Sound input creates an analog electrical signal that is combined in the transmitter with a powerful carrier signal

Analog signal

Carrier signal

Audio signal plus carrier

Speaker recreates sound

Radio receiver filters out carrier signal

Combined waveform is transmitted

view of the transmitter, but also by electrical conduction through the earth itself or by reflection off an electrically charged layer of the atmosphere, the ionosphere (Figure 6.1).

Lee De Forest paved the way to radio by inventing the vacuum tube in 1906. After further improvements by inventor Howard Armstrong, the vacuum tube permitted a weak signal to be both amplified and precisely modulated by controlling the flow of electrical charges inside a small glass enclosure shaped something like a lightbulb.

AM is short for **amplitude modulation,** which means that the sound information is carried in variations in the height, or amplitude, of the radio wave. In an AM radio system, the electric current that comes out of a microphone or an electronic recording device is combined with a high-frequency electromagnetic carrier wave that corresponds to the frequency of a particular radio channel. The AM radio band was fixed at 535—1605 kHz in 1941 (the k is a symbol for 1000), then extended to 1705 kHz in 1988. For example, the carrier wave is 540,000 Hz if you have your radio tuned to 540 on the AM dial. The combined wave is amplified and fed into a radio transmitter, which is essentially a giant electromagnet. The combined electromagnetic wave induces a weak electric current inside your radio antenna. Then the carrier frequency is removed, and the original audio is recovered, amplified, and sent to the speakers.

In 1933, Howard Armstrong, now an RCA engineer, developed **FM, or frequency modulation.** In FM radio, the sound information is carried by variations in the frequency of the radio wave around the central carrier frequency, which is 101,700,000 Hz if you are tuned to FM101.7. Compared to AM, FM has a greater frequency range and less static, so stereo broadcasting was begun in the FM band. The FM channels are wide enough so that two slightly different versions of the broadcast can be carried. These are electronically combined inside your receiver to produce the two separate signals you hear in your left and right speaker. (AM stereo is in service, but it is much less widely used.) Because FM signals can travel only in the line of sight, FM is limited to about a 30-mile range. That is much less than AM stations that, "on a good night," can be heard hundreds of miles away because AM frequencies bounce off the upper atmosphere and can travel great distances over the horizon.

In the 1950s, transistors, and later, integrated circuits (see Chapter 12) replaced the tubes in radios. Transistors performed the same functions as the tubes, making it possible to use a weak electrical signal to control a large flow of electrical charges, but in a much smaller package. The pocket-size transistor radios of the 1950s were the first practical personal music players.

■ FIGURE 6.1
How AM radio broadcasting uses radio waves The announcer's voice is converted to electricity by the microphone. This electrical signal is then combined with a powerful, high-frequency carrier signal and transmitted to the home receiver. The receiver filters out the carrier and re-creates the original electrical analog signal, which the loudspeaker converts back to sound energy.

AM or amplitude modulation carries information in the height, or amplitude, of the radio wave.

FM or frequency modulation carries information in variations in the frequency of the radio wave.

Why Is Radio Spectrum Scarce?, Part II

Returning to our experiments with electromagnetism (Part I, Chapter 5) we left our science teacher Ms. Kotter after she had demonstrated the operation of electromagnetism. Then Ms. Kotter sprinkled some of the iron filings on a piece of cardboard, reconnected the electromagnet to the battery, and showed you that she could move the filings around the surface of the cardboard by passing the magnet underneath it. This proved that electromagnetic fields act at a distance, just as a radio transmitter affects the antenna on your radio from miles away.

If your school's science budget was up to it, your teacher went one step further. She hooked up the coil of wire to a meter that measured electric current and moved a magnet back and forth through the middle of the coil. As the magnet moved, the needle on the meter twitched, showing that a changing magnetic field induced an electric current in the wire. This is what happens inside your radio antenna and also in the playback head of your tape recorder, converting a magnetic field back to electricity.

If Ms. Kotter had borrowed some gear from the local college's electrical engineering department, she could have continued with a demonstration of the *electromagnetic spectrum.* The spectrum is a means of classifying electromagnetic radiation according to its frequency. The electrical current in your home is at the low end of the spectrum, 60 Hz. The sounds in our stereos are between 20 and 20,000 Hz, the range of frequencies that can be heard by the human ear.

If we created a visual representation of a pure tone at any of these frequencies on our borrowed gear, it would resemble the dollar sign "$" lying on its side; we call that shape a wave (a *sine wave,* to be exact). We refer to the height of the wave as its *amplitude,* and the number of times that it goes through the complete cycle (tracing one hump facing down and one hump facing up) in a second is the *frequency.* The *phase* refers to the point in the cycle at which we begin.

The radio frequencies used in our consumer electronics devices are organized into bands. For example, AM radio is in the High Frequency band; VHF television (channels 2–13, see Chapter 8) takes its name from the Very High Frequency band—that's also where FM radio is located. Similarly, the UHF (channels 14–69) are in the Ultra High Frequency band. Cell phones and satellites use yet higher frequency bands. Light is part of the spectrum, too.

Communication channels are assigned according to the frequency of their carrier waves. But additional frequencies clustering around the carrier are needed to encode the audio or video information, and the more space we have for each channel, the more information we can transmit. The total range of frequencies needed is the *bandwidth* of the channel. Our telephones have a bandwidth of only 3100 Hz, whereas AM radio channels are 10,000 Hz, compared to 100,000 for FM radio and six million for television.

What makes the spectrum scarce? Some parts of the spectrum are better than others. For example, the AM radio spectrum is highly desirable because waves can travel thousands of miles, while FM signals can barely peep over the horizon. At higher frequencies, transmissions may be absorbed by water droplets and so fade out when it rains. Plus, many of the older services are "spectrum hogs:" FM radio channels are 100,000 Hz wide, but they deliver only two 15,000 Hz channels to your ears. And, there are many other uses for the spectrum besides consumer electronics; two-thirds of the spectrum is reserved for the military and other government users. Finally, to prevent interference, we have to geographically separate transmitters operating on the same frequency. All that makes the spectrum both scarce and valuable.

Note: Part I of this box, "Experiments with Electromagnetism," appears on page 133 in Chapter 5.

High Definition Radio

High Definition Radio (formerly known as Digital Audio Broadcasting) transmits audio that has been converted to computer data, as in a CD recording, over the air from earthbound radio transmitters to special digital receivers. This increases the quality of the sound and makes radio signals less susceptible to fading. "Near CD quality" sound is the result, leading to the "high definition" label, borrowed from high definition TV (see Chapter 8). The digital signal also includes information about the music so that listeners may set their radios to "seek heavy metal" if they so desire and see the name of the station and the tune they are listening to on their display. The digital signals can also pack additional channels of information, such as news updates and alerts about travel and weather conditions.

HD radio has been on the air since 1997 in Europe, but U.S. broadcasters are just now introducing it. To protect their vested interests, they insisted that the new service be transmitted in the same frequency band and on the same channel (the approach is called "in band, on channel") as their current stations, while maintaining the conventional analog service. The trick is to transmit the digital signal at such low power that it is not detected by conventional analog receivers. That was no mean feat, especially in the AM band where there was little bandwidth available to encode the digital signal. So, it took several years to perfect.

Satellite Radio's Technology

The broadcasters must hurry if they want to remain the leading source of live sound. XM Radio and Sirius transmit music via satellite to compact receivers via wafer-shaped antennas that can be placed on the roof of a car, bypassing earthbound radio stations entirely. Both XM and Sirius operate on two or three **geosynchronous satellites** to achieve full coverage of the U.S. market. Local repeaters mounted on the tops of buildings and hills, operating curved frequencies as the satellites enable XM and Sirius's signals to be available even if the view of the satellite is blocked by buildings or mountains. That is also what allows satellite radio to insert local traffic and weather reports—and potentially local ads, into their transmission.

Internet Radio's Technology

Internet radio began with experimenters in 1993 who used early technologies like MBONE (IP Multicast Backbone on the Internet). Full-time stations started in 1995 when hobbyists, ad agencies, and regular broadcast radio stations began to create Internet radio stations. More radio stations started putting their signals on websites, but many web radio stations are completely independent from broadcast radio stations and are available only on the Internet. Some represent small "pirate" radio stations, which broadcast on the air when they can and also on the web. Hundreds of radio stations feed their programming to the World Wide Web through sites such as Yahoo.com, in an effort to reach out-of-town listeners and people at work. There are many "Internet only" channels that cannot be found on the air. Near-CD-quality stereo can be had if you have a fast enough network connection. Internet streaming technologies (see Chapter 9) make it possible to listen to programming in real time instead of downloading and saving prerecorded files. Wireless Internet connections are becoming available (Chapter 9) that offer the potential of replacing your car radio or personal stereo with a wireless Internet receiver, or playing music over your cell phone or personal data assistant (for example, Palm Pilot). However, the recording industry would like to nip those developments in the bud as we will explore in the "Media Literacy" section or at least profit from them.

Webcast

Webcast or Internet radio stations use varying technologies for "streaming" a continuous transmission (composed of digital bits) over the Internet (as opposed to downloading individual files, like MP3 music files). One of the first streaming audio technologies was developed by RealNetworks, but currently one of the most common ways to distribute web radio is via streaming MP3 technology, using the relatively standard MP3 music format. Depending on the source, interested listeners will need RealNetworks software or an appropriate MP3 player, like Winamp for Windows or iTunes for Macintosh. Internet radio

Geosynchronous satellites are satellites whose rotation matches that of the earth so they stay in a fixed position relative to the earth's surface.

A webcast is a broadcast on the World Wide Web.

streams have opened a new front in the music piracy "wars" that pit the Internet community against the likes of Steve Jobs of Apple and the RIAA grants he fronts for. Freely available programs will automatically break up the incoming streams into individual tracks and record them on your computer, or share them with your favorite online community.

INDUSTRY: RADIO GROUPS AND MUSIC LABELS

Radio in the Age of the New Media Giants

Radio lives in a contradictory time of countervailing trends. New digital technologies seem to allow many more new entrants in music distribution and radio. However, economic and regulatory changes have also encouraged unprecedented concentration of the ownership of a few major players (in terms of hits, sales, and profits) all across the radio industry.

Radio stations were once owned by many kinds of individuals and small groups. Since the 1996 Telecommunications Act deregulated ownership, concentration of station ownership in the hands of new, nonlocal groups has increased dramatically (Table 6.2). The difference in scope between the early 1990s and the late 1990s was astonishing. In 1992, the largest radio ownership group was Infinity with 22 stations (*Broadcasting*, Nov. 16, 1992). In 1999, the largest group, Clear Channel (484 stations) bought the next largest, AMFM (460 stations), creating a new behemoth that had 1200 stations in 2004, about one-tenth of *all* American radio stations.

The goal for these large groups is to achieve national coverage. Clear Channel now boasts that it can offer potential advertisers as much national coverage via its radio stations as can television networks. After the effective dissolution of national radio networks in the 1950s, the ability to sell nationwide advertising coverage had shifted to television networks. National advertisers, such as Nike, had to assemble shifting groups of radio stations by local ad purchases to achieve national exposure on radio. Groups can now own multiple radio stations in a single market, too, so they can offer a national advertiser exposure on several different formats, such as country, classic rock, and urban R&B. In fact, although Clear Channel only owns 10 percent of all stations, it takes in about 20 percent of the overall advertising revenue and attracts about 25 percent of total listeners nationwide—about a third of the population. Clear Channel now owns most of the stations in many cities and towns, a growing example of *horizontal integration*. This shows that it can not only offer attractive packages and coverage to advertisers, but also dominates the formats and genres that most people listen to.

These groups also want to achieve *economies of scale*. Spreading costs across several stations enables groups to buy or create programs, buy supplies and equipment in bulk, and share management and consultant costs, plus lowering costs for local advertisers. Groups like Clear Channel created most of their local announcements—even news and weather—from centralized production facilities using a few announcers and managers to cover a number of stations.

Regulations in the 1996 Telecommunication Act also permit much more *cross-ownership* across industries. So Cox (cable), Disney (film), and others acquired radio station groups, too. Most of the top media groups are involved in music or radio businesses in some way. Most of the major film studios were involved in the music recording and distribution business. Regulations in effect until the 1980s prevented those studios from owning broadcast stations or networks, or vice versa. Now as studios like Disney acquire networks such as ABC, they also get involved in the radio business, integrating broadcast distribution with their existing music production, an example of *vertical integration*. Other new conglomerates with origins in television, for example, Viacom, have acquired networks like CBS, with radio

Table 6.2 Top Radio Industry Ownership Groups

Radio Group	Number of Stations Owned in 2004	Number of Stations Owned in 1999	Revenues 2003 in Millions
Clear Channel	1200	484	3423
Cumulus Broadcasting	301	232	292
Citadel Communications	213	108	366
Infinity Broadcasting	180	163	2186
Entercom	104	42	495

Source: "Inside radio," *WSJ Research; Broadcasting and Cable, 2004;* on the Internet at http://www.broadcastingandcable.com

groups. Others, such as Cox, with origins in newspapers, have acquired a number of stations. However, a number of the top ten radio ownership groups, like Clear Channel, Infinity, Entercom, Citadel, Emmis and Cumulus, are based primarily in radio (Broadcasting and Cable, 2004) which reflects *horizontal integration* (see Chapter 2).

Inside Radio Stations

Radio stations vary greatly in the size and complexity of their staff. However, they all have to take care of certain basic functions: administrative (payroll, accounting, purchasing), technical (engineering, transmitter operation, maintenance of FCC logs), programming (local, news, music playlists, network or syndicated programs, promotion of programs), and sales (local sales, relations with national and regional sales firms). While most of these have traditionally been done locally with at least a small staff, with the growth of ownership groups most of these functions are increasingly done by a centralized group staff, which covers a number of stations.

The manager oversees planning, audience development, ratings, and sales. The program director supervises the air sound, playlists, DJs, and announcers. There is usually a music director who plans the playlists. Producers are usually required for anything more complex than simple announcing, such as talk shows and drive-time shows. Many stations also have a news director. And someone has to keep the station on the air, so there has to be an engineer on duty. Commercial stations have a sales manager and an advertising sales staff. Because almost 75 percent of radio advertising has usually been local, the advertising sales staff is crucial for selling local advertising. However, the growth of large ownership groups gives them greater chances to sell regional or national advertising.

When it comes to working with national advertisers who might want to sell national spot ads in the local market, that function is delegated to *advertising rep* firms. The reps work on behalf of local radio stations to sell ads to national advertisers, although large radio station groups are now getting directly involved in these transactions as well.

Some of the traditional networks still carry news and other national programming. Syndication (see Chapter 2) is also an important factor in the radio industry. *Syndicators* are organizations that produce programming for resale to other media outlets. For example, all Infinity stations carried Infinity's syndicated Howard Stern show, and Infinity also syndicated the show to other stations in other markets. (As noted earlier, Howard Stern left Infinity in 2004 to go to satellite only radio Sirius to avoid FCC restrictions on his show.) There are 20 to 25 main syndicators, such as Mediamerica, New York, which has Patrick Buchanan and Rush Limbaugh.

Noncommercial Radio

Despite the predominance of commercial radio, many stations are licensed for noncommercial formats and purposes. They tend to focus on education, classical music, jazz, independent rock, a variety of ethnic immigrant music, news, and public affairs. Most are owned by universities or other educational groups, although quite a few are owned by foundations, local nonprofit groups, and others. If more **lower-power** licenses are eventually offered by the FCC, the diversity of ownership among noncommercial radio will probably increase greatly, as many community groups currently excluded from ownership would start broadcasting. (Some of those broadcast now as pirate stations, but FCC enforcement shuts down most unlicensed broadcasters relatively quickly. Others would move from Internet-only radio to broadcasting.) Most noncommercial broadcasters are FM stations, typically at the lower end of the dial. There are relatively few noncommercial AM stations, since most AM licenses were granted before the FCC started reserving a few licenses in each market for educational and noncommercial groups.

Public broadcasters are roughly one-third of all noncommercial stations, compared to a larger number of student-run stations at universities, and a smaller number of religious stations. Mostly they program content that would not be considered commercially viable, although a few student-run stations that program rock and pop music are actually competitive in local listener ratings, so they could attract advertising. Most depend on a mix of government, institutional, and listener support. Public stations tend to have more news, and more public affairs discussion, than most commercial stations, although many AM stations and some FM stations now program a mix of news, syndicated talk shows (like Don Imus), sports talk, and local call-in talk shows.

Some public stations program music that is not commercially viable, depending on the market. Over a third of public stations program a great deal of classical music; others program jazz, older pop music, like 1930s–1940s big band, and, on many college stations, folk, indie rock, noncommercial rap, and so forth. There are also a number of noncommercial stations that program to religious audiences or in languages spoken by too few local residents to support commercial broadcasting. Some large cities may have several noncommercial stations specializing in different formats and audiences.

The economics of noncommercial radio have always been difficult. Before 1990, public radio stations tended to depend quite a bit on both program support from the Corporation for Public Broadcasting and financial support from federal and state governments. Since 1990, the funding for those national resources has been steadily cut back, so public stations have come to depend more on their sponsoring institutions (including many colleges and universities), other supportive local institutions, and direct contributions from listeners. Some public stations have run out of financial support to the point where their sponsoring institutions sold their license to a commercial owner.

GENRES AROUND THE DIAL

Radio Formats

Rigid musical programming formats dominate many stations. They focus on an hourly cycle of music, advertisements, station promotions, short news items, traffic reports, and weather reports. We can visualize this hourly cycle as a **format clock** in the shape of a 45 rpm record (Figure 6.2). This hourly schedule shows the DJ when to play certain kinds of music, when to read a news item, when to play prerecorded ad spots or promo-

---

Lower-power stations have more limited transmission power and cover smaller areas than regular FM stations.

Public broadcasters aim to serve public interests with information culture and news.

Format clock is an hourly radio programming schedule.

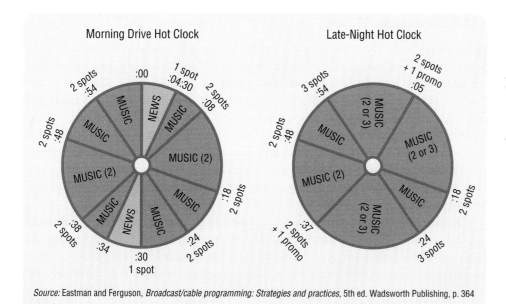

Morning Drive Hot Clock

Late-Night Hot Clock

Source: Eastman and Ferguson, *Broadcast/cable programming: Strategies and practices,* 5th ed. Wadsworth Publishing, p. 364

■ **FIGURE 6.2**
Clock Concept of Formats
Radio programmers and disc jockeys often use a clock concept to program what will be played in an hour: music from different lists, spots or ads, news and weather, and so on.

tions (*promos*), when to read ad copy, and when to bring in another announcer for news, weather, sports, or traffic.

This hourly schedule includes just enough news, sports, weather, and talk to meet the audience's general interests, but focuses on music. The key programming element, therefore, is the music director who selects the music that fits into the various parts of the hourly schedule to capture and hold the audience's attention. The music director creates a playlist of songs, organized by categories. A typical Contemporary Hit Radio (CHR) station has a playlist of a few top songs that might be repeated almost hourly at various points on the clock, interspersed with a few songs that are rising into popularity and a few others that are fading but still popular. Depending on the station, the disc jockey either plays exactly what the music director specifies or picks songs within a fairly narrow range. In larger, more competitive markets or among stations owned by national groups, music selection is often centrally decided; in smaller markets, stations rely more on record company promoters to determine what is likely to be popular with their audience. Although the format clock is most associated with Top 40 radio (or CHR in contemporary terms), similar repetitive patterns may be found at country and western, urban contemporary, and even classical stations.

The format clock is no longer followed as religiously as it once was. For example, many stations have turned to a menu of talk and humor lightly interspersed with music during the morning drive-time hours, while focusing more on music later in the day. Others vary their music blocks to provide "30 continuous minutes of commercial-free music" or "12 in a row" in hopes of attracting audiences during commercial breaks at other stations.

These blocks may be commercial-free but not *promotion*-free, as radio stations seem to be constantly promoting themselves. The various on-air contests, station identifications, listener call-ins, dedication lines, and concert promotions are a vital part of radio programming, too, to build listener loyalty and get them to put that station on the preset buttons of their car radio.

The Role of Radio Ratings

Inside the radio business, many professionals see their advertisers as the real customers. Clear Channel, for example, boldly states that it is in the business of selling audiences to advertisers, not the radio or music business. In order to persuade those advertisers to buy time on their stations, they rely on audience research to show how large their audience is and, more important for many advertisers, who the audience is. This kind of pragmatic audience research is called **ratings** studies. They estimate how many people are listening to a station at a certain time. Ratings also break down the audience by key demographics that are particularly important to advertisers, so that they know whether the people that their ad is reaching are older or younger, male or female, Anglo, Latino, or African-American, and so on.

Radio ratings are gathered from scientifically selected random samples of listeners, much like local TV station ratings and derived (see Media and Culture, Chapter 8). Members of the sample are recruited by phone and sent paper listening diaries to fill out, recording the stations they listened to at various times of the day. These results are used to compute the *ratings of* the stations, that's the percentage of persons with radios who are listening to the station and *shares,* the proportion of persons actually using their radios at a given time. The Arbitron Company collects the data from 294 radio markets (from New York to Casper, Wyoming), and distributes them to local stations and advertisers who subscribe to their service in the form of rating books delivered four times a year. Arbitron also runs a national rating service called RADAR, for network radio programming, and a survey of online radio stations, Comscore. The paper diaries present some accuracy problems, especially when you consider that a great deal of radio listening takes place in moving automobiles, so automatic, electronic personal people meters are being developed.

Ratings can be crucial for establishing the importance, or more specifically, the commercial attractiveness, of a new format or audience group. For example, while Latino audiences are virtual majorities in many cities, in others, it is not clear whether there are enough people interested in Latino music to attract advertisers and justify a commercial station focusing on them. In this kind of case, audience ratings research can help show whether a new station has a viable audience. Good ratings in one city for a new format, like "jammin' oldies" or "adult alternative," may lead other commercial broadcasters to try the format.

Music Genres and Radio Formats

As we have seen, radio programmers, especially those on FM, increasingly look for targeted formats that cater to specialized audiences. Radio station formats often mirror musical genres that draw specific audience segments. Increased competition for audience segments has also increased the importance of research. When deciding which music format to adopt, stations increasingly rely on consultants who poll local radio listeners to determine which new format or format variation is likely to draw the biggest audience. This is becoming increasingly true of large ownership groups who own up to half a dozen stations in a single market. They use research very carefully to avoid overlap in the audiences that they reach and to ensure that they reach the audience segments that are the most attractive to their advertisers.

In fact, stations are frequently targeted to some audience groups that are smaller than others but sufficiently attractive to advertisers that both advertisers and radio programmers prefer to focus on them. This is apparent in Table 6.1 (page 160), which shows dra-

Ratings measure how many people are listening to a station.

matically that although Top 40, or Contemporary Hit Radio, draws the fourth highest national share of radio listening, it has fewer stations than eight other formats, including country, news/talk, adult contemporary, oldies, adult standards, rock, Hispanic, and religious, most of which have lower listening shares nationwide. However, in specific local or even national advertising markets, the audiences for those other formats may well have greater purchasing power and be much more attractive to advertisers, and, hence, to programmers.

Music genres evolve with their audiences, and many radio formats have changed quite a bit in the last decade. For example, starting in the late 1990s, many stations went to an "alternative rock" format, including some nationally distributed package formats like the "Hot Adult Contemporary" format "Mix 107" (or whatever the frequency of the local affiliate is). They would play alternative-oriented current hits mixed with some older and some new music. After alternative began to lose its appeal as a genre, these stations tended to refocus on either modern rock to target a more youthful audience, or other forms of hot adult contemporary to capture a slightly older audience.

In the meantime, other formats were rising, like "jammin' oldies," a mixture of 1960s soul, 1970s funk, and rhythm and blues. This format could reach across African-American, Latino, and Anglo-American audiences more successfully than many other formats. It also managed to bring in both younger and middle-aged audiences. So it reached an interesting breadth of people for its advertisers.

Formats often subdivided. Country split into hit/contemporary, classic/traditional, and *ranchera* (Mexican-American country music) branches. Christian formats grew quickly and then subdivided into traditional gospel and contemporary divisions, with the latter varying to include country, rock, and even rap-related branches.

These are mostly FM formats. Because of AM's broader signal reach, many stations in sparsely populated smaller towns adopt a broad-based middle-of-the-road, country-western, talk, or oldies format. And AM increasingly caters to minority groups, such as Latinos, as the dominant formats move to FM.

Talk Radio

Music is not the only game on radio. As stations specialize, news, talk, weather, and sports information grow in importance. A number of audiences, like adult men, and to a somewhat lesser degree adult women, are strongly attracted to news, sports, and talk, so station owners and advertisers who wish to pursue that audience tend to consider using this format. For example, "shock jocks" like Don Imus appeal strongly to 18–35-year-old blue-collar men, so a station (or its advertisers) wishing to reach that group would think hard about running Imus or someone similar. So the news and talk general area is subdivided into a number of niches. Some stations do 24 hour news and weather. Most of those are national network news stations, but a very few do primarily local news. Some stations do talk and music during what is often called drive time while many are commuting to or from work. Many stations carry nationally syndicated talk shows, such as those featuring Rush Limbaugh, Don Imus, Dr. Phil, Howard Stern, and Dr. Laura Schlesinger. These shows are highly divided between shock jocks who appeal to younger men, and talk hosts like Dr. Phil who appeal more to women. As we write this, Dr. Phil has just visited the small town of Elgin, Texas, near Austin, and local papers showed him being greeted by screaming female fans, mostly in their twenties.

Talk radio is probably best known for a number of highly visible major syndicated talk shows, but there are a number of more specialized shows, such as sports talk shows focused on a specific city. For example, both college and professional sports teams often have local or regional talk shows, often with coaches or popular local sportscasters, which specialize in talk about particular teams.

On the AM band, where sound quality is not quite as high as on FM, many stations emphasize news, talk, and sports. However, a number of FM stations also feature a mixture of talk, call-ins, music, news headlines, and weather—aimed at a broad audience during morning and afternoon commuting hours (drive time). Morning shows on major stations increasingly reflect this more "talky" drive-time format. As the syndicated talk formats gain more of an audience, many FM stations that had focused on music find themselves changing to talk formats because those draw a more lucrative audience. For example, despite the popularity of hip-hop among younger audiences, a number of hip-hop stations just shifted to a syndicated talk format to target a demographic group among young and middle-aged men that was more highly sought by potential advertisers.

National Public Radio

Many public stations get much of their programming from a few key national sources: National Public Radio (NPR), Public Radio International (PRI) and, for a few, the Pacifica Network. NPR provides an afternoon news program called *All Things Considered,* a morning news program called *Morning Edition,* and other programs to a large group of affiliated public stations. The creation of these network programs depends on fees from affiliates, some funding from government sources, program sales, educational institution funding, foundation funds, corporate underwriting (sponsorship), and individual listener donations or sponsorships. Foundations and corporations both tend to offer funding for specific kinds of programming and news, so NPR has to be attentive to potential conflicts of interest between following ideal journalism criteria in selecting stories and pleasing a foundation that wants more stories on the environment or labor issues. However, since two-thirds of NPR's funding comes from station dues, and stations are increasingly supported by listener contributions, pleasing listeners is the ultimate requirement. According to reviewers like Aufderheide (1996), that tends to make stations cautious about news and programming, wanting to interest listeners but not offend anyone. Conservative listeners and the George W. Bush administration pressured NPR, criticized by some as too liberal in point of view, to provide more "balanced" content.

Radio Programming Services

The economics of radio programming have changed again to favor centralized, syndicated, or networked programming. A number of different sources exist from which to choose. Many stations now subscribe to national, regional, or state networks for news and sports (including the regional networks on which college sports are broadcast).

Music-oriented stations also carry syndicated programs such as concert specials (like the *King Biscuit Flower Hour*) or Top 40 hit countdowns. Locally programmed, "live" DJ formats are usually the most popular, particularly during drive-time hours when a mix of local weather, traffic, and news is most appealing.

However, for an increasing number of station owners, locally programmed stations are a risky venture. Many stations buy complete, packaged music services designed by outside experts who look at the prospective audience, consider the format options, and evaluate what has worked in similar markets. This approach has reduced the DJ's auton-

She Has Done Thousands of Interviews

© Tom Bullock/Courtesy of NPR

■ **RENÉE MONTAGNE**

Name: Renée Montagne

Current Position: Co-host, *Morning Edition,* on National Public Radio

Born: In California

Education: BA in English from the University of California, Berkeley, Phi Beta Kappa.

First Experiences: She began her career as news director of San Francisco's community radio station, KPOO, while still at university.

First Job: She worked as a reporter/editor for Pacific News Service, in San Francisco.

Big Break: From 1980 to 1986, she worked in New York as an independent producer and reporter for NPR and the Canadian Broadcasting Corporation. In 1990, she traveled to South Africa to cover Nelson Mandela's release from prison, and continued to report form South Africa through 1992.

Career Expansion: She served as correspondent and occasional host since 1989 on *Morning Edition.* She worked for NPR's Science, National, and Foreign desks. For two years, she co-hosted with Robert Siegel on *All Things Considered.*

Most Notable Achievement: In 1994, she and a team of NPR reporters covered South Africa's first historic presidential and parliamentary elections, which won the Alfred I. DuPont-Columbia Award.

Method: she has done thousands of interviews: with Kurt Vonnegut on how he transformed surviving the World War II firebombing of Dresden into the classic anti-war novel *Slaughterhouse Five;* National Guardsmen on how they handle the holidays in Iraq; and Toni Morrison on the dreams and memories she turned into novels.

Recent Moves: She traveled through Afghanistan, interviewing farmers and mullahs, women and poll workers, the President and an infamous warlord for a series on the country's 2004 elections.

omy considerably since the more freewheeling days of the 1950s and 1960s, when DJs often selected which records to play. Currently, over a fifth of all U.S. stations use a satellite-delivered, syndicated service as their main source of programming.

A variety of radio *programming services* are available. The most complete are satellite-based networks, like ABC Radio's Satellite Music Network, that deliver news, music, and other entertainment and even sell national advertising. Those are the easiest options for an owner, who simply affiliates with a network and carries its programming, like old-fashioned network affiliates. Format syndicators provide a full music program but do not sell commercial ad time for the station or provide news or other information services. Full program-service companies, such as Westwood One, provide completely automated formats, such as "The Oldies Channel" and "Soft AC (adult contemporary)." Full-service automation is popular because of the wave of mergers sweeping the radio industry. Non-local owners are less likely to feel that they know the peculiarities of the market and are more likely to rely on relatively safe, nationally standardized formats. Locally programmed automation systems are also cheaper; for example, a fully programmable system that handles up to 300 CDs, as well as tape machines for commercial and announcement inserts, costs under $10,000.

MEDIA LITERACY: THE IMPACT OF THE AIRWAVES

One of the most important issues to understand, in order to be media savvy or "literate," is who makes the decisions on radio content. Radio seems very diverse, with dozens of stations in most areas. However, how large and diverse is the group of people making key radio content decisions?

Who Controls the Airwaves?

Early government regulators such as the 1920s Secretary of Commerce Herbert Hoover, hoped that industry self-regulation would be adequate to allocate radio frequencies and avoid frequency interference between stations. However, new stations started using frequencies at will, resulting in substantial frequency interference between stations. The Federal Radio Commission, which standardized frequency allocation, was followed by the comprehensive Federal Communications Commission Communications Act of 1934. However, the FCC's "public interest" standard for reviewing and renewing licenses has proven too vague to provide a basis for denying license renewal to misbehaving broadcasters. For example, radio personality Howard Stern frequently violated rules about indecency on the air, incurring substantial fines, but the repeated violations have not resulted in the denial of license renewals for any of the stations that carry his show. However, increasing FCC pressure in 2004 caused him to move to satellite radio in 2006.

The FCC had enough power to compel compliance with the rules on transmitter power, height, and frequency use that it imposed to avoid frequency interference. In the past, the FCC created rules about ownership, **concentration** and **cross-ownership,** obscenity and indecency in radio content, and the role of networks and affiliates. The Telecommunications Act of 1996 eliminated the national limits regarding ownership; it replaced the old cap of 20 FM stations and 20 AM stations with local ownership caps, which means that a major group like Clear Channel can own up to eight stations in many markets. Under the 1996 Act, a single owner can own up to 8 radio stations in a market with 45 or more commercial radio stations, 7 radio stations in a market with 30–44 radio stations, 6 radio stations in a market with 15–29 radio stations, and 5 stations in markets with less than 15 radio stations. However, such limits have been challenged in the courts. They were reviewed by the FCC in 2003, but further relaxation of limits was blocked by Congress in 2003.

Concentrating Ownership, Reducing Diversity?

This striking concentration of ownership threatens diversity of content. Fewer radio station owners than ever are local residents of the areas their stations serve, which presumably limits their ability to understand local interests. Fewer owners are minorities or female.

Fewer stations are programmed locally because, **group owners** often supply programming from a central source. For example, one of the major groups, Clear Channel, started to program all of its southern stations from one central facility in Austin, Texas, even providing voicing for local weather and ads. The local stations are automated and play just the prerecorded programming. Clear Channel now follows that pattern in many areas.

The counterargument is that concentrated ownership may actually provide more format diversity. When one group owns six to eight stations in a market, it will target each one at a different interest group. For example, Clear Channel bought six stations in Waco, Texas. Three of them had very similar country formats. Clear Channel changed one to album-oriented rock and targeted the others to distinct country audience segments. One

Concentration of ownership occurs when media are owned by a small number of corporations.

Cross-ownership is ownership of different kinds of media.

Group owners own a number of broadcast stations.

2002 FCC effort to look at the diversity of music played examined the top songs played by a large sample of radio stations in March 1996 (before the 1996 Act) and March 2001 in top markets. It found only modest changes in diversity, with a slight decrease in the diversity of songs within the same format across local markets, and a slight increase in the diversity of songs within the same format within each local market.

What is even more problematic is that news and information content are also centrally programmed and lack genuine local input or diversity. This seems to go against the principle of maximizing localism that has, in theory, guided FCC licensing decisions since the 1934 Communications Act. A poignant point in case was a train accident in Minot, North Dakota one night. Local residents tried to call the radio station to warn residents to evacuate only to discover there was no one "there" at the remotely controlled "local" station.

In 2003–2004, an effort to increase the amount of concentration of ownership permitted by the FCC encountered an unexpected groundswell of public opposition. What many groups objected to was precisely the decrease in local control and local input that the growth of groups like Clear Channel seemed to imply. Enough individual citizens and groups complained to their congressmen that the Congress instructed the FCC not to change the rules, and the FCC decided not to fight to change them (see Chapter 14 for more information on how this process works).

After people realized that few noncommercial stations had emerged from the initial scramble for AM licenses in the 1920s and 1930s, some FM frequencies were reserved for noncommercial and educational use. Frequencies are reserved in each market, typically at the lower end of the FM band. This provision has made both experimental college stations and independent foundation stations possible, like the Pacifica stations in California, and it laid the basis for the current National Public Radio. At least this element of diversity remains unaffected by the consolidation of commercial ownership that is underway.

However, the rise in group ownership creates new concerns. The Chain Broadcasting rules protect affiliates, not owned-and-operated stations. Now that thousands of stations are owned and controlled by single corporations, they could use their market power to control the fortunes of popular music acts or syndicated commentators. Since Clear Channel, for example, controls both many music stations and national concert promotions in most areas, it acts as a gatekeeper and refuses to run ads for concerts promoted by competing stations. It has great power over which music groups get a chance to be heard.

© AP/Wide World Photos

■ **ALTERNATIVE TO MAINSTREAM**
Groups like the Dave Matthews Band can start with a small but loyal following of radio and concert listeners and generally become more widely heard and widely popular as they get more airplay on more kinds of station formats.

You Can't Say That on the Radio

Freedom of speech continues to be a focus for radio broadcasting. In contrast, the recording industry has traditionally been lightly scrutinized. It has been considered analogous to publishing in that it doesn't involve use of a scarce public resource, such as the airwaves; it has a large degree of competition; and exposure to recorded music is, in principle, entirely voluntary.

Obscenity and *indecent* speech are continual issues. The recording industry exercised a certain degree of self-censorship up through the 1960s. Groups that used **obscene speech**

Obscene speech depicts sexual conduct in a way that appeals to sexual interests in a manner that is "patently offensive" to community standards, and lacks serious artistic, political, or scientific value.

or graphic sexual references were usually excluded from the major labels. This situation changed greatly in the late 1960s, as many of the major rock groups carried by major labels began to use more graphic language and explicit themes. This trend continued until challenged by groups of parents and others concerned about exposure to recordings that contain violence, sexist and racist imagery, and graphic language. In 1989, Tipper Gore, wife of then Senator Albert Gore, led a group that pushed for warning labels about explicit lyrics on record and CD covers. A number of record labels now place such warnings on their covers, but the effectiveness of these warnings has been questioned. Some think the warnings simply attract more attention. This debate was renewed again in 2001 when rapper Eminem was nominated for a Grammy music award for an album with lyrics that many critics considered not only obscene, but violent and abusive to women. They felt that the Grammy award was rewarding antisocial behavior.

Radio has been more closely scrutinized under the rationale that the airwaves are a scarce resource to be used in the public interest. The FCC has standards restricting obscene or **indecent speech.** Up through the 1970s, certain words could not be used, and broadcasters were held responsible even for call-in programs to make sure that prohibited language was not broadcast. Comic George Carlin developed a comedy routine in that era about "Filthy Words," which featured words you couldn't say on public airwaves. Those prohibitions were challenged in court (see Chapter 14), but the FCC still restricts speech that is considered indecent—that is, that uses graphic language pertaining to sexual or excretory functions. The FCC prohibits such language during daytime and evening hours but has made the late-night hours between 10 P.M. and 6 A.M. a "safe harbor" for more explicit kinds of speech. Despite the prohibition, "shock jocks" such as Howard Stern routinely violate the rule, are fined, and consider paying the fine a cost of doing business. Thousands of radio stations play music by stars like Eminem, whose lyrics probably also violate those rules, but music has been less scrutinized by the FCC than verbal comedy or commentary. In 2004, due to Congressional pressure, the FCC imposed stiffer fines and penalties for indecency. Stations and networks protested these punishments as censorship and Howard Stern started calling for President Bush's defeat in the 2004 election to protest the change in policy. However, FCC pressure continued and Howard Stern announced he will move to satellite radio to avoid FCC controls. Some conservative activists suggested extending broadcast indecency rules to satellite radio and cable TV.

STOP & REVIEW

1. What kinds of radio networks exist now?
2. How are radio formats related to music genres?
3. What are the target audiences for some of the main radio formats?
4. Why does the concentration of radio ownership cause concern?
5. What copyright challenges are raised by Internet radio?

Breaking or Promoting Internet Radio

Reuse of **copyrighted** music, syndicated talk shows, and other intellectual property has been a major issue for the radio industry. The licensing of recorded music for play over the radio is complex. Copyright law requires payment for performance of work copyrighted by an artist, including the playing of a recording over the radio. Two main music-licensing groups—the American Society of Composers, Authors and Publishers (ASCAP) and Broadcast Music Incorporated (BMI)—serve as intermediaries between recording artists and radio stations. These two traditional groups have been joined by the Radio Music License Committee, which represents radio stations in negotiations with ASCAP. Radio stations get licenses for the music listed by the music-licensing group in return for

Indecent speech is graphic language that pertains to sexual or excretory functions.

A copyright is a legal privilege to use, sell, or license creative works.

a fee, usually 1 to 2 percent of the station's gross income. ASCAP or BMI then pays the copyright holders, according to how often each song is played.

In 2002, a very thorny negotiation took place over the royalties to be paid for music played on Internet radio stations. The result required Internet stations to compensate not only artists, like regular radio, but also recording companies, which regular radio does not have to do. The Radio Music License Committee has negotiated royalty levels for radio stations with ASCAP which should make Internet radio operations and costs more predictable.

SUMMARY AND REVIEW

WHAT WERE THE KEY DEVELOPMENTS THAT LED TO RADIO BROADCASTING?

Marconi pioneered radio as a form of two-way communication. The development of the vacuum tube by De Forest was crucial. It permitted continuous sound-wave transmission and reception, beyond the on/off transmission that had sufficed for transmission of coded messages in wireless telegraph systems. Other crucial developments included better microphones, amplifiers, and tuners and more powerful transmitters.

HOW DID RADIO BROADCASTING AFFECT THE RECORDING INDUSTRY?

At first, the sales of the recording industry fell off, as people moved to purchase radios instead. Over the long run, the recording industry came to rely on radio to make people aware of artists, and recordings that they could purchase.

WHO FORMED THE MAIN RADIO NETWORKS?

The main radio networks were put together by David Sarnoff at RCA/NBC and William Paley at CBS.

WHAT KINDS OF PROGRAMMING CHARACTERIZED RADIO NETWORKS DURING THEIR HIGH POINT?

Network radio relied largely on music but also carried news, sports, comedy, variety shows, soap operas, dramas, suspense, and action adventures as well. Many of those genres moved to television after 1948.

WHEN AND WHY DID RADIO NETWORKS DECLINE?

After television coverage and audiences began to grow, around 1948, network radio began to lose much of its audience to television. Some of the types of entertainment it had relied on worked better for the mass audience with a visual component on television. Radio came to rely more on music, which could be programmed locally by disc jockeys playing records.

WHEN DID FM RADIO BEGIN TO INCREASE IN IMPORTANCE? AND WHY?

FM radio began to increase as more receivers became available in the 1960s. It also prospered as FM stereo became widely available and appreciation of music quality increased among the audience, making FM the main radio medium for music.

WHAT KINDS OF RADIO NETWORKS EXIST NOW?

Some of the traditional networks continued, like ABC. New networks were created by new ownership groups, such as Infinity, around popular syndicated shows, such as Howard Stern's. Large ownership groups like Clear Channel use a number of nationally programmed formats, which are the main new networks. National Public Radio also emerged as a significant news and public affairs programming service, linking most of the nation's noncommercial, or public, radio stations.

WHAT ARE THE MAIN TECHNICAL DIFFERENCES BETWEEN AM AND FM RADIO TRANSMISSION?

AM refers to amplitude modulation. The sound information is carried in variations in the height, or amplitude, of the radio wave. FM stands for frequency modulation. The sound information is carried in variations in the frequency of the radio wave. In general, AM signals carry farther than FM, which travels strictly in the line of sight, so there is more potential for frequency interference among AM stations. Therefore, fewer AM licenses can be granted in the same cities. FM has higher-fidelity sound characteristics than AM (a greater frequency range, cleaner sound, and less static), so stereo broadcasting was begun in FM.

HOW IS THE INTERNET AFFECTING RADIO?

Many radio stations are now transmitting their music, news, and other programs over the Internet to reach new audiences, both in their regular coverage areas and distant, but some stations had to close because they couldn't afford to pay royalties to record companies and recording artists.

WHAT ARE RADIO FORMATS?

A format is a particular radio programming strategy oriented around a playlist of music and focused on a particular genre or audience. Common examples are Contemporary Hit Radio/Top 40, R&B, and modern rock.

HOW HAVE RADIO FORMATS CHANGED SINCE THE DECLINE OF RADIO NETWORKS?

Radio programming became decentralized as local stations pulled away from networks. Stations began to decide on their own formats, responding to local audiences and local competition from other stations. As more stations entered the market, formats focused on segmented audiences. Nationally programmed music services focused on single formats are becoming very common.

WHAT IS THE TOP 40 FORMAT?

Top 40 is characterized by playing only top single records, usually the Top 40 on record sales charts. Today it is known as Contemporary Hit Radio.

HOW HAVE RADIO FORMATS EVOLVED SINCE 1970?

Radio formats have tended to reflect the evolution of pop and rock music since 1970. They have followed the segmentation of the audience and fragmentation of the music genre. This trend has been accentuated by a steadily increasing number of FM stations, which have had to specialize to find audiences.

WHAT ARE THE TOP FORMATS NOW ON FM? ON AM?

On FM, the main formats are news/talk, country, religious, adult contemporary; adult standards, oldies, classic rock, Spanish Contemporary Hit Radio; alternative; and urban contemporary, usually focused on African-American music, rap, hip-hop, dance, and Hispanic music. Several patterns developed on the FM stations reserved for noncommercial alternatives: classical music; experimental rock, indie rock, and folk, found largely on college stations; and news and public affairs. AM stations tend to emphasize news, call-in talk shows, and talk and sports. AM stations also tend to serve smaller towns and rural areas, where the population is less dense and where a broad-based, middle-of-the-road, country-and-western, or oldies format makes more sense.

WHAT ARE THE KEY COMPONENTS OF RADIO INDUSTRY ORGANIZATION?

The main elements of industry organization are national ownership groups, like Clear Channel; national music program services, like Westwood One; national business services, like ratings organizations; and local stations.

HOW ARE RADIO STATION AFFILIATES RELATED TO NETWORKS?

Affiliates in broadcasting are stations that contract to use the programming of a network and to share advertising and advertising revenues with it. Networks also have owned-and-operated stations (O&Os). Group owners own a number of broadcast stations. Sometimes they also provide them with common programming, as a traditional network would. New kinds of networks are emerging that provide programming for stations for a fee or for shared advertising. Companies like Westwood One can provide ready-made programming for dozens of formats.

WHAT WAS CHANGED BY THE COMMUNICATIONS ACT OF 1934?

The Communications Act of 1934 defined the broadcast band, standardized frequency designations, and created a more powerful regulatory body, the Federal Communications Commission (FCC). The FCC devised more systematic procedures for granting radio licenses and rules on transmitter power, height, and frequency use. The FCC imposed rules about ownership, concentration and cross-ownership, and the role of networks and affiliates.

WHAT CAME OUT OF THE CHAIN BROADCASTING HEARINGS?

Chain broadcasting refers to radio networks and their control over talent and over affiliated stations. After the Chain Broadcasting hearings, held between 1938 and 1941, the FCC ended network control over affiliates' program selections.

WHAT WAS CHANGED BY THE TELECOMMUNICATIONS ACT OF 1996?

The Telecommunications Act of 1996 changed FCC rules about station ownership limits. It eliminated previous station ownership limits. For radio, there are no national limits, and local ownership caps increase with market size. This considerably increased concentration of ownership, which raises issues about content diversity, localism, and minority ownership.

WHAT ARE THE ISSUES INVOLVED IN CONCENTRATION OF RADIO OWNERSHIP?

A few large ownership groups now own as many as half of all stations in many cities. This clearly reduces the localism of ownership, which may then reduce responsiveness to local interests. Group stations are increasingly programmed at a distance, including programming of "local" news. Diversity of both music and news may well be reduced, although ownership groups claim that they actually increase the diversity of music formats available in a market.

WHAT ARE THE LIMITS ON FREEDOM OF SPEECH IN RADIO BROADCASTS?

Up through the 1960s, certain obscene words could not be used, and broadcasters were responsible for ensuring that they were not used. Those prohibitions were successfully challenged in court, but the FCC still restricts speech that is indecent. The FCC prohibits such language except during late-night spots that are a "safe harbor" for more explicit speech.

MEDIA CONNECTION

For web links, quizzes, and key term flash cards, visit the **Student Companion Website** at http://communication.wadsworth.com/straubhaar5.

 For unlimited easy access to additional and exclusive online study, support, and research tools, log on to **1pass** at http://1pass.thomson.com using the unique access code found on your 1pass passcode card.

 The **Media Now Premium Website** offers *Career Profile* videos, *Critical View* video news clips, and *Media in Motion* concept animations. You'll also find Stop & Review tutorial questions, a sample final exam, and much more.

InfoTrac College Edition is a fully searchable online database offering anytime, anywhere access to more than 20 years' worth of articles from nearly 5,000 diverse and reliable sources.

 vMentor provides live, one-on-one online tutoring to connect you to experts who will assist you in understanding the concepts covered in your course.

Interested in a job in radio? In the Career Profile video for this chapter, Matt Staudt of Alice 97.3 in San Francisco (http://www.radioalice.com) talks about his job as executive producer of the station's Morning Show.

When Spiderman swings to the rescue he continues a tradition of filmic storytelling that goes back over 100 years. This chapter traces that tradition from silent films to modern blockbusters with computer animation characters. It examines the major film genres, technological changes, studio and industry organization, and the issues of content ratings, concentration, and control.

HISTORY: GOLDEN MOMENTS OF FILM

The early years of film were marked by experimentation with content and forms, major technological innovations, and disputes over who could use, control, and benefit from the inventions. The first challenge was to capture motion on film.

Can horses fly? In 1877 Leland Stanford, a California railroad millionaire and founder of Stanford University, bet $25,000 that a galloping horse actually lifts all four hooves off the ground at the same time. The hooves flew too fast to settle this by merely looking at a horse with the naked eye, and the best still photographs of the day were also ambiguous.

Photographer Eadweard Muybridge came up with a conclusive means to settle the bet. He made a series of still pictures of a galloping horse, mounted them on a rotating cylinder, and then gave the cylinder a spin. The picture of the horse seemed to "move," but more slowly than in real life. At last it could be seen that at a certain point in each stride, all four hooves did in fact leave the ground at the same time (Brockway, Chadwick, & Hall, 1997). Muybridge took advantage of what's known as *persistence of vision,* in which a brief afterimage is left on our retinas. The next trick was to find a useful way of recording and showing events in motion.

1888   Edison develops motion picture camera

1900   Nickelodeon era

1915   *Birth of a Nation* is first feature film

1927   *The Jazz Singer* is first "talkie"

1946   Peak of film box office—90 million attend weekly

1948   Television competes; major studios have to divest their theater chains

1968   MPAA movie ratings introduced

1977   *Star Wars* highlights focus on big-budget blockbusters

1995   *Toy Story* first major release computer-generated film

1997   *Titanic* becomes highest grossing film of all time

1997   DVD introduced

1999   Netflix introduced; first flat rate DVD rental plan

2005   D2D theaters grow rapidly

In 1888, Thomas Edison invented the first functional *motion picture* camera. Edison also invented a projector in 1892 (see "Technology: Making Movie Magic," page 193). The French Lumière brothers came up with the idea of projecting movies on a screen for all to see. The pace of competition was quick. The first successful premieres by the Lumières and Edison were in 1896. By 1900, New York City had 600 Nickelodeons, simple movie players that showed short films for a nickel. For a while, most films simply showed short black-and-white, silent depictions of actual events in motion, such as horse races. By 1903, some films were developing more of a story line and plot. *The Great Train Robbery,* made by Edwin S. Porter in 1903, was the first *story film,* or *movie,* and was very popular. At first, audiences ducked when the train robber's gun fired.

Edison wanted to create a standard by licensing his technology, but he was competing with the somewhat superior Biograph camera and projector technologies, run by the American Biograph and Mutoscope Company. In 1909, Edison and Biograph agreed to pool patents under the Motion Picture Patents Company (MPPC) to establish a single motion picture standard using the best technologies available. The MPPC tried to collect a fee from every film and distribute it to the inventors on the basis of the number of patents each held. Independent producers consequently started to use bootleg equipment and moved their base of operations far away from New York, where the MPPC companies were based. The independent producers chose Hollywood, California, for its weather and space for studios. The industry became centered in Hollywood after 1915, and the old MPPC companies based in New York lost their control.

Larger screens for better image quality made more complex action sequences possible. Filmmakers put dialog into titles on screen to make the narration more complex. In 1915, film director D. W. Griffith took a major step forward in film form and technique with the controversial drama *Birth of a Nation.* Griffith used well-produced outdoor battle scenes, close-ups, and cuts between different simultaneous sequences of action, such as the threat to an imperiled heroine and the rescuers riding to save her, to increase dramatic tension. It was the first full-length **feature film.** (Films over 1½ hours long became known as *feature films.*) It was the most popular film in the United States for over 20 years. However, the film, set during and after the Civil War, features Ku Klux Klan members as its heroes and was used by the Klan as a recruiting film. Although the film was revolutionary in form, it was racist in content and was boycotted by the NAACP in

Feature films are longer story films, usually over 1½ hours.

its initial release. Concerned it would incite violence, several states banned the film, an early instance of film censorship (See Chapter 14). At this early stage, no national policy about film content existed, so states exercised censorship, that would probably be disallowed by courts now. Soon after, in the 1920s, the industry started self regulation. (See the Motion Picture code on page 205 and regulation vs. self regulation in Chapter 14.)

In this silent film era, from 1903 to 1927, film storytelling developed considerably. Films were still black and white, and silent, but these very limitations forced them to be creative, using the actors' expressions and gestures, as well as subtitles, to tell the story. It also made the audience use its imagination. The music for the film was live at first. Early filmmakers drew on novels, paintings and illustrations, vaudeville, and circuses as models. Movies became longer, as audiences came to expect the medium to tell more complex stories (Knight, 1979).

Hollywood has had several "booms" or "golden ages" of prosperity, artistic success, and widespread cultural impact. These periods have been followed by "busts," when the film industry lost parts of its audience to newer media technologies, but the first golden age was the age of silent film.

Silent Films Set the Patterns

Silent films established classic genre formulas for telling stories on film that are still followed today. Because producers of silent films had to rely on visuals, with only subtitles' brief written dialog added, these films were oriented toward action and lavish sets. For example, *The Great Train Robbery* featured action and suspense, and *Birth of a Nation* showed battles, chases, and historical scenes. The genres they relied on are alive and well today; witness action adventure (the *National Treasure*, 2004) and historical costume dramas (*Troy*, 2004). Table 7.1 describes the main silent-film genres.

Table 7.1 Early Film Genres

Silent Film Genres

- Westerns, such as *The Great Train Robbery* (1903)

- War movies, with battles and character conflicts, such as *Birth of a Nation* (1915)

- Horror, including the original *Dracula, Nosferatu* (1922)

- Romances, love stories such as *The Sheik* (1921)

- Physical comedies, with car crashes and pratfalls (such as the Keystone Cops shorts) or facial expression and body language (such as Charlie Chaplin and Buster Keaton films)

- Historical costume dramas, with fictionalized plots, such as D. W. Griffith's *Intolerance* (1916)

- Documentaries, such as *Nanook of the North* (1921)

- Action/adventure, such as Douglas Fairbanks' *Thief of Baghdad* (1921)

- Melodramas, such as *The Perils of Pauline* (1914)

Early Sound Film Genres

- Crime dramas, with cops, gangsters, and violence, such as *Little Caesar* (1930)

- Animation, such as *Snow White and the Seven Dwarfs* (1937)

- Screwball comedies, with glamour and light humor, such as *It Happened One Night* (1934)

- Character studies, such as *Citizen Kane* (1941)

- Detective movies, with complex heroes, such as *The Maltese Falcon* (1941)

- Suspense, such as Fritz Lang's *M* (1931)

- Monster movies, such as *King Kong* (1933)

- Horror movies, such as *Dracula* (1931)

- Musicals, such as *Flying Down to Rio* (1933)

- War films, such as *Wings* (1931)

- Film noir, "dark," skeptical films, such as *Double Indemnity* (1944)

- Serials, such as *Buck Rogers* (1936–1940)

Stars and Studios

From their new base in California, several **major film studios** developed a strong industrial production capability, producing movies almost on an assembly line, leading later critics to begin to talk about *cultural industries* (Horkheimer and Adorino, 1972). Studios developed their own complete teams of actors, writers, directors, technicians, and equipment that enabled them to produce large numbers of successful feature films.

As more movies were produced, film studios discovered that certain actors and actresses could attract viewers no matter what the movie was about. The **star system** was born. The dashing and romantic Rudolph Valentino (*The Sheik,* 1921), Lillian Gish (*Intolerance,* 1916), Mary Pickford (*Madame Butterfly,* 1915), and Charlie Chaplin (*The Gold Rush,* 1925) became such attractions that their names appeared above the title of the film on theater marquees. The importance of the star actor or actress was linked to the rise of the *studio system.*

Though silent, early movies were visually powerful enough to create both adoration and controversy. Some movies in the 1920s shocked much of the audience with sexual themes, partial nudity, and depiction of a fast urban life, as in *The Jazz Age* (1929), where both men and women "partied" hard. Stardom made the private lives of these early movie actors more visible, and some stars' lives were scandalous to many viewers. In a notorious case in 1922, silent film comedian Fatty Arbuckle was accused, wrongly, as it turned out, of brutally raping and murdering an aspiring actress. In response to this and other incidents, the industry decided to impose self-censorship before it was censored by the government or others. In 1922, the studios created the Motion Picture Producers and Distributors of America, known as the Hays Office. It created voluntary content guidelines, the **Motion Picture Code.** The

Major film studios like Fox or Disney integrate all aspects of production and distribution.

The **star system** was the film studios' use of stars' popularity to promote their movies.

Motion Picture Code of 1930 (Hays Code) was a self-regulation of sex on screen by the motion picture industry.

Catholic Church, B'nai Brith, and National Education Association all pushed for a Production Code that forbade scenes that gave a positive portrayal or image of "crime, wrongdoing, evil, or sin." Hays soothed public complaints but imposed a tough internal censorship that bridled the creativity of industry writers, directors, and actors (Knight, 1979).

Look Who's Talking

Attempts were made almost from the beginning of film to make the moving pictures talk. Edison's talented assistant Thomas Dickson experimented with movie sound before 1895. The studios were initially reluctant to invest in sound technology, as were the movie houses. Eventually, however, one of the then-small studios, Warner Brothers, made the commitment to develop sound technology and created *The Jazz Singer* in 1927. It featured two sections of recorded music and included singing that was synchronized with the film so that the singer's lips moved when they were supposed to. *The Jazz Singer* also had a little bit of recorded dialog, which fascinated the audience. Unfortunately, *The Jazz Singer* also was an example of American racism: rather than featuring an African-American performer, the film used white singer Al Jolson playing the jazz singer in "blackface" makeup.

© Bettmann/CORBIS

■ **FILM LEGENDS**
Stars were important to the success of the film medium. Douglas Fairbanks and Mary Pickford (bottom row) were so big that they started their own studio, United Artists (with Charlie Chaplin and D. W. Griffith).

"Talkies" effectively ended the golden age of silent movies. Acting became less overstated and stylized, since plot could be carried by dialog and not just by expression and gesture. The actors' vocal quality became critical. Studios suddenly had to become skilled in the use of sound effects and music. The crisis for actors and studios used to making silent films was captured well in the musical classic *Singing in the Rain* (1952). Some actresses and actors did not have the vocal quality or more subtle acting skills to survive. Talkies required an influx of new talent, such as Fred Astaire, actors who came largely from vaudeville and Broadway.

The use of dialogue created new possibilities for both drama and humor. However, the need to use fixed microphones made the first talkies much more static than the best silent films. Still, the audience preference for talking pictures was clear. Because audiences liked talkies, they made more money for the producers of the movies. By 1933 nearly all films had sound.

When these movies with sound came into vogue, new genres emphasized the advantages of the new medium. Another golden age of movies created extravagantly produced musicals, with lavish visuals, dancing, and singing. A series of films by the elegant dancing team Ginger Rogers and Fred Astaire, starting with *Flying Down to Rio* in 1933, put music and motion together.

Comedies became more verbal, with jokes and sophisticated bantering added to their basic repertoire of slapstick and sight gags. Several comedy subgenres were created. The zany comedies of the Marx Brothers, such as *Night at the Opera* (1935), poked fun at authority. Screwball comedies, such as *It Happened One Night* (1934), featured Katharine Hepburn, Cary Grant, and other big stars in elegantly set and clever but silly stories.

Talkies are motion pictures with synchronized sound for dialogue.

Sound, dramatic visuals, and action were combined in increasingly complex formulas that often addressed concerns of the day (or at least of the decade). Crime stories, such as *Little Caesar* (1930), reflected a real-life increase in organized crime that grew with the prohibition of alcohol. Another genre was the classic detective film, such as *The Maltese Falcon* (1941), directed by John Huston, which featured Humphrey Bogart. A key genre variation on these detective films was the **film noir,** "the dark film," which tended to be more skeptical, even cynical, and had antiheroes instead of the simpler heroes of earlier films. Classics of this genre include *Double Indemnity* (1944).

Suspense and mystery stories, such as Alfred Hitchcock's *The 39 Steps* (1935), constitute another major genre of Hollywood films. Historical epics were another specialty. The most successful film of the 1930s was *Gone with the Wind* (1939), set in the South during the Civil War, with a melodrama-like cast of archetypal characters including the swaggering, handsome hero Rhett and the strong-willed heroine Scarlett.

After the Japanese attack on Pearl Harbor in 1941 and the German declaration of war on the United States, World War II films such as *Bataan* (1943) reflected and promoted American patriotism (Gomery, 1991). The war was such a pivotal experience for so many Americans that World War II films persisted long after the war was over. Heroic World War II movies like *Saving Private Ryan* (1998) were still being made in the 1990s. By the late 1960s, the growing negative public reaction to the Vietnam War changed the nature of war films to a more critical view.

Similarly, the western became a means for exploring the American myth and American character. The director John Ford, for example, created a number of classic westerns. They gradually changed from the optimistic view of cowboys and cavalry soldiers exemplified by *She Wore a Yellow Ribbon* (1949) to films such as *Cheyenne Autumn* (1964), which began to consider the perspective of Native Americans as "good guys," with a different slant on the American conquest of the West. Table 7.1 on page 184 lists the main early sound film genres that took shape in the 1930s and 1940s.

The Peak of Movie Impact?

The cultural impact of movies in America in the 1930s–1940s was extraordinary. Most people went to the movies at least weekly if they could afford it. They got news information from newsreels, such as Fox's *Movietone News* and *March of Time* newsreels, which provided much of the information people had about the rest of the world before television news. They waited from week to week to see what would happen next to Flash Gordon or other heroes of the serials that played before the feature. The Depression kept some people away (revenues did sag at first after the economic crash of 1929), but most people tried hard to find the money for the movies. Hollywood responded with a number of imaginatively escapist films to help people forget their troubles. The pure fantasy of *The Wizard of Oz* (1939) is an enduring example of brilliant 1930s escapism.

Film noir were "dark" moody American films of the 1940s often focused on detectives or similar themes.

The Studio system in Hollywood put all aspects of a film together in one production and distribution company.

The Studio System

Movies made a lot of money. As profits went up and movies became a profitable business, a merger wave took place. The Great Depression killed off many small producers and nearly 5000 independent movie theaters (Gomery, 1991). Their misfortune actually strengthened the economic situation and control of a few big studios, and it concentrated production decisions in the hands of a very few studio executives, a reality that came to be known as the **studio system.**

By 1930, a fairly stable pattern of studio organization emerged. There were five major studios: Paramount, Loews/MGM, Warner Brothers, Fox, and RKO. All five shared several key characteristics. These studios owned their own distribution chains of movie theaters. They owned extensive production facilities. They relied on teams of stars and directors who made several movies together for them. They developed both prestigious feature films and **B-movies,** which were cheaper and not so prestigious but made consistent profits as the second feature at local theaters. Control over production, distribution, and exhibition enabled studios to make sure that their movies were distributed and played widely, but it constituted a form of **vertical integration** that ultimately drew the attention of federal regulators to the concentration of power in the studios.

However, each studio also had its own distinctive style. Paramount was the most profitable and powerful studio, with over 1000 theaters. It relied on proven directors such as Cecil B. DeMille (known for extravagant epics such as *The Ten Commandments,* 1956) and stars like crooner Bing Crosby and comedian Bob Hope. Loews/MGM had impressive facilities: 27 soundstages on 168 acres. It sought prestige with new Technicolor musicals, but it also made a lot of money with B-movies such as the *Tarzan* adventures. Twentieth Century Fox combined two studios, developed new stars such as Tyrone Power and Betty Grable, and also made money with documentaries including *March of Time* and Movietone newsreels. Warner Brothers went from marginal status in the 1930s to number three in 1949 by promoting comedies, genre films such as Errol Flynn's *The Adventures of Robin Hood* (1938), and cartoons starring Bugs Bunny, Elmer Fudd, and Daffy Duck.

RKO, Radio-Keith-Orpheum, produced some quality films, notably *King Kong* (1933), Fred Astaire and Ginger Rogers musicals, and *Citizen Kane* (1941), but made most of its money from its movie houses and from cheaper, more predictably profitable B-movies.

The minor Hollywood studios of the 1930s and 1940s included several that are now major players: Universal, Columbia, and United Artists. These studios struggled because they did not control their own distribution and exhibition networks. They also made most of their money with B-movies. Universal Pictures' only real successes in the 1930s and 1940s were low-budget productions such as Abbott and Costello comedies, Flash Gordon serials, Woody the Woodpecker cartoons, and horror movies (for example, *Dracula,* 1930). Columbia Pictures was a small, independent producer that rose to make classic Frank Capra movies, such as *It Happened One Night* (1934), but made more money from westerns with Gene Autry and Three Stooges shorts. United Artists was founded by silent-era stars—Mary Pickford, Douglas Fairbanks, and Charlie Chaplin, along with D. W. Griffith. It prospered most in the 1920s when these founders were still creating movies. Another two studios were even smaller, Monogram and Republic. Republic was famous for a time as a producer of action serials, whose *cliffhangers* and action sequences have been liberally borrowed by the likes of Steven Spielberg in his *Indiana Jones* movies. Republic was also the first home of cowboy hero John Wayne.

The studio system peaked after World War II in 1946–1948. The war ended the economic limits imposed on movie production by the Great Depression. Right after

LOONEY TUNES characters, names and all related indicia are trademarks of and © Warner Bros. (s03)

■ **ONE FROGGY EVENING (1957)**
Beyond Disney: Chuck Jones (1912–2002) added many innovations and a wry sense of humor to animation at Warner Bros.

B-movies are cheaply and quickly made genre films.

Vertical integration is when companies with the same owner handle different aspects of a business, such as film production and distribution.

■ BEST FILM EVER?
Orson Welles's *Citizen Kane* popoularized a number of filmmaking techniques, including new camera angles and types of shots.

Theatrical films are those released for distribution in movie theaters.

Gross is the total box office revenue before expenses are deducted.

Concentration of power by integration of many aspects of media into one company creates concerns about political control and loss of diversity.

Fin-Syn, or Financial interest in Syndication, rules kept TV networks from producing or owning entertainment programming.

World War II, returning soldiers and sailors joined the masses of people attending the movies weekly. The year 1946 was the peak of audience exposure and financial success for **theatrical films** in the United States. Around 90 million Americans went to the movies every week to see movies like *It's a Wonderful Life* (1946). In 1947, the U.S. film industry **grossed** $1.7 billion, a figure that sank to $900 million by 1962, reflecting competition from television (Mast & Kawin, 1996).

Film Faces Television, 1948–1960

By 1948, the film industry faced significant competition from a new technology: television. Film attendance also declined as returning World War II veterans started families and moved to the newly established suburbs, far away from downtown movie theaters (Gomery, 1991). Hollywood first responded with drive-in movies and later, in the 1970s, shifted to new movie houses in suburban shopping centers. After 1948, television quickly cut into Hollywood's theatrical box office receipts. The film industry suffered a severe, concurrent blow to its theater-based revenues. The government had become concerned with the **concentration of power** in the Hollywood system, where studios both produced movies and controlled distribution. In 1948, the government ordered studios to get out of at least one aspect of film business: production, distribution, or exhibition. Studios challenged the decision, but it was confirmed by the Supreme Court (*United States v. Paramount Pictures,* 1948).

The four biggest studios—MGM (Metro Goldwyn, Mayer), Warner, Paramount, and Fox—struggled to readjust after agreeing to sell off their theater chains. Paramount and United Artists sold off their exhibition chains. MGM/Loews struggled for almost a decade in the courts to avoid separating the company's Loews theater chain from its MGM studio. They finally split in 1959, and MGM shakily emerged as a separate studio entity. Ironically, this forced divestiture of theatrical distribution took place at a point when studios were losing their dominance. Almost every small town went through the shock described in *The Last Picture Show* (1971), as thousands of small-town theaters disappeared.

The film industry began to realize that if it couldn't beat television, maybe it had better join it. Disney started producing programs specifically for television: *Disneyland* for ABC (1954–1957), followed by *Mickey Mouse Club* (1955–1959). Warner Brothers and Paramount both made much of their money in the 1950s and 1960s by producing series for television and distributing films to it (Gomery, 1991). The networks began to order most of their programs from studios or other outside producers since it was then cheaper to buy programming from companies that were already geared up to create it (Sterling & Kittross, 1990). Later, television networks were forced to buy most of their programs from the studios because of government rules that limited how much network programming the network itself could create or own. Those rules on financial syndication, the **Fin-Syn** rules, were designed to diversify the sources of television production.

After 1961 film was more common on television, as "Saturday Night at the Movies" (NBC) topped the ratings. Television networks have been using movies strategically ever since to compete with each other. Airing movies became an even more important way for

© MGM/Photofest

© New Line/courtesy Everett Collection

UHF and independent stations—even many PBS stations—to compete with network programs.

As audiences got used to television, they demanded something different from movies. Part of the film industry response was in technological innovation. Although Technicolor had been invented in 1917, it spread slowly with films such as *Gone with the Wind* and Disney cartoons. By the early 1960s, nearly all films were in color.

Another relatively successful technological innovation aimed at competing with TV was wide-screen film. CinemaScope had been developed in the 1920s, but it took hold only under encouragement from the head of the Fox studio in the early 1950s. Studios finally embraced the new wide-screen idea, but outfitting theaters proved expensive and took quite a long time. Hollywood also tried to compete with TV by mounting lavish, big-budget spectacles such as *Ben Hur* (1959). However, extravaganza movies could also backfire, as did Fox's *Cleopatra,* which cost $30 million in 1963 and didn't come close to breaking even.

The movie industry also tried to capitalize on the fact that it could include more controversial material than TV could. This strategy meant including sex, such as in the James Bond thriller *Goldfinger* (1964), or social issues like racial prejudice, in films like *Guess Who's Coming to Dinner* (1967). However, by the 1960s the power of the movie studios was declining. Independent producers gained more of a role in producing movies for studios, which they then distributed. For their own in-house activity, film studios began to spend much of their time producing series for television, and the studio system, which had flourished in its golden era, died.

Studios in Decline

Although movie studios suffered in the 1950s, only RKO actually went out of business. Most changed hands. Most struggled through a cycle of lean years with few hits and fat years when a hit saved the day; *The Godfather* (1972), for example, made Paramount an unprecedented $1,000,000 a day for its first month.

Columbia and United Artists in some ways fared better than the larger studios by not having to adjust to the loss of theater businesses. Warner and Columbia Pictures made television series. Universal was acquired by MCA and also went into television production.

■ TITANIC HIT

Titanic became the all-time box office draw in 1997, reviving Hollywood's faith in big-budget pictures. *The Passion of the Christ* in 2004 was an example of attracting audiences with graphic violence connected to a religious theme.

United Artists capitalized on distributing movies, such as John Huston's *The African Queen* (1951), for talented independent producers. Disney moved into the studio ranks with animated films and its Buena Vista production and distribution company, which produced family fare epitomized by *Mary Poppins* (1964).

As independent producers gained more power, several things happened to American movies. Audiences changed, becoming younger, more cosmopolitan, and more interested in sensation and social observation. The values and current interests of teenagers and college students began to dominate films (Mast & Kawin, 1996).

New directors pushed into Hollywood from outside the studios and the star system, some from 1960s *underground films,* some straight from film school, some from TV commercials. These new directors transformed traditional Hollywood genres, often by increasing the use of sex, violence, and social controversy such as Francis Ford Coppola (*The Godfather,* 1972) did. Directors like Woody Allen (*Annie Hall,* 1976) tended to create much more offbeat, personal films, some of which turned out to be major commercial successes.

As suggested above, films in the 1960s also became more political and topical. For instance, although *M*A*S*H* (1970) was set during the Korean War, it was filled with the antiwar sentiment many Americans harbored about the Vietnam War. Films such as *Taxi Driver* (1976) explored the underside of city life, whereas *The Graduate* (1967) explored the angst of growing up in the suburbs. Films reexamined American myths, including cowboys and the West in the hyper-violent *The Wild Bunch* (1969) and the hard-bitten detective in *Chinatown* (1974).

Rebellion against the repressive Victorian-era morality that had inspired the Hays Office was definitely part of the change American society underwent in the 1960s. The Hays Office itself closed down in 1945, although the code technically remained in force until 1966. Meanwhile, local censors were muzzled by free speech rulings from the U.S. Supreme Court. Movie producers continually pushed the limits of what was acceptable, which led to new calls from concerned parents that raised the specter of government censorship. Instead, the industry again opted for self-regulation, this time in the form of content ratings administered by the Motion Picture Association of America (see page 205).

Even as films seemed to turn inward to focus on American culture in the 1960s and 1970s, they were still selling very well abroad. The studios had joined together as the

Motion Picture Export Association of America (MPEAA) in the 1930s and had taken control of much of the international film distribution business. Exports were one of the things that continued to keep Hollywood profitable throughout the 1950s and 1960s.

In the 1970s–1990s, filmmakers such as Steven Spielberg (*ET,* 1982) rediscovered that film has a visual intensity well beyond that of television, especially in the darkened movie house with a big screen. Thus action sequences, striking landscapes, and special effects became competitive advantages for movies. As more sophisticated Dolby and Surround Sound systems emerged, intense sound also characterized the movie theater experience.

Hollywood Meets HBO

By the late 1970s and early 1980s, the film industry began to take increasing advantage of cable TV and rented videotapes as new distribution channels. Cable TV boomed as a source of viewing alternatives to network television, particularly after the launch of nationwide service by Home Box Office (HBO) in 1975 (see Chapter 8), which relied almost exclusively on feature films for its content. The new satellite-based cable super-stations WGN, WOR, and WTBS used quite a few old films. Independent stations, usually on UHF, also began to show more old movies and reruns of hit series from syndication services. These developments helped the film industry regain some of the revenue that it had lost to network television in the 1950s and 1960s.

Videocassette recorders (VCRs) diffused very quickly, as they became more widespread in American homes throughout the 1980s. Prices dipped to under $100 by 2001, when over 90 percent of American homes had acquired a VCR. People used VCRs to record and replay favorite shows off television or cable as well as to view movies rented from video stores. The video rental business started with small independent rental shops, which bought video stock from distributors. It later consolidated decisively, with independents shrinking, with some supermarkets and other stores renting videos as a sideline, and with massive video rental and sales chains like Blockbuster taking most of the business.

The spread of video rentals ultimately contributed both to the blockbuster phenomenon and to *audience segmentation.* Even today, many people rush to the video store to get the latest hit movie on tape or DVD. By contrast, other people walk straight by what the industry calls "top renters" to find Japanese animation, old cowboy movies, old *Star Trek* episodes, or whatever else captures their attention. As a result, a lot of B-movies now go straight to video, where loyal fans are waiting for yet another teenage beach sex comedy or crazed android from the future.

In general, the film industry progressively began to produce for more narrowly focused audiences. After the mass audience had moved to television, film had to aim at more specific groups. For **first-run distribution** to movie theaters, most films were increasingly targeted at a specific audience, the 15- to 24-year-olds who still went out to film theaters. On the other hand, one or two blockbuster movies such as *Jaws* (1975) could ensure a studio's financial health for years by reaching a wide audience. Thus, audience segmentation pits Hollywood's continuing urge to create blockbuster movies that capture a mass audience against its desire to maximize profits. *Star Wars* (1977) is usually regarded as the turning point in a return to spectacular, big-budget blockbuster filmmaking. Filmmakers hurried to take advantage of the latest special effects, often raising costs (see Profile: George Lucas, page 192). The star system also returned with a vengeance, which also raised film costs as stars such as Tom Cruise could get over $20 million for a film.

By the 1970s, *made-for-TV* movies became increasingly common. These movies could be turned into TV or cable TV series if they were popular, as was *Buffy the Vampire*

First-run distribution for films is to movie theaters.

■ GEORGE LUCAS

PROFILE

George Lucas

Occupation: Screenwriter, film director, producer, and media entrepreneur

Born: May 14, 1944, in Modesto, California

Education: University of Southern California's film school

Big Break: He met Francis Ford Coppola through a scholarship sponsored by Warner Brothers Studio. They formed American Zoetrope, a film company that let Lucas direct *THX 1136* (1971). This gave him enough momentum to make *American Graffiti* (1973), which cost under $1 million, made over $50 million, and made Lucas a millionaire.

Big Achievement: Probably his masterwork was his next film, *Star Wars* (1977), which he wrote and directed for his new company, Lucasfilm Ltd.

Inspirations: To write and visualize *Star Wars,* he tried to make an archetypal hero story.

He studied fairy tales, ancient mythology, and the myth studies of Joseph Campbell. He also borrowed liberally from other mythic action films, World War II movies about aircraft carriers and fighters, westerns, Errol Flynn's swashbuckling sword fights, Buck Rogers and Flash Gordon movie serials, and comic books.

Next Moves: Lucas made a *Star Wars* trilogy that also included *The Empire Strikes Back* (1980) and *Return of the Jedi* (1983). The third installment of a second trilogy, *Attack of the Clones,* debuts in 2005.

Expansions: He expanded Lucasfilm into postproduction facilities and multimedia research. He went into other companies and technologies. Industrial Light and Magic was formed in the 1970s to do cutting-edge special effects. Skywalker Sound is a state-of-the-art recording studio that does postproduction for filmmakers and mixing for the music industry. LucasArts did research and development to create games on CD-ROM.

Slayer (1997). Made-for-TV movies often did surprisingly well against other movies and series. Audiences and revenues for cable channels in the 1990s were such that "made-for-cable" movies became relatively common on channels such as HBO and TNT, surpassing the number of "made-for-TV" movies.

Now, new technology and market forces again transformed the movie industry. Home video has become a driving force with revenues from video store rentals and direct sales of videos and DVDs (known as *sell through*) outstripping box office receipts two-to-one. Large video rental chains demanded a share of the profits from filmmakers. The cost of producing major films skyrocketed as producers raced to outdo each other with spectacular computer-generated special effects. In hopes of spreading those costs over larger and larger audiences, the industry began to internationalize both with respect to its ownership—which now included foreign investors such as Sony Corporation and Rupert Murdoch—and with respect to its audiences.

While moviemaking at the major studios began to gravitate more toward genres (for example, science fiction, action adventure) that could "translate" well across cultures, there was a revival in independent filmmaking outside of the major studios. Some directors, like John Cassavetes, had survived as independents for years. Now many others joined them. Computer technology for editing and high-quality, low-cost digital cameras drove down the cost of "small films" and offered the prospect of a renaissance in filmmaking apart from the financial pressures of the block-buster mentality that gripped Hollywood. It helped that some inexpensively made films, like *The Blair Witch Project* (1999), also made considerable profits. Video rental chains promoted independent films with special packaging in many of its stores. But the idea of **independent film** is relative. The Independent Film Channel in 2004 featured "My Big Fat Greek Wedding," which to date has grossed over $220 million, produced by Tom Hanks's small company, Playtone. Some prefer to use the label *independent* for much smaller films.

Over 300 independent feature films are made on average each year, often starting as film school projects and sometimes funded through relatives' credit cards. These films circulate at an increasing number of film festivals around the world, hoping to strike gold, like *Napoleon Dynamite* (2004), produced by filmmakers who were recently students in Utah, which hit big at the Sundance Film Festival and was widely distributed. However, they still depend on studios for distribution.

STOP & REVIEW

1. What was the studio system?
2. Which were the main studios?
3. What were some of the main silent film genres?
4. What genres came in with talking films? Which were prominent in the 1930s and 1940s?
5. Why did studios want to own their own distributors and movie theater chains? Why did federal regulators force the studios to divest themselves of their movie theater chains in 1948?
6. When did the studio system decline? Why did it decline?
7. What effect have new distribution technologies, such as video and cable, had on the film industry?

TECHNOLOGY: MAKING MOVIE MAGIC

Eadweard Muybridge's first motion picture of a galloping horse used a rather unwieldy recording system—the horse's hooves triggered trip wires on 700 still cameras to yield a mere 60 seconds of action. Edison's *kinetograph* in 1888 was a close relative to his *phonograph* (see Chapter 5), in that the pictures were recorded a frame at a time on a hand-turned revolving cylinder with a light-sensitive surface. Soon the cylindrical photographic plates gave way to strips of the newly invented Kodak film.

Edison's 1892 kinetoscope was the first playback mechanism for the masses—but for only one viewer at a time. The Lumière brothers originated the movie projector in 1895 by shining a light through the strip of picture transparencies and enlarging them with an optical lens. If the frames were changed fast enough (20 frames per second was about right), the viewer had the sense of continuous motion. This was because the afterimage of each frame persisted just long enough for the next frame to appear.

Apart from some advances in film processing and developing, basic motion picture technology did not change much over the next 25 years. As movies got longer, it became necessary to replace the hand-cranked projector with an electric motor. The actors' words appeared printed on the screen, not spoken, and a live organist played theme music in the theater.

Movie Sound

Edison invented a movie sound system in 1913 but the first successful *talkie* was *The Jazz Singer* (1927). *The Jazz Singer*'s sound was supplied by AT&T Bell Labs scientists, who synchronized a record with the film. Soon a way was found to record the sound on an optical track right on the film. A photoreceptor picked up variations in the light shining through the sound track and reproduced them as weak electric currents that were fed into an amplifier and then the movie theater's speakers. The latest Digital Theater Sound (DTS) systems harken back to the old AT&T system, except that digital CDs hold the

Independent film is made by a wide variety of people outside the control of the major studios.

sound and are synchronized with the images via digital codes printed on the film, yielding multidimensional digital surround sound. Surround sound systems are now proliferating in home theaters to simulate the sound of the theater experience.

Making Movies Look Better

Early inventors also improved the visual aspects of film. First, the film exposure rate was increased slightly, from 18 or 22 frames per second in early films to 24 frames per second. This increase eliminated the jerkiness that was apparent to some viewers. Film also got wider, growing from 16 mm to 35 mm to 70 mm. The additional width of the film expanded the field of vision for filmgoers in the interest of imparting a better sense of reality. Wide-screen CinemaScope was popular in the early 1950s, but it gave way to Panavision, which is still used extensively (Gomery, 1991).

Color films originated around 1910, but color scenes had to be painstakingly tinted by hand, frame by frame, on each print. Color films did not become widely available until the CinemaScope process of color photography debuted in 1939. Another color process, Technicolor, was introduced in 1922, but its patent owners restricted its spread until 1950, following a U.S. government antitrust suit. Most films were in color by the 1960s.

Special Effects

Early audiences were easy to fool with simple *stop-action* effects. If you showed them a magician climbing into a box and closing the lid, stopped the camera long enough for the magician to exit, and then restarted the film to show an empty box, early moviegoers were convinced that the magician had magically escaped. Later, the actors were filmed against the backdrop of another film projected from behind. This technique, called **rear projection,** gave the impression that actors in the studio were really paddling a boat in the rapids or engaging in other dangerous stunts. And many a model train and toy boat were sacrificed to simulate real-life cataclysms.

Modern special effects are often traced back to the 1933 classic *King Kong.* The big ape was actually an 18-inch furry doll with movable limbs that were painstakingly moved one frame at a time. When Kong grabbed our heroine, Fay Wray, she was filmed in the clutches of a life-sized mock-up of a giant gorilla's arm. *King Kong* was the first film to use a technique called **front projection.** When our heroine appeared struggling on the top of the Empire State Building, a building model was shot with a miniature movie screen on its roof, onto which pictures of the real Fay struggling were projected. *King Kong* also relied heavily on the already-familiar rear projection, as well as a technique in which live actors were filmed against a neutral backdrop and then **composited** with a background shot of, say, a charging dinosaur. The background was **matted,** or blacked out, in the areas where the actors would appear so that the two images could be superimposed. Stop action, compositing, matting, and scale models are still the staples of many special-effects sequences today. Look at the production documentaries that are included on DVDs such as *The Lord of the Rings* or other recent films for examples.

The Digital Revolution

The computer is taking over in special effects. *Star Wars* used computer-driven cameras to construct multilayered space battles. In an update of Muybridge's pioneering technique, computer-controlled still cameras shot the spectacular slow-motion action scenes in *The Matrix.* One of the first noteworthy uses of *computer animation* was in a 16-minute

Rear projection effects have images projected behind performers who are in the foreground.

Front projection lets actors be photographed in front of an image so that they appear part of it.

Compositing is merging several layers of images that were shot separately.

Mattes are background paintings or photographs that are combined with performers in the foreground.

You Ought to Be in Pictures

One of the biggest barriers to aspiring auteurs has always been the cost of producing a student film. Doing it the "old-fashioned way," using 16 mm photographic film, rented cameras and sound equipment, and traditional editing and film processing techniques, could set the young film artist and her family back $30,000 or more, even if her "film school buddies" wrote the scripts, performed, and directed for free pizza. No more.

What does it take now? The MiniDV format yields results comparable to 16 mm film in many settings, with twice the resolution of old-fashioned analog video cameras. The cameras can be had for less than a thousand dollars and use the same Charge Coupled Device (CCD) technology in their image sensors (see Chapter 8) that high-end digital video cameras do. Some have still image recording capabilities and use the same storage media (for example, Compact Flash or Memory Sticks) that digital still cameras do, so you can take your production stills with the same camera. The latest models boast "near broadcast quality" megapixel (that is, millions of picture dots, or pixels, per frame) resolution, 20X optical zoom, three CCDs for improved color, and sufficient light sensitivity to film in total darkness—some in a device the size of a pack of cigarettes. The 60-minute cassettes are less than $5 apiece and, like any other videotape, can be erased and reused if the actors fluff their lines. MiniDVs are designed to be consumer electronics gadgets that will take the place of the old analog camcorder, so the production quantities and features are always going up and the prices going down.

Moving digital images create a lot of data so it has to be compressed. DV cameras use a method based on the JPEG standard used for still photos you see on the Internet rather than the MPEG-2 standard found in other video applications (see Chapter 8), but the two can be converted. Or, you can download the compressed files to your computer for editing. Universal Serial Bus (USB) and IEEE 394 (more popularly known as FireWire) are standard connections on both MiniDV cameras and the latest personal computers. The multigigabit disc drives also found on most personal computers nowadays provide adequate storage for short films (an hour of film takes up 13 billion bytes), but you will need lots of RAM and a video graphics card, too. For editing, home computers using Adobe Premier or Apple's Final Cut Pro will do. Home computer sound editing products also do an acceptable job on the sound track.

So, if you can borrow a MiniDV camera from a gadget-loving relative and get your friends to work for free pizza, your student film can now be produced for a few hundred dollars. For truly professional results, you could upgrade to the higher-resolution DVCAM (Sony) or DVPRO (Panasonic) formats, but those cameras cost 10 times as much.

If you want someone besides your film school buddies to see your project, you may need to have it transferred to film; that can cost thousands of dollars. However, many film festivals now project "films" in video, and many of the commercial outlets for short subjects (for example, European television and the Independent Film Channel on cable) are video venues. There are also sites on the Internet (for example, AtomFilms) that will distribute short works online, either as downloads or streamed files (see Chapter 9). If you fancy actually making money on your film in theaters, then you will have to pay for the film transfer, at least until the new digital projectors become more common.

---

segment of the 1982 Disney film *Tron*, which took place inside a computer-generated virtual world. In 1995, Pixar Animation's *Toy Story* became the first full-length computer-animated hit film. No one had to draw each frame, or cell, of animation as in all previous animated movies.

Increasingly, computer-generated monsters and sets are filling in for scale models. Sometimes computer images stand in for real actors in dangerous action sequences, such as the "people" falling off the *Titanic* as it slipped beneath the waves. The waves were computer-generated, too. Computer effects are also what made it possible for makers of *The Lord of the Rings* to use a live actor to create motion for the character Gollum but then change his appearance to something much less human. *The Polar Express* (2004), made extensive use of the *motion capture* technique, in which motion sensors are attached to a live actor (Tom Hanks, in that case) and the output fed into a computer so that the animations realistically reproduce the gestures and expressions of the actor. Another 2004 film, *Sky Captain and the World of Tomorrow,* pushed computer special effects in another dimension. *Sky Captain's* actors were real, but they performed on empty sets and had the retro-style robots and settings filled in by computer.

Special effects are glitzy, but the real computer revolution in Hollywood is taking place behind the scenes, during the **postproduction** process when films get their finishing touches. Film editing used to involve unspooling miles of raw film footage and manually cutting and splicing to make a master copy. Now the filmed sequences are transferred to computer media where they can be accessed at random and spliced with the click of a mouse—a process known as **nonlinear editing.** Not only is this faster, but it also allows the editor to be more creative in playing "what if" in the editing suite.

Celluloid film itself is becoming obsolete with the advent of digital cameras that record high-quality images directly in digital formats—with no chemical film processing required. In fact, they don't call it "filming" anymore; now it's "image capture." George Lucas' *Attack of the Clones* was the first major production to use **digital video** for image capture.

Now that computers have become involved in all aspects of moviemaking, "desktop" filmmaking is fast becoming a reality. Small groups of talented people can shoot films in video and edit them on personal computers with off-the-shelf software without Hollywood actors, directors, cameras, sets, or key grips (see "Technology Demystified: You Ought to Be in Pictures," page 195). Digital filmmaking lowers costs, opening the film industry to student filmmakers and diverse artistic visions. The Internet is beginning to serve as a distribution mechanism for the digital filmmakers, removing the last analog stop in film production and perhaps also the last financial barrier to the solo film artist-auteur. In fact, we already have virtual film studios, such as Pixar Animation Studios, run by Steve Jobs, cofounder of Apple Computers, which has become known for its various hit movies produced entirely with digital animation inside computers, starting with the *Toy Story* series, and recently including *The Incredibles* (2004).

Movie Viewing

What will the movie theater of the future be like? The odds are that it will be nothing like today's. Movies have always tried to stay a step ahead of the competition by offering an aesthetic experience that cannot be duplicated by its competitors, so look for bigger screens and ever more sophisticated digital sound systems.

The old movie projector is being replaced by new digital light projectors that show digitized movies stored on compact discs. Look for them to be linked by satellite in time for the premiere of the next *Star Wars* saga, eliminating the time and expense of hand delivering copies of new films to the theater. They literally do it with mirrors. The digital light projectors, or *DLPs*, as they are called, have microchips with millions of tiny mirrors on their surface. The mirrors are adjusted thousands of times per second to reflect tiny dots, or *pixels*, of red, green, and blue light onto the movie screen. DLPs may also convert theaters back into venues for live entertainment, something we haven't seen much of since the days of vaudeville. Digital cinema has been slow to catch on, in part because they cost several times what a conventional projector does. And the DLP projectors have lower resolution, about 1300 lines compared to 4000 lines for conventional film.

But don't look for the "feelies," "stinkies," or "tasties" that science fiction writers have predicted since the 1930s. The sensory modalities of touch, smell, and taste are now better understood, and computer interfaces are being developed to stimulate each one. However, that will probably occur in computer-based virtual reality environments that may require users to wear helmets and body suits with sensor arrays. This is the antithesis of the shared

Postproduction includes editing, sound effects, and visual effects that are added after shooting the original footage.

Nonlinear editing uses digital equipment to rearrange scenes to make the master copy.

Digital video is recorded, edited and often transmitted in digital form as used by computers.

© Walt Disney Productions/Photofest

■ **MONSTROUSLY DETAILED**
The lavish animation, including details of individual hairs, in *Monsters, Inc.* (2001) was a giant step forward in computer animation. The Pixar Studio under Steve Jobs has specialized in creating entirely digital animated films.

environment that makes moviegoing a social event. Back in the 1950s, 3D (three-dimensional) movies fizzled for three important reasons that may still stand in the way: They made many movie patrons nauseated, the 3D glasses got in the way if you tried to smooch your sweetie, and they looked silly.

Still, 3D movies are likely to reappear at some point, only without the cardboard glasses and the airsickness bags. Laser light has potential for creating lifelike, moving three-dimensional images. Pass the virtual popcorn, please.

While the movie theater may never die, movies are increasingly viewed in the home. A breakthrough in videotape technology, called *helical scanning,* making it possible to record movies on small spools of tape led to the home videocassette recorder in 1975. Now VCRs have largely been replaced by an array of digital recording technologies, including the DVD and digital video recorders, or DVRs. (See Chapter 8.) The latest DVRs also support more downloads from the Internet. Indeed, the attention of the movie industry is increasingly focused on the personal computer, with an online movie battle looming to rival the fracas over music downloads. On the pirates' side we have Bit Torrent and Groupster, two new wrinkles in file sharing. Bit Torrent scatters fragments of large video files across multiple computers, making it faster to "share" the lengthy files. That also frustrates "spoofing," the uploading of corrupted files by movie industry operatives. Groupster aims to defy copyright law by streaming videos between closed groups of friends, a "private performance" that evades copyright laws. The industry has responded with a variety of pay services such as Netflix, Movielink and Starz! Ticket. But there is a catch, the legal services all employ digital rights management technology which not only prevents copying the movies for your friends, but also "self-destructs" your copy after a limited period—usually 24 hours. With half of all Internet homes now on broadband connections, movie downloads are threatening the home video stores.

THE FILM INDUSTRY: MAKING MOVIES

The Players

Today, the film industry is a high-volume mixture of large and small players that continue to shift and evolve. There are eight major film producers: the old-time studios—Columbia, Fox, MGM, Paramount, Universal, and Warner Brothers—along with Buena Vista (Disney) and TriStar (Sony). In Chapter 8 we will see that five of these, Warner, Fox, Paramount, Buena Vista, and Universal, are part of vertically integrated corporations that dominate video and film production and distribution. Each produces 15 to 25 movies per year, combining for about two-fifths of the almost 500 feature films released annually in the United States (MPAA, 2004). At the height of Hollywood's fame in 1946, the major studios each produced 40 to 50 movies each year. The major Hollywood studios currently invest an average of about $48 million per film, plus an average of $31 million in advertising per film, plus high overhead to keep the studio organizations running, so the stakes are very high and the pressure to produce big hits is enormous. One new studio, DreamWorks, started by Steven Spielberg in 1995, seemed to be gathering steam with major hits like *American Beauty* (1999) and *Shrek* (2004). With films like *Shrek I* and *II,* DreamWorks has become the main competitor to Pixar Studios in popular

animated films. Pixar has primarily worked as an animation production group to be distributed by Disney, but
they have not renewed their contract with Disney, and
may be moving to become another studio on their own.

Independent Filmmakers

There are many independent film companies, like Tom
Hanks's Playtone, and Drew Barrymore's Flower Films,
which actually produce most of the movies that the
major studios distribute. These are not to be confused
with an extensive, much less formal network of independent filmmakers. These "indies" usually produce
films for much less than the major studios or the major
independent production companies, often only a few million dollars. A classic pattern is
that new filmmakers eke out a hodgepodge of financing for their first film. If their film
succeeds, they might get studio backing for subsequent films. For example, going back to
film history, Spike Lee made *She's Gotta Have It* (1986) for $200,000, but after that film
made $7 million, Columbia produced his next, *School Daze* (1988). Since more and
more festivals show short features, a new pattern can be seen in *Napoleon Dynamite,*
which attracted support from Viacom/MTV for full feature-length production after a
short film-school version was a hit at the Sundance Film Festival.

Table 7.2 Top Six Studio Owners	
Media Group	Main Movie Production Companies
Time Warner	Warner Bros., New Line
Walt Disney	Buena Vista, Miramax, Touchstone
Universal-NBC	Universal, PolyGram Films
Viacom-CBS	Paramount
Sony	Columbia, TriStar

Source: Variety's Global 50: http://www.variety.com/index.asp?layout=global50

The system for independent filmmakers is quickly becoming more organized. People
willing to back films now scout major film schools and short-film festivals to see what
new filmmakers look promising, perhaps to invest limited funds in a first film. Once new
filmmakers have their first feature film, they can try to get it shown at a variety of festivals. There are both national festivals, such as the Sundance Festival in Park City, Utah,
and regional festivals, such as South by Southwest, in Austin, Texas. Likewise, across the
country, various organizations run specialized film festivals, presenting film series focused
on LGTB (lesbian, gay, transgender, and bisexual), Jewish, and Asian content, for example, or by filmmakers belonging to these cultural groups. Hundreds of independent
feature films are produced every year now, some as film-school projects, many completely
independent. The problem is getting them distributed.

Distribution gives the studios a stake in many of the independent films that they distribute, but it also gives them more control than independent filmmakers think is healthy. For
example, Miramax creator Harvey Weinstein sold his company to Disney and thus had years
of bitter conflict with Disney studio management, despite the profits both sides have made
from the deal. However, maneuvers around studios to arrange distribution of a film are also
possible. Cable and video release rights, which are often arranged before production, can
help finance nonstudio productions by known independent producers. Steven Soderbergh
began this trend as he financed his innovative independent film *sex, lies and videotape* (1989)
primarily by selling the video rights to RCA/Columbia Home Video (Mast & Kawin, 1996).

Independent filmmakers and smaller or independent production houses have grown in
power since the 1960s (they now account for over half of the movies that are distributed)
but they have a shaky existence, often doing only as well as their latest films. Independent
studios Carolco, which produced the *Terminator* movies, and Orion, which had *Dances
with Wolves* (1990) and others, hovered on the brink of bankruptcy in 1992 until they were
bought by Ted Turner. However, Disney-owned film company Miramax had essentially
become another major studio by 2000, with a string of international coproductions, like
Shakespeare in Love (1998) or *Amelie* (2001), and increasingly mainstream Hollywood
productions, like *Bridget Jones's Diary* (2001).

Film Distribution Windows
Films are now released in a
series of "windows" to a variety
of media.

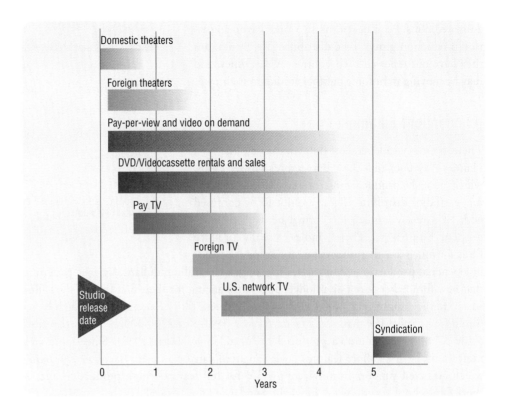

Film Distribution

The major studios are increasingly part of industry conglomerates. They still control most film distribution, as they have since the 1920s. If a studio produces a film, then that studio handles its distribution to theaters and video, cable TV, and overseas releases. Independent filmmakers also must turn to a film studio or some other distribution company to make those connections and get the film distributed.

Films are distributed to a series of **windows,** or times linked to specific channels. The archetypal distribution for a major film might be theatrical distribution, then international theatrical distribution, pay-per-view, pay cable, videocassette and DVD rentals and sales, network exhibition, basic cable networks, and finally syndication (Figure 7.1). Increasingly, all the domestic steps have an international parallel. In general, there are many more film distribution options now than in the heyday of studio control. Many films are not seen as being worth the promotional costs for theatrical release and go straight to video for distribution in stores and on cable.

Theatrical distribution of films is in fact growing again, after years of decline. There were less than 18,000 screens for films in the United States in 1980, but almost 36,000 in 2003. The U.S. theatrical part of distribution earned $9.5 billion at the box office in 2003. However, home video has grown even more. Americans spent over $22 billion in total on home video in 2003, according to the Video Software Dealers of America (http://www.vsda.org).

In between studio distributors and local rental shops are a group of distributors, including CBS/Fox Video, RCA/Columbia Home Pictures, Vestron, TriStar, Orion, and dozens of others. The retail side of video is the most complex and changeable. Chains, such as Blockbuster Video, dominate. Other retailers, particularly "Big Box" retailers like Wal-Mart, now have racks of DVDs and videos for sale. And home video sales are fast becoming a staple of online commerce on the Internet. Both rentals and sales of DVDs

Windows are separate film release
times for different channels or media.

Netflix It

Americans seem to have a boundless appetite for watching movies, and an equal interest in finding new ways of getting to those movies. They also have a rapidly increasing fondness for ordering things online. Maybe it was inevitable that someone would put those two forces together. Still a new company like Netflix can put ideas together to create a stunningly successful new business.

Like many successful ideas, Netflix combines familiar desires and habits with new technology. Like Amazon and many other successful examples of e-business, Netflix builds on the familiarity of an old-fashioned mail-order catalog, which has been around since the Sears Catalogs in the 1890s brought rural people and others far from new things in stores into the emerging American consumer economy. It builds on the efficiency of the U.S. mail and delivery services. (The lack of such reliable delivery holds back on-line catalogs in many countries.)

Netfix lets customers rent all the movies they want by mail for a fixed monthly fee. Users pick movies online and add them to a queue of choices that are mailed out when they are available. It removes several disincentives offered by rentals from stores, such as the need to actually go to the store to get movies and then return them.

However, like other new services with a technological twist, older services have begun to offer approximations of Netflix's idea that keep much of the new concept, but using the old technology. Hollywood Video and others began to offer unlimited rentals for a monthly fee. Netflix also has to face other competitors. There are direct competitors who copy their service. There are both legal and illegal Internet download services. And there are pay-per-view film services over cable and satellite television. This is a crowded and competitive landscape. However, Netflix's success seems to reinforce the point that many customers like services which are innovative but still reasonably familiar, supplying products by mail with an interface, an online catalog, that is also by now known to many.

---

are now driven in part by extra scenes added back in and extra features, such as documentaries about aspects of the making of the film. *The Lord of the Rings* films managed to sell two or three different DVDs of each film to some buyers by releasing more extra scenes, extra features, and longer previews of the next movie in the series with each successive DVD release.

TELLING STORIES: FILM CONTENT

Film, more than any other medium other than perhaps printed novels, is centered around storytelling, the creation of striking and memorable narratives that draw people in to spend fairly high amounts of money to see them, often repeatedly.

Team Effort

Much more than in fiction writing for novels, songwriting, or even television production, creating film content or stories is an ensemble or group effort. While audiences tend to think of movies in terms of which actors star in them, filmmaking is probably more driven by directors, producers, and writers, not to mention visual designers, photography directors, music directors, film editors, special effects people, and casting directors. Even less obvious but just as critical are script readers, development executives, market researchers, focus group services that examine ideas and plots, studio finance people who package various sources of money together, marketing strategists who plan promotional campaigns, and release strategists who assemble theaters so that films can open "big," and so forth.

Many people add to the substance of a film's contents. A memorable, award-winning film, like *Lost in Translation* (2003), is based on strong performances by actors like Bill

Making a movie is an ensemble process involving the creative talents of many people.

© Frank Micelotta/Getty Images

Murray. But it also depends on the casting of less well known actors, striking visual design, original cinematography, memorable music, sound effects, and the central role of the director in orchestrating all of these processes and the people who perform them. While the number of Academy Awards may seem endless, it is interesting to think about how all these people contribute creative elements to the final film content. The complexity and organizational, and financial demands of putting all these people and their roles together in a finished film is one reason that the Hollywood studios dominated film production for so long and are still central to the production of most major films, performing most of the business, finance, and marketing functions that give the artists budgets to work with.

Most often, the controlling hand on film production and storytelling is the director. Sometimes directors are simply hired to oversee a process envisioned by a producer, who typically lines up the financing, story developers, scriptwriters, director, and sometimes major stars. However, the most memorable films usually reflect the artistic vision of a director who selects and directs the people who actually act, shoot the film, create the special effects, and so on. The most strongly creative directors often write or cowrite the scripts or story concepts for their films.

Many films start with a writer's draft film script, which is circulated among studios, producers, directors, and even leading actors, looking for interest. Thousands circulate, hundreds get optioned for a serious look, but few get made. Sometimes scripts emerge as films with remarkably little change. More often film scripts go through revisions, including the addition of other writers, and are often changed substantially by directors on the scene of production or in the final editing.

Finding Audience Segments

The history section of this chapter describes the earlier genres that laid the foundation of current moviemaking formulas. These are still present, but an explosion of new film genres began in the 1950s and continues today as filmmakers experiment with new ways to attract audiences. Table 7.3 lists several more recently evolved film genres.

New genres proliferate in search of audience segments. However, the basic ones are the kinds of genre categories that you find labeling the aisles of video stores: comedy,

TABLE 7.3 Recently Evolved Film Genres

- Youth rebellion movies, such as *The Wild One* (1954)

- Spy stories, with gadgets and action, such as James Bond in *Goldfinger* (1964) or *The Bourne Supremacy* (2004)

- Romantic comedies, with varying degrees of sex, such as *Pillow Talk* (1959) or *Eternal Sunshine of the Spotless Mind* (2004)

- Science fiction, such as *Forbidden Planet* (1956) and *I Robot* (2004)

- Slasher movies, such as *Friday the 13th Part VII* (1998)

- Rock music movies, such as *A Hard Day's Night* (1964) and *Hedwig and the Angry Inch* (2001)

- "Black" movies, such as *Superfly* (1972) or *The Visit* (2001)

- Spanish-language movies, such as *El Mariachi* (1992) or *Y tu mamá también* (2001)

- Coming-of-age movies, in which teenagers discover things about themselves, such as *The Breakfast Club* (1985) or *10 Things I Hate about You* (1999)

- Antiwar movies, such as *Apocalypse Now* (1979) or *Three Kings* (1999)

- Sword and sandal movies, with swords and muscles, such as *Conan, the Barbarian* (1982) or *Troy* (2004)

- Disaster movies, such as *The Towering Inferno* (1974) or *The Perfect Storm* (2000)

drama, action, horror, science fiction, classics, family, westerns, animation, documentary, and foreign. These genres continue to dominate, as filmmakers blend classic genres to reach very broad audiences both in the United States and abroad. The blockbusters favor genres in which American big budgets and special effects can be used to best advantage: action-adventure, crime, horror, drama, and science fiction. (See "Media and Culture: Igniting Documentaries with *Fahrenheit 9/11*," page 204.)

Film content has become more diverse in part because film audiences have become more diverse. However, films are often still made to maximize the box office earnings of the initial theatrical distribution (Table 7.4). The initial *box office* is what gives a film its "buzz,"

Table 7.4 Top 10 Worldwide Movie Earners of All Time

Film	Company/Year	Director	Box office gross (in millions)	Gross domestic/ overseas
Titanic	Paramount, 1997	James Cameron	1,845	600.8/1244.2
The Lord of the Rings: The Return of the King	New Line, 2003	Peter Jackson	1,118.9	377.0/741.9
Harry Potter and the Sorcerer's Stone	Warner Brothers, 2001	Chris Columbus	976.5	317.6/658.9
The Lord of the Rings: The Two Towers	New Line, 2002	Peter Jackson	926.3	341.8/584.5
Star Wars: Episode I—The Phantom Menace	Fox, 1977	George Lucas	924.5	431.1/493.4
Shrek II	Dream Works, 2004	Andrew Adamson	918.5	441.2/477.3
Jurassic Park	Universal, 1993	Steven Spielberg	914.7	357.1/557.6
Harry Potter and the Chamber of Secrets	Warner Brothers, 2002	Chris Columbus	876.7	262.0/614.7
The Lord of the Rings: The Fellowship of the Ring	New Line, 2001	Peter Jackson	871.4	314.8/556.6
Finding Nemo	Pixar, 2003	Andrew Stanton	864.6	339.7/524.9

Igniting Documentaries with *Fahrenheit 9/11*

Walking through a grocery store in Texas in 2004, you could see something that few would have expected before this in a sale rack of eight DVDs aimed at the widest possible general public, two were documentaries, *Supersize Me* and *Fahrenheit 9/11*. Before 2004, few documentaries were ever shown in theaters in general distribution and even fewer were considered box office hits.

Several documentaries began to push open the door. Michael Moore's documentary about gun violence, *Bowling for Columbine,* came out in 2002, and has earned $22 million in theaters, plus more on video. A more traditional wildlife documentary, *Winged Migration,* came out in 2003 and made almost $12 million. *Supersize Me* (2004), a documentary critique of fast food impact on health, made $11.5 million. And Michael Moore's *Fahrenheit 9/11* (2004) made $119 million, and created both industry and political controversy.

Even before *Fahrenheit 9/11* opened on June 25, 2004, critics complained that advertising for it constituted political advertising against President Bush. The film critiques both President Bush's handling of the 9/11 terror bombings as well as the Bush family's close relationship with the Saudi royal family and other Arab world oil industry powers, including the family of Osama bin Laden, head of al Qaeda. For example, Moore charges that the Bush administration permitted members of the bin Laden family residing in the U.S. to be secretly airlifted out immediately after 9/11 even though many other Middle Easterners were being almost randomly taken into custody.

Moore has shown an increasingly sure hand at making funny but biting political documentaries that do well at both the box office and on video. *Fahrenheit 9/11* was made with Miramax, part of the Disney group, even though top officials at Disney, like Michael Eisner, had been afraid the project would be too political. In fact, Disney refused to distribute the film, although the publicity generated by that probably helped promote it to audiences. Lion's Gate Films profitably distributed the film. Disney was not alone in its caution, Warner Brothers refused to distribute a documentary on the Iraq War that David O. Russell, the director of Three Kings (1999), wanted to release with the film on DVD.

Fahrenheit 9/11 did prove politically charged and polarizing. Some film critics, like Manohla Dargis of the *Los Angeles Times* (June 27, 2004), called it propaganda, although Dargis points out that that is not necessarily a bad thing. The Motion Picture Association of America gave it an "R" rating, even though the filmmaker contested the rating, which made it harder for teenagers to view. The film won the Palme d'Or, at the Cannes Film Festival, which boosted its popularity, particularly outside the United States, where the film was often well received. Inside the U.S., observers tended to conclude that the film polarized potential audiences. Those who were inclined to be critical of President Bush, particularly over Iraq, likely had their intensity of feeling reinforced by the film. Those who supported President Bush used Moore's criticism as a reason to support the President. Moore claimed that he had heard from soldiers in Iraq that *Fahrenheit 9/11* was widely shown on bootlegged copies, even though the film was officially forbidden among military there.

Whatever the impact that *Fahrenheit 9/11* might ultimately have on U.S. politics and society, it is safe to say that it made the movie industry look at documentaries in a whole new way. *Variety* magazine, the trade paper of the industry, devoted a number of stories in 2004 to the impact of the idea of the documentary as a new form of box office hit. It will be interesting to see if other documentaries can leverage its success to get better financing and distribution from Hollywood. Aside from the four mentioned above, only twelve other documentaries had made over $3 million since 1988. So Hollywood is interested, but cautious. Stay tuned.

Sources: www.boxofficemojo.com, Variety.com

its momentum. Thus studios still tend to make movies for people who go out to the movies. This makes the typical movie theatergoer, who is younger and more tolerant of sex and violence, disproportionately influential in decisions about what kinds of movies are made. Almost half of film viewing at theaters is by people aged 12 to 29, a third of whom go to movies at least once a month, compared to a fifth of all older adults (http://www.mpaa.org).

Films are now viewed primarily on television, cable, or home video. The average amount of time spent watching films on video has increased dramatically in the last decade. Over 90 percent of American homes have a VCR, and over half have a DVD player. Over three-quarters of Americans rent videotapes or DVDs at least occasionally. By 2003, over half rented DVDs. Many also buy, for a total of $14 billion of tape/DVD sales in 2003 (MPAA, 2004).

The interests of these Americans are more diverse than those who go to movie theaters. For example, young adults, especially those with young families, are among the heaviest renters, and children's videos are the most popular genre. Some sequels to popular animated features, like *Land Before Time* (1998), which was followed by eight subsequent videos culminating with *Land Before Time IX: Journey to the Big Water* (2002), were released on video only. The average household spends over $210 per year renting and buying videocassettes or DVDs.

STOP & REVIEW

1. How do independent filmmakers differ from studios?

2. What is currently the typical distribution cycle of a film?

3. What has been the effect of home video on the movie industry?

4. What has been the impact of the foreign purchase of film studios?

MEDIA LITERACY: FILM AND YOUR SOCIETY

The film industries are embroiled in a number of policy and social issues that affect how they conduct business and the kinds of content they create.

Violence, Sex, Profanity, and Film Ratings

For years, one of the most powerful forces in the entertainment industry has been the Motion Picture Association of America (**MPAA**). The MPAA, composed of the major film studios, has been a significant player in American culture and politics.

After years of debate and what seemed to be an increase in the number of movies with profanity, explicit sex, and violence in the 1960s, the Motion Picture Association of America instituted a rating system in 1966 to give people an idea of what they might encounter in a film, to avoid outside regulation by letting people make more informed choices. After some further modifications over the years, the **MPAA rating** categories are now as follows:

G—For all ages; no sex or nudity, minimal violence

PG—Parental guidance suggested; some portions perhaps not suitable for young children, mild profanity, non-"excessive" violence, only a glimpse of nudity

PG 13—Parents strongly cautioned to give guidance to children under 13; some material may be inappropriate for young children

R—Restricted; those under 17 must be accompanied by parent or guardian; may contain very rough violence, nudity, or lovemaking

NC-17—No one under 17 admitted; formerly rated X; generally reserved for films that are openly pornographic, although some mainstream films receive this rating.

Many people have debated the appropriateness and utility of these ratings. Some argue that as a form of industry self-censorship, the ratings violate freedom of speech for filmmakers. Others argue that, as with music lyric advisories, the ratings simply excite the interest of younger viewers. Many observe that the restrictions imposed on teenagers by R and NC-17 ratings are not enforced by theaters, whose managers are aware that teens are the main moviegoers. Indeed, enforcing the rule would be hard; in multiplex movie theaters, people under 17 often buy a ticket for a PG movie, then go into an R-rated one. There is also category creep. Films that might once have been rated R now squeak through with a PG-13.

The ratings system also allowed filmmakers to continue to produce films with sexually explicit and violent content, because they can argue that audiences are alerted to avoid

MPAA (Motion Picture Association of America) is a trade organization that represents the major film studios.

MPAA ratings is a movie rating system instituted in 1968.

Ratings Breakdown Over 17,000 films have been rated since 1968, with over half (57 percent) being R-rated—while PG and PG-13 films make up another third. PG-13 and R represent over 87 percent of all films rated in 2001.

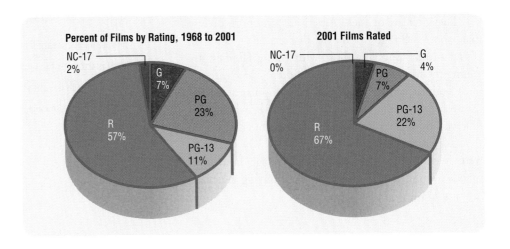

such material. Ratings have not decreased the numbers of violent or sexual films. Since 1968, 57 percent of all films have been rated R. However, many parents have expressed appreciation for the ratings, which do give them something to work with in guiding children's viewing, perhaps more inline with the TV content ratings (see Chapter 8).

Viewer Ethics: Film Piracy

Illegal use of copyrighted intellectual property has been a serious issue for the film industry. (Also see Chapter 14.) Estimates of financial losses to studios and other film copyright holders resulting from illegal copying or piracy are in the hundreds of billions of dollars, both in the United States and abroad.

Films have been relatively easy for many people to copy ever since videotape technology came into wide use in the 1980s, and the introduction and early popularity of VCRs unnerved the movie industry, which feared that illegal copying or piracy would keep people from paying for either a movie ticket or a video rental. The MPAA initially tried to suppress the diffusion of videotape technology, fearing massive piracy. When that attempt failed, the MPAA put a great deal of energy into demanding the enforcement of laws against illegal video copying of movies, both in the United States and abroad. As the law enforcement crackdown began to reduce piracy, and as more people started renting legitimate copies from a rapidly expanding set of video rental outlets, the MPAA studio producers began to realize that video was more of a gold mine than a threat.

The film industry hopes to discourage illegal film copying on videotape at the consumer level. Consumers may make a videotape copy of a film that is being broadcast or cable-cast for their own use. However, they may not sell or rent that copy to anyone else. A consumer may not copy a film from one VCR or DVD onto another. This is why all videotaped films have an FBI warning against illegal copying at the beginning of the tape. Increasingly, too, both videotapes and DVDs of films have technological safeguards against copying. The MPAA is also currently concerned about use of TiVo-style digital video recorders to copy broadcast and cable films and hopes to implement technical and/or legal means to prevent it.

Another big issue in piracy is illegal copying by people who intend to sell or rent the illegal copy. That defrauds copyright holders of rentals or sales that they might otherwise have from potential consumers who rent or buy the illegal copy instead of the legal one. Only legal copies provide royalties to the copyright holders, compensating them for the expense and work that went into the movie. Thus the film industry, via the MPAA, has pushed law enforcement officials both in the United States and abroad to enforce copyright laws by pursuing large-scale, commercially oriented pirates. Those who are illegally copying tapes on a large industrial scale are the ones principally targeted by enforcement efforts, although the MPAA is also going after file sharing of films between individual computers over the Internet.

The MPAA has had remarkable success in getting most governments to crack down on film piracy. The U.S. government has helped apply pressure on other governments to enforce the existing international copyright agreements. Nearly all governments have signed the Berne Copyright Convention, which covers video piracy.

New issues arise in protecting intellectual property that exists in digital form since it is easier to pirate digital material because a computer can be used as the main copying tool. That is fast becoming true of movies as well, now that entire films can be placed on a digital video disc that can be played by a computer or a digital TV receiver. And Internet hackers have already learned how to crack discs' copyright protection and "share" movie sites over the Internet. The movie theater is another front in the anti-piracy war. Films now include flashing colored dots that carry identifying information about the print so that the studios can track down pirates who surreptitiously tape first run movies at the cineplex. Other technologies, including night vision goggles, are used to look for hidden cameras in the audience on premier nights.

■ **SPIDEY VS. THE PIRATES**
Spiderman can defeat movie bad guys but still loses to pirates at home and abroad.

Film Preservation

Although scholars now widely recognize film as a major art form in its own right—the modern-day equivalent to great novels or paintings by the masters—the sad fact of the matter is that our film heritage is literally crumbling to dust all around us. The biggest problem is that the nitrate film stock that was in use until the early 1950s is chemically unstable. First the image fades, and then the film stock itself gets sticky and finally turns to dust—sometimes even exploding in the vaults through spontaneous combustion. Already, most of the film from the silent era has been irretrievably lost, and the film classics of the 1930s are in danger. The solution is to transfer the films to "safety stock" with a shelf life of 200–300 years, but there is a backlog of over 100 million feet of film that will take 15 years to copy at the present rate—by which time many precious film moments will be lost forever.

But recent movies have their own special problem: colors fade after as little as five years in storage. You can see this vulnerability as you watch older films on TV—all the colors seem dull or brown. There is no obvious solution here, although copying to digital storage media may eventually save the day. However, the color films must first be "separated" into red, green, and blue color masters, a very expensive process indeed.

You may have heard of *film colorization*—a process by which computers create colors for old films—but that can only be a last resort. That approach is anathema to film historians since they feel it has been used to despoil (some of them prefer the term "mutilate") black-and-white film classics such as *It's a Wonderful Life*. The fact that film colorizers are able to claim a copyright and turn a profit on the new color works only further infuriates film preservationists who decry the commercialization of masterpieces of classic film.

Movie Co-Production, Saving National Production or the New Cultural Imperialism?

It worries many countries that Hollywood films tend to dominate their viewing screens. Hollywood films can take up to 90 percent or more of screen time in many countries, perhaps even more of video and DVD rentals. So countries are increasingly anxious to find ways to get more national production. (For more on the history of why U.S. films dominate, see Chapter 16.)

One phenomenon that is blurring and perhaps also partially solving the issue is an increasing tendency for Hollywood to participate in complex co-productions with other countries—for example, *The Lord of the Rings* films. A recent UNESCO (2003) study cited them as an example of how Hollywood films dominate, but are they in fact Hollywood films? The basis for the films is J.R.R. Tolkien's novel trilogy of the same name, which the author seems to have originally intended as a mythology for Great Britain, his home country (*The Letters of J.R.R. Tolkien,* 1981). Critics such as John Garth (2003) argue that the story and some of the characters come very directly from his experience in the British Army in World War One. The director, the main screen story adapters/writers, the special effects people, and a number of actors are from New Zealand, where the films were shot, edited and the special effects created by a New Zealand company. Most of the lead actors were British or American. Financing and distribution came from Hollywood. One can argue whether the sensibility is essentially that of a Hollywood blockbuster. Fans of the books have scrutinized the films closely to see if the original story has been overwhelmed, and opinion from them is mixed. The films have helped create a burgeoning film industry in New Zealand.

Other major films like *The Last Samurai* were shot there, and other British novels like C.S. Lewis' *Narnia* books are being made into films there.

A number of other current examples abound. After the recent success of a number of Mexican films, Hollywood is actively looking in Mexico for scripts, directors and actors for co-production. The same is true with India and Brazil. Critics in those countries are wondering whether some of their best and brightest are being seduced into making films that are directly co-produced using Hollywood money and formulas, or less directly borrowing Hollywood formulas to eventually gain global distribution by Hollywood distributors, who control global distribution (see Chapter 16). However, other critics and viewers are happy that Hollywood money, distribution, and formulas are facilitating the revival of filmmaking by national directors.

One way of looking at this is as a new wave of U.S. cultural imperialism (see Chapter 16), with U.S. ways, if not literally U.S. movies, continuing to dominate the world. Or one can view it as a complex globalization where the U.S. and other countries interact with each other, even though the U.S. still tends to dominate the overall output and flow of films. This interaction is also called *glocalization,* the local adaptation of imported ways of doing things, a combination of global and local (Robertson, 1995).

Sources: The Letters of J.R.R. Tolkien, edited by Humphrey Carpenter. Boston: Houghton-Mifflin, Boston, 1981, p. 144. John Garth. *Tolkien and the Great War: The Threshold of Middle-Earth.* Boston: Houghton-Mifflin, Boston, 2003.

STOP & REVIEW

1. What movie genres are most dominant now?

2. How have film audiences changed in the last two decades?

3. How are films targeted now?

4. Why were film ratings developed? What are the pros and cons of ratings?

5. Have vertical and horizontal integration in the film industry affected content diversity?

6. What copyright and piracy problems does the film industry face?

However, digital technology should eventually end one of the most serious affronts to cinematic artistry—the practice of "panning and scanning" films for television. Movies are basically "too wide" for the television screen, so the broadcaster either has to put black bands at the top and bottom of the picture (known as letterboxing) or move the TV camera back and forth across the movie image, focusing on only one part of it at a time. The new digital High Definition Television (HDTV, see Chapter 8) systems should put an end to that, since they offer wider screens that match the movie image.

SUMMARY AND REVIEW

WHO INVENTED THE MOTION PICTURE CAMERA?

Thomas Edison, in 1888, although others competed by 1900.

FOR WHAT INNOVATIONS IN SILENT FILMS IS D. W. GRIFFITH RESPONSIBLE?

D. W. Griffith pioneered using a large screen, well-produced outdoor battle scenes, moving shots, and close-ups. His 1915 *Birth of a Nation* was the first feature film.

WHAT WAS THE STAR SYSTEM?

Rudolph Valentino, Lillian Gish, and Charlie Chaplin were such attractions that their names appeared above the name of the film on movie marquees. The studios rose on the basis of this star system, using the stars' popularity to promote their movies.

WHAT WAS THE STUDIO SYSTEM?

The studio system consisted of production companies that employed the complete set of facilities and people required to make and distribute movies. The major movie studios grew by developing a stable of actors, writers, and directors who worked for them over a period of years.

WHICH WERE THE MAIN STUDIOS?

The main Hollywood studios were United Artists, Paramount, MGM (Metro Goldwyn Mayer), Fox, Warner Brothers, Universal, Columbia, and RKO.

WHAT WERE SOME OF THE MAIN SILENT-FILM GENRES?

The silent-film genres included westerns, war movies, science fiction, romances, physical comedies, and historical costume dramas.

WHAT CHANGED WITH TALKING PICTURES?

Talking pictures created a sudden change, starting with *The Jazz Singer* in 1927. Acting became less overstated and stylized. The actors' voices and the use of sound effects, as well as music, became important. Talkies required an influx of new talent, which came mostly from vaudeville and Broadway.

WHAT WERE THE MAIN FILM GENRES OF THE 1930S AND 1940S?

In the 1930s, movies emphasized their new attraction, sound, by creating a series of extravagantly produced musicals, with dancing and singing. The other main genres of the 1930s and 1940s were comedies, crime dramas, suspense, mysteries, historical epics, film noir, and detective movies.

WHEN DID THEATRICAL FILM ATTENDANCE BEGIN TO DECLINE?

Theatrical film attendance and the revenue of studios at the box office began to decline after 1946, as television viewing made strong, steady inroads into film theater attendance.

HOW DID HOLLYWOOD AND ITS FILMS CHANGE AFTER THE ADVENT OF TELEVISION?

The film industry was closely tied to theatrical chains, and television quickly cut into their revenues. However, as small theaters closed all over America in the 1950s, the film industry began to realize that it couldn't beat television. Disney started producing programs for television in 1954, and other studios followed. All began to license films for showing on television, and many eventually produced made-for-TV movies.

WHEN DID THE STUDIO SYSTEM DECLINE?

By the 1960s, the power of the movie studios was declining. Independent producers gained more of a role in producing movies, and film, studios began to spend much of their time producing TV series.

HOW DID CABLE TELEVISION AFFECT THE FILM INDUSTRY?

Movie channels like HBO provided an important new distribution channel for films, and cable channels began to commission new made-for-cable films.

HOW DID HOME VIDEO (AND DVD) AFFECT THE FILM INDUSTRY?

Video (and DVD) has become the most profitable distribution channel for films.

WHO INVENTED THE MOVIE CAMERA AND PROJECTOR?

Thomas Edison invented most of the major components of the camera, whereas the Lumière brothers in France discovered the principle of projecting light through the transparent filmstrips.

HOW HAS FILM BEEN IMPROVED?

Film has been improved by increasing the number of frames or images per second, making the image wider, and adding color.

HOW HAVE FILM SPECIAL EFFECTS CHANGED?

Mechanical models, as in the classic 1933 *King Kong*, have been made more sophisticated and ultimately replaced by computer-generated images. Superimposition of images and the use of background mattes have also been made more sophisticated by computers.

HOW DO INDEPENDENT FILMMAKERS DIFFER FROM STUDIOS?

The major film producers are the old-time studios—Columbia, Fox, MGM, Paramount, Universal, and Warner Brothers—along with Buena Vista and Miramax (Disney), and TriStar (Sony). Each produces 15–25 movies per year. Independent film companies work alone or with majors. Individual independent filmmakers, or "indies," usually produce fewer films and for much less money than the majors—often a few million dollars.

WHAT IS CURRENTLY THE TYPICAL DISTRIBUTION CYCLE OF A FILM?

Typical distribution for a major film might now be theatrical distribution, international theatrical distribution, pay-per-view, pay cable, videocassette/DVD sales, network exhibition, basic cable networks, and finally syndication. It is increasingly common for all the domestic steps to have an international parallel. There may be some variations as when basic cable networks outbid a broadcast network for rights, for instance. Many films seen as not being worth the promotional costs for theatrical release go straight to video stores and cable.

WHAT ARE THE MAIN FILM GENRES?

The basic ones are the kinds of genre categories that you find in video stores: comedy, drama, action, horror, science fiction, classics, family, westerns, animation, and foreign.

WHY WERE FILM RATINGS DEVELOPED? WHAT ARE THEIR PROS AND CONS?

After years of debate and what seemed to be an increase in movies with explicit language, sex, and violence in the 1980s, the MPAA instituted a ratings system to give people an idea of what they might encounter in a film. Some critics argue that as a form of industry self-censorship, ratings violate freedom of speech for filmmakers. Others argue that the ratings simply draw the interest of younger viewers. The restrictions on teenage viewing of films rated R and NC-17 are often not enforced by theaters, because teens are the main moviegoers.

WHAT ARE THE ISSUES REGARDING FILM PIRACY AND COPYRIGHT?

Piracy, or illegal copying of film, increased since the use of VCRs became widespread, and has cost the industry hundreds of billions of dollars in revenue. The Motion Picture Association of America pushes for enforcement of copyright laws to curb piracy. New digital technologies, such as digital video disc (DVD) and file sharing across the Internet, threaten to increase copying again via computers.

MEDIA CONNECTION

For web links, quizzes, and key term flash cards, visit the **Student Companion Website** at http://communication.wadsworth.com/straubhaar5.

 For unlimited easy access to additional and exclusive online study, support, and research tools, log on to **1pass** at http://1pass.thomson.com using the unique access code found on your 1pass passcode card.

 The **Media Now Premium Website** offers *Career Profile* videos, *Critical View* video news clips, and *Media in Motion* concept animations. You'll also find Stop & Review tutorial questions, a sample final exam, and much more.

 InfoTrac College Edition is a fully searchable online database offering anytime, anywhere access to more than 20 years' worth of articles from nearly 5,000 diverse and reliable sources.

vMentor provides live, one-on-one online tutoring to connect you to experts who will assist you in understanding the concepts covered in your course.

In the Career Profile video for this chapter, Joe Mendoza talks about being president and owner of Falcon Lighting, a lighting and grip company in California.

Can new hit shows bring back the "lost" primetime audiences that ABC, CBS and NBC once had to themselves? We'll see how the Big Three evolved into a new big five that dominate both broadcast and cable television today. We will also see why some critics have called television content "a vast wasteland" and review efforts to improve television as well as criticism that TV is worse than ever.

A HISTORY OF TELEVISION

TV Pioneers

The television medium's transition from an inventor's daydream to a cultural phenomenon took place in a relatively short span of years. In 1922, 14-year-old Philo Farnsworth rode a tractor over an Idaho hay field and had the idea for an electronic "image dissector" that could cut an image into a series of lines like the rows of his field (Horvitz, 2002). Using primitive mechanical sets, Charles Jenkins of the United States and John Logie Baird of Great Britain made the first experimental transmissions in 1925. The British Broadcasting Corporation had the first electronic television service in 1936. Regular broadcasts for electronic receivers in the United States started in 1939 (Abramson, 1987; Udelson, 1984).

The technical standards for television that are still in effect today (see page 225) were set by a group of TV manufacturers, the National Television Systems Committee (NTSC), in 1941 (the FCC also adopted commercial radio's economic model that year). However, the United States' entry into World War II in December put television on hold.

1925	First television transmission	**1975**	HBO goes on satellite
1948–1952	TV freeze, cable TV is born	**1976**	WTBS, first basic cable service
1953	Color TV introduced	**1987**	Fox television network debuts
1961	Newton Minow calls TV a "vast wasteland"	**1996**	Telecommunications Act triggers merger wave
1967	Public Broadcasting Act	**1998**	Broadcast networks lose dominance
1972	FCC opens cities to cable	**2007–2009**	Planned transition to digital TV

After the war ended in 1945, lingering doubts about television's viability were quickly erased. TV cameras improved, and AT&T's new **coaxial cable** and **microwave** technologies made networks technically possible.

The Freeze 1948–1952

TV grew so fast that it soon became evident that there weren't enough channels to serve all major cities. So, the FCC put a "temporary" freeze on new stations in 1948 while it came up with a new allocation plan, but the thorny issue of color television standards prolonged the freeze for four years. The 108 stations approved before the freeze went on the air, as the number of TV sets in use skyrocketed until they were in about a third of all homes (Sterling & Kittross, 1990). Many smaller cities were left out in the cold by the freeze, though, and that spawned cable television (see Chapter 12).

The 1952 FCC rules, the Sixth Report and Order, finalized the frequencies for the **VHF** (very high frequency) television band (channels 2–13), opened the new **UHF** (ultra-high frequency) band (channels 14–83, later reduced to 14–69), and set aside channels for educational broadcasting. Only VHF stations prospered, though, because they had more power than UHF and because the FCC did not require UHF tuners in all new TV sets until 1964. The VHF allocations effectively limited the number of national television networks to three because most cities had only three VHF channels available.

The development of network television also owes much to the foresight of two radio pioneers (see Chapter 6), David Sarnoff at NBC and William Paley at CBS. They were willing to invest in the fledgling medium and to put the talent and advertisers developed by their radio networks at the disposal of early television producers. In the early years, ABC was led by Leonard Goldenson, a former movie executive who was the first to bring the work of Hollywood production companies to the small screen.

The Golden Age

Television back then was much different from today. The pictures were in black and white (color television, introduced in 1953, was slow to catch on), and screens were small. Early TV cameras gave live shows a dull, gray look. Most of the shows *were* live, or else shot on film, because videotape didn't appear until 1956. Most programs originated in New York, and stations beyond the reach of the coaxial cables that fanned out from Manhattan showed poor-quality kinescopes that were filmed from the television

Coaxial cable is the high-capacity wire used for cable television transmission.

Microwave transmits information between relay towers on beams of high-frequency radio waves.

VHF is the very high frequency television band, channels 2 to 13.

UHF stands for ultra-high frequency, channels 14 to 69.

screen and shipped to **affiliates** for rebroadcast. Viewers nudged finicky antennas to tweak their reception. Changing channels meant leaving your seat; remote controls didn't appear until 1955.

Although the quality of the picture was inferior to today's, the quality of some of the programming was perhaps superior. The late 1940s and early 1950s are called television's "Golden Age," largely a tribute to live drama anthologies that were popular then. Unlike today's predictable episodic dramas, the anthologies had a different story line and cast each week and often dealt with disturbing subject matter. Rod Serling's *Twilight Zone* series is the best example of the Golden Age style that can be found while channel surfing today.

News and public affairs programs were also hallmarks of the Golden Age. Nightly network news broadcasts began in 1948. The early newscasts were crude by today's standards, but early public affairs programs had an immediate impact on public debate. *Meet the Press,* which first went on the air in 1947, is the longest-running TV program of all. In one of television's finest moments, CBS news correspondent Edward R. Murrow exposed the anticommunist "crusade" of the early 1950s as a campaign of innuendo and half-truths.

Serling, Murrow, and the other Golden Age pioneers fought a losing battle to make television artful and informative. Instead, commercialism and Hollywood production values became the hallmarks of network television as NBC, CBS, and ABC came to rule the airwaves. NBC originated the first network television broadcast in 1946 and also the first network prime-time lineup two years later. CBS and NBC succeeded by importing popular programs from their radio networks. Network television's first big star was comedian Milton Berle. People bought televisions—and stopped going to movie theaters on the night he was on—just so they could see him. Still, network television wasn't profitable at first, but huge profits from **owned-and-operated stations (O&Os)** in major cities sustained the Big Three. By 1956, 95 percent of all stations carried Big Three programs. In 1952, television network advertising revenues surpassed radio's; by 1955 TV topped magazines and newspapers as well. Meanwhile, movie attendance dropped to half of its peak in 1946. After a weak fourth network, Dumont, died in 1955, the Big Three reigned supreme across the media landscape (Sterling & Kittross, 1990).

Television's current commercial model also emerged in those years. In another carry-over from radio, early shows had a single advertiser, the shows were often named after their sponsors, and advertisers played an active role in developing their content. The commercial pitches were not neatly packaged into commercial breaks. The next "act" in a variety show might be a chorus dressed like Texaco service station attendants, singing the company's jingle. Or, "plugs" might be woven into the scripted dialog. Sylvester "Pat" Weaver, president of NBC Television, introduced longer programs, including periodic specials he called "spectaculars," and the *Today* and *Tonight* shows. The longer shows were too expensive for any one sponsor, so Weaver introduced *participating sponsorship,* in which multiple sponsors shared a show, and *spot advertising,* in which the sponsors purchased minute-long "spots." That helped the networks seize control over programming from the advertisers while allowing them to increase their advertising rates.

© The Kobal Collection/CBS-TV

■ **LUUUUUUUCY!**
Comedienne Lucille Ball was a popular star in TV's Golden Age and a pioneering female executive behind the scenes.

Affiliates contract with networks to distribute their programming.

Owned-and-operated stations (O&Os) are stations owned and operated by networks.

■ **FIGURE 8.1**

FIGURE 8.1

How Ratings Are Computed

Ratings are computed by dividing the number of homes watching a show by the total number of TV households. Shares are computed by dividing by the number of households using TV at a particular time.

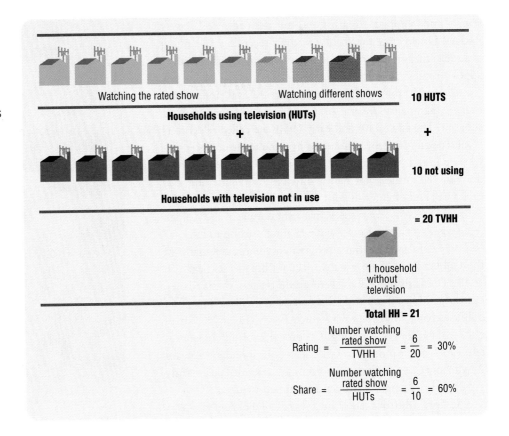

Watching the rated show   Watching different shows   **10 HUTS**

Households using television (HUTs)

+   +

10 not using

Households with television not in use

= 20 TVHH

1 household without television

Total HH = 21

$$\text{Rating} = \frac{\text{Number watching rated show}}{\text{TVHH}} = \frac{6}{20} = 30\%$$

$$\text{Share} = \frac{\text{Number watching rated show}}{\text{HUTs}} = \frac{6}{10} = 60\%$$

The Golden Age Gets Canceled

The Golden Age died as audiences shifted and **ratings** ruled (Figure 8.1). By 1956 TVs were in two-thirds of American homes and the broader audience didn't appreciate the highbrow drama anthologies as much as the well-educated, urban, East Coast early adopters had. Sponsors wished for more upbeat lead-ins to their snappy commercial jingles. Ratings services migrated from radio early on (see "Media and Culture: Going by the Numbers," page 217) and the introduction of overnight ratings in 1961 added urgency to competition for audiences. The multiple sponsorship model focused attention on "buying" audiences by the thousand (the **cost per thousand**), and programs that appealed to uncommon tastes had prohibitively high costs on that basis.

Ratings are one half of the formula for economic success; low production costs are the other half. Situation comedies, or sitcoms, cost less than drama or variety shows, and the 1951 hit *I Love Lucy* proved their appeal. Cheaper still were quiz shows that eliminated scripts and professional actors—and those shot to the top of the ratings in the mid-1950s. Television executives also turned to Hollywood for more efficient productions. ABC ordered the first series from a film studio, *Disneyland,* in 1954. Western movies were popular then and ABC recycled its sets and unemployed movie actors to produce shows like *Maverick* and *The Rifleman* on the cheap. By 1957 nearly all entertainment production had moved west to major studios or independent production companies, leaving only network news and soap operas behind in New York.

Into and Out of the Wasteland

As television became more important, criticism of the medium also grew. In 1958 it came to light that greedy sponsors had rigged popular TV quiz shows to improve their ratings,

Ratings measure the proportion of television households that watch a specific show.

Cost per thousand is how much a commercial costs in relation to the number of viewers that see it, in thousands.

Going by the Numbers

With so much of our popular culture centered around television, the questions of why some shows are cancelled while others live and what shows are made in the first place are important ones. To answer those questions, we need to understand television ratings, since that is how the success of commercial TV and cable programs is judged.

Since 1950, A. C. Nielsen Company has dominated television audience measurement with its audimeter technology that electronically records when the television set is on and which channel it is tuned to. By installing the audimeters in the television sets of a representative national sample of homes and matching the tuning information to logs of local station programming, it was possible to calculate the number of homes in the sample whose sets were tuned into a particular program at a particular time. From that, the percentage of television homes that watched, say, *I Love Lucy,* during a particular quarter hour could be calculated and that percentage, called a rating, could be compared with other shows.

The households that participate in ratings studies are randomly selected from master lists of all the homes in the United States (or, in some studies, by calling randomly selected phone numbers) so that every home has an equal chance of being included. That makes the sample statistically representative of the population from which it is drawn. These are the same basic techniques employed in the public opinion polls that are used to predict election outcomes.

Figure 8.1 (page 216) shows how television ratings are calculated. A television household is any home with a (working) television set. There are about 120 million of those in the United States. A HUT is a Household Using Television; about 60 percent of all TV households are usually HUTs during prime time. A rating is the percentage of all television households tuned in to a particular program. Each rating point represents about 1,200,000 households. A share is the percentage of HUTs watching a program: thus, it is based on only the homes actually watching television at a particular time.

Advertisers perform an additional computation to arrive at the cost per thousand (or CPM, as it is known). They multiply the rating by the number of households each rating point represents and divide that into the cost of buying a commercial spot in the corresponding program. So, if *ER* has a 20 rating, that translates into 20 million television households, or 20,000 lots of 1000 homes each. If a 30-second spot on *ER* costs $400,000, we divide that by 20,000 and arrive at a CPM of $20. Generally, advertisers select the programs that have the lowest CPM.

After a series of mergers and acquisitions, the A. C. Nielsen Company has morphed into Nielsen Media Research and is owned by a Dutch company, VNU. The old-style audimeters that recorded only household-level viewing have given way to People Meters that record individual viewing for national rating reports, called the National Television Index (NTI). The 5000 People Meter families are prompted by a flashing red light to push buttons on a box to indicate who is in the room at that moment. The old-style audimeters are still in use in 55 metered markets where they provide overnight ratings based on samples of 400–500 households per market.

To compile local TV ratings and audience demographics in each of the 210 local television markets, Nielsen mails viewing diaries to random samples of homes contacted by phone. Family members record all the programs they watch during a particular week in the diaries. The local surveys are conducted during the four annual sweeps months of November, February, May, and July, and their results are used to set local TV advertising rates. You may have noticed that the programs are a little better and the local news stories are a little more sensational during those months as broadcasters compete for attention in the Nielsen homes.

The accuracy of ratings is a growing concern. Minorities are seriously underrepresented in rating studies. Only about a third of all the homes contacted participate in diary studies and many "fudge" their answers by writing in programs they would like Nielsen to think they watch, but don't actually tune in. Viewers in People Meter homes, especially young children, tire of pushing buttons and are undercounted. The ratings of shows starring minority characters also do poorly in people meter homes. Inaccurate ratings can disenfranchise important groups of viewers who are undercounted and see their favorite shows disappear. In the bigger picture, ratings disenfranchise anyone whose political views or tastes in entertainment differ from the mainstream. Some critics think that homogenizes both public discourse and popular culture, reducing both to the "lowest common denominator;" that is, the uninvolved and uniformed. This is a growing concern as Nielsen rolls out local people meters in major markets to replace the local market paper diaries—and to eventually replace "sweeps" with year-round ratings.

So, the search is on for a "passive" meter that will automatically record individual viewers such as by sensing their body heat or by "recognizing" their faces with digital pattern recognition. Advanced systems might tell advertisers when viewers are paying attention to the TV set, when they are smiling at the program, or when their eyes are tracking the image of their product. Personal meters might be carried by individuals and automatically record viewing outside the home.

ROLE MODEL?
Were the violent protests of the 1960s inspired by the violent TV shows of the 1950s?

© Everett Collection

causing a national scandal. The Big Three commanded 90 percent of the prime-time audience with a predictable mix of variety shows, sitcoms, and shoot-'em-ups that varied little from year to year or from network to network. In 1961 FCC Chairman Newton Minow called American television a "vast wasteland" of mediocre, uninformative programs.

Television news continued to have its defining moments throughout the 1960s: The Kennedy-Nixon debates, Kennedy's funeral, Vietnam War coverage, the moon landing. But still the question of how to improve television entertainment programming loomed. Perhaps the Big Three's *oligopoly* (see Chapter 2) had to be broken, beginning with their stranglehold on television production.

The networks dominated their relationships with movie studios and independent producers, successfully demanding large shares of the off-network **syndication** revenues that came from selling reruns to local stations. The FCC imposed the Financial Interest in Syndication Rules (known as *Fin-Syn* for short) in 1970 to push the networks out of the syndication business. The FCC's 1970 Prime Time Access Rule closed the 7 to 8 P.M. time slot to network programming. And, in 1975, the Justice Department put limits on the number of hours of entertainment programming the networks could make in-house.

These moves shook up the television industry. Studios profited from syndication and were even willing to take a loss on shows during their first runs in expectation of syndication profits later. The new rules also benefited producers of first-run syndication who filled the 7 to 8 P.M. time slot with cheap-to-produce shows like *Wheel of Fortune*. Independent UHF stations found they could pull audiences away from the Big Three with first-run syndication. By the mid-1970s most homes finally had UHF tuners and many UHFs turned into successful independent stations that competed against network affiliates with a mix of reruns, live sports, and old movies.

Another approach to breaking the Big Three's oligopoly was to provide a noncommercial alternative. The FCC's 6th Report and Order allocated 242 channels nationwide for noncommercial educational TV. The first such station, KUHT in Houston, signed on in 1953. But no mechanism for public funding was provided. Early public broadcasters had to rely on funds provided by educational institutions, grants from private foundations, and the proceeds of on-air auctions (beginning at KQED in San Francisco in 1955). The Public Broadcasting Act of 1967 established the Corporation for Public Broadcasting (CPB) to finance programming from federal tax funds, followed in 1969 by the Public Broadcasting Service (PBS), to distribute programs to public stations. Major PBS stations, such as WGBH in Boston, emerged as program producers. PBS added some new viewing choices, notably *Sesame Street* in 1969, and British imports, including *Upstairs, Downstairs* (PBS, 2004).

The Rise of Cable

Thanks to public broadcasting and local independent stations, by the early 1970s many viewers enjoyed a half dozen choices. However, further expansions would push the boundaries of the available broadcast channel allocations and also the capacity of local

---

Syndication is rental or licensing of media products.

advertising markets to support additional "free" channels. Thus, new distribution technologies and economic models might be required.

Cable television got its start in small cities in Oregon and Pennsylvania that did not have TV stations prior to the freeze on new stations in 1948 (see Chapter 12). After the freeze ended in 1952, cable television continued to spread throughout small towns that were too remote to pick up television signals off the air. Enterprising local businesses would perch antenna masts atop tall buildings or nearby mountains to pull in signals from cities just over the horizon, then redistribute them via *coaxial cable* to their customers in each town. To reach truly remote communities in the West and Midwest, cable operators built networks of *microwave* antennas that picked up broadcasts from urban TV stations and relayed their signals to smaller communities. However, these **distant signals** television stations imported from faraway cities threatened local independent UHF stations since they often carried the same types of programs. To protect UHFs, the FCC ruled that cable systems **must carry** nearby broadcast signals and banned cable from the 100 largest major markets in 1966.

Without original programming, however, cable TV did not appeal to enough suburbanites and city dwellers to justify the expense of building cable systems in their neighborhoods anyway. And, without access to large urban audiences, there was no way to justify the development of original programming for cable. One solution to this programming quandary was to offer movies and live sporting events on special channels that required an additional monthly fee, a fee that was split between the cable operator and the program providers—that model became known as **pay TV.**

The FCC reversed its ban on urban cable systems in 1972 and mandated that each new cable TV system have at least 20 channels. That decision, along with the development of satellite distribution, opened the way for the hundreds of channels we enjoy today. It provided the channel space for Home Box Office (HBO) to create the first national *pay TV network.* HBO made a splash in 1975 by transmitting the Ali-Frazier boxing match, the first pay program distributed by satellite to home viewers. It followed with a steady stream of recent Hollywood films.

Ted Turner pioneered advertising-supported cable channels by retransmitting a local independent station he owned in Atlanta via satellite in 1976. It evolved into the WTBS **superstation.** Turner profited by selling advertising at premium rates to advertisers who wanted to reach a national audience. Since the superstation derived considerable revenue from its advertising, Turner could charge cable operators much less than HBO could, literally pennies per month instead of dollars per month. Cable operators included the superstation as part of the basic monthly charge for service, a practice that popularized the term basic cable. WGN from Chicago and WOR (later WWOR) from New York also appeared via satellite in short order.

Networks that were available only on cable also began to appear. The first were the Christian Broadcasting Network (CBN, later known as The Family Channel), the Cable Satellite Public Affairs Network (C-SPAN, the industry sponsored public service information channel), and the Entertainment and Sports Network (ESPN). By 1982 there were three dozen satellite networks available on cable. In 1980 Turner launched a second

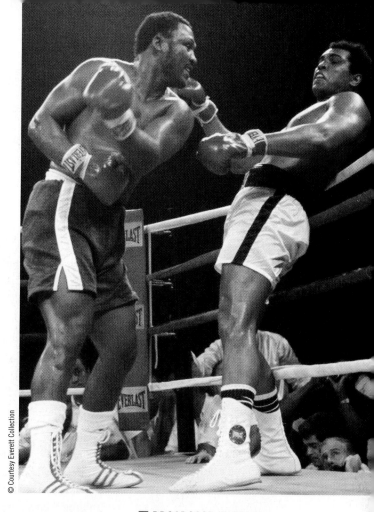

© Courtesy Everett Collection

■ **BROADCAST KNOCKOUT**
The Ali-Frazier fight was the first national pay TV event from HBO.

Cable television transmits television programs via coaxial cable or fiber.

Distant signals are cable channels imported from major television markets.

Must carry is the policy that requires cable companies to carry local broadcast signals.

Pay TV charges cable customers an extra monthly fee to receive a specific channel.

A **superstation** is a distant signal that is distributed nationally via satellite.

■ TOP RATED

The *Roots* miniseries was one of the top-rated TV shows of all time and pioneered a new genre.

network, the Cable News Network (CNN), which became a staple of cable channel lineups everywhere. These channels amplified the appeal of basic cable service, giving rise to a new concept in TV programming—**narrowcasting,** or devoting an entire channel to one particular genre (for example, popular music, MTV) or audience segment (for example, African-Americans, BET). This strategy would gradually erode the mass audience for broadcast network television in years to come.

With new channels and the lure of pay cable revenues, large cable companies that owned multiple cable systems, **multiple system operators (MSOs)** (see Chapter 12), contended for cable franchise rights in the top 100 cities. In 1984 the FCC further fed the cable boom by removing rate regulation. The new urban cable systems, most with 50 or more channels, opened new slots for yet more cable networks, and rate deregulation meant that cable operators could readily generate the money to pay for them.

The *1984 Cable Act* also forced cable operators to accept a little competition of their own, to share programming channels with new wireless technologies. Since cable didn't appear in some large cities until well into the 1980s the FCC authorized over-the-air subscription television. Back then, anyone who could afford a six-foot backyard **television receive-only (TVRO)** dish could receive all those cable channels for free—at least until cable networks started scrambling their transmissions and charging the dish owners. An early attempt at a **direct broadcast satellite (DBS)** service, United Satellite, failed in 1985 when many cable networks refused to license their programming. It would be another 10 years before DBS became viable.

Another new technology of the 1970s that was expected to compete with cable actually benefited it. The first home videocassette recorders, or VCRs, appeared in 1975, and video stores spread like wildfire in the 1980s. It was feared that home video would lure people away from pay TV channels, but many viewers just added rented videos to their existing entertainment options. Some even increased their television viewing by *time-shifting* programs such as daytime soap operas, and by building libraries of movies taped from pay TV.

Narrowcasting targets media to specific segments of the audience.

Multiple system operators (MSOs) are cable companies that operate systems in two or more communities.

Television receive-only (TVRO) was a backyard satellite system that let individual homes receive the same channels intended for cable systems.

Direct broadcast satellites (DBS) transmit programs via satellite directly to home antennas.

The Big Three in Decline

With business prospects dimming, the Big Three all changed owners in the mid-1980s. The new owners slashed staff to improve profitability, and many of the cuts fell on the networks' news operations (Auletta, 1991).

Ironically, just as the Big Three declined, new broadcast competitors emerged. Cable TV extended the audience coverage and economic viability of UHF stations, and the number of TV stations one corporation could own increased from 7 to 12 in 1985. Profits from the revitalized UHF O&Os bankrolled programming. Film studios were in a good position to enter the network business with their in-house production units, and the profits accumulated from syndication, flowing from the *Fin-Syn* rules. In 1987 Australian media magnate Rupert Murdoch started the Fox television network, using his Twentieth Century Fox film studios as a base. The Fin-Syn rules were lifted in 1993 so

Table 8.1 The Top 10 TV Shows of All Time (Excluding sports)

Rank	Program	Network	Rating	Share	Date
1	*M*A*S*H* Special (Last Episode)	CBS	60.2	77	2-28-83
2	*Dallas* (Who Shot J.R.?)	CBS	53.3	76	11-21-80
3	*Roots* Part VIII	ABC	51.1	71	1-30-77
4	*Gone with the Wind*—Part 1	NBC	47.7	65	11-7-76
5	*Gone with the Wind*—Part 2	NBC	47.4	64	11-8-76
6	Bob Hope Christmas Show	NBC	46.6	64	1-15-70
7	*The Day After* (Sun. Night Movie)	ABC	46.0	62	11-20-83
8	*Roots* Part VI	ABC	45.9	66	1-28-77
9	*The Fugitive* (Last Episode)	ABC	45.9	72	8-29-67
10	*Roots* Part V	ABC	45.7	71	1-27-77

Source: Nielsen Media Research-NTI, Jan. '61–June 17, 2001. Available at http://www.tvb.org/rcentral/mediatrendstrack/tvbasics/basics12.html

that networks were once again allowed to produce and syndicate their own entertainment programs. That encouraged more new networks. Warner started The WB network; Viacom built UPN around stations it owned. For Spanish-speaking viewers there is Univision, founded in 1992. They were joined in 1998 by PAX TV.

Now the regulators reined in the Big Three's biggest competitor. The 1992 Cable Act forced cable programmers to offer their services on an equitable basis to competing distribution systems. The Act changed the *must-carry rules* so that broadcasters could demand compensation from cable.

The former Big Three struggled as their tried-and-true programming formulas became unprofitable. The producers of long-running series like *ER* and sports leagues demanded ever-higher fees, to the point that costs could no longer be recouped from advertising. And still ratings declined. The top rated shows of all time have not seen a new addition since the early 80s (see Table 8.1). In 1998, for the first time, the Big Three attracted less than half of the prime-time viewing audience (Figure 8.2). Only profits from the networks' O&Os kept them afloat.

Instead of innovating with new programming, the networks turned the clock back to the 1950s. As they had in the past, they tried to offset declining ratings with lower production costs. So-called "reality" programs such as *Cops* and *America's Funniest Home Videos* were cheap to produce because they relied on "found" material, such as home videos and police footage. Other reality shows like *Survivor* and prime-time quiz shows economized by featuring unpaid amateurs competing for prizes. *Survivor* and *Big Brother* also represented a new approach, licensing a format that

© NBC/Courtesy Everett Collection

■ WHAT'S NEW?
Network TV continues to recycle old ideas and familiar faces, as in the spin-off series, *Joey*.

Big 3 in Decline Audience viewing shares for the Big Three are half what they were in the mid 1980s.

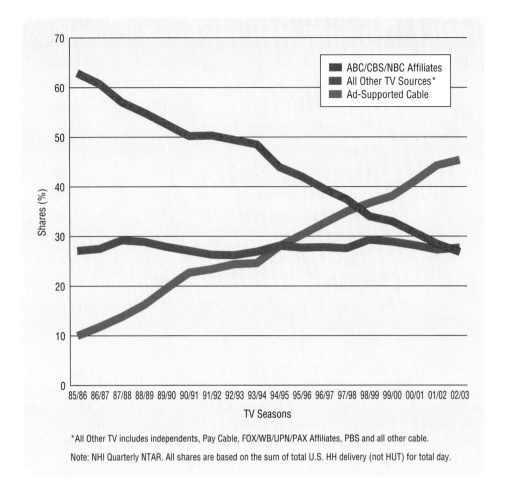

*All Other TV includes independents, Pay Cable, FOX/WB/UPN/PAX Affiliates, PBS and all other cable.

Note: NHI Quarterly NTAR. All shares are based on the sum of total U.S. HH delivery (not HUT) for total day.

had proven successful in other countries. True innovation was stifled by a complex pattern of relationships among producers, networks, and the media conglomerates who owned them. Increasingly, new series were approved for development more on the basis of their corporate parentage than for their potential to please viewers. Broadcast networks also had to contend with innovative offerings on cable, such as *The Sopranos* on HBO. For the first time, cable programs attracted audiences on the same scale as the broadcast networks.

Television in the Information Age: The Big Five

Efforts to bring television into the Information Age have altered television industry ownership patterns. The Telecommunications Act of 1996 relaxed media ownership rules and triggered a merger binge that married broadcast to cable television. Disney, Viacom, News Corp, Time Warner, and NBC Universal are the new "Big Five" that now dominate television. In 2003, Congress moved to liberalize TV ownership restrictions further, paving the way for a new round of acquisitions and mergers.

A worldwide race to make television digital poses new challenges to the television industry. In 1998 the first of a new generation of digital **high-definition television (HDTV)** stations went on the air, but digital broadcasting was a slow starter as stations, cable systems, producers, and consumers balked at the cost of the transition. The FCC jump-started the transition by mandating that all new large-screen TVs (34 inches or larger) sold after July 2004 (followed by smaller sets in 2007) must have

High-definition television (HDTV) is digital television that provides a wider and clearer picture.

■ **IDOLATRY**
American Idol rides the crest of the reality TV craze.

digital receivers built into them and by getting cable operators to agree to carry up to five HDTV channels.

On other fronts, though, digital television advanced rapidly. A new generation of Direct Broadcast Satellite (DBS) systems was launched in 1995. DirecTV and the Dish Network delivered hundreds of channels of crisp digital pictures over dishes about the size of a large pizza. Cable operators responded with their own digital offerings that spawned a new wave of specialized programming services and brought high-speed Internet connections to the home. Meanwhile, consumers came to appreciate the quality of digital TV through the rapid spread of DVD players.

By the mid 2000s, it was clear that although the broadcast networks might long survive, cable was getting the upper hand. Long-running broadcast hits like *Frasier* left the air with no heirs apparent while popular cable series like *The Sopranos* drew ever-bigger audiences. Reality TV supplanted scripted dramas and comedies that had long been network mainstays. The uproar over an "accidental" exposure of a breast during a Super Bowl halftime show forced the networks into a defensive posture in their competition with sexy cable programs for young audiences. Popular interactive TV forms like *American Idol* challenged assumptions about what the television viewing experience should be. Another form of interactive video, the *digital video recorder* (*DVR*), posed the threat of massive "commercial zapping" and the end of commercial broadcast television as we know it. Still, broadcast networks showed signs of life in the 2004–2005 season with new scripted shows like *Lost* and *Desperate Housewives*. Meanwhile, local TV stations looked forward to a digital renaissance of their own by offering multiple channels of local news and sports as well as network HDTV programs.

TECHNOLOGY: INSIDE YOUR TV

From a Single Point of Light

Whether they are originated by broadcast or cable, analog or digital, all television pictures are formed by a single point of light that races back and forth and up and down the television screen so fast that it fools the eye into seeing a full moving image. TV uses the same optical illusion exploited by motion pictures (see Chapter 7), persistence of vision. In 1884 Paul Nipkow of Germany had the idea of **scanning** an image by breaking it up into a series of light spots that moved in a linear progression across the field of vision. Mechanical sets designed by Jenkins and Baird in the 1920s used Nipkow's principle. The pictures were formed by shining a light through perforations in a rapidly spinning disk. The result was a crude, flickering picture in which only the outlines of moving images could be seen.

Don't try this at home! But, if you were to disable the circuits that steer the point of light across the screen you could unmask the "magic" of television: The entire television picture would collapse into a single point of light that would flicker in the transition from darkly lit scenes to bright ones (the changes from pixel to pixel would be invisible, owing to the persistence of vision). The light is produced by a beam of electrical charges that are "shot" from an electron gun at the rear of the picture tube. When they hit the inner surface of the tube, they cause the coating of the tube to give off a glow. The more electrons there are hitting the surface at a given instant, the brighter the glow is. Vladimir Zworykin invented the all-electronic receiver tube that first used this technique.

Recalling our experiments with electromagnets in Chapters 5 and 6, we know that a moving electric charge and magnetic fields interact with one another. Electromagnets circling the neck of the picture tube direct the beam across the screen in successive rows

Scanning means making TV pictures out of a series of separate picture lines.

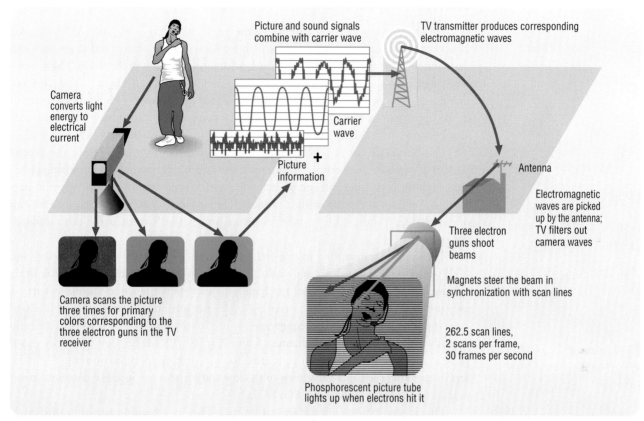

Camera converts light energy to electrical current

Picture and sound signals combine with carrier wave

TV transmitter produces corresponding electromagnetic waves

Carrier wave

Picture information

+

Camera scans the picture three times for primary colors corresponding to the three electron guns in the TV receiver

Antenna

Electromagnetic waves are picked up by the antenna; TV filters out camera waves

Three electron guns shoot beams

Magnets steer the beam in synchronization with scan lines

262.5 scan lines, 2 scans per frame, 30 frames per second

Phosphorescent picture tube lights up when electrons hit it

to create each full-screen picture from top to bottom, one *pixel,* or picture element, at a time. That feat is duplicated 30 times a second. Each frame of the picture is made up of 525 lines, but that is divided up into two sets (or fields) of 262 and a half lines, and the two halves of the picture are combined, or *interlaced,* to complete the picture.

These standards were established in 1941 by the National Television Systems Committee (NTSC), which also set the ratio of the width of the picture to its height (the *aspect ratio*) at 4 to 3. The only significant modification over the years was the introduction of color television in 1953. The color picture tubes fired three electron guns simultaneously—one each for red, green, and blue—at corresponding color dots on the screen. The eye blends these colors to make various hues (Benson & Whitaker, 1990). French and German engineers made improvements in color broadcasting in the 1960s and incorporated them in SECAM and PAL standards that are incompatible with America's NTSC.

To this point, we have been describing conventional cathode ray tube (CRT) receivers, but CRT receivers with screens larger than 34 inches get quite heavy and bulky owing to the sheer size of their glass picture tubes. There are several new display technologies to choose from when in the market for a digital HDTV receiver. *Liquid crystal display (LCD)* screens have three tiny, light solid state devices at each pixel that control the flow of light through miniature red, green, and blue filters. LCDs are available both in flat screens and rear projection systems. Flat screen *plasma displays* have three miniature fluorescent lights located at each pixel that are activated by grids of invisible wires running across the screen. For the home theater crowd, *Digital Light Processing* (*DLP,* see Chapter 7) technology is making its way into consumer video projection systems. Another projection system option is *LCOS (liquid crystal on silicon).* Both promise better resolution, brighter colors, and less bulky consoles than conventional projection systems.

■ **FIGURE 8.3**
Broadcasting a Television Signal
A broadcast television signal goes from the camera to the transmitter, through the air to the antenna, to the TV set.

Television Transmission

What fires the electron guns? The television broadcast signal works like AM radio (see Chapter 6), except that variations in the high-frequency carrier correspond to the light and dark values of the picture instead of to the loud and soft portions of the audio. These *luminance* signals, as they are called, are recovered from the carrier inside the TV set and fed into the electron gun (Figure 8.3). TV sound is added by a separate FM radio signal carried in the upper part of the television channel. The color, or *chrominance,* information rides along on a separate carrier that is superimposed on the black-and-white picture signal.

The home TV set is synchronized with the transmitter to reproduce the precise pattern of pixels in their proper locations on the screen. Horizontal synchronizing pulses are sent at the beginning and end of each line. Vertical synch pulses indicate when to start a new set of lines at the top of the screen. While the electron gun moves back to the top of the picture, it shuts off for a brief instant, a time period known as the *vertical blanking interval (VBI).*

Television is transmitted in two frequency bands, VHF (very high frequency) and UHF (ultra-high frequency), and each channel occupies a total bandwidth of 6 MHz (Figure 8.4). (The M is a symbol for 1 million, and Hz is the abbreviation for hertz, a measure of the frequency of the signal, in cycles per second.) There are 12 VHF channels, channels 2 to 13, in the frequencies 54–72, 76–88, and 174–216 MHz. FM radio is sandwiched in between TV channels 6 and 7 at 88–108 MHz. (You can verify this if there is a channel 6 on the air in your area. You can pick up its audio on some FM radio sets by cranking the tuner way down to the low end.) There are 56 UHF channels, channels 14 to 69, between 470 and 806 MHz.

That is how local broadcasts are transmitted. The first television networks used coaxial cable and microwave technology (see Chapter 12). In the 1970s, satellite became the standard means of linking both cable and broadcast networks to their affiliates and for transmitting feeds of local news and sporting events back to the networks' head ends. Now fiber-optic networks are used, too.

Making Pictures

Now, back to the studio. The camera tube was the center of a patent dispute between Philo Farnsworth and television's co-inventor Vladimir Zworykin. The best features of both their inventions were combined in the image orthicon picture tube ("immy" for short, the origin of the "Emmy" designation for awards in television excellence, incidentally) in 1946, and that made TV pictures acceptable for wide public consumption.

Most TV cameras nowadays use solid state components called charged coupled devices (CCDs) to make pictures, instead of glass tubes. In CCD cameras, each pixel is represented by a miniature solid state component that converts light to electricity. The electrical voltages associated with individual pixels are transmitted one at a time according to the NTSC scanning pattern. Color cameras separate the incoming light from the scene into three separate color components, each with its own CCD.

Video Recording

British television inventor John Logie Baird made crude video recordings on 78 rpm records in 1928, but practical video recording lay 30 years in the future. Magnetic audiotape was introduced in the late 1940s, but television contained so much more information than audio that mountains of tape would have to move across the recording head at impossible speeds. The solution was to use multiple recording heads. In 1956, videotape

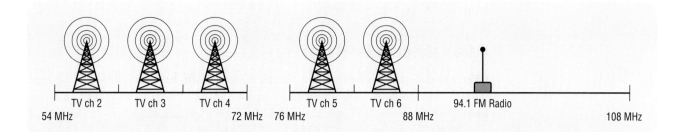

TV ch 2   TV ch 3   TV ch 4   TV ch 5   TV ch 6   94.1 FM Radio

54 MHz   72 MHz   76 MHz   88 MHz   108 MHz

■ FIGURE 8.4

TV Spectrum TV channels are arranged so that each is 6 MHz wide. FM radio is tucked in between TV channels 6 and 7.

made its debut on the *Jonathan Winters Show.* Videotape made lucrative reruns of live shows possible, was more efficient to edit than film, and was indistinguishable from live TV, so it soon became the medium of choice.

Early video recorders required huge reels of two-inch tape. The key development that paved the way for the home Videocassette recorder (VCR) was *helical scanning.* It stores video tracks on a slant (imagine cutting up tape into short segments and pasting them together slantwise), so the length of the tape could shrink to manageable proportions. Today's Video Home System (VHS) players rely on this technique (Benson & Whitaker, 1990).

Digital video disc (DVD) players store compressed digitized video on higher-capacity versions of the familiar audio compact disc (see Chapter 5). New generations of DVDs are now on the horizon. DVD+ R DL discs will allow you to record (that's the +R part) today's videos on one side of a double-layered (that's the DL part) DVD, nearly doubling (to 8.5 gigabytes) the amount of storage. HDTV recording will require improved laser and video compression technologies (see Chapter 12) to put movie-length high-definition features on a single disc, up to 50 gigabytes in all. There are two competing standards, Blu-ray (backed by Sony) and HD DVD (backed by Toshiba), which could lead to a costly "format war" that could leave unlucky consumers with useless machines. Another drawback is that the new HDTV sets have antipiracy technology built into them that may make it impossible to record programs off the air without paying a fee.

Digital video recorder or DVR, systems (also known as personal video recorders or PVRs) cross a VCR with a computer hard drive, continuously storing compressed digital video as it is transmitted. The TiVo brand name is often associated with these, but most of them are now being rented by cable TV and direct broadcast satellite companies rather than sold. DVRs let viewers make their own instant replays and pause and rewind programs in progress. While few ever mastered the intricacies of programming their VCRs, the DVR interfaces are easy to learn and the machines can "remember" the shows you want saved. With the assistance of current TV schedules downloaded via phone or cable TV connections, they can track down your favorites when their time slots shift, tape the entire run of *American Idol,* and even omit the reruns. DVRs also make inferences about your viewing pleasures and offer their own selections: The *Idol* fan may soon find her DVR also recording *Star Search* for her. The technology also makes it possible to skip the commercials, a feature that threatens the existence of both commercial broadcasters and basic cable channels.

Or, you may have an entertainment server in your future that stores and plays all of your digital media throughout your home. Cable operators are beginning to offer an all-in-one set-top box that includes a cable tuner, DVR, cable modem, MP3 jukebox, and DVD player. Other companies, including Sony and Microsoft, are building disc drives and network connections into their game consoles so that they can be transformed into a central storage and control system that will take the place of your stereo, TV, and VCR. Consumer electronics manufacturers hope to popularize "place shifting" with these technologies. That's the ability to record digitally and send the video anywhere in the home over high speed networks.

Video Production Trends

Over the years, cameras have steadily shrunk in size and can be carried anywhere. Rugged portable cameras (and, increasingly, home videos shot by viewers) have greatly expanded coverage of live events from the studio to floors of political conventions, to the helmets of football players. Electronic news gathering (ENG) systems transmit the news footage back to the studio via remote microwave antennas mounted on mobile vans. Other footage arrives in the newsroom via satellite, and the incoming digital video files are stored on video servers, which are massive computer disc drives. Reporters and news editors view the files and compose and edit stories while sitting at computer workstations that are linked to the video server through high-speed local area networks (see Chapter 12) that interconnect all the computers in the newsroom.

These systems take advantage of digital film production techniques (see Chapter 7) that have been adapted to television. The transition to high-definition TV may well mark the final convergence of film and video production, making it feasible to shoot feature films on video. Nonlinear editing had a great impact on video production by speeding up postproduction and lowering costs. Digital graphics, special effects, and computer animation are also becoming routine. For example, many TV stations have virtual news studios in which the reporters perform on an empty stage and computer graphics fill in the set. Increasingly, digital production techniques are migrating from specialized studio equipment to personal computers so that what once required a professional editing suite may soon take place on an ordinary desktop.

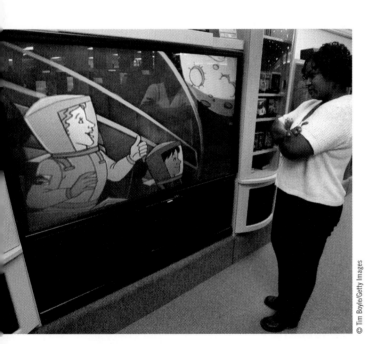

■ BIGGER AND BETTER?
Consumers are still wondering if the wider and clearer pictures of HDTV are worth the cost and hassle.

Here Comes Digital Television

The goal of digital television is to improve the quality of the picture. Digital video that matches NTSC's quality is called standard-definition TV (SDTV), whereas high-definition television (HDTV) provides pictures suitable for large-screen home theater systems. In many respects, digital television is already here, in DBS systems, digital cable services (see Chapter 12), DVDs, and DVRs. Those systems encode video in digital form for transmission or storage, then convert it back to conventional analog TV to display it on our "old-fashioned" NTSC-standard TV sets. What remains is to make over-the-air broadcast signals digital.

HDTV doubles (to 1080) the number of vertical scan lines, widens the picture to match the 16 to 9 aspect ratio of movie screens, and adds six-channel "surround sound." That generates over six times as much data as SDTV (see Technology Demystified: Inside HDTV). To provide extra bandwidth, the FCC gave each broadcaster a second channel in the UHF band, but a major string was initially attached. By December 31, 2006, (or by whatever date 85 percent of homes can receive an HDTV signal, whichever comes last) broadcasters were to turn in their old analog channels and vacate the VHF band! But the FCC has backed off that deadline hoping that its mandates for placing digital tuners in new TV sets will trigger the 85 percent adoption level within a couple of years after the original deadline.

TECHNOLOGY DEMYSTIFIED ■■■■■■

Inside HDTV

There is much more to digital television than meets the eye. Behind the wider and clearer picture lies a complete change in the way television programs are made and transmitted to the home.

The output of the camera is digitized using the same basic techniques of sampling and quantizing we learned about in relation to music CDs, back in Chapter 1. (You might wish to review that discussion, on page 8). But video contains a lot more information than audio, so the information is sampled much more often than for musical recordings, 13.5 million times per second. Our eyes are less sensitive to color information than they are to light and dark (luminance), so the color components are sampled less frequently. Still, the data spills out at about a quarter billion bits per second,

Next, the signal must be cut down to a size that can be transmitted over a standard TV channel, which can carry only 19 million bits per second. In Chapter 12 we will see that this is done by removing redundant information within and between frames of the television picture. The compression uses a process called MPEG-2, after Motion Picture Expert Group, which developed it. (The MP3 music files on the Internet reflect the audio portion of this standard.) The picture comes out of the MPEG encoder chopped up into chunks, or packets, of 1500 bits apiece, and 313 of these segments make up a single frame of the picture.

The next step actually adds to the length of each packet by appending data that helps to detect and correct errors that may occur during transmission. The data stream modulates a carrier signal in the UHF band in much the same way that a modem sends data over a phone line (see Chapter 12, page 372). However, there is more bandwidth, or capacity, in the UHF channel, so data can be transmitted at much higher speeds.

The transmission is not limited to HDTV pictures, however. Broadcasters can pack multiple conventional TV channels into the same channel space and can also include streams of Internet data. In fact, broadcast executives look to supplemental digital services to provide new sources of revenue that will offset the immense costs of switching to digital television. For example, they might offer a new form of pay TV by offering downloads of (legal) copies of movies to your computer or DVR.

The viewer must have a device that reverses the data encoding and compression processes to create a signal that can be fed into his or her TV tube. HDTVs have that built in, but owners of conventional sets will have to buy a set-top box. Those viewers won't get an HDTV picture on their sets, though; those old TVs are locked in to the NTSC standard. With the aid of the set-top boxes they will be able to receive a standard-definition television (SDTV) picture, although that will mean either cutting the edges off the picture or putting black bands (called "letterboxing") at the top and bottom to make the wide screen image fit the narrow NTSC screen.

Consumers are beginning to warm up to HDTV sets, even the expensive new LCD or plasma flat-screen versions, but there are some drawbacks. Some viewers are turned off by the "cliff effect," finding that they cannot receive any digital pictures at all in areas that have marginal conventional reception (see "Technology Demystified: Inside HDTV"). Cable operators promise to carry only a few high-definition signals and high-definition DVDs are still in the future, forcing HDTV owners to put up rooftop antennas if they want to receive all the high-definition programs available. But sooner or later we all will come around and either buy new HDTV sets or digital converters for our old ones. We'll have to, because analog television signals as we know them just will not be there anymore.

Digital television also brings with it multicasting, that is, transmitting multiple standard-definition signals simultaneously on a single TV channel. Broadcasters haven't quite decided what to do with multicasting yet. Some are thinking in terms of 24-hour local news channels, others in terms of data services; others are considering pay channels and a form of interactive TV (see next section).

Interactive TV?

This brings us to the question of interactive television. The idea of "talking back" to your TV and having it respond is nothing new. Time Warner experimented, and failed, with an interactive cable system called "Qube" back in the 1970s and tried and failed again in

■ IS THIS INTERACTIVE TV?
British viewers can chat with each other about BBC programs as they view.

© Courtesy of BBC Sports

the early 1990s. Conceptions of interactive programming have had a certain sameness over the years: interactive quiz shows, audience participation gimmicks, selectable alternative endings to dramas, alternative camera angles or in-depth statistics for football games, ordering products by "clicking" on their on-screen images.

Perhaps the most prevalent form of interactive TV in the United States today is the DVR that we discussed earlier, but its interactivity is ultimately limited to selecting content and to very limited forms of modifying the content (essential to our definition of interactivity, back in Chapter 1) such as "zipping" commercials and getting instant replays. *American Idol* presents another limited example: the votes that viewers send in via cell phone and text messages have a significant effect on content, but the results are delayed by a day. For "true" interactivity, those changes should take place in real time; imagine a version of *American Idol* where viewers can "boo" a contestant off the stage before Simon Cowell gets his claws into him—or where the audience has a "shut up, Simon" button!

British viewers (see World View in Chapter 12) already have interactive television. In the United States, cable operators continue to show mild interest in the concept but are wary of Time Warner's costly failures. Broadcasters could add interactive content, perhaps broadcasting it inside "multicasted" digital television signals and using phone connections for the return channel. Microsoft's Xbox game console is another possible way to put interactive TV capability into homes.

STOP & REVIEW

1. Why did the FCC freeze television licenses from 1948 to 1952?
2. Where did the television networks come from?
3. List the main competitors to broadcast television.
4. How does a television picture tube work?
5. What is high-definition television (HDTV)?

INDUSTRY: WHO RUNS THE SHOW?

Once-clear separations between the companies that produce, distribute, and exhibit television programs locally have been erased by industry deregulation and a wave of mergers and buyouts. Here we will concentrate on the pieces of those conglomerates that absorbed the conventional television business.

Table 8.2 The Big Five

Name	Broadcast TV	Production Studios	Cable TV	Other
AOL Time Warner	The WB	Warner Brothers Hanna-Barbera	HBO, Cinemax, CNN, Headline News, TNT, Turner Classic Movies, TBS, Cartoon Network #2 cable MSO	AOL, *Time, Sports Illustrated* magazines, Atlanta Braves
Disney Corporation	ABC Television, 10 O&Os	Disney Studios Buena Vista Touchstone	ESPN, Disney Channel, ABC Family, Toon Disney, SoapNet, Classic Sports Network, pieces of Lifetime, E!, A&E, and History Channel	Disneyland, ESPN magazine, 62 radio stations, Mighty Ducks
Viacom	CBS, UPN, 16 CBS O&Os, 18 UPN O&Os, 5 others	Paramount Studios, CBS Productions, King World Productions	Showtime, Spike TV, MTV, MTV2, Noggin, VH-1, Nickelodeon, BET, Comedy Central, TV Land, CMT, Flix, Sundance Channel	Blockbuster home video Simon & Schuster, Infinity (184 radio stations)
News Corp	Fox, 34 O&Os	20th Century Fox	FX, Fox News Channel, Fox Movie Channel, Fox Sports, The SPEED Channel, National Geographic Channel, Madison Square Garden Network	Newspapers, satellite TV, HarperCollins
NBC Universal	NBC, Telemundo, part of PAX, 14 NBC O&Os, 15 Telemundo O&Os	NBC Universal Studios	MSNBC, CNBC, Bravo, Mun2TV, Trio, USA, Sci-Fi	5 theme parks

Source: Who Owns What, http://www.cjr.org/tools/owners/

Inside the Big Five

The Big Five that dominate television today are Time Warner, Disney, Viacom, News Corp, and NBC Universal. These top companies are vertically integrated conglomerates that combine video production, national and local distribution, and other media properties under a single corporate umbrella (see Table 8.2). Their top managers come from the field of finance rather than entertainment (see Media Profile, Richard Parsons).

The force behind the urge to merge is *synergy,* getting multiple benefits from integrating production and various forms of distribution. For example, by ordering TV shows from their own production companies, the conglomerates save on production costs for their first-run television programs and profit directly from subsequent off-network syndication. Syndicating productions from their studios to their own cable channels and O&Os is far more lucrative than licensing programs from others, since the profits from both sides of the business stay "in the family." The conglomerates also cross-promote their holdings. For example, CBS can promote its youth-oriented shows on MTV now that both are part of Viacom, while MTV could refuse ads for the Fox network.

The various production and distribution assets are also chips in negotiations between conglomerates. For example, if Time Warner wants the right to carry ABC/Disney's O&Os on its cable systems, then it must agree to provide space for Disney's cable programming services on its cable systems nationwide. Disney can pressure Time Warner to renew shows it produces for the WB in exchange for renewing programs that Warner Brothers makes for ABC. Until acquiring Universal Studios in 2004, NBC was at the mercy of the other Big Five. For example, it had no real leverage with Warner Brothers Studios when negotiating the cost of *ER,* which Warner produces for NBC.

Content Creation

The way that television programs are produced varies somewhat according to genre. Each reflects a slightly different economic model.

Entertainment.   Production companies hire the directors, actors, and technicians and shoot and edit television entertainment programs. The networks contract with production companies for the rights to the first runs of the shows and typically pay fees that cover two-thirds to three-fourths of the initial production costs. The production companies may profit from the syndication rights by selling them in off-network syndication. For example, each

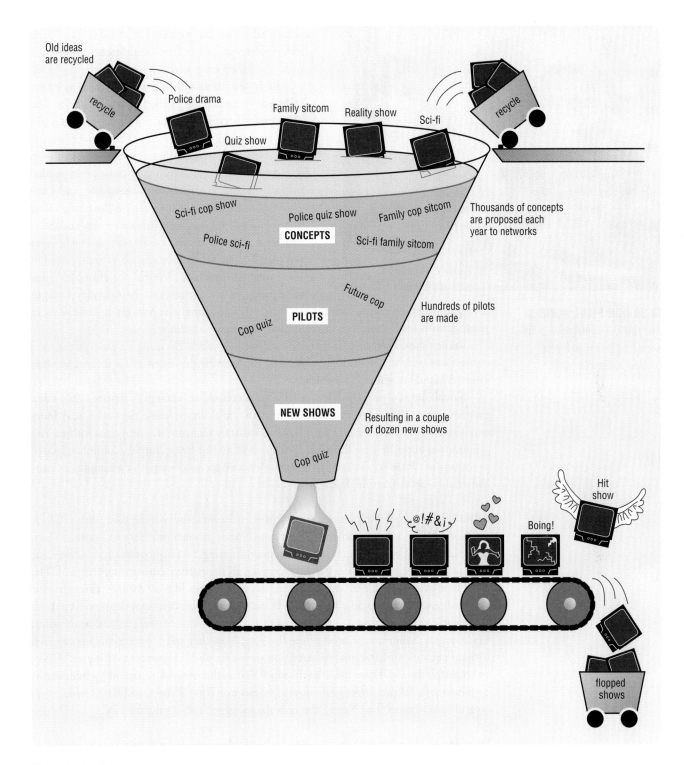

FIGURE 8.5

TV Program Development Familiar TV program genres are continually recombined and recycled into new concepts. The most promising concepts are made into pilot shows, and a few of those survive to be the new shows we see each year.

episode of *The Simpsons* is worth about $4 million in syndication fees when re-run on local stations. However, with the abolition of the Fin-Syn rules in 1993 and the recent merger craze, most network entertainment programs are now either produced in-house or co-owned by the networks. The rest are usually purchased from production companies

Courtesy Everett Collection © Columbia Tristar/

■ SO OUR PILOT BOMBED
Seinfeld is an example of a hit show that tested poorly for preview audiences.

associated with other members of the Big Five. Many independent producers have been forced out of business, and others have joined forces with the Big Five.

Each year thousands of concepts for new entertainment programs are pitched to the networks. The concepts are tested in phone surveys (for example, "How interested would you be in a show featuring young New Yorkers searching for romance and jobs in the big city?"). Several hundred of those are expanded into scripts under contract to the networks, and a few dozen of those are made into sample programs called *pilots.* The pilot shows are tried out on test audiences who view them in auditoriums or on cable television systems. This is an inexact science at best. Some of television's all-time hits (*Seinfeld,* for example) failed their previews, but the test numbers do play a role in determining which pilots reach the air. However, some programs now get air time without pilots or with low test ratings through their corporate connections.

Reality shows represent a different economic model. By using amateur actors and doing away with scripts and elaborate sets, they can be produced at far lower cost than scripted dramas or situation comedies.

Not all the new program ideas go to network television, though. First-run syndication programs are rented to network O&Os, network affiliates, cable networks, and independent stations. The Big Five each have subsidiaries that produce programs for first-run syndication, but others are associated with movie studios (for example, Columbia TriStar, producers of *Wheel of Fortune*) or major television group owners (for example, Tribune Entertainment, makers of *Andromeda*).

Network News. News programs are journalistic endeavors, and we refer the reader to Chapters 4 and 15 for a discussion of those aspects of news production. Here we consider them in the context of other types of television programming. News programs have little value in syndication, so their producers have to make all the money during their first run. The Big Three produce the evening news and magazine shows like *60 Minutes* through their own in-house news divisions. The networks cut many of their correspondents, and cut back on investigative reporting to reduce costs during the rounds of mergers and acquisitions that brought them into the orbit of the Big Five. Now they rely more on footage supplied by local network affiliates, foreign television networks, and independent "stringers." CNN has replaced the Big Three (and specifically CBS) as the network of record by building its own international news operation, now a key piece of Time Warner, and Fox is building its own news operation (Fox News) that now draws bigger audiences than CNN.

Local News. Most programs produced by local television stations are either newscasts or magazine-format shows. Local news is a major profit center, so much so that most stations run two hours or more of it per day. Stations profit from the news because it is popular both with local audiences and local advertisers and the revenues go directly to the local station—they are not shared with the network or a program syndicator. The news expansion has also been fueled by the ready availability of news footage, both that obtained from networks via satellite and from the station's own local electronic news-gathering capacity (Live! From Newschopper Five!). Production costs have declined over the years as equipment has gotten cheaper, although those cost savings are easily erased by the purchase of news helicopters, portable satellite uplinks, and the conversion to HDTV equipment.

© Mark Richards/Photo Edit

Sports. The networks also maintain their own sports divisions that supply the announcers, equipment, and staff for broadcasts of sporting events. However, they can't just walk into the stadium and set up their cameras; they have to buy the rights to the broadcasts from the sports leagues, and pay dearly for the privilege. For example, ABC pays the National Football League over a half billion dollars a year just for the rights to Monday Night Football and then spends another $3 million to produce the actual telecasts. ABC loses up to a quarter of a billion dollars a year on the deals, despite attracting large numbers of 18- to 24-year-old males valued by advertisers, and also despite having local affiliates kick in over $30 million a year to defray costs.

Public TV. Most PBS programs are produced by PBS stations in Boston, San Francisco, Los Angeles, New York, and Washington, D.C. Independent producers, notably Sesame Workshop (the producers of *Sesame Street,* formerly known as Children's Television Workshop), and the British Broadcasting Corporation (*Masterpiece Theater*) account for the rest. The Corporation for Public Broadcasting (CPB) funnels taxpayers' money to fund PBS programming, currently about $400 million a year. PBS now follows a centralized programming decision-making model, not unlike the commercial networks, under which programming executives in Washington decide which series to develop and air on PBS stations. Producers depend on a mix of funding from CPB, PBS member station contributions, corporate underwriting, public contributions, and foreign network cosponsorship. Contributing corporations and foundations are acknowledged in **underwriting** credits, those on-air announcements that express appreciation for financial support and describe what the donors do, but aren't commercials, not really.

Cable Production. National cable networks follow the same content acquisition strategies as the national broadcast networks, but local production is rather limited. Many cable systems produce their own **local origination** programming. The most elaborate operations resemble television stations, producing local news and sports for advertising-supported channels that are programmed by the cable operator. These are sometimes organized at a regional level to spread production costs across multiple cable systems. Most cable systems also maintain **community access** channels over which the operator has no direct control. Their productions are staffed by employees of the local educational or governmental institutions that create the programs, or sometimes by individuals who want their own cable shows. These local productions are thus subsidized by community groups, whereas the facilities used to produce them are financed by franchise fees (see Chapter 12) paid by the cable operator to the municipal franchise authority.

National Television Distribution

Television programs are distributed nationally by either networks or syndicators. Broadcast and cable networks differ somewhat in the ways they finance national distribution.

Commercial Broadcast Networks. CBS, NBC, and ABC have been joined by Fox, The WB, UPN, PAX, and Univision. These eight commercial broadcast networks all develop

Table 8.3 Top 10 Cable Networks

Rank	Network	Subscribers
1	Discovery	88,600,000
2	C-SPAN (Cable Satellite Public Affairs Network)	88,400,000
2	USA Network	88,400,000
4	ESPN	88,300,000
5	TNT (Turner Network Television)	88,000,000
5	CNN (Cable News Network)	88,000,000
5	TBS (Superstation)	88,000,000
8	Nickelodeon	87,600,000
8	A&E Network	87,600,000
8	Lifetime Television (LIFE)	87,600,000

All subscriber figures as of April 2004.

NOTE: Figures may include noncable affiliates and/or subscribers. Broadcast viewership is not included.

Source: http://www.ncta.com/Docs/PageContent.cfm?pageID=281

Table 8.4 Top 5 Pay Services

Network	Subscribers
Home Box Office	27,200,000
Showtime	12,000,000
Starz	12,000,000
Cinemax	11,800,000
The Movie Channel	10,800,000

Source: John M. Higgins, (2004) "Premium Networks Take a Hit," *Broadcasting & Cable* 134(6): 1

Pay-per-view charges viewers for each showing of a program.

and schedule programs for national audiences, distribute them to their local affiliates via satellite, and profit from the sale of spots to national advertisers.

Profits are hard to come by in network television. The Big Three each generate over $3 billion in advertising revenues per year, but profits are drained by huge payments for sports rights, production fees for entertainment shows, and multimillion dollar salaries for news correspondents and late-night comedians, plus the same taxes and routine operating expenses that all media firms incur (see Chapter 2). The networks also pay affiliate compensation fees to local TV stations that can run over $10 million per year in major markets, although that practice is changing. Television network operations routinely incur huge net losses, some soaring into the hundreds of millions of dollars. The network TV losses are offset by profits from other lines of business, including their hugely profitable O&O stations and cable networks.

Basic Cable Networks.   Over 300 basic cable TV networks are delivered via satellite, but the Big Five media conglomerates control many of the leading ones. Basic networks derive their revenues from national advertising revenues and *affiliate fees.* The affiliate fees are paid by cable operators, on a per-subscriber basis (these range from $1.75 per month per subscriber for ESPN to a few cents per month for C-SPAN). Many basic networks also make local advertising spots available that local cable systems sell to local advertisers. The largest basic cable networks (Table 8.3)—Discovery, C-SPAN, USA, and ESPN—are found on virtually all cable systems. There are about six dozen regional basic cable networks (for example, Madison Square Garden Network, New England Cable News).

Superstations like TBS, WGN, and WWOR are a special case in that they are also local television stations in their home markets but sell ads primarily to national advertisers. Some systems import distant signals besides the satellite-delivered superstations; often they are stations from nearby major television markets.

Pay Services.   Home Box Office is by far the largest pay TV network, followed by Showtime, Starz, Cinemax, and The Movie Channel (Table 8.4). Pay TV networks derive their revenues exclusively from affiliate fees. With only one revenue stream, those fees are substantially higher than for basic services. A small cable operator might charge its subscribers $10 per month for HBO and pay half of that back to HBO. Large cable multiple system operators (MSOs) have the market power to negotiate discounts, so they may pay HBO only about half of what the small cable company does.

Pay-per-view programming is also delivered by satellite and financed by affiliate fees, predicated on the number of pay-per-view orders. The main program categories for

PPV are sports, especially boxing and professional wrestling; recent films; and adult programs. The spread of digital cable has brought with it many new pay-per-view options, with some systems offering dozens of movies each night. New *video-on-demand* systems expand choices to include classic movies as well as recent movie releases.

Public Broadcasting.   The Public Broadcasting Service (PBS) is careful not to call itself a network, but it performs many of the same functions, notably developing and distributing a lineup of programs nationally via satellite. There are no advertising sales, but PBS does funnel money to national program development.

Syndication.   Local stations fill out their schedules with syndicated programming, particularly during the daytime and the 7–8 P.M. time slot set aside by the Prime Time Access Rules. These include first-run syndication programs, licensed directly to local stations, and off-network syndication, reruns of programs that previously aired on network television.

Syndicators obtain the rights for programming and then license the programs to local stations. Syndication is increasingly dominated by the Big Five (for example, Kingworld, a subsidiary of Viacom syndicates *Oprah*), but affiliates of lesser media conglomerates, such as Hearst Entertainment Distribution, and independent companies also play a role. Stations may pay for the programs outright (cash), pay a reduced price and show some advertisements or commercial spots arranged by the syndicator (cash plus barter), or pay nothing but give the syndicator more commercial minutes to sell to national advertisers (barter). Syndication contracts have an exclusivity clause so that only one station per market will have the right to show a particular program. Many of these deals are made at the annual convention of the National Association of Television Program Executives (NATPE), which functions as a bazaar for syndicated programming.

© The Kobal Collection

■ **SYNDICATED**
Longtime syndication hit *Wheel of Fortune* is licensed directly to local TV stations.

Local Television Distribution

Local distribution of television was once the exclusive province of the local TV station. Now, cable television and satellite systems also play a role; we will learn more about them in Chapter 12. A television station is an organization that holds a federal license to create or organize programs for a specific community and transmit them on its assigned channel. There are currently 1300 local commercial TV stations nationwide, and they may be categorized according to their ownership arrangements and relationships to national networks.

Group-Owned Stations.   Many stations are operated by companies with multiple broadcast properties, called *group owners*. Group owners benefit from economies of scale in management, programming, and advertising sales. To prevent monopolization, limits were set on the number of stations one group could own. The limits changed over the years. A cap on coverage equaling 35 percent of the television audience was set by the Telecommunications Act of 1996, but that has been increased to 39 percent by Congress. Duopolies, that is, ownership of two stations in the same market, is permitted in large markets but not in smaller ones, and triopolies are prohibited. *Local management agreements* also allow group owners to manage local stations they do not own on a contractual basis. Cross-ownership rules that prevent newspapers and cable companies from owning television stations in the same markets are also in place.

The Big Five (with the exception of Time Warner), are also group owners. Their owned-and-operated (O&O) stations are concentrated in major markets where they are major profit centers for their parent. The other major group owners are mainly offshoots of lesser media conglomerates such as the Hearst Corporation with 27 stations.

Network Affiliates. A common misconception is that the TV networks own all their local outlets. However, aside from the network O&Os, currently about 100 stations in all, local distribution of network programs is carried out by affiliates. These are individually owned or group-owned stations that have contractual arrangements with a network to show its programs locally.

Network affiliation is desirable because of the ratings draw of network prime-time shows. Local stations profit from the sale of local ad spots that run during network programs. A little over half of station revenues come from local ads, including those placed in locally produced or syndicated programs as well as the local ad availabilities in network shows. The other half of the revenue comes from ads placed through the station by national and regional advertisers. These are arranged through *rep firms* that act as intermediaries between local stations and advertisers based in other cities.

Network affiliation has been especially profitable over the years because the Big Three paid their affiliates to take their shows, a practice called *affiliate compensation.* That was to maintain the loyalty of affiliates and to encourage them to carry (or clear) network programs without preemption. However, the declining profitability of broadcast networks and competition among group owners to win network affiliations in major markets has reversed the flow of cash. Now, the networks are starting to charge the affiliates for programming, and bidding wars have erupted among group owners for the right to represent the Big Three in major markets.

Independent Stations. Independent stations are not affiliated with any network. Independents buy most of their programming from syndication services and sell their advertising in the local, regional, and national spot markets. Relatively few independents remain now that there are eight networks in operation.

Down at the Local Station. Local stations vary in size from a couple of dozen to several hundred employees, as a function of the size of the markets they serve. Regardless of size, all commercial television stations have a common set of key roles (Table 8.5) organized around the basic tasks of obtaining and transmitting programs that will attract audiences and, with them, advertisers.

The program director arranges contracts with networks and syndicators and is responsible for filling the overall broadcast schedule. Local news programs are an important source of profits and so account for most of the local programming resources. Stations employ news directors, assignment editors, news writers, on-air personalities, and remote camera crews to produce their news shows. Promotion managers draw audiences with on-air promotions ("plane crash coverage, live at 11!") and use advertising and public relations to make the station more visible in the community.

Advertising sales are the lifeblood of every commercial television station. The sales director manages a staff of account executives who make sales calls to local advertisers. They carry rate cards that list the charges for advertising according to the time of day and length of the commercial spot. The sales director also contracts with a rep firm to sell blocks of commercials through national and regional advertising agencies. The traffic

Table 8.5 Local Television: Key Personnel

Job Title	Job Description	Helpers
Station Manager	Overall responsibility for management, financial performance, planning, community relations	All other managers, front office staff of secretaries
Chief Engineer	Keeps the station on the air, monitors FCC standards	Transmitter engineer, studio technicians
Program Director	Selects and schedules programs, negotiates for syndicated programs	Syndicators
Promotion Director	Plans and directs on-air and off-air community promotions	Graphic artist, copywriter
News Director	Responsible for local news programs	Assignment editor, writers, announcers
Production Director	Produces the station's programs	Producers, directors, production crew
Sales Manager	Sells advertising time	Account executives, national rep firm
Traffic Manager	Schedules commercials	Advertising agencies
Director of Finance	Controls the station's finances, monitors the budget	Accountants and bookkeepers
Research Director	Analyzes and compiles reports on ratings, commissions local research	Ratings services

Source: Sherman (1995)

manager makes sure the commercials air at their proper times. Stations contract with Nielsen Media Research to provide ratings data that they use in their sales presentations. Large stations employ their own research directors who analyze the ratings and conduct local market studies, such as evaluations of local news anchors.

Stations also employ engineers to keep the station on the air and maintain the transmitter and studio equipment. The finance department keeps track of revenues and expenses for the benefit of the station manager, who has overall responsibility for the profitable operation of the enterprise.

Noncommercial Stations

There are over 350 public television stations. There are community stations that rely on individual and corporate contributions and educational stations, usually affiliated with local colleges or universities, that also receive funding from state or local governments. Public broadcasting operations are similar to those of commercial broadcasters, but they are run on a nonprofit basis. PBS stations must pay for the programming they receive from PBS and also for any syndicated programs. In place of the advertising sales force found in commercial stations, public stations have managers in charge of staging on-air membership and auction drives and soliciting contributions from private individuals and local foundations. They also seek corporate underwriting of local and national programs.

Television Advertisers

Each year advertisers spend about $54 billion on broadcast advertising and another $14 billion on cable. Broadcast television ratings have declined over the years, but network television continues to draw a disproportionate share of advertising because it still represents the most efficient way to reach the largest number of potential consumers at a single time. There are several basic types of TV advertisers with differing needs:

National advertisers sell general-consumption items, such as soft drinks. They buy blocks of advertising time from national broadcast networks during the up-front season. That's the time each spring when the networks sell time on the next season's shows. Time that is not sold then goes into the *spot market* and later into the scatter market, for last-minute ad sales.

National spot advertisers and regional advertisers sell products with more limited appeal, such as surfboards or snow tires. They buy spots through advertising rep firms from both network affiliates and independent stations.

Local advertisers, such as automobile dealers and supermarkets, buy slots in locally produced shows or those allocated by the networks to their local affiliates during network programs.

GENRES: WHAT'S ON TV?

Broadcast Network Genres

As we know, genres reflect a negotiation between the artist and the audience as to what is engaging or entertaining. In television, advertisers and network accountants are very much parties to that negotiation, however. We saw throughout the history of television that genres evolved to pursue audiences that interest advertisers and also in response to the changing economics of production. Recently, reality shows proliferated as conventional prime-time entertainment formulas and became more and more expensive to produce. With no scriptwriters or high-priced actors to pay, the reality genre is a far more profitable alternative. But, almost anything that appeals to 18- to 34-year-olds stays on the air while shows with older audiences are canceled. So now scripted dramas like *Lost* that appeal to young adults are staging a comeback.

The currently popular genres are situation comedies (sitcoms), dramas, action-adventure, reality shows, newsmagazine shows, and movies. Current examples of each genre, along with their early television ancestors and predecessors in other media are shown in Table 8.6. The table also shows some of the major genre variations. For example, dramas may be subdivided into medical, legal, and police dramas. Other variations hinge upon the interplay of plot and character development. In many shows, the characters are static and only the situations change from week to week (for example, *Will and Grace*) while in others the characters continually develop and stories revolve around their interactions (for example, *Desperate Housewives*). In yet others the weekly stories are woven into continuing plot lines (for example, *ER*).

What explains the continual variation of genres over time and the general programming trends that yield a bumper crop of forensic examiner shows like *CSI* one year, but fewer hospital dramas and situation comedies in aother? We'd like to think that the best minds in Hollywood are always at work thinking up original ideas for enticing new programs and that when their ideas hit a responsive chord in the audience, a new genre is born. The truth is that television programming ideas are highly derivative, and not just in the United States, but the world over (see World View: While You Were Watching American Idol). Many a program development meeting in Hollywood begins by asking "what's hot" (for example, "detective shows with bloody corpses" and "hospital dramas with gaping wounds") and ends up blending two or more hot topics together into an "original" concept (for example, *CSI*). If that concept is a hit, they spin it off

■ **ACTION**

Lost is an action-adventure show with dramatic elements.

Table 8.6 Prime-Time Television Genres

Genre	Origins	Early Example	Current Example	Genre Variations
Situation Comedy	Radio comedy skits, "screwball" movie comedies	*I Love Lucy*	*Will & Grace*	Family, workplace, buddy, cartoon
Drama	Live theater, radio and movie dramas	*Dragnet*	*ER*	Crime, medical, law, romance, soap opera
Action-Adventure	Radio serials, westerns, gangster movies	*The Rifleman*	*Lost*	Detective, science fiction, western, police
Reality	Radio interviews, movie documentaries	*Queen for a Day*	*Survivor*	Talk shows, home video, police footage
Movies	Live theater, vaudeville	*Monday Night at the Movies*	*ABC Big Picture Show*	TV movies, miniseries
Game Shows	Radio quiz shows	*21*	*Jeopardy*	Quiz, celebrity guessing games
Newsmagazine	Newspapers, radio news, movie newsreels	*See It Now*	*60 Minutes*	Newsmaker interviews

into derivative shows (for example, the Miami and New York versions of *CSI*). The use of one-shot pilot tests to evaluate new ideas and the tendency to cancel programs that are not immediate ratings hits further works against the survival of truly original concepts.

Population trends also factor in to please advertisers. That is especially true of demographic trends among 18- to 34-year-olds, whom advertisers hope will become loyal lifetime consumers if they view programs that carry the advertiser's ads while in early adulthood. So, in times when young adults are mostly singles starting careers in the Big City, we see programs about urban singles, like *Friends*. If young adults start forming families in droves, the *Friends* get married (or at least have children) and we see more family situation comedies like *Malcolm in the Middle*. If twenty- and thirty-somethings start moving out of the city, we see shows like *Desperate Housewives* set in the suburbs.

Genres are also shaped by the types of people who tune in at different times of the day, or dayparts. For example, early morning shows such as *Good Morning America* target a broad range of adults. Then soap operas and talk shows take over, targeting housewives, older people, and college students. After school we find cartoons for children and adolescents, then switch to news and game shows when the parents get home.

Weekly viewing and lifestyle patterns come into play on the weekends. The "kidvid" block of cartoon programs occupies Saturday mornings when many children are in the audience. Sports fill the weekend afternoons to catch workers on their days off.

© Everett Collection

■ LOOKS LIKE A NEW GENRE
Combine a cop show with a hospital show and you get a forensic investigation show, like *CSI*.

While You Were Watching *American Idol* . . .

American television is often criticized for its lack of originality, but is television better anywhere else? You be the judge. While you were watching *American Idol* and the final episodes of *Friends* and *Frasier* the top-rated shows in May 2004, these were the top shows from countries around the world (leaving out sports, news, and specials).

Country	Title	Blurb
Australia	*Survivor All Stars*	The same CBS series we saw, exported.
Canada	*Friends* series finale	We know the plot: six young New Yorkers seek careers and relationships in the big city.
China	*Lucky 52*	A game show similar to *Jeopardy.*
India	*Aap Beeti*	Supernatural thriller with a social message. Buffy meets Joan of Arcadia.
Mexico	*Mariana de la Noche*	A telenovela: A miniseries in soap opera style. Mariana marries Ignacio but Marcia, her foster aunt, wants him, too . . . .
Russia	*The Land of Love, the Land of Hope*	A Russian telenovela.
Holland	*Rijdende Rechter*	*The People's Court,* Dutch style.
Spain	*Cuentame Como Paso*	Soap opera about an extended family in post-war Spain (post Spanish Civil War, that is).
United Kingdom	*Hell's Kitchen*	A reality show in which celebrity guests learn how to cook. *Celebrity Mole* meets *Survivor,* in the kitchen.
South Africa	*The Bold and the Beautiful*	Sally gets the 411 on Brooke's wedding from Stephanie. The same soap we see on CBS.

As you can see, much of the world has no original ideas to offer us because they are watching the exact same shows, or variations on them, that we do! Prime-time soap operas seem to be the one genre that U.S. viewers are short on, but at least we have *Desperate Housewives.* In Chapter 16 we will re-examine the similarities and differences in TV worldwide.

Source: http://www.radiotv.org/audiencesTV.html

What's on Cable?

Cable networks elevated counter-programming to an art form by chipping away at the network prime-time audience with specialized target audience programs. Cable networks also used *bridging* to good advantage, scheduling programs to run past the hour and half-hour marks that bound broadcast network shows. Headline News and The Weather Channel follow the programming clock model found in radio, scheduling recurring segments at the same time each hour. General-audience cable channels such as USA Network maintain a balance of programming intended to attract a broad audience throughout the day, translating the broadcast television daypart strategy to cable.

Cable is well known for niche channels dedicated to particular interests or groups of viewers. Academics call this *narrowcasting.* Although this term is not much used in the industry itself, it nicely contrasts cable's approach with the broadcast networks' mass audience appeal. Narrowcasting confounds what we learned about media economics in Chapter 2. Advertising sales are predicated on reaching the largest possible audience at the lowest possible cost, so how can cable programs that appeal to small audiences survive? Advertising-supported cable networks supplement their income from **affiliate fees** paid by local cable systems. And, advertisers will pay a premium if the audience includes a high proportion of viewers interested in their products. A computer company may find a higher concentration of potential customers viewing a cable TV show about computers than among viewers of a broadcast situation comedy, for example. Cable networks economize by using "recycled" material (for example, classic TV shows), free material (World War II combat footage), or original material that is inexpensive compared to prime-time broadcast entertainment programming (for example, professional wrestling).

Genre channels extend particular genres to channel-length format, for example, CNN (all news), and ESPN (all sports). As the channel capacity of cable systems climbs, the genre channels diversify into subgenres. For example, the "news" category includes channels dedicated to regional news (Northwest Cable News), local news (NY1 News), repeated-on-the-half-hour news (Headline News), sports news (ESPNEWS), weather news (The Weather Channel), entertainment news (E! Entertainment Television), business news (CNBC), international news (CNN International), and news programs from countries around the world (SCOLA).

Other channels are built around audience characteristics; they are target audience channels. For example, Black Entertainment Television schedules music videos, black college sports, and public affairs programming for African-American viewers. Women (WE), children (Nickelodeon), and Hispanics (Univision) are among the other demographic target audiences. Others might better be described as lifestyle channels. Their programs are aimed at people who share a common interest or way of life, on channels for people who enjoy the outdoors (The Outdoor Channel) as well as for homebodies (HGTV).

PBS Programming

PBS stations are not as ratings driven as commercial television, but they still need audiences to attract donations, corporate underwriters, and voter support for continuing government subsidies. PBS stations focus on more cumulative (or "cume") ratings that reflect program viewership over a week or a month. This gives PBS the freedom to specialize in different genres from commercial broadcasters. Documentaries, highbrow cultural programming, and drama anthologies could not survive on network television but pull in enough occasional viewers to keep public broadcasting viable. Individual PBS stations have scheduling flexibility, since they are not required to run national programs at a specific time, unless the programs are specifically tagged for a time slot at PBS headquarters.

Programming Strategies

The underlying assumption of program scheduling is that television viewing is a deeply ingrained habit and that most people, most of the time, sit (or lie) down to watch television as opposed to specific programs. Thus, the key to ratings success is to be the least objectionable choice among the many programs offered at a particular time of the day.

Program executives build ratings by maintaining a consistent flow of viewers from one program to the next, and the tactics they use fill a colorful vocabulary (Eastman, 1993). They may schedule programs in blocks of the same genre (for example, edgy

Affiliate fees are monthly per-subscriber fees that cable programming services charge local cable operators for their programs.

family comedies *The Simpsons* and *Malcolm in the Middle* back-to-back) that appeal to the same audience segment. They will lead off a time block or lead in to a promising new show with a proven show like *CSI* in hopes that the weaker ones that follow will inherit the audience. A new show's chances can also be improved by following it with a highly rated established show like *ER* as a *lead out,* or by inserting it between two strong shows; that's called *hammocking.* If there aren't enough established programs for that, a strong show may be placed in between weaker ones; that's *tent-poling.* Local stations rely on *stripping,* running the same program in the same time slot every day of the week, and *checkerboarding,* rotating programs in a particular time slot.

The competitors try to disrupt audience flows. *Stunting* includes changing the time slot or length of a program, adding high-profile guest stars, running intensive promotions, or scheduling specials to make some of the viewers "flow" away from their usual programs and disrupt established viewing habits. They may go head to head with the competition by scheduling a program in the same genre as the competition's, such as running a hospital drama opposite *ER.* Or they may counter-program with an offering from a completely different genre that caters to a different audience, such as going against *Monday Night Football* with a sensitive drama. In this light, PBS might be seen as a counter-programming network.

However, in the new media environment these techniques are losing their effectiveness. Now network programmers constantly shift schedules from week to week, quickly pull new shows that aren't instant hits, and sometimes insert reruns into the lineup to build ratings for a program. Short-run series like Stephen King's *Kingdom Hospital* are also on the rise. Time-honored programming customs like fall preview week and sweeps months (when the rating services conduct studies in all TV markets) are eroding.

Stung by the continuing loss of viewers to niche-oriented cable channels, broadcast network executives are imitating their cable competitors by appealing to select target audiences. The WB, for example, specializes in shows like *Grounded for Life* calculated to appeal to young females. UPN features shows starring African-American actors such as *Girlfriends, Half and Half,* and *Eve* that are top-rated shows among black viewers. Univision's soap opera series *Cristina* and *Maria de la Noche* are the highest rated in Hispanic households.

STOP & REVIEW

1. What are the Big Five media conglomerates?
2. Why is it hard to make a profit from network television?
3. List the leading prime-time network genres.
4. What are the strategies networks use to maintain audience flow?
5. Describe the narrowcasting strategy.

MEDIA LITERACY: OUT OF THE WASTELAND?

Today there are hundreds of viewing options where once there were only three. But have we really left the "vast wasteland" of repetitive, mindless, and uninformative programming that Newton Minow described 40 years ago?

The New Television Hegemony

Limits on television station ownership are again a controversial issue now that both the old numerical limits have been lifted and the new (as of the Telecom Act of 1996) national coverage limits have been raised, to 39 percent of all TV households. Companies can also own two stations in major markets and manage stations that they do not own. Rules against multiple TV network ownership (for example, Viacom owning both CBS and UPN) and cross-ownership of television stations, local cable systems, and newspapers are also under question.

Why restrict ownership at all? Wouldn't an unregulated marketplace of ideas with an abundance of channels provide multiple points of view? The problem is that excessive **horizontal integration,** might limit the diversity of content. The Big Three (and now CNN) all cover basically the same stories, in about the same order, with similar footage, and with a similar slant. And what if a single company controlled all the leading television, radio, cable, Internet, and print news outlets in your hometown?

© NBC/Courtesy Everett Collection

Certainly there are many more sources of news and entertainment than ever. The Fox News Channel has emerged as an ideological alternative in network news, supporting the diversity-through-abundance argument. But now, **vertical integration,** as well as horizontal integration, threatens diversity. The objectivity of the news is undermined by corporate interests and the commercialization of news content. The bottom line is that political views, cultures, and viewing tastes that differ markedly from the mainstream are still not found on television. On the entertainment front, vertical integration among studios and cable and broadcast networks limits the originality of prime-time programming and shuts out independent producers.

Another way to preserve diversity would be to require television to cover controversial issues or to give advocates of opposing views the right to reply. That is what the Fairness Doctrine once required broadcasters to do. But in 2000 the Supreme Court struck it down. Perhaps the doctrine is truly obsolete in a new media environment that features talking heads on both the left and the right. However, minority party candidates still have difficulty getting their message out, and the media still select the issues and candidates that they wish to cover.

Many of the diverse viewpoints are expressed on cable channels that economically disadvantaged viewers may not be able to afford. News is more ratings driven than ever, so public service obligations of broadcasters are more likely to be fulfilled by "happy news" visits to children's hospitals than by hard-hitting discussions of the health insurance issue.

Is Television Decent?

Janet Jackson's "wardrobe malfunction" during the 2004 Super Bowl halftime show sent a shock wave through the executive suites of the broadcast networks. Although they work under the same "safe harbor" rule as radio, limiting indecent content between 10 P.M. and 6 A.M., the networks had been pushing the boundaries of decency for years in an effort to compete with cable television. Each year shows like *NYPD Blue* would

Horizontal integration is concentrating ownership by acquiring companies that are all in the same business.

Vertical integration is concentrating ownership by acquiring companies that are in related businesses.

Diversity in Television

Diversity on the screen and diversity behind the screen are logically related. It takes diverse people to make diverse images. So we ask, how diverse are television ownership and television employment?

Women and minorities are drastically underrepresented in the ranks of TV station owners and board members, and minority television station ownership is declining. The FCC once had rules to encourage minority ownership, but these were abolished by federal courts as imposing racial quotas. Minorities own only 1.9 percent of the nation's TV stations, even though they constitute over a fourth of the total U.S. population (NTIA, 2000). The merger wave in the television industry left women and minorities behind since they do not enjoy equal access to financing for station acquisitions, and every time the limits on broadcast ownership are raised that threatens minority ownership. In 2003, the FCC's new equal opportunity rules went into effect, raising new hopes for equal representation in TV and radio management ranks. However, the rules only require monitoring of minority employment and outreach efforts for minority applicants, and minority groups complain that the FCC has not applied the rules when evaluating TV station license renewals.

Minorities have historically been underrepresented in front of the camera. The fall 1999 television season had so few minority actors that there were threats of boycotts by minority groups like the NAACP and La Raza. Roles for African-Americans increased after that, but other minorities remain underrepresented. For example, Hispanics account for 11 percent of the U.S. population but only 3 percent of the roles on television (Mastro & Greenberg, 2000). Most of the minority actors are found in roles in racially segregated programs that are shown in blocks targeted primarily to minority audiences (Wynter, 1998), and this trend is increasing (Children Now, 2002). The good news is that the trend has increased the level of representation of minority characters to match and even exceed their numbers in the general population (Glascock, 2003) However, even shows that feature minorities in positive leadership roles in an integrated environment, such as the police lieutenant character on NBC's *Law and Order,* may perpetuate a subtle form of racism in which minorities are acceptable only as "regula-

tors" who do society's dirty work. Other groups, including Asian-Americans and Native Americans, are almost invisible on television.

Minority representation in front of the screen, as well as on it and in back of it, has now become an issue. In 2004 the Nielsen ratings changed their method of measuring audiences in the country's major markets, switching from paper diaries to electronic measurement. Viewership of programs featuring minority characters dropped substantially, leading to calls to boycott the ratings on the grounds that too few of the electronic meters were being placed in minority homes. Inaccurate ratings could cause the cancellation of shows featuring black performers and reverse the trend to increase diversity on the screen.

Females are also underrepresented, although this, too, is improving over time (Glascock, 2001). Female actresses still play traditional female roles in television programs and their commercials. For example, women who appear in computer commercials on television tend to be clerical workers rather than business professionals or managers (White & Kinnick, 2000). The male characters in children's shows are active, dominant, and aggressive (stereotypically male traits), whereas females are stereotypically deferential, dependent, and nurturing (Barner, 1999). While some television moms (for example, on FOX's *Malcolm in the Middle*) play more assertive roles than they did in 1950s TV hits like *Leave It to Beaver,* there are still plenty of Marge Simpsons who perpetuate the image of stay-at-home mother.

Diversity in television matters. First, all of society benefits from diverse points of view, and one of the best ways to guarantee that is to have owners, managers, producers, and performers drawn from all segments of society. Second, children take their cues from television. Seeing a predominance of white males in powerful TV roles may give minority and female children the mistaken impression that it is their "place" in society to be subservient and submissive.

Broadcasters respond that they are in the business of entertainment and making money—that it's not their job to cure all of society's ills. However, this ignores the prominence of television and also, perhaps, the broadcasters' obligation to operate in the public interest.

show a little more breast and buttock (oops, can we say that in a family textbook?) and introduce a new swear word to the TV lexicon. Jackson's prime-time "exposure" to a national audience was so shocking that, for once, network executives did not even try to hide behind the First Amendment. Instead, they started reworking scripts of shows under production and instituted tape delays on live broadcasts so that offending words and images could be deleted.

What especially attracted the broadcaster's notice was Congress's threat to up the fines for indecency, then $27,500, and to count each broadcast as a separate incident. So, instead of CBS Television paying a single fine, that would be multiplied by 15, the number of O&O stations CBS has. And, each of its affiliates would have to pay fines of its own. Plus, the uproar threatened the broadcasters' claim that they are committed to wholesome family entertainment.

Broadcasters began to complain more loudly that it is not fair that they are subject to decency restraints that cable is not. The rationale for that policy is that broadcasts enter the household unbidden, over the public airwaves, whereas viewers must pay to receive cable. So, if anyone finds cable indecent they can either choose not to subscribe or buy lock-out devices that will screen out indecent channels. However, with either cable or satellite subscriptions now in 85 percent of U.S. homes, that argument is getting a bit shabby.

The newfound passion for decency could lead us back to the bland, unrealistic shows of the 1950s, where even married couples slept in separate beds. There were some ironies in the Super Bowl incident, too. The same broadcast carried some rather explicit ads for "male sexual dysfunction" products. A short time later the FCC did an about-face, ruling that when Bono had used the "f-word" as an adjective during a Golden Globes awards show it was indecent, whereas before the Super Bowl incident it was not. The chilling effect of the Super Bowl incident began to spread. Some stations refused ads for a movie about sex researcher Alfred Kinsey while others rejected a network telecast of *Saving Private Ryan* for fear of incurring FCC fines. However, by the end of 2004 the networks fought back, airing a sexy promotional ad for *Desperate Housewives* during Monday night Football featuring (an apparently naked) Nicolette Sheridan, and initiating a legal appeal of the fines for the Super Bowl incident. And, heck (can we say that?) you couldn't even see Jackson's [bleep] without HDTV. The point is, whose arbitrary standards of indecency will we impose on everyone?

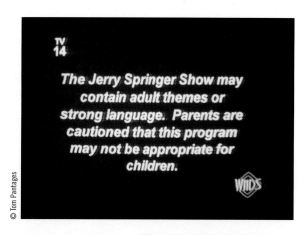

© Tom Pantages

■ VIOLENCE WARNING
Parental advisories such as these are voluntary ratings supplied by the networks to help parents control children's viewing. They also help to stave off criticism about excessive violence on television.
TVY—All Children
TVY7—Directed to Older Children
TVG—General Audience
TVPG—Parental Guidance Suggested
TV14—Parents Strongly Cautioned
TVM—Mature Audiences Only

Children and Television

What about the children who watched the shocking Super Bowl half-time show? The incident once again inspired calls to censor objectionable content on television that might be seen by children. Usually, regulatory efforts run up against the First Amendment and its protection of free speech, so industry self-regulation has been the inevitable outcome. The outcry over the Super Bowl incident was so overwhelming that, for once, the industry took immediate action to police itself. However, self-regulation has never been effective in the long run, and television continues to be an oversexed medium in the eyes of many parents.

For their part, broadcasters insist that it is up to the parents to mind their own children. To help parents do their part, the Telecommunications Act of 1996 required that new television sets sold in the United States include a "*V-chip*" that enables viewers to block programming, via an electronically encoded system that works off voluntary content ratings supplied by the networks. However, less than 10 percent of parents actually use the V-chip, and only about half consult TV ratings to decide what children can watch (Kaiser Family Foundation, 2001).

Another alternative to censorship is to ensure a supply of educational children's programming; that was the objective of the Children's Television Act in 1990. The act mandated that TV broadcasters serve educational and informational needs of children.

However, the FCC wrote rules broadly enough to allow *The Flintstones* to be counted as educational. After years of quibbling over what was "educational" and what was "specifically designed for children," a quantitative standard of three hours per week of children's programming was set (Kunkel, 1998). However, industry follow-through has been unenthusiastic and has not met the spirit of the rules, perhaps not even the letter of the requirements.

Historically, violence on television has been a bigger concern than sex. In Chapter 13 we will review research indicating that the violence children see on television can cause them to be violent in later life. Researchers estimate that the average child sees many thousands of acts of violence before reaching adulthood. Ironically, their calculations never include sports, even though a single football play may contain more acts of violence (defined as the use of physical force against another human being) than an entire week of prime-time police dramas. Shouldn't the Super Bowl be rated TV14 for excessive violence? And, if so, was more harm done to the children by the football game than by the halftime show?

The Fate of Public Broadcasting

Another way to preserve diversity is to have the government subsidize it. That is the premise behind public broadcasting. PBS stations have indeed provided valuable alternatives over the years, ranging from the *News Hour* to *Sesame Street.*

Nonetheless, PBS repeatedly comes under attack. Conservative politicians denounce a perceived liberal bias in PBS programming. In the past, conservative critics tried to eliminate federal funding, currently about $400 million per year, but they have been appeased somewhat by the addition of right-leaning public affairs programming to the PBS lineup. Others charge that PBS features elitist programs that appeal to an educated and affluent audience. Advocates of the free-market approach to broadcast policy point out that cable television, and now the Internet, provide the cultural, news, and educational fare that were once found only on public stations, at no cost to the taxpayers.

In response, PBS has diversified its funding sources. Many PBS programs today rely on enhanced underwriting in which corporate sponsors are given on-air acknowledgments for their charitable contributions to program development. The PBS website hawks videos and merchandise tied into its national programs. PBS schedules have been expanded to include old movies and syndicated offerings like *The Lawrence Welk Show.* It's also expanding its core programming mission with the new digital PBS Kids channel, featuring reruns of *Mr. Rogers* and other public broadcasting favorites. Other PBS stations are using their digital multicasting capability to offer local news and extended coverage of government proceedings. A greater emphasis on local public affairs may also provide a new mission in an era in which the TV screen is dominated by global media corporations.

However, some of these efforts have alienated some of PBS's longtime supporters who object to creeping commercialism and a dilution of its core mission. Politicians will continue to meddle unless some formula is developed to make PBS financially independent, such as an endowed trust fund or dedicated tax. So, public broadcasting continues to face an uncertain future.

Can Free TV Survive?

Others question the continued existence of commercial broadcasting. They argue that commercial broadcasters have never lived up to their obligations to serve in the public

Television and the Days of Our Lives?

If films are larger than life, television seems more intimate, the very stuff of our daily life. Television seems to influence our daily routine more than any other medium. In the 1950s, people began to eat their dinners off TV trays so they could watch the tube during dinner. Now students schedule their studying around *Desperate Housewives,* and *American Idol* got families to reschedule vacations.

Anthropologists observe how people see television as an essential part of their daily life, and television programmers have tried hard to see that that continues. Some of the more successful "new" television genres, talk and reality shows, play up this connection to daily life, looking in on the daily lives captured on screen of the MTV's *The Real World, Road Rules,* and *The Simple Life.*

This focus on daily life in television studies corresponds to changes in social theory. Social and cultural theorists, from Fernand Braudel to Anthony Giddens, have focused our attention on how people live their daily lives and how it reflects the choices they make. What we do and watch day-to-day reflects who we are. We might tell the Nielsen television researchers that we prefer *Masterpiece Theater,* but we actually watch *Days of Our Lives* and professional wrestling. Scholars like David Morley look at the patterns of daily life to see how television is affecting us and whether we are accepting or rejecting its messages. Feminist scholars, like Charlotte Brunsdon, look at how women watch soap operas to resist and cope with the pressures on women in society.

Television is often the source of some of the main narratives of our lives, the topics we talk about with our friends, family, and coworkers. Horace Newcomb called television a cultural forum, one of the places where important forces like race and gender, and issues like fear of terrorism or crime, get discussed in very broad ways. That happens both in the obvious places like news and talk shows, as well as in dramas, comedies, and reality shows. For example, Newcomb grew up in the South while racial segregation was still in place. He observed that new ideas about race came into the discussion in the South in part through national television programs, both news and drama. They began to treat

© Bettmann/CORBIS

■ **TV DINNER**

Television has had a profound influence in our daily routines since the 1950s.

race differently, leading many Southerners to talk about race in new terms that they were seeing on television.

At another level, Raymond Williams talked about the flow of television, that television is not just a series of discrete programs, but more of a continuous flow of experience. Both academic and industry researchers try to understand how television holds the audience over from one program to another (Williams, 1989). Since the 1950s, television programmers have been trying to convince us, "Don't Touch That Dial" and hoping that if we really like *Will and Grace,* we will also stick around to watch what comes next. But the early natural flow of television declined with the remote control, ended with the enormous multiplication of channels brought by cable and satellite television, and is now totally defeated by the DVR.

interest with quality local news and community affairs programming. Another basic premise of broadcast regulation, localism, has been lost in the merger craze that saw many locally owned stations sell out to group owners. Commercial television occupies valuable spectrum space, and the industry has profited enormously from its free use of that scarce public resource.

Broadcasters are an extremely powerful lobby in Washington, though. No congressperson wants to risk alienating the local TV stations that will cover the next election. Commercial broadcasters also make the politically powerful argument that their programming is offered free of charge to the public, ignoring the fact that we all pay for the "free" programs through the products we buy.

However, there is another, more serious, threat to "free" commercial broadcasting that comes from within: The basic business model of producing programs for large audiences and then selling those audiences to advertisers is no longer viable. As we have seen, fees for entertainment and sports programs have skyrocketed, while commercial broadcast audiences have shrunk. The DVR, which can make it easy to fast forward commercials, is a huge threat. Although, so far DVRs seem to have had little impact on the recall of television commercials and have even increased overall television viewing (and commercial exposure) in the homes that have them. Some in the industry wonder if the future of prime-time entertainment is represented by pay channel offerings like *The Sopranos,* and the end of "free" TV. One proposal is to use the multicasting capability of broadcasters to offer an over-the-air pay service to compete with cable and satellite. Others have proposed a $250 per year tax on DVRs to make up for the lost advertising revenue.

STOP & REVIEW

1. What are the current rules governing television station ownership?
2. How can we clean up violence and sex on television?
3. How diverse is television?
4. What are the pros and cons of helping public broadcasting to survive?
5. What are the threats to "free" commercial broadcasting?

SUMMARY AND REVIEW

WHO INVENTED TELEVISION?

Philo Farnsworth was awarded the patent for television. Vladimir Zworykin shares the credit for the invention of TV cameras and receivers. John Logie Baird of Great Britain and Charles Jenkins of the United States made the first television transmissions in 1925. Electronic television service began in Britain in 1936 and was introduced to the United States in 1939. In 1941 the National Television Systems Committee (NTSC) mandated black-and-white television standards that are still in use, specifying 525 lines per frame and 30 frames per second.

HOW DID THE BIG THREE NETWORKS DOMINATE TV?

NBC, CBS, and ABC brought their programs, stars, audiences, and advertisers with them from radio. During the FCC freeze, most cities had only one or two stations and NBC and CBS were the top affiliation choices. ABC rebounded when it ordered programs produced by Hollywood studios. UHF stations were too few and their signals too weak to support a fourth network.

WHAT WAS THE GOLDEN AGE?

Early network television featured variety shows, drama anthologies, and quality public-affairs programming seldom seen today. Top actors and writers based in New York tackled serious dramas. Shifting audiences, creeping commercialism, Hollywood production values, and quiz show scandals spelled the end of the Golden Age.

HOW DID VIEWING CHOICES EXPAND BEYOND THE BIG THREE?

FCC Chairman Newton Minow called television a "vast wasteland" of bland programming in 1961. The Corporation for Public Broadcasting and the Public Broadcasting Service were established to provide an alternative source of programming. The Fin-Syn rules and other regulatory measures limited the amount of television programming that the networks could produce and own. Independent UHF stations began to prosper after UHF tuners were required in new television sets and the FCC opened up the major cities to cable television. That paved the way for pay services like HBO and advertising-supported basic channels like WTBS.

HOW DID NEW TELEVISION NETWORKS DEVELOP?

In 1987, Rupert Murdoch started the Fox television network. Cable TV helped Fox, since most Fox affiliates were independent UHF stations, which cable brought to most homes with excellent picture quality. Fox also pursued younger viewers beloved by advertisers. The WB, UPN, and PAX networks followed.

WHAT IS THE IMPACT OF CABLE ON BROADCAST TV?

The proportion of viewers who tune in to prime-time broadcasts from ABC, CBS, and NBC has declined dramatically in recent years. Cable households are heavy viewers of television, and over half of viewing in cable households is now devoted to channels available only on cable.

HOW IS NETWORK TELEVISION CHANGING?

Now, broadcast networks are part of vertically integrated media conglomerates that also include movie studios, cable networks, and other media assets. The Big Five media conglomerates (Time Warner, Viacom, Disney, NBC Universal, and Fox) have replaced the Big Three as the dominant players in the television industry. Old program formulas are proving too expensive to sustain, so the networks are searching for new financial and programming models.

HOW DOES TELEVISION WORK?

The camera tube breaks images down into scanning lines, which can be scanned by an electron beam. The beam causes a discharge of energy that turns into electrical voltage variations. The lines of resolution (525 for NTSC) are the lines per frame scanned by the electron beam. A picture tube, or cathode ray tube, fires an electron gun at dots on the inside of the screen; the dots glow with varying intensity to create an image. Electromagnets are used to steer the beam of electrons as it retraces the same pattern generated by the TV camera.

WHAT IS DIGITAL TELEVISION?

Television is making a transition to digital broadcasting that is scheduled to be completed in 2007. High-definition television (HDTV) sets will display sharper, wider pictures. Broadcasters may also transmit standard-definition television (SDTV) pictures to viewers who add digital adapters to their conventional NTSC receivers. New digital recording and storage options are appearing, including digital video disc (DVD), DVRs, and video-on-demand systems.

WHERE DO COMMERCIAL PROGRAMS COME FROM?

Companies owned by the Big Five dominate the production of network television and cable programs, the production and distribution of first-run syndicated programming, and the syndication of off-network reruns of network programs. Lesser media conglomerates and a dwindling number of independent producers and syndicators account for the rest. National broadcast, cable, and satellite networks transmit programs to the public. The broadcast networks own their own stations (O&Os) in major markets and rely on affiliates to broadcast them elsewhere. Independent stations are those without network affiliation. Cable channels reach the home through local cable television systems or through direct broadcast satellite.

WHAT ARE THE MAIN TELEVISION GENRES?

Sitcoms, dramas, action-adventure, movies, news, and reality shows are the main genres in network prime time today. Conventional genres are becoming too expensive to be profitable. Genres that appeal to 18- to 34-year-olds predominate, as that group is highly valued by advertisers.

WHAT STRATEGIES DO TV PROGRAMMERS USE?

Programming varies to reflect the varying composition of the audience during different parts of the day. Program executives schedule programs to maintain audience flow from one program to the next and to disrupt the flow of viewers on other networks. Many cable networks follow a niche programming, or narrowcasting, strategy in which they schedule programs that are all of the same genre or that are designed to appeal to specific target audiences.

WHAT ENCOURAGES DIVERSITY IN TELEVISION?

Horizontal and vertical integration in the television industry threaten the diversity of ideas. Limits on television station ownership and on cross-ownership of media have been relaxed over the years. Companies can now also own or manage more than one station in a single market. Policies that encourage minority and female ownership and employment in the television industry or that mandate fairness in the coverage of important issues can also increase diversity. Marketplace forces might produce diversity on their own by providing many competing alternatives. However, the growing dominance of the Big Five media conglomerates calls this policy into question.

WHY CAN'T THEY CLEAN UP TV?

The First Amendment frustrates efforts to censor violent or sexual content, so industry self-regulation is ultimately the only option. Cable has even fewer restrictions than broadcast TV on the premise that parents can simply discontinue their subscriptions or purchase lock-out devices if they find its content objectionable.

WHAT IS THE FUTURE OF BROADCASTING?

Public broadcasting continues to be the target of critics who find it too liberal, too elitist, or simply an unnecessary public expense. Public broadcasters are attempting to diversify their funding base but in so doing incur criticisms that they are yielding to commercial pressures and losing focus. Commercial broadcasters are a powerful influence in Washington. However, there are growing doubts about the value of preserving local broadcasting in light of broadcasters' reluctance to cover controversial public issues and their occupation of valuable portions of the communications spectrum. The economic model for broadcast network television is failing.

Use the Media Now CD-ROM for access to digital learning materials that bring to life concepts and issues addressed in this chapter. The CD's features include Career Profiles—short videos that present current media professionals talking about their jobs and industries.

MEDIA CONNECTION

For web links, quizzes, and key term flash cards, visit the **Student Companion Website** at http://communication.wadsworth.com/straubhaar5.

 For unlimited easy access to additional and exclusive online study, support, and research tools, log on to **1pass** at http://1pass.thomson.com using the unique access code found on your 1pass passcode card.

 The **Media Now Premium Website** offers *Career Profile* videos, *Critical View* video news clips, and *Media in Motion* concept animations. You'll also find Stop & Review tutorial questions, a sample final exam, and much more.

 InfoTrac College Edition is a fully searchable online database offering anytime, anywhere access to more than 20 years' worth of articles from nearly 5,000 diverse and reliable sources.

vMentor provides live, one-on-one online tutoring to connect you to experts who will assist you in understanding the concepts covered in your course.

Interested in a career in television? In the Career Profile video for this chapter, Josh Springer, a producer for a public television station, explains how he got his start in the industry.

9

Internet cafés like this one are but one of the ways the Internet has impacted our culture. No study of the communications media these days would be complete without including the Internet. This chapter traces the history of computer media from their early origins in the nineteenth century to the latest developments on the World Wide Web.

HISTORY: SPINNING THE WEB

Most of us think of the Internet as a very recent development, dating back to the last decade of the twentieth century. In fact, the origins of computers and their networks can be traced back over 175 years, to the early nineteenth century. They finally evolved into the Internet as a direct result of the global military conflicts in the mid-twentieth century.

The Victorian Computer Age

The early ancestor of the Internet was the electric telegraph. American Samuel F. B. Morse started the first commercial telegraph in 1844 (see Chapter 12). The Associated Press newswire was the first electronic information service, in 1848, and thus the earliest precursor of today's World Wide Web.

Computers also date back to the nineteenth century. In 1822 Charles Babbage, professor of mathematics at Cambridge University in England, created the difference engine, a mechanical computer. Despite the patronage of Lady Ada Byron Lovelace, who is sometimes credited with being the first computer systems analyst, Babbage's computer

1844	Morse's telegraph, data network forerunner	**1993**	Mosaic, first Internet browser
1966	SABRE, first civilian computer network	**1995**	Amazon.com popularized e-commerce
1969	ARPANET established	**2000**	Dot-com bust
1972	Alto, first personal computer	**2004**	Apple iTunes popularizes pay content
1986	NSFNET opens Internet for civilian use	**2004**	e-Activism
1991	Internet opens to commercial users; HTML developed; the World Wide Web is born		

was never finished (Evans, 1981; Wulforst, 1982). Computers would wait another 100 years to be developed into useful inventions.

Computers Go to War

John Vincent Atanasoff of Iowa State University is credited with inventing the electronic computer in 1939, on the eve of World War II (1939–1945), although he, too, failed to assemble a complete working model. In 1943, the British secret service used the first all-electronic digital computer (named *Colossus*), designed by computer pioneer Alan Turing, to crack Nazi secret codes. The first general-purpose computer, the electronic numerical integrator and calculator (ENIAC), completed in 1946, was enlisted in the Cold War, running calculations for the first hydrogen bomb. ENIAC's inventors, J. Presper Eckert and John Mauchly, made UNIVAC, the first civilian computer, in 1951.

The Ancestors of the Internet

Another precursor of the Internet was also an instrument of war: the SAGE air defense system, dating from the early 1950s. The first **modems** fed bomber counts into phone lines that connected the first **wide area network (WAN)** to SAGE's computer memory.

One of the first civilian data networks was American Airlines' SABRE airline reservation system. It was started in 1966 to coordinate ticketing between travel agents and airlines across the country. Today, it is known to web users as Travelocity.com.

The first **local area network (LAN)** linked computers at the Livermore, California, atomic weapons laboratory in 1964. The plan was to continue weapons research at Livermore and other labs even if civilization was wiped out in a nuclear war. ARPANET, the Advanced Research Projects Agency Network, was designed to link the weapons research centers. It was the direct predecessor of today's Internet. Anyone who has ever struggled with an Internet connection will appreciate its famous first words, in 1969. The operator typed "L . . . O . . ." (trying to tell the person at the other end to *LOG* IN), but the system crashed before the message could be completed!

Making Computers Smaller and More Fun

In the days before the personal computer, the networks were connected to room-size systems, called mainframes, mostly produced by computer giant IBM. Users pecked at "dumb" terminals that were little more than keyboards connected to a display screen,

Modems convert digital data to analog signals.

Wide area networks (WANs) connect computers that are many miles apart.

Local area networks (LANs) link computers within a department, building, or campus.

© Bettmann/CORBIS

■ **FIRST COMPUTER**
Babbage's difference engine was the forerunner of today's computers. It was designed in 1822 to create mathematical tables.

© Courtesy of Apple Computer, Inc.

with no on-board computing capability. In the early 1960s "mini" computers, about the size of an office desk standing on end, came out. The experimental Alto computer, developed by the Xerox Corporation in 1972–1974, was the first personal computer. It boasted a mouse, and a high-speed local area network connection called Ethernet, invented by Bob Metcalfe.

The first commercially available personal computer, the Altair, was practically useless at first—all the user could do was play at imitating the patterns of flashing lights on its control panel. But the Altair inspired a young computer hacker from Seattle by the name of William Gates to write a programming language for it, BASIC, and to found Microsoft Corporation. It also inspired young Steve Jobs to build the first Apple II in 1977.

And then there was Pong, the first computer video game in 1972. A form of electronic Ping-Pong, it started as a wildly popular arcade game that later came out on a dedicated home player unit. People started using their personal computers to play games, too, and games soon emerged as the most popular home computer application (Calica & Newson, 1996).

The Birth of Online Services

Videotex was an immediate precursor to today's consumer information services on the web. Telephone lines connected the users' "dumb" terminals to central mainframe computers that stored the information. Early systems used television sets as their display units (hence the "video" part of the name) and were limited to text (the "tex" part) and crude graphics. The world's first commercial videotex service, Prestel, was launched in Great Britain in 1979 (Bowman & Christofferson, 1992). AOL founder Steve Case came up with his Big Idea, to make online services easy to try and easy to use, while struggling with an early videotex service in 1982.

The popularity of the Internet's communication functions trace back to *Bulletin Board Systems (BBSs),* many operating from closets and spare bedrooms of computer enthusiasts. BBSs sparked interest in the exchange of e-mail, posting opinions online, and uploading and downloading of computer information (Rafaeli & LaRose, 1993) that soon migrated to the Internet.

Videotex is the delivery of textual information to consumers over telephone networks.

The Web Is Born

In 1984, Apple's Macintosh introduced high-resolution graphics and **multimedia** to personal computers. The new graphics capabilities overwhelmed storage capacity of the floppy disks of the day, though. By 1988 compact discs used in home music systems were adapted to computers, establishing compact disc read-only memory (CD-ROM) as the first interactive multimedia.

In 1987, Apple began shipping an application called "Hypercard" with each new Macintosh. Hypercard popularized the *hypertext* concept, the "linking" function that makes it possible to navigate by "mouse clicking" on keywords or icons. However, that idea was not an Apple original. Presidential science advisor Vannevar Bush first proposed a system for storing and accessing information through associative links back in 1945.

The marriage of videotex, hypertext, computer graphics, interactive CD-ROM, and multimedia personal computers created the environment in which the World Wide Web was born. The initial vision for the Internet was spelled out by J. C. R. Licklider of the Massachusetts Institute of Technology in 1962 (Leiner et al., 2002; Cringely, 1998). He foresaw a global network of computers through which data and programs could be accessed from any point on the network. Licklider fulfilled his vision as the first head of the Defense Advanced Research Project Agency (DARPA), which funded ARPANET. The fundamental mode of communication for the Internet, packet switching, was developed by Paul Baran in the United States in the mid-1960s.

After a somewhat inauspicious start in 1969 (see above), the Internet rapidly added connections at major universities. Nineteen seventy-two was a breakthrough year. ARPANET had its first public demonstration, and that was also the year that e-mail was first introduced and when the network acquired its name and essential character, too. The term "internetting" was introduced to describe a new concept, open network design, that would allow diverse networks to talk to one another. Thus, the idea of a "network of networks" that still characterizes the Internet today was born. The basic rules, or protocols, for communication between networks were also laid out at that time, and these evolved into the *transmission-control protocol/Internetworking protocol* (TCP/IP), largely through the efforts of Vinton Cerf, and TCP/IP became the "official" protocol of the Internet in 1983. Another Internet pioneer, Jon Postel, contributed the system of naming and numbering addresses on the Internet.

The ARPANET had gradually spread from weapons researchers to other users at major universities. A number of other "closed" networks were growing in parallel in the 1980s, including an e-mail system for university professors (BITNET) and a popular discussion group system (USENET). To build a common infrastructure to support academic research nationwide, these networks were merged into NSFNET and put under the National Science Foundation (NSF) in 1986. At that time, many of the details of the design of the Internet were finalized and the foundation for the backbone network that would link regional networks together was laid.

In 1991 the Internet was opened to commercial users, and the NSF started withdrawing its financial support. Programmers at the University of Minnesota came out with a program named after their school mascot, Gopher, that first brought hypertext online, although it could link text files only. Also in 1991, Tim Berners-Lee of the CERN laboratory in Switzerland observed that researchers were hampered by the necessity of reformatting documents every time they moved between computer systems. He wrote the **hypertext markup language (HTML)** to solve that problem and the first primitive web browser to display textual documents. That was the basis of the World Wide Web.

A group of students at the University of Illinois led by Mark Andreessen released the first graphical Internet browser, Mosaic, in 1993 so that the average computer user could

Multimedia systems integrate text, audio, and video.

Hypertext markup language (HTML) is used to format pages on the web.

© AP/Wide World Photos

■ THE FATHER OF THE WEB
Tim Berners-Lee originated HTML and gave us the web.

view the wonders of the web, in color and with pictures. Their university wasn't interested in commercializing the product so Andreessen and his colleagues rewrote it for their own private company as Netscape.

By 1995, Netscape had over 50 million users, the operation of the net was turned over to commercial providers, and online services like America On Line (AOL) began offering Internet access. The Internet craze was in full swing. The web proved to be the "golden application" that propelled home computer ownership to new heights. Over the next five years, the Internet blossomed into an international network for entertainment, interpersonal communication, information, and commerce.

Governance of a burgeoning international network that had started life as a United States Defense Department research project, later to become an NSF science project, began to pose some problems. The ruling bodies of the Internet, notably the Internet Architecture Board and the Internet Engineering Task Force (see page 275) gradually expanded to include international representatives. The important task of doling out domain names, the addresses on the web, was in the hands of a private company, Network Solutions, under contract to the U.S. government. In 1998 ICANN (Internet Corporation for Assigned Names and Numbers) was formed as a nonprofit private corporation to oversee the assignment of the .com, .net, and .org domain names, and to develop new ones.

Content restrictions also became an issue. A portion of the Telecommunications Act of 1996, the Communications Decency Act, was written to ban "indecent" material, such as naked female breasts, from the Internet. That law was ruled to be unconstitutional, but efforts continue to restrict sexually explicit material in the United States. France apparently had no problem with breasts but tried to ban material considered politically obscene: souvenirs from Nazi Germany. China attempted to ban criticism of its government, and Cuba and North Korea prohibited Internet access to prevent their citizens from learning of the world beyond their iron curtains.

The heady days of the dot-com boom gave rise to new media companies that have since become household names, at least in "tekkie" homes. Jeff Bezos started Amazon.com in 1995 as an electronic bookstore before evolving into an online megamall. Internet auction house eBay first made its mark that same year as a marketplace for oddball collectibles, such as the Pez candy dispensers sought by the wife of founder Pierre Omidyar. Yahoo!, the brainchild of Jerry Yang and David Philo, two grad students from Stanford, began in 1994 as an online search engine before being supplanted by Google (the work of two other Stanford grad students, Sergey Brin and Larry Page, who started their company in 1998) and evolving into an advertising-supported *portal*. To some it seemed only a matter of time before the tiny, but interactive, banner ads on sites like Yahoo! would replace conventional advertising.

Other Internet pioneers did not fare so well. Steve Case's American On Line (AOL) introduced tens of millions of homes to the web and is still the leading Internet service provider, but it has faded into the background of the Time-Warner media conglomerate that it merged with in 2000. Netscape was soon supplanted by Internet Explorer on the strength of Microsoft Corporation's dominance of the home computer market and was absorbed by AOL. In 2000, the "dot-com boom" gave way to the "dot-com bust" as investors soured on Internet stocks, online consumers tired of the novelty of clicking on banner ads, and the general economy weakened. That year also marked the emergence of the Napster music sharing service, but that was closed down by court order in 2002 for violating copyright laws.

Media in the Internet Age

After the turn of the twenty-first century, the web matured and began to converge with conventional media. Consumer interest in online information, entertainment, and electronic shopping, or **e-commerce,** reached levels comparable to the early days of radio or television. Home computer ownership surpassed 75 percent (NetRatings, 2004), although many minority and low-income families were still unconnected (NTIA, 2004). And, profitability returned as many Internet start-ups shut down, leaving online ad and e-commerce revenues to be divided among the survivors. New models for Internet advertising (see Chapter 11) emerged, ranging from animated ads that literally jumped out of their boxes and moved across the screen, to short promotional films featuring "name" celebrities, to *sponsored link* ads that appear alongside search engine results.

To reach the millions of eyeballs now glued to the web, conventional media rolled out web versions of their products, invested in Internet properties, and incorporated online content into their signature products. Interactive television and online newspapers aimed to integrate web content with the conventional media consumption experience within the framework of conventional advertising-supported media. Cable TV systems offered Internet service and joined telephone companies to route calls over it. Broadband connections to the Internet skyrocketed, reaching 40 percent of U.S. homes in 2005. That spurred the electronic media to think about ways of distributing their products over the web and to clamp down on Internet pirates who "shared" music and movies for free.

The mid-2000s may yet prove to be era in which the old media gained dominance over the Internet. The entertainment industry resorted to heavy-handed tactics to curb the flow of free online entertainment, such as suing file sharers and their universities and imposing stiff copyright fees on Internet radio stations. Meanwhile, the wildly successful Apple iTunes service introduced millions of Internet users to the concept of paying for online entertainment content that was once available for free. With its carefully cultivated underdog image, few noticed that in the process Apple had jumped into bed with the old media and resorted to many of the same monopoly tactics that made Microsoft infamous. Broadband Internet connections and iTunes thus paved the way for successful pay entertainment services to follow. Still, the Internet continues to assert its unique advantages over the old media. In the wake of a tsunami disaster in the Indian Ocean in 2004, the Internet provided both a channel for news and images leaving the stricken region and a conduit for an unprecedented wave of individual charitable donations from Internet users the world over. An influential national survey showed that Internet usage was reducing television viewing (Nie & Ebring, 2005). So, the battle between old media and new media continues to rage in cyberspace.

TECHNOLOGY: MOORE'S LAW

Computers and their networks progress at an astounding rate. According to *Moore's Law,* processing capacity in computer chips has doubled about every 18 months since the late 1960s (Moore, 1996). That is why new personal computers are obsolete as soon as they come out of the box. And according to Metcalfe's Law (after Bob Metcalfe, one of the

E-commerce (electronic commerce) completes online purchases and financial transactions on the web.

founders of the Internet), the value of the Internet increases rapidly with the number of users. That drives continual Internet technology growth.

Inside Your Computer

As you may have learned in your high school computer class, the evolution of computers is traced through their *central processing units* (CPUs), where all the actual data processing takes place. First-generation computers, like ENIAC, used old-fashioned vacuum tubes like the ones in early radios (see Chapter 6). The second (1960s) generation used transistors, and the third (1970s) generation had integrated circuits with thousands of transistors on a single silicon computer chip. Today's personal computers are fourth-generation computers with very large-scale integrated (VLSI) chips with millions of components each. The latest mainframes are fifth generation; they use parallel processing units working in tandem. In the search for artificial intelligence some computers have CPUs that mimic the structure of the human brain.

Computers also need short-term memory to "remember" what they are doing and to hold the programs currently in use. Integrated memory circuits store the 1s and 0s of computer data in an array of tiny rechargeable batteries. The CPU charges up the "battery" when it wants to store a 1 and discharges for a 0. Personal computers hold hundreds of millions of bytes in their short-term random access memory (RAM) units. Each **byte** consists of eight of the tiny batteries, each representing a single *bi*nary computer dig*it*, or bit. But all those electrical charges die as soon as we turn our computer off.

Long-term memory saves our data for another day. Hard disk drives store data magnetically on a rigid, rapidly spinning disk so that the recording head can quickly move to any point to retrieve data. Floppy disks use a flexible plastic disk instead of a hard, rigid one. The three-inch floppies that carry about a million and a half bytes of data are fast becoming extinct, but high-tech versions of removable magnetic memory disks like the Zip drive will store nearly a billion bytes of data. Read-only memory (ROM) stores the basic instructions needed to start, or "boot up," the computer in solid-state circuits that activate whenever the computer is turned on. Compact disc read-only memory (CD-ROM) stores billions of bytes of data in patterns of tiny pits on the surface of a plastic disc, just like a music CD (see Chapter 5). Digital Versatile disc (DVD) drives are common; they hold up to 25 times as much data as conventional CDs. Most new personal computers have a recordable CD drive (CD-R) that allow users to record their own data, such as music files downloaded from the web, or rewritable ones (CD-RW). Now storage technologies for home video and home computers are converging rapidly. For example the new DVD+R DL recorders (see Chapter 8) will store up to 8.5 billion bytes of data on a double-layered DVD disk. Another high-tech bauble combines style with storage: miniature storage devices, called thumb drives or jump drives, carry billions of bytes of data on a key chain.

Convergence came to display technologies long ago. The cathode ray tube (CRT) display came along in the 1960s. It's just like a TV picture tube (see Chapter 8) except that each frame of the image is constructed from a single top-to-bottom scan of the picture tube, instead of by interlacing two partial scans as the television does. The LCD displays (also in Chapter 8) now making their way into home theater systems originated in laptop computer screens.

On the input side, each key on the keyboard sends out a string of digits in the ASCII (American Standard Code for Information Interchange) code when you press it. The mouse originated at the Stanford Research Institute in 1968.

A **byte** is (usually) eight computer bits. Each byte can represent a single numerical digit or letter.

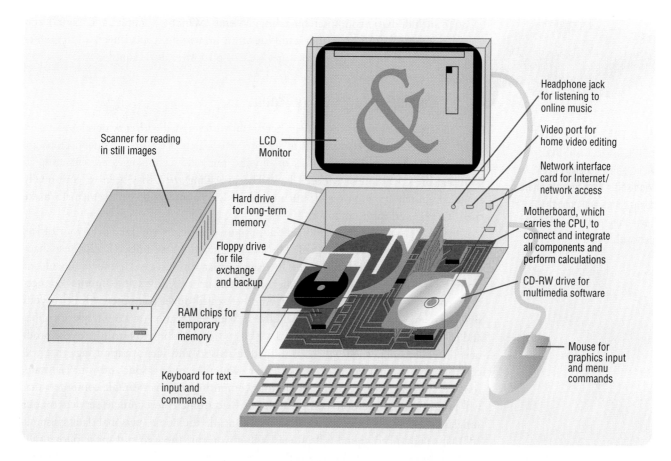

Scanner for reading in still images

LCD Monitor

Headphone jack for listening to online music

Video port for home video editing

Network interface card for Internet/ network access

Hard drive for long-term memory

Floppy drive for file exchange and backup

Motherboard, which carries the CPU, to connect and integrate all components and perform calculations

CD-RW drive for multimedia software

RAM chips for temporary memory

Mouse for graphics input and menu commands

Keyboard for text input and commands

■ **FIGURE 9.1**
Components of Today's Personal Computer System
Personal computer systems include the central processing unit (CPU), the monitor, input devices (keyboard and mouse), and data storage (hard disk and floppy disk).

Computers are sprouting new plugs to connect us with our multimedia world (Figure 9.1). The standard telephone modem jack has been joined by a wider one, called an RJ-45 jack, for high-speed Internet connections. The wide (about ½ inch) rectangular ones are Universal Serial Bus (USB) ports that connect a wide range of peripherals from printers to external storage devices. The tiny rectangular plugs are IEEE 1394 ports, more commonly known as FireWire, for rapid uploads from your digital still camera or digital video cam.

Software

Back in 1946, to shift ENIAC from calculating artillery shell trajectories to working on the hydrogen bomb, technicians had to move electrical cords and mechanical switches by hand. There was no *software*.

Early software was in machine language, written in 1s and 0s that drove the binary circuits inside the computer. FORTRAN, released by IBM in 1955, used recognizable words, such as "RUN" and "GO TO" and was the first high-level language. BASIC (beginner's all-purpose symbolic instruction code), came out in 1965. Young William Gates wrote a version of it for the Altair that gave Microsoft its start. Programs that use pictures and symbols to issue commands are graphical user interfaces (GUIs). Although popularized by Apple Computer, GUIs originated with Xerox's Alto computer back in 1972–1974.

Today, most personal computer and web applications are written in a language called C++. Application programs are the ones that actually perform functions for users. These

■ IS THAT A COMPUTER IN YOUR GAME CONSOLE?

Video-game consoles like Microsoft's Xbox include Internet connections and enough computing power to double as personal computers.

include basic computer operating systems (Windows, Apple, and Linux) and "productivity suites" that combine word processing, spreadsheet, and graphics applications in a single package—Microsoft Office, for example.

Computer Technology Trends

The future of the Internet is inextricably intertwined with new developments in the computers connected to it. Integrated circuits etched on silicon chips are nearing limits imposed by the laws of physics, but new technologies are emerging to continue the operation of Moore's Law. The prevailing trend has been to continually make computers more powerful, but now there is a countervailing movement to make them simpler and more compact.

In the "less is more" scenario special-purpose computers will take over your office, living room, and even your kitchen. The latest digital video recorders (DVRs; see Chapter 8) connect your television to the Internet so that you can receive movie downloads from the web. Or, video-game consoles with built-in hard drives and Internet connections could be the wave of the future. Another scaled-down computer will be in your stereo system, and perhaps another will live in your refrigerator (to keep track of recipes and to monitor your ice supply). Everyday objects from clothing to furniture to the products on your pantry shelf will have miniature sensors and identification tags that will connect them to your home network ("Dear owner: the milk is sour and your jeans are, too"). A tantalizing aspect of this ubiquitous computing trend is wearable computers that will project communication, computation, and electronic entertainment services on our sunglasses and respond to voice commands. Outside the home, personal data assistants (PDAs) or advanced digital cell phones will let you surf the web and make phone calls over the Internet while you are on the move and interface with your car's information systems. With all those specialized computers around, the ones in our dorm rooms and offices might be stripped down to Internet appliances that do little more than connect us to the web and download the software we need at the moment.

In the "more is better" case, multimedia computers will add new sound and video processing capabilities until they become home entertainment servers sitting at the middle of a high-speed computer network that distributes entertainment and information throughout your home. For example, a new version of Windows is designed to let you operate your home stereo, DVD player, and stereo through a personal computer acting as your home media server. A capacious hard drive will let you store all of your MP3s and record TV shows like the new digital video recorders (see Chapter 8) and retransmit them to all the rooms in your home.

Inside the Internet

Protocols are rules for data communication.

TCP/IP (transmission-control protocol/Internet protocol) is the basic protocol used by the Internet.

To understand trends in Internet technology, we need to recall that there are many varying patterns of communication, or **protocols** that are the basic building blocks of Internet applications. There are over 100 protocols associated with the Internet, known collectively as **TCP/IP (transmission-control protocol/Internet protocol).** (Figure 9.2) Many govern the inner workings of the network, rules for addressing, routing, error checking, and acknowledging messages. Some of the protocols that are readily apparent to Internet users include:

- *Mail.* The *simplified mail transfer protocol (SMTP)* is for sending e-mail between host computers on the Internet. The *Post Office Protocol (POP)*

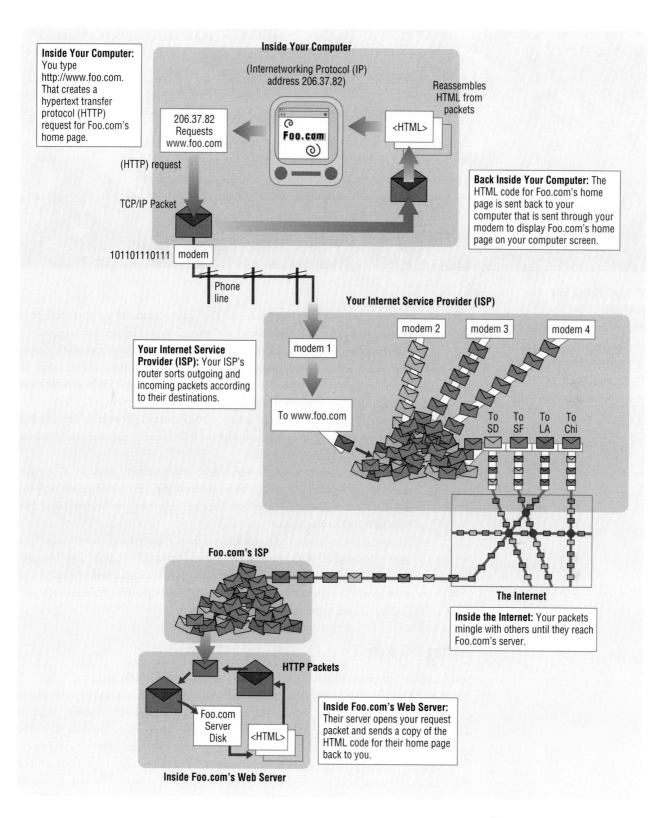

Inside Your Computer: You type http://www.foo.com. That creates a hypertext transfer protocol (HTTP) request for Foo.com's home page.

Inside Your Computer

(Internetworking Protocol (IP) address 206.37.82)

Reassembles HTML from packets

206.37.82 Requests www.foo.com

Foo.com

<HTML>

(HTTP) request

TCP/IP Packet

Back Inside Your Computer: The HTML code for Foo.com's home page is sent back to your computer that is sent through your modem to display Foo.com's home page on your computer screen.

101101110111 modem

Phone line

Your Internet Service Provider (ISP): Your ISP's router sorts outgoing and incoming packets according to their destinations.

Your Internet Service Provider (ISP)

modem 2   modem 3   modem 4

modem 1

To www.foo.com

To SD   To SF   To LA   To Chi

The Internet

Inside the Internet: Your packets mingle with others until they reach Foo.com's server.

Foo.com's ISP

HTTP Packets

Foo.com Server Disk

<HTML>

Inside Foo.com's Web Server: Their server opens your request packet and sends a copy of the HTML code for their home page back to you.

Inside Foo.com's Web Server

■ **FIGURE 9.2**
Inside the Internet   Information is sent over the Internet using the TCP/IP protocol.

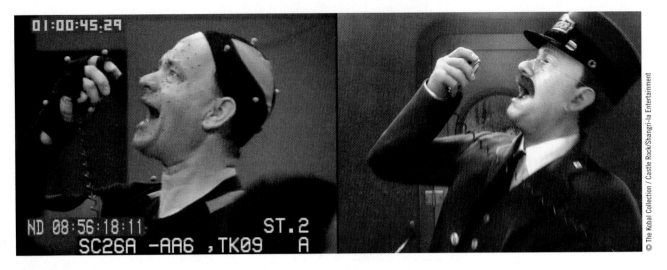

■ CAPTURING THE VIRTUAL YOU

By donning motion capture gear like that worn by Tom Hanks during the making of *The Polar Express*, actors can be positioned in virtual reality environments.

connects users to their mail servers. The *listserv* protocol governs electronic mailing lists (listservs) that "broadcast" e-mail to special-interest groups.

- *File Transfers.* The *file transfer protocol (FTP)* governs how electronic documents and computer programs are transmitted across the Internet, such as when web pages are uploaded to a web server by using FTP. The **hypertext transfer protocol (http)** handles file transfers over the web.
- *Locators.* The *Domain name service* (DNS) translates web addresses that people use (such as http://www.msu.edu) into the addresses that the Internet uses (such as 35.9.7.102).
- *Conversation. Internet relay chat (IRC)* lets Internet users send instant messages by typing back and forth to one another. The *Usenet* protocol is for asynchronous discussions in which users make postings in online discussion forums called newsgroups.
- *Remote Access. Telnet* logs into computers from remote locations to access files and programs. *PPP (point-to-point protocol)* and *SLIP (serial line interface protocol)* are protocols for accessing the Internet through phone lines.
- *Document Display.* The *hypertext markup language (HTML)* governs the display of web pages on the screen.

Surfing the Web

Several of these protocols work together when you go surfing on the web.

Web pages are stored on disk drives on dedicated computers called *web servers* connected to the Internet. The servers may be ordinary personal computers connected to a modem and running special software that lets remote users access the data, but that makes for very slow downloads. Large commercial sites use high-powered computers connected to high-speed *digital carrier lines* (such as *T1s* or *T3s*; see Chapter 12) so that they can store gigabytes of data and serve thousands of users at once. The web page files include *html tags* (see "Technology Demystified: Make Your Own Web Page from Scratch!" on page 267) that your browser software (for example, Internet Explorer) uses to display the text and graphics on-screen.

When you request a web page by typing its *Uniform Resource Locator (URL)* into your browser or by clicking on a hyperlink, the *DNS* protocol translates the address of the web page you ordered into the numerical form of the address and sends the request to your modem. The request is formatted using the *hypertext transfer protocol (http)*. The

Hypertext transfer protocol (http) is the Internet protocol used to transfer files over the web.

Make Your Own Web Page from Scratch!

Everybody knows how easy it is to be a web page author these days—you just select the "save as web page" option in your favorite word processing program. You can actually make a web page from scratch, without *any* special software, if you are willing to learn a little hypertext markup language (HTML). Knowing your way around HTML code is a valuable skill if you want to make your living in the Internet industry because those programs that make things easy for you also create "bloated" HTML code that professional web developers disdain. Basic HTML knowledge also comes in handy if you want to fix "broken" code on your own web pages. So let's see how easy it is:

```
‹html›‹p›THIS IS MY WEB PAGE‹/p›
‹p›This is my lost dog Skippy.
‹a imgsrc="skippy.gif"›Skippy‹/a›.‹/p›
‹p›‹a href=www.ibm.com>
P.S. I dig computers.‹/a›‹/p›
‹/html›
```

will produce the simple web page you see on page 269, with a link to the IBM web page at http://www.ibm.com. Those expressions inside the angle brackets are the *tags;* they are the instructions that tell your computer how to display the elements of your web page. For example, p starts a new paragraph; /p indicates the end of the paragraph. The imgsrc command identifies the graphics file we want to put on our page. Now save your file as "plain text." Finally, rename your HTML file index.html.

Unfortunately, XHTML (see page 269) complicates things a bit. You have to add <head> and <body> tags at the beginning of the document and include a <title>. You also need something called a document type declaration (DTD), to let the browser know what type of web page you have. And, the <html> tag must indicate what form of XML you are using and the language (for example, "en" for English). But our simple web page will still work without all of that. HTML tutorials are available on the web, and you can easily copy the commands from other people's web pages by simply clicking on View Source on your web browser's top-line command bar and copying the instructions into your file.

Whether you are writing your own HTML code or taking the easy way out, you have to get pictures scanned into computer-readable format. If you have a photo of Skippy, it's best to use the .JPG (short for JPEG, the Joint Photo Expert Group standard for compressing digital photographs) format. If you have a hand-drawn "wanted poster," use .GIF instead; it's better for illustrations (and you can't just change the file extension, you actually have to reformat the file). Many one-hour photo stores also give you the option of getting your pictures on disc, although you may have to change formats.

Web design programs provide a "publish" button when you want to send your files to your web server, but you can do that the old-fashioned way, too. Inside your web browser's URL window just fill in ftp:// followed by the location of the place on your web server where you want the file to be located (you get that from your Internet service provider).

SLIP or *PPP* protocols govern the transfer of information between your computer and your **Internet service provider (ISP).**

Your request is a short message, but the web page you receive in return may be quite lengthy, and that could tie up both the server and the network connection. So, before sending the page you requested on its way, the server breaks it up into a number of *packets* of about 1500 characters (or about 12,000 bits) each. (This paragraph has about half that many characters, including the spaces.) The server appends a header with dozens of bits of information that indicate how many packets are in the message and the sequence number of each packet, along with the result of a mathematical calculation that is used to check each packet for errors that might occur during transmission. The rules for doing all that are called the *transmission-control protocol,* or *TCP.*

The packet of data and the TCP information are then placed in a digital "envelope" that has your Internet address (known as your *IP address*), the address of the server, and instructions about what to do about packets that get delayed for some reason. That is done according to the Internet protocol (IP). Taken together, these two sets of rules are referred to as TCP/IP.

Then the TCP/IP packet is sent to a network switching device called a *router.* Routers are like postal clerks. They check the IP address on each packet and select the best path for

Internet service providers (ISPs) are the companies that provide connections to the Internet.

it through the Internet *backbone* network. Along the way, the packets pass through several routers and some packets may be diverted to alternate routes depending upon which path is the least congested at a given moment. The TCP/IP packet containing the requested web page is ultimately directed to your ISP's router, then into the ISP's modem at the other end of your local telephone connection, and finally into your own modem.

Your computer reassembles the packets according to the sequencing information (the TCP part), checks for errors, and requests replacements for any corrupted packets. Then all the addressing and sequencing information is stripped away, and the parts of the original HTML file are merged together and sent to your browser. The **browser** displays the page for you according to the instructions it finds in the HTML file. Then you see the web page.

Internet Trends

The future of the Internet is shaped in part by changes in network transmission technology that we will examine further in Chapter 12. Our main focus here is on trends in Internet protocols. The most important point to bear in mind here is that the Internet's packet switching protocol is well on its way to taking over the world of the media. Everything from music (MP3s, Chapter 5), to telephone calls (Voice over IP, see Chapter 12) to video (see below) is being transmitted over the Internet, and more is to come.

Networks. Briefly, the major network technology trend is toward broadband connections capable of millions of bits per second that are on their way to every home and work cubicle (see Chapter 12). Cable modems have the early lead over Digital Subscriber Line (DSL) connections in the broadband race. At 56,000 bits per second, your old computer modem is an obsolete slowpoke. To keep up with all the MP3 and digital video files that broadband users download, the connections in the Internet backbone are also being upgraded to fiber-optic cables that carry billions of bits per second.

The other major network trend is wireless. Third-generation (3G) cell phones make it possible to check your e-mail and surf stripped-down web pages with your phone. The addition of geopositioning satellite (GPS) capabilities to the phones will deliver site specific information, such as a guide to nearby restaurants—or spam about special offers from the convenience store on the next corner. *WiFi* (more formally known as IEEE802.11) offers wireless broadband access, but only if you stay in one place. A growing number of college campuses, airports, Internet cafés, home users, and even entire cities are installing WiFi "hotspots" for broadband access. If the limited rage of WiFi hotspots frustrates you, watch for new WiMax services that will cover entire cities from powerful, centrally located transmitters. And, if you want your 3G cell phone (or your portable MP3 player or digital camera) to "talk" to your PC without a wire, there is a third technology, called Bluetooth, for wireless connections across your table top.

Streaming. Along with faster broadband connections, streaming technology is what will someday relieve us from the frustration of slow downloads. Streaming makes the Internet "play" like a radio or TV. The originating server sends a continuous stream of short files, each with a small segment of the audio or video, and each segment plays as it arrives. (Live webcams and Internet telephony use the same technique.) High-tech music fans who are tired of the hassle and danger of music downloading are learning how to record the streams for later playback. One such product, Replay Radio, boasts that it is TiVo for your Internet radio, complete with access to a thousand stations all over the world—and the ability to skip the ads. Even after the files are cut down to size, a major compromise

Browsers are the computer programs that display information found on the web.

with the Internet's packet switching protocol is necessary, though. Corrupted segments may be dropped instead of waiting for corrected packets to arrive. That approach is known as the User Datagram Protocol (UDP). To keep up with the web's growing video capabilities, video search engines are beginning to appear. Some envision a day when these replace the TV remote control and TV Guide as the gateway to the world of video.

New Languages. Also adding much "coolness" to the web are variations on the basic hypertext markup language (HTML) (see "Technology Demystified: Make Your Own Web Page from Scratch," page 267). When you see web pages with dazzling animated sequences, you might be experiencing *DHTML* (the "D" is for dynamic), an HTML extension that controls the position and motion of graphic objects on your screen. There is a stripped-down version called the Wireless Markup Language (WML) for wireless Internet devices like digital cell phones. Voice recognition technology is also being introduced so web users can navigate and ask for assistance with spoken commands.

XML ("X" for eXtensible) lets programmers define their own tags. Tags are the commands that tell your browser how to display the document, for example, where to locate a picture on the screen and how big it should be. The price for a zircon ring could be identified with a price designation in XML, whereas an HTML tag would just specify format (for example, font size) without reference to content. Your computer can search XML pages for the price information, extract it, and make a custom display just for you, perhaps one comparing zircon ring prices from all over the web. XML is a "meta language" from which tags for specific applications can be made. For example, NewsML is an XML variation that standardizes the presentation of audio and video clips and interactive features alongside Internet news stories. XHTML is a new version of the original HTML language that makes web pages conform to the rules of XML, so that (eventually) web pages will look the same regardless of which browser you are using.

When you see a gray box that says "application loading," that means a Java program is downloading to your computer. Java Scripts are written with a subset of the Java language. They can change the appearance of buttons as your mouse "rolls over" them and perform other interactive tricks. At e-commerce sites, your credit card and order information is funneled to the web store's computer with another type of interactive program, Common Gateway Interface (CGI) scripts.

© David Young-Wolff/PhotoEdit

■ **FUTURE TV?**
Streaming video could evolve into an alternative to your TV set.

■ **MY WEB PAGE**
The HTML code on page 267 creates this web page.

Plug-ins.   These are "helper programs" that work along with browser software to play audio and video (for example, RealPlayer®, Windows, or QuickTime players), activate animations (Flash), or display documents (Acrobat). Others display 3D images or accessorize your MP3 playbacks with improved sounds or images that dance on your screen. These are large programs that must be downloaded and installed before the features will work, but the more popular (and less proprietary) ones eventually get built into new versions of web browsers.

As multimedia web content expands, media players are another way to speed things up, by further compressing media files that are sent over the Internet. The new MPEG4 standard cuts files to a sixth of the size of MPEG2 (MP3 is the audio component of MPEG2; see Chapter 5) files used on home video DVDs and in digital cable systems. New media players from RealNetworks, Apple, and Microsoft incorporate this technology. However, the new media players come with another feature that consumers may not appreciate, *digital rights management.* These systems provide for the **encryption** of content with a secret code that can prevent users from recording or replaying content for which they have not paid the copyright holder.

Tracking.   Some other web innovations also aren't so cool if you are concerned about your privacy. **Cookies** are tiny files that some websites deposit on visitors' hard drives. That's how sites recognize visitors and greet them by name without making them log in every time. But cookies can also track and collate information between sites without the user's knowledge, and third-party cookies placed by companies that monitor web advertising may do so without the user's knowledge. (If you want to check your cookies, open Internet Explorer 6, click on Tools, Internet Options, Settings, View Files.) Cookies can be controlled through the security settings in the latest browser programs. IE6 also incorporates the Platform for Privacy Preferences (P3P) that automatically "reads" the privacy policies of participating websites and accepts cookies only from those that comply with strict privacy standards, such as not collecting personally identifiable information. However, few sites supply that information in a form that P3P can read.

Web bugs are tiny (one-pixel) or invisible (for example, matching the background color of the web page) images that are embedded in HTML code. When your browser pulls them up, the server that stores the invisible images receives a notification. These bugs can follow your tracks inside a website and also track you to other web pages. They can also extract identifying codes from cookies stored on your computer that identify you uniquely at the sites you have registered. And your e-mail can be bugged too, letting the sender know when you open it and also if you forward it to someone else!

However, even when there are no cookies or web bugs present, your privacy is not assured. That's because the basic operation of the Internet's TCP/IP protocol routinely uses your Internet address to route information. When you switch from one website to another, the site you leave receives information about where you are going and the next one you visit also "knows" where you were last.

Yet another privacy threat is *spyware* (sometimes also called adware). These are programs that are downloaded to your computer when you install other applications from the Internet, such as music file sharing programs. The spyware not only monitors your surfing behavior, but also causes ads to pop up on your screen in the hopes of directing you to e-commerce sites. Your online safety is also threatened by security "holes" in your browser or operating system software. These allow hackers to get access to personal information stored on your computer or to use your computer to launch spam at other users. Windows and Internet Explorer are the most vulnerable because they are so ubiq-

---

Encryption means writing a message in a secret code.

Cookies are small files that websites leave on their visitors' computers.

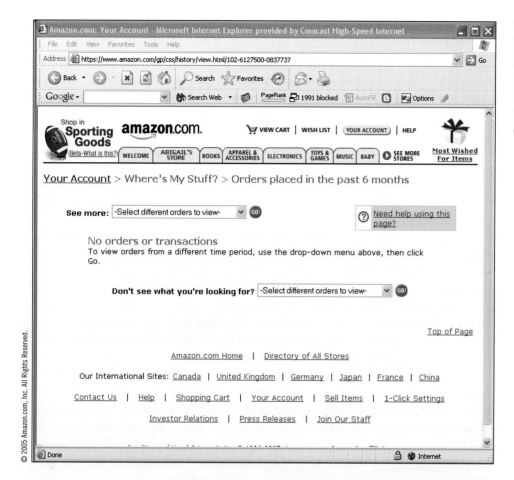

YOUR SECURITY IS A LOCK
Look for the https (at the upper left) and the lock icon (at the bottom right) to be sure that you are on a secure Internet connection.

uitous. Hackers don't bother with the Apple operating system or the Firefox browser, so some users switch to them just escape the hackers.

Encryption. Internet encryption protocols have come to the forefront in the battle between college students and the media industry over the "sharing" of media files. The industry is adding encryption to streaming music files and to prerecorded DVDs and CDs that the students try to "crack." For their part, the students encrypt the music and video files that they send through file "sharing" services so that the industry's copyright lawyers can't prove piracy. Encryption is also essential to protect credit card transactions in e-commerce and is also becoming an issue in efforts to crack down on terrorism and other criminal activities.

Digital encryption methods involve scrambling the digits in a message so that only the recipient can read them. A simple method would be to add a 1 to each digit (so that 1001 becomes 0110). But computers are adept at ferreting out simple patterns such as these, so complex formulas called encryption algorithms are used. The algorithm plugs a unique string of random numbers (called the key) into the formula to encode and decode the message. Even then, if we used the same key for all of our messages it would eventually be easy to crack the code. So, there has to be some way to change the key for each message and to share that key with our correspondent (using a public key) without meeting him or her in a dark alley and exchanging a secret code that only the two of us share (that's called a symmetrical key). We also want a private key, known only to us. But, if we sent that key over the Internet, someone could intercept it!

1. What were the contributions of Charles Babbage, John Vincent Atanasoff, and Eckert and Mauchly to the early development of the computer?

2. How did the personal computer come about?

3. How was the World Wide Web born? Who were its pioneers?

4. What are the important components of computer systems, and how do they function?

5. What are some new web technologies?

One popular approach to resolving this dilemma is to combine the different types of keys; this is found in the popular Pretty Good Privacy (PGP) protocol incorporated into many e-mail programs. We code the document with a symmetric key that only we and our correspondent know and that is good only for a single session. Then we encrypt the symmetrical key with a public key that our correspondent sends us but which requires his or her own private key to decode. First we decode the symmetrical key by using the public key and our own private key; then we use that to decode the message.

Online credit card transactions are encrypted using a similar method called the secure socket layer protocol. You can tell when you are at a secure website because the address window shows https (think "s" for security) instead of http and a tiny padlock icon appears in the lower corner of your browser frame. Although no encryption method is foolproof, when you see that symbol your transaction is at least as safe as handing your credit card to a department store clerk and far safer than reading it over the phone to a complete stranger! Most security problems occur after your credit card number is stored on a vendor's server, not while it is being transmitted.

In fact, commonly available encryption protocols are so effective that they pose a national security threat: even the most powerful computers can't easily crack coded messages between would-be terrorists and criminals. So, law enforcement officials periodically put forward proposals that would require users to give the government copies of their private keys.

Internet 2 is a project involving over 200 universities that conducts experiments with the next generation of Internet technology and gives us a preview of more things to come. High-speed connections (250 megabits per second) will transform today's grainy Internet videos into HDTV for high-quality video conferences and distance education applications as well as entertainment. Multicasting will make it possible to connect thousands of screens to the same content, an Internet version of cable television. A growing number of universities are using the high-speed network to deliver cable television channels to their students' computers instead of their television screens even as the students use it for superfast downloads of "shared" music and video files. And, the annoying skips and pauses encountered when streaming audio or video content today will be a thing of the past.

An update to the basic Internet protocol, IP version 6, is also part of the plan. It will extend the length of Internet addresses so that more can be made. The current TCP/IP protocol will run out of addresses after "only" about four billion have been issued. If we issue addresses in all of the world's languages, that could soak up billions more (see "World View: What's in a Name?", page 277). And, what happens when your car, your TV set, and your toaster need their own IP addresses? IP version 6 (we currently use version 4) will have the capacity for trillions of addresses.

THE INDUSTRY: DAVID VS. GOLIATH

Internet 2 is a new, faster version of the Internet.

The Internet industry has several major sectors. Hardware manufacturers make the computers and network gear, and software publishers make the programs that run on them. Content providers develop web pages, and Internet service providers (ISPs) provide access to them. Telephone, cable, and satellite companies (see Chapter 12), provide the infrastructure of the Internet backbone and also home connections. Their representatives also sit on the governing bodies that oversee the operation of the Internet and set its technical standards. Each industry sector has giant firms but also many innovative small ones that sometimes overturn the Goliaths with bold new ideas.

Computer Toy Makers

The hardware sector includes makers of computers (further subdivided into supercomputers, mainframes, minicomputers, workstations, and personal computers), computer storage devices (such as disk drives), and their peripherals (such as printers and modems). The Internet also relies on specialized network gear that directs packets of Internet data to their proper destinations. In the personal computer market, Dell and Hewlett-Packard are the leaders. The two companies that started the personal computer trend, Apple and IBM, are now minor players, and IBM's personal computer operation was sold to a Chinese company in 2004. Sun Microsystems and Silicon Graphics are the leaders in producing the powerful workstations that graphic designers and media special effects specialists use. Cisco Systems is the leading maker of network gear for the Internet.

Where Microsoft Rules

Software manufacturers develop applications for personal computers, an industry several times the size of another well-known "software" industry, motion pictures. Microsoft dominates personal computer operating system software (that is, Windows) and also many application categories, including word processing (Microsoft Word) and web browsers (Internet Explorer). Software manufacturers resemble book publishers in that sales are made through retail outlets that offer titles from many different publishers. Much of the software that winds up in the hands of consumers is bundled with computer hardware at the time of purchase. Increasingly, though, software is bought and downloaded over the Internet, an important component of electronic commerce.

A great deal of software is *freeware* or *shareware.* This is software, such as the Linux operating system, for which the authors do not claim copyright protection or whose developers lack a sophisticated distribution network and hope that users will pay voluntarily. As for Internet browsers and plug-ins distributed for "free," they are still part of a moneymaking scheme. Their creators profit from the sale of other programs that make new content and the specialized software that runs the servers on the Internet.

AOL and Company

Internet service providers (ISPs) connect users to the Internet and provide e-mail accounts. Some, such as industry leaders America Online and Microsoft Network (MSN), create original content and so combine the roles of ISP and content provider (see below). Others, such as Earthlink (and thousands of small local providers across the country) are purely ISPs in that they provide access but little in the way of content aside from portal pages that welcome their users with the news of the hour when they log on. ISPs usually lease high-speed connections to the Internet backbone from telecommunications carriers such as MCI or local phone companies or are affiliated with companies

© Getty Images

■ **WHERE'S THE COFFEE?**
Internet cafés offer temporary ISP service and computer access for a fee.

with their own networks. Major long-distance carriers, most local phone companies, and a growing number of cable TV operators also offer ISP services. Currently there are about 10,000 ISPs in the United States in all (http://www.thelist.com, 2004), although many are small local operations.

To understand the ISP business, let's start with a local mom-and-pop operation. Their basic business model is resale of telecommunications services. They lease a high-speed phone line (such as a T1; see Chapter 12) and connect it to the Internet with a packet switching device called a router. They need a server that will host user web pages and handle e-mail but that could just be a personal computer with lots of *RAM* and a huge hard disk. The server software is shareware. On the inbound side is a pool of modems that accept incoming calls from subscribers. Then they obtain a domain name from an Internet registry service (see below) and they are in business. As long as the monthly subscription fees cover the monthly charges for the T1 and the inbound local lines, pay mom and pop reasonable salaries, and pay the up-front investment, the ISP turns a profit. The entry costs may only be a few thousand dollars for the server and the installation of the phone lines. If mom is the computer expert, she tends the computers and phone connections and provides tech support while pop takes orders and sends out bills. If business gets too good and their subscribers start complaining about busy signals, they add more local phone lines, T1s, RAM, and staff to increase capacity.

What does online Goliath AOL have that mom and pop haven't got? All of the basic mom-and-pop functions turn into separate divisions inside AOL: marketing, customer service, billing, and technical operations. Now, AOL has Time Warner to produce unique content, something mom and pop cannot match. AOL has 23 million subscribers that attract advertisers and "partners" who pay millions for the right to be, for example, AOL's exclusive airline. Those are revenue sources that mom-and-pop operations do not enjoy.

One thing AOL does *not* have is an extensive in-house engineering department to oversee the technical operation of its network. It *outsources,* or subcontracts, that to concentrate on providing service and content. There are a wide variety of other outsourcing options available. Hosting services provide space for other companies' web pages on their servers. Ad servers such as DoubleClick.com will take charge of advertising sales and automatically insert the ads on their clients' sites. Other firms will run customer service or make the content of the web pages on a contractual basis.

Content Providers

Web pages are often made by in-house design departments. Some of the largest are the multimedia design departments at old media titans such as Disney, but new media companies such as Amazon.com and AOL have in-house staffs, too. Another model is to reformat content produced for the old media side of the business, as they do at the *New York Times,* but even that requires dozens of employees with web design skills.

There are also thousands of independent design firms and web developers (see http://www.1234-find-web-designers.org/) who blend the creative talents of graphic design professionals with the technical skills of webmasters and computer programmers. Interactive ad agencies are another source of web creation expertise. Web design firms once congregated in a few locations around the country, including the "south of Market street" (SOMA) neighborhood in San Francisco, Silicon Alley in New York City, and in the Los Angeles area. However, the dot-com "bust" of the early 2000s nearly emptied those areas out, and since then web design has cropped up nearly everywhere. Traditional graphic design, advertising, and public relations firms have also entered the market as have web hosting companies that provide server space for clients and that will design and maintain the site itself for an additional fee.

We also need to include the many sources, ranging from the National Weather Service to the author of the local elementary school lunch menu, who create the raw information that others shape into information services. In a sense, anyone who has ever posted her or his own "home page" on the World Wide Web is a content provider.

Internet Organizations

Who runs the Internet backbone (officially known as the very high-speed Backbone Network Service, or vBNS), the network that connects ISPs, web servers, and individual computers around the world? It is a not-for-profit, cooperative enterprise of major regional networks, such as the MERIT network in Michigan. The Internet is made up of high-speed digital carrier lines that are leased by the regional networks from long-distance carriers. At the local level, the ISPs lease or own high-speed phone lines that connect their local users to the Internet. The larger national ISPs maintain their own high-speed networks, interconnecting with the rest of the Internet only at regional Network Access Points (NAPs).

One of the most important issues is the assignment of addresses and domain names. In 1998, an international not-for-profit organization, the Internet Corporation for Assigned Names and Numbers (ICANN), was entrusted with this task. ICANN oversees private companies that replaced a single firm, Network Solutions, Inc., that previously had the job. Now ICANN decides who gets the rights to domain names and charges an annual fee to the domain owners for the privilege.

ISOC (the Internet Society) is a nongovernmental international membership society that promotes the orderly use and development of the Internet. It is modeled after the professional associations that college professors belong to—a throwback to when the Internet was a research network run by major universities. The Internet Architecture Board (IAB) is a committee within the Internet Society that makes important policy decisions about operations and future developments. Its members are, for the most part, employees of large corporations (such as Microsoft) that have important financial stakes in the Internet. Technical matters are overseen by the Internet Engineering Task Force (IETF) through its various working-group committees.

CONTENT: WHAT'S ON THE INTERNET?

The Internet has some characteristic forms of content that we have called "genres" in previous chapters. However, these concepts are still couched in the technical terms of protocols and domains.

The World Wide Web's content can be characterized according to the various domains (see "World View: What's in a Name?," page 277) that are appended to **uniform resource locators (URLs).** URLs are the jumbles of letters, "slashes," and "dots" that indicate the network addresses of content stored on web servers. An example is www-DOT-msu-DOT-edu (http://www.msu.edu) which will get you to the home page of Michigan State University (MSU). The .edu part indicates that the page belongs to the *edu*cation domain. The various top-level domains each have their own characteristic types of content, but .com is where most of the "sizzle" is found (see Table 9.1). We'll begin by considering types of content that fit well with the conventional mass media functions of surveillance and entertainment introduced in Chapter 2, and then go on to consider some of the newer forms.

Uniform resource locators (URLs) are the addresses of web pages.

Table 9.1 Top 10 Web Properties

Parent Name	Unique Audience (in thousands)	Time Per Person HR:min
Microsoft	89,110	01:21:44
Time Warner	79,235	04:01:47
Yahoo!	76,729	01:59:42
Google	55,137	00:19:56
eBay	36,496	01:47:34
United States Government	34,903	00:21:06
RealNetworks	23,731	00:33:28
Amazon	23,327	00:16:18
InterActiveCorp	23,032	00:17:55
Walt Disney Internet Group	20,597	00:35:39

Source: http://www.nielsen-netratings.com/news.jsp?section=dat to&country=US. For the month of February 2005.

Electronic Publishing

Electronic publishing includes online versions of conventional print publications, as well as information published only on the Internet, but with a difference. Even stodgy "old media" such as the *New York Times* (http://www.nytimes.com) reorganize content for the Internet crowd (such as the online *Times'* Circuits section, with articles about computer media) and add links to other sites, searchable indices of past articles, online forums, and multimedia extensions, including audio and video files and computer simulations. The online *Times* even has links to the cartoons and TV listings disdained by the staid printed version. A growing number of online publications, including the commentary magazines *Slate* and *Salon,* have no offline counterparts.

Other sites publish information that expands upon specific features of conventional publications (for example, the weather forecast) or contain volumes of information conveniently indexed in interactive form. Again, old media companies such as The Weather Channel (http://www.weather.com) and CNN (http://www.cnn.com) are among the most popular destinations. Others provide directories of useful information, such as Internet service providers (http://www.thelist.com). You can also find online encyclopedias (http://www.encyclopedia.com) and dictionaries (http://www.dictionary .com) for general reference.

Corporate sites run by large companies (for example, http://www.ibm.com) usually confine themselves to publishing information about themselves, their products, and their services once published in paper product brochures, annual reports, and press guides. But many, including Hewlett-Packard (http://www.hp.com), offer useful information to consumers and professionals in their fields of interest. Many, notably Cisco Systems (http://www.cisco.com), a manufacturer of network gear for the Internet, include electronic commerce storefronts to sell their wares to consumers or to other businesses.

Government information is also growing in importance, with U.S. government web pages among the most popular domains on the web. At all levels of government, there is

What's in a Name?

Domain names are the addresses that we use to find places on the Internet, and they work the same all over the world. The last part of the name, known as the top-level domain, can tell you a lot about the nature of the website you are visiting. Here is how to decode them.

.edu is meant for educational sites, including colleges and universities.

.gov is for government agencies.

.org is for nongovernment, not-for-profit organizations.

.mil is set aside for military organizations.

.net is for Internet service providers (ISPs).

.com is short for "commercial."

These six domains are not the only ones you will find if you surf the Net. Outside of the United States, domains are assigned according to country. For example, .it is for Italy, and .fr is for France. .int is for international organizations like the International Telecommunications Union. There is also .us for the United States, a domain name used by many city governments and public schools. Countries with catchy domain names are gaining thousands of "virtual citizens." Tonga's .to domain lends itself to memorable constructions such as welcome.to and sell.to, and many of Tuvalu's .tv addresses are rented out to the television industry. Other countries such as American Samoa (.as) have had their domains hijacked by profiteers, raising the issue of national sovereignty rights in domain names. Other countries want domain names that do not rely on the Roman alphabet, such as the Chinese and Arab countries. They have to use numeric URLs for now. Catalonia, a fiercely independent region of northern Spain, had been denied use of the .cat domain because it is a region and not a country and decided to use .net instead of .es (the domain name for the rest of Spain).

To relieve a worldwide shortage of domain names, ICANN has proposed several new ones, including .info and .biz for general use and .pro for professionals such as lawyers and doctors. The domain of .name can be used for personal web pages, .museum for museums, .aero for airlines, and .coop for business cooperatives. The new .kids domain is restricted to wholesome content just for children.

a growing trend toward *e-government*, so that citizens can find public information about everything from where the fish are biting to how to file for unemployment. An increasing number of applications and transactions with government agencies can also be completed online.

Entertainment

Entertainment sites also carry leading old media names such as Time Warner and Disney. Some, like the sites run by broadcast TV networks (http://www.cbs.com), are extensions of offline products that repackage or promote old media content. Others add new interactivity to old media, such as "play along" versions of popular TV shows like *CSI*. Yet others have a distinctive online identity (http://www.disney.com). A common thread is interactivity, with celebrity chat rooms and short media clips among the leading attractions.

Efforts to put conventional television and movie content on the web have met with only limited success thus far due to the long download times required for video files and the poor quality of streaming video. Adult entertainment is the lone exception thus far,

EverQuest: The Shadows of Luclin by Sony Online Entertainment Inc.
© EverQuest: The Shadows of Luclin by Sony Online Entertainment Inc.

■ **WHERE IS THE DUNGEONMASTER?**
Multiuser dungeons (MUDs) like EverQuest feature lifelike figures called avatars.

but we can't talk about that in a PG-rated textbook! However, the spread of broadband Internet connections and the prospect of Internet 2 are making online entertainment more viable. A new version of the TiVo digital video recorder records lengthy video files off the Internet for you while you are away from your computer, perhaps solving the downloading problem. Short video programs are available to subscribers to AOL's high-speed service, but anyone with a broadband connection can sample videos at http://www.winamp.com after downloading their free plug-in player.

However, there are millions of streaming radio stations in cyberspace, including many that can be heard only on the Internet and also many that are the personal stations of single individuals. Launchcast (Yahoo!), AOL Radio Network, and Microsoft Online Radio are the Internet radio leaders, offering links to hundreds of streaming music channels each. While all the genres of broadcast radio may be found on the net, Internet radio is a real boon to fans of musical genres that broadcasters find unprofitable or those who want to tune in to the world. For example, http://www.anetstation.com is a blues station from Antarctica. And, you don't have to tie up your computer while you listen. A growing number of options connect your stereo directly to the net.

Online Games

Online games are also entertaining, but their intense interactivity puts them in a category of their own. If you are tired of beating everyone else in your dorm at *NFL Fever,* you can look for new opponents online through the Xbox's Internet connection. Sony's Playstation and Nintendo's Game Cube are following suit. Other game sites try to replicate the experience of a TV quiz show.

Meanwhile, the staple of online gaming, Multiuser Dungeons (MUDs, also known as role playing games) have evolved from text-based fantasy games ("now the dungeon master enters the room and sees the magic key, now he turns to the princess and . . .") to elaborate multiuser communities that interact by clicking on graphical objects, called MOOs (for *M*UD, *O*bject *O*riented). Sorcery and magic themes are still popular. One, *EverQuest,* has over 60,000 online at a time and is sometimes called "evercrack" for its addictive qualities.

A variety of other themes are popular, including action-packed "shooter" and flight simulator games, variations on classic card and board games, and puzzle games. Online casino and poker games that allow real world (and also, in the United States, really unlawful) bets to be made are also the rage, especially among those with gambling addictions.

Portals

Portals combine directories, interpersonal communication, and information into an all-purpose, customizable "launch pad" that users will visit first whenever they go on the Internet. Portals greet registered visitors by name and keep track of their favorite types of content.

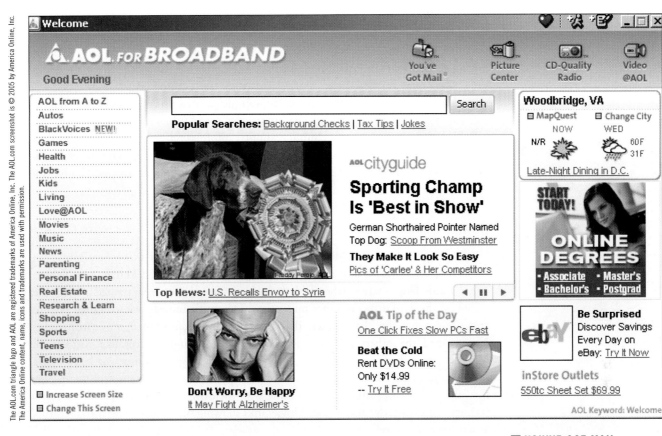

Portal content is organized around familiar categories such as news, entertainment, travel, computing, health, and personal finance. Interpersonal communication features include e-mail services, chat rooms, and discussion groups. Portals compete with one another with new customer services; some will keep track of appointments or remind you of anniversaries. In that respect, they fill the surveillance function (see Chapter 2), once the province of newspaper headlines and television news broadcasts, with a new personal twist. Advertisers see them as the web's equivalent to the electronic mass media. Leading portal sites include Yahoo! and those of Internet service providers such as AOL and MSN.

Search Engines

Search engines such as Yahoo! and Excite have been transformed into portals, but other sites maintain their primary identity as search engines. These are a new media form, although obvious print precursors may be found in library card catalogs, *The Reader's Guide to Periodical Literature,* and the local phone book.

These include index sites that allow users to search the Internet with keyword searches (such as google.com) and people finders (like switchboard.com). Google has emerged as the giant among search engines, so much so that turning up near the top of its search results is the key to success for many websites. Another search engine, Ask Jeeves, is also among the top 10 web properties (see Table 9.1). Students everywhere especially appreciate search engines of databases such as *InfoTrac, Lexis-Nexis,* and *Proquest* that connect them directly to articles they can cite in their term papers, without a trip to the library.

■ YOU'VE GOT MAIL

And you also have entertainment, information, shopping, and everything else on the Internet with America Online and the many other portal sites on the web.

Communities

Communities include chat rooms and listservs, instant messenger services, and the online forums that let users post their opinions, ask questions, and contribute to online discussions. Web rings are closed circles of related pages (for example, the Woody Allen web ring) that all refer to one another (http://dir.webring.com/rw lists many of these). In terms of media functions, these represent the interpretation and values transmission functions.

The interests range from technical computer information, to bizarre sexual practices, to news from exotic places around the globe. Others have evolved into online clubs and support groups. They have also become a staple of online college courses. Google and Yahoo! index communities online.

Downloading

File "sharing" sites are a wildly popular variation of community sites where music and video files, and also musical tastes and criticism, are shared. Best known was Napster, where music fans "shared" (the music industry preferred the term "pirated") MP3 files stored on the hard drives of other music fans. The music industry closed down Napster and similar sites, on the premise that they illegally circumvented music copyrights. Napster and the others gave way to peer-to-peer sharing services like KaZaA and Madster, where the file exchanges occur directly between users, without ever being stored on a central server where the music industry's copyright lawyers might find them. Now the "old media" companies are responding with their own pay service versions of music (iTunes and Rhapsody) and movie (MovieLink) showing sites. Now Napster has returned as a pay service as well.

Download sources also include the home pages of leading software manufacturers and CNET's download.com. There you can purchase new software, and download updates and plug-ins for your existing programs. They also have freeware that can be downloaded completely free of charge as well as shareware programs that can also be downloaded for free with the good faith expectation that you will pay to become a registered user at some later date.

Blogs

Weblogs, or *blogs* for short, are a cross between a personal web page, personal diary, an online directory, and a newspaper editorial page. They may record personal observations about the events of the day or record the events in one person's life.

Many blogs are organized around special themes with the hope of attracting like-minded web surfers (see http://www.blogwise.com for an index to several thousands of these). Many are written by professional journalists in their off-hours, offering yet another source of commentary on the web. Perhaps the best known is http://www.Wonkette.com (a.k.a. Ana Marie Cox). Specializing in titillating gossip from Washington, D.C., Wonkette has won minor celebrity status, covering the 2004 political conventions for MTV. Millions of web surfers have their own blog—and so can you (see Chapter 4). Blogs reached new heights in 2005 by carrying images of the aftermath of a tsunami that devastated the Indian Ocean region. This popularized a new form: the video blog.

Electronic Commerce

Electronic commerce sites perhaps belong in a category of their own. They are more like retail stores than conventional media enterprises, sites where you shop for products and

Media, the Internet, and the Stories We Tell about Ourselves

Not long after the Internet started being used by mass numbers of people in the United States, Jon Katz wrote in *Wired Magazine* about the impact of the Internet on the presidential election of 1996. The main impact then, he wrote, was that the Internet had enabled all the fringe groups to find and reinforce each other. So, if you really thought Bill Clinton was secretly controlled by little green men from Alpha Centauri, you could find like-minded souls on the Internet. That reflected a prevailing view that the Internet was going to fragment society into lots of small segments that did not share much.

In that regard, many thought that the Internet was the very essence of a new *post-modern* society. One of the main points of post-modernism is that society is gradually losing its big stories that almost everyone knows, its *meta-narratives.* For example, most people until at least the 1960s were familiar with a variety of Biblical ideas and expressions, even if they were not believing Christians or Jews. Now a writer or speaker cannot really assume that people in his audience will be familiar with those once-common sayings and concepts. Similarly, most people going through the educational system until the 1970s or 1980s had read a good deal of Shakespeare, so that many of his lines have become common phrases. Those are also now less widely familiar in the United States. Both of these sources contained a lot of what was considered common wisdom about what was important and how to live. Many of those meta-narratives were taught by parents, schools and churches, but many of their specific elements and references had also been carried across society by traditional mass media, like newspapers, magazines, and the big three television networks that almost everyone watched until the 1980s.

Post-modern theorists like Lyotard observed that one of the primary reasons for the breakdown in consensus over the main stories guiding our society was the fragmentation of people's experience with media. As media proliferated, people had more choices, so fewer shared common sources of ideas. People listened to different music, listened to talk shows of very different opinions, read different novels, and watched television shows with different spins and focuses. Within universities and high schools, people also argued furiously over what ought to be read and taught, so no one could assume that people had read the same things in their freshman English courses or their introductions to literature. So overall, even before the Internet, people were receiving increasingly wildly diverse ideas from fragmented media.

© Raymond Depardon/Magnum Photos

■ CULTURAL DIVERSITY OR FRAGMENTATION?
Michel Foucault is one of the originators of the post-modern school.

Many of the post-modernists consider this rather liberating. With less uniformity of media, it will be harder for anyone to exercise *hegemony* over ideas, to create and enforce an ideological consensus that limits freedom of thought. However, some sociologists, like Todd Gitlin in *The Twilight of Common Dreams,* worry that the consensus necessary for addressing social problems is breaking down into factionalism.

Some scholars are wondering, however, whether this supposed fragmentation is taking place. Looking at the Internet, for example, Edward Herman and Robert McChesney argue that since so much of the web traffic goes to the same large corporate media sites, the Internet does not have much potential for really breaking down the hold of the main media on the audience. They see news and information on the web dominated by the same faces with the same hegemonic intent (see Chapter 2).

complete purchases. E-commerce businesses that make sales directly to consumers are known as *b to c* (business to consumer).

Most follow the familiar catalog shopping model, except that the product information and order blank are online. Many sites are what the retail trade calls category killers: they specialize in one line of products, such as children's toys (for example, eToys). Others imitate shopping malls by carrying many different types of products, like Amazon.com, which is much more than an online bookstore. Many are pure e-tailers that exist only online. Many are online offshoots of brick-and-mortar retailers like Wal-Mart (and shopping mall chain KB Toys in the case of eToys) that are called clicks and mortar operations. In the aftermath of a giant meltdown in Internet stocks in 2001, many of the pure e-tailers (like the original eToys operation) closed up shop, but more and more conventional retailers are going online to incorporate the web in their overall marketing effort. Many are finding that customers shop for products on the web before coming into their real-world stores to actually buy them; other customers shop in the real world stores and return home to make their purchases online.

Other sites depart from the catalog shopping model. Services as well as products are sold online, with the Internet taking the place of the travel agent (for example, Expedia) and the hotel clerk (hotels.com). Auctions such as eBay (sometimes called *c to c,* for consumer to consumer) let visitors bid on collectibles and yard-sale items offered by other visitors. Reverse auctions like priceline.com let shoppers name the price and sellers bid to meet it. Or, shoppers can buy things from other people by tuning into newsgroups that specialize in buying and selling goods. There are e-commerce sites that don't actually sell anything but act as clearinghouses for comparative shopping information (for example, for automobiles at http://www.autobytel.com). Others have product directories, coupons, and buyer incentive programs.

By far the biggest category of e-commerce doesn't want your business, not unless you *are* a business. Business to business (or *b to b*) sites sell products to other firms. Network equipment manufacturer Cisco Systems became one of the biggest corporations in the world with that business model. There are also online shopping malls for business supplies and services, and some of the biggest corporations are organizing online bazaars for their suppliers and customers. The watchword is *disintermediation,* eliminating distributors that serve as intermediaries between manufacturers and their customers.

What Makes a Good Web Page?

Although 291 million people worldwide actively use the Internet, they don't use it very long, averaging only about six hours per *week,* as opposed to the four hours a *day* the average U.S. adult spends watching television (NetRatings, 2004). E-mail is the most common activity (see Table 9.2) and the most time-consuming. The web has millions of sites to choose from, and visitors spend an average of less than a minute on each page within a site. So an important goal of web page designers is to make people stay longer.

Table 9.2 Most Common Internet Activities	
Activity	**Percent Internet Users**
e-mail or messaging	88
Product/service search	76
News, weather, sports	66
Product/service purchases	52
Health-related search	42
Playing games	38
Government-related search	36
Online banking	28
Media (TV, movies, radio)	22
Job search	19
Financial transactions	6
Online course	6

Source: Based on all Internet users age 15+ NTIA, 2004.

Some of the techniques thought to increase user involvement are borrowed from old media, including contests and giveaways (borrowed from radio), continual updates of content (à la the newsbreaks on network television), and episodic storytelling (from television). Graphic designers adapt eye-catching colors and attractive layouts from magazine layouts. Content counts, too, although web surfers prefer short items, about a screen's worth, to lengthy articles. Portal sites borrow their basic "everything you need to start the day" strategy from newspapers. Other inducements to stick to e-commerce sites are drawn from retail promotions, including coupons, sales, and celebrity appearances. And if we can't beat TV, why not *be* TV? That's the premise of AOL's new broadband service, to lengthen visits by sharing movie clips and music videos.

There are other strategies unique to the web. Framing is the practice of surrounding pages with a border that includes a logo from the web page you started from. Interactive programs are also unique to the web. Many an Internet user has gotten hooked on a site by playing online computer games; participating in MUDs, chat rooms, or newsgroups; or even just compulsively answering e-mail. That's why portal sites incorporate these features.

Another strategy is personalization of content to individual users. In a sense, the website gets to know its visitors, responding to and even anticipating their needs. After establishing a personal relationship, visitors linger longer and return more often. Abandoning the site would incur the cost of reentering detailed personal information at a new portal, selecting from its content options, and waiting for it to learn our innermost desires by tracking our surfing behavior.

What websites are the stickiest of all? In terms of the number of minutes spent per visit, sites that feature online games, auctions, stock trading, free e-mail, and portal services are the most successful.

But perhaps the amount of time users spend at a site should not be the primary criterion for a "good" web page, though. That reflects "old media" thinking tied to the need to deliver eyeballs to advertisers. What about "coolness?" Coolhomepages.com collects ratings from other web page designers. From that perspective, the key to having a cool web page is lots of empty dark space (or blank white space) with small print, intriguing Flash animations, and large graphic design spaces. Among popular websites that you may have heard of, the Apple Computer home page (with lots of white space) gets high marks, whereas those with lots of text and useful information cluttering things up get no respect.

Another school of thought is that the amount of time spent on a page is an indication of *bad* design. Usability researchers (for example, http://www.useit.com) hold stopwatches on users and train cameras on them as they surf web pages. They try to identify and correct confusing features that slow users down. Designing web pages around tasks, giving all the pages in a site a consistent look and feel, supplying site navigation aids, and minimizing download times are key design considerations. In this approach, "cool" web pages with artistic designs and slow-loading animations that don't help users complete a well-defined task are bad designs. But "uncool" designs with lots of text and buttons all over the place also tend to flunk their usability tests, so at least the designers and the usability engineers can agree on that.

STOP & REVIEW

1. List the major Internet protocols and the major types of content on the web.

2. What makes web pages "sticky"?

3. Who are the leading makers of computer hardware and software?

4. What is the difference between a content provider and an Internet service provider?

5. What are the major divisions of labor in an ISP organization?

6. Who runs the Internet now?

MEDIA LITERACY: WHO SHALL RULE THE INTERNET?

As wider and wider segments of the world population come in contact with the Internet, pressures mount to rein in what some see as corrosive anarchy but others view as inalienable freedom. Internet privacy and intellectual property issues (see Chapter 14) grow in importance. What governance model will eventually emerge?

Internet as a Robber Baron?

What if the owners of Internet companies take a page out of the book of John D. Rockefeller and other Industrial Age "robber barons" by using the network as a tool to create monopolies? Software giant Microsoft Corporation was found guilty of that in 2000. A federal court found that Microsoft abused its market power by bundling its Internet browser software with its Windows operating system (which controls 95 percent of the market), a practice that drove competing browser makers (Netscape) out of business, creating excessive horizontal integration. The European Union is also after Microsoft. In 2004, EU regulators ruled that Microsoft must sell a version of Windows without the media player built in so that competing media players have a chance.

Microsoft chairman Bill Gates might respond that the Information Age is like no other, that the fast pace of technological change makes monopolies impossible—just look at the rise and fall, and the return, of Apple computer, for example. Meanwhile, Gates is investing in an astounding array of ventures in other areas of the "convergence business," including cable television, video games, and photo archives activities that raise new fears of excessive vertical integration. But with Old Media companies like Time Warner and Disney among the top destinations on the Internet, Gates might argue that they are a greater threat to dominate the new media.

A Corporate Hegemony?

Even if no one company dominates the Internet, corporate control is still a possibility. Although the Internet can be characterized as a collaborative, cooperative effort on the part of computer professionals around the world, the historical involvement of the U.S. government and the growing role of U.S. corporate giants cause concern. Critics fear that the corporatization of the Internet—the increasing influence of commercial interests on its governance and growth—will make it just another means of perpetuating the economic status quo (McChesney, 1996). Thus, some advocate putting the key administrative functions in the hands of not-for-profit international organizations such as ICANN. The companies that set the technical standards for this transition stand to profit immensely and could form powerful transnational monopolies that operate against the best interests of consumers, beyond the reach of the laws of nation states.

Aside from their sheer economic might, **copyrights** and **patents** (see Chapter 14) are the most important tools that corporations have to control the Internet. The Copyright Term Extension Act of 1998 was the key weapon the recording industry used to fight Napster. The record companies would prefer to limit music distribution to secure sites like iTunes and Rhapsody that can charge users for each copy. While they accuse college students of being "pirates" and ask their universities to act as copyright cops, perhaps it is the recording industry executives who are acting like buccaneers. Afraid that they couldn't profit sufficiently from distributing music new ways on the web, they had their

A **copyright** is a legal privilege to use, sell, or license creative works.

A **patent** gives an inventor the exclusive right to make, use, or sell an invention for 17 years.

industry lobbyists and lawyers use bare-knuckle tactics to ensure that they could keep plundering music fans the old-fashioned way. The courts ruled that peer-to-peer networks like KaZaA were not breaking the law because the indices listing the songs were on the computers of users, not KaZaA's. The recording industry responded by having their friends in Congress propose legislation that would make it unlawful to in any way "induce" another person to infringe copyrighted material; they hope that will allow them to close down the peer-to-peer networks as well.

Now the corporate attorneys are going after images. Anyone who uses an image of Mickey Mouse on his web page risks getting a nasty letter from Disney's lawyers. Bill Gates has obligingly endowed the new Windows Media player with "digital rights management" capabilities that will make it easy to crack down on piracy, but also to interfere with the fair use rights of consumers—for example, making it impossible to make back-up copies of music files. New copy protections on DVDs and digital TV sets will be in place to make sure that your fair use rights are impossible to exercise there, too.

Another copyright enforcement tactic is to prevent "deep linking," the practice of bypassing a website's front page (and also its advertising) to link directly to content buried within. If corporate attorneys succeed in having that outlawed it would cripple the essential nature of the web, the ability to hyperlink from one page to another. Thus far the U.S. courts have upheld deep linking, but a growing number of sites are implementing user agreements that prohibit the practice when users register at the site.

The Ruling Class?

Another danger is that the Internet will become the exclusive province of a privileged, computer-savvy ruling class, further widening the digital divide between rich and poor. Whites are much more likely to use the Internet than are Hispanics or African-Americans. Although more and more minority famililes have Internet access, the 20 percentage point gap between white and African-American families did not close between 2001 and 2003, belying claims that this so-called "digital divide" is closing. In addition, households with incomes of $75,000 a year or more are nearly three times as likely to use the Internet as those living in poverty (NTIA, 2004).

The disparity does not exist because minority families don't want computers; more whites than minorities give "don't want it" as their reason for not being on the Internet. Low income is a factor: Hispanics and African-Americans are twice as likely as whites to list "can't afford it" as the reason for being unconnected (NTIA, 2002). Lack of relevant content is another issue. Many nonusers feel there is nothing on the Internet they need. Others have trouble getting started. Low-income communities lack the helpers and training resources that are available to aid middle-class users. And, even as low-income users begin to catch up, high-income households are moving up to superior high-speed connections.

Other demographic differences between users and nonusers are disappearing as the web goes mainstream. More females than males now use the web, eliminating the gender gap in Internet access, although the quality of access to computer resources is still unequal (AAUW, 2000). Web users are still younger than nonusers and also better educated. Senior citizens, people with a high school education or less, and central city residents are also among the "have-nots" (NTIA, 2004).

Some of the disparities in Internet access between ethnic groups and social classes are beginning to disappear in the United States. Among children 8 to 18, the percent who go online in a typical day is virtually the same for whites, African-Americans and Hispanics (Kaiser Foundation, 2004). However, programs that have subsidized access in public schools and libraries are under attack, and both minority and low-income Internet users have a high degree of reliance on public computers. So, it is too early to conclude that the digital divide is a problem that has been solved. As broadband access spreads new "broadband" gaps between whites and minorities, rich and poor, urban and rural are cropping up. This is one instance where the United States lags the rest of the world, ranking near the bottom of the world's top economies in broadband penetration (ITV, 2003).

The danger is that as public institutions move online, bringing everything from driver's license renewals to voting with them, the poor will be disenfranchised. In the long run, inferior Internet access will also mean inferior access to employment and educational opportunity, deepening the cycle of poverty that costs all citizens dearly, both in this country and worldwide (see Chapter 16).

■ CLOSING THE GAP
Before the digital divide can close, more minority households will have to see scenes like this one.

Government?

Government intervention is one answer to threats of corporate abuse or class conflict. However, government control is inherently difficult to impose on a medium that freely crosses international boundaries.

Governments also like to tax what they control, which could retard the growth of the Internet. Thus far, the United States government is resisting the temptation to tax web access and federal law prohibits states and cities from taxing the monthly fees charged by Internet providers. However, the taxation urge is strong at the state level where e-commerce sales are beginning to cut into sales taxes that are the states' primary source of revenue. Online stores are required to collect sales taxes on purchases made by customers in the same state, but that applies only to the state in which the Internet subsidiary is located. If you buy a product from an out-of-state website, you, the customer, are supposed to pay the appropriate sales tax to your own state. However, few people are that honest and thus far states have only gone after purchasers of big ticket items. Plans for a uniform tax code that would simplify tax collection by retailers are in the works, though, so the tax-free/tax-cheating days of the Internet may soon be past.

On the other hand, the job of running the Internet is becoming too big to entrust to volunteer labor, as is now often the case. Essential Internet functions are overseen by technicians who work on the Internet as a sideline while holding down other full-time jobs. On one fateful day, the volunteers managing the Internet accidentally erased most of the addresses on the network so that most web pages were temporarily inaccessible. The Internet's current caretakers tend to be more technical than political in their orientation.

This situation is certain to invite the intervention of national or international political institutions. In 2003 the United Nations convened the first World Summit on the Information Society. The summit's action plan called upon the nations of the world to promote the development of the Information Society for the benefit of all, emphasizing core values of diversity, security, and education. However, it stopped short of recommending international initiatives or governance structures that might attain these goals.

It is tempting to look to the government for solutions to some of the social problems of the web. For example, the lack of equal Internet access might be addressed by establishing Universal Service policies like those for telephones (see Chapter 12). The Communications Decency Act was an attempt (although an unconstitutional one; see

Chapter 14) to ban pornography sites on the Internet. The Child Online Protection Act cracked down on sites that obtained personal information from children. There are repeated calls for new laws that will safeguard the privacy of adult Internet users as well, updating the *Electronic Communications Privacy Act* and other privacy legislation for the Internet age.

However, too much government involvement could have frightening implications for our civil liberties. Law enforcement officials also want the power to snoop on private communications sent in secret code (see below). The U.S.A. Patriot Act, passed in the immediate aftermath of the 9/11 terror attacks, enlists Internet ISPs as government informers. It initially endowed the FBI with sweeping powers to snoop on Internet users nationwide without obtaining warrants in local jurisdictions, although that provision was later struck down by the courts in 2004. The Homeland Security Act empowers government agents to sift through e-mail and Internet traffic logs to detect "patterns of terrorist activity."

And how will governments resolve conflicts between themselves? Efforts to stamp out smut on the Internet in America could undermine free-speech rights in other countries with more liberal mores. Other governments censor political ideas, such as when a French court banned online auctions of Nazi memorabilia and demanded that eBay remove the items (it refused). U.S. media giants want to wipe out "file sharing" services, but U.S. copyright protections are stronger (some might say excessive) compared to other countries. By basing their corporate headquarters, servers, and computer programs in countries with weaker protection, it might be possible to evade U.S. laws. Online gambling is another example. Operators set up Internet casinos and "bookie joints" in Third World countries where such activities are legal, allowing gamblers all over the world to have a "piece of the action" and avoid paying taxes on their winnings. Recently, the World Trade Organization sided with countries like Antigua where these activities are legal and accused the United States of unfair trade practices in attempts to cut off American gamblers.

The United States plays a dominant role on the Internet today, but that is changing fast. That's why ICANN (see earlier discussion) was set up with an international board. But thus far ICANN's leadership has been ineffective and the U.S. government threatens to terminate its contract. What governmental body could fill the void?

Terrorists and Criminals?

One area where more government involvement could be welcome is improving the safety of the Internet—we might call that *i*-Safety. The Internet harbors terrorists, and no sophisticated espionage techniques are required. The September 11, 2001, terrorists sent plain-text messages from public terminals in their local libraries to help coordinate the attacks. They also "surfed the web" to obtain public documents containing sensitive information about national landmarks, airports, and nuclear power plants as they selected their targets. That has resulted in a major cleanup of such information online. However, Homeland Security still fears a "digital Pearl Harbor" in which the Internet could be used to hack into vulnerable systems that control the nation's power and electrical supplies.

And, terrorists may also be using Internet-based identity theft schemes, sometimes called *phishing,* to finance their operations. That's when you get a legitimate-looking request from, say, someone with the web address of citisecure.com to give them your Citibank account number so they can track down fraud at the bank. In reality the information goes to an offshore website run by terrorists who use the information to plunder your account.

The Internet has also become a tool for ordinary criminals who use it to break into secure computer systems to steal information and wreak havoc. The worst fears of online shoppers were realized when a hacker managed to steal credit card numbers from CD Universe, a large e-commerce site. The malicious "fun" of spreading viruses over the Internet, soliciting sex from minors in chat rooms, and pitching fraudulent schemes via e-mail are other popular Internet crimes. Denial of service attacks threaten the operation of the Internet by bombarding websites with bogus requests that jam their servers and slow the Internet backbone.

Spamming occurs when direct marketers or outright con artists do mass e-mailings to the unwary user, often with names and addresses garnered from chat rooms or newsgroups. Many Internet users do not realize that they place themselves directly in the crosshairs of direct marketers who employ harvesting programs to automatically extract e-mail addresses at those sites. Personal web pages are another fertile hunting ground for spammers. Spam victims can use **filtering** utilities in their e-mail software to screen some of the junk. The new CANSPAM law makes it a crime to send spam, and it is beginning to have some impact. But, the spammers are adept at using phony accounts, routing replies through offshore servers, and even taking over the computers of unwary users to mount their attacks.

Theft is not the only criminal activity that makes us unsafe online. Armed with an interactive medium that integrates mass communication and personal communication, twisted minds can reach out directly to the impressionable—or be contacted by them. Indeed, there are horror stories of child molesters contacting their prey through Internet chat rooms, marriages ruined by online love affairs, and murderous Internet fantasies enacted in real life. One youth was found guilty of a hate crime for sending harassing racist e-mail to Asian-Americans whose names he plucked off Internet discussion groups. Efforts to control antisocial behavior by regulating content create a classic confrontation between free expression and public morality.

Unfortunately, many of the measures law enforcement might use to assure our *i-*Safety also infringe upon our privacy rights as citizens. We, the users of the Internet, also play a role in making the Internet safer. When is the last time you updated your virus protection, downloaded updates to your operating system software, or decided not to open an e-mail attachment that you weren't expecting?

STOP & REVIEW

1. Who should run the Internet?
2. How could digital media "robber barons" manipulate the information superhighway to their advantage?
3. What is the digital divide?
4. What are some of the major threats to privacy on the Internet?
5. How do terrorists use the Internet?

Spamming is unsolicited commercial e-mailing.

Filtering software automatically blocks access to websites containing offensive material.

SUMMARY AND REVIEW

WHAT WERE THE EARLY ORIGINS OF THE INTERNET?
Charles Babbage created plans for the difference engine, a mechanical precursor of the modern computer, in the 1820s. Samuel Morse's telegraph was the earliest precursor of today's computer networks. Early telegraph wire services such as the Associated Press were the forerunners of information services on the web.

WHAT LED TO THE COMPUTERS OF TODAY?
The first electronic computer was designed, though not successfully built, by John Vincent Atanasoff in 1939. Data processing needs in World War II resulted in the construction of the first working digital computer, Colossus, and the first programmable computer, ENIAC, developed by Eckert and Mauchly. The SAGE system, which produced breakthroughs in

computer memory, data communications, and display technologies, was also inspired by military needs. Advances in integrated computer memory circuits made it possible to construct small-scale computers. The Altair was the first personal computer, although the Apple II was the first machine of its kind that would be recognizable to today's PC user. College dropouts Steve Jobs and William Gates share the credit for key developments in personal computer hardware and software, and computer giant IBM gave personal computers their initial boost into the workplace.

WHAT ARE THE ORIGINS OF THE WEB?

Today's Internet began in 1969 as ARPANET, a computer network using the TCP/IP protocol to transmit messages between defense-related research labs. It slowly evolved to serve wider groups of academic and organizational users before being opened up to all computer users in 1991. The World Wide web represents one of the most successful protocols used on the Internet, the hypertext transfer protocol (http). It was the culmination of developments in computer graphics, hypertext, and consumer videotex services that crystallized with the creation of the HTML language in 1991.

WHAT ARE THE COMPONENTS OF A PC?

The computer's central processing unit is where data are processed and calculations carried out. Short-term memory holds the programs, or software, that run the computer and saves the results of the calculations on a temporary basis. Long-term memory, in the form of floppy or hard disks, makes it possible to save programs and information after the computer has been turned off. Computer interfaces, such as the cathode ray tube, keyboard, and mouse, let the user interact with the computer programs. A modem is a device that makes it possible to send programs and files of data between computers over telephone networks.

WHAT ARE SOME FUTURE DIRECTIONS?

One is to make personal computers simpler, perhaps yielding "ubiquitous computers" that will be found in many everyday devices such as TV sets and household appliances. The other direction is the design of more sophisticated multimedia computers that will replace all of the other communications media found in the home today. Both scenarios foretell the evolution of the web into a multimedia network that will carry radio, TV, and phone conversations. New web programs including XHTML, Java, and special-purpose plug-ins expand the interactive capabilities of the Internet. An upgrade of its backbone capacity, known as Internet 2, the spread of high-speed access options for home users, and new wireless technologies will expand the capabilities of the Internet.

HOW IS THE INTERNET INDUSTRY ORGANIZED?

Computer hardware companies such as Dell make the computers. Software companies such as Microsoft manufacture common computer applications, but again there are many specialized niches for particular types of software, and other companies specialize in designing custom software for specific users. Content providers are the companies that create information for the web and multimedia applications, whereas Internet service providers make the actual physical connections to the Internet. No one entity owns or controls the Internet or the web. They are run by a patchwork of voluntary organizations, including the Internet Corporation for Assigned Names and Numbers (ICANN) and the Internet Society.

WHAT'S ON THE INTERNET?

Internet content can be defined in terms of the major varieties of protocols that are used, which include e-mail, file transfers, chat, locators, remote access, and document display. The web is an example of the latter. Web pages may be categorized by their domain names (such as .com and .edu; see "World View: What's in a Name?," page 277) or by the nature of their content. Portals, e-commerce entertainment sites, and information are the leading categories today, but new genres are continually emerging.

WHO RUNS THE INTERNET?

The high-capacity backbone that interconnects major Internet nodes is operated by long-distance carriers, and local connections to those nodes are handled by information service providers (ISPs) and local telephone companies. ISPs provide basic Internet connections and sometimes also provide content (as in the case of America Online), but most content providers are independent. A variety of nonprofit organizations help run the Internet, including the Internet Society, the Internet Engineering Task Force, and the Internet Corporation for Assigned Names and Numbers.

WHAT SOCIAL ISSUES SHAPE THE INTERNET?

Most computer media issues revolve around the control of the Internet. Some proposed policies are aimed at keeping the Internet open and diverse, such as by protecting individual privacy, preventing monopolization by corporate interests, providing equal access for all, and keeping it free of taxation or direct control by national governments. Others would clamp down on cyberspace by restricting pornography, encryption, and hate speech or by strictly enforcing the intellectual property rights of copyright and patent holders.

MEDIA CONNECTION

For web links, quizzes, and key term flash cards, visit the **Student Companion Website** at http://communication.wadsworth.com/straubhaar5.

 For unlimited easy access to additional and exclusive online study, support, and research tools, log on to **1pass** at http://1pass.thomson.com using the unique access code found on your 1pass passcode card.

 The **Media Now Premium Website** offers *Career Profile* videos, *Critical View* video news clips, and *Media in Motion* concept animations. You'll also find Stop & Review tutorial questions, a sample final exam, and much more.

 InfoTrac College Edition is a fully searchable online database offering anytime, anywhere access to more than 20 years' worth of articles from nearly 5,000 diverse and reliable sources.

vMentor provides live, one-on-one online tutoring to connect you to experts who will assist you in understanding the concepts covered in your course.

In the Career Profile video for this chapter, Bob Baxley, director of Search at Yahoo!, talks about working on interaction design for web applications.

PUBLIC RELATIONS

How can we draw atten-
tion to our favorite cause?
This chapter describes
professional public rela-
tions—the organized
effort to gain favorable
action on behalf of one or
more goals or objectives
of an institution or organization. In this chapter,
we trace the origins of
the practice, examine the
current structure of the
industry, and describe
the major trends and
issues that are transforming the public relations
industry within the information society.

This chapter is by **Don Bates,** managing director, Media Distribution Services (MDS), which is headquartered in New York, N.Y. Mr. Bates has taught graduate and under-graduate courses in public relations and marketing at the New School University and the New York Institute of Technology. He currently teaches in the master's degree "Strategic Communications" program at Columbia University.

HISTORY: TO INFORM AND PERSUADE

Edward Bernays, whom many have considered the founder of modern public relations, wrote, "The three main elements of public relations are practically as old as society: informing people, persuading people, or integrating people with people. Of course, the means and methods of accomplishing these ends have changed as society has changed." (Bernays, 1961).

Civilization and Its Public Relations

For Bernays and other historians of the practice, professional **public relations** has always gone hand in hand with civilization. Whether they were promoting their image as warriors or kings, leaders of ancient civilizations such as Sumeria, Babylonia, Assyria, and Persia used poems and other writings to promote their prowess in battle and politics. In Egypt much of the art and architecture (statues, temples, tombs) was used to impress on the public the greatness of priests, nobles, and scribes. In ancient Rome, Julius Caesar carefully prepared the Romans for his crossing of the Rubicon in 49 B.C.E. by sending

Public relations are organized activities intended to favorably influence the public.

1900	The Publicity Bureau of Boston established as first public relations firm	**1950**	PRSA Code of Professional Standards adopted
1913	Ludlow Massacre establishes value of corporate public relations	**1965**	PRSA Accreditation established
1923	Edward L. Bernays publishes *Crystallizing Public Opinion,* first book on professional public relations	**1970**	International Association of Business Communicators (IABC) founded
		1989	*Exxon Valdez* crisis becomes PR nightmare
1929	Bernays stages Torches of Freedom march to promote smoking	**1998**	Association Council of Public Relations Firms founded in United States
1948	Public Relations Society of America (PRSA) founded	**2002**	PRSA promulgates Universal Accreditation
		2004	Sarbanes-Oxley Act goes into effect

reports such as "Caesar's Gallic Wars" (52 B.C.E.) on his epic achievements as governor of Gaul. Later, the teachings of Jesus and his apostles took center stage in the battle for religious dominance in the public mind. Once the Christian church took shape, it relied on eloquent speeches and letters, such as Paul's epistle to the Romans, to win converts and guide the faithful. Great documents of liberty crystallized the power of **public opinion.** For example, the *Magna Carta*—the thirteenth-century English charter of rights and liberties—inspired the U.S. Constitution.

The word **propaganda** originated in the Catholic Church. In the seventeenth century, it set up its *Congregatio de Propaganda Fide,* the "congregation for propagating the faith." In doing so, it explicitly acknowledged the need for a third party to facilitate communication between government and the people (Bernays, 1961). Along with the spread of new knowledge in new forms—such as translations in the fifteenth century of the Bible from Latin into everyday languages, mass-printed books, and newspapers— came an explosion of public communications. In 1792 the National Assembly of France created the first government-run propaganda ministry. It was part of the Ministry of the Interior, and it was called the Bureau d'Esprit or "Bureau of the Spirit." It subsidized editors and sent agents to various parts of the country to win public support for the French Revolution.

The American Way

England's rebellious American colonies produced a host of public relations experts, including Paul Revere, Benjamin Franklin, John Peter Zenger, Samuel Adams, Alexander Hamilton, James Madison, and John Jay. Adams has been called the great press agent of the American Revolution for fashioning the machinery of political change. Hamilton, Madison, and Jay are credited with winning ratification of the Constitution by publishing letters they had written to the press in 1787 and 1788.

These letters became known as the Federalist Papers. The other great documents produced by the founders of the United States—the Declaration of Independence, the Constitution, and the Bill of Rights—may all be seen as masterworks of public relations in addition to being masterworks of political philosophy and democratic governance.

Public opinion is the aggregate view of the general population.

Propaganda is the intentional influence of attitudes and opinions.

Many American legends are the result of public relations campaigns. For example, the story of Daniel Boone was created by a landowner to promote settlement in Kentucky. And Davy Crockett's exploits were largely created by his press agent, Matthew St. Clair, to woo votes away from President Andrew Jackson. The master of all nineteenth-century press agents was Phineas T. Barnum. Showman par excellence, Barnum created a wave of publicity stunts and coverage that made his circus, "The Greatest Show on Earth," an irresistible draw in every city and town it visited after its inception in 1871.

Age of the Robber Barons

It was in the last two decades of the nineteenth century and the early years of the twentieth century that professional public relations bloomed. The hard-bitten attitudes of businessmen toward the public were epitomized in 1892 by the cold-blooded methods of Henry Clay Frick in his attempt to crush a labor union in the Carnegie-Frick Steel Companies plant in Homestead, Pennsylvania. The employees' strike was ultimately broken and the union destroyed by the use of the Pennsylvania State militia. Brute force won the battle for immediate control, but public opinion, framed in the struggle of the workers, won the war (Cutlip, Center, & Broom, 1985). Corporations quickly learned the value of combating hostility and courting public favor through professional public relations.

© The Granger Collection, New York

■ **BORN ON A MOUNTAINTOP**
An early public relations success in the United States was Davy Crockett, many of whose feats were inventions of his press agent, Matthew St. Clair.

Corporations also learned the value of publicity in attracting customers and investors. Companies across America established press bureaus to manage the dissemination of news favorable to themselves and unfavorable to their competitors. The "battle of the currents" between Westinghouse (advocate of alternating current, or AC, power transmission) and Thomas A. Edison's General Electric (advocate of direct current, or DC, transmission) is one of the earliest examples of how public relations was first conducted in the United States by powerful economic interests. Using former newspapermen as their publicists, the companies fought each other tooth and nail for media attention, political influence, and marketing advantage.

Trade associations also caught the public relations fever in the late 1800s. The Association of American Railroads claims it was the first organization to use the term *public relations* in its 1897 *Year Book of Railway Literature*. In the 1900s, public relations evolved from individual press agents and publicists to counseling firms that offered their services as experts in the field. The nation's first publicity firm, The Publicity Bureau, was founded in Boston in 1900.

The early decades of the 1900s also saw the emergence of public relations departments in the offices of large local, national, and international charities. By the 1970s, most charitable enterprises of any significance had in-house PR operations and/or outside PR counsel. These operations were much smaller than those in the corporate world, but their role was equally important. They helped to communicate their organizations' purposes, practices, and performance with the goals of building public awareness, raising money, influencing legislation, recruiting volunteers, and otherwise currying public support for their interests.

SAVE YOUR CANS
Help pass the Ammunition

MCCLELLAND BARCLAY USNR

PREPARE YOUR TIN CANS
FOR WAR
1 REMOVE TOPS AND BOTTOMS
2 TAKE OFF PAPER LABELS
3 WASH THOROUGHLY
4 FLATTEN FIRMLY

© The Granger Collection, New York

■ BULLET THEORY

World War I showed the power of public relations in getting citizens involved in the war effort.

A front group works on behalf of another organization whose direct involvement might be controversial.

PR Pioneers

Ivy Ledbetter Lee was perhaps the most famous of the early public relations practitioners, and with good reason. A former Wall Street reporter, Lee became a public relations counselor with George Parker in 1904, although he didn't use the term public relations until more than a decade later. He believed that business had to tell its story honestly, accurately, and openly in order to win public understanding and support. He developed a publicity policy of "the public be informed" in contrast to the infamous statement of financier William Vanderbilt, "the public be damned." John D. Rockefeller, Jr., asked for his advice in handling the so-called Ludlow Massacre that began in 1913 in southern Colorado when some 9000 people went on strike. In April 1914, an accidental shot led to a battle in which several of the miners, two women, and 11 children were killed. With the family name being pilloried across the land, Lee had Rockefeller, Jr., visit mining camps after the strike was over to see for himself the conditions under which miners worked. He also advised John D., Sr., who was being attacked by muckrakers as an arrogant capitalist, to let the public know about his charitable contributions, which he had kept secret. In the end, Lee died in relative disgrace for putting his considerable skills to work in getting the Soviet Union recognized in the United States in the 1930s and in assisting Nazi-owned businesses (Hiebert, 1966).

Edward L. Bernays and his associate and wife, Doris Fleischman, were among those who competed with Lee for prominence. Bernays is credited with coining the term *public relations counsel* in his first book on the subject, *Crystallizing Public Opinion,* originally published in 1923. Bernays viewed public relations as an art applied to a science. He and his colleagues went well beyond publicity in their roles as consultants to business, government, and not-for-profit enterprises. In 1917, during World War I, Bernays joined the Committee on Public Information, also known as the Creel Committee, which was organized to help sell war bonds and generally promote the war effort.

One of Bernays' most famous campaigns was the 1929 Torches of Freedom March in which he had 10 carefully chosen women walk down Fifth Avenue smoking cigarettes. The women were advancing feminism while setting the stage for a surge in smoking by women. What the public and the press didn't know was that Bernays was a consultant to the American Tobacco Company at the time, raising an ethical issue that still confronts the public relations profession today—who's really directing the communications and why? Bernays also created many of what have become known as **front groups,** such as the Trucking Information Bureau and the Better Living Through Increased Highway Transportation, to pursue private interests with the support and assistance of the general public. Two recent books view Bernays as the father or master of "spin," the art of intentionally manipulating public opinion in support of one's products, services, ideas, or issues without regard for truth or reality (Ewen, 1996; Tye, 1998).

Public Relations Matures

In the 1930s and 1940s, several organizations were founded to represent the interests of public relations practitioners, culminating in 1948 in the formation of the Public

■ PR MESS
Scenes of oil-covered dead sea
creatures created a public
relations disaster for Exxon after
a 1989 oil spill.

■ PR GUY
The President of the United States performs a public relations function whenever he addresses the nation.

Relations Society of America (PRSA). Today, the PRSA remains the world's largest public relations membership association with more than 20,000 members, primarily in the United States.

By the late 1960s, public relations had matured into a full-blown professional enterprise, comprising in the United States several hundred public relations agencies, large and small, and more than 100,000 individual practitioners in business, government, and not-for-profit enterprise. Part of the driving force for this growth at this time was the great burst of political turbulence that engulfed the world. Part was also the burgeoning consumer movement that sought to protect the average person against unsafe products, unsanitary working conditions, unfair pricing, and other breaches, real and alleged, of the expanding social contract that said, in effect, the "Customer is King." Corporations found themselves crafting "Bills of Rights" for their customers, recasting their credit agreements in "plain English," and instituting numerous other reforms to guarantee consumer satisfaction. Colleges and universities were particularly affected, as their campuses became hotbeds of social action. Like business and government, they, too, had to pay attention to their "publics" or suffer the consequences.

In the 1980s and 1990s, business and government became the primary targets for initiatives aimed at curbing air pollution, water pollution, deforestation, and the general threat of ecological disaster caused by global warming and the destruction of the world's natural habitats. The *Exxon Valdez* oil spill off the coast of Alaska in 1989 was an environmental catastrophe that sparked a public relations calamity for the entire oil industry. Here, too, public relations practitioners were called upon to assist in addressing these highly charged issues and, more important, in communicating what their employers or the activist organizations they represented were doing to improve matters.

This period also witnessed the growth and extension of consumer activism around issues such as unfair labor practices and unbridled corporate expansion and market control. By 2000, these issues had become lightning rods for public concern about the almost unbridled success and globalization of such mega brands as Wal-Mart and McDonald's. In 2004, for example, Wal-Mart became the subject of an enormous amount of media scrutiny, including two lengthy network TV news documentaries devoted to analyzing the company's power as the world's largest retailer.

Down the years, ethical and legal breaches of conduct led to the promulgation in 1950 by PRSA of a Code of Professional Standards. Since these guidelines were introduced, more than 200 colleges and universities in the United States have begun offering undergraduate and graduate degrees in public relations in which the courses emphasize ethical issues and concepts such as credibility and accountability.

Nonetheless, enforcement has been lax, principally because of the difficulties involved in trying to prosecute breaches of conduct by individuals who work in an unlicensed profession protected by freedom of speech and related Constitutional privileges. Enforcement became so challenging and costly that in 2000 PRSA completely revised its Code so that its power to expel a member for transgressions applies only if he or she has been "sanctioned by a government agency or convicted in a court of law." Now, the Code is framed as a self-directed teaching tool that expresses the "universal values that inspire ethical behavior and performance" (see "Media and Culture, Society of Professional Journalists' Code of Ethics", page 470).

The New Millennium Meltdown

And then there was the boom and bust of the dot-com bubble in the late 1990s followed in 2001 by the 9/11 terrorist attacks, and in 2002 by the greed-induced

Cross-Border Campaigning

With the transformation of larger PR firms into global entities, particularly firms from the U.S., there has been a corresponding increase in promotion and publicity campaigns across national and regional borders that not too many years ago would have been handled by local firms in the target countries because of their familiarity with the local language and culture.

Since English has increasingly become the default language for international business, cultural and linguistic barriers have become less critical when dealing with business publics. However, if you can communicate in the local language, you can promote and publicize things much more effectively to the local market.

Examples abound, but two from U.S.-based Ketchum PR exemplify this trend and suggest equally impressive campaigns that in the near future will be aimed at and directed within the U.S. by PR firms headquartered in other countries.

In March 2002, a few months after the release of *Harry Potter & The Philosopher's Stone,* Ketchum PR handled the global launch of the film's DVD and VHS versions. The launch took place in the UK, however, where Harry Potter was written and its author lived, and it was pitched from there to media in other countries. Suffice it to say, the firm took advantage of the unmatched promotional opportunities available in the United Kingdom. The core event featured the Hogwarts' Express steam train from the film.

Cast members and invited celebrities and their children took the train from a depot outside London to the city's Kings Cross station. Platform 1 was transformed into Platform 9¾, as in the film, complete with a Hogwarts'-themed enclosure, which became the venue for the launch party. A select number of 50 media from around the world were given group interviews with the cast.

In the end, the campaign generated 1150 print articles, 21 website features, 37 radio features and 6 TV features. The cumulative audience in the UK alone was 37,981,000 for TV, 389,585,109 (circulation) for print with a potential readership of 1,246,672,349, and 81,423,600 for radio. Most important, 1.2 million units of the video versions were sold the first day, breaking all records for such sales.

A survey by Pfizer, the makers of Lipitor, the world's leading cholesterol-management drug, exposed cholesterol's global reach and underscored the urgency of giving cholesterol education a global stage.

Working for Pfizer, Ketchum leveraged the 2002 Winter Olympics as a global platform and Olympic gold medal athletes as its messengers. Partnering with the International Olympic Committee, it hosted a global press event at the Olympic Museum in Lausanne, Switzerland. Olympic gold medalist Mark Spitz, swimmer extraordinaire, briefed consumer media on key messages. Pfizer affiliates worldwide were provided with cholesterol-education information for use with local media.

Millions worldwide were exposed to Pfizer's messages. The No. 1 key message, "Go for the Goal," appeared in 83% of coverage. Fifty percent of coverage contained more than six key messages, and 100% of the coverage was favorable for Pfizer and Lipitor.

In many ways, the trend toward more frequent cross-border and global PR initiatives is an important step forward in the evolution of cultural cooperation between and among different countries. But it is also a trend that could inflame national passions and create public and private tensions about issues such as cultural imperialism and world domination, particularly by the U.S., although in the decades ahead countries such as China or those of the European Union could find themselves similarly challenged as they grow in global power.

---

meltdown of ethics and governance in companies such as Enron and WorldCom. For the public relations industry, the response to these national and world crises was a mixed blessing.

While many practitioners, particularly in large corporations and public relations agencies, were chastised for not doing enough to persuade companies to come clean sooner about their financial deceptions, there was at least as much praise heaped on other practitioners for all that they did during and after 9/11 to help corporations, government agencies, and nonprofit organizations communicate with the American public and the world about what had happened, what was being done to put things back in order, and what to expect in the near future.

Looking back, professional public relations has more than fulfilled its role in society despite the many setbacks that seem to go hand in hand with the practice from time to time. What began as mainly a U.S. enterprise in the early 1900s has grown, almost inexorably, to become a global enterprise, far surpassing what even the most visionary of its early proponents imagined. Worldwide, there are probably another 100,000 professional practitioners along with scores of national PR associations that represent their interests.

PR practitioners have prospered as the issues with which they concern themselves have grown in magnitude and impact. And following national and international trends, the profession has moved from being a largely all-white, all-male preserve to an ethnically diverse, gender-integrated industry.

PR TOOLS AND TECHNOLOGIES

Public relations practitioners do their work with a variety of tools and technologies, using everything from pencil and paper to PDAs and the Internet—that is, using whatever will assist them in efficiently and effectively creating, delivering, and tracking their communications on behalf of clients and employers.

The Tried and True

Certainly since the early 1900s, when professional public relations as we know it today took shape, the dominant tools have been printed **news releases, pitch letters,** and **press kits.** Releases are used to convey general news and information to editors and reporters. "Pitch" letters are used to invite more extensive coverage of a particular story, usually as an exclusive for those to whom they are sent. Paper press kits usually include cover letters and news releases with information about whatever is being promoted (for example, a product, service, campaign, or event), plus any number of supporting materials such as brochures, biographies, photos, and business cards.

The New and Newest

A **news release** summarizes news and information in a form and style that is preferred by the media.

Pitch letters are designed to interest editors and reporters in covering a topic from a given perspective or "angle."

Press kit is a collection of promotional materials.

Although conventional tools and technologies continue to dominate the practice of public relations, they are fast being supplanted by tools and technologies that build on the latest advances in video, audio, and computer communications. Their various forms have given public relations practitioners unprecedented opportunities for reaching handfuls or millions of people more personally and directly than only a generation ago would have seemed impossible.

Video News Releases (VNRs), are ready-to-air television news stories that are provided to news programs free of charge for their use during news broadcasts. They are the television equivalent of print news releases, and a surprising amount of video you see on television news programs today is from video news releases. They are used most

■ **VIDEOCONFERENCING** ■
Video conferences distributed by satellite are an important public relations tool, such as this one to promote John Madden's NFL video game.

frequently for health care, consumer, technology, travel, and business stories. Although they can be expensive to make ($20,000–$30,000 each), the publicity that VNRs generate in small, medium, and large markets is often extensive, especially when compared to what an organization would have to spend on paid advertising to gain comparable airtime and attention.

For example, when the Federal Drug Administration approves a new drug, it is all but mandatory that the drug makers in question provide newsrooms with manufacturing shots and sound bites so that the story can be reported adequately and accurately. When Pfizer introduced Viagra, the footage was used on more than 2000 individual broadcasts, according to Douglas Simon, president & CEO of D S Simon Productions, which produced and distributed the VNR. Nielsen Media Research's SIGMA system has been a boon to VNR producers, allowing them to electronically track what stations aired the VNR and report this information to clients.

VNRs should be no longer than 90 seconds to two minutes in length and include separate audio tracks for the interview sound bites and voice-over so stations can substitute the voice of their own reporter. The shorter the segment, the more likely stations will air it in its entirety. They should also include additional footage and sound bites called B-Roll, which offers the station more flexibility in fitting your story into its newscast.

VNRs are distributed by satellite and tape and have also benefited from the Internet and digital transmission. By using their own digital video servers, news producers can call up VNRs—along with related stories from their networks and other news sources—then incorporate what they want into their news broadcasts. Accompanying text documents provide additional background. Recent breakthroughs include online editing sessions, which allow producers and clients to review and approve VNRs almost on the fly, and use of streaming video to put VNRs on company and organization websites.

Edited B-Roll (Outtake) Packages are a form of VNR. These include three to five minutes of unedited video footage, along with printed scripts known as "slates," which help to facilitate editing. They are distributed to TV stations in much the same way as VNRs. B-Rolls cost less than VNRs and often can work for quick turnaround projects. Macy's generated nationwide publicity in advance of its Thanksgiving Day parade with a B-Roll project on the test of its new balloons.

© Sergei Karpukhin/Reuters/Landov

Webcasts are a form of broadcast production that incorporates *streaming video* and audio. Typically, they are used to deliver a live press conference or other event to the computer screens of target audiences. They are frequently used to meet information distribution requirements for publicly traded companies. In the case of the media, a reporter or producer can watch from his or her desktop, viewing not only video but text and photos; participate in interviews if they are part of the package; then download the satellite or Internet feed to get excerpts for use in their on-air coverage.

Webcasts still remain a supplement to VNRs and SMTs, but their use and impact are increasing as the Internet expands as a "first source" of news and information for media and the average citizen. Most webcasts are also filed for "on-demand" requests so that they can be viewed by people who may have missed the original broadcast or by producers who may want to use some of their content later on for other purposes.

Satellite Media Tours (SMTs) allow your spokesperson to be interviewed live on 15–25 television stations across the country during a brief three- or four-hour period. Before their widespread use, spokespeople would travel from city to city to do in-studio appearances. It was costly and time-consuming. With an SMT, a celebrity or company spokesperson spends a few hours in a broadcast studio or on location being interviewed by news anchors while the interview is shown live to viewers. Interviews typically last two to three minutes. Stations also have the option of taping the interview for later use or editing excerpts into a news program.

Beyond their logistical efficiencies, key benefits of the SMT are more control of your message, especially during the live interviews, and a certainty before the actual date of the SMT of where your segment will be broadcast. Unlike a VNR, SMT bookings are secured in advance and should be pitched the media four to six weeks in advance. They are less effective for short lead-time projects unless the media interest would be over-whelming. As part of the SMT, videotape of the product or service can also be transmitted to interested stations as a B-Roll package or rolled-in live during the interviews.

E-SMTs, or satellite media tours via the Internet, have little to do with satellites and a whole lot to do with computers. Like webcasts, they provide an easy way for public relations clients to allow the media and others "virtual attendance" and participation in press

PR ONLINE
The PR Newswire website indexes press releases from around the world in both text and video form, seen here.

conferences, where they can watch the event in progress and e-mail questions before, during, and after the event.

Interactive News Releases are sent via e-mail or posted on a website for general viewing by the public or in a press-only password-protected area. Besides addressing the who, what, when, where, and why of the release's topic (the 5 Ws), there are usually one or more "hot links" that direct recipients to associated information such as brochures and photos that are on the sender's server or the server of the vendor that produces the releases and/or stories. Increasingly, the content of these releases appears in the e-mail window proper, obviating the need for conventional "attachments" which often carry computer viruses.

Electronic Press Kits (E-Kits) are the e-mail or Internet version of traditional printed press kits except that they can contain all of the bells and whistles associated with Internet interactivity. They are also produced as CD-ROMs. E-kits can be as simple or as sophisticated as the creator's imagination. Typically, they include a "home page" that lists a variety of interactive links to files of information such as news releases, executive biographies, product photos, facility videos, and PowerPoint or audiotape presentations. E-kits are often found on major corporate websites. They are also used as supplements to or replacements for printed press kits.

The beauty of both the interactive news release and electronic press kit is that they can be updated "on the fly" as circumstances dictate. With their printed counterparts, the alterations either couldn't be made or a new printing would have to be requisitioned, requiring several days for production.

Blogs or web logs (see Chapter 4) spread news, rumors, attacks, and opinions so fast that they demand nearly impossible reaction times from PR practitioners. Many PR practitioners are therefore forced to monitor at least some of the major blogs—those that carry news and target specific industries or subjects—to see what they're publishing that might impact their employers or clients. In practice, everyone with access to the Internet can have a blog, so their importance as vehicles for both defying as well as delivering public relations messages will only grow.

Blogs are online commentaries, usually in the form of personal "diaries."

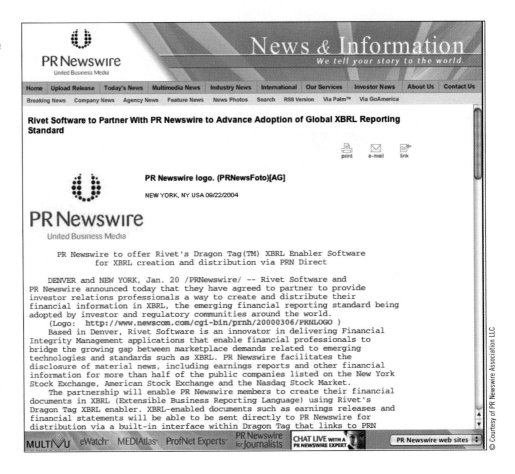

Online Advocacy Systems such as ARENA from Legislative Demographic Services allow organizations to organize and manage online campaigns that engage employees, investors, customers, and other key stakeholders in promoting their interests. With these systems, constituencies can be mobilized in minutes to write local elected officials arguing for or against a particular piece of legislation, "pitch" editors and reporters with strategically designed news stories, get out the vote in statewide elections, and help combat social issues such as poverty and environmental damage.

Essentially, advocacy systems allow for the application of innovative legislative affairs tactics to traditional community relations outreach. For example, Entergy Corporation, which provides electric power in the southern states and operates nuclear power plants in other areas of the country, uses its advocacy system for assisting low income families to pay their residential heating bills, and for educating local communities about nuclear power and what the company is doing to protect its facilities against a possible terrorist attack.

Entergy enrolled volunteers and administered web surveys to track the actions they were willing to undertake. Using web pages and online seminars, the volunteers were trained to become skilled advocates who can speak with the media, make phone calls to elected officials, and deliver public testimony in government hearings. With these systems, the communications can be archived and the actions taken can be evaluated for return on investment and other criteria.

Online Media Databases are loaded with information on the tens of thousands of reporters and editors in the United States and around the world. These databases can be used to research individual records, print address labels, and send "blast" faxes and e-mails. Among the largest online databases—with more than 300,000 contacts by name and editorial "beat"—are Bacon's and Burrelle's/Luce, but other companies have begun

Cyber Smear

There is another, more sinister side to the Internet, as has been pointed out by public relations counselor Don Middleberg, chairman and CEO of Middleberg Euro RSCG, a U.S.-based international public relations firm. "In our new media age," he adds, "it is possible for almost anyone to single-handedly wreak havoc, create controversy, or mar the image of your company by using the great equalizer—the Internet. A lone, disgruntled employee (or a small group of Internet-savvy people) can rapidly disseminate his or her message as loudly and effectively as a multibillion-dollar company." Mark Weiner, CEO of Media Link, a firm specializing in providing research on companies' reputations, says that "'Cyber smears' include boycotts, scams, rumors and false reports, all passed along by mass e-mails, disparaging gossip on message boards and on websites." Sometimes the smears are "urban legends," as was the case for Tommy Hilfiger (the false rumor that he appeared on the Oprah Winfrey Show and commented on regretting the appeal of his clothing to minority consumers spread). Fake coupons (for free products from McDonald's and Starbuck's, among others) also travel the internet. Other times the activities are more sophisticated and aggressive.

Ford Motor Co. found itself in the midst of an Internet attack by a group of cyber citizens demanding the recall of 26 million cars and trucks that it claimed were dangerous. The Association of Flaming Ford Owners (AFFO) posted a website (http://www.flamingfords.com) describing an alleged fire hazard. The group also sent out a mass e-mail to 8500 domain managers, promoting the site and asking them to add links back to the "Flaming Ford" site.

McDonald's has also experienced a cyber crisis. The McInformation Network is an activist group dedicated to "breaking the chains of censorship by multinational companies." The group created the anti-McDonald's website McSpotlight (http://www.mcspotlight.org) to provide the press and public with information on the "McLibel" trial, a libel suit that has been underway since 1990 when McDonald's sued two people in London who published, on the Internet, a fact sheet entitled. "What's Wrong with McDonald's." Another example of these anticorporate sites is Chasebanksucks .com. There are also consumer advocacy sites like fight-back.com and Public Citizen (www.citizen.org) that draw attention to alleged corporate misdeeds, as well as numerous opinion sites such as Epionions.comand complaints.com, where consumers post comments and reviews.

Cases where libel may be involved present more problems, Middleberg also notes. "Lawyers will want to take action, but this may not be the best way to handle the situation. Because there have been few precedents and rulings concerning libel and the Internet, it is unlikely that your company will win such a suit. In addition, the case will likely

■ PR NIGHTMARE
Public relations professionals worry that the Internet perpetuates negative images long after a disaster. The *Exxon Valdez* oil spill took place in 1989, but it is still a focal point of sites on the web.

be expensive and may very well draw unwanted media attention to the crisis." As a preemptive measure, more and more corporations are developing and maintaining their own blogs.

to develop and offer similarly designed databases. Chief among these companies are PR Newswire, Business Wire, and Media Distribution Services (MDS). In addition, there are scores of smaller databases targeted to specific media such as Hispanic Americans, African-Americans, and gays.

Journalists can use some of these databases to make discreet requests for information or assistance concerning stories they are covering, and PR practitioners and others can respond accordingly. Trade and professional associations are imitating this trend by offering their own online connections to their members as well as related news and information. For example, Media Resource from Sigma Xi, the Science Research Society, helps reporters and writers find reputable sources of scientific information at no charge.

Online Tracking and Monitoring Systems help PR practitioners track what the media, competitors, customers, and others are saying about their employers or clients. To do this, they use companies that literally "clip" news and feature articles. The resulting stacks of clips become evidence of accomplishment.

Although hard copy is still preferred by most PR practitioners, the trend is clearly toward hiring companies that employ sophisticated tracking software. Burrelle's/Luce and CyberAlert, for example, monitor media coverage throughout the World Wide Web and deliver summaries of the stories they find to their clients' desktops. They also monitor blogs and logs, even though the veracity of what many of them publish is highly questionable. CyberAlert, for example, monitors more than 30,000 web message boards, forums, and discussion groups, more than 60,000 UseNet news groups, and more than 100,000 web blogs that have been vetted for their news content.

The Power Punch

E-mail is fast becoming the preferred method among PR practitioners for contacting the press one-on-one with "pitch" letters. Its use for distributing news releases has also grown but not as significantly because large numbers of editors and reporters don't want releases by e-mail unless they ask for them. They don't like the imposition of unsolicited material, and they are afraid of computer viruses that frequently come with e-mail attachments. Those who like e-mail like opt-in e-mail feeds or "wires" that deliver hyperlinked summaries of releases targeted to their editorial interests. From the summaries, they can click to the full text and/or download photos, audio, or video.

Another e-mail innovation is Instant Messenger (IM) software, which allows PR practitioners to communicate live with the media and other audiences who are online at the same time they are. One advantage is that IM doesn't leave the same kind of electronic trail that e-mail does. Another advantage is that PR people can keep their IM addresses more private than their public e-mail addresses and share them only with trusted contacts.

E-mail has also been a boon to practitioners charged with public affairs and government relations. In 2004, both candidates for the U.S. presidency used the technology for communicating with their constituents and others. The Kerry campaign chose e-mail to announce John Edwards as his running mate, and Bush's campaign manager used e-mail to challenge accusations by Kerry's campaign manager. Both parties also used e-mail as a fund-raising tool. Kerry attracted more than $80 million over the Internet with e-mail as a principal means of thanking those who gave and for asking for more.

During the primary campaign, President Bush's 2004 e-campaign director, Michael Turk, said that "E-mail is a critical component of what we do. We have more than 7 million subscribers to our e-mail list and reach out to them with information, calls to action, and to actively engage in volunteer activities. The ability to deliver that kind of targeted information to voters does not exist in other media."

G. Simms Jenkins of Brightwave Marketing wrote that "We should expect to see increased usage of e-mail marketing in both national and local politics as candidates continue to recognize the value of this timely, highly personalized, low-cost medium."

Online Press Rooms

Most major corporations have press rooms on their websites. A good example is Verizon, whose site (http://newscenter.verizon.com/) makes it easy for editors and reporters to access news announcements and find staff contacts when they are seeking information or comment. Most online press rooms also have archives of earlier releases, photos, fact sheets, and related supporting materials. In addition, some companies and their public relations firms have established "dark" sites that can be uploaded at a moment's notice to serve as specialized press rooms should a crisis occur that requires an immediate response. For example, if a car manufacturer suddenly had to recall some of its vehicles, it could use one of these "dark" sites to launch its version of the story within minutes of hearing about the recall. Being proactive, they are able to reach the media and other audiences in almost real time and thereby minimize media inquires for basic facts about the situation. These crisis-preventive sites are also used to quell or otherwise control rumors.

STOP & REVIEW

1. When are video news releases more effective than printed ones?

2. How have new electronic media outlets such as the Internet changed the practice of public relations?

3. What are some of the functions that personal computers perform in modern public relations agencies?

4. What are some of the high-tech approaches that are used to influence political opinion?

INSIDE THE PR INDUSTRY

Public relations practitioners often use advertising, direct marketing, and related tools and techniques to promote their client's or employer's interests, but these are not part of the PR function per se. They have different purposes and require specialized expertise and knowledge for their execution. Understanding the difference helps to keep the public relations function in perspective and avoid client misunderstandings about what to expect from PR and what to pay for the services involved. Given its complexity, it's not surprising that definitions of the practice of public relations abound. Following are the two that summarize the most commonly held views in the industry:

> "Public relations is the management function that identifies, establishes, and maintains mutually beneficial relationships between an organization and the various publics on whom its success or failure depends." (Cutlip, Center, & Broom, 1985)

> "Public relations helps our complex, pluralistic society to reach decisions and function more effectively by contributing to mutual understanding among groups and institutions. It serves to bring private and public policies into harmony." (Public Relations Society of America, 2005)

In more practical terms, "on the job," the public relations unit, whether one person or many, has a wide range of responsibilities.

The Functions of Public Relations

A public relations practitioner or department advises and counsels the organization on communications questions affecting its client's or employer's publics and serves as an

Table 10.1 Specialties or Functions of Public Relations

Activity	Description
Publicity or media relations	gaining press coverage through news releases, press conferences, and other materials
Promotion or selling	developing and disseminating print and audiovisual materials, arranging exhibits and displays, and providing promotional giveaways
Community relations	working with community groups and other key community interests that can influence public attitudes and public policies
Government relations	assisting or influencing state, local, or federal government action on problems involving legislation, regulation, and related activity
Public information	developing and disseminating print and audiovisual materials whose purpose is to inform, educate, and assist
Special events	planning and managing internal and external events such as ground breakings, ribbon-cutting ceremonies, tours, and open houses aimed at attracting public attention
Employee relations	assisting management in informing staff at all levels about personnel policies and practices, labor relations, contracts, benefits, and other issues that involve the health and welfare of the labor force
Issues management, reputation management, crisis communications	identifying and helping to manage the big issues that affect institutional success, such as air and water pollution (the environment), foreign competition, ethnic diversity, plant closings or relocations, public censure, and corporate malfeasance
Lobbying	working with legislators and their legislative aides to influence the content and course of legislative action that affects institutional practices, through contributions to political action committees (PACs), campaign contributions, and other direct assistance not included as part of more conventional government relations efforts

early-warning system on emerging issues related to its success. It also provides technical support for other management functions with an emphasis on publicity, promotion, and media relations. Most conspicuously, it acts as a gatekeeper with the press, legislators, and government officials.

Among the many functions that PR practitioners perform, publicity and **media relations** are arguably the most important. Upwards of 70 percent of the average practitioner's week is devoted to working with the press to encourage news and feature coverage of his or her client's or employer's interests. This involves the full range of media relations assignments:

- Strategize, plan, and coordinate media relations and publicity.
- Prepare and disseminate news releases, press kits, and press alerts.
- Call, write, fax, and/or e-mail editors and reporters.
- Work with public relations services that assist them in their endeavors—for example, vendors that print, mail, fax, e-mail, and "wire" information to the press.
- Evaluate media relations and publicity results.

Public relations is usually organized into several key categories that are classified according to target audience and the nature of the activity (Table 10.1). How much time and money an organization puts into these functions depends on the level of need. Organizations facing big issues and big problems tend to do more. Organizations with less of a need may devote their time and energy to only one or two areas. Over time, however, every organization makes use of most PR functions, except perhaps for lobbying, which most nonprofit organizations and most smaller, less visible enterprises don't engage in.

Media relations focuses on establishing and maintaining good relations with the media.

Table 10.2 The Many Publics in Public Relations

For businesses	For not-for-profit enterprises	For government agencies
Shareholders/investors	Contributors/donors	Taxpayers/voters
Customers/consumers	Clients/consumers	Legislators
Employees	Volunteers	Related government agencies
Suppliers	Employees	Employees
Financial institutions	Members	Community activists
Legislators	Suppliers	
Community activists	Legislators	
Educational institutions	Community activists	
Print/broadcast media	Print/broadcast media	

The Publics of Public Relations

Public relations activities are addressed to one or more of the many publics that can influence an organization's success: customers, employees, shareholders, donors, the press, and so on (Table 10.2). When public relations practitioners refer to "publics," they mean the audiences they communicate with as part of their daily work. Depending on the needs and interests of the institutions they represent, a particular list of publics could be extensive.

For example, the typical multinational corporation has to deal with customers, banks, legislators, regulators, unions, employees, stockholders, investors, competitors, suppliers, community neighbors, trade associations, and the press in order to conduct its business.

In contrast, the average nonprofit organization may deal with only a few publics besides the press: for example, employees, donors, legislators, and volunteers. The first column of Table 10.2 shows the key PR publics for most for-profit institutions. Normally, the publics are targeted with a mix of PR tools and techniques, many of which are used in conjunction with related, but independently developed, marketing, advertising, and human resources initiatives.

Good vs. Bad PR: A Commentary

Good public relations has many benefits: improved credibility and accountability, stronger public identity, more favorable press coverage, greater sensitivity to public needs, improved employee morale, larger market share, increased sales, and better internal management. Bad public relations can exist as well, often because the people in charge of the function do their jobs poorly or because the company or organization they are employed by operates outside the bounds of the public interest.

Perhaps management allowed the production of faulty products, permitted pollution of the firm's surroundings, or illegally manipulated the price of the company's stock. In these instances, public relations may help to soften the fallout (negative press coverage, public outrage, regulatory punishment), but only a change in management policy or practice will truly make a difference. If one cliché dominates public relations thinking, it is this: "You can't make a silk purse out of a sow's ear."

The classic example of poor PR in recent years was Exxon's handling of the 1989 disaster in which one of its tankers, the *Exxon Valdez,* ran aground near Valdez, Alaska, spilling 250 million gallons of crude oil. It was the largest spill ever in North America,

affecting more than 1200 square miles of ocean, damaging some 600 miles of coastline, and killing as many as 4000 Alaskan sea otters along with thousands of sea birds and other precious wildlife. In the aftermath, Exxon's chairman at the time, Lawrence Rawl, decided not to visit the site, an action that was interpreted by area residents and the public-at-large as arrogance of the first order. He also didn't comment on the event for a full week, and the company established its media center in New York, not in Valdez where the action was.

In the end, Exxon got pilloried in the press for its unresponsiveness, and public sentiment turned against the company. After all was said and done, the disaster cost the company more than $2.5 billion in cleanup costs, legal judgments, and other expenses. More recently, major drug companies have seen their stock prices plummet in response to bad public relations about the dangerous side effects of arthritis drugs like Vioxx.

■ BAD PR
The Vioxx controversy is a recent, yet classic, example of how bad publicity can hurt major corporations.

Elements of Successful Public Relations

The practice of public relations is based on research and evaluation, including public opinion polls, readership surveys, mail questionnaires, telephone interviews, focus groups, and literature searches. Of necessity, then, good public relations begins with a serious assessment of public attitudes. Without adequate background on the people you are trying to reach and how they think, it is difficult, if not impossible, to communicate effectively. More specifically, without research and evaluation you cannot design programs that will change or modify the views of your target audiences.

Second, public relations is a planned effort, not a hit-or-miss proposition. Planned means managed. Managed means based on overall organizational objectives, not just the public relations unit's views. Planned effort begins with a written action plan for a year or more ahead that allows for changes and contingencies along the way. This plan must have the approval of top management. It schedules needed publications and communications, such as a monthly newsletter, the annual report, and speeches and presentations for special events. More important, the plan sets up a timetable and strategies aimed at achieving overall goals for the program (see "Media and Culture: A Year in the Life of a Public Relations Campaign," page 312).

Third, public relations has the goal of public support. The public might support a for-profit organization by purchasing products, investing in stock, or voting for or against specific trade regulations. Public support for a not-for-profit organization might take the form of donations of money or material, volunteer assistance, or paid memberships. For a government agency, it might mean legislative influence, taxpayer cooperation, or public participation. (See Figure 10.1.)

Over time, the public relations unit makes use of most of the print, electronic, and face-to-face communications available in our society. These are the tools and techniques (Table 10.3) that help organizations to reach their publics (Table 10.4). They are the vehicles that carry information back and forth between private and public interests.

The workhorse of public relations, the press release was invented in the late 1800s. Written in the form of a conventional news story, a release presents the point of view of the organization that disseminates it. Newspaper editors and reporters often use facts, quotes, and other information from releases to amplify their stories or support their accuracy and credibility.

Table 10.3 Public Relations Activities

Annual reports	Letters to editors	Satellite broadcast media tours
Advertorials	Meetings	Seminars
Audiotapes	Newsletters	Speakers' bureaus
Audiovisual presentations	News releases	Special events
Blogs or logs	Novelties	Speeches
Brochures, flyers, circulars	Open houses	Sponsorships
Compact discs	Opinion polls	Streaming video
Computer demonstrations	Paid advertisements	Surveys
Conventions	Photographs	Teleconferences
Editorials	Plant tours	Videoconferences
Electronic press kits	PowerPoint presentations	Video news releases
Event sponsorships	Press conferences	Videotapes
Exhibits and displays	Press kits	VIP visits
Feature articles	Product placements	Webcasts
Interactive news releases	Public demonstrations	Websites
Legislative alerts	Public service advertisements	Workshops
Legislative testimony	Radio news releases	

Table 10.4 Key PR Publics and PR Tools Used to Reach Them

PR publics	PR communications (examples)
Customers/clients	Special events, newsletters, billing inserts
Employees/managers	Newsletters, employee videos, company websites
Stockholders/investors	Earnings releases, annual reports, annual meeting
Legislators/regulators	Letters, research reports, personal contacts
Print/broadcast media	News releases, press conferences, press interviews

Early in the twentieth century, Ohio Bell Telephone discovered that if it handed out "canned" news in this form, newspaper reporters would stop going to telephone rate hearings to get the information in person (Bleifuss, 1994), thereby minimizing uncomfortable inquiries about the rates and related matters.

The traditional format (one or two pages of double-spaced text with standardized spelling and punctuation) was developed to satisfy the needs of editors for space in which to edit the text, and typesetters who required certain kinds of editorial markings in order to follow the flow of individual pages while typesetting the text. With more and more releases distributed via e-mail and more and more print media moving to digital printing, the format of press releases has become far less important for recipients.

A Year in the Life of a Public Relations Campaign

Suppose an electrical power utility decides to implement a community-wide program to help clean up local waterways, with the goals of educating the public about environmental pollution, improving the quality and safety of waterside recreation, getting local legislators and the press to view the utility as a good corporate citizen, and persuading more customers to look kindly on its services and rates. Public relations would have the primary responsibility for keeping the cleanup in the public eye, taking reasonable advantage of the situation to get credit where credit is due for the utility. The utility's public relations unit might plan the following:

- A website specially designed for the program and featuring hard news, editorials, photos, background on environmental pollution, calls for action, downloadable program materials, list server entry, press entry, hyperlinks to sponsoring organizations, and so on.
- A press conference to announce the launch of the program, combined with delivery and follow-up of press kits that include news releases, project descriptions, resource lists, and cleanup priorities.
- Speeches that the CEO and other top executives would give throughout the year to local business and community groups.

- Posters, flyers, and other prepackaged information to recruit volunteers from local schools, churches, and community groups and to excite and motivate employees about the benefits of the program and their role in making it successful.
- Public service announcements for use in free airtime on local television and radio stations.
- Paid ads and advertorials promoting the utility's role in launching the cleanup effort and promoting the utility as a good corporate citizen that runs a well-managed business but whose primary concern is serving the public interest and all of its customers equally.
- Kickoff special events such as cleanup parties, a parade through town, meetings of public officials, and an essay or art competition.
- A press and information bureau to track cleanup activities and report the results to the community via news updates, awards, and other forms of recognition.

PR Jobs

Although public relations is the preferred generic term in most corporations, the function is also known by other designations that may appear in an organizational chart or in the titles of practitioners. Among the most popular are public affairs, corporate communications, and corporate relations. In specific industries such as public utilities, you might find the terms consumer affairs or community relations; in not-for-profit and government organizations, public information or marketing communications. In addition, the function may be subdivided further to reflect specific jobs, such as investor relations, financial relations, fund-raising, charitable contributions, and media relations.

Today, all leading corporations have public relations departments of one sort or another. The same goes for major not-for-profit organizations such as colleges, hospitals, and national charities. Government also has similar operations, though they are usually called public affairs offices or public information offices.

To assist these entities, there are more than 4000 public relations firms, most with a relative handful of employees, but scores with 50 or more. The top 10 or so firms each have 1000–2000 or more worldwide. Currently, the PR counseling industry generates revenue in excess of $8 billion worldwide, $4 billion in the United States alone.

According to the Bureau of Labor Statistics, public relations is one of the fastest growing fields that does not require a master's degree or higher. In 2002, the last time its figures were updated, public relations specialists held approximately 158,000 jobs, up from 122,000 in 1998, and about 11,000 public relations specialists were self-employed. Most of these people are concentrated in large cities where press services and other

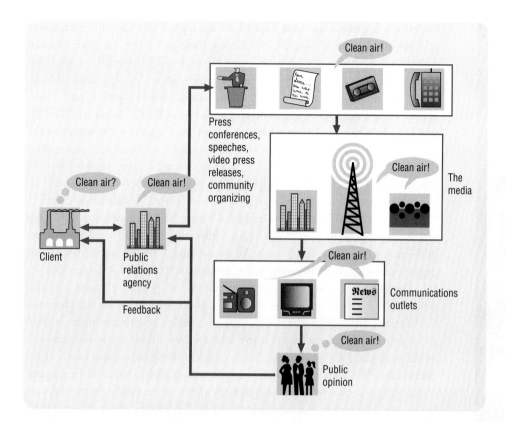

PR Campaign Public relations agencies organize communication events such as press conferences, speeches, and telemarketing campaigns to alert communications media organizations to important issues so that the subsequent media coverage will sway public opinion in favor of the client. Opinion polls and direct responses from the public provide feedback to the client and the agency.

communications facilities are readily available and many businesses and trade associations have their headquarters.

Beginning practitioners start in the area of publicity and media relations, writing and editing news releases, contacting reporters and editors, and generating press coverage. Seasoned practitioners are more involved in planning and management and more sophisticated issues such as government relations and crisis communications. When these practitioners write, it is most often speeches, proposals, and presentations. When they work with the media, it usually involves broader editorial issues and higher-level contacts. (See "Profile: Helen Ostrowski," page 316.)

Salaries in the PR field begin around $20,000–$25,000 and can rise as high as $300,000 or more at the top of the largest corporations and agencies. In *PR Week*'s 2004 salary survey, the average salary was $63,590, down from the prior two years owing to the slow economy, and ranged from $48,444 for nonprofit practitioners to $80,650 for utilities and power industry practitioners. By title, the salaries for senior managers ranged from $90,914 to $133,691.

Besides salaries, there is an increasing use of bonuses, stock options, and other corporate-style benefits to add to the public relations practitioner's compensation package. Owners of PR firms, of course, can pay themselves as little or as much as they like based on the profitability of their business. The owners and principal of many of the top PR firms are millionaires.

Professional Resources

Some 160,000 people in the United States work full-time in public relations. Aside from their job titles, public relations professionals are characterized in terms of the organizations they belong to and the publications they read. Although the Public Relations Society of America (PRSA) has dominated the public relations industry for most of its history,

competing organizations have formed to serve particular specialties or power groups within the profession. Chief among these groups are the International Association of Business Communicators (IABC), the National Investor Relations Institute (NIRI), and Women in Communications Incorporated (WICI). There are also several invitation-only organizations for senior practitioners, such as the Arthur Page Society and Women Executives in Public Relations (WEPR). In 1998, the Council of Public Relations Firms was established to represent the business and professional interests of the PR agencies in the United States. And there has been a comparable growth in professional societies worldwide. (See "World View: Cross-Border Campaigning," page 299.) Besides the European-based International Public Relations Association (IPRA), which acts as a kind of clearinghouse for practitioners outside the United States, there are membership associations along the lines of the PRSA, although significantly smaller, in most of the major countries of the world. All are devoted to improving the practice of public relations. The IPRA website lists more than 80 of these organizations.

The growing power and professionalism of public relations are also reflected in the development, over the past 30 or so years, of several respected publications that cover the field. Besides weekly newsletters such as *Jack O'Dwyer's Newsletter, Bulldog Reporter,* and *PR News,* there are magazines such as *PR Strategist, PR Services,* and *Communication World,* newspapers such as *PR Tactics* and *PR Week,* and research journals such as *Public Relations Review* and *Public Relations Quarterly.* Newsletters such as *Interactive Public Relations Report* have come into being to serve the interests of the growing ranks of new media and technology specialists.

There is also an expanding list of websites covering public relations, almost all of them accessible without charge. Included among these are on-linepr.com (hundreds of listings and hyperlinks to PR, marketing, and advertising sites worldwide), prplace.com (PR resource compendium), prwatch.com (PR industry critic), and silveranvil.org (PR case studies).

MEDIA LITERACY: IN WHOSE INTEREST?

Issues affecting public relations include the conflict between private and public interest, professional ethics, professional development, and the use of research and evaluation.

Private Interests vs. the Public Interest

Publicity is an appropriate pursuit of private as well as public institutions in a free society. Just like individual citizens, corporate entities have the right to speak on their own behalf and to promote their interests under the law. However, their voices may sound louder than the average citizen's since they have professional public relations experts and Washington lobbyists, and make multimillion-dollar contributions to advocacy organizations that amplify their views. And the major news media cannot be relied upon to be objective arbiters since they, too, are part of large multimedia conglomerates that are often reluctant to offend their largest corporate advertisers. Furthermore, it is very tempting for journalists to rely heavily on slickly written press releases when creating their news stories. Many wonder whether this gives large corporations undue influence in public affairs and the ability to dominate society in the interests of their corporate owners. (See "Media and Culture: The Sarbanes-Oxley Act," page 317.) It

■ **STREET FIGHTING WOMAN**
Disgruntled corporate employees sometimes take their grievances to the streets to attract attention to their cause.

© AP/Wide World Photos

The Velvet Ghetto

First identified in the 1980s, the velvet ghetto continues to be where many female public relations practitioners live today. Women now dominate employment in the field, in part because of affirmative action policies, the need to provide a "woman's viewpoint" to appeal to female publics, the perception that public relations is suited to women, and also the fact that PR jobs pay better than other positions open to women. However, female practitioners earn only 60 percent of what men do in comparable positions, so a competing explanation is that women are a "better buy," that they will work for lower pay than men while helping to improve the corporation's overall affirmative action profile (Grunig, Toth, & Hon, 2001).

In most media industries there are patterns of employment discrimination against women. At first glance the public relations field seems to be a notable exception, so much so that male practitioners have sometimes charged reverse discrimination. But some think the opportunities for women, particularly in the corporate ranks, are a reflection of a deeper pattern of sex discrimination that has been called a "velvet ghetto." Female public relations employees are well represented and well paid but are unable to break the "glass ceiling" between them and powerful upper management jobs, although of late there have been notable promotions (see "Profile: Helen Ostrowski," page 316).

For most of the history of modern public relations, those doing the day-to-day work came from the ranks of newspaper reporters and editors, jobs that were formerly dominated by males. Today, the field attracts individuals from a wider variety of backgrounds, virtually all of them college graduates with degrees in the liberal arts, large numbers of whom studied journalism, marketing, public relations, mass communication, and English. Some of these are academic fields in which women traditionally have been well represented, and that, in turn, has opened up new opportunities for women to enter public relations. The management ranks are still male dominated, but that is changing as college-educated females rise in the ranks and their salaries begin to match those of their male counterparts.

raises the policy issue of limits on donations to political groups. It also raises ethical issues. How far should public relations professionals go to reach journalists? How accepting of professional publicity materials should journalists be?

Thus, there is a natural tension between corporate interests and the public interest. This tension can be seen and heard daily in the press when corporations are charged with corruption, environmental pollution, undue political influence, and restraint of trade—in sum, with using their money, power, or influence in ways that compromise or undermine the public interest. In recent years, the agenda of issues has expanded to include critical social issues.

Sometimes large corporations commit offenses so visible that they are unable to manage public opinion. On November 4, 1996, the *New York Times* published a story accusing senior company officials of a major corporation of "belittling the company's minority employees with racial epithets," such as "black jelly beans," in private meetings. Some of these conversations had been recorded clandestinely, fueling a $520 million lawsuit against Texaco on behalf of 1500 African-American employees. Within hours of the first story, the American media exploded with a frenzy of damning coverage. The cost to Texaco was $176 million to settle the discrimination lawsuit. It also initiated a corporation-wide effort to eliminate racism in the workplace.

Every day, however, in contrast to stories like Texaco's, the press also gives large amounts of favorable coverage that directly advances corporate interests—strong company earnings, successful government initiatives, noteworthy charitable events. Much of the background for these and related stories, particularly in the business press, comes from PR representatives who send news releases and pitch letters to editors and reporters suggesting angles that they and their publications or stations might take. These representatives also make countless phone calls to the media. They organize press briefings, press luncheons, and other "contacts" to stay in touch with editors and reporters for offensive as well as defensive purposes.

PROFILE

Chief Executive Officer Porter Novelli International

Name: Helen Ostrowski

Education: B.A. Humanities, New York University

Current Job: Global chief executive officer, Porter Novelli International

Job Responsibilities: Direct all aspects of global public relations agency

Previous Positions: President, Americas; regional director, Northeast/Midwest Region; general manager, N.Y. Office; EVP, Health Care, N.Y. Previously, held various management positions with health-care public relations agencies. Spent 15 years on the corporate side at American Cyanamid Company (corporate public affairs) and Schering Plough (international pharmaceutical PR and corporate internal communications)

Management Style: Consensus-building style to inform decision making and gain support, with strong focus on high-performance expectations.

Most Notable Achievements (PR and Other): Editor of 1982 *NY Walk Book,* a hiking guide to New York and New Jersey—hiking is a passion, as is sailing. Professionally, working on interferon, the first bioengineered drug, and handling public relations for the American Society of Clinical Oncology.

How She Got to the Top: Secretary at American Cyanamid, and was assigned to the public affairs group

Where Do You Go from Here?: "I think after a long career in public relations, capped by heading a great firm, my next step will be to do something radically different (and spend time with my husband!). I'm not sure what it will be, but likely either teaching or something with children."

■ HELEN OSTROWSKI

© Courtesy of Porter Novelli

And, if public opinion isn't enough to win the day, lobbyists attempt to directly affect votes on legislation affecting major corporations by making donations to the campaigns of politicians who enact the legislation. For example, the communications and electronics industry, led by Microsoft and AT&T, donated nearly $130 million to political campaigns in the 2000 elections (Opensecrets.org, 2001). After President George W. Bush won the White House in 2000, a number of media commentators speculated that such donations, coupled with a generally less aggressive overall approach to antitrust enforcement, helped win Microsoft more favorable treatment by the new administration.

In general, the issue for the media and society's institutions when it comes to media relations and publicity boils down to one word—power. The media have an obligation to cover institutions as objectively as possible, but their own corporate interests sometimes interfere with that obligation. The corporations, in turn, have an obligation to operate in the public interest, but that is often subordinated to the profit motive, and they have the economic power to impose their views on others through their public relations resources.

Public relations practitioners have to worry about what the public wants as much as what their employers want. Consequently, they live with a divided sense of self. They are both makers of messages and messengers. But most practitioners seem to relish their role despite its inherent difficulties. They understand the importance of the role that public relations plays in society, and they are willing to tolerate criticism in order to accomplish their goal.

The Sarbanes-Oxley Act: Making Corporate America Conform to Ethical Behavior?

What is it?

Signed off in 2002, the Sarbanes-Oxley Act is a piece of U.S. compliance legislation with global implications, designed to prevent financial malpractice and accounting scandals such as the Enron debacle. It is named after Sen. Paul Sarbanes, D-Maryland, and Rep. Michael Oxley, R-Ohio, the main architects of the legislation.

What does it involve?

The Act covers governance issues, many concerning the types of trade that are allowed within a company. For example, the Act forbids personal loans to officers and directors. Former WorldCom boss Bernie Ebbers had taken considerable loans from his company shortly before it became the center of a corporate scandal. Other measures regulate the responsibilities of audit committees that check a company's compliance. The Act also offers protection to whistleblowers.

While much of what the Act purports to do is common sense, the actual challenge is ensuring the law is observed and that compliance can be demonstrated. The most common area of focus is the archiving of all communications and the creation of transparent and auditable systems for recording transactions, dealings, and any kind of business correspondence. Applications such as instant messaging are also being singled out as areas that need to be secured and made clearly accountable.

How do companies comply?

Most companies are working with accredited auditors and consultants. These firms test compliance and search for material weaknesses—flaws that would fail the SOX test—so there is a lot of shareholder trust to gain from filing for SOX compliance.

Even if nothing bad ever happens, companies cannot afford to be remiss with their compliance. Noncompliance will probably mean heavy fines—which as yet have not been outlined or defined—and a serious loss of shareholder trust and brand value. Large financial institutions will probably be able to pay fines easily, but the loss of face and the ensuing PR disaster of public naming and shaming could be colossal.

Hiding the Truth?

Professional public relations practitioners occasionally undermine their personal and professional ethics when they work for an organization, institution, or individual that does something unethical or illegal that ends up in the press and by extension the public is lied to and/or manipulated by the perpetrator. The lie may be relatively venial and have few or no consequences, but frequently the lie is grave enough to have major implications; for example, for employees who lose their jobs, for stockholders who lose their hard-earned investments, or for people who lose their lives.

A recent example was the failure in the late 1990s of Bridgestone/Firestone and Ford Motor Co. to warn the public and their customers about structural weaknesses in tires installed in the Ford Explorer. The companies then remained silent or uncaring for many weeks after the failures became public knowledge. More than 140 deaths and more than 500 injuries have been attributed to accidents in the vehicles equipped with the faulty tires.

The public relations practitioners who worked for these companies didn't initiate the actions that led to the fiascoes, but they certainly played a major role in perpetuating the pattern of deception by promoting the companies' actions and then defending them as innocuous when they became public and the damage had been done.

Corporations are not the only offenders. In 2005 the U.S. Department of Education came under fire for providing payments to conservative African-American talk show host Armstrong Williams so that he would plug the department's policies to minority audiences. The payments, made through a major public relations firm, were not voluntarily disclosed prior to their exposure in the press. This constituted an unethical public relations practice and also possibly illegal government-sponsored propaganda.

Although there are accepted codes of ethics that guide the practice of public relations (see Chapter 15), the pressure on many practitioners to give unequivocal support to their employer's actions, even when those actions may be unethical and possibly illegal, remains a critical challenge for the profession.

Professional Development

Other issues for practitioners involve professional development and personal growth. Clearly, there is a need for practitioners to become more sophisticated about how to use new technology for communications purposes. They also have to learn more about the basics of business, how it is structured, and how it is managed. Since most practitioners enter the field after studying liberal arts or after having worked in journalism and publishing, they have little knowledge of how corporations and small businesses operate.

To communicate profit-and-loss issues for their clients, they need to get up to speed as quickly as possible. There is also a great concern in the field about maintaining the high standards in writing and thinking that have been the foundation of the practice's success over the years. Senior practitioners, in particular, complain about how difficult it is to find employees who are strong, journalistically oriented writers.

There has also been tremendous growth in the numbers of local, national, and international public relations conferences, seminars, and workshops sponsored by professional associations, universities, and for-profit enterprises. These meetings cover everything from the basics of public relations to trends and issues driving the management of organizational communications. And the PRSA has developed a Universal Accreditation program to judge an individual practitioner's understanding and knowledge. It also has a Fellows program to recognize long-term involvement in, and major contributions to, the practice of public relations.

Although the Accreditation and Fellows programs have no legal status, they are viewed as measures of professional integrity and success. In this sense, they open doors to jobs, promotions, and industry leadership. More generally, they underscore the public relations field's interest in improving the value of what practitioners do as communicators in the information society.

Use of Research and Evaluation

A general criticism often leveled against the industry is that practitioners need to conduct more research and increase their evaluation of the impact and effectiveness of their efforts. Although both activities are included in the traditional public relations planning process, research and evaluation are still used scantily in helping to define the goals of programs and activities and later in measuring their effectiveness.

Part of the reason for the limited use is money. Most public relations budgets allocate little money for anything beyond the essentials. These budgets focus largely on tactical, not strategic, thinking. To move forward in this area, practitioners need to integrate research and evaluation into their plans and budgets. They also need to educate top management on the value of research and development in designing and delivering more effective messages and programs.

In addition to providing clearer direction for programs, research helps build the theory and practice

STOP & REVIEW

1. What are some of the important elements of ethical behavior in public relations?
2. What is the role of evaluation in public relations?
3. Why is professional development especially important in the public relations field?

of public relations, linking the field to other mass communication functions in the process. Major research techniques in public relations include environmental monitoring (assessing the corporate climate), audits (evaluating an organization's standing with its publics), and readability studies (analyzing a publication's effectiveness). A few of the most prominent research firms are Echo Research (out of Great Britain), KD Paine and Partners, CARMA, and Delahaye Medialink. Typically, they are engaged by large organizations to assist in measuring and evaluating PR success. They use the full range of criteria, including message content, audience exposure, market share, geographical distribution, return on investment, positive versus negative impressions, and related factors.

In the absence of research and evaluation, public relations' effectiveness is compromised and the practitioner's credibility and accountability suffer. Unless you know where you are going and have some expectation of results, you will never really know whether you have succeeded. And unless you can point to hard data substantiating the impact of your programs, the client or employer will always be suspicious of promises and recommendations.

SUMMARY AND REVIEW

HOW DID PUBLIC RELATIONS DEVELOP?

In a sense, professional public relations is as old as history itself. The rulers of ancient empires, political propagandists, and the propagators of the world's great religions were among the first to use public relations techniques. In this light, the Federalist Papers, the Bill of Rights, and the popularization of frontier heroes such as Daniel Boone and Davy Crockett may be seen as examples of successful public relations campaigns. Modern public relations evolved in the late nineteenth century as large corporations sought to defend their interests in the arena of public opinion. The first independent public relations counsel was established in the early 1900s. Ivy Lee was an early practitioner who worked to improve the image of the industrialists of the late nineteenth century. Edward Bernays is widely regarded as the originator of the current professional practice. Mass-persuasion propaganda campaigns during both world wars were also influential in expanding the scope and effectiveness of public relations.

HOW ARE CHANGES IN COMMUNICATIONS MEDIA ALTERING PUBLIC RELATIONS?

Expansion in the number of media outlets, especially in newspaper publishing and cable television, has expanded the opportunities for public relations professionals to present their message to the public. Video news releases were developed to help place public relations stories in television newscasts. Satellite networks and videoconferences afford new opportunities to deliver highly targeted press briefings. Electronic mail, mass calling, web pages, and facsimile are also being applied in modern public relations practice. And new tools such as interactive news releases and electronic press kits are becoming more popular. Meanwhile, the internal operations of public relations organizations are being transformed by the adoption of personal computers to automate many routine public relations tasks and to gain access to relational databases and online information services that offer public relations information. Public relations techniques used in political campaigns are also taking advantage of advances in computer and telecommunications technology, giving politicians new opportunities to circumvent mass media channels and state their case directly to the public.

WHAT ARE THE KEY ELEMENTS OF SUCCESSFUL PUBLIC RELATIONS?

Public relations campaigns succeed to the extent that they promote mutual understanding between the organization that sponsors the campaigns and one or more of the publics on which the organization depends to achieve its goals. Although it is a distinct function, public relations often relies on the successful execution of related pursuits such as advertising and marketing for its campaigns to succeed. Evaluation and attention to ethical standards are two other key elements.

WHAT ARE SOME OF THE TECHNIQUES USED IN PUBLIC RELATIONS?

The techniques used to reach the public depend on the nature of both the public relations message and the public or publics to which they are addressed. Annual reports, press releases, speeches, teleconferences, news conferences, advertorials, and public tours are some of the techniques commonly used on behalf of corporate public relations clients. Not-for-profit groups and government agencies rely more on unpaid forms of promotion, such as public service announcements and door-to-door canvassing by volunteers.

HOW IS THE PUBLIC RELATIONS INDUSTRY ORGANIZED?

Most large organizations have their own public relations departments, although they go by various names, including public affairs and public information. There are also thousands of independent public relations firms that supplement corporate PR departments or perform these services for smaller firms. Public relations may also be categorized in terms of functions, including media relations, promotion, community relations, government relations, public information, special events, employee relations, issues management, and lobbying. Public relations professionals are often members of such organizations as the Public Relations Society of America and the International Public Relations Association.

WHAT ARE SOME CRITICISMS OF PUBLIC RELATIONS?

Critics contend that professional public relations is an organized attempt to mislead the public and to represent the interests of large corporations at the expense of the public good. In the past, public relations campaigns have stooped to such tactics as concocting fictitious news events and creating phony organizations to promote their causes. Now public relations practitioners subscribe to codes of ethics as one approach to understanding the implications of and avoiding such abuses.

WHAT DOES IT MEAN TO BE A PUBLIC RELATIONS PROFESSIONAL?

Today's public relations professionals hold college degrees in fields such as liberal arts, journalism, marketing, mass communication, and English. Also, more than 200 colleges offer programs in the field of public relations. Practitioners seek accreditation from professional societies such as the Public Relations Society of America and follow the society's voluntary ethical standards. They keep up to date by reading professional publications aimed at the public relations field. They also participate in continuing education programs to develop their abilities throughout their careers.

WHAT IS THE ROLE OF RESEARCH AND EVALUATION IN PUBLIC RELATIONS?

Research helps public relations practitioners improve the effectiveness of their activities, and evaluation helps them determine how effective they have been. Environmental monitoring, audits, readability studies, trend analysis, and evaluation activities such as soliciting feedback from public relations clients and publics are examples of research and evaluation methods.

MEDIA CONNECTION

For web links, quizzes, and key term flash cards, visit the **Student Companion Website** at http://communication.wadsworth.com/straubhaar5.

 For unlimited easy access to additional and exclusive online study, support, and research tools, log on to **1pass** at http://1pass.thomson.com using the unique access code found on your 1pass passcode card.

 The **Media Now Premium Website** offers *Career Profile* videos, *Critical View* video news clips, and *Media in Motion* concept animations. You'll also find Stop & Review tutorial questions, a sample final exam, and much more.

 InfoTrac College Edition is a fully searchable online database offering anytime, anywhere access to more than 20 years' worth of articles from nearly 5,000 diverse and reliable sources.

vMentor provides live, one-on-one online tutoring to connect you to experts who will assist you in understanding the concepts covered in your course.

What's it like to work in public relations? In the Career Profile video for this chapter, Julie Crabill, senior account executive at Edelman Public Relations, discusses her day-to-day job functions.

11

This chapter was written by **Daniel A. Stout, Ph.D.,** Associate professor of journalism and mass communications at the University of South Carolina. Formerly the manager of special advertising projects at the *Houston Chronicle,* he has published numerous articles on advertising and mass communication. He presently serves as founding co-editor of *The Journal of Media and Religion.*

Although the goal of advertising has always been to inform and persuade, it is undergoing dramatic changes as a form of communication. This chapter describes some of the economic, cultural, and technological events that ushered in the era of contemporary advertising, and examines the evolving structure of the advertising industry, current advertising strategies, and media literacy as it relates to advertising.

HISTORY: FROM MINOR INDUSTRY TO META-INDUSTRY

It is often thought of as a twentieth-century phenomenon, but some form of **advertising** has existed for centuries. Since the time when people began living in small groups and villages, attempts have been made to persuade others to purchase or trade goods. Some archaeologists, for example, must have been disappointed when their translations of ancient Greek and Egyptian stone tablets revealed solicitations to stay at particular inns for the night or listed goods for sale! Signage on the walls of ancient cities of Greece and Rome also marketed tangible goods such as food and wine. Another basic form of advertising occurred centuries later when town criers filled the streets of Europe. They told the citizenry about the "good deal" to be found "just around the corner."

With the introduction of the printing press in Europe in 1455, and later the dawning of the Industrial Revolution in the eighteenth century, businesses accessed ever-larger markets for their goods. The printing press also spawned a new form of advertising, the *handbill.* The advantage of handbills over signs and town criers was that the message

Advertising is communication that is paid for and is usually persuasive in nature.

1704	First classified ads	**1980**	Era of creativity begins
1833	Penny Press originated	**1990s**	Era of integrated marketing
1849	First formal ad agency	**1994**	Internet banner advertising
1860s	Most magazines carry advertising	**2000**	Internet advertising slumps
1895	Image ads common	**2003**	Internet advertising revives, especially on Google
1926	First radio network		
1960s	30- and 60-second TV commercials dominate advertising	**2004**	Database marketing expands

could be copied efficiently and distributed to many people in a relatively short time, and the content could be expanded to include as much description as was thought necessary to promote the transaction. Flyers and hand-distributed leaflets are still much in use today, particularly by local retailers and candidates for political office. Printing also enabled the first newspaper advertisements, which began around 1625.

Advertising in America

The earliest newspaper ads in America were classified ads published in the *Boston News-Letter* in 1704 (Sandage, Fryburder, & Rotzoll, 1989). An example of advertising from the colonial period is the following ad, which appeared in Benjamin Franklin's newspaper, the *Pennsylvania Gazette.*

To be SOLD A Plantation containing 300 acres of good Land, 30 cleared, 10 or 12 Meadows and in good English Grass, a house and barn lying in Nantmel Township, upon French Creek, about 30 miles from Philadelphia, Enquire of Simon Merideith.

Franklin expanded the space devoted to advertising and was the first to apply creative writing skill to advertising copy. He was also the first to include illustrations alongside the copy.

Later, the Industrial Revolution played an integral part in the rise of modern advertising. The convergence of capitalism, railroads, and, later, electricity, and the appropriation of abundant natural resources led the United States to a situation where more products could be manufactured than consumed. This created a need for sophisticated, persuasive messages that stood out in a competitive environment.

Benjamin Day's *New York Sun* originated the concept of the mass circulation newspaper, or Penny Press, in 1833. From that point on, we see advertising emerging both as a form of persuasive communication, bought and paid for by the advertiser, and later as an economic engine with the potential to support the media enterprise financially.

■ **EARLY PRINT ADVERTISING**

Advertising increased toward the end of the eighteenth century as more products were mass-produced and more people became potential consumers. This ad for Cook's Virginia tobacco appeared around 1720.

© The Granger Collection, New York

The Rise of the Advertising Profession

In examining the history of advertising, it is necessary to acknowledge the work done by its practitioners. The earliest advertising professionals were essentially advertising agents, who wholesaled advertising space on behalf of publishers. The best-known advertising agent from this era was Volney B. Palmer, who started in the advertising business in 1842 and coined the term *advertising agency* in 1849. Palmer represented some 1300 newspapers and originated the commission system, under which publishers paid a fee on completion of an advertising sale. Palmer also offered a wider range of services than other agents. He not only sold advertising space but also produced the ads, delivered them to the publishers, and verified their placement.

In 1865, similarly, George P. Rowell, considered to be the founder of the advertising agency as we know it today, began contracting with local newspapers for a set amount of space and then brokered the space to clients. This arrangement made Rowell something of an independent "middleperson" who had to cater to both publishers and advertising clients. Rowell advised his clients on which newspapers to select for their needs.

Political propaganda also played an important role in the evolution of modern advertising. During World War I, advertising found its voice directed away from the materialistic needs of the average citizen and toward the good of the country as a whole. This campaign—in which Albert Lasker, an advertising pioneer and managerial genius, played an important role—included activities designed to build public sentiment for the war effort as well as appeals to the homefront to curtail unnecessary consumption and to "buy war bonds" instead.

The Rise of Broadcast Advertisers

As shown in Chapter 6, the 1920s witnessed the rise of a powerful new mass medium for advertising: the radio. Radio came of age as an advertising medium in 1926 when RCA purchased a chain of radio stations from AT&T, including WEAF in New Jersey, and established the National Broadcasting Company. The creation of the radio network concept provided national advertisers with an unprecedented means of distributing messages to prospects across the nation simultaneously (Fox, 1984). The new medium was designed to bring news, information, and entertainment to the public at large and depended exclusively on revenues received from advertisers (see Chapter 6).

The years following World War II saw the explosive expansion of television as an advertising medium, especially after the establishment of national television networks in 1948. Television quickly grew to compete with other forms of mass communication as the key creative medium for national advertisers. The combination of sight and sound gave advertisers the ability to demonstrate products to millions of viewers in a dramatic way. Soon, TV personality John Cameron Swazey was attaching watches to outboard motor rudder blades and snowplow treads in order to prove that "Timex takes a licking but keeps on ticking." Other commercials showed that Bic pens could still write after being shot through blocks of solid oak with high-powered rifles, and that Samsonite luggage was undamaged after being dropped from an airplane. Although magazine advertising was also a growing medium, television enjoyed the ability to demonstrate products.

© The Granger Collection, New York

■ ADVERTISING AS WAR

During World War I, advertising turned from promoting consumption of goods to getting citizens involved in the war effort by buying war bonds.

Hard Sell vs. Soft Sell

A defining moment in advertising occurred in 1905 when John E. Kennedy, a copywriter working in partnership with Albert Lasker at the Lord & Thomas advertising agency in New York, redefined advertising as "salesmanship in print." Before then, advertising copy was usually brief and hyperbolic, and most ads sought a mail-in response from the reader. This *hard-sell* approach to advertising as a mediated sales tool used persuasive techniques and introduced the "reason why" philosophy to copy preparation (Wells, Burnett, & Moriarty, 1995). The *soft-sell* approach was pioneered at about the same time by Stanley Resor and his copywriter Helen Lansdowne at the J. Walter Thompson agency. This approach tended toward an emotional rather than a rational appeal. The soft-sell approach became so prevalent by the 1980s that this period is often referred to as the **era of creativity.** That is, advertising during this time was as much about entertainment as it was about marketing. Saturn advertising is a contemporary example of the soft-sell approach in automobile advertising. From magazine ads to TV commercials to in-store displays, messages feature Saturn buyers describing how the car reflects their values; all ads have a conversational style that is relaxed and friendly. Instead of making a glitzy sales pitch, owners are depicted at home or at work simply talking about the quality of the product and the fair price.

The "Big Five" Traditional Media

For most of the twentieth century, advertising appeared primarily in five media: newspapers, magazines, radio, television, and outdoors (that is, billboards). The newspaper is considered the "shopper's medium" where readers clip coupons and learn what local retailers have on sale. Magazines and radio are "niche" media, reaching specialized audiences. Kraft Foods might place an ad in *Southern Living* or *Chocolatier* to reach upscale women; stores such as Old Navy and Nike Town could place ads on hip-hop radio stations to engage teens aged 14–18. Outdoor advertising can reach large numbers of people repeatedly in major cities. Television, through sight and sound, is excellent for image building and demonstrating new products. While these five media remain important in the advertising mix, there are many more options today.

The Era of Integrated Marketing Communication (IMC)

Today, advertisers choose from a wide array of media—from Internet animated banner ads to movie trailers on DVDs. This situation has created a phenomenon known as **integrated marketing communication (IMC),** which encourages the use of virtually all communication channels available to the advertiser. IMC is the "practice of unifying all marketing communication tools—from advertising to packaging—to send target audiences a consistent, persuasive message that promotes company goals" (Burnett & Moriarty, 1998).

While traditional advertising has long been the most common form of marketing communication, it no longer dominates the way it once did. For example, in recent years the ready-to-eat cereal industry has done more **sales promotion** (coupons, sweepstakes, sampling, and so on) than advertising. In the era of IMC, traditional media are not the only options, and the media used ultimately depend on the needs of the advertiser. For example, Oakley, one of the most successful manufacturers of sunglasses and sports eyewear, attributed much of its success to the nontraditional medium of stickers. Consumers were so eager to be associated with the prestige of the Oakley brand that they were willing to purchase stickers and place them on their car windows, motorcycles, and

In the **era of creativity** advertisers emphasized entertainment as well as information.

Integrated marketing communications (IMC) assures that the use of all commercial media and messages is clear, consistent, and achieves impact.

Sales promotions are specific features like coupons to directly spur sales.

Its cleaner, brighter **Taste** means cleaner, brighter teeth! **New Pepsodent,** the only tooth paste containing **Irium,** removes the film that makes your teeth look dull— uncovers the natural brilliance of your smile!

Pepsodent

Pepsodent

A PRODUCT OF LEVER BROTHERS COMPANY

Use Pepsodent twice a day— see your dentist twice a year

■ **SEX SELLS**

This toothpaste ad from the 1950s is an example of the soft sell, emphasizing the product's taste and sex appeal over its ability to prevent cavities.

other possessions. Today, companies do not restrict themselves to advertising but instead try to find that combination of marketing, public relations, sales promotions, and direct marketing that best achieves their goals (Elliott, 2001).

ADVERTISING EVERYWHERE

Advertising is an expanding phenomenon with a widening set of uses and effects. Once the exclusive domain of sellers and retailers, advertising is so widespread that doctors, lawyers, and educators utilize it every day. Advertising's center of gravity has expanded from the business sector to the culture at large. Hospitals now have marketing plans, and universities think of themselves as "brands." Advertising appears in public schools and educational materials in ways that would not have been permitted even 20 years ago. Global commercialization of media has lead to an increase in national and multi-national advertising. Advertising firms are also consolidating globally, as major global firms buy up or partner with major local firms.

Advertising by religious groups is also a growing trend, as denominations from Judaism to Buddhism advertise in a variety of media. (See "Media and Culture: Religious Branding," page 329.) Similarly, other not-for-profit organizations, social and political, utilize increasingly strategic advertising. While it's not a new advertiser, the U.S. Armed Services provides yet another example of advertising's increased presence in our lives. At press time, the ongoing military action in Iraq has led the military to increase the prevalence and sophistication of its advertising for recruits. Although advertising is still essential to the selling of goods and services, it is no longer just a "for profit" phenomenon.

STOP & REVIEW

1. How would you describe "advertising" as a form of communication?
2. What role did the Industrial Revolution play in ushering in the era of modern advertising?
3. Which advertising techniques were influenced by war propaganda?
4. How does Colonial advertising of the late 1700s differ from advertising today?
5. What has been the effect of integrated marketing communication (IMC)?

TECHNOLOGY: NEW ADVERTISING MEDIA

The technology of advertising has developed side by side with the technology of the mass media. We will not recount these developments here since they are covered in Chapters 3 through 9, but will instead focus on the ways in which information technologies are starting to transform conventional advertising forms.

Advertising in Cyberspace

No development in the last decade has drawn more speculation in the advertising industry than the Internet. Advertising on *blogs* (chat rooms in e-newsletter format), **intermercials** (ads appearing before the ISP connects to Internet), and **buttons** (miniature banner ads) are just a few recent developments. Some claim the Internet is not only an excellent way to reach diverse audiences, but is also a way of extending the effectiveness of traditional media such as newspapers, magazines, radio, and television (Kaye & Medoff, 2001). For example, magazine advertisements for the cereal Smart Start also appear on the Kellogg's website. Experts project a steady increase in spending on Internet advertising to reach $10 billion in 2006 (Pricewaterhouse, 2004).

Intermercials are ads that appear before the ISP connects to the Internet.

Buttons are miniature banner ads.

Religious Branding: Secular Marketing Techniques Used by Denominations

"Religious retailing" and "religious marketing" are names for an expanding yet controversial form of advertising. Annual sales of religious books, music, gifts, and jewelry are now over $3 billion (Haley, White, & Cunningham, 2001) and stores such as Wal-Mart and Target often have separate sections for religious products. Contemporary Christian music (CCM) is one of the fastest growing categories of the music business (Perry & Wolfe, 2001). The brand WWJD (What Would Jesus Do?) is a popular jewelry and clothing line in the southern United States.

Despite this success, religious marketing is controversial. According to a study by Haley, White, & Cunningham (2001) consumers are divided about whether marketing is an appropriate means of religious worship. This issue surfaced recently when makers of the top-grossing film *The Passion of the Christ* rolled out a line of products that included a Passion Nail Necklace, Passion Pocket Coin, and Passion Pocket Card, and a variety of framed photos and images from the movie. For users, such products are a valid form of religious worship and a means of affiliating with a particular community. Critics, however, observe *symbol flattening* or the dilution of an icon's religious significance through excessive reproduction. They claim that the image of the cross, for example, is so widespread that few understand its historic significance.

Regardless of one's position on this issue, advertising professionals will have to study religious markets more than they have in the past. Religious symbols must be used cautiously and respectfully. For example, the social marketing campaign "What would Jesus drive?" was designed to promote responsible fuel consumption but was also controversial. It is vital that advertisers do extensive pretesting before executing such campaigns.

Perhaps the most interesting aspect of the Internet is its interactive nature. Whereas traditional media (such as television, magazines, and newspapers) are finite sources of information, the Internet is a responsive and flexible data source through the two-way exchange of messages. The website for Hallmark cards exemplifies this unique feature. A "reminder service" is available whereby customers are asked for friends' and relatives' names and birthdays and are later contacted through e-mail when it's time to send that person a greeting card. These Internet features allow advertisers to communicate with consumers in nontraditional ways, thus enabling advertisers to grow personalized consumer relationships that build strong ties to the brand (Duncan & Moriarty, 1997).

One recent development on the Internet involves **viral marketing.** This form of advertising involves marketing teams engaging participants in conversation about products in chat rooms and on message boards. The advertisers' strategy is to stimulate brand-related discussion and hope that others will carry it on, spreading word of the product like a virus to new customers. Some forms of viral marketing involve hiring individuals to use a company's products (for example, clothes, sunglasses, jewelry, and so on) and converse with others about the product during the course of a day.

The medium also has its critics. The tiny banner ads that have been the staple of Internet advertising since 1994 are limited in their ability to convey product information or alluring product imagery. Their **click through rate,** the percentage of viewers who click on the ads to visit the advertiser's home page, has dropped to a third of 1 percent as web surfers either ignore the banners or use software to automatically strip, or block, them from the pages they view. This has resulted in recent experiments with new sizes and formats of web advertising. For example, the Internet Advertising Bureau introduced new size options for Internet advertising in 2001 (Tedeschi, 2001). Internet ads now fill more of the web page and may appear in the middle of pages instead of the top and

Viral marketing is from specific people spreading ideas about products in chat rooms or similar fora.

Click through rate is the percentage of readers who click on the ad to visit the advertiser's page.

© Eveready Battery Company, Inc. 2004.
Reprinted with permission.

bottom margins. Internet *pop-up* and *pop-under* ads also spring up before the reader's eyes during browsing. Search pages like Google have advertiser-sponsored links. Such ads have gotten mixed reactions from consumers.

Despite these challenges, it appears that Internet advertising is here to stay. One indicator of this is the growing presence of the youth market on the web. A recent survey reports that 25 million teens (12–17) use the Internet and by 2007, 86% of them will be online (Born to, 2003). The Internet has now overtaken television as the medium of choice for teens, suggesting that this medium holds great promise in years to come.

An infrastructure for the purchase of Internet advertising is also a good sign for the future. Advertisers can now reach consumers efficiently through a system of online ad networks. Companies such as DoubleClick and ValueMedia partner with thousands of websites to create Internet ads that reach millions of users. DoubleClick regularly provides data of particular use to advertisers such as demographic profiles of Internet users. Beyond that, the organization helps advertisers measure the effectiveness of their Internet campaigns. They achieve this by identifying loyal customers, tracking their web surfing behavior, and communicating with them in relevant and cost-effective ways. Another company, Plurimus, analyzes web user data obtained from Internet service providers.

They Have Our Number

Information technologies have created and are continuing to create new ways of building relationships between consumers and brands. **Database marketing** makes this possible on a grand scale. Advertisers store information about consumers so that messages can be personalized in the future. Database marketing is a radical departure from mass media advertising as we know it today, more akin to direct marketing or the early direct response ads of the 1800s than the mass-market product advertising that dominated the twentieth century.

Database marketing is used when advertisers store information about consumers so that they can personalize messages.

One need not look further than a local grocery store for a starting point of database marketing. When we apply for discount cards or check-cashing privileges, we customers fill out a questionnaire giving personal information (address, occupation, income, product preferences, and so on) that is stored in a database along with a record of our purchases. The information is aggregated into national databases and then sold to advertisers, who in turn store the information in their databases. If a consumer regularly buys chocolate chip cookies but hasn't been to the store in recent days, the database is programmed to mail a discount coupon for the customer's favorite cookie brand. Alternatively, coupons might be issued directly at the checkout counter. Or, have you ever wondered why retailers ask for your phone number when you pay by check? It's not so they can track you down if your check bounces; your bank knows where you live, after all. That phone number is the key to matching information about that purchase with all your other purchases and with your personal information. If you use a credit card, it's even easier for them to track your purchases.

Database marketing relies on a process known as *data mining,* or the ongoing compilation and analysis of pertinent data for the purpose of updating marketing strategies as consumer needs evolve. Data mining appeals greatly to both media and advertisers since it enables much more targeted advertising, perhaps individual targeting, based on the compilation of information such as purchasing habits, online reading preferences, subscription information, product registration information, online movements across pages or click patterns, and personal credit histories.

Portal websites such as Yahoo! help advertisers take advantage of databases by creating high levels of Internet traffic for them. Consumers registered at the site enjoy messaging, e-mail, news, games, and commercial and other services. Portal databases then offer registered users links to products of interest. For example, if a visitor accesses information on watches, they're immediately given options to link to specific watches on sale at Wal-Mart, Target, and other stores.

Lands' End, Inc., which sells clothing and related merchandise via catalogs, has a highly developed database system in place. Customers create a 3-D model of themselves by providing critical measurements, which are stored in the database until applied to the individual's personal Virtual Model. Once a virtual model is created the customer can use it to "try on" items and outfits to see how they will look on his or her body. Outfits can be stored and recalled for later reference. Use of these database tools is even more widespread now that Land's End goods are available through the Sears website as well.

The Land's End customer data file is so extensive that when an order is phoned in, the operator is able to "call up" the individual from the database and identify all the items he or she has ever purchased including clothing sizes and style preferences. The customer service representatives at direct marketing operations like these even know who you are before you say "hello." A variation of the Caller ID feature found on consumer telephones identifies your telephone number and brings up your file while the sales rep's phone is still ringing.

The Internet raises database marketing to a new level that many consumers may find somewhat disconcerting. Through the use of cookies (see Chapter 9), small computer files deposited on consumers' computers as they surf the Internet, advertisers can track visits to websites and exposure to advertisements. Over time, information can be matched across sites and identified with individual consumers, even those who are careful to avoid revealing personal information on the web. From the advertiser's perspective this has the advantage of greater efficiency, limiting ad exposure to the most likely prospects and reducing duplicate exposures. Internet users are not the only ones giving up detailed personal information to advertisers.

The new digital video recorders (for example, TiVo) that record TV programs on computer disks so that viewers can rewind and fast-forward TV programs in progress also record detailed viewing information and upload the information as part of the subscription service that comes with the devices. Consumers can fight back by fast-forwarding through the commercials, but that fact is also recorded, perhaps targeting the consumers for a direct marketing pitch through another medium. Many models of DVRs no longer permit fast-forwarding, and newer TiVo units display advertiser logos while they are in fast-forward mode. Consumers have consistently complained that TV commercials interrupt the entertainment experience; these developments seem to address this weakness.

This situation is one reason advertisers try to achieve **permission marketing,** or the condition where Internet advertising and e-mail contact is welcomed, not resented. Seth Godin, author of the book *Permission Marketing,* argues that privacy is not an issue if the consumer has entered into a mutually beneficial conversation with the seller. According to Godin, e-commerce marketers and consumers must build a mutually beneficial relationship over time through the Internet. This requires ever-greater incentives that must meet the changing needs of consumers if permission marketing is to be effective.

Advertising and E-Commerce

E-commerce refers to the broad range of commercial transactions and purchases taking place on the Internet. Consumers can visit websites with comparative product and pricing information, ask questions, read reviews from other consumers, and even complete their purchases. It is both an impulse and a directional technology. The impulse potential arises from the growing number of browsers or "surfers" who respond to commercial messages on a whim as they use the Net for other purposes. For example, a reader of a book review in the online version of the *New York Times* may impulsively decide to click on the Barnes and Noble ad to order a copy. The Net becomes a directional medium when consumers decide to purchase a particular product and then go to a company's website to do so.

Spam, or unsolicited commercial e-mail, is another form of Internet advertising that is wearing out its welcome with consumers. Direct marketers, or spammers as they are known, automatically "harvest" e-mail addresses by the millions from unsuspecting consumers who frequent chat rooms or discussion groups or post them on their personal web pages. The more aggressive spammers send their messages through multiple servers, or disguise their true origins to defeat filtering by consumers' own e-mail programs. However, these actions are illegal under the **Canspam Law.** This federal law, known as the *Can-Spam Act of 2003,* regulates commercial e-mail and authorizes the Federal Trade Commission (FTC) to create a set of regulations for spam and empowers the agency to enforce them (See Chapter 14). Nonetheless, spam technology often includes *web bugs* (see Chapter 9) in the e-mails that automatically notify the sender if the message has been opened. This type of tracking technology isn't limited to e-mail and is also used during web surfing. In the battle for Internet privacy, consumers have developed some high-tech tactics of their own, such as *anonymizers* that let them surf the web without fear of being traced.

More New Advertising Media

Not only will Internet advertisers reach consumers at home and in the workplace, but through wireless Internet, or Internet *telephony,* interactive communication can occur

Permission marketing is when the consumer authorizes and welcomes contact from advertisers on the Internet.

Canspam Law regulates commercial e-mail.

anytime and anyplace (see Chapter 12). Outside work and home, the information center of the future is a telephone with Internet capability; it allows consumers to order products on the go and receive commercial e-mail from local retailers. For example, as one drives along the highway, a call is received from a favorite fast-food restaurant just ahead, informing the driver of current menu specials and discounts.

Satellite radio such as Sirius is also extending the reach of advertisers. Radio signals are no longer confined to conventional signal transmission but can cover vast areas equal to the broadcast coverage of satellites. Consumers also listen to the radio on the Internet.

Digital video recorders (DVRs) are another technology forcing new approaches for advertisers. Over 75 percent of advertising professionals feel that DVRs will have a significant effect on the creation of alternative TV advertising methods (Ad Pros, 2004, p.1). They give consumers control over what they choose to watch and a means of fast-forwarding through TV commercials. Therefore, 55 percent of advertising professionals believe that new ad formats such as **advertainment,** content sponsorship and product placement will gain popularity (Ad Pros, 2004, p. 1). However, they also agree that the 30-second TV commercial will continue as a popular option for advertisers.

This ability to circumvent commercials through interactive TV systems, digital video reorders, and remote controls has led to unique forms of **product placement,** in which products are written into the program's script or format. Oprah Winfrey, for example, gave away 276 Pontiac G6s to her studio audience during the normal course of the show (see "Media & Culture: *Oprah!* Talk Show or Marketing Vehicle?," page 334). Participants on the show *Survivor* are often rewarded with Doritos and Mountain Dew. On *American Idol,* judges and contestants drink Coke and wear Old Navy clothes. The point is, if people aren't watching the commercials, the advertising must appear where they are watching. Even a candidate for governor in Indiana during the 2004 elections used this strategy by creating a reality TV show to solicit votes (Baar, 2004).

The fear of losing advertising revenue is so great that a second generation of product placement has emerged. Products don't just appear in the show but are now significant elements of the plot (Nussenbaum, 2004). An early example was a *Seinfeld* episode in which Junior Mints were incorporated into the story line, and during recent seasons of *The Apprentice,* episodes revolved around one or two brands, such as M&Ms. Perhaps the most aggressive example of this new form of product placement is *The Days,* featured on ABC but developed by the private company MindShare, a "media agency," essentially a hybrid media and advertising agency. The program tells the story of a family in Philadelphia, and the characters use Unilever products such as Dove soap, Wisk detergent, and Skippy peanut butter. As the story unfolds, the products are important devices in depicting the scenes of real life.

The oldest form of advertising, the outdoor sign, is also undergoing a high-tech makeover. *Digital imaging technology* imposes signage onto stadium and arena walls that does not exist outside of the television screen, the same basic technique that superimposes a visible first down line on the screen for football fans. These virtual ads reach large audiences and can be changed quickly and efficiently. Other developments in the outdoor industry include application of electronic message boards, which enables the placement of billboard-like ads in malls and other indoor venues. *Tri-face* or revolving signs give more advertisers the chance to promote themselves in sports arenas. For example, the sign next to the basketball floor at a major arena revolves to reveal a new advertiser every few minutes or so.

The movie theater is also emerging as an important advertising category. Most moviegoers don't seem to mind commercial messages if they provide relaxation and fun.

Advertainment combines advertising into the entertainment content.

Product Placement is the practice of inserting commercial products, usually for a fee, in entertainment such as movies or television programs.

Oprah! Talk Show or Marketing Vehicle?

Since the candy product Reese's Pieces appeared in Steven Spielberg's 1982 film *ET,* commercialism has penetrated artistic and entertainment media that were previously off-limits. "Product placement" is when companies pay to have their products featured in movies or television programs. A more recent example is the bottles of Coca-Cola that can be found everywhere on the set of the hit show *American Idol.* Product placement was taken to a new level when all 276 members of the studio audience of *Oprah!* were awarded new Pontiac G6s. As the host shouted, "Everybody gets a car! Everybody gets a car! Everybody gets a car!" marketing executives and media critics were already debating the merits of this controversial media event. Is this type of commercial event the wave of the future? Is the line blurring between advertising and conventional TV programming?

Representatives of GM claim the event is already a success. According to Mary Kubitskey, advertising manager for Pontiac, traffic at the car's website has increased dramatically (Freeman, 2004). Winfrey's credibility with millions of women often translates into record sales for books, CDs, and other products. Yet there is considerable ambivalence about this type of in-program promotion from both business and social perspectives. Tom Klipstine, a former corporate public relations executive at GM, suggests that people often remember the event, but not the product. "The main question for this campaign is, was the association worth over $7 million? For Oprah, it is a definite yes. But for Pontiac it is just the beginning of an association with Oprah and only time will tell."

What, then, is strategically defensible and responsible product placement? The following questions might be helpful to advertisers as they consider product placement in their marketing communication program:

1. Is it consistent with the goals of the company's marketing plan? In other words, what is the product placement designed to achieve?
2. How will success of the product placement be measured? It is reasonable to expect that the product placement will result in increased sales or product awareness, for example.
3. Does it undermine the artistic and entertainment value of the media content it becomes a part of? Are the writers confident that their goals have not been compromised? Does it fit naturally into the format of the media vehicle? If not, confusion and controversy are likely to follow.
4. Have such promotions been planned and studied carefully before they are implemented? Ideas for product placement should be pretested with targeted consumers in focus groups and interviews.
5. How often should companies engage in product placement? Are there risks in doing this kind of marketing too often?

Theater advertising has expanded from conventional preshow spots and slides, and *trailers,* or *previews,* for upcoming new releases, to commercials only slightly modified from their original television forms, to "talking" popcorn bags, advertiser-sponsored text messaging, and video-enabled cell phones in the lobby so patrons can play games. This is an example of how advertisers can capture audiences in positive entertainment environments. One of the fastest growing segments, theater advertising spending, recently passed the $350 million mark (Stanley, 2004, p. 49). Similarly, *video game advertising* is on the rise. Advertising expenditures on in-video game advertising, a form of product placement, and *advergaming,* a game featuring commercial brands, are projected to reach $260 million by 2008, up from $79 million in 2003 (Kerner, 2004).

Other advertisers are experimenting with kiosks, stand-alone computer terminals that provide in-depth product information right at the point of sale. Through new software programs, a company's website can be accessed at a kiosk in a retail outlet. The "intel-

STOP & REVIEW

1. What is "database marketing," and how is it changing advertising today?
2. How might new technologies affect the practice of advertising in the future?
3. What is "permission marketing"?
4. Why is "data mining" so important in advertising?
5. What does it mean to "grow" consumers rather than "talk at" them?

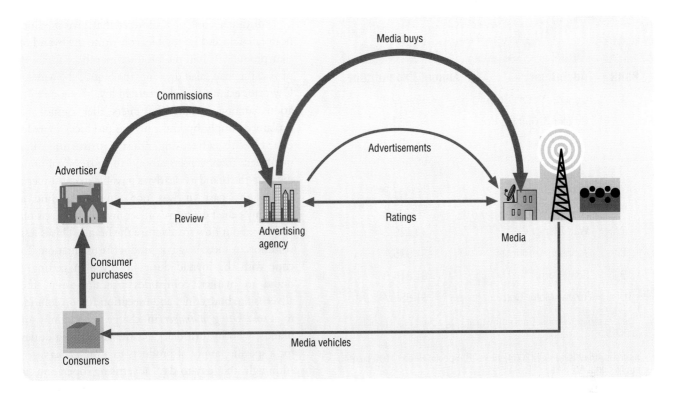

How Advertising Works
Advertisers pay commissions to agencies to create ads, then review their work. Advertising agencies buy time on media, and place ads according to ratings data. The media reach the public with the ad, and they buy the advertisers' product (or not).

ligent shopping cart" has made its appearance, complete with a computer display that directs the consumer to product locations and special promotions throughout the supermarket. Some grocery chains are installing, over their checkout lanes, television monitors that telecast news of in-store specials and messages from brand advertisers. Finally, the cost of computer chips that can synthesize the human voice is dropping quickly, raising the specter of the "talking cereal box" shouting advertising slogans at us as we walk down the supermarket aisle.

INSIDE THE ADVERTISING INDUSTRY

Someone must identify the need for an advertising message—and foot the bill for the campaign that results. This initiator is the advertiser. Then the message must be created. Here the responsibility may either be retained by the advertiser or be subcontracted to an advertising agency. Next, the message must be placed in one or more of the **advertising media,** each of which has its own organizational form and structure. **Research organizations** then help all concerned evaluate and measure the target group, the message content, and the media vehicles under consideration. As a means of understanding the structure of the industry, readers can follow the development of an advertising campaign from the moment of its conception by an advertiser to its presentation to the public by examining Figure 11.1.

Advertising media are the communication channels that carry messages to consumers.

Advertisers

The top categories of advertising expenditures are automotive, retail, business and consumer services, and entertainment and amusements. All told, over $85 billion is spent on advertising in the United States each year. Leading national companies such as General Motors and Procter & Gamble lead the list of major advertisers (Table 11.1).

Research organizations compile statistics about consumers and their media habits and evaluate advertising messages.

Table 11.1 Top 10 Leading National Advertisers*

Rank	Advertiser	Annual Expenditure
1	General Motors Corp.	$3,429.9
2	Procter & Gamble Co.	$3,322.7
3	Time Warner	$3,097.3
4	Pfizer	$2,838.5
5	Daimler Chrysler	$2,713.5
6	Ford Motor Co.	$2,233.8
7	Walt Disney Co.	$2,129.3
8	Johnson & Johnson	$1,995.7
9	Sony Corp.	$1,814.8
10	Toyota Motor Corp.	$1,682.7

*Dollars are in millions. Ranked by total U.S. advertising spending in 2003.

Source: *Advertising Age* (2004, June 28) Special Report. 100 Leading National Advertisers. P. S-2.

All dimensions of a product that give it value, both tangible and intangible, constitute the **brand** of that product. While the product may be something physical such as salad dressing, the brand, "Newman's Own" for example, evokes certain loyalties and affiliations among certain consumers that cannot be explained simply by knowing the product's ingredients. How the advertising industry is structured and organized, then, centers around the goal of communicating the brand as clearly as possible to consumers.

In the past, it was not unusual to find a company's chief executive officer involved in decision making about how to advertise the brand. This is less common in today's age of product segmentation. To cope with the myriad duties involved in getting a brand to market, companies typically assign the advertising, budgeting, and execution responsibilities to a *marketing manager* in charge of a family of brands, who in turn delegates the advertising duties for a specific family of products to a *brand manager.* Although the day-to-day advertising operation is normally handled by the brand manager, ultimate approval of the advertising budget is typically handed down from the marketing manager level or higher.

In a large company that sells a product for a national audience, the advertising process begins when the marketing manager calls for a meeting with the advertising manager of the firm to discuss advertising goals, deadlines, and expectations for the coming year. The creation of the advertising message is generally not performed by the company itself but instead is delegated to an advertising agency (see Figure 11.1). An advertising agency can provide an outside, objective perspective that companies can't get internally. The advertising manager invites a number of agencies to make presentations and, when one is selected, acts as a liaison between the firm and the agency.

For a local retailer, the process is much simpler. Typically, the owner determines approximately how much to spend on advertising in the coming year, writes the ads, and arranges to have them placed in local newspapers, on radio stations, or in other local media. This is not to say, however, that the selection of the target for the ad or the development of the message is any less important. It is just that the process unfolds on a somewhat lesser scale than in a national program.

Local retailers also take advantage of *co-op advertising support* from national companies. For example, a retail store that buys a product such as Colgate toothpaste gets an allowance for advertising from the Colgate-Palmolive Company. Ready-made print ads are also provided for the retailer to use. In other words, a good share of local advertising is actually paid for by national advertisers.

While the positions of brand manager and advertising manager remain important in most companies, there is a growing necessity for all marketing employees to know something about advertising. As business consultant Regis McKenna puts it, "Marketing is becoming an integrated part of the whole organization, rather than a specific function" (Kuchinskas, 2000, p. 136). This is the reason why in some companies, the vice president of marketing is often a person skilled in *marketing communication,* as are the marketing managers and brand managers (p. 136).

A brand consists of all the dimensions that identify and give unique value to a product or company.

Table 11.2 Elements of an Advertising Plan

Element	Purpose
Situation analysis	Explains where the company is, how it got there, and where it wants to be in the future. It identifies relevant problems that must be addressed by advertising and gives a detailed description of the consumer and the product.
Objectives	Those things we want the advertising campaign to achieve. Most advertising plans include both business objectives ("Increase unit sales by 25,000 during the next year") and communication objectives ("Achieve 65 percent awareness of the product within the target market"). Objectives differ according to the nature of the product, competition, consumer demand, and available budget.
Target market profile	A description of those individuals who would be the most likely to purchase the product. The target profile usually includes demographics (the target's age, sex, ethnicity, and income) and psychographics. Psychographics are lifestyle descriptions of the consumer's attitudes, interests, and opinions.
Positioning statement	A short paragraph explaining how the company wants the consumer to perceive the product. A lot of things can be communicated (price, quality, convenience), but what is the most important thing the advertising has to convey? A recent campaign for Southwest Airlines positions the product as a friendly airline whose discounted fares offer "freedom to move about the country." The advertising is light and humorous and consistently conveys this theme.
Creative strategy	Part of the plan that describes the specific theme and approach of the advertising. In other words, the creative strategy is a description of what the advertising will actually look like. In national campaigns, the strategy contains a big idea or a fresh and interesting way to make a point about the product. The big idea for Little Caesar's Pizza is an animated Caesar character in a Roman toga who utters, "Pizza, Pizza!" in all ads to communicate that you always get two pizzas for the right price.
Media plan	Lists the communication vehicles that will carry the advertising. Should television be used? Why or why not? If Internet advertising is rejected, what are the reasons? A good media plan ensures that enough of the right people are reached at an efficient price.

Inside the Advertising Agency

Most major companies do not want to plan and produce advertising campaigns themselves. Their business is to produce and sell a product, be it tennis shoes, soft drinks, or dog food. Therefore, a variety of advertising agencies have grown up at local, national, and international levels to plan and produce ad campaigns for them.

Agencies are organizations of businesspeople and talented individuals (see "Profile: Advertising Visionary, Scott Remy," page 338) who create and place **advertising plans** (see Table 11.2) for their clients. As we noted earlier, the first advertising agent, Volney B. Palmer, came on the scene over 150 years ago. Eventually Palmer and other media brokers offered more and more services, such as designing advertisements.

Today, full-service agencies complete virtually all elements of an advertising campaign including research, strategic planning, and generation of creative ideas for ads. Examples of major full-service advertising agencies include Ogilvy & Mather (now a subsidiary of the WPP Group), which produced many memorable campaigns and slogans, such as "At 60 miles an hour, the loudest noise in this new Rolls-Royce comes from the electric clock." These companies employ **account executives,** who act as liaisons between the agency and the client. They mobilize and coordinate all of the agency's work on the advertising campaign.

The **advertising plan** is a written document outlining the objectives and strategies for a product's advertising.

Account executives are the liaisons between the agency and the client.

Advertising Visionary

© J. Walter Thompson

Name: Scott Remy

Early Years: Grew up in Las Vegas, Nevada

Position: Senior Partner and Group Management Director, J. Walter Thompson, Chicago.

Style: An ambitious, talented, and good-humored advertising veteran, Remy describes himself as a "compassionate driver and emphatic achiever who makes things happen but leaves people their dignity."

Most Notable Achivements: With brilliant ad campaigns to his credit such as Nestle, Blockbuster Video, General Mills, Clorox, and Heinz, Remy says his greatest achievement is "being successful in my career while holding on to my personal values and maintaining my family as a priority."

Most Dubious Achievement: While he literally dumped one of his clients: "One time I took a prospective client golfing, and took a turn too hard and sent him tumbling out of it [golf cart]."

Entry Level: A gifted Elvis-inspired guitar player, Remy sought out a career that combined creativity with "a sense of normalcy" in terms of family stability. After dabbling in college journalism, PR, and other communication disciplines, he deemed advertising his destiny and pursued it with a vengeance. As a student, Remy was recruited by several top ten agencies and was offered an account executive position just before graduation. His assertiveness and practical application of advertising helped him succeed in his initial interviews and throughout his career.

Inspiration: "The best moments are when you win a new piece of business and every-body works their tails off trying to make this happen. You have to do it fast, it has to be good, it has to be really well put together—quickly, and you're in competition. The thrill and the adrenaline and the rush that comes from doing that and then seeing it come to fruition is really, really cool."

How He Got to the Top: To succeed long term in advertising, Remy recommends that you have "the ability to shrug off defeat and disappointment" and "the ability to deal with multiple people in different ways." Advertising practitioners must deal with creative, business, and sales people as well as a host of consumer mentalities that are as diverse as the products they purchase. "You have to have a strong sense of yourself, but you also need to be versatile and be able to get into other people's worlds and lives and talk to them in their own language."

Where Does He Go from Here? Remy is leading the transition from the traditional advertising mindset to the present era of new technology. "We probably shouldn't even call ourselves ad agencies anymore because that indicates the old model of TV, magazines, mass media. Throw it out there and you can reach people. Well, those days are long gone. Now it's all about communication planning . . . and it's more than just a website. You find people on cell phones now; you get people on their Palm Pilots; everywhere you turn, technology has allowed people to stay more connected to messages, and you have to be there at the very beginning. If you're just an old-fashioned advertiser with a couple of ads, it's real easy to ignore you."

Source: Interview conducted and summarized by Shellie Frey, Brigham Young University.

Agencies are experiencing considerable change stimulated by both new technology and the trend toward efficiency. A decade ago, agencies handled advertising in traditional media such as newspapers, magazines, television, and radio. Today, clients insist that they have expertise in direct marketing, online advertising, sales promotion, and public relations. Here are the major departments within a typical ad agency:

real conversation: priceless

© Courtesy of MasterCard

The Creative Department.   A key element in the advertising plan is the creative strategy, or what the advertising will say in order to achieve the objectives of the campaign. Using the research data as a foundation, copywriters and graphic designers in the creative department begin work on a creative concept or "big idea." *Concepting* is the act of saying something in a unique way but at the same time ensuring that the message is "on strategy" with what needs to be communicated for the product to sell. A classic example is the campaign for Energizer Batteries featuring the battery-powered "Bunny," whose power supply is so much better than competing brands that the toy seems to work endlessly. The creative concept is to show what appears to be a normal commercial for another product; the mechanical bunny rolls across the screen, interrupting the ad in an unexpected and humorous way. This campaign, which has been running for a number of years, is a classic example of concepting in that it is both attention-getting and informative in terms of a unique product feature. More recent examples of great concepts include Capital One's "What's in your wallet?" campaign as well as the "priceless" ads by MasterCard.

A variety of creative professionals may be involved in the ad's execution: writers, artists, art directors, musicians, graphic designers, content or subject experts, and researchers. What emerges after a period of creative incubation is not a single clear-cut solution to all of the client's problems, but rather several executions, one of which will be able to survive the critical client review process. Once an execution gets approval from the client, the assignment is given back to the creative department for final production.

The Media Department.   Meanwhile, the agency's **media department** is hard at work selecting media to carry the client's message, given the budget available. The account executive works constantly to keep all parties up-to-date on one another's progress. After the client and the media buyer approve creative and media recommendations, a specialist within the media department initiates negotiations with media suppliers for the purchase of specific media vehicles to carry the advertising message. It used to be that the media department dealt only with traditional media (for example, television, radio, newspapers, magazines, and billboards). Today, however, ads are placed in a wide range of nontraditional media as well, from ads on plastic cups to commercial trailers in movie

Media departments negotiate on behalf of the advertiser to buy space from media companies.

Table 11.3 Advertising Spending by Media

Media	Jan–Sept 2003 (Millions)	Jan–Sept 2004 (Millions)	% Change
Newspapers (local)	$16,649.5	$17,752.4	6.6%
Network TV	$14,438.2	$16,463.1	14.0%
Magazines	$13,524.3	$14,879.0	10.0%
Spot TV	$11,284.0	$12,343.3	9.4%
Cable TV	$9,035.2	$10,489.5	16.1%
Internet	$4,446.1	$5,593.2	25.8%
Local radio	$5,357.1	$5,457.0	1.9%
B-to-B magazines	$3,802.7	$3,859.5	1.5%
Syndication	$2,471.0	$2,898.5	17.3%
Hispanic media	$2,726.3	$2,872.6	5.4%
Newspapers (national)	$2,238.4	$2,454.6	9.7%
Outdoor	$2,041.5	$2,400.8	17.6%
National spot radio	$1,924.6	$1,875.1	2.6%
FSI's 7	$1,017.2	$1,065.4	4.7%
Sunday magazines	$974.7	$1,053.1	8.0%
Network radio	$735.0	$754.2	2.6%
Local magazines	$234.3	$258.5	10.3%
Total	$92,899.9	$102,469.6	10.3%

Source: TNS Media Intelligence/CMR Strategy multimedia ad expenditure database <marketingtoday.com/research/1204/first_9_months_2004.htm>. Retrieved February 12, 2005.

theaters. New technologies are forcing media departments to consider new options, especially on the Internet. Another trend is better communication between the media and creative departments. The best media placements occur when media buyers understand the overall strategy and creative concept.

Advertising Media

The main economic base of many American media is advertising. For commercial radio and television stations, it is by far their most important source of revenue, whereas newspapers and magazines depend on a combination of newsstand sales, subscriptions, and advertising. Table 11.3 shows advertising expenditures across various media. In selecting media, advertisers consider whom they want to reach, what kind of message or information they want to communicate, and the costs of various media.

Advertisers try to reach the largest number of people in the target audience at the lowest possible price. The costs of various media depend on several factors: the size of the audience, the composition of the audience (age, wealth, education, and so on), and

Table 11.4 Strengths and Weaknesses of Advertising Media

Medium	Strengths	Weaknesses
Newspapers	Intense coverage Flexibility Prestige Dealer or advertiser coordination	Short life Hasty reading Moderate to poor reproduction
Magazines	Market selectivity Long life High reproduction quality Prestige Extra services	Inflexible to coverage/time Inflexible to copy changes Low overall market penetration Wide distribution
Television	Mass coverage High impact Repetition Prestige Flexibility	Fleeting message Commercial wearout Lack of selectivity High cost
Radio	Audience selectivity Immediacy Flexibility Mobility	Fragmentation Transient quality of listenership Limited sensory input
Internet	Cost-efficient Personal Interactive	Loss of privacy Low reach Technical expertise required

the prestige of the medium. In general, media with larger audiences can charge more for accepting and carrying advertisements. However, a smaller, more specifically focused audience can sometimes be even more valuable to an advertiser than a larger, more heterogeneous one. Comparisons among vehicles are made on a cost per thousand (CPM) basis—that is, on the basis of the cost of reaching a thousand members of the target audience for the ad. This efficiency comparison is determined by dividing the cost of each ad by the size of the audience it delivers, in thousands.

The general goal is to try to reach the largest number of people in the target audience for the lowest dollar investment (Martin & Coons, 1998), but many other factors may also be considered, including the inherent characteristics of different media. Table 11.4 lists some of the strengths and weaknesses of various advertising media. The nature of the target audience also affects media selection. Often media advertisers want to reach a broad general audience. Some advertisers want to sell products, such as soap or soft drinks, that might interest virtually everyone in a mass audience. Other advertisers might use a general-audience medium if it has a high impact on a particular group they want to reach. For example, although a very broad audience watches prime-time network television, ads are often placed there for products aimed primarily at seniors, such as denture adhesive cream. Television may reach a larger proportion of older people than any other *audience segment.* An advertiser that wants to sell athletic shoes to teenagers will pick just the television shows and radio stations that appeal selectively to teenagers.

Table 11.5 Research Services and the Audience Data They Provide

Medium	Company	Audience Report Content
National television	Nielsen Media Research	Ratings for programs on the national TV networks
Local television	Nielsen Media Research	Ratings for programs broadcast by local TV stations
National radio	Arbitron	Ratings for network programs by local radio stations
Local radio	Arbitron	Ratings for stations broadcasting in the local market
Newspapers	Audit Bureau of Circulation	The number of newspaper copies sold
Magazines	Simmons/ MRI Research	Ratings for the top magazines in the United States
The Internet	Nielson Net Rating	Demographic profiles of Internet users

Research

An integral part of the entire advertising process is research. Those involved with marketing research collect and analyze data about product sales and factors that affect consumer opinions about products. In the advertising agency, account executives depend on research analysts and account planners to provide in-depth consumer profiles and key information about the competition. In other words, they try to get into the head of the consumer and obtain a deeper, more thorough understanding of what drives him or her to buy products.

Media research experts work for both the media industry and the media departments of the advertising agencies to give them information about patterns of exposure to the mass media. Media research encompasses:

- Ratings for radio and television broadcasts
- Circulation figures for magazines and newspapers
- Profiles of the users of consumer products
- Media usage habits
- Qualitative studies that gauge audience reactions to specific media vehicles
- Reports on annual advertising expenditure levels of the leading national brands
- Copy tests that evaluate the effectiveness of ads under development

Examples of research companies and the audience information they provide are shown in Table 11.5. Audience measurement studies are sufficient to tell us whether the advertising message is being exposed to a target group and roughly what numbers are involved, but it does not provide insights into how or why the advertising is able to communicate successfully. For this purpose, we need a second dimension of audience research, one that enables the advertiser to talk directly with the target group. Because this research focuses on individuals and what "drives" them, it is often referred to as

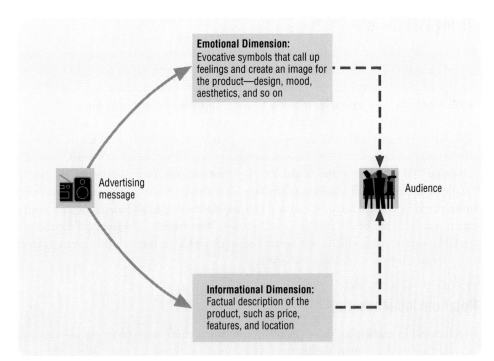

■ FIGURE 11.2
Emotion or Information?
All communication has informational and emotional dimensions. In order to cut through the clutter of competing messages, advertising often emphasizes the emotional as much as the informational.

Emotional Dimension:
Evocative symbols that call up feelings and create an image for the product—design, mood, aesthetics, and so on

Advertising message

Audience

Informational Dimension:
Factual description of the product, such as price, features, and location

motivational research. Examples of this form of audience research include focus groups and mall intercepts.

Another form of advertising-related research, **copy testing,** is used to assess the effectiveness of advertisements while they are still under development. For example, a test ad might be inserted in television programs in selected markets, and researchers might contact respondents by phone on the day after it appears to determine whether they can recall seeing the ad. More sophisticated methods allow direct comparisons of ads by doing "split runs" of magazines in which alternative versions of the same ad are sent to different households. Cable television systems can also be used in this way to provide comparisons of alternative treatments for television commercials.

ADVERTISING'S FORMS OF PERSUASION

Advertising must communicate important information about products (such as price, features, channel of distribution, and the like), but it also requires a creative way of stating these facts that cuts through the clutter of competing advertisements and gets the attention of consumers. As shown in Figure 11.2, all messages have an informational dimension and an emotional dimension. Because advertising has to get the attention of audience members who are usually not interested in the message, how the message is conveyed is just as important as what is said. In this section we look at advertising as a form of communication in terms of both its style and its content. First, we offer an explanation of *continuity of theme.* Next, we explain how advertisers integrate symbols of popular culture. Then a discussion of relationship marketing and direct marketing is followed by a list of other forms of advertising communication. Finally, *buying motives* or consumer needs are discussed as the keys to advertising success, as are demographic issues, diversity, and global advertising.

Copy testing evaluates the effectiveness of advertisements.

Mining Pop Culture

One way in which advertisers align themselves with consumers is through the art and entertainment of popular culture. By borrowing familiar symbols in the culture, advertisers promote consumer identification with the product. Commercials for the iPod from Apple Computer, for example, recently featured hip-hop dancing and music. Also, the recent "Do it eBay" theme was featured in ads with on-stage music and dancing comparable to elaborate contemporary Broadway theater productions. The use of popular culture in advertising is nothing new, however. In the 1960s, for example, the Coca-Cola campaign "I'd like to buy the world a Coke" featured folk music and reflected young people's concerns about achieving harmony and world peace. Ultimately, advertising turns out to be a reflection of social and cultural norms due to a tendency to communicate in the language of the familiar. The Vietnam War provided the political context for the Coke commercial, which itself became as much a plea for friendship between peoples as it was an advertisement for a soft drink.

Relationship Marketing

In **relationship marketing,** advertisers and consumers communicate one-to-one through personalized media such as the Internet, direct mail, or the telephone. One of the most significant business trends in recent times, relationship marketing goes beyond one-way channels of mass media. Computers, for example, make personal and relevant messages possible in an interactive fashion. Companies use databases to personalize messages, with an emphasis on talking with consumers and "growing" them rather than sending out the same message to everyone.

The telephone continues to be an important instrument for relationship marketing. Credit card companies, such as American Express, often study the demographic characteristics and buying habits of each individual cardholder in order to identify specific products that fit specific lifestyles (such as life insurance, special hotel accommodations, luxury gift items, and the like). In order to personalize transactions and build relationships, QVC, the home shopping network, often features telephone callers discussing, on the air with the show host, their product-related experiences.

Relationship marketing is successful when brand loyalty is achieved. This is the goal of automobile dealers that create a time line for each car purchased. Three months after the initial purchase, a letter or e-mail is fired off reminding the new owner that it is time for a tune-up. As the car gets older, additional letters are sent, offering a wide variety of discount services, up to and including special offers on a new car purchase.

Direct Marketing

Although direct marketing was an aspect of most ads in the last century, more recently it has become a discipline unto itself. The main goal of this form of marketing communication is to sell a product quickly, making a visit to a retail store unnecessary. More and more, direct marketing techniques and advertising techniques are beginning to converge, especially as the advertising industry turns to new, more interactive forms. Many advertising agencies now have direct marketing departments, whose activities are rapidly growing in importance.

Direct marketing differs from conventional advertising in that it concentrates the marketer's resources on the most likely prospects, rather than sending a message to a wide

Relationship marketing is when consumers develop a strong preference for brand through one-to-one communication.

Direct marketing is a form of advertising that requests an immediate consumer response.

■ ADVERTISING THE
OBVIOUS
Advertising gives the consumer
new information and often does
so with humor and surprise.

audience in the hope that at least some of the prospects will receive it (Nash, 1992; Sirgy, 1998). Direct marketing also has a quality of immediacy, because recipients of the message are asked to take direct action, such as placing an order over the phone or returning a printed order blank by mail. Although direct marketing messages do not have the same "glitz" as mass media advertising, they do have two major advantages over other forms of advertising: (1) they can be customized to individual consumers, using personal forms of address and bits of personal information gleaned from computer databases, and (2) their effectiveness can be measured so that they can be continually fine-tuned.

Direct marketing encompasses a wide variety of communications media and includes e-commerce. It has long been popular with book publishers, record clubs, and magazines, but now it is coming into favor with a full range of advertisers. Direct mail ("junk mail") solicitations, catalog sales, and telemarketing are perhaps the most obvious forms of direct marketing activities. However, anyone who has ever called a toll-free number to order the "the greatest hits of the sixties," returned a magazine subscription form, entered a magazine contest or sweepstakes, sent in a donation to a TV telethon, or redeemed a coupon clipped from the newspaper has also responded to a direct marketing appeal.

Infomercials are also a form of broadcast direct marketing. These are program-length, made-for-television presentations whose sole purpose is selling the featured product or service. The infomercial concept has been taken to its logical conclusion in the form of entire cable networks devoted to hawking products through toll-free numbers—the home shopping channels.

The Internet can also play a role in direct marketing. Suppose, for example, that a car salesperson wants to build a list of long-term customers. If first-time car buyers' information is entered into a database, it can be used to contact them via e-mail when the next car purchase is likely. Some salespeople e-mail car photos, descriptions, and prices. Purchases can then be made directly via the Internet.

The direct marketing industry relies on many of the same creative and media professions that advertising does, but it has some unique disciplines of its own as well. For

Infomercials are paid television programs that promote a product.

■ SELLING THE SWOOSH
Tiger Woods' image helps sell a variety of products, including Nike.

Brand loyalty is the consumer's propensity to make repeat purchases of a specific brand of product.

The buying motive explains the consumer's desire to purchase particular products.

example, there are firms that specialize in compiling and matching computerized telephone and mailing lists, others that specialize in assembling direct-mail packages, others that receive only toll-free calls, and others that just open return mail and complete (or "fulfill") the orders.

Research also takes on a distinctive character in direct marketing campaigns. Direct marketers are able to gauge the results of their advertising appeal, as well as the appropriateness of the media chosen, by counting the dollars in the cash register at the end of the day. This direct cause-effect measure allows the advertiser to try out various approaches and see their results immediately without resorting to the various media research services.

Targeting the Market

Here are some ways in which advertising can be used to try to affect actions taken by members of the target market:

Give new information. This includes announcements by advertisers regarding new products or product improvements, sweepstakes or contests, and other items of a newsworthy nature. The government-funded advertising campaign on the use of condoms to help prevent the spread of the AIDS virus is an example.

Reinforce a current practice. Advertisers who currently enjoy a dominant position in a product category and need to make consumers less receptive to competitive appeals are the primary users of this type of message. This is one of the most efficient uses of advertising, because it addresses the "heavy user" of the product who does not need to be convinced of its merits. In this case, the advertiser tries to increase **brand loyalty,** the propensity to make a repeat purchase of the product. A recent example would be the "The One and Only Cheerios" slogan that simply reminds consumers of the reliability of the product's quality.

Change a predisposition. This approach is exemplified by the often annoying ads that take on a competing product head-to-head. It is also the most difficult type of ad to execute successfully because it needs both to address and to change the purchasing habits of those who regularly use a competitor's product. (Furthermore, the competitors often answer with their own campaign.) Advertisers tend to be satisfied when they succeed in raising brand awareness, or the consumer's ability to identify the product. An example was a Kleenex bath tissue campaign using data from "touch tests" to argue that its Cottonelle brand was "softer than the leading premium brand."

Understanding Consumer Needs

Whatever communication approach is used, all advertising must appeal to a **buying motive** to be successful. Table 11.6 lists 15 consumer needs, or motives, to which most advertising appeals. The copywriter selects a creative approach that is unique and addresses some consumer need. For example, Dove is positioned as a cosmetic, not a soap, and Southwest Airlines is presented as the carrier that "frees" the economically minded flyer to "move about the country." The Internet site, Yahoo! markets itself not as a search engine, but as a "life engine," providing several services quickly and conveniently. The most effective advertising communicates the need clearly and repetitively.

Table 11.6 Consumer Needs Appealed to by Advertising

Achievement	The need to accomplish difficult tasks
Exhibition	The need to win the attention of others
Dominance	The need to hold a position of influence
Diversion	The need to have fun
Understanding	The need to teach and instruct
Nurturance	The need to support and care for others
Sexuality	The need to establish sexual identity
Security	The need to be free from threat of harm
Independence	The need to make one's own choices
Recognition	The need to receive notoriety
Stimulation	The need to stimulate the senses
Novelty	The need to do new tasks or activities
Affiliation	The need to belong or win acceptance
Succorance	The need to receive help and support
Consistency	The need to achieve order

Source: Adapted from Settle, R., and Alreck, P. (1986). *Why They Buy* (New York: Wiley), 26–28.

THE CHANGING NATURE OF THE CONSUMER

How are consumers changing? This is the question that drives **demographic segmentation,** which categorizes people on the basis of the personal and household characteristics that the U.S. Census Bureau tabulates, such as age, sex, ethnicity, and income. Trends in these areas are very important to advertisers. For most advertisers of consumer products, women between the ages of 18 and 49 are the primary target group; they make the most purchases in supermarkets and department stores.

Of all demographic variables, age and ethnicity are of considerable importance to marketers at the present time. Census data, for example, reveal a growing senior market. Just as the 25–34 and 35–44 age groups have been essential to advertisers, the 50+ segment that is growing will be extremely important in years to come. This is likely to have dramatic effects on future marketing strategies. Given their leadership roles in business, government, and other fields, seniors are often opinion leaders who influence what others buy. Children (5–12) and teenagers (13–17) total about 22 million in North America, making them important segments for advertisers (Feather, 2000).

In addition, ethnicity is a demographic category that advertisers are studying. About 30 percent of the population belongs to an ethnic minority group (Racial, 2005, p. 1). According to the Census Bureau, non-Latino whites will comprise only 40 percent of the U.S. population by 2010 (p. 1). The Latino-American population is the fastest growing, followed by Asian-Americans and African-Americans. These developments remind advertisers that consumer markets are not homogenous and that messages must be sensitive to the needs of emerging segments.

Demographic segmentation is based on social or personal characteristics, such as age, sex, education, or income.

LIVE IN A PLACE WITHOUT BILLBOARDS

An important principle of advertising is unity. All elements from headline to photography should accomplish a marriage of image and words.

Importance of Diversity

Taking into account the diversity of consumer groups, some companies have an ethnic plan so that advertising is inclusive and relevant to all consumers. There is inevitable diversity within target markets, and they shouldn't be thought of as a single homogeneous group. Latinos, for example, come from North America, Latin America, and South America. Consumers of Peruvian descent have different buying habits than those from Mexico, for instance. And, contrary to popular perception, not all Latinos prefer advertising in Spanish.

Prior to 1980, African-Americans were rarely featured in television commercials (Dates & Barloe, 1997). Although black celebrities such as Michael Jackson, Lionel Richie, and Bill Cosby began appearing in commercials by the 1980s, it remained evident that advertisers were using "black celebrities, but few black faces" (p. 93). In other words, despite the fact that African-Americans are found in all professions from technical to managerial, advertising tends to reflect the stereotype that successful African-Americans are often portrayed as sports or popular music stars. There is a great need for a wider range of diverse portrayals of minorities (see Chapter 13).

How advertisers portray women has also been controversial. In an extensive review of the scholarly literature on the subject, Wood (2005) concludes that women are consistently underrepresented and are less likely to be depicted in professional occupations. Women also tend to be portrayed as taller and thinner than average, a practice that raises the question of whether advertising encourages a feeling of dissatisfaction with one's own body. Researchers disagree, however, about whether these images actually create unrealistic expectations for young women and cause body dissatisfaction. Holmstrom (2004), for example, reviewed the findings of numerous studies and concluded that thin women may have minimal to no effect on viewers, and that images of overweight women appear to have a positive impact on women's body image. The issue remains, however, that there may be vulnerable audiences among teens and that advertisers should be sensitive to these groups.

Global Advertising Blunders:
When Advertising Gets Lost in Translation

Advertising across borders is a growing phenomenon. Multinational organizations (MNOs) design campaigns that appear in many countries throughout the world. For example, McDonald's has restaurants in 90 countries with an advertising strategy for each. Translating campaigns, however, can be challenging. Product names and slogans in one country can mean something altogether different in another. Here are some examples of significant blunders resulting from inadequate understanding of various cultures:

- Rolls Royce got into trouble when it introduced its Silver Mist model. The word *mist* in colloquial German means "manure."
- A campaign for Schweppes Tonic Water appeared in Italy as "Schweppe's Toilet Water."
- On billboards across Mexico, chicken mogul Frank Perdue was featured alongside the slogan, "It takes a hard man to make a chicken aroused."
- McDonald's translated Big Mac into "le Gran Mec" in France, only to discover that the phrase means "the big pimp."
- Ads for United Airlines in Japan contained a map with an important island missing. This omission made the headlines of major newspapers.
- GM tried to sell its Chevrolet Nova in South America, overlooking the fact that *no va* means "doesn't go" in Spanish.
- In China, Coca-Cola was introduced as *ke-ke-ken-la,* which means "bite the wax tadpole" in some dialects. Also, Kentucky Fried Chicken's slogan, "finger-lickin' good," was understood by Chinese consumers to mean "Eat your fingers off."

Such examples suggest the need for better-trained international marketing executives. Firms are increasingly interested in college graduates with some background in international studies. International business is an emerging area in MBA programs at major universities. These programs stress not only the importance of knowing foreign languages, but also a sense of the local culture where business is conducted. Global advertisers of the future must understand how products are perceived from within a culture, placing less emphasis on mass-market approaches that ignore local norms, values, and traditions.

Compiled from:

Ricks, D. (1999). *Blunders in International Business,* 3rd ed. Malden, MA: Blackwell.

Marketing Translation Mistakes. Retrieved September 21, 2004, from the World Wide Web: http://www.il8nguy.com/translations.html.

Global Advertising

Technology and political change have given rise to a new business environment where international marketing opportunities abound. The Internet, in particular, makes it possible for businesses to reach foreign markets inexpensively; advertising is conducted online without high overhead costs. The global business climate is also the result of political initiatives such as the North American Free Trade Agreement (NAFTA), the General Agreement on Tariffs and Trade (GATT), and its successor the World Trade Organization, which create new opportunities for international trade.

International advertising is expanding due to more aggressive competition from foreign businesses that create pressure on U.S. companies to explore international markets. Global

Table 11.7 Top 10 Global Advertisers

Rank	Advertiser	Headquarters
1	Procter & Gamble	U.S.
2	Unilever	Europe
3	General Motors Corporation	U.S.
4	Toyota Motor Corporation	Japan
5	Ford Motor Company	U.S.
6	Time Warner Inc.	U.S.
7	DaimlerChrysler AG	Europe
8	L'Oreal S.A.	Europe
9	Nestle S.A.	Europe
10	Sony Corporation	Japan

Source: Datamonitor (5 April 2004). Compiled from *Advertising Age,* TNS Media Intelligence, IBOPE, and others. List last updated: 5 April 2004. <datamonitor.com>. Retrieved February 12, 2005.

campaigns of Toyota, Nestle, and Unilever, for example, force U.S. businesses to beef up the international components of their marketing plans. As shown in Table 11.7, five out of the top 10 international advertisers are based outside the United States.

Although international advertising requires knowledge of other cultures, many global campaigns are not clearly translated into various languages (see "World View: Global Advertising Blunders," page 349). According to Ricks (1999) Procter & Gamble showed a husband and wife in the bathroom together in an ad for Camay Soap. Japanese consumers, however, are often offended by such depictions. In another campaign, Nike featured people from around the world stating their slogan "Just do it" in various languages, but a Samburu tribesman was actually saying "I don't want these, give me big shoes." Such mistakes reinforce the need for in-depth research and planning to ensure that global messages reflect the values and traditions of the countries they appear in.

MEDIA LITERACY: ANALYZING ADVERTISING

What constitutes effective advertising? How can one use advertising optimally in both professional and family settings? A thorough understanding of advertising effects may take years to comprehend, but there are basic frameworks of analysis that beginning students of advertising can utilize immediately. According to Kubey (1991), media literacy is the ability to "appreciate, interpret, and analyze the media" (p. 1). For advertising, this can be done at two levels. First, there is the professional level where advertising is assessed according to how well it gets the attention of consumers and keeps them interested; this is media literacy from the perspective of the designer of messages. The other area involves those critical skills necessary to make advertising a positive force in everyday life; this involves literacy of the consumer who must sort out the difference between useful and undesirable aspects of advertising.

Hidden Messages

It is now nearly 50 years since advertising critic Vance Packard published *The Hidden Persuaders* (1956) in which he called attention to some of the more underhanded tactics advertisers and their agencies used to sell their wares, including the embedding of hidden subliminal messages that supposedly unconsciously stimulated buying. Some claim that when American Express placed pop-up ads in recent movies, the company was engaging in a subliminal strategy. Media literacy is the means by which citizens defend against such tactics and see through attempts to manipulate.

Implicit Messages

Advertising does more than just sell products; it also promotes a materialistic way of life. This view holds that advertising, taken as a whole, implies that happiness is achieved by consuming material goods. That is, the long-term impact of advertising has been to reinforce a market economy and create a consumer culture in which the acquisition of goods and services is the foundation of societal values, pleasures, and goals. Examples include lifestyle advertising for alcoholic beverages, which often situates products in luxurious settings. The emphasis is as much on the wealthy lifestyle of the user as on the product itself. That has certain ideological implications. One is that it reinforces the legitimacy of the current capitalist system. Gaining wealth within that system is seen as the top priority, rather than addressing inequities or the environmental damages of the system. Second is that people are led to think of themselves primarily as consumers rather than citizens. Rather than being encouraged to think in political terms, reinforcing political involvement, people are simply encouraged to earn and spend more.

Americans are the targets of an astonishing number of commercial messages. It is estimated that the average consumer is exposed to some 5000 advertisements each day (Pappas, 2000, p. 1). Debate has raged over the ultimate effect of these images. Some scholars express concern that this volume of advertising encourages "false

■ **COUNTER-ADVERTISING**
Adbusters tries to counter the effects of consumer culture—but TV networks won't accept their ads.

needs" in consumers. This situation was the impetus for the creation of the popular magazine *Adbusters,* which is devoted entirely to criticism of consumer culture. Social critic Stewart Ewen (1976) argues that advertising creates an ideology of consumption by promoting a materialistic way of life. When advertising trades in the core function of a product (a shoe's comfort and durability) for a lifestyle appeal (shoe as symbol of a desirable lifestyle), it promotes a "culture of consumption" in which consumers subscribe to the idea that problems can be solved by simply acquiring products (Featherstone, 1991; See Chapter 13). However, other observers have questioned whether advertising creates a consumer culture or is, rather, simply a by-product of our consumer impulses. The brief format of advertising may also seem to promote the instant-solution approach to life. That is, the short dramas of 30-second commercials often show physical or social ills quickly remedied with a few painkillers or a shot of mouthwash.

If mindless consumption is bad for society, what can be done? One approach is to make consumers more aware of excessive consumption through the promotion of an annual "Buy Nothing Day," which falls on the day after Thanksgiving. Never heard of it? That's not surprising, since the major television networks refuse to run advertisements paid for by the event's promoters.

Privacy

The current era of integrated marketing presents new ethical dilemmas. Privacy is of great concern to consumers as databases are used to store personal information. Citizens are often outraged about the sale of this data to other companies resulting in a mountain of unwanted mail and e-mail. For this reason, responsible companies engage in permission marketing, informing website visitors about how the information will be used. TRW, for example, spent $30 million in recent years updating their website and computer systems to address consumer concerns about privacy (Duncan, 2005, p. 259).

Deception

In order to preserve their good name, most advertisers go to great lengths to avoid deceptive advertising. However, blunders can occur especially when a third party—the advertising agency, prepares advertising.

Just such a problem occurred when Volvo was found to have "rigged" a commercial that apparently demonstrated the car's ability to withstand the weight of a heavy truck placed on its roof. Other vehicles were not as fortunate and suffered severe damage. However, a production company hired to film the spot had reinforced the Volvo, and weakened the other vehicles. When this fact came to light, Volvo was forced to pay a fine, and the company immeasurable damage to its credibility. More recent examples of deceptive investigations include ads by Publisher's Clearing House announcing winners of cash prizes and the FTC's crack down on deceptive advertising for long distance telephone services.

Sometimes, however, deception is less obvious. *Puffery* is when advertisers make exaggerated claims that can't be proven. This softer deception ranges from small-business claims such as "Best pizza on the planet" to national slogans such as Wal-Mart's slogan, "Always the low price. Always." These claims raise a number of compelling questions about truth in advertising. At which point should an advertiser be required to substantiate such claims? From the perspective of social responsibility, advertisers must also ask whether particular consumer groups are vulnerable to puffery (for example, children, seniors) and assure that groups are not taken advantage of.

The Federal Trade Commission (FTC) and other government agencies regulate deception, but the most effective regulation comes from within the industry. The Children's Advertising Review Unit (CARU), for example, is comprised of industry professionals who promote responsible children's advertising and to respond to concerns raised by consumers.

Children and Advertising

Young children are thought by many parents and researchers to make up a vulnerable audience. According to Schudson (1984), vulnerable audiences are those who lack sufficient resources to make informed decisions about advertising appeals. Organizations such as the Center for Media Literacy and Citizens for Media Literacy encourage audience members to develop critical skills to analyze media at a young age. Although the effects are not fully understood, several studies explore whether (1) preschool-age children have difficulty explaining the intent of commercials, (2) children exposed to advertising make frequent requests for products to their parents, and (3) parental discussions of advertising increase children's comprehension of commercials (see John, 1999; Rajeev & Lonial, 1990).

Policy makers are particularly concerned with the issue of how well young children (of preschool age) can explain the purpose of commercials. Children watch cartoon shows such as *Digimon* and *Batman Beyond* only to be confronted with toy products under the same names. Recent controversies also include the educational programming of "Channel One," a television channel with news and information, as well as advertising, placed in schools and targeted at children. This raises the question of whether advertising should be aired in public schools. Other advertisers offer "free" Internet service in exchange for the opportunity to run ads at the bottom of the screen on schoolroom computers. The 1996 Telecommunications Act exhorted advertisers to use the rating system developed by the television industry when designing commercials aimed at children.

For their part, advertisers remind us that children have always had a desire for information about products available to them. Parental supervision also plays an important role in how children come to use advertising in everyday life. This view suggests that children also learn from advertising and that exposure to it helps prepare them to cope with the complexities of society. Parents can play an important role by explaining ads as they watch them with their children. The exercise of "talking back at the television" is a chance to explain advertising techniques and help children understand how advertising differs from other types of mass communication.

Product Placements

As advertisers seek new ways to reach consumers, the lines between advertising and noncommercial content are blurring. One example of this is *product placement,* (see "Media and Culture: *Oprah!* Talk Show or Marketing Vehicle?," page 334). Another is the *advertorial,* that looks like news content but is actually a commercial message. In print, advertorials are designed to look like magazine articles. On television, they might come in the form of talk shows such as the program *Jack LaLane's Power Juicer,* that features celebrity guests and a studio audience. Media literacy implies an awareness of these techniques and the ability to identify commercially sponsored material. Consumers should look closely for identifying messages such as "Advertising" or "Paid-For Program."

© Bettmann/CORBIS

■ YOU'VE (NOT) COME A LONG WAY BABY
Sex-role stereotypes have been around a long time. This vintage ad for Lucky Strike cigarettes reflects the "this is beautiful" stereotype found in many modern ads. Also note the deceptive claim about the health benefits of smoking.

SUMMARY AND REVIEW

WHAT ARE THE MAIN EVENTS IN ADVERTISING HISTORY?

Advertising has been around in some form since ancient times. The Industrial Revolution and the rise of new information technologies are the most influential events ushering in the modern era of advertising. With the Industrial Revolution came a competitive environment that required advertising to be persuasive as well as informative in order to break through the clutter of competing messages. Radio, television, and computers have played major roles in commercial communication. Today, advertising is a meta-industry that permeates virtually all sectors of society from medicine to religion.

WHAT HAS BEEN THE IMPACT OF THE COMPUTER ON ADVERTISING?

Computers allow advertisers to build databases and store information; so personalized messages can be sent via the Internet. Database marketing helps build deeper relationships with consumers. Data captured from users of the Internet provides detailed profiles of media usage as well as consumer behavior, providing an unprecedented opportunity to target advertising efficiently, but also threatening the privacy of users.

WHAT IS INTERACTIVE ADVERTISING?

Interactive advertising permits a direct response from the customer to the advertisement. The customer could respond to a button on the Internet or certain kinds of digital TV to directly order goods or services. Truly interactive advertising goes further to permit the customer to call up ads and additional information. Ads would be customized based on information supplied about the customer's identity and interests.

HOW ARE ADVERTISING CAMPAIGNS COORDINATED?

Marketing managers and brand managers who work for major advertisers budget and plan advertising strategies that will help them introduce new products or increase the sales of existing products. They work with an advertising manager to coordinate their companies' overall advertising efforts. Once a campaign is planned, they might contact one or more advertising agencies to execute the plan.

HOW ARE CAMPAIGNS ORGANIZED INSIDE AN ADVERTISING AGENCY?

The account executive is the liaison between the advertiser and the advertising agency staff. The account executive coordinates the activities of the creative department, which creates the ads, and the media department, which determines where the ads will be placed. Copywriters conceive of creative ideas and write the ads. The agency's media buyer negotiates with the media.

WHAT IS THE ROLE OF RESEARCH IN THE ADVERTISING PROCESS?

Advertisers rely on market research to help them understand the target market. In the agency, account planners ensure that there is a strong connection between research findings and the final advertising message. Researchers use data about who watches or reads media, but also use sophisticated breakdowns by audience segment and psychographics to target advertising, The Internet permits new, even more detailed forms of research and data-gathering, but also raises potential privacy issues.

WHAT ARE THE DIFFERENT TYPES OF COMMUNICATION USED IN ADVERTISING?

Advertising is generally designed to achieve one of three basic goals: to provide new information (brand awareness), to reinforce a current practice (brand loyalty), or to change an existing predisposition. Advertising genres are further categorized according to the type of buying motive they appeal to. Advertisers have identified 15 needs, or buying motives, to which most messages appeal.

WHAT IS DIRECT MARKETING?

With direct marketing, the recipient of the advertising message is asked to make a direct and immediate response to the ad, such as by mailing in a printed order blank or dialing a toll-free number to place an order. Telemarketing, home shopping channels, infomercials, and catalog sales are other common examples. The popularity of direct marketing is likely to increase in the future as the spread of interactive technologies such as the Internet makes it easier to place orders in direct response to advertising.

HOW ARE ADVERTISING AUDIENCES CHANGING?

The number of seniors is growing, as are several ethnic groups. Advertisers in the future must have a thorough knowledge of diverse markets. The Hispanic market will be the largest ethnic group in the United States, in terms of both population and buying power, by 2010. The African-American population is younger and growing faster than Anglo-Americans. It is also possible that Asian-Americans could be among the top three segments in terms of purchasing power by the year 2010.

IN TERMS OF ADVERTISING, WHAT DOES IT MEAN TO BE MEDIA LITERATE?

In terns of advertising, there are professional and consumer levels of media literacy. Professionals must communicate in a way that gets attention of the consumer, maintains interest, and motivates purchase. Consumers must be aware of implicit messages, teach children critical skills, and know the distinction between the world presented by advertising and actual society.

MEDIA CONNECTION

For web links, quizzes, and key term flash cards, visit the **Student Companion Website** at http://communication.wadsworth.com/straubhaar5.

 For unlimited easy access to additional and exclusive online study, support, and research tools, log on to **1pass** at http://1pass.thomson.com using the unique access code found on your 1pass passcode card.

 The **Media Now Premium Website** offers *Career Profile* videos, *Critical View* video news clips, and *Media in Motion* concept animations. You'll also find Stop & Review tutorial questions, a sample final exam, and much more.

InfoTrac College Edition is a fully searchable online database offering anytime, anywhere access to more than 20 years' worth of articles from nearly 5,000 diverse and reliable sources.

 vMentor provides live, one-on-one online tutoring to connect you to experts who will assist you in understanding the concepts covered in your course.

Although a career in advertising can be demanding work, it offers opportunities for creativity and client relations. In the Career Profile video for this chapter, Liddy Parlato talks about how she got her start in this industry.

12

Cell phones are the latest infrastructure technology to transform our lives. In this chapter we will examine the development of the telephone, cable TV, and satellite networks that are the infrastructure of the Information Society. We will see how breakthroughs in infrastructure technology made the electronic media we enjoy today possible. We'll also review efforts to make these networks accessible to everyone.

HISTORY: BETTER LIVING THROUGH TELECOMMUNICATION

If you asked the average college student (see Media & Culture: "What My Cell Phone Means to Me," page 359) what the most exciting and life-transforming development in the New Media was today, you might be surprised to hear that it is not the Internet, their DVD player, or their iPod, but their cell phone. In this chapter we will see how changes in the communication infrastructure often have astounding effects on the lives of the people who use them and the societies they live in.

The New Media of Yesteryear

Most great civilizations create an **infrastructure** to communicate at a distance, the essence of telecommunication. The ancient Greeks and Romans had fire towers to carry messages from distant outposts of their civilizations. The Yorubas of eastern Africa had a network of drummers. The Anasazi people of the American Southwest "broadcast" fire signals from atop high plateaus in the twelfth century C.E. In Napoleon's day, mechanical signal towers sent dispatches across France (Holzmann & Pherson, 1994).

The infrastructure is the underlying physical structure of communication networks.

1844	Telegraph service begins	**1975**	HBO's first satellite transmission
1876	Bell invents the telephone	**1984**	AT&T divests local operating companies
1934	Communications Act regulates telecommunications	**1996**	Telecommunications Act opens up competition
1948	First cable systems	**2002**	Telecom "meltdown"
1962	First communications satellite, first digital phone network, first pagers	**2004**	Local phone competition rules struck down
		2005	SBC acquires AT&T

Library of Congress

■ LIGHTNING LINES

The telegraph transformed communications in the business world in the late 1880s. Here telegraph wires span a busy New York City street.

Samuel F. B. Morse's telegraph was an early forerunner of the Internet. The first words Morse sent in 1844, "What hath God wrought?" only slightly exaggerated the importance of his invention. By 1859 telegraph lines spanned the United States, and in 1866 they reached Europe via undersea cable. Historian Daniel Czitrom (1982) called them "lightning lines" both for their speed of transmission and for their transforming effects. Businesses coordinated far-flung branches. Newspapers gathered the news of the world. Ordinary citizens kept in touch with family and friends. Together with the railroads, the telegraph made national economies and a national culture possible.

The next technological leap came when speech teacher and inventor Alexander Graham Bell accidentally spilled some acid on his lap one day in his lab in 1876 and called out for his assistant, "Mr. Watson, come here, I want you." The apparatus on his table magically relayed his words over wires into the next room. Mr. Watson came running, and the telephone was born (Brooks, 1976).

These nineteenth-century "new media" have interesting parallels with today's. With its combination of interpersonal communication and information services, wasn't the telegraph the Internet of the nineteenth century (Standage, 1998)? Radio, in the sense of audio mass communication, might be traced back to February 12, 1877, when Alexander Graham Bell demonstrated his invention in Salem, Massachusetts, and had Mr. Watson deliver a speech from Boston to the assembled lecture audience over a leased telegraph line. Much early speculation about the telephone centered on multichannel mass media functions like conveying news and music to the home (LaRose & Atkin, 1992).

The Rise and Fall of Ma Bell

Vertical integration is when a company owns related businesses in the same industry.

The company that Bell founded set a pattern for **vertical integration** that communication conglomerates both envy and emulate—and that regulators still struggle to control—even today. Soon after the Bell Telephone Company was established in 1877, it acquired West-

What My Cell Phone Means to Me

Throughout history, telecommunications have had transforming effects on the people who use them and the societies they live in. What impact will cell phones have on us and our culture? Why not ask college students about that? They are members of the first cell phone generation. Accordingly, we convened small groups of students to discuss the meaning of cell phones in their lives.

Many of the comments restated the obvious benefits that cell phone companies stress in their marketing campaigns: convenience, safety, and staying in touch anytime, anyplace. However, some of these take a unique twist in lives of college students: being able to make calls when roommates tie up the (wire-line) phone, coordinating pit stops between cars while on road trips. The positive effects centered on increasing social interaction and the ability to participate in more social activities. On the negative side, students were annoyed by repeated calls from people they didn't want to hear from, the increased pace of their social lives, and a loss of spontaneity. Some also found that their social interactions tended to become limited to other people with cell phones.

Comments like these resonate with concerns about the effects of communication technology on society. One point of view is that Americans are becoming less involved in organized social activities, that they too often go "bowling alone" in the words of one social critic (Putnam, 2000). To the extent that cell phones stimulate and coordinate social activity, they could help reverse that trend. However, other critics fear that new media offer us too much choice in the content we consume and the associates we seek out, breaking our sense of living in a shared culture. If we limit our social contacts only to others with cell phones, or on our text messaging buddy list, that trend could accelerate. Whether cell phones ultimately improve or destroy social contact will of course depend upon which of these opposing tendencies becomes the dominant one.

---

ern Electric, an electrical equipment manufacturing firm, the third cornerstone of a vertically integrated monopoly that also included its local and long-distance networks. In its early years Bell ruthlessly used its **patent** rights and later its market power to undercut its competitors. Bell also refused to interconnect competitors with its long-distance network.

In 1910 the company, now named American Telephone and Telegraph, AT&T, acquired the Western Union Telegraph Company, raising the specter of a national telecommunications monopoly. Under threat of an antitrust suit, AT&T cancelled the deal, promised to mend its ruthless ways, and offered to provide quality service for all, the principle of **universal service.** This agreement, the so-called Kingsbury Commitment, was formally enacted into law by Congress in the Graham Act of 1921. That exempted AT&T from the **Sherman Antitrust Act** and validated the notion of a "natural monopoly"—that is, it only made economic sense to have a single phone company serving an area. On the state level, concerns about monopoly power led to *rate of return* regulation. That shielded telephone subscribers from excessive monopoly prices while assuring stockholders a steady return.

With rates in check and interconnection with the long-distance network assured, the telephone slowly expanded from the circles of wealthy tradespeople and professionals who owned them at the turn of the twentieth century (Fischer, 1992). The telephone became a lifeline to rural families and helped spur population movement from the cities to the suburbs. AT&T continued its dominance, but now with such a friendly face that it seemed almost motherly, winning it the nickname "Ma Bell."

In the 1920s AT&T again stepped out of bounds in efforts to control the new media of that day. It established the first radio network around its WEAF radio station (see Chapter 6) in an attempt to dominate radio. In the film industry, Western Electric sound equipment allowed Al Jolson to utter "You ain't heard nothin' yet" on screen in 1927 (see Chapter 7). Also that year AT&T conducted a public television demonstration. Again

A **patent** grants the exclusive rights to an invention to its inventor.

Universal service is the principle that everyone should have access to infrastructure networks.

The **Sherman Antitrust Act** (1890) prohibits the restraint of free trade.

■ "HOY!"
Here Alexander Graham Bell inaugrates the line between New York and Chicago in 1892.

made mindful of the threat of government intervention, AT&T refocused on telephone service.

During the Great Depression (1929–1939), telephone subscriptions declined but the company paid dividends to stockholders (mostly Republicans) while laying off thousands of workers (mostly Democrats). That placed communications policy on the agenda of Democratic President Franklin Roosevelt. The Communications Act of 1934 defined AT&T as a **common carrier.** That required AT&T and other telephone companies to offer service on an equal basis to all paying customers, and prohibited them from having any financial interest in the content. AT&T also had to submit financial reports and rate notifications with the new **Federal Communications Commission (FCC).**

The FCC soon launched an antitrust investigation that dragged on for almost 50 years. The basic problem was that it was virtually impossible for competing equipment manufacturers to make sales within the Bell System, and it appeared that Western Electric's prices were too high, fattening local telephone rates for consumers. A 1956 Consent Decree forced AT&T to license its patents fairly (including the transistor, invented in Bell Labs in 1947) but left the monopoly intact. Cracks slowly appeared, such as the Hush-a-Phone decision that established the right to connect "outside" equipment (a rubber earpiece in that case) to AT&T's network. Competition for long-distance calls opened up in 1977 when Microwave Communications, Inc. (MCI) was allowed into the business. A second antitrust case ended in the Modified Final Judgment (MFJ) in 1984. That forced AT&T to sell off, or divest, its local phone companies. The local exchanges were parceled into seven **Regional Bell operating companies (RBOCs)** that retained the right to the Bell trademark. Ma Bell was dead.

Cutting the Wires

Where did our cell phones come from? Wireless telecommunication dates back to Marconi's wireless telegraph in 1896 (see Chapter 6). As we saw in that chapter, radio was primarily a two-way communications medium for the first 25 years of its existence, before radio broadcasting dominated the airwaves. While radio communication was wireless in those years, it wasn't very mobile. Such bulky equipment and lengthy antennas were required that only large ocean going vessels, like the *Titanic,* had mobile radios. The first land-based mobile radios in the United States were two-way radios installed in Detroit police cars in 1921. Mobile radios advanced rapidly during World War II (1939–1945) as they became commonplace in tanks and airplanes. The first hand-held personal communication devices also appeared on WWII battlefields, in the form of the walkie-talkie. They were the work of Canadian inventor Al Gross who went on to pioneer Citizen's Band (CB) radio and the telephone pager (Bellis, 2000).

After World War II, wireless **microwave** systems replaced telephone cables on highly trafficked routes between major cities. These systems were fixed in place, not mobile, anchored to tall towers. They carried thousands of simultaneous telephone calls between cities rather than between individual mobile handsets. Microwave technology also inspired science fiction writer Arthur C. Clarke to come up with the idea for **satellites** in 1945. They are essentially microwave transmitters launched into space, beginning with AT&T's Telstar satellite in 1962.

Common carriers provide service to all on an equal basis.

The **Federal Communications Commission (FCC)** regulates communication in the United States.

Regional Bell operating companies (RBOCs) are the local telephone operating companies that AT&T divested in 1984.

Microwave systems transmit information between relay towers on highly focused beams of radio waves.

Satellite systems send information back and forth to relays in orbit around the earth.

Our Wireless World

Although Americans are beginning to catch up, they are still behind the rest of the world in their utilization of cell phones and in the advanced wireless technology available to them. The reasons are varied: The FCC was slow to approve the technology allowing other nations (notably Scandinavian countries) to get a head start. The unique "called party pays" approach in the United States deters users from keeping their cells switched on and may inhibit casual calls, limiting their usefulness. It's also true that other countries had greater incentives to adopt cell technology. In most of the rest of the world local calls are charged by the minute and long-distance rates are relatively high. Cell phone operators bypassed wire-line networks to offer substantial savings. And, in many countries wire-line phones simply were not widely available. For whatever reasons, Americans still have a lot to learn about going wireless.

In the Far East and Europe the cell phone has become a vital part of popular youth culture. Ring tones of the latest hits are downloaded so widely and updated so often that they are a major factor in promoting new music. One Scandinavian band achieved fame by having a "hit" ring tone before it ever released a record. Fans kicked off their concerts by playing back the ring tone in unison. With Internet access still relatively limited and expensive (owing again to those charges for local calls) short message service (SMS) messages fill the communications niche occupied by Internet instant messenger service in the United States. SMS messages are also used in interactive television shows; for example, to pick the winners in the European music contests that were the original model for *American Idol*.

In developing countries such as Venezuela the cell phone provides new groups of people with access to modern communications. Until recently phone companies there were inefficient state-run monopolies, and there were often years-long waiting lists to get a new line installed. Many poor neighborhoods were simply not connected at all or else their residents did not have the necessary consumer credit to qualify for a phone. Prepaid cell phones are proving to be a widely popular and affordable option. They not only connect people with their family and friends but also with educational and job opportunities and serve as a significant status symbol in poor neighborhoods.

There are other lessons about cell phones that Americans might hope not to learn. It's an eerie feeling to walk down a city street in Italy where seemingly everyone is waving their hands in the air and talking passionately to an invisible someone, but not to you. *Bonjourno*, anyone?

Mobile telephones for personal use have been around since 1947, but early systems had limited capacity, which meant long waiting lists for new customers and busy signals for subscribers. Paging systems were introduced in 1962 to relieve some of the pent-up demand. In 1975 citizens band (CB) radio service opened up to general use, but did not allow private conversations and had limited range. The demand for mobile communications still mounted, prompting the FCC to reallocate TV channels 70 to 83 for analog cellular radio service in 1978. However, the FCC was slow to authorize the new cellular service, which wasn't available in the United States until 1982.

A second generation of digital wireless phones came along in 1995. The new cell phones were lighter and made mobile data communications more accessible but otherwise didn't evolve quite as expected. Although wide-scale competition was planned, AT&T and its Bell Operating Company offspring soon dominated. The FCC declined to select a technical standard, resulting in three mutually incompatible systems. Meanwhile the rest of the world settled on a European standard (GSM, short for *Global System for Mobile communications*) and enjoyed lower prices, wider availability, and more rapid innovation as a result. This left the United States lagging behind the world in telecommunications (See WorldView: Our Wireless World) for perhaps the first time since the invention of the telegraph, a reminder of the importance of technical standards.

THE BROADBAND INFRASTRUCTURE

AT&T provided the **broadband** infrastructure for network television, **coaxial cable** connections that linked television stations, beginning in 1946. By 1951, the first national television network using a combination of coaxial cable and microwave was in place. Later, in the 1970s, broadcast networks switched to satellites to deliver their programs to their affiliates. Satellites also distributed cable television programming services, beginning with HBO in 1975 and WTBS in 1976. In 1995 **direct broadcast satellite (DBS)** systems like DirecTV began beaming television programs directly to the home through pizza-size antennas.

Local distribution of television in areas without broadcast signals launched the cable television industry in 1948. Cable thrived in small cities and towns for the next 20 years, but the FCC blocked it from large cities in 1966 (see Chapter 8). In 1972 the FCC reversed the ban, and major cable **multiple system operators (MSOs)** like Tele-Communications Inc. (TCI, now owned by Comcast) and Warner Cable (later to become part of Time Warner) raced to wire major urban markets.

The first **fiber-optic** telephone cables debuted in 1977, and over the next decade they began to replace coaxial cable and microwave connections in voice, data, and video applications. In the late 1990s cable operators converted to fiber-optic cables, paving the way for dozens of new digital television channels and two-way Internet and telephone services.

The Government Steps Aside

The growth of new infrastructure industries helped convince the government to deregulate telecommunications and let marketplace competition reign. Under the **Telecommunications Act of 1996** local telephone companies could offer cable TV and long-distance service, and long-distance and cable companies were allowed in the local telephone business (Baldwin, McVoy, & Steinfield, 1996).

The Telecommunications Act triggered a merger frenzy among infrastructure companies intent on offering "one-stop shopping" for all types of communication and making themselves big enough to compete globally. For example, Bell Atlantic and NYNEX, two of the seven RBOCs divested by AT&T in 1984, combined to control local phone service from Maine to Virginia, then gobbled up the largest remaining independent telephone company, GTE, and renamed themselves Verizon. Major carriers ran up mountains of debt to pay for their acquisitions.

The multichannel television market is another problem area. Cable TV rate increases have greatly exceeded the rate of inflation since the Telecom Act deregulated prices. Some competition has emerged from the DBS industry, where DirecTV and Dish now serve 15 percent of U.S. homes with digital multichannel service. However, the satellite broadcasters are required to pick up and retransmit local TV stations under a law enacted at the request of the broadcasting industry. That cut into profits and forced DirecTV into the clutches of global media baron Rupert Murdoch, owner of News Corp and the Fox Network.

Long distance is perhaps the biggest success story, with hundreds of competitors slashing rates to half their 1996 levels. Internet telephony (calls placed over the Internet instead of conventional phone networks) is an innovative technology that further cuts costs. The RBOCs began entering the long-distance business in 1999, providing new competition.

The average cost of local telephone service also declined slightly as competitors began to enter local telephone markets in the early 2000s. Taking advantage of econom-

---

Broadband systems carry multiple channels of video, audio, and computer data simultaneously.

Coaxial cable is the high-capacity wire used for cable television transmission.

Direct broadcast satellites (DBSs) transmit television signals from satellites to compact home receivers.

Multiple system operators (MSOs) operate cable TV systems in two or more communities.

Fiber-optic systems use light instead of electricity.

The Telecommunications Act of 1996 opened the U.S. telecommunications industry to competition.

ical bulk leases of local phone lines brought about by the Telecom Act, a wide variety of firms ranging form long distance giant MCI to small local Internet service providers found they could resell the lines they leased from RBOCs and still realize a profit for themselves while yielding bargains for consumers.

The competition has gotten a little too hot for some. Former industry leader AT&T bought, then sold, its cable television operation to another large cable company, Comcast, when the expected profits from cable telephone service were slow in coming. Many telecommunications firms bet too heavily on the Internet during the dot-com boom of the 1990s (see Chapter 9) and drastically overbuilt new fiber-optic networks. Others plunged huge sums into acquiring licenses to run digital cellular networks in major cities. Stocks tumbled and companies and their senior executives tumbled with them as the boom turned to bust at the turn of the twenty-first century. Almost overnight, MCI WorldCom went from being one of the biggest success stories of the Information Age to being its biggest bankruptcy as the telecommunications industry collapsed in a worldwide meltdown. In response to shrinking profits, AT&T commenced its withdrawal from the consumer long distance business in 2004, and agreed to merge with Southwestern Bell in 2005. Thus, the Telecom Act began to break communication conglomerates as well as make them.

Competition no longer seems to be an easy answer to the challenge of providing an affordable communications infrastructure. As competitors began to drop, long-distance prices began to creep back up. Local competition was dealt a severe blow in 2004 when the courts struck down a key provision of the Telecom Act that required the RBOCs to open themselves to competition by leasing their lines to competitors at discounted rates. That could increase both local and long distance rates for consumers (see "Media Literacy: Service for Everyone?," page 383).

However, other recent developments still point the way toward meaningful competition and, eventually, a radical transformation of the communications infrastructure. *Number portability* for cell phones came into full effect in 2004, making it possible for consumers to switch cell phone carriers—or from wire-line to cell phone service—while retaining their old telephone numbers. Comcast Cable announced that it would soon begin offering telephone service in all of its major cable systems using Internet-based technology. Also in 2004, new wireless broadband technologies began to make headway. Thus, the promise of affordable one-stop shopping for all of our telecommunication needs may still be kept, but the question of what companies and what technologies will fulfill it is still unanswered.

© Adam Rountree/Bloomberg News/Landov

■ **SAD STORY**
Bernard Ebbers led MCI WorldCom into bankruptcy and became a symbol of the meltdown in the telecommunications industry.

STOP & REVIEW

1. What were the origins of the telephone and telegraph?
2. Why did the government want to break up AT&T?
3. What did the AT&T divestiture do?
4. How did mobile phones get started? Satellites? Cable?
5. What was the impact of the Telecommunications Act of 1996?

TECHNOLOGY: INSIDE THE INFRASTRUCTURE

New infrastructure technology makes it possible to carry more information faster and to more locations than ever. By tracing infrastructure technology back to its roots, we can better understand today's technology.

Applied Electromagnetism

An appreciation of Morse's telegraph—and all of the electronic media that followed—begins by harking back to an experiment popular in many grade schools (see Chapters 5 and 6). The teacher wraps wire around a big iron nail and hooks the wire up to a battery. Then she flips a switch that sends electricity flowing through the wire, and the nail instantly turns into a magnet that can pick up other nails. When she flips the switch off, the nails drop dramatically back to the table. Morse's telegraph operated on the same principle, except that the telegraph key acted like the teacher's switch, turning the flow of electricity on or off, and the magnet caused a thin strip of metal to click up and down many miles away as it became magnetized and demagnetized. The pattern of clicks spells out the letters of the alphabet in Morse Code. For example, the letter A is a short click (called a dot) followed by a long click (called a dash).

Electromagnetism also explains what happened when Alexander Graham Bell called out to Mr. Watson. The air pressure waves from his voice hit a flexible membrane. A short wire was attached to the membrane, and as Bell shouted, the wire bobbed up and down in a beaker of acid, varying the electrical resistance in the circuit in response to Bell's voice. That was the variable resistance transmitter that was the basis for Bell's patent. The wire was connected to an electromagnet in the next room, which tugged at a flexible steel reed in response to the varying current. As it vibrated, the steel reed generated air pressure waves that sounded like Bell's voice. The acid was banished after it ruined Bell's trousers, but varying an electrical current in response to sound pressure waves is still the basic function of all microphones.

The earliest phones were attached to dedicated telegraph lines (there were no switches), connecting two points a few miles apart (there were no means to amplify the signals). Users shouted "Hoy! Hoy!" to alert the party at the other end, who shouted back "Hoy! Hoy!" (Bell disdained the use of "hello" for all his years.)

The alerting problem was soon solved by Watson, who invented an electromagnetic device that gave the telephone its ring, but the other limitations were the subject of continuing development. The solutions eventually found their way into mass media systems, including motion pictures, radio, broadcast TV, cable TV, and satellite (Fagen, 1975).

Do You Hear Me?

One of the first inventions to emerge from AT&T's labs was the repeater amplifier. It used the *audion tube,* a 1906 invention by Lee De Forest that also was a key development in radio broadcasting. Early long-distance callers had to shout into the telephone, but no one could shout all the way from New York to San Francisco! In the first transcontinental call in 1915, Bell again had the honor of uttering the first words: "Hoy! Hoy! (he still refused to say "hello") Mr. Watson? Are you there? Do you hear me?" Watson did.

Will Everybody Please Get Off This Line?

In the 1880s telephone poles with up to 30 crossarms literally darkened the skies. Phone conversations filled with static because early systems had only one wire, using the earth

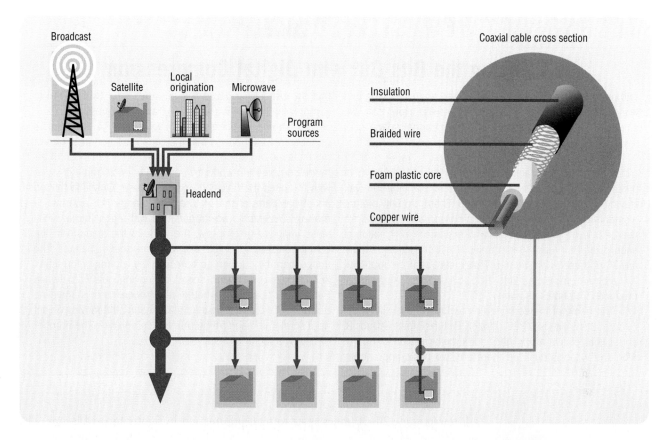

Cable TV   The cable headend feeds broadcast, satellite, microwave, and local origination signals into a coaxial cable distribution networks of trunks, feeders, and drops to individual homes.

to complete the electrical circuit. The introduction of electrical power systems that same decade created intolerable noise. That forced phone companies to use a pair of wires for each call, and that crowded the poles even more. A search began for a way to put multiple telephone conversations on a pair of wires, a search that continues today.

Multiplexing.   Multiplexing systems, introduced in 1918, combined telephone conversations with high-frequency *carrier waves* to be sent over telephone wires, just as multiple radio channels are transmitted simultaneously through the air (see Chapter 6). At the receiving end the carrier wave was removed and the original phone calls recovered.

Coaxial Cable.   As the name implies, coaxial cable has a single long wire running down its central axis and a second electrical conductor that is wrapped around it like a long metal tube. This arrangement keeps unwanted signals from entering the cable and also prevents the cable signals from leaking out and interfering with other communications. After World War II, AT&T began to use the medium in high-capacity trunk systems that carried phone calls between major cities. Coaxial cable also has the capacity, or *bandwidth,* to carry video, and it was soon applied in the transcontinental connections that linked TV networks to their affiliates. Local cable systems also used it to distribute television signals from their **headends** to individual homes (Figure 12.1).

Microwave.   World War II radar detection systems were also adapted to telecommunications. *Microwave* entered the public telephone network in 1948. Thousands of calls at a time were multiplexed on adjacent channels sent through the air. However, instead of broadcasting in all directions, microwave systems used directional antennas located atop

Headends are where signals are fed into the local cable network.

Squeezing the Bits Out with Digital Compression

Without digital video compression we still might be living in a world with "only" 50 television channels. How can we squeeze five digital channels into the channel space of a single analog channel?

As we learned back in chapter 8, each frame of a TV picture is made by tracing 525 horizontal lines, but 45 of those are lost in what's called the vertical blanking interval, leaving 480 that we can actually see. There are 640 picture elements (*pixels,* for short) on each horizontal line, and if we use 24 bits to encode the color and brightness information of each pixel, then each frame takes 8 million bits, and there are 30 of these each second. That means that an hour-long TV program translates into 900 billion bits. And HDTV produces four times as many.

The name of the compression technique used in digital cable and satellite is MPEG (Motion Picture Expert Group) 2, and it is a relative of the MP3 audio compression standard. After the video is digitized there are two basic approaches that are used to squeeze the bits out, *intra* (within) frame compression and *inter* (between) frame compression.

Intraframe compression is a lot like MP3. It subtracts unnecessary information that the senses do not miss, except here it is redundant visual information that is removed. Interframe compression works by comparing each frame of video with the ones that follow it and precede it. Only information about the parts of the picture that change (for example, a moving soccer ball) are transmitted with each frame, while static images (for example, the walls of the stadium in the background) are updated only when the scene changes. The image can be further compressed by storing information about the direction and speed of moving objects between frames (for example, whether the soccer ball is traveling upward or downward) instead of recreating the moving object from scratch in each frame. All that compresses the number of bits by a factor of better than 50 to 1.

tall towers some 20–30 miles apart to send information in tightly focused beams. The signals received at each tower were amplified and relayed to the next one down the line, making it possible to extend networks thousands of miles.

Microwave was also useful for television. Microwave links were part of the first coast-to-coast television connection in 1951. Cable TV companies used it to import broadcast signals from distant cities that were beyond the reach of the tallest antennas. HBO used microwave before switching to satellite. Microwave is still used today by local TV stations to transport signals to their transmitters and to gather live news footage from mobile vans.

Satellite. In 1945 science fiction writer Arthur C. Clarke proposed that three microwave transmitters circling the planet could cover the globe if their orbits (geosynchronous orbits 22,300 miles high) were such that their rotation speed matched that of the earth. Another World War II innovation, the ballistic missile, made this feat imaginable. The first communications satellite, Telstar I, went into orbit in 1962. The first words were less than momentous: "Will everybody please get off this line?" There were so many dignitaries listening in that the circuit overloaded.

In satellite systems a powerful microwave transmitter, or *uplink,* beams the signal from, say, the network control center run by CNN in Atlanta to a microwave receiver (called a *transponder*) aboard an orbiting satellite. The satellite transponder retransmits the signal to *downlinks* back on earth—to dishes located at the headends of local cable systems, for example. Large backyard satellite antennas called Television Receive Only (TVRO) dishes could also pick up the signals, but they were scrambled and dish owners had to pay to get them unscrambled.

During the 1970s, satellite technology replaced terrestrial (earth-based) microwave and coaxial cable networks on international phone routes and in television networks (Hudson, 1990). Rocketry improved so that more powerful (and heavier) satellites could be launched, shrinking the size and cost of the receiving dishes down to those used in today's Direct Broadcast Satellite (DBS) systems. Digital compression technology (see "Technology Demystified: Squeezing the Bits Out with Digital Compression," page 366) expanded satellite capacity by squeezing five digital television channels into the spectrum space formerly occupied by one standard analog channel.

Digital Carriers. Also in 1962, the first digital telephone call was made back on earth. The new digital carrier system, known as a *T1,* converted voices to digital pulses (see Chapter 1) and reconstructed a simulated voice for the listener on the other end. By taking turns transmitting short digital voice samples from multiple calls, 24 simultaneous conversations were combined on a single copper wire circuit (Millman, 1984). When used for data instead of phone calls, T1 lines carry 1.5 million bits per second. T1s connect many **Internet service providers (ISPs)** and popular websites to the Internet. For those with an even greater need for speed, there is the T3, which transmits 45 million bits per second.

Fiber Optics. Alexander Graham Bell patented a "photophone" that used light to transmit phone calls in 1880. Electrical signals from a telephone made a light flicker, and as the blinking light fell on a photoreceptor that converted light to electricity, the original signal was recovered. Long strands, or fibers, of glass were found to conduct light over longer distances, but still the light faded too rapidly. The laser, invented at Bell Labs in 1958, ultimately held the key to practical fiber-optic systems by producing intense beams of pure, concentrated light.

The first commercial fiber-optic systems were installed in 1977 as replacements for T1s. Fiber-optic carriers proved ideal for computer data since they were immune to the electrical interference that plagued copper wire systems such as the T1 and thus were relatively error free. Their method for sending information, turning the light source on and off, was well suited to the 1s and 0s of data communication. Optical fiber signals travel hundreds of miles before they fade and have to be regenerated, further reducing errors. Optical carrier (OC) systems in the Internet backbone reach speeds of billions of bits per second. And, the speed of optical networks, including those already installed, doubles about every 18 months as engineers devise new ways to combine multiple light sources (and thus multiple data streams) in a single strand of glass.

Number, Please?

Switching equipment is another key component of the telecommunications infrastructure. Switches direct information to its intended destination and let users take turns using expensive transmission circuits.

Manual Switching. Millions of telephone operators would be needed to handle today's telephone traffic if calls were still manually patched together with electrical plugs as they once were. Today there are far fewer operators than in the 1920s before automatic switching.

Automatic Switching. Early automatic switches were close relatives of the jukebox. Mechanical arms rotated and jiggled up and down, touching tiny electrical contacts connected to subscribers' telephone wires. Beginning in 1951, long-distance calls could be dialed automatically from the home. Large organizations find it profitable to install their own switches, called *private branch exchanges (PBXs). Key systems* are an economical alternative for smaller companies. In 1965, AT&T crossed the telephone switch with a computer to produce the first digital switch. The giant clattering electromagnetic switches

Internet service providers (ISPs) provide connections to the Internet.

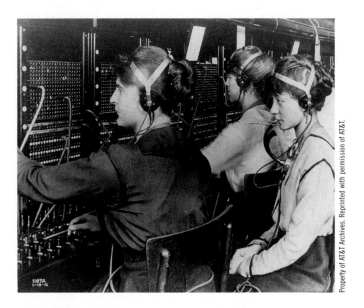

and swarms of technicians that once filled telephone exchanges have been replaced by refrigerator-size electronic switches humming quietly to themselves in the dark.

Intelligent Networks. Once, all of the transactions necessary to establish and terminate a telephone call (*signaling,* in telephone jargon) passed through the same connection that the voices did. This tied up lines for many seconds just to establish a connection, even if it turned out that the line was busy. Enterprising college students, including Steve Jobs of Apple Computer fame, found they could place free calls by emulating the tone used to turn long-distance billing on and off.

New intelligent networks use a separate data network that "checks ahead" for a busy, so you no longer have to hang on the line while intermediate connections are established. This also enables caller ID, which connects the intelligent network to a digital display on the subscriber's telephone, and the follow me feature that automatically redirects calls. College students again have to pay for their long-distance calls (unless they place them free on the Internet!, see below).

NUMBER, PLEASE

Before automatic switching, live operators completed all calls by moving plugs around their switchboards.

Packet Networks. **Packet switching** divides data streams into chunks, or *packets,* and mixes the data from many users together into a shared, high-speed channel rather than dedicate a separate channel to each pair of users. In other words, the messages are switched around instead of the circuits. Each chunk of data carries an address so the packets can be reassembled (see Chapter 9). This approach is used in the *TCP/IP* Internet protocol.

Packet switching is also found in internal data networks that organizations run for themselves: *local area networks* (LANs). LANs are high-speed networks that connect all of the computers in a building or campus to allow them to share hardware (such as high-speed printers) and software (such as customer service applications), and communicate with each other (via e-mail) and the outside world (via Internet gateways; see Figure 12.2). Ethernet is a common standard for such networks. It typically uses coaxial cables like the ones found in cable TV systems and transmits data at a rate of 10 million bits per second. This is a common networking scheme for college computer labs and dormitories as well as businesses. LANs that use fiber-optic or "fat" telephone cables (the ones with extra-wide connectors, known as RJ-45) and now wireless connections can be found with data transmission speeds ranging up to billions of bits (gigabits) per second.

Voice calls can also be digitized and divided into packets. Such calls may be terminated to conventional phone lines, or they can be completed between computers connected to the Internet, allowing for free long-distance calls. Internet telephony is revolutionizing the technology and the economics of the telecommunications industry. Since Internet (IP) protocols are used, Internet telephony also goes by the name *voice over IP,* or VOIP for short. By integrating voice communication and Internet access in the same network, it will eventually be possible to replace expensive telephone switches with cheap, generic packet switching equipment. For example, New Zealand plans to turn off its conventional (circuit-switched) telephone network and replace it with an Internet-based voice network in 2010. In the United States cable TV operators like Comcast are leading the way with local telephone service based on voice over IP.

Packet switching breaks up digital information into individually addressed chunks, or packets.

© Rob Casey/Getty Images

■ **BLINKING LIGHTS**
Fiber-optic systems carry
information at gigabit speeds
with few errors.

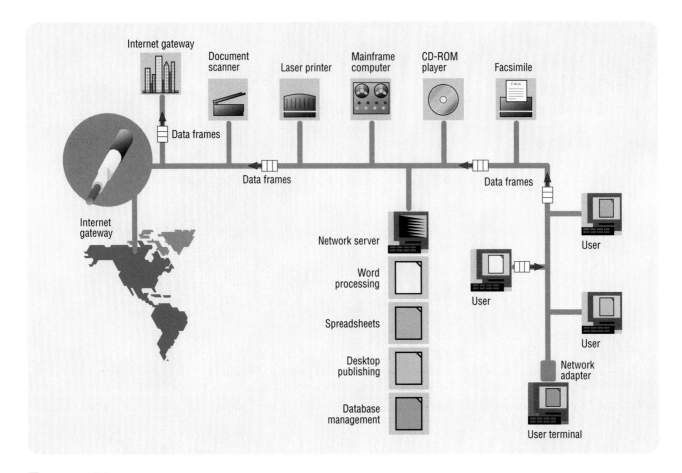

Internet gateway

Document scanner

Laser printer

Mainframe computer

CD-ROM player

Facsimile

FAX

Data frames

Internet gateway

Data frames

Data frames

Network server

Word processing

Spreadsheets

Desktop publishing

Database management

User

User

User

Network adapter

User terminal

■ **FIGURE 12.2**

LAN Local area networks allow multiple users to share peripheral devices such as printers and to access software stored on a shared file server.

Cable Converters. Cable TV companies don't have the same switching problems telephone companies do. Their networks carry the same channels into every household, and the set-top *converters* merely select one channel at a time. They are called converters because they convert the signal from the channel it is transmitted on inside the cable network to channel 3 (or 4) on your TV set.

Pay channels present a problem since they must be scrambled. In the early days a technician had to pay a visit to install, or uninstall, the scrambling device every time customers changed their pay services. Addressable converters surmounted this problem by turning themselves off and on in response to digital codes broadcast through the system. Each converter has its own unique address so channels can be turned on and off without sending a technician. Coaxial Cable Analysts introduced the first such system in Columbus, Ohio, in 1973. The same technology can authorize specific programs as well as entire channels—that's how pay-per-view programming is controlled.

Becoming Digital

The basic way to transmit computer data is to turn on a tiny electrical voltage to represent a 1 and to turn off the voltage to represent a 0. Unfortunately, telephone systems must reject certain electrical pulses to avoid confusion with the pulses that old-fashioned rotary phones use to dial numbers and to work within other technical limitations of this nineteenth-century invention. How can we send computer data through the public telephone network, then?

Phone Modems. The **modem**, or **modulator-demodulator,** converts digital pulses to signals that can be accepted and processed by the phone system as if they were sound. But, they are limited to a top speed of 56,000 bits per second (see "Technology Demystified: Whistling Your Computer's Tune, or, How Modems Work," page 372).

Digital Subscriber Line. Telephone companies are pushing **digital subscriber line (DSL)** technology for high-speed Internet access. DSL can transmit digital video as well as data and voice at millions of bits per second over standard telephone lines. Unlike conventional modems, DSL requires a change in the connections inside the telephone company's central office switch and, sometimes, modifications in local telephone network cabling as well.

Digital Cable. Digital compression techniques (see "Technology Demystified: Squeezing the Bits Out with Digital Compression," page 366) now push coaxial cable to new limits. Five digital channels can now be squeezed in the same space required for one analog TV channel. In 1998 major MSOs began to upgrade their systems to hundreds of channels. For the cable subscriber, this means a new level of service that comes with a set-top box capable of decompressing and displaying the digital signal on a conventional analog set. Newer digital televisions can also display the signals with a built-in box.

Some digital cable systems offer *video on demand.* These systems store movies on a huge computer disk drive at the headend. Viewers can make requests from a lengthy menu of movies and pause and fast-forward the movie. Multiple users can access the same movie file at the same time, in much the same way that you can have multiple files "open" simultaneously on a personal computer.

Cable Modems. Using transmission techniques similar to their telephone cousins, **cable modems** carry data to Internet users right alongside HBO and CNN (see "Technology Demystified: Whistling Your Computer's Tune, or, How Modems Work," page 372). They take advantage of the greater transmission capacity of cable to send data at speeds ranging up to 10 million bits per second—nearly 200 times as fast as conventional phone lines. Most home users opt for more modestly priced services offering "only" about a half million bits per second. Satellite companies have their own version of cable modem service that sends web pages through home satellite receivers.

Broadband Power Line. Why not use the third wire you have coming into your home, your electrical power line, for data transmission? That is the promise of broadband power line (BPL). Until recently, electrical interference from power transmission posed serious problems, but the technical barriers have been overcome and in 2004 the FCC approved the technology for use in the United States. By taking advantage of a network that is already installed—in the walls of your home as well as the streets of your neighborhood— BPL could mean low cost broadband connections for everyone, and competition for telephone and cable companies.

Communicating Anywhere

Mobile communication uses techniques very similar to radio broadcasting (see Chapter 6) except that mobile services operate in different portions of the **communications spectrum** than broadcasters do and use far less powerful transmitters. The airwaves are crowded so wireless communication has to be extremely efficient.

Mobile Telephone. The original mobile telephone service operated from a single central antenna and handled only 46 simultaneous conversations in any one city. This meant

Modems (*modulator-demodulators*) convert digital data to analog signals and vice versa.

Digital subscriber line (DSL) sends high-speed data over existing phone lines.

Cable modems connect personal computers to cable TV systems.

The communications spectrum includes the range of electromagnetic radiation frequencies that are used in wireless communication systems.

Whistling Your Computer's Tune, or, How Modems Work

To transmit data, modems must use the same sound frequencies that we use to talk. Or whistle. We humans can transmit data, just not as fast. For example, to send a 1, whistle a high note (wheet). To send a 0, whistle a low-pitched note (whoot). Or, we could make a loud whistle (WHOOT) a 1 and whistle softly (whoot) for a 0. (Try it! 1000001 = WHOOT, whoot, whoot, whoot, whoot, whoot, WHOOT—that's the letter A in computer talk!). The pitch is also known as the *frequency,* whereas loudness is more properly known as *amplitude.* There is another property of pure tones, their *phase.* When you hook your stereo speakers up wrong and they sound tinny, that is because they are out of phase.

If you whistle very quickly you might reach five bits per second, although no human listener could keep up. Computers can perform hundreds of millions of tasks per second, including whistling, but the phone system can't "hear" frequencies higher than 3500 cycles per second (or Hertz, abbreviated Hz). So, we can't change the phone signal at a rate (known as the *baud rate*) of more than 3500 times per second. To be on the safe side, we generally limit the baud rate to 2400. If we indicate only a single bit with each change, that would mean a top speed, or *bit rate,* of 2400 bits per second.

The trick is to transmit more than one digit each time, so we change the signal by combining variations in amplitude, frequency, and phase. For example, we could make a loud, high-pitched note (WHEET) correspond to 00, while a soft low note (whoot) would be 11 (and wheet=01, WHOOT=10). Now we could whistle up the letter A as follows: WHOOT-WHEET-WHEET-whoot (we added an extra 1 at the right to fill out an eight-bit character, or *byte*). Now our bit rate is double the baud rate; that would bring us up to 4800 bits per second. We could use intermediate levels of amplitude and frequency (modems actually use amplitude and phase, but that is harder to whistle) to indicate more and more digits every time we change the signal. Noise in the telephone line limits this to 12 bits per baud, that yields 12 x 2400 = 28,800 bits per second. By using digital compression to squeeze out repetitive strings of data we can push that up to 33,600.

The so-called 56K modems operate on a different principle. They try to fool the phone network into thinking that you have a digital phone line. Recalling our discussion of digital phone transmission in Chapter 1, that means that they send seven bits of information 8000 times a second, 7 x 8000 = 56,000. However, the FCC limits that to 53,000 in many areas to prevent electrical interference with standard phone calls. If you live in a crowded neighborhood or too far from the phone company's central office, your line may go through a digital carrier system that defeats the digital trickery. In that case your top speed drops back to 33,600 bits per second.

© Chris Cooley/Terry Wild Studio

■ NEED FOR SPEED

Cable modems offer fast Internet access—but you have to share the connection with your neighbors.

How do the new digital subscriber lines overcome these limitations? They use the same old phone wires, but the phone company installs a new computer card for your line in its central office. That removes the 3500 Hz speed limit. Freed of that restriction, standard phone wiring can handle 750,000 Hz, and by transmitting multiple digits every time we change the signal, we attain speeds of up to 18 million bits per second, enough for several digital television channels. But that's only if we have a direct connection to the central office and don't live more than two miles from the nearest one.

Cable modems work much like phone modems, except that the frequencies they use are farther up in the electromagnetic spectrum, well beyond the range of our hearing. The cable operator packs the data into unused television channel slots so that it travels to your home right alongside HBO. Cable modem speeds vary from as much as 10 million bits per second down to 200,000. The channel space that your cable modem service occupies is shared by other cable modem users in your neighborhood, as many as 500 other homes near you.

that the forty-seventh caller did not receive a dial tone, which happened often as the subscriber base grew and multiple users contended for the limited number of channels.

Pagers. *Pagers* are miniature radio receivers that monitor a channel "piggybacked" on top of an FM radio station or satellite channel. They wait for a unique numerical code that is their signal to "go off." *Digital pagers* transmit the number to call or a brief message ("Don't forget the milk") by appending digital codes to the paging signal. In two-way paging the recipient can send a brief return message ("skim or regular?").

Cellular Phones.   Cellular takes its name from dividing large service areas into clusters of small zones, or cells, each only a few miles across (see "Technology Demystified: How Your Cell Phone Works," page 374). The transmitters in each cell are relatively weak, so it is possible to reuse their frequencies in nearby cells without causing interference. As the user moves, the call is handed off to the next cell in the network and automatically reassigned to a new channel. The first-generation cell phones used analog transmission.

Digital Cellular.   Second-generation cell phones are digital. They use smaller cells—some only a few hundred yards across. Digital compression is used to shrink the streams of digits and save network capacity. Digital transmission techniques make it possible for several users to share each channel. Smaller cells and digital transmission methods expand capacity and lower costs compared to conventional analog systems. Most of the countries of the world adopted a common standard for second-generation phones called GSM (short for Global System for Mobile communications), but U.S. operators built networks using two other competing standards as well that were incompatible with each other and also with GSM. Networks using GSM technology are only now making a belated bid to dominate the U.S. market.

Now the world's mobile carriers are making the transition to *third-generation* (3G) phones that cross a telephone with a handheld computer, with a built-in web browser and e-mail service. They can complete mobile electronic commerce transactions by simply pointing and clicking the cell phone at what you want to buy, whether it's a gas pump or a restaurant menu. Based on their popularity in the Far East, U. S. operators expect the most compelling application for 3G users will be sending still snapshots and video clips to each other over our cell phones. When fully developed, 3G networks promise broadband transmission speeds of millions of bits per second, enough to send full motion color pictures through your cell phone, to download your favorite music files, and to effortlessly surf the web on portable computers.

However, a competing technology variously known as *General Packet Relay Service* (GPRS) or 2.5G is stealing some of the third generation's thunder. Unlike conventional cell phones (and also conventional wire-line phones) that have to establish a dedicated connection before you can start talking, the GPRS phones are "always on." They use a variation of packet switching (see Chapter 9) that sends tiny chunks of information through the air with the address of the receiver's cell phone on each one. The 2.5G phones can surf stripped-down web pages or can be connected to laptop computers to Net-surf at up to double the speed of conventional phone modems.

GPRS is also well suited for SMS (*short message service*) messages. These are short (160-character) text messages that appear on your digital cell phone screen. These are all the rage with teens in Europe and the Far East. They have been slower to catch on in the United States, perhaps because American teens had gotten used to text messaging in Internet chat rooms before these phones appeared. The SMS messages can also be used to complete mobile e-commerce transactions and to implement a crude form of interactive TV in which home viewers use their cell phones to vote for their favorite *American Idol* contestant. SMS is also used to download personalized ring tones and pictures to today's cell phones.

© PR Newswire/SPRINT

■ CAN YOU SEE ME NOW?
The new third-generation cell phones make two-way video calls a reality.

How Your Cell Phone Works

To imagine the structure of a cellular phone network, think of a honeycomb. It is made up of six-sided geometrical shapes (hexagons) arranged in neat rows. The hexagons are the cells, and in the center of each cell is a radio transmitter that "broadcasts" in the frequency range set aside for cellular radio service. The next time you ride an interstate highway, look for elongated pyramids alongside the road made out of metal tubing (they look a little like the Eiffel Tower) topped by triangular antenna arrays that look a lot like a wedge of cheese. Those are the cellular radio towers, and they are connected by wires to each other and with the rest of the public phone network through a mobile telephone switching office. Each tower has many different channels to carry calls, and those same channels can be reused at other towers that are one layer of cells removed in the hexagonal pattern—that's what makes cellular radio much more efficient than the old mobile phone systems.

When you turn on your cell phone it lets the nearest antenna know you are there. Then, when a call comes in for you, the system pages your cell phone, it rings, and if you answer your cell phone it negotiates with the nearest cell site to determine which channel to put you on. Similarly, when you place a call your cell phone requests a channel for you and transmits the number you send.

Each cell is only a few miles across, and in a speeding automobile you may cross a cell boundary every few minutes. When that happens, the cell you are leaving automatically "hands off" your call to the next cell, which assigns you a new channel so you can continue talking.

Digital cell phones use digital compression to reduce the size of the channels that are required. They also take advantage of multiplexing to further expand capacity, but two different approaches are used in the United States (and a third in Europe and most of the rest of the world) that make digital phones from competing systems incompatible. One approach, the same one used in T1 carriers, assigns each caller to a designated time slot on a particular channel and then makes callers "take turns" transmitting brief streams of data on the same channel. The other approach (invented by 1940s movie star Hedy Lamarr) scatters the digital fragments of your conversation over many channels but attaches an identification code to each one so that they may be snatched from the air and reassembled into a phone conversation.

© PR Newswire/MEBLINK WIRELESS, INC.

■ WIRELESS WEB

Motorola's Talkabout is one of the many devices available for checking e-mail on the go.

WiFi is short for wireless fidelity.

Wireless Internet Options. Cell phones from all three (and a half) generations can be connected to computers for wireless Internet access, but first-generation (2400 bits per second) and second-generation (9600 bps) connections were painfully slow. That problem will be solved when 3G networks come to your town, but the rollout is slow and still plagued by the problems of spotty coverage and incompatibility between systems, at least in the United States. Fourth generation systems are already on the drawing boards. Mobile high definition TV phones are planned.

Some computer buffs aren't waiting for mobile phone companies to solve their wireless Internet access problems for them. They are installing wireless Internet transmitters (called "hotspots") on their rooftops and desktops. It is also a handy way of networking multiple computers in a single home without poking holes in the walls for cables. The rooftop version is formally known as *IEEE802.11* (after the standard from the Institute for Electrical and Electronic Engineers that defines the service), or more simply as **WiFi.** WiFi sends the Internet's TCP/IP packets through the air to wireless receivers at speeds of 10 million bits per second, so it is a broadband system. Several new WiFi varieties are entering the market, boasting speeds of 100 million bits per second, and the ability to move from hotspot to hotspot without losing the connection.

Many areas have wireless broadband Internet services operating outside of the frequencies dedicated to WiFi service. Some of these networks use a new standard called

WiMax but there are also proprietary approaches; Verizon has one called EVDO, for example. Unlike WiFi systems, these operate in regions of the electromagnetic spectrum where powerful transmitters are allowed. That makes it possible to cover entire cities with a single transmitter and to serve areas, such as small towns and vacation resorts, where low population densities make other high-speed options uneconomical.

The desktop version of wireless networking is called Bluetooth (it's named after a tenth-century Danish king with dental issues). It links your digital cell phone to your personal computer, or to wireless printers, scanners, and digital cameras. It has a range of only about 30 feet and a top speed of under a million bits per second (although a newer version tops 2 million bits per second), but even so it is not limited to use around the house or the office. Bluetooth could also connect your cell phone to your car's information system (which you will soon have to get) or to mobile commerce applications, like the "intelligent wireless gas pump."

LEO Satellites. Earth-based mobile systems are challenged by new satellites that fly in low earth orbit (LEO). The lower orbits mean smaller and cheaper receivers with a small whip antenna instead of a dish. However, low-flying satellites constantly change their position so dozens are needed to ensure coverage. Others fly in somewhat higher orbits and are called middle earth orbit (MEO) systems. Another popular satellite technology is the GPS (geo-positioning satellite) system that locates lost boaters, drivers, and hikers by comparing the strength of signals received from three or more satellites turning overhead.

Motorola launched a satellite mobile phone service, Iridium, in 1998. It was an initial flop, thanks to airtime charges that ran several dollars per minute, brick-like handsets, and the necessity of taking the phones outdoors to make a call. Prices have dropped to the dollar-per-minute range and handsets now fit in a coat pocket, but these remain niche services beloved mainly by arctic explorers and roving CIA agents. Satellite-based broadband Internet services could be a different story but also have been slow to develop. The largest of these, DirecWay, a subsidiary of DirecTV, offers a 500kbps service for slightly more than the cost of a cable modem.

INFRASTRUCTURE SERVICES

Digital technology brings a growing array of telecommunications services to the consumer. One basic strategy is to provide "one-stop shopping" for all of the customer's communication needs. Indeed, that strategy did much to drive mergers and acquisitions among cable, telephone, and Internet companies.

Wire-Line Services

Basic local telephone service has the acronym *POTS,* for *plain old telephone service.* The basic POTS functions—dial tone, transmission, and switching—are unchanged since the 1890s. These are delivered via conventional phone wires, so we call them wire-line services. Computerized switching added options like touch-tone dialing, call waiting, speed dialing, three-way calling, and call forwarding in the 1970s.

There are many new options. Phone companies have a variety of "package deals" that combine optional services like caller ID and Internet access with differing rate plans for local calls. Calling plans offer a trade-off between the size of the minimum monthly payment and the number of free local calls allowed: the fewer free calls, the lower the monthly fee. Phone companies also offer line maintenance service, but if you feel comfortable plugging in a modular phone jack, that may be an unnecessary expense.

TECHNOLOGY DEMYSTIFIED ■■■■■■

Our Internet Connection Options

In the previous section we examined Internet options from telephone, cable, and wireless infrastructure providers. Which ones can you get, and which can you afford?

A good place to start is with the list of Internet service providers in your area, from http://www.thelist.com. But the list relies on companies to volunteer information, and what you see is not always up-to-date or accurate, so it still pays to check around on the latest services and rates once you narrow the field a little. For cable modem information, call your local cable television company or try Cable Data Com News (http://www.cabledatacomnews.com/cmic/cmic72 .html).

Digital subscriber line and Integrated Services Digital Network are perhaps the hardest to track down, because their access is dictated at the level of the local telephone exchange, not necessarily by city, county, or state. Try 2Wire's DSL locator for a quick check on DSL (http://www.2wire .com/links/areacode) availability.

StarBand (sold through the DISH Network) and DirecWay (from DirecTV) are satellite options. You can get them anywhere you live, as long as you have a rooftop with a clear view of the southern sky (where their satellites are).

Terrestrial wireless networks are another option. Nextel and Sprint have extensive coverage in many urban areas. To see what your wireless broadband options are, visit http://www.bbwexchange.com/wisps/.

If your local phone service costs too much, you do have options. Some areas have *Competitive Local Exchange Carriers* (CLECs), including your local cable television company, which may offer lower rates. Other consumers give up their (wire-line) telephones to take advantage of cell phone rates that include packages of "free" minutes. Qualified low-income households can take advantage of *lifeline service* that provides discounts on local service.

Custom local area signaling services (CLASS) include automatic redialing of the last party you called, or the last party that called you, and a second-number option (one line answers to two different numbers, sometimes known as the "teen line"). Other features act like a private social secretary. Caller ID and voice mail are the most popular of these. You can also select parties who will ring through, or reject calls from those (such as telemarketers) who don't identify themselves. Some features, such as automatically redialing the last party who called (an aggressive way to discourage crank callers), can be activated on a per-call basis without monthly fees. The intelligent network also automatically looks up the address associated with the number when you call for help—that's enhanced 911—or call you if there is danger near—reverse 911.

Digital subscriber lines (DSL) are your telephone company's entry into the broadband Internet market. They boast data speeds from 128,000 to as many as 18 million bits per second over conventional phone lines. The closer you are, the faster the connection. DSL service includes a full-featured telephone link so that users can talk on the phone and connect to the Internet at the same time. Unlike cable modem service, DSL is a dedicated connection so that a slower DSL line may sometimes perform better than a nominally faster cable connection (see "Technology Demystified: Our Internet Connection Options," above).

Wireless Services

Cell phone customers have a bewildering range of options. The basic variables are whether the cell phone itself is included in the deal, whether long-distance minutes are included or charged at a per-minute rate, the size of the basic monthly fee, and the number of "free" monthly minutes that are included. Other packages include Internet access, CLASS services, and "free" SMS (short message service; see page 361) messaging. But there are many hidden charges that can fatten your bills, such as roaming charges (incurred when you travel outside your local operator's system), premium charges for peak (daytime) calls, activation and disconnection charges, and steep directory assistance charges. Your choices are further clouded by ever-changing "special introductory offers." Fortunately, to sort through your options there are online comparisons of services available in your area (http://www.getconnected.com and http://www.letstalk.com).

There is also the prepaid option if you don't want to tie yourself to a long-term deal. You can buy cards from your cell phone company in set amounts that prepay your calls at an agreed-upon rate. You can also buy disposable prepaid phones with a set amount of air time already paid for.

Since the United States lags behind other countries in cell phone technology we can predict the new options American consumers will have by looking at what is already available elsewhere. Camera phones are here, but those downloads are slow and expensive. The advent of high-speed 3G cell phones will change that and make roving full-motion video conferences possible. Ring tones are also relatively slow and expensive on 2.5G networks; higher speeds will improve that option and also make it easier to download and play recorded music. Mobile commerce (m-commerce for short) will let you point and click your cell phone at the gas pump or refill your money card while on the run. Or how about a "buddy list" for your cell phone so you can broadcast text, voice, and images to your inner circle?

There are also a growing number of wireless options that are not based on cell phone networks. WiFi is spreading from "techie neighborhoods," coffee shops, and airport terminals to cover entire communities. In some areas bands of WiFi enthusiasts (and municipalities) band together to provide free service, but increasingly you pay by the hour for connections. In the technology section we also discussed satellite and terrestrial wireless Internet service options, which are cost-competitive with both wire-line and wireless telephone options.

One option you don't have, at least if you live in the United States, is to make the calling party pay when they call you on your cell phone. That is the norm worldwide and may be an important reason why the United States lags behind other countries.

Long Distance

Long-distance calls are still generally (this is getting to be a very complex issue; see pages 378–380) placed by a completely different company from the one that provides your local service, a long-distance carrier. When customers sign up for local telephone service, they can designate one company as their primary long-distance carrier. Those nagging sales calls from long-distance companies are intended to persuade people to change their designated carriers. Dial-around long-distance services, the ones that make you dial "ten-ten," or an 800 number bypass the designated carrier.

Local toll calls, those that stay within the same area code but that are still billed by the minute, are also competitive now. Consumers must designate a separate carrier for these calls as well. The same company that provides local service can carry the calls, but competing companies may offer lower rates.

Long distance has long been billed by the minute with the rate depending upon the time of day and the day of the week, but that is changing fast. Newer calling plans offer a flat per-minute rate for all calls or a certain number of "free" minutes in exchange for a minimum monthly fee. The cheapest long distance calls of all are placed through VOIP providers like Vonage. Although you can make your computer your telephone, many

Courtesy of AT&T

■ PLACING YOUR CALL

Long distance networks are monitored at network control centers like this one.

users find it convenient to place calls through a conventional-looking phone instrument that is either connected to the Internet through a cable modem or the conventional phone network. Vonage and other VOIP providers can pick up the call from your local telephone company and switch it through the Internet where it rings through to a conventional phone on the other end. For totally free long distance calling on the Internet you have to arrange in advance with your calling partner and have their Internet (IP) address, rather than their telephone number, handy. No one should be paying more than a dime a minute these days, and some rates go as low as two cents a minute.

There is one notable exception. Pay phones charge as much as *two dollars* a minute and tend to be located where there are vulnerable populations, such as college students away from home for the first time, who have no phones of their own and perhaps also no idea of current competitive rates. To avoid exorbitant charges, many travelers use a calling card so that calls are billed through their designated primary carrier, at a substantial savings over pay-phone rates.

Toll-free calls are also provided by long-distance carriers. These are so popular that the original block of 800 numbers is exhausted, so now 888 and 877 prefixes are also used. These are not really free calls. The charges are reversed and callers ultimately pay for them in the price of the products they order. There are also personal 800 numbers, a popular option with college students, since it allows them to call home and automatically bill their parents.

Cable Services

In Chapter 8 we described the various cable-service options of basic, pay, and pay-per-view television, and above we encountered some new ones, including digital cable, video on demand, and cable modem connections. Now, many cable operators offer local phone service as well. Cable telephony provides POTS and custom calling services, just like any local telephone company does, except that your conversation is carried on the same coaxial cable that brings you CNN and HBO, often using the latest VOIP technology.

Cable operators also bundle their services just like phone companies do, except they call the bundles *tiers*. By law, they must offer a basic tier of service that includes all the local TV stations. Many offer additional tiers of basic service, combined with packages of multiple pay channels and the new digital cable services. Now Internet, cable modem, and phone services are added to the package.

However, there is growing recognition that customers have become more sophisticated, so now the search is on for bundles of services that will appeal to particular target market segments. Putting this in terms we have used in other chapters, this is the shift from *mass marketing* to *niche marketing*.

THE INDUSTRY: THE TELECOM MOSAIC

The infrastructure industry is a complex one thanks to historic restrictions on the types of businesses that companies could enter. Industry organization is changing in the wake of the Telecommunications Act of 1996, but a complicated, almost bewildering, mosaic of firms has emerged thus far.

Too Many Telephone Companies!

Telephone companies can be roughly divided into three categories based on the scope of the calls they were traditionally allowed to carry: international, long-distance, and local

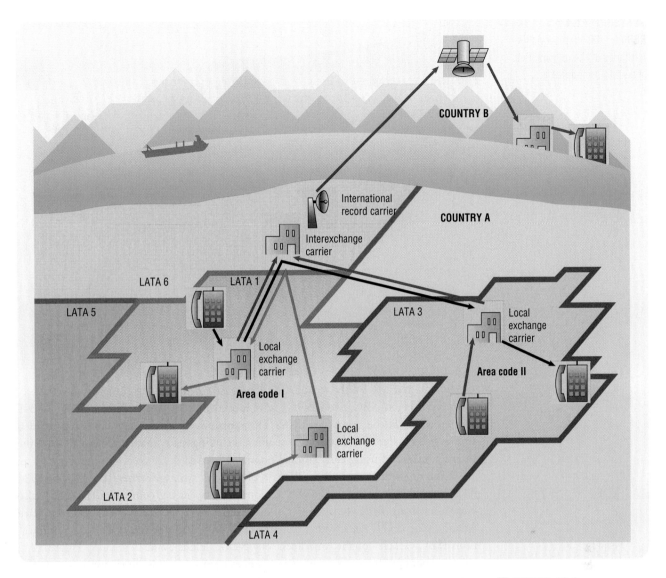

International
record carrier

Interexchange
carrier

COUNTRY B

COUNTRY A

LATA 6   LATA 1

LATA 5

LATA 3   Local
exchange
carrier

Local
exchange
carrier

Area code II

Area code I

Local
exchange
carrier

LATA 2

Local
exchange
carrier

LATA 4

■ **FIGURE 12.3**

LATA   Calls within a LATA are
completed by a local exchange
carrier. Calls between LATAs are
handled by interexchange or
long-distance carriers whether or
not both parties are in the same
area code. International calls are
handed off to international
record carriers.

(Figure 12.3, above). The distinctions are becoming quite ragged because the Telecommunications Act was intended to eliminate them. For example, Verizon, a local telephone company, now provides long-distance service to many of its customers as well and is now the third-ranking consumer long distance company as well as the second largest cell phone company nationwide.

International record carriers (IRCs) handle long-distance calls between countries. Once, every nation had a single international long-distance carrier. That was AT&T in the United States. Now MCI and Sprint compete with AT&T for international traffic, and many other countries have also instituted competition in international long distance.

Interexchange carriers (IXCs, in telephone industry jargon) carry domestic long-distance telephone calls. Long-distance calls include those that are made between area codes (such as between Grand Rapids, area code 616, and Detroit, area code 313) and those completed within area codes that cross *local access and transport area* (LATA) boundaries. These boundaries were set during the AT&T divestiture to demark local from long-distance calls. Adding to the confusion are new overlay area codes, such as 679 in Detroit. These are added in cities where all the available phone numbers have been exhausted. They require users to dial the area code to complete a local phone call.

AT&T and MCI only account for about a third of the U.S. long-distance households. Verizon and SBC, two RBOCs, have moved ahead of MCI. With the SBC-AT&T merger, SBC will be the largest IXC. The remaining long-distance market is divided among 700 smaller long-distance companies, including many that complete calls over the Internet instead of using conventional phone networks.

Local telephone service is the domain of the *local exchange carriers* (LECs). The 1984 AT&T divestiture established seven Regional Bell operating companies (RBOCs), also known as "baby Bells" or *telcos* for short, which have merged to four: Verizon (Bell Atlantic plus NYNEX), Qwest (formerly U.S. West), Southwestern Bell Communications (SBC, which bought Ameritech and Pacific Telesis), and BellSouth (Figure 12.4, above). About 1400 local independent telephone companies survive that were never affiliated with the Bell system. The largest of these, GTE Corporation, joined forces with Bell Atlantic to form Verizon. Now that there are competing local carriers, these incumbent LECs are known as ILECs.

Competitive local exchange carriers (CLECs) compete with the incumbent local exchange carriers. One of the main thrusts of the 1996 Telecom Act was to make it possible for the alts, as they are sometimes known, to provide competition in the local loop where the RBOCs still had monopolies. There are dozens of CLECs in every state (your state **public service** or **public utilities commission** is a good place to check for your options). Many went into business at the height of the dot-com boom to offer high-speed DSL connections, then quickly went out of business when boom turned to bust. The more successful ones, including one operated by Time Warner, cater primarily to large businesses.

AT&T and MCI also provide local service in areas where the local phone companies have opened their networks to competition. They do not own the local lines themselves, but rather lease them at a discounted rate from the local phone company and then resell them to the public. However, a recent court decision (see "Media Literacy: Service for Everyone?," page 383) may put an end to this practice.

Public service commissions regulate telecommunications at the state level.

The King of Cable

Name: Brian L. Roberts

Education: Wharton School, University of Pennsylvania

Position: President, Comcast Cable

Style: Warm family guy in private. In business, as *Fortune* magazine said, he's a "stone cold killer."

Greatest Achievement: At a 1997 meeting with Microsoft Chairman Bill Gates, Gates wondered aloud what would make the industry build digital cable systems faster. Brian asked, "Why don't you buy 10% of the industry?" And Gates did buy 10%—of Brian's company.

Most Dubious Achievement: His dad (sins of a dynastic family fall on the son) invented the music video channel by turning a camera on a goldfish bowl and playing music in the background.

BRIAN L. ROBERTS

Inspiration: His father, Comcast founder Ralph Roberts

Entry Level: Brian was born into one of cable's great "ruling families" but had to climb his way to the top in his daddy's firm, literally. His first job was "pole climber," a cable installation technician who climbed telephone poles to hook up customers in Trenton, New Jersey.

How He Got To The Top: He moved up through progressively important jobs inside Comcast. He was named president in 1990, replacing his father, who moved up to chairman.

Where Does He Go from Here? Now he wants to challenge the telephone giants by offering telephone service over his cable networks. Or, has he bitten off more than he can chew?

Source: "The first family of cable," *Fortune;* New York; Oct. 29, 2001; John Helyar; 137–142; "The cable guys," *Time;* New York; July 23, 2001; Adam Cohen; 32–33.

Cable Companies

Most systems are owned by cable multiple system operators (MSOs). Comcast is by far the largest with over 21 million subscribers. The top 5—Comcast along with Time Warner, Charter Communications, Cox Cable, and Adelphia—collectively control over two-thirds of all cable homes. Large MSOs use their market power to negotiate substantial discounts on programming fees and equipment purchases. They also set corporate-wide policy on local programming and pricing and marketing strategies and often make decisions about which cable networks are carried on local systems.

In some 9500 individual communities, local systems pick up broadcast and satellite signals and relay them to subscribers in their respective franchise areas. Cable programming services charge the local cable operator monthly fees for the right to deliver their programming to the home. Many systems sell advertising slots on basic channels to local advertisers in their communities. Home shopping channels pay cable operators a commission on the sales generated in their franchise areas. The parent MSO expects each local system to turn a profit from its subscription and advertising fees and home shopping commissions after paying out programming fees, local operating expenses, taxes, and the municipal franchise fee.

In most states, cable is regulated at the municipal or county level. New Jersey and Connecticut opted for statewide regulation. Local regulation is usually delegated to a city

■ PIZZA, ANYONE?
A pizza-size satellite dish on the outside means that Direct Broadcast Service (DBS) television may be found inside.

employee who is advised by a local cable commission. These commissions monitor the performance of their cable companies when local franchises come up for renewal. Cable operators are assessed a franchise fee by the municipality. The standard fee is 5 percent of total revenues after taxes. Those fees are passed directly through to cable subscribers; they are itemized as the "franchise fee" on the monthly bill.

Mobile Carriers

Mobile carriers include various paging and radio telephone services, but cellular radio is the biggest. Analog cellular networks have two competing providers in each market, but one is usually the local wire-line telephone company; that makes the RBOCs major providers. The largest cell phone company is Cingular, a joint venture of Verizon and Vodaphone (a British cell phone company) that recently bought up the former number one, AT&T Wireless. Sprint PCS, T-Mobile, and Nextel also have national cellular networks. In 1995, the FCC opened a new block of mobile telephone frequencies for a digital personal communication service, or digital cellular, and expanded the number of licensees from two to five in each market in order to increase competition. Now mobile phones are becoming popular enough—and cheap enough—to provide some competition in the local exchange.

Satellite Carriers

Most of the leading broadcast and cable networks are distributed by two dominant carriers, Pan Am Sat and GE Americom. They build, launch, and maintain the satellites and lease transponders to the likes of CBS, CNN, and PBS. Direct broadcast satellite (DBS) operator DirecTV contracts with Hughes Satellite, and the Dish Network uses EchoStar for its satellite networks. Together, DirecTV and EchoStar count a fifth of the homes in the United States as subscribers. INTELSAT and INMARSAT are two international consortia that handle television, voice, and data traffic. The former specializes in transmissions to fixed ground stations, and the latter provides mobile service. Comsat is the U.S. representative in both consortia.

Private Networks

Finally, many large organizations operate their own private networks. These include connections between their own internal *local area* networks (LANs) and phone networks (PBXs) and public networks and also high-capacity links (for example, T1s) between their major locations. In some cases, the organizations build and operate the transmission systems end-to-end. In other cases, they lease dedicated circuits that only they can use from telecommunication carriers. For example, the major television networks lease satellite circuits from satellite carriers to distribute programming to their owned-and-operated and affiliate stations. Another arrangement is the virtual private network (VPN) wherein they lease capacity from telecom carriers on the carriers' own networks, but not dedicated physical links. Some of the private networks are quite extensive, covering thousands of locations in dozens of countries and employing hundreds of workers to run and maintain them.

STOP & REVIEW

1. How were each of the limitations of the first telephones overcome?
2. What are the important trends in mobile communications?
3. What are the basic options for home Internet access?
4. Define and distinguish the following terms: IXC, LEC, CLEC, RBOC, IRC.
5. What is the function of a cable MSO?

■ **UNIVERSAL SERVICE?**
The promise of affordable telephone service for all has still not been kept for all Americans. Many people still have to rely on pay phones to make their calls.

MEDIA LITERACY: SERVICE FOR EVERYONE?

The main issues confronting society regarding the infrastructure industry still revolve around fulfilling the Kingsbury Commitment (see page 359): how to provide affordable service to all.

The Political Economy of Telecommunications

The Telecommunications Act of 1996 was intended to untangle ownership rules and line-of-business restrictions and let free market forces prevail. The hope was that industry structure would remain fluid and that competition and continuing technological change would drive down prices. Many would argue that the promise of competition is still largely unfulfilled. The principal result has been growing vertical and horizontal concentration in the telecommunications, computer, mass media, and information industries.

The Telecom Act dangled the "carrot" of entry into the long-distance arena over the heads of the RBOCs, if they would open their local monopolies by leasing facilities to competitors at reasonable rates. Most states now allow the RBOCs in the long-distance business. However, in 2004 a federal court struck down the requirement to offer the discounts. That means that competitive providers who do not own their own local networks, but rather lease them from RBOCs, may eventually be driven out of business. With the RBOCs already competing in the long-distance business and without the ability to become "one stop" telecommunication providers in the wake of the new ruling, it is likely that many long-distance companies may leave the residential long-distance business to concentrate on more profitable business customers. Indeed, that was one of the factors that forced AT&T into a merger deal with SBC in 2005.

That could wipe out the only benefit that consumers have experienced from the Telecom Act thus far: lower long-distance rates. Local phone rates have also dropped recently, but may rise again as competition dwindles. And, cable companies will be tempted to subsidize their entry into the local phone business by jacking up cable television rates—increases that have greatly exceeded the rate of inflation since the passage of the Telecom Act.

Whose Subsidies Are Unfair?

The infrastructure industry is riddled with subsidies for corporations and certain classes of users. Most are vestiges of old regulations, but they are difficult to root out.

Before it was broken up in 1984, AT&T diverted revenues from long-distance to subsidize local telephone service with the regulators' blessing. After the divestiture, *access fees* were built into long-distance phone bills. The fees flowed back to local carriers through a four-cent-per-minute charge added to long-distance calls. When per-minute long-distance rates dipped into the single digits, it was because access fees were shifted from long-distance calls to monthly charges on local phone bills. Now universal service fees have returned to long-distance bills with a vengeance, only in the form of a 7–12 percent surcharge tacked onto your long-distance bill instead of per-minute charges.

There is one privileged group that does not have to pay access fees—Internet service providers (ISPs). They operate millions of telephone lines through which their subscribers dial in to the Internet. Some argue that this unfairly burdens people without computers, forcing them to subsidize Internet users. Some policy makers want a modem tax that would equalize the burden, but others fear that this would only drive low-income homes—and many libraries and schools—away from the Internet. And, even the slightest rumor of a modem tax galvanizes the Internet community to deluge Congress with abusive e-mail.

Internet telephony rips through a complex fabric of public subsidies. As Internet data, they are transformed in the eyes of the Federal Communications Commission from "basic" telecommunication services that should contribute fees to universal service programs to "enhanced" information services that have no such obligations. International Internet calls evade the surcharges that countries impose on calls that cross their borders. Those who still call on public phone networks must offset these lost revenues, subsidizing Internet users who use the same networks.

Some users are subsidized as a matter of social policy. Low-income households get special low phone rates. Rural subscribers pay the same rates as city residents even though it costs much more to serve them. Now there is a move to "de-average" telephone rates so that they will match the true cost of service. That sounds fair, doesn't it? But it may drive many rural residents off the network. And, all residential phone subscribers are subsidized by businesses. Should that subsidy be eliminated, too? Ouch. Subsidies always seem unfair until it is *our* subsidy that is taken away.

Preserving Universal Service

How should we ensure affordable phone access for all? Telephone access is a necessity in low-income households, a reality recognized by public assistance programs, which include telephone service among the basic utilities covered by welfare payments. The low monthly rate offered through *lifeline service* is another option to assist low-income households. However, the rise in local telephone rates since the AT&T divestiture limits telephone penetration in low-income households, and many also have credit problems that prevent them from obtaining telephone service (Mueller & Schement, 1995). Thus, although phones are found in 94 percent of all American homes, that figure falls to 85 percent in African-American homes. And, in rural areas some phone companies now refuse to connect remote homes.

How will universal access be assured in a truly competitive environment? Won't new companies naturally cater to businesses and well-off consumers who yield the greatest profits? The Telecommunications Act of 1996 pledges to maintain the concept of *universal service*. However, mechanisms for subsidizing it—such as making all telecommunications companies pay into a common fund—have yet to be finalized.

The Internet raises the question of expanding the definition of universal service beyond basic telephone service to data communications, computers, and information services. In 1998, the E-Rate program was established by the FCC to grant discounts of up to 90 percent for Internet access technologies such as T1 lines to libraries and schools.

Nine out of 10 public schools are now connected to the Internet as a result. But the initiative does not provide maintenance or training, nor does it extend access to the homes of the disadvantaged, and it has become scandal-ridden.

The costs of all universal service schemes are ultimately passed back to the consumer, bringing the problem of affordable access full circle. Some policy makers believe that universal service fees are incompatible with the free market philosophy of the Telecommunications Act and that disadvantaged populations would be better served by the more competitive prices that an unregulated market should theoretically provide. But will they?

Who Owns the Airwaves?

Historically, licenses to use communication frequencies were awarded by the FCC in competitive proceedings to the companies that were best qualified to operate in the public interest (see Chapter 14). Now that free markets are "in" and regulation is "out," auctions have replaced competitive licensing. Licenses for the new digital cellular systems were handled this way, for example. Less government bureaucracy is needed to monitor the new system, and the proceeds from the auctions go into the public treasury, so theoretically they reduce the tax burden for all.

However, auctions also mean less government influence in achieving important social goals such as equitable access and diversity. The auction proceeds have been unpredictable and subject to speculation. Some "winning" bidders have been bankrupted by the exorbitant sums they paid, whereas other auctions have seen valuable spectrum space go for bargain-basement prices. The new policy has also been applied unevenly and perhaps unfairly. When broadcasters were given new channels for digital television service, they received the frequencies at no charge and with few "strings" attached.

The United States is facing a severe shortage of frequencies for mobile communications. The FCC wants to open TV channels 60 to 69 for mobile applications, but the broadcasters who currently occupy that part of the spectrum are demanding billion-dollar sums. The FCC would also like to reallocate 40 more TV channels when broadcasters give them up in the transition to digital broadcasting, in 2007. But broadcasters are dragging their feet, prompting the FCC to consider imposing spectrum usage fees if they hold onto them after the deadline. Another possibility is to open up a secondary market for communication frequencies so that companies that are underutilizing theirs could lease them out for other purposes. Spectrum space for wireless communication is also limited by military needs. For example, the new WiFi wireless Internet services interfere with military radar. Military applications occupy about 60 percent of the usable communications spectrum overall.

All of Our Circuits Are . . . Destroyed

An information society is inherently dependent on the functioning of its communications infrastructure. The September 11, 2001, terror attacks demonstrated both the vulnerability and the resiliency of the telecommunications infrastructure. The World Trade Center was a major hub for telecommunications. The falling towers destroyed telephone switching equipment serving 175,000 customers in lower Manhattan, cell phone and broadcast antennas atop the Twin Towers, and fiber-optic links in the Trade Center's basement that carried Internet traffic from as far away as Washington, D.C.

Still, emergency 911 phone service never went down, and portable cell phone towers were quickly trucked in to restore service near Ground Zero. The disaster proved that packet switching, a system that had been originally designed to survive a nuclear war, could indeed effectively reroute Internet traffic around damaged areas. When long-distance phone

lines became jammed with callers trying to reach relatives in Manhattan, AT&T technicians were able to open lines for outgoing calls with a few taps on their keyboards. Verizon technicians were also able to quickly reroute lines for use by government and emergency officials (Guernsey, 2001).

However, the same network control centers that helped manage the 9/11 emergency are themselves potential targets. Accessing telephone company computer systems is the dream of hackers and terrorists alike.

© Matthew McDermott/Corbis Sygma

■ **EMERGENCY 9/11**
The World Trade Center attacks highlighted the vulnerability of American's telecommunications infrastructure.

Big Brother Is Listening

The 9/11 attacks also produced some changes in telecommunications surveillance laws. As any devotee of television cop shows knows, law enforcement can listen in on phone conversations and read your e-mail only if they have a warrant from a local judge that establishes a probable cause (that is, that probable evidence that a crime will be discovered) for their search. About 1300 wiretaps a year are authorized in the United States for criminal investigations, mostly for drug-related crimes. However, information about the time and destination of calls (sometimes called trap-and-trace information) is considered less private and is easier to obtain—law enforcement merely has to certify that it is needed for an investigation, with no hearing or probable cause required. The police, the FBI, the Drug Enforcement Administration, and the 19 other federal agencies can also sweep entire telephone exchanges and zero in on individual voices or key words. Ordinary telephone subscribers can activate the call trace feature that automatically forwards the telephone number of harassing callers to the authorities.

Digital technology complicated telephone surveillance. If the police tap an Internet connection, all they hear is computer noise, not "I'll send you the plans for the nuclear power plant next Tuesday." Copper wires are easy to tap since they radiate electromagnetic energy that can be readily intercepted, but fiber-optic lines are untappable without physically cutting into them. This led law enforcement officials to request—and receive—special access ports to digital networks in the telephone central offices and to devise the Carnivore system to sweep through e-mail.

In the aftermath of the September 11 attacks Congress passed the U.S.A. Patriot Act (see also Chapter 14), which significantly expanded the scope of surveillance. Trap-and-trace authority has been extended to the Internet so that now law officers can demand to see records of the websites you visited and even track the search terms you type into Google without obtaining a warrant. The FBI and the CIA can now conduct nationwide roving wiretaps without going through local courts or even naming specific suspects. The law seems to contain loopholes that would allow domestic law enforcement agencies to circumvent restrictions placed on them by claiming the search is covered by the Foreign Intelligence Surveillance Act, under which warrants are issued in secret. Similarly, national security agencies might circumvent the limits on them by obtaining information from domestic law enforcement agencies. The Act also includes a new definition of "domestic terrorism" that might be broad enough to include legitimate protest activity (EFF, 2001). Although we all hope these measures will help crack down on terrorists, civil libertarians fear this legislation could usher in a future society, patterned after George Orwell's *1984,* that will routinely monitor the movements and words of all citizens.

Private Lines

So we can't be sure the government isn't listening in on our conversations, but what about our nosy neighbors? The Electronic Communication Privacy Act (ECPA) generally assures us that our wire-line conversations cannot be tapped or recorded without our permission or legal authorization.

However, the issue of telephone privacy is a complex one, depending upon the technology we use and where we use it. If we use a cordless phone, we lose our legal right to privacy. That's because the frequencies that cordless phones use are in the easily accessible FM radio spectrum and are readily intercepted.

If we use a cell phone the electronic transmission is protected even though older model scanners can tune in. By law, newer scanners can't access the cell phone frequencies. That law was enacted precisely to preserve the expectation of cell privacy. But if we carry on our cell phone conversations in a public space we may lose that expectation. In addition to being rude, we are making public utterances that can be intercepted and recorded, and a sensitive microphone might also pick up the voice of the person we are talking to through our handset.

A new privacy threat comes from cell phone locator services. Cell phone providers have been required to deploy technology that makes it possible to pinpoint the location of cell phones. That's so that emergency 911 calls can be traced back to their origin. But cell phone companies eager to cash in on their investment may sell information about your location to nearby businesses ("Hello, there is a sale on zircon rings just around the corner from you!") or to suspicious spouses or nosy neighbors.

On the plus side, the Federal Trade Commission has finally gotten around to establishing a do-not-call list under the Telephone Consumer Protection Act, passed back in 1991. Now you can sign up online to have your phone number protected from telemarketing calls. Violators face fines of $11,000 per call. However, nonprofit organizations, pollsters, market researchers, and companies that you have a prior relationship with (such as your long-distance company) are exempt.

STOP & REVIEW

1. What has been the impact of the Telecom Act?
2. What are the main issues in spectrum allocation?
3. Why are phone calls completed over the Internet so cheap?
4. How is universal service implemented in the United States?
5. How secure are the infrastructure networks we rely on?
6. Is digital technology a help or a hindrance to law enforcement?

SUMMARY AND REVIEW

WHAT WERE THE EARLY ORIGINS OF TODAY'S TELECOMMUNICATIONS INFRASTRUCTURE?

Morse's telegraph and Bell's telephone were the first electronic communications networks. They spawned newspaper wire services and audio information services that were the first electronic mass media.

WHAT ROLE DID AT&T PLAY?

Bell founded the company that was to become American Telephone and Telegraph (AT&T). AT&T's effort to monopolize the infrastructure by buying the Western Union Telegraph Company led to government regulation that shaped the entire telecommunications industry for decades. Important interventions included the Communications Act of 1934 and the Modified Final Judgment (MFJ) of 1984 that forced AT&T to divest itself of the companies (Regional Bell operating companies, RBOCs) that provided local telephone service, while retaining its long-distance network.

SUMMARY AND REVIEW

HOW DID WIRELESS TELECOMMUNICATIONS DEVELOP?
Although mobile telephone service dates back to 1946, early systems were plagued by insufficient capacity. Paging services originated in the early 1960s to meet some of the demand for mobile communication. In 1978 cellular radio service was introduced in the United States, expanding the capacity of mobile telephone networks.

HOW DID CABLE SPREAD THROUGHOUT THE UNITED STATES?
Cable television started as a community antenna service for rural communities in 1948. It expanded into suburban areas beginning in 1972, reaching the largest cities in the early 1980s.

HOW WERE THE TECHNICAL LIMITATIONS OF THE FIRST TELEPHONES OVERCOME?
The first phones were very limited in their range, connectivity, and ease of use. Amplifiers and carrier systems overcame the limitations of distance and untangled the maze of wires that darkened the skies over major cities. The capacity of telephone networks has continually improved with microwave, satellite, and fiber-optic transmission systems. Meanwhile, advances in switching technology gradually reduced the labor intensiveness of the telephone network and made it possible for telephone subscribers to dial numbers anywhere in the world automatically. Digital communication first came to the telephone in 1962, making possible further improvements in capacity and transmission quality and ultimately leading to such "intelligent network" services as caller ID.

HOW ARE CABLE TELEVISION PICTURES TRANSMITTED TO THE HOME?
The cable operator's headend picks up transmissions from satellite, microwave, broadcast, and local studio sources. The channels are combined electronically and transmitted over a coaxial cable network to the home. A set-top converter is used to recover the channels and play them on the home television receiver. Pay TV signals may be scrambled so that only homes that pay an additional monthly fee may receive them. New addressable cable systems make it possible to electronically authorize the reception of entire pay channels or specific programs, a type of distribution called pay-per-view.

WHAT ROLE MIGHT WIRELESS COMMUNICATIONS PLAY IN THE FUTURE?
Digitization has also meant vast improvements in the capacity and quality of wireless networks for mobile communications. Third-generation (3G) systems should make wireless Internet access commonplace. IEEE802.11b (WiFi) is a competing wireless Internet technology. New satellites with low earth orbits and the opening of new frequencies for terrestrial communication make wireless technologies possible contenders in the battle to build the information superhighway.

WHAT TELEPHONE SERVICES ARE AVAILABLE TODAY?
Local telephone service extends beyond plain old telephone service. Custom calling features made possible by the intelligent network, such as caller ID, give users a large measure of control over their communications. Digital subscriber lines (DSL) are aimed at heavy Internet users. There is a growing variety of options in both long-distance and mobile calling plans that allow subscribers to trade off monthly minimum fees for the number of "free" calls they are allowed.

HOW IS THE INFRASTRUCTURE INDUSTRY ORGANIZED?
Telephone companies are classified according to the scope of the calls they are permitted to carry. Local exchange carriers (LECs) can carry local calls, whereas interexchange carriers (IXCs) carry domestic long-distance calls, and international record carriers (IRCs) carry international calls. Local access and transport areas (LATAs), established under the terms of the AT&T divestiture, distinguish local and long-distance calls. Competitive local exchange carriers (CLECs) are a new type of telephone carrier permitted to carry local telephone calls in competition with an established local exchange carrier.

HOW IS THE CABLE INDUSTRY ORGANIZED?
Most local cable systems are owned by multiple system operators (MSOs) and purchase their programming from the various basic, pay, and pay-per-view networks, predicated on monthly per-subscriber affiliate fees. The local systems also sell advertising on basic cable channels. Some MSOs own interests in programming services as well as in the local systems that distribute them to the public. Regulatory oversight is provided by local cable franchise authorities and the FCC.

WHY IS THERE A TREND TOWARD MORE COMPETITION?
Policy makers hope that competition will mean lower prices and more advanced and faster services for the telecommunications consumer. They believe that competition is the best way to create the so-called information superhighway and preserve the universal service principle.

WHAT IS THE SIGNIFICANCE OF UNIVERSAL SERVICE IN THE INFORMATION AGE?
Universal service is the promise of affordable telecommunications access for all. However, that promise has not been achieved for minority and low-income populations. Telecommunications deregulation now threatens access in rural areas as well and has made universal services a promise without a definitive plan of action.

WHAT IS THE SIGNIFICANCE OF THE TELECOMMUNICATIONS ACT OF 1996?

The aim of the Telecommunications Act was to remove most of the regulations that apply to telecommunications infrastructure industries and replace regulation with competition. However, the immediate impact of the act was to trigger a wave of consolidation within the industry while local telephone companies continued to resist competition.

WHAT CHALLENGES DOES THE INFRASTRUCTURE POSE FOR SOCIETY?

Society must decide how to allocate scarce resources, such as the communications spectrum, to competing interests. The growing reliance on the information infrastructure makes society increasingly vulnerable to technical disruption of telecommunications providers. Advanced digital technology also poses barriers to the legitimate electronic surveillance needs of law enforcement officials while at the same time raising the specter of excessive snooping on ordinary citizens.

MEDIA CONNECTION

For web links, quizzes, and key term flash cards, visit the **Student Companion Website** at http://communication.wadsworth.com/straubhaar5.

1pass™ For unlimited easy access to additional and exclusive online study, support, and research tools, log on to **1pass** at http://1pass.thomson.com using the unique access code found on your 1pass passcode card.

 The **Media Now Premium Website** offers *Career Profile* videos, *Critical View* video news clips, and *Media in Motion* concept animations. You'll also find Stop & Review tutorial questions, a sample final exam, and much more.

 InfoTrac College Edition is a fully searchable online database offering anytime, anywhere access to more than 20 years' worth of articles from nearly 5,000 diverse and reliable sources.

 vMentor provides live, one-on-one online tutoring to connect you to experts who will assist you in understanding the concepts covered in your course.

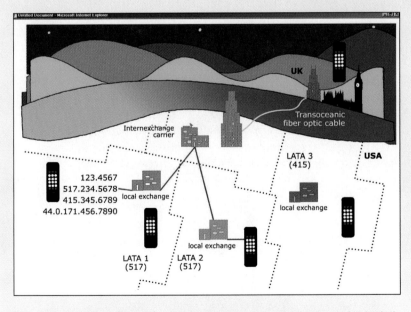

For an animated look at how the LATA zones discussed in this chapter work, watch the Media in Motion animation of them on the website.

13

Video games are fun, but are they bad for you? The impact of media violence on children is one of the controversial issues about the relationship between media and society that we will examine in this chapter.

Why do we spend thousands of hours every year with the communications media, and what is the cumulative impact of that exposure on ourselves and our society? In this chapter we review the research methods, theories, and key findings that attempt to answer those questions and examine the broader implications of media consumption for society at large.

BASHING THE MEDIA

"Media bashing" is a recurring ritual. Media critics point to new evidence of harmful media effects in the endless stream of violence, sex, and hate that they see pouring forth from the media. The talk shows and editorial columns buzz, and Congressional hearings are held. The media criticize the research, blame the parents, say it's not their job to fix society, retreat behind the First Amendment (see Chapter 14), and promise to regulate themselves better. Then the debate simmers down until the next study comes out. What does the research really tell us, and how much can we rely on it?

The latest round came after the breast-baring incident involving singer Janet Jackson before a Super Bowl halftime show audience that included millions of young children. The sense of public outrage was so great that, for once, the contrite television executives

1898	Newspaper publisher William Randolph Hearst summons the United States to war— "Remember the Maine!"	**1975**	Under FCC pressure, broadcasters adopt the "family hour" to provide wholesome early-evening TV programming
1932	U.S. movie industry institutes voluntary censorship	**1986**	Meese Commission reports on the effects of pornography
1933–1945	Nazi propaganda machine holds Germany in thrall	**1990**	Children's Television Act mandates broadcast television programming specifically designed for children
1954	U.S. Senate holds hearings on the effects of television violence on juvenile delinquency		
1960	Klapper concludes media have limited effects	**1998**	TVs equipped with V-chips are introduced
1972	U.S. Surgeon General releases research report on television and social behavior	**2004**	Breast exposure during Super Bowl halftime show triggers media cleanup

Source: Liebert & Sprafkin, 1988

parading before Congress took immediate action. They temporarily reduced the sexual content of prime-time TV scripts and added delays to live broadcasts like the Super Bowl so that indecent content could be "bleeped" in time in the future. The FCC and Congress also acted to increase the fines for broadcasting indecent content and to expand the interpretation of what was indecent, without stopping to ask what harm had actually been done. However, the FCC had to stop short of banning sexual content entirely, since that would infringe on the free-speech rights of broadcasters. By the following fall, the television networks were once again pushing the boundaries of sex on TV shows like *Desperate Housewives*. The FCC also had nothing to say about the intensely violent content that preceded and followed the halftime show and which arguably poses a much greater threat to the children in the audience: the football game itself!

Media effects are changes in cognitions, attitudes, emotions, or behavior that result from exposure to the mass media. The term is often used to denote changes in individuals that are caused by exposure to the media. However, broader impacts on society, as opposed to individual effects, are also of concern to us. And, not all scholars see a cause and effect relationship between media use and human behavior. We will use the term *media impacts* in the broader sense to encompass these varying aspects of the complex relationship between media and society. In this discussion, exposure to the media may itself be considered an impact, since the time we spend with the media itself reflects an effect on our daily lives, a decision to engage in media consumption behavior at the expense of time that might be spent on other activities.

STUDYING MEDIA IMPACTS

There are a variety of approaches for studying such impacts. All the methods have strengths and weaknesses that we need to understand to evaluate their contributions to the media and society debate. First, we will consider some of the contrasting general approaches to understanding media impacts; then we will consider four systematic methods for obtaining evidence of those impacts: content analyses, experiments, surveys, and ethnographies.

Media effects are changes in knowledge, attitudes, or behaviors resulting from media exposure.

Contrasting Approaches

There are several, widely varying basic approaches to interpreting media impacts. These include deductive versus inductive reasoning, critical versus administrative research, and qualitative versus quantitative research.

Many social scientists begin with a theory based on the law of cause and effect. They derive, or deduce, predictions about media impacts from their theories of human behavior and culture and then empirically test these predictions through systematic observation. Their results either support the theory or refute it, which leads to new theoretical paradigms. Thus, they follow the *scientific method.* Mass media exposure is usually viewed as the "cause," or **independent variable.** Exposure to media content is seen as the trigger for mental processes and behaviors that are the "effects." These effects—such as antisocial or prosocial behaviors—are called **dependent variables** (Wimmer & Dominick, 2002). Of course, if we are interested in the prior question of what causes media exposure, then media use becomes the dependent variable and the factors that may cause that exposure such as our gender, our personality, and our beliefs about the benefits of media exposure become the independent variables.

Other scholars observe peoples' real-life interactions with media and with each other and then induce, or infer, theories about those interactions. These include most ethnographers and also many *critical theorists.* Paul Lazarsfeld (1941), one of the pioneers in communications research, was the first to point out the difference between what he called *administrative research,* which takes existing media institutions for granted and documents their use and effects, and *critical research,* which criticizes media institutions themselves from the perspective of the ways they serve dominant social

Independent variables are the causes of media effects.

Dependent variables are the consequences, or effects, of media exposure.

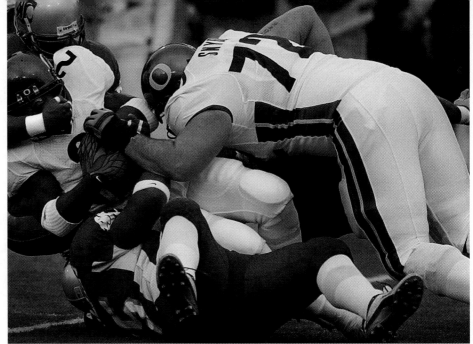

NONVIOLENT?
Despite many sequences in which players are targets of force initiated by other players, football games don't "count" in studies of TV violence.

groups. Most of the research described elsewhere in this chapter, even that which results in "criticism" of the media for excessive sex or violence, falls into the administrative research category, because it fails to critique the basic foundations of existing media institutions. Instead, critical theorists favor interpretive and inductive methods of inquiry drawn from such fields as history, feminist studies, cultural anthropology, Marxist political economic theory, and literary criticism (see Chapter 2).

Some social scientists use quantitative methods to enumerate their findings and analyze statistical relationships between independent and dependent variables. Other scholars infer the relationships from qualitative methods, such as by studying the symbols in media content or observing behavior in natural settings. Yet others believe it is important to combine both sets of methods and look for insights offered by both approaches and points of agreement between them.

Content Analysis

Content analysis characterizes the content of the media. Researchers begin with systematic samples of media content and apply objective definitions to classify its words, images, and themes. For example, what if researchers want to find out whether television has become more violent over the years? They might select a *composite week* of prime-time programming by drawing programs from different weeks of the year to represent each of the shows in the prime-time schedule. They would develop objective definitions of violence, such as "sequences in which characters are depicted as targets of physical force initiated by another character." Trained observers would then classify each of the scenes in the sample of shows and compare notes to make sure that their definitions were consistent. Then the researchers would record the number of violent acts per hour and compare the results with those of previous studies (Gerbner et al., 1994).

Content analyses create detailed profiles of media content and identify trends in content over time. However, they cannot be used to draw conclusions about the effects of the media because the audience often perceives media in a different way than the researchers—or the producers of the content—do. Content analysis is a time-consuming task, so researchers sometimes take only a limited sample (such as one week's worth of prime-time television shows) from major media outlets. That obviously doesn't reflect the

Content analysis is a quantitative description of the content of the media.

full range of content that the audience sees. The definitions can be problematic, too. For example, if a character in a situation comedy slaps another character on the back (which would be a sequence in which a character is the target of physical force initiated by another character) and they begin laughing, is that violence? What if a character is hurt by a hurricane instead of another person? What about a football tackle? According to some definitions these are violent acts; according to others they are not.

A recent content analysis of television violence (Federman, 1998) overcame many of these problems. With multimillion-dollar funding provided by the cable television industry, the researchers examined three entire television seasons, rather than a single composite week, and included 23 different cable television and broadcast networks. They also were very sophisticated in their definitions of violence, examining the context of violent acts—for example, whether the violent behavior was rewarded or punished—rather than simply counting the number of gunshots and body blows.

The researchers found that television continues to be very violent. In all three TV seasons, three-fifths of all prime-time programs contained violence and they averaged over six violent incidents per program per hour. They estimated that preschoolers who watch two hours of television daily witness 10,000 violent acts each year. Most of these involved "high-risk" portrayals that children are likely to imitate, such as violent acts committed by attractive characters in realistic settings in which no harmful consequences are shown. In contrast, only one in 20 programs had antiviolence themes.

Experimental Research

Experimental research studies media effects under carefully controlled conditions. Typically, a small group sees a media presentation that emphasizes one particular type of content. For example, preschool children are shown violent cartoon shows, and their responses are compared with those of preschoolers exposed to media that lack the "active ingredient," for example, nonviolent cartoons.

Experimental subjects must be randomly divided between these groups-such as by flipping a coin—to minimize the impact of individual differences among subjects. If they were not assigned randomly—if the children were simply asked to pick which kind of cartoon they would like to see—the aggressive children might volunteer for the violent ones, and the results would therefore reflect the nature of the children rather than any effect of the media content. The same goes for sex, age, social status, and other variables that might affect the outcome. The randomization process cancels out their effects by putting equal numbers of boys and girls, rich and poor, in each group.

Perhaps the most influential media effects experiments were conducted by Albert Bandura (1965) and his colleagues at Stanford University. They showed preschoolers a short film in which a child actor behaved aggressively toward a Bobo doll, an inflatable doll the size of a small child with the image of a clown printed on its front and sand in its base so that it rocked back and forth when hit (today's children sometimes call them "bop dolls"). The actor in the film, whom Bandura called the model, punched the doll in the nose, hit it with a mallet, kicked it around the room, and threw rubber balls at it. This aggressive sequence was repeated twice in the film.

All of the children saw that part of the action. However, there were three different endings to the film, and the children were randomly divided into groups that each viewed a different one. Children in the "model-rewarded condition" saw an adult actor reward the aggressor with verbal praise, soda, candy, and Cracker Jacks. In the "model-punished condition," the adult scolded the model and spanked him. A third group of children in the "no-consequences condition" saw only the opening sequence.

Experimental research studies the effects of media in carefully controlled situations that manipulate media exposure and content.

© Courtesy of Albert Bandura

▇ TAKE THAT, BOBO

In Bandura's classic experiment on imitation of violence, children were shown a movie (top four frames) of a model hitting a "Bobo" doll. If children saw the model rewarded for this behavior, they treated the doll similarly (middle and bottom rows).

Generalizability is the degree to which research procedures and samples may be generalized to the real world.

Validity is the degree to which we are actually measuring what we intend to measure.

After the show, which the children were told was a TV program, subjects were led to a playroom equipped with a Bobo doll, a mallet, some rubber balls, and assorted other toys. As adult observers watched, many of the children in the model-rewarded and no-consequences conditions imitated the aggressive acts they had seen; those in the model-punished condition tended not to do so. However, even the children in the model-punished condition had learned how to perform the behaviors. When adults offered them candy, they started beating up the Bobo doll, too.

The researchers concluded that the punishment the children experienced vicariously in the model-punished condition inhibited their aggressive behavior. However, the most important finding of the study was that the no-consequences condition also produced imitation. This suggested that mere exposure to television violence—whether or not the violence was visibly rewarded on-screen—could spur aggressive responses in young children.

The value of such a carefully controlled design is that it rules out competing explanations for the results (such as the possibility that subjects who saw the violent endings were more violent children to begin with). Only the endings of the film (also known as the *experimental treatments*) were varied among groups, so that any subsequent differences among them (such as the beatings the subjects inflicted on their own Bobo dolls) could be attributed to the differences in the media content.

However, the small and unrepresentative samples used in experimental studies, which often consist of college students in introductory classes or the small children of university professors, raise questions about **generalizability,** the degree to which the results apply to other populations and settings. The measures that are used (written responses to a questionnaire or highly structured experimental tasks) and the conditions under which the experiments are conducted do not reflect the real-world situations of ultimate interest, such as behavior in an actual child's playroom or on a school playground. This is the issue of *ecological validity.* More generally, **validity** is the degree to which research findings and methods reflect the true phenomena under study, without distortion. For example, college entrance exams are valid predictors of future performance in college only if those who score high on the exams also perform well in college later on. Or, to assess the validity of a paper and pencil measure of aggression, we might compare the results with observations of aggression on the playground. A related concept is **reliability,** the degree to which our methods produce stable, consistent results. For example, if we re-administered a college entrance exam or the aggression measure to the same group of students a week after the first administration, we would expect the individual scores to remain about the same. Researchers have to provide evidence of both validity and reliability when reporting their results.

The experimental treatments may also be unrealistic in that (1) they often involve much more intense sequences of content than are likely to be encountered in the real world, and (2) they are often presented as disjointed segments that do not show the context of the actions. For example, in studies of pornography effects, excerpts from several pornographic films are edited onto a single tape. The edited sequences have a lot more "action" than the original films, which intersperse the sex scenes with some token plot and character development. Moreover, experimental subjects, often recruited from first-year college courses, may be exposed to content that they might not normally see, and that may exaggerate the effects (Anderson & Meyer, 1988).

© Spencer Grant/PhotoEdit

Survey Research

Survey methods also play an important role in media research. For example, researchers interested in the effects of violent video games might administer a questionnaire to a random sample (see "Technology Demystified: The Science of Sampling," page 398) of U.S. schoolchildren. Media effects are inferred by statistically relating the independent measures of media exposure ("How many violent video games have you played in the last week?") to the dependent variable of interest (such as self-reports of violent behavior: "How many fights did you have last week?"). If those who play a lot of video games also get in a lot of fights, and those who do not play many video games are relatively nonviolent, we would say that the two variables are **correlated.**

Survey studies are more generalizable than experimental studies, because their samples may represent larger populations, such as all U.S. schoolchildren in our example. Even if the samples are not strictly representative of a larger population in a statistical sense, they may still add to our understanding of media effects. For example, instead of randomly sampling all U.S. schoolchildren, a very expensive undertaking, we might conduct our survey in several school districts chosen to include children from diverse backgrounds. By extending research to more realistic settings and more diverse populations than in experimental studies, surveys can increase our confidence in the generalizability of the findings. They can also account for a wider range of factors than just media exposure, such as peer pressure to play violent games and religious beliefs that discourage them.

However, survey research provides ambiguous evidence about cause and effect. In our example, it is possible that aggressive children like to play violent video games. In other words, violence causes the playing of video games instead of the other way around.

Reliability is the extent to which a result is stable and consistent.

Correlated means that there is a statistical measure of association between two variables.

Survey studies make generalizations about a population of people by addressing questions to a sample of that population.

TECHNOLOGY DEMYSTIFIED ■■■■■■

The Science of Sampling

Headline: Survey finds 10 percent hooked on the web. "How can that be?" you ask yourself, "*all* the people I know are Internet junkies." The answer to this riddle is the key to the science of sampling. Clearly, one's circle of friends does not adequately represent the opinions of the entire country. Survey researchers could talk to absolutely everyone, conducting a census, but that is prohibitively expensive. By using probability sampling, researchers can get accurate results with far fewer respondents. Telephone interviews are a particularly efficient way to conduct surveys, so let's see how sampling is done for them.

The ideal is to start from a complete sampling frame, a list that includes all members of the population under study. The other important point is to sample the list randomly, so that everyone on the list has an equal chance of being selected. We could cut up all of the phone books in the country, cull the duplicate listings, pack the individual listings in a giant revolving metal drum, and start picking numbers. That would take a drum the size of a cement mixer and would overlook the many homes with unpublished numbers, though, including a large proportion of city dwellers. It also leaves out people who moved since the last phone book came out, and they tend to be young, low-income, and minorities. Researchers, therefore, use random-digit dialing in which a computer generates random telephone numbers so that all telephone subscribers have an equal chance of getting a call.

By following this procedure, researchers can get an accurate response by contacting a relatively small sample, and they can estimate the precision of their findings and also the probability that they are in error. For example, a sample of 400 homes yields a 3 percent margin of error (or *standard error* as it is more properly known) for a question that 10 percent of the respondents say "yes" to (for example, "Are you addicted to the Internet?"). That means the "true" proportion is likely to be somewhere between 7 percent and 13 percent, 10 plus or minus 3. If researchers replicated the survey many times to check its accuracy, the odds are that the results would fall within the range of sampling error 95 percent of the time. The beauty of this approach is its efficiency. The opinions of the entire country can be represented by a few hundred respondents. However, to cut the margin for error in half in our example (to 1.5 percent), surveyors must quadruple the sample size.

These neat calculations overlook a messy problem with surveys; however, the growing number of people who refuse to cooperate with them, or the problem of nonresponse bias. Cooperation rates have plummeted from 80 percent in early phone survey studies to 30 percent recently, and telephone technology trends (for example, caller ID, see Chapter 12) point toward further problems with nonresponse bias.

Some researchers are turning to mail surveys, door-to-door interviews, and web surveys instead. However, these techniques have their own sampling problems. Well-designed mail surveys can achieve the same response rates as phone interviews, but only by paying respondents monetary incentives that may bias the results. And, the sad fact is that 20 percent of the adult population is functionally illiterate and can't read them. There is no comprehensive list of web users and no efficient way to randomly generate e-mail addresses, so probability sampling is impossible there. Door-to-door interviewing still yields high response rates but cost 10 times as much as phone interviews. So, researchers have to economize by cutting their sample sizes, and that increases their sampling error.

It is also possible that both violent behavior and video game use are both caused by some unexamined third variable, such as lax parental supervision. This is the sort of situation in which experimental studies or ethnographic research (see below) might help to sort out the ambiguities.

In media effects research, the most valid surveys are longitudinal studies that survey the same subjects repeatedly over a number of years. Huessmann (1982) asked the parents of eight-year-olds to identify their children's favorite TV programs and asked the children's playmates to rate the children on their antisocial behavior. They recontacted the same families five and 10 years later and re-administered the survey. If the youngsters who watched a lot of television are more violent as teens than the ones who watched relatively little television as children, then we can conclude that childhood television exposure does indeed encourage violent behavior later in life. If some of the teens in the follow-up surveys have subsequently reduced their television viewing but remain violent people, we can rule out the competing explanation that "violent people like violent television." In other words, we can be fairly certain that television causes violent behavior, and rule out the competing explanation that violent people like to watch violence. In fact, that is what Huessmann and his colleagues concluded, although the relationship was found only among boys.

However, very few survey studies are repeated over time; most are just "one-shot" studies that compare media exposure and behavior but ignore the direction of any causal relationship. Even longitudinal studies cannot account for the influence of variables the researchers leave out, such as parental supervision, that might explain both violence and television viewing. We should also note that other longitudinal studies of TV violence have found no effects (Milavsky et al., 1982). Still others have yielded rather puzzling results, including a later study by Huessmann and his associates (Huessmann & Eron, 1986) that showed a violence effect for girls but not for boys. Furthermore, a pattern of inconsistent findings emerged from similar studies in Poland, Finland, Israel, and Australia. This raises the possibility that media effects may not be generalizable across cultures.

■ A HOUSE OF MIRRORS
Focus groups are conducted in front of two-way mirrors that let researchers observe and film the proceedings.

Ethnographic Research

Ethnography is a naturalistic way of looking at the impacts of communications media. It adapts the techniques anthropologists use to look at cultures in a holistic way. Ethnography places media in a broad context of media users' lives and cultures. Sherry Turkle (1995) combined observations of people using the Internet in natural settings like libraries and school computer labs with in-depth explorations conducted in her own office. She assembled a picture of how people use the medium to explore their own identities and create new ones. Other researchers join online communities as participant observers to examine social life in cyberspace.

Focus groups are another way of capturing people "in their own words" through guided group interactions. A group of six to 12 people is gathered in a conference room and led by a skilled moderator as they explore topics of interest to the researcher. Behind a two-way mirror sit microphones, TV cameras, and researchers taking in every word. These are free-flowing, but guided discussions that produce long transcripts rather than neat statistical tables. Social scientists use them to explore new research topics and to help generate questions for surveys. Ethnographers also use them to produce the raw data needed to formulate inductive theories of media processes; for example, to understand the information needs of minority and low-income Internet users. Focus groups have significant flaws, however. Focus group recruiters place hundreds of calls to find a single person willing to come out in the dark of the night to visit a focus group facility, even when they offer substantial monetary incentives. The handful who show up in no way represent the general listening, viewing, or web surfing public. The other problem is with group dynamics. The same discussion process that generates profound insights can also veer into unique concerns that ordinary people would never reach on their own.

Ethnography is a naturalistic research method in which the observer obtains detailed information from personal observation or interviews over extended periods of time.

Although ethnographers sometimes use questionnaires, ethnography is often seen as an alternative to survey research. Surveys make it possible to compare many people through standardized questions, but they may impose response categories on the respondents. That approach yields standardized responses that are easier to tally, but ethnographers value letting people speak in their own words, using their own concepts and categories. Surveys force people to choose among predetermined responses, which raises the issue of validity. Does the forced choice reflect what the respondent really meant to say? Ethnographers let the participants in a study speak in their own words, although the researcher still has to select what to report and interpret what the subjects' words mean.

Ethnographies can yield great depth of information about a particular place at a particular time, but they do not permit much generalization. Although ethnographers try to record information so thoroughly and accurately that others would reach the same conclusions from their data, such reliability, or reproducibility, is hard to achieve. Moreover, ethnographers can get so close to their respondents that they sometimes influence the events they are observing, and bias results. If a researcher got so close to her subjects that they asked her what websites *she* wanted to visit, for example, that could bias the results.

Thus, the different types of research methods tell us different things. Content analyses often show that the media are filled with violence and sex, for example, but tell us nothing about the actual effects on the audience. Experimental studies often find evidence of effects, even from extremely short exposures of 15 minutes or less, but cannot assess how other factors may reduce or enhance those effects. Survey studies use larger, more representative samples than experimental research but seldom reach unambiguous conclusions about the effects of media exposure. Ethnographic studies provide deep insights, but the results are sometimes too subjective and particularistic to duplicate. It is important to explore these issues with a variety of different methods.

THEORIES OF MEDIA EXPOSURE

What medium will I choose today? A video game, iPod, or a textbook? *Media Now* or *Introduction to Calculus?* You obviously picked *Media Now,* but why? To understand media impacts, we need to understand how the media work their way into our lives. Are we uncritical consumers of everything big media companies send our way, or do we actively select content? Theories of media exposure attempt to explain the processes we use to make our daily media consumption decisions.

Uses and Gratifications

The **uses and gratifications** perspective dominates thinking about media consumption behavior. This theory is based on the premise of an active audience (see "Media and Culture: The Active Audience," page 401). Users actively seek out media that meet their needs for new knowledge, social interaction, and diversion.

The various media satisfy differing needs. For example, interpersonal communication is one of the important gratifications that people expect of the Internet (Papacharissi & Rubin, 2000). The websites that fulfill these expectations are thus likely to earn longer visits and repeat viewings. Entertainment needs are more likely to be addressed by Hollywood films or television situation comedies.

Uses and gratifications theory (Palmgreen & Rayburn, 1985) focuses on the match between the gratifications we seek and those we actually obtain from the media. Elihu

Uses and gratifications is the theory that media are actively selected to satisfy our needs.

The Active Audience

Just how powerful are the media relative to their audiences? Some believe that the media have an enormous influence on audiences. For example, Adorno and Horkheimer (1972) saw powerful media propaganda as an explanation for the Holocaust and other brutal acts during World War II. And today, some see the media as powerful carriers of ideology that impose the interests of ruling groups on vulnerable audiences (Chomsky & Herman, 1988), such as by convincing young children that shiny toys are the key to happiness.

The power of the media is limited by processes of selective exposure, selective attention, and selective perception that have been well studied by social scientists. However, this idea of a selective audience parallels a popular notion in **cultural studies** that media and audiences are both powerful. The communication process is a reciprocal activity involving the joint creation of meaning between the author or producer and the person who receives the message and makes sense of it (Downing, Mohammadi, & Sreberny-Mohammadi, 1990). Stuart Hall (1980) redefined encoding as creating a message with verbal, visual, or written codes or symbols that someone else decodes with her or his own understanding of those codes. From this perspective communication involves the exchange of meaning through the language and images that compose the shared culture of participants. The receiver of the communication plays an active role, filtering messages through the lens of his or her own social class, culture, significant groups, and personal experiences (Morley, 1986).

One view of the audience reception process builds on the idea of *reading*. Media producers create texts. Here, "texts" include radio programs, music, television shows, and films as well as printed texts. And, reading is not literally the reading of words but our interpretations of the media. Creators of media content have a preferred reading that they would like the audience to take out of the text. However, the audience might reject it, negotiate some compromise interpretation between what they think and what the text is saying, or contest what the text says with some alternative interpretation (Morley, 1992). The audience response depends on what they, their family, and their friends already think about things. For example, a Republican Party member watching a Republican political ad will agree with it, a Democrat will disagree with it, and an Independent might agree with part and reject part.

Katz (see Media Profile on page 393) is one of the originators of this approach. For example, if we tune in to *Law and Order* expecting to see gripping police drama and this week's show features some tense scenes in the "interview room," our expectations are met and we are likely to come back next week. Another viewer's expectation might be for a pleasant diversion, in which case the same scenes might arouse unwelcome tension and cause him to switch channels. According to this theory, we arrive at our media consumption decisions by performing a mental calculation in which we compare the gratifications we obtain with those we seek from all of the media alternatives available to us, taking into account all of the needs (for example, for diversion, information, companionship) that are relevant to us at a given moment.

Our media behavior changes all the time because the gratifications we seek from the media are in a constant state of flux. We encounter new media that raise new expectations. Our life situation may change and with it the criteria we use to select media. At some stages of our lives we may seek media that entertain; at other times information may be more of a priority. And, the different media vary with respect to the gratifications they provide us. For example, television is associated with entertainment, whereas the Internet is more related to information seeking (see Table 13.1).

Cultural studies argues that media and audiences work together to define culture.

Learning Media Behavior

Uses and gratifications parallels **social learning theory** (Bandura, 1986) to some extent, except that our expectations are said to form around outcomes of behavior rather than the gratification of needs. The outcome could be the feeling of joy we experience after

Social learning theory explains media effects in terms of imitating behavior seen in the media.

Table 13.1 Uses and Gratifications of Television and the Internet

I watch TV . . .	I use the Internet . . .
Because it entertains me	Because it's easier
Because it's enjoyable	To look for information
Because it relaxes me	To get information for free
Because it is a pleasant rest	Because it is a new way to do research
Because it allows me to unwind	Because it is enjoyable
When I have nothing better to do	Because it is entertaining

Sources:
1. Rubin, A. (1983). Television uses and gratifications. *Journal of Broadcasting, 27,* 37–51.
2. Papacharissi, Z., & Rubin, A. (2000). Predictors of Internet use *Journal of Broadcasting & Electronic Media, 44,* 175–196.

seeing the latest Tom Hanks movie. The next Tom Hanks movie that comes along may attract us, too, because we expect a similar outcome. Likewise, if we find his new movie upsetting, we may pass up the one after that altogether. Uses and gratifications would call that enjoyment a gratification; social learning theory calls it an outcome. In social learning theory our observations of the experiences of others are also important. For example, if we see smiling people coming out of a Tom Hanks movie, we may want to see it too. We also learn by listening to what others have to say about the media, including people in our daily lives and media critics.

Social learning theory adds to the uses and gratifications theory in many other ways. It explains the avoidance of media, as in "I'd better not let Mom catch me reading *Playboy,* or I'll be grounded." Here, the expectation of a negative consequence dictates usage. Media behavior is also determined by our own inner self-regulation (LaRose & Eastin, 2004): "I'm not watching *Survivor* tonight because I am disgusted with how much of a couch potato I am." Much media behavior is governed by habit, in which we suspend active observation of our own media consumption and just "automatically" turn to the sports page or begin our day by checking our e-mail. In the extreme, self-control may completely fail those who habitually rely on media to relieve negative feelings, which results in media addictions, such as addictions to pornographic sites on the Internet.

Another factor is our perception of our own competency to consume the media, or our self-efficacy. If you've ever put down a book thinking, "That's too deep for me," self-efficacy influenced your media behavior. Self-efficacy strongly influences how computer media are used, especially by new users. What computer user has not had an attack of computer anxiety, or a fear of using computers, after an especially frustrating day at the keyboard?

Computer-Mediated Communication

Uses and gratifications and social learning theory have also been applied to understanding the use of electronic media for interpersonal communication. For example, we use the telephone because it provides enjoyable social interaction and the ability to complete social and commercial transactions (LaRose, 1999).

A great deal of the research on mediated interpersonal communication takes place in organizations, where computer networks are used for all forms of electronic communication. Hence, this field of study is known as *computer mediated communication,* and includes media that we may not immediately associate with computer networks, such as video teleconferencing, and others that are obviously mediated by computers, such as e-mail.

An important concept is *presence,* "a psychological state in which virtual [that is, computer generated] objects are experienced as actual objects" (Lee, 2004, p. 37). Social presence refers to the experience of social actors through the social cues provided in various communication media. E-mails that consist only of printed words are said to have low social presence, which theoretically makes them suited only for routine exchanges of information. Two-way videoconferences have high social presence since they convey important social cues in voice intonations and facial expressions and live interactions flow in both directions. These features supposedly make them suitable for more sensitive tasks like negotiating business deals and firing employees. However, e-mail gets used for just about everything nowadays despite its low social presence. How can that be? Even a "lean" medium like e-mail can be used effectively in tasks requiring social cues as parties learn about each other through repeated exchanges (Walter, 1996).

STOP & REVIEW

1. What are some of the concerns about the impact of media on society that lead to "media bashing"?
2. Contrast the inductive and deductive approaches to studying the effects of the media.
3. What is a media effect?
4. What is the purpose of content analysis?
5. In what ways are experimental studies superior to survey studies? In what ways are they inferior?
6. What do ethnographers do?

THEORIES OF MEDIA IMPACTS

Above we considered theories about why people use the media. Next we examine theories of the consequences of media usage for the individual (Figure 13.1).

Media as Hypodermic Needle

The United States was seemingly driven into war with Spain in 1898 by sensational coverage concocted by newspaper publisher William Randolph Hearst (Chapter 4). His papers trumpeted the sinking of the U.S. battleship *Maine* in Havana harbor (the true cause of which remains unknown to this day) and alleged atrocities by Spanish soldiers so loudly that the thirst for war became unquenchable.

This event made the mass media seem extremely powerful, capable of swaying minds with the impact of a speeding **bullet** or a hypodermic injection, images that led to theoretical models of the same names. Later, radio speeches by Nazi leader Adolf Hitler seemed to play a vital role in sparking the Holocaust of World War II. American film propagandists began the systematic study of the most convincing propaganda techniques. Experimental studies of **persuasion** begun during World War II identified the types of verbal arguments (one-sided versus two-sided appeals, and fear appeals versus reasoned arguments) that are the most convincing (Hovland, Lumsdane, & Sheffield, 1949).

The **bullet model**, or hypodermic model, posits powerful, direct effects of the mass media.

Persuasion is the use of convincing arguments to change people's beliefs, attitudes, or behaviors.

The Multistep Flow

Survey studies of social influence conducted in the late 1940s presented a very different model from that of a hypodermic needle in which a **multistep flow** of media effects was evident. That is, most people receive much of their information and are influenced by the media secondhand, through the personal influence of opinion leaders (Katz & Lazarsfeld,

The **multistep flow** model assumes that media effects are indirect and are mediated by opinion leaders.

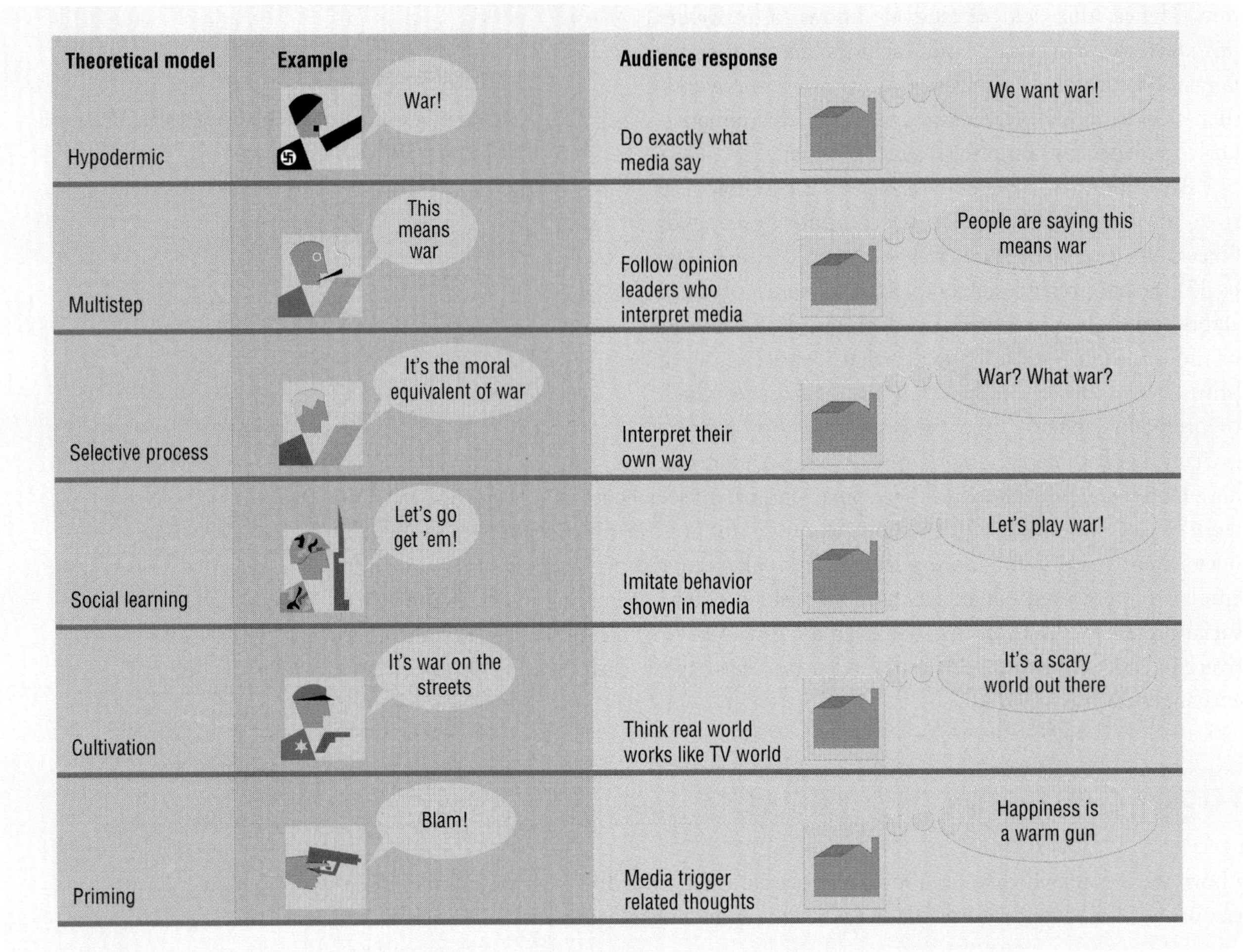

Theoretical model	Example	Audience response	
Hypodermic	War!	Do exactly what media say	We want war!
Multistep	This means war	Follow opinion leaders who interpret media	People are saying this means war
Selective process	It's the moral equivalent of war	Interpret their own way	War? What war?
Social learning	Let's go get 'em!	Imitate behavior shown in media	Let's play war!
Cultivation	It's war on the streets	Think real world works like TV world	It's a scary world out there
Priming	Blam!	Media trigger related thoughts	Happiness is a warm gun

FIGURE 13.1
Theories of Media Effects
There are a number of alternative theories about how to understand mass media effects.

1955). The opinion leaders themselves are influenced by more elite media rather than everyday mass media channels. For example, political opinion leaders might take their cue from *The Nation,* a magazine devoted to political commentary for an elite audience. In the second step, the opinion leaders share their opinions with members of their immediate social circles; say, the "Friday night regulars at the country club," but only after some modification and adaptation to the norms of that circle. The club members belong to other social groupings (including their families, coworkers, and members of other clubs to which they belong) that are influenced in turn by them, and so on. Eventually, social influence radiates outward in society to people who never heard of *The Nation.* But at every step in the process, social influence is modified by the norms of each new social circle it enters and by conflicting views that originate from other elite sources as well as popular mass media sources such as *CNN.* The point is that although the media have some influence, the process of persuasion is primarily a social one.

Selective Processes

Another theme of the media effects studies that followed World War II was that the selective reception reduces media impact. Audiences exercise *selective exposure:* They avoid messages that are at odds with their existing beliefs. Thus, those who take the "pro-war" position in the terrorism debate are not likely to read a newspaper editorial advocating peace. Even when people expose themselves to discordant content, they distort it with *selective perception.* Thus, pro-war supporters who watch a TV interview with an antiwar advocate are more likely to find additional "proof" that their position is correct than to be converted to the cause of peace. Selective retention means that people's memories are also distorted, so that months later someone may remember that her side won a war debate when in fact her side was humiliated (Sears & Freedman, 1972).

In 1960 Joseph Klapper published an influential review of postwar research on the effects of the mass media. Klapper concluded that the media were weak, able to deliver only a few percent of the voters in an election, and able to gain only a few points' worth of market share for advertisers. Even these **limited effects** registered only at the margins, he said, primarily among the uninterested and the uninformed (Klapper, 1960).

Social Learning Theory

Within a few short years, Klapper's conclusions seemed unsatisfactory. In the 1960s, social critics cast about for explanations for mounting violence, political unrest, and a decline in public morality, especially among young adults. Television seemed a likely cause, because the young people belonged to the first "TV generation" that had grown up with the medium, and TV was loaded with images of violence and sex. About the same time, a new theory of mass media effects, social learning theory, lent credence to these claims. Previously, we applied this theory to media consumption behavior, but it originally entered the field of mass communication research to explain the effects of television. The theory explained that viewers imitate what they see on TV through a process known as observational learning. The "rewards" that television characters receive for their antisocial behavior, including not just the loot from their robberies but also their very appearance on a glamorous medium such as television, encourage imitation. On the other hand, when the bad guys on TV get caught and go to jail, this presumably inhibits viewers from imitating them. The more we identify with a character—the more that it resembles us or someone we would like to be—the more likely we are to imitate his or her behavior. The Bobo doll experiments we examined previously validated this theory.

Cultivation Theory

Another explanation emerged from a group of researchers led by George Gerbner at the University of Pennsylvania. They theorized that heavy exposure to television imparts a worldview that is consistent with the "world" of television (Gerbner et al., 1994). According to **cultivation theory,** heavy television viewers are likely to overestimate their own chances of being victims of violent crime, for example. The viewers who adopt this distorted worldview might tolerate violence in their communities and families and in their own behavior.

Limited effects holds that the effects of the mass media on individuals are slight.

Priming

Priming is another theory (Berkowitz, 1984) in which the activation of one thought activates related thoughts. Seeing the Roadrunner cartoon character bash the hapless coyote with a hammer makes us more likely to bash our little brother after the show, or so the theory goes. Incidental cues may unleash the aggression. The next time we see a hammer and little brother is standing near—look out!! Children may store "scripts" about how to respond with violence that they learn from the media in long-term memory and then act out those scripts when a real-world event triggers that memory (van Erva, 1990). This

Cultivation theory argues that mass media exposure cultivates a view of the world that is consistent with mediated "reality."

Priming theory states that media images stimulate related thoughts in the minds of audience members.

theory offers a possible explanation for lurid "copycat" crimes, such as setting a subway token booth aflame with flammable liquid, just like a scene in a movie (Leland, 1995). Currently we might use this theory to explain a rash of real-life injuries resulting from people imitating professional wrestling moves in their back yards.

Agenda Setting

In Chapter 2 we described agenda setting as a process through which public figures and important events help to shape the content of the media. *Agenda setting* theory also describes the effects of that process on the media audience: the rank ordering that the audience assigns to important issues of the day tends to match the amount of coverage that the media give those issues (Wanta, 1997). For example, it has been found that political campaign press coverage affects the types of issues discussed in online discussion groups (Roberts et al., 2002).

Catharsis

The *catharsis hypothesis* argues that media sex and violence have positive effects by allowing people to live out their antisocial desires in a mediated fantasy world (Feshbach & Singer, 1971). This theory was popular in the 1930s and 1940s before it was widely believed that the media were responsible for society's ills. Recently this hypothesis has resurfaced in a critique of the research about the effects of television violence (Fowles, 1999).

Critical Theories

Critical theorists question the theories used in media effects studies as well as the methods used. We examined some of the major critical theories in Chapter 2. Critical studies of media impacts, such as violence, focus less on behavioral effects on individuals and more on large-scale cultural impacts, such as permitting some groups to practice violence against other groups. Other critical scholars also focus on Freudian-style psychological interpretations of motives and implications.

For example, a critical analysis of John Hinckley's attempted assassination of Ronald Reagan in 1980 examined the way in which Hinckley "read" (or interpreted) a violent movie (*Taxi Driver*) and mingled it with his fantasies about actress Jodie Foster and former actor Ronald Reagan (Real, 1989). By noting that Hinckley committed his act of violence on the eve of the Academy Awards ceremony, Real wove an explanation of how the would-be assassin was trying to communicate his unrequited love for Foster.

Or, critical theorists might examine changes in the way in which violence toward indigenous Americans was portrayed in Westerns from the 1930s, when violence against "Indians" was uncritically accepted, to the 1960s, when that violence began to be challenged in film treatments, such as *Little Big Man*. Similarly, critical approaches to the study of advertising emphasize the ways that advertising promotes a general pattern of consumption—as opposed to the consumption of specific products, which is the focus of administrative advertising research—in a way that draws people into a capitalist economic system that may not benefit them. Likewise, a critical look at the political effects of mass media might bypass campaign advertisements entirely and instead examine the hidden political messages about obedience to authority, class structure, and gender relations contained in such "nonpolitical" programs as *Sesame Street* and *The Simpsons*. Thus, the critical theorist is able to examine broad questions about the relationship between culture and society that may elude the social scientist.

Note that in interpretations such as these, the ebb and flow of cause and effect between media and society is not a one-way street. In a sense, the media themselves are the "effects" of class domination or racial prejudice. And, the media are only a part of a broader system of exploitation. It's insufficient to examine them in isolation from the cultural fabric into which they are woven.

Cultural studies scholars are most likely to see culture as an interaction between audiences and media, not a one way effect. Rather than talking about how communication effects are limited by selective perception, some critical theorists would state that audiences are active "readers" of media "texts." They would focus on the prominence of the audience instead of on the source of the media messages (Morley, 1992). Critical theorists speak of "group mediation" (Barbero, 1993) or "interpretive communities" of groups who are similar in education, occupation, wealth, and family background (Lindlof, 1995), whereas social scientists use the term *multistep flow* to describe the way in which social interactions affect perceptions of the media. Likewise, critical theorists have relabeled the SMCR model (Chapter 1) the "linear model" or "transmission paradigm."

MEDIA AND ANTISOCIAL BEHAVIOR

Antisocial behavior is contrary to prevailing norms for social conduct. That includes unlawful actions, such as murder, hate crimes, rape, and drug abuse, as well as behaviors that most members of society find objectionable even if they are not illegal, such as drunkenness and sexual promiscuity.

Violence

The effects of violence on television have received far more attention by researchers than any others. Effects on children are a special concern, because youngsters have trouble distinguishing between the real world and the world of the small screen. To the child's mind, if the coyote character in the Saturday-morning TV cartoon recovers instantly from a bash on the head, then the same should be true for little brother. With short attention spans, young children are unlikely to associate the legal consequences that emerge in dull courtroom scenes at the end of the show with the eye-catching shootout at the beginning. Children spend a great deal of time with television, much of it unsupervised by parents, so the potential exists for great harm to impressionable young minds.

Television is indeed packed with violence—three-fifths of all prime-time shows include it, at the rate of 4.5 violent acts per program (Signorelli, 2003)! Children's television shows have even more violence than other programs, glamorize it just as much, and trivialize it even more (Wilson et al., 2002). Literally thousands of experimental studies, many patterned after Bandura's Bobo doll study, demonstrate that children can imitate violence they see. Televised violence prompts children not only to carry out parallel acts of aggression but also to perform other, novel forms of violent behavior; it predisposes them to select violent resolutions to conflicts in their daily lives, and even primes them to engage in violent acts (Anderson et al., 2003). Also, children will imitate violence even if it is not explicitly reinforced on television (Liebert & Sprafkin, 1988). The strength of these effects is comparable to those associated with such well-documented public health hazards as lead poisoning and cigarette smoking (Bar-on et al., 2001). Most of the research has focused on fictional violence in prime-time dramas, but in the post-9/11 world there is growing concern that violent news programs may also be harmful to children (van der Molen, 2004).

Some still reject experimental studies on the grounds that they are conducted under unrealistic conditions (Anderson & Meyer, 1988; Milavsky et al., 1982). Field

Antisocial behavior is behavior contrary to prevailing social norms.

experiments conducted in real-life settings also demonstrate the effects of media violence (Paik & Comstock, 1994), but when natural observations of violent behavior are used instead of relying on respondents' own imperfect memories, the results are mixed (Wood et al., 1991). One field experiment found evidence of a catharsis effect that reduces violent tendencies through exposure to fantasy violence (Feshback & Singer, 1971).

Survey studies also tend to show a relationship between violent behavior and viewership of violent television (Paik & Comstock, 1994). Adult viewers who watch violent programs are likely to hold worldviews that match the TV portrayals they see (Gerbner et al., 1994), a result consistent with cultivation theory. That is, if we see a lot of violence on TV, we are more likely to expect violence in our own lives. However, these relationships are relatively weak ones (Morgan & Shanahan, 1997). They may be statistical artifacts or may be due to factors other than exposure to television, including the differing social characteristics of heavy and light viewers (Hirsch, 1980).

More convincing are longitudinal panel studies in which television viewing at one time is related to violence exhibited at a second time that is days, months, or even years later. Earlier (page 398) we mentioned panel studies by Huesmann (1982, 2003) and his associates that indicated that television viewing at an early age is related to violent behavior later in life. Recent research suggests that the effects continue to mount even in later years (Johnson et al., 2002). The violence that teens see on television may also affect their violent behavior. However, violence on television is not the most important factor contributing to violence in society. Family and peer influence, socioeconomic status, and substance abuse are more important (U.S. H.H.S., 2001).

So, the effects of television violence remain controversial. It is probably safest to conclude that exposure to antisocial television portrayals can have at least short-term effects in promoting violent behavior. Most researchers would add that there are probably long-term effects as well, especially on children. If this is true, recent attempts to label violent content are long overdue, but unfortunately the content labels voluntarily supplied by television networks underrepresent the amount of violence in program content (Kunkel et al., 2002). Moreover, the labels may not be effective unless accompanied by improved parental supervision or automatic content filtering. Simply labeling the programs as violent actually attracts more young viewers to the "forbidden fruit" (Bushman & Cantor, 2003). Parental mediation can make a difference. Providing brief negative evaluations of violent characters can reduce the effects of violent television (Nathanson, 2004).

Prejudice

Sexism, racism, and other forms of intolerance may also be promoted by the media. Media portrayals encourage **stereotyping,** the formation of generalizations about a group of people on the basis of limited information. Stereotypes are harmful when they become rationalizations for treating others unfairly. Furthermore, negative stereotypes may be internalized by members of the groups to which they are applied, undermining their own self-respect. Media are very effective at creating stereotypes because they are sometimes the only source of information we have about other groups and because they often present a distorted view of those groups.

For example, content analysis of current children's television programs shows that women are underrepresented and are stereotypically deferent and nurturing, whereas males are shown as active and aggressive (Barner, 1999). Since the 1970s, women have begun appearing in higher-status jobs on television and in somewhat fewer stereotypically female occupations (for example, secretary and nurse). However, the percentage of women shown working outside the home has changed little through the decades, the

© Ted Horowitz/CORBIS

■ **CHILD'S PLAY?**
The research shows that violent video games provoke violent behavior in children.

Stereotyping is the making of generalizations about groups of people on the basis of limited information.

men on TV are still more likely to be employed than the women, and there are still fewer female than male roles overall (Signorelli & Bacue, 1999). The reinforcement of stereotypes begins with programs aimed at toddlers: *Barney and Friends* and *Teletubbies* portray female characters as caregivers and followers (although male roles are more flexible, Powell & Abels, 2002).

To the male viewer, this might make it seem acceptable to treat women as inferiors. For their part, women may feel diminished because of their underrepresentation on TV. They may internalize the common media stereotypes that beautiful women are more valued and that women should sacrifice their careers for their families (Signorelli, 1989). Also, experimental studies have shown that young girls exposed to a heavy dose of TV shows that portray women in traditional sex roles limit their own career aspirations to traditionally female occupations (Beuf, 1974; Freuh & McGhee, 1975). There are fewer sex-stereotyped female portrayals these days (Glascock, 2001), but it is still relatively rare to see women portrayed in traditionally male-dominated occupations (Signorelli & Bacue, 1999). Gender stereotypes can also make us dissatisfied with our own bodies. Exposure to TV ads that portray women as sex objects makes women want to be thinner and men want to be larger than they actually are (Lavine, Sweeney & Wagner, 1999) whereas stereotyped TV commercials make women have less interest in traditionally male-dominated subjects (for example, mathematics; Davies et al., 2002). As with violence effects, the impact of sex-role stereotyping can be counteracted by parental interventions that provide contradictory information (for example, "lots of girls do things besides paint their nails and put on make-up," Nathanson et al., 2002, p. 928).

The life aspirations of minority children are also affected by the limited media portrayals of minorities (Clark, 1972). The level of representation of minority characters on network television now matches and even exceeds their numbers in the general population (Glascock, 2001). But, racially stereotyped portrayals persist; for example, African-Americans are still more often portrayed as lazy and Latinos as flashy dressers compared to whites (Mastro & Greenberg, 2000). Racially stereotyped television portrayals of minorities may also make white viewers view minorities in more negative ways, such as making them more willing to see African-Americans as criminals (Ford, 1997).

Stereotypes are spreading in the new media, too. Internet newsgroups and chat rooms are notorious for abusive treatment of female participants, especially in the early days of the web when few females were online—forcing many to assume fake male identities. There are numerous examples to be found in popular CD-ROM games such as *Myst* (save the helpless princess!), and "adult entertainment" sites on the web offer blatantly sexist content (Dietrich, 1997).

Media stereotyping affects all groups in society. Blue-collar families are underrepresented and are often portrayed in a way that denigrates their lifestyles (consider *The Simpsons*). The same is true of homosexuals, persons with disabilities, the homeless, the mentally ill, and seemingly any group that deviates from a mainstream society dominated by professional, "straight," healthy, and wealthy white males. We can easily summon to mind stock images of serious college students ("nerds" in media lexicon), millionaires, lawyers, and police that have little in common with their real-world counterparts. To

© AP/Wide World Photos

■ **UNDOING STEREOTYPES**
Female executives like Anne Sweeney, president of the ABC Television Group, may hold the key to reducing gender stereotypes in front of the camera as well as behind it.

some extent, the media cannot function without stereotypes. They are the "picture in our heads" (Lippmann, 1922) that stories are made of, a type of conceptual shorthand that allows viewers to recognize characters immediately and connect with their situations.

It is when the negative stereotypes spill over from the flickering screen into our daily lives that they become a concern. In the wake of the September 11 terror attacks, there is the danger that we may be unduly influenced by media images of Muslims and Arabs as terrorists and warmongers. Arab stereotypes have long been present in popular media (Shaheen, 2003). This might lead us to be prejudiced against Arabs or to back policies that punish them unfairly. Indeed, this situation is one in which the media images could be especially powerful. They highlight serious intergroup conflict in the starkest terms and provide the only information that many viewers have about members of a relatively small minority group. These are conditions in which media stereotypes can have very corrosive effects.

Sexual Behavior

Sex in the media erupted as an issue in the 1920s, in the aftermath of a wave of Hollywood sex scandals. Hollywood imposed strict self-censorship standards that now seem ludicrous in retrospect: no cleavage, no navels, separate beds for married couples, no kisses longer than four seconds, cut to the clouds overhead if sex is imminent. When Elizabeth Taylor said the word "virgin" in a 1954 movie, it caused a sensation. Since then, producers and publishers have continually pushed the limits to reap financial benefits at the box office and the newsstand, although now in the wake of the infamous Super Bowl halftime breast exposure incident, the pendulum may be swinging back.

The last decades have seen a dramatic increase in highly explicit pornographic material through magazines, home video, and now the Internet. At the same time, social norms have become more harsh against behaviors once tolerated but now labeled as date rape and sexual harassment. These two trends are clearly on a collision course, raising anew the question of the effects of sex in the media.

Experimental studies show that when males are exposed to explicit pornography, they are more likely to express negative attitudes toward women, to think that relatively uncommon sexual practices (such as fellatio and anal intercourse) are widespread, and to be more lenient with rape offenders in hypothetical court cases. In experiments that examine the combined impacts of pornography and violence, a common procedure is to seat the male subjects at an apparatus that supposedly delivers electrical shocks to a female in the next room. (The shocks are simulated, and the females are confederates of the experimenter who are trained to act as though they are being shocked, so no one really gets hurt.) The males are more likely to administer electric shocks (sometimes even supposedly lethal ones!) after exposure to pornography (Allen, D'Alessio, & Brezgel, 1995). However, this may apply only to violent pornography, in which the female models are subject to coercive or sadistic behavior, and then only when women are shown to be enjoying the abuse (Felson, 1996).

In the 1980s, a presidential commission (the so-called Meese Commission) spearheaded a cleanup of pornography to remove coercive and violent portrayals (Attorney General of the United States, 1986). Did the Meese Commission go far enough? Feminists also campaign against any pornography that is degrading to women—anything that portrays women as subservient or unequal sex partners, shows them as faceless sex objects, or involves bodily invasion by nonhuman species or inanimate objects. Canadian antipornography laws reflect this stricter definition of pornography.

Others argue that the Commission went too far. Out in the real world, the availability of pornography in a community does not seem to be related to the incidence of

ABC/Danny Feld, © ABC/Courtesy: Everett Collection

■ **SEX ON TV**
Sexy shows like *Desperate Housewives* have been linked to the sexual behavior of their viewers.

rape in the same area (Gentry, 1991). Sex offenders do not have any more exposure to pornography than anyone else. However, they are more likely to consume pornography before engaging in sex and are highly aroused by material that matches the nature of their criminal sexual activities (Allen, D'Alessio & Emmers-Sommer, 1999). One way to interpret these contradictory findings is that pornography, even when consumed at high levels, does not promote sexual aggression in most men. However, among those who are at "high risk" for sexual aggression (for example, men who are impulsive or hostile by nature), pornography exposure greatly adds to that risk (Malamuth et al., 2000).

But perhaps the relatively mild sexual portrayals found on television, in which sexual intercourse is at most strongly implied by showing "after" pictures of actors between the sheets, is a bigger threat to society than hard core pornography. Adolescents who watch a lot of television sex are twice as likely as those who see little of it to engage in sexual intercourse in the year following their exposure (Collins et al., 2004). Perhaps that makes television an important contributing factor to unwanted teen pregnancies.

Drug Abuse

A generation ago there was concern that movies such as *Easy Rider* glorified the drug scene and contributed to illegal drug use among college students. The media generally bowed to these concerns, if only because drug films were not as profitable as those featuring violence and sex, and because distributors of illegal drugs cannot buy advertisements for them!

The abuse of legal drugs is quite another story. Cigarette ads have long been banished from television by law. The ads can no longer glorify smoking by showing happy, glamorous people (or cuddly cartoon characters) puffing away; the Surgeon General's warnings about the hazards of smoking must be displayed; and there can be no imagery that obviously is designed to appeal to children. Hard liquor distillers long avoided television (although this is now changing), but beer and wine commercials are one of the leading sources of advertising revenue for television, and so are ads for over-the-counter drugs, and restrictions on prescription drug ads have been relaxed so that they, too, can appear on television.

Advertisers claim that these ads do not boost overall consumption levels and affect only the relative market share the various brands enjoy. However, studies of children and adolescents indicate that advertising exposure is related to consumption of both alcohol (Grube, 1995) and cigarettes (Pierce et al., 1998). Meanwhile, young children exposed to over-the-counter drug commercials look at drugs as a way to solve their personal problems, a habit that might carry over to illicit drugs (Atkin, 1985).

Critics have long contended that some of the ads are secretly targeted to young viewers through characters (such as the wisecracking amphibians in Budweiser beer ads and Joe Camel) that are carefully crafted to appeal to impressionable young viewers at an age when they are vulnerable to initiating lifelong addictions. Recent revelations of secret cigarette industry marketing studies on children have shown that the critics were right. But depictions of cigarette smoking in the movies may also encourage young people to smoke (Pechmann & Shih, 1999). Now attention has turned to antismoking campaigns directed at teens and children. Campaigns that attack the motives of the tobacco industry have proven effective (Farrelly, 2002), but antismoking ads produced by the industry itself actually improve attitudes toward the industry. And, ads critical of the industry are prohibited under the terms of a settlement with the tobacco industry that set aside billions of dollars for smoking prevention.

Tobacco industry apologists like to argue that theirs is a legal product and they have a right to advertise it, even if some children get in the way. After all, fast food may be harmful. Why don't we ban hamburger commercials aimed at children? Maybe we should. Now some critics have begun to argue that fatty foods are indeed addictive like a drug. There is a well-established association between television viewing and obesity in children (Gortmaker et al., 1996).

The Impacts of Computer Media

The spread of the Internet turns society's attention to the effects of the new media. New social effects of the Internet are being "discovered" all the time. Some fit into conventional categories of media effects, although others do not.

Antisocial Behavior. What are the effects of the new media? Experimental studies show that violent computer games appear to be every bit as harmful as violence on television (Anderson, 2004). Indeed, one recent study found that video games have an even greater ability to desensitize children to violence than either television or experience with real-life violence (Funk et al., 2004).

The Internet also brings pornography into the home and the classroom, and a recent survey shows that a quarter of children aged 10–17 have had unwanted exposure to sexual material on the Internet and a fourth of those were very upset by the experience (Mitchell, Finkelhor, & Wolak, 2003). Sadly, some of the unwanted exposure comes from devious porn site operators who try to build traffic to their sites by using variations on popular sites frequented by children. At one time, typing in Dinsey.com, as opposed to Disney.com led children to an adult website, for example. However, the dynamic nature of the Internet has thus far frustrated attempts by social scientists to measure its effects, or even catalog its content. One study of interactive computer pornography found that it had no effect on either attitudes or aggressive behavior toward women among college freshman males (Barak & Fisher, 1997).

Computer Anxiety. Other research has focused on dysfunctional uses of the computer itself rather than on the effects of its content. Computer anxiety, also known as cyberphobia and computerphobia, is a debilitating fear of the computer (Kernan & Howard, 1990). It afflicts up to a third of the adult population; people with the most extreme cases suffer from nausea, vertigo, and cold sweats. Their anxiety has several possible origins, including the fear that they will cause damage by pushing the wrong key, concern over the social effects of the computer (such as compromising privacy), fear of personal failure, and an "out of control" feeling that nontechnical persons may experience when faced with a complex technical system. Women and people with relatively low mathematical skills are especially likely to suffer from computer anxiety. Computerphobes do poorly on computer tasks and in computer classes and are dissatisfied computer users. Internet self-efficacy (Eastin and LaRose, 2000) is the opposite of computer anxiety. Self-efficacious users use the Internet more and get more out of it.

Addiction. At the other end of the spectrum are Internet addicts (Grohol, 1996). Computer media have an interactive quality that responds to the user's every move. Sometimes they do what we wish, but other times not, and the results are highly variable. That keeps us coming back for more—the same pattern of reinforcement that prompts addictive behaviors like gambling. Parents complain about children seemingly becoming addicted to a particular game, and some researchers would agree (Griffiths, 1998). Heavy Internet users show signs of tolerance, craving, and withdrawal, all signs of addiction (Brenner, 1997). There is also anecdotal evidence of adults bankrupting themselves from fees paid to interactive gaming or adult entertainment sites on the web. The problem may spread as activities with well-established addictive qualities, such as gambling and fantasy sports leagues, go online. Addictive qualities of virtual reality systems are sometimes

The Grand Online Casino: Outstanding Casino games and Real Money Gambling since 1997.

openly touted by developers who promise a "better high than drugs." However, recent research suggests that "symptoms" of Internet addiction, such as an inability to control one's use or a mounting need for more web surfing, are merely indications of the formation of media habits (LaRose, Eastin, & Lin, 2003). Relatively few Internet users are in danger of having their lives destroyed by the web, the true indication of a serious behavioral addiction.

Psychologist Sherry Turkle (1995) prefers the metaphor of seduction to that of addiction. She stresses that the holding power of the computer comes not from what is external (like a drug) but rather from what is within people, what they learn about themselves through their infatuation with computer media. What attracts them is its ability to provoke self-reflection, to extend their minds into artificial worlds that adapt to the needs of each user. In this view, habitual computer users are drawn by their ability to control the world inside the computer, to achieve the illusion of intimacy, to gain confirmation of a sense of selfhood, and to express themselves in their own style.

COMMUNICATIONS MEDIA
AND PROSOCIAL BEHAVIOR

Prosocial behavior is in a sense the opposite of antisocial behavior. It includes behaviors and positive qualities that we want to encourage in our children and our society: cooperation, altruism, sharing, love, tolerance, respect, balanced nutrition, contraceptive use, personal hygiene, safe driving, improved reading skills, and so on. We can also include in this list discontinuing antisocial behaviors, such as deciding to quit smoking, drinking, reckless driving, or unsafe sex. Prosocial media fall along a continuum based on the relative mixture of entertainment and informational content. They range from transmitting

Prosocial behaviors are those that a
society values and encourages.

heavily sugar-coated, subtle messages to explicit, direct educational efforts.

Efforts to promote prosocial media are the flip side of "media bashing" that we outlined earlier. Instead of criticizing the media for sex and violence, only to have them retreat behind the First Amendment, why not encourage them to produce more wholesome and educational programs? The Children's Television Act of 1990 does just that. It mandates that programs designed specifically for children be aired as a condition for broadcast license renewals (see Chapter 14). After years of wrangling over just how much children's programming is enough, what "specifically designed for children" means, and even who children are, meaningful guidelines were finally passed in 1996 (Kunkel, 1998).

© James Leynse/Corbis SABA

Information Campaigns

Information campaigns use the techniques of public relations and advertising to "sell" people on prosocial behaviors. They seek to achieve specific changes in their audience, such as heightening public awareness of a health or social problem and changing related attitudes and behaviors. They usually adopt an informal and entertaining style to attract an audience. Perhaps the most familiar manifestations of information campaigns are the public service announcements that populate late-night television, such as the recent anti-smoking campaign in which famed screenwriter Joe Eszterhas recounts the gruesome details of his throat cancer.

Information campaigns have a spotty record of success. Experimental studies show that some campaigns do affect the awareness, attitudes, and the behaviors of their audience. Campaigns can succeed if they have clear objectives and sharply defined target audiences and if they find relevant ways to overcome indifference (Rice & Atkin, 2000). Social marketing, an integrated marketing communication approach (see Chapter 11) to behavior change, combines media, interpersonal influence, and carefully managed efforts to introduce recommended products directly into the lives of the target audience. This approach has achieved considerable success in the health communication field (Maibach & Holtgrave, 1995). In a safe-sex campaign, public service ads might be combined with posters in nightclubs and with volunteers who circulate on dance floors to distribute condoms.

Even when well designed, some information campaigns face too many obstacles to have much impact. Many rely on free advertising space (hence, their appearance late at night) and consequently have difficulty reaching their audiences. The public interest groups that produce information campaigns too often expend all their resources in developing the media materials, leaving little for paid media placements directed to their target audience.

And, not all information campaigns are effective to begin with. They are often created by advertising professionals who contribute their time in exchange for a chance to showcase their skills. The results are often eye-catching and memorable ("My name is Joe Eszterhas. Cancer makes you cry and then it kills you.") but not enough to overcome

Information campaigns use the techniques of advertising in an attempt to convince people to adopt prosocial behaviors.

selective reception. Or, they may fail to activate the social networks that apply personal influence. A common mistake is to use strong fear appeals when targeting teens. Unfortunately, the teens who engage in the target behavior are also likely to have low self-esteem, which means they will discount or deny the message rather than take it to heart. The adults behind the campaigns think strong fear appeals are great ("Yeah, hard hitting. That'll teach them!"), but the target audience just makes a joke out of them.

Antidrug campaigns offer another example. Informing children about the risks of drugs can also have the unintended effect of making drug use seem more prevalent and therefore more socially acceptable to them. One widely touted drug education program, Project D.A.R.E., was found to be ineffective at best (Lynam et al., 1999) and at worst may have encouraged drug use.

In other cases, campaigns may have foggy objectives or uncertain target audiences, or they may have too many objectives, trying to satisfy multiple agendas ("We want users to stop using, potential users to stop thinking about it, and their parents to drum both messages into their children's heads"). Campaign developers seldom have the resources to fund the detailed research that goes into successful product commercials. And, they try to achieve much more than product advertisements, which merely aim to increase awareness of a brand name or a new product. Information campaigns often target deeply ingrained habitual behaviors, a goal that is generally unattainable through advertising alone.

Informal Education

Without a "captive audience" of classroom students, informal education efforts must artfully combine the elements of education and entertainment. The best-known example is *Sesame Street.* Since its inception in 1969, *Sesame Street* has proved to be a popular and effective means of readying children for school (Fisch & Truglio, 2001).

Sesame Street is also an example of a phenomenon that plagues prosocial media-the unintended effect. *Sesame Street* was originally designed to close the gap in school readiness between minority and majority children. Unfortunately, it does just the opposite. Middle-class, white children who watch the show learn more about "words that begin with b" than low-income minority children, and the knowledge gap (see page 422) between the two widens as a result (Cook et al., 1975).

What about the prosocial effects of entertainment media? Do couch potatoes soak up valuable information from TV quiz shows? Do children imitate altruistic behavior from Sponge Bob cartoons as readily as they pick up violent behavior from the violent coyote? We call these effects *incidental learning* because they are side effects of exposure to entertainment. Relatively little research has been done on the prosocial effects of entertainment media. Content analyses of television entertainment programming reveal frequent examples of prosocial behavior, although these instances may be overwhelmed by glorified depictions of aggression (Greenberg et al., 1980). According to some studies, prosocial programs can be highly effective (Huston et al., 1992; Friedlander, 1993). For example, an episode of *Friends* in which a broken condom led to an unwanted pregnancy proved to be an effective form of sex education (Collins et al., 2003).

Distance Education

The delivery of courses through the mass media is more formally known as *distance education.* Television is a familiar distance learning medium for college students at large universities who watch lectures live or on tape via closed-circuit television or cable systems in their rooms. As deadly as televised lectures sometimes are, they are as educationally effective as "live" classroom instruction (Johnston, 1987). When shown to "nontraditional" students (usually older, working adults) who cannot come to campus for lectures, telecourses sometimes prove more effective than conventional instruction. That is probably because adult learners are often better motivated and more knowledgeable than on-campus students and because they usually take only one course at a time.

The goal of distance education is to make instruction more accessible to the learners at more locations, at different times, and in small groups. But there is also often a hidden administrative agenda: greater economic efficiency through economies of scale (Tiffin & Rajasingham, 1995). That sounds good, too, but what it really means is extending the back of the lecture hall electronically to enclose hundreds more students. The drawback is the lack of any meaningful intellectual relationship between student and teacher and the reduction of knowledge to packets of information that can be consumed electronically (Newman & Johnson, 1999).

The latest trend in distance education is putting courses on the World Wide Web, the virtual university. Many online courses are just expanded course outlines or lecture notes published on instructors' home pages. Another approach borrows from the telecourse model by placing audiotapes or videotapes of classroom lectures on the web, and these appear to be as effective as classroom lectures (LaRose, Gregg, & Eastin, 1999). Another model uses e-mail, newsgroups, and chat rooms to conduct live virtual seminars, which may be even more effective than conventional instruction (Schutte, 1997). Other courses immerse learners in a compelling learning environment that is a cross between a video game and a trip to the zoo, and these interactive multimedia courses also appear to be educationally effective (Yaverbaum & Nadarajan, 1996). Critics contend that the online instructors are unprofessional and that in the process higher education is devalued into a commercial product and the university is reduced to being a brand name (Confessore, 1999).

In K–12 schools, observers worry that multimedia glitz may sacrifice education for entertainment and that investments in computers aren't paying off. Students seem to be motivated by computers, but that apparently has not led to better test scores or better attendance. Many computers remain locked up in labs, and many teachers don't know how to use them. Students do learn when everyone in class has a computer, but not when students have to compete for scarce "seat time" on shared computers (Bulkeley, 1997).

The Impacts of Advertising

If the media have such mixed success in influencing behavior, why is there so much advertising? (For more on advertising, see Chapter 11.) The answer is that advertisers are happy to achieve rather limited impacts. Most advertisers take our consumption behavior as a given. They merely seek to strengthen our *brand awareness* so that we think of their product when we are in the store and maintain brand loyalty so that we will keep coming back for more. Thus, automobile manufacturers do not waste their money convincing us that we need a new car. But they do try to make us think of their product when we are out shopping for a car and convince us to come back to them for our next one (Jeffres, 1986).

Does advertising work? Even with these relatively modest goals, many advertising campaigns are a flop. Sometimes they are outgunned by more powerful campaigns from competitors. Many other factors influence consumer purchases, including special promotional offers, the price of the product, its availability, the way it is packaged, and—let us not forget—consumer needs and the actual merits of the product. Any of these can negate the effects of the most polished advertising campaign. Sometimes the campaign is simply ineffective. Part of the problem lies with the way ads are tested. If they are highly memorable, they are deemed successful. Only much later do the advertisers find out whether they sell more hamburgers or athletic shoes.

■ OLD JOE
Cigarette advertising influences impressionable minds and may encourage young children to acquire an unhealthy lifelong habit.

It is unclear exactly how advertising works even when it is successful. The *hierarchy of effect* is a common notion in advertising research that states that purchase decisions follow a set series of steps: first comes awareness, then interest, then decision, followed by the action of actually buying the product. But there are many competing hierarchies, including some in which action comes first, as in the case of an impulse buy. One recent review of the literature concluded that none of the proposed hierarchies is especially compelling (Vakratsas & Ambler, 1999).

The impact of television advertising on young children is of great concern because most children first come into contact with the consumer society through TV. Young children have a difficult time understanding commercials. They confuse the commercials with the programs and react uncritically to advertising messages (Liebert & Sprafkin, 1988). Advertisers can exploit young viewers by using the hosts of children's shows to hawk their products, selecting deceptive camera angles to make tiny toys appear child-size. They prompt children to parrot advertising slogans to wear down their parents: in a study of Christmas lists, two-thirds of seven- and eight-year-olds asked for products that were advertised on TV (Buijzen & Valkenburg, 2000). Exposure to television advertising is also related to children's materialism and, when their purchase requests go unfulfilled, also to family conflict and life dissatisfaction (Buijzen & Valkenburg, 2003). Cereal commercials promote unhealthful confections by placing toys in the packages instead of nutrition. Even more serious are the effects of advertising for harmful adult products, such as cigarettes. Before he was forced out of advertising by the new tobacco advertising code, "old Joe Camel" in the Camel ads was highly memorable and highly effective in promoting brand awareness among children (Difranza et al., 1991).

There are many successful advertising campaigns, and the best ones can yield substantial increases in market share. However, the average commercial campaign is likely to register an increase in sales of only a few percent. These modest gains nonetheless translate into millions of dollars for mass market products. New advertising research methods that make it possible to match detailed records of television viewing with computerized records of purchase behavior obtained from supermarket scanners show that advertising may have a long-term impact as well. Heavy exposure to successful ad campaigns impacts purchasing behavior one and two years later (Lodish et al., 1995).

Is advertising good for society? Overall, about 3 percent of the total amount that consumers spend for goods and services goes into advertising. In some product categories, cigarettes and soft drinks; for example, most of the cost of the product is advertising cost. When manufacturers establish brand loyalty, they can charge more for their products. However, advertising also makes consumers aware of alternative products and special offers, and it generally promotes competition, which helps to keep consumer prices down. Overall, it appears that advertisements are a slight "bargain" for the consumer (Jeffres, 1986).

The Impacts of Political Communication

Like it or not, political campaigns have largely evolved into advertising campaigns, the candidate being the "product." The techniques of market research and mass persuasion have been applied with a vengeance to politics. The political caucus has given way to the focus group.

What is the net effect of the political ads that glut the airwaves just before an election? The ads are most likely to impact those who are relatively unaware of an election and its issues, but are also likely to discourage highly aware voters from seeking other types of information (Valentino, Hutchings, & Williams, 2004). However, since unaware voters are also unlikely to vote, the overall impact may be minimal. According to the multistep flow model (page 404), undecided voters who do vote are likely to be swayed by the people around them rather than by advertising.

Political communication researchers have largely given up trying to understand how to sway votes, concentrating instead on more complex interactions between voters, the media, and political systems (Iyengar & Reeves, 1997). For example, newspaper readership (although not television news viewership) and engagement in political discussion fosters involvement with local political issues (Scheufele et al., 2002). For their part, political practitioners have turned to negative ads in the hope of cutting through voter apathy, but overall these are ineffective, too (Lau et al., 1999). The campaign coverage that appears in the media, including news stories, opinion polls, public appearances by the candidates, debates, and editorial endorsements, is inherently more effective than political advertisements. That's because authoritative media sources are generally more credible, or believable, than politicians, and credible sources are more persuasive. Also, recall an earlier discussion (in Chapter 2) of the gatekeeping, framing, and agenda setting functions of the mass media; their ability to define what the important issues are. In this light, the media may have their most profound impacts on public opinion between political campaigns rather than during them. Debates have some impact on perceptions of the candidate's character, but only strengthen confidence in pre-existing voting choices rather than change votes (Benoit & Hansen, 2004). However, debates do have a leveling effect when it comes to voter information about the candidates (Holbrook, 2002).

The less important the election, the more important political coverage becomes. This is because voters are unlikely to be aware of candidates or issues outside of the presidential race and one or two other high-profile contests. Most Americans cannot name their own member of the House of Representatives, let alone the name of the challenger or the positions either candidate takes on the issues. Because people are naturally unwilling to vote for an unknown quantity, this often gives incumbents and candidates with names such as "Kennedy" and "Trueheart" a natural advantage. Issues have turned into TV "sound bites." In this vacuum, advertising can be effective since it is effective in establishing name recognition.

The commonly held beliefs, attitudes, and misconceptions about the issues of the day are what we call public opinion. Like candidate preferences, public opinion is also shaped through interpersonal influence. The publicity attached to polls may help mold public opinion through a process called the spiral of silence (Noelle-Neumann, 1984). That is, when we believe that our opinions match the rising tide of public opinion; for example, when we see poll results that support our own opinions, our beliefs are strengthened. Conversely, when we sense that we hold an unpopular belief, a "red" voter in a "blue state" for example we remain silent. Because one of the ways we gauge how popular our own opinions are is by hearing the same opinions voiced by others, a self-perpetuating cycle begins that eventually suppresses the less popular view.

Media coverage does affect voter participation. In minor elections where as few as 10 percent of the eligible voters turn out, if the media focus on an otherwise obscure race,

© James A. Finley/Reuters/Landov

■ **POLITICALLY EFFECTIVE?**
The research shows that debates between the candidates change surprisingly few votes.

voter participation may soar. If the coverage selectively galvanizes unified blocs of voters, this can have a major impact on the election results. However, politicians learned in the 2004 presidential elections that door-to-door get out the vote drives are more effective than mediated ones. Overall, voter participation is falling off and media coverage seems to be playing a part (McLeod, Kosicki, & McLeod, 1994). The media seem to define the issues and the candidates and are creating a crisis in citizenship that has turned election campaigns into publicity campaigns (Bucy & D'Angelo, 1999). The real issues are reduced to sound bites and catchy visual images for the TV camera's benefit. The campaign is treated like a sporting event, and candidates are defined by the media's obsessive dissection of their "character" issues. With no real engagement in the issues, it is perhaps not surprising that the electorate often responds with apathy.

The Internet inspires dreams of political rebirth by providing a new medium for political movements and civic engagement (Davis, Elin, & Reeher, 2002) and stimulating voter turnout (Tolbert & McNeal, 2003). There is a growing e-government movement whose goals are to expand access to public services and coalition building (Ho, 2002). Websites attract political donations at far less cost than conventional methods, making it cost-effective to raise money from "grassroots" donations as small as a few dollars. Political candidates also use their websites to keep in touch with the faithful and blitz reporters with e-mail. Online voting is making an appearance, and it might reverse the long-term decline in citizen participation once problems with voter fraud and access are overcome (Westen, 1998). Meanwhile, the power of the mainstream media to set the public agenda is being contested by bloggers, the amateur political reporters of the web (Ashbee, 2003; see also Chapter 9).

But the Internet could also destroy political discourse. It is used as a recruiting tool by hate groups that would like to suppress diverse opinions (Bostdorff, 2004; see also "World View: International Web of Terror"). Public discussions on-line have run afoul of depressing realities such as public indifference and uncivil behavior (Schmitz, 1997). The Internet is not accessible to all. That limits its value as a medium of political communication or as an electronic voting booth in an egalitarian society. Information technology can also record and store so much information about us that social control could become absolute (Gandy, 1993). For example, who would check out a book (or a website) about Marxism knowing that a record of that transaction might become permanently attached to one's personal database and be used in some future "witch hunt" for communist sympathizers?

STOP & REVIEW

1. Name three theories that contend that mass media have strong effects.
2. What are some of the factors that weaken media effects?
3. Does television cause violence, or doesn't it? Explain your answer.
4. Name some examples of prosocial effects of the media.
5. What are the characteristics of successful public information campaigns?
6. Discuss the effects of advertising.

UNDERSTANDING SOCIETAL IMPACTS

Societal effects could be viewed as the aggregate of individual effects across large groups of people, the whole being equal to the sum of its parts. However, individual effects do not translate directly into broad social impacts, and indeed different theories have been proposed to explain the broader implications of the media (see Chapter 2). The important issues related to media and society reflect issues that confront society at large. They are at the root of many of the controversies that swirl around the media, and indeed underlie many of the political debates in a free society. Indeed, we abandon the use of the term "media effects" at this point, since that is closely associated with social science research on the media and the individual, and instead consider broad "social impacts."

Communications Media and Social Inequality

One of the thorniest issues confronting society is inequality between social groups as defined by wealth, race, and gender. What are the roots of social inequality in society? As societies become more complex, they become more stratified—more divided into unequal social groups or classes (Braudel, 1994).

People may be categorized both in terms of their monetary wealth, or economic capital, and in terms of differences in their education and family backgrounds—their cultural capital (Bourdieu, 1984). Differences in both economic and cultural capital help perpetuate social inequality. As we saw in Chapter 9, gaps in Internet access still remain between income, racial, and education groups over time (NTIA, 2004), a phenomenon known as the digital divide. We saw that efforts to close the divide focus primarily on making up differences in economic capital by subsidizing computers and Internet connections in poor neighborhoods.

However, equal access does not necessarily translate into social equality according to the *knowledge gap hypothesis.* The gap is between the information "haves" and the "have-nots." The information-rich "haves" are those with superior levels of education and access to libraries and home computers. The "have-nots" are the information-poor who have inferior levels of education and resource access, and tend to be the economically poor as well (see Figure 13.2). The knowledge gap hypothesis states that the dissemination of information benefits both groups but that it will benefit the information-rich

The Information Gap According to the knowledge gap hypothesis, the introduction of new information technologies will help both the information-rich and the information-poor get richer, in terms of the information they possess, but the rich get richer faster, causing the information gap to widen.

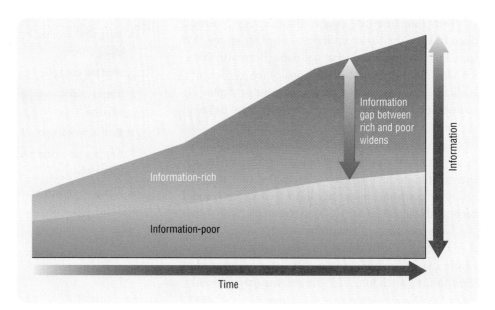

more, thereby widening the disparity between the two. Many studies have documented that information gaps are widened by the media (Gaziano, 1997), even by such well-intentioned efforts as *Sesame Street* that are specifically designed to close the gap. But, involvement may help to close the gap: those who are motivated to seek out information on a particular issue engage in more active information processing and learn more (Eveland, Shah & Kwak, 2003).

When access is unequal, the gaps get wider still. For example, privileged upper classes have easier access to print media because they can afford them more readily and also have more leisure time in which to consume them. Inequalities in access to information technology widens the gap between rich and poor (Stoll, 1995; Haywood, 1995). The knowledge gap hypothesis suggests that efforts to close the digital divide (by placing computers in the schools, for example, or making e-mail available to all) will be at least partially self-defeating. That said, it will be difficult to close the knowledge gap short of changing the fundamental inequalities in society. One approach is community networking, which offers Internet access and content to disadvantaged groups through government agencies, schools, churches, or residential communities (Borgida et al., 2002). The premise is that community-based resources tailored to local needs by community members themselves will close the gap. However, the substitution of Internet services for "real" public services may help justify cuts in public services while making the poor more reliant on a technology that they have difficulty accessing (Virnoche, 1998).

Media and Community

What impact do communications media have on our most intimate and valued relationships? Television usage may lower community involvement (Brody, 1990), and virtual communities on the Internet may displace face-to-face relationships (Spretnak, 1997). People tend to treat communications media as though they were people, talking back to their television sets and giving their computers affectionate nicknames (Reeves & Nass, 1996). These interactions are a poor substitute for interpersonal relationships.

As psychologist Sherry Turkle asks, "Is it really sensible to suggest that the way to revitalize community is to sit alone in our rooms, typing at our networked computers?" (Turkle, 1995, p. 235). At some point, we would no longer be a nation of Americans, or even of Anglo-, African-, Asian-, or Hispanic-Americans, but a disjointed collection of cults and splinter groups. The Internet perhaps accelerates this trend in modern society by divorcing social relationships from physical reality and moving them beyond our local community (Robins, 1996).

At one point it was thought that the Internet caused depression and social isolation among heavy users (Kraut et al., 1998). The researchers carried out a field experiment in which they introduced Internet access into homes and found that heavy teenage Net surfers exhibited more signs of depression than light users and also showed increased stress and loneliness. The investigators argued that weak social ties formed on the Internet displaced "real" relationships, with harmful side effects on psychological well-being. They called this finding the Internet paradox; they found it paradoxical that a social technology such as the Internet—that is used mainly to send e-mail—could reduce social involvement and lead to loneliness and depression. However, later research on the same group found that the negative effects disappeared as users became better acquainted with the Internet, although community involvement declined (Kraut et al., 2002). On the other hand, a national survey found that Internet use decreased the time spent socializing (Nie, Simpson, Stepanikova, Zheng, 2004).

Another study (Jackson et al., 2003) focusing on low-income urban households found an initial improvement in well-being after three months, but that effect disappeared after 16 months. However, the most surprising finding of the latter study was that low-income respondents used the Internet for hardly any communication at all. The researchers explained that was simply because so few low-income homes have computers that there was no one else to talk to. Thus, a further Internet paradox is how to resolve these two conflicting bodies of research. This can be done by replicating the studies to make sure they produced reliable and generalizable results and then probing for new variables that might resolve their apparent contradictions. At this point in the search for the answer to the Internet paradox, it appears that online communication strengthens and complements real-world communication rather than replaces it, although that may be true only for those who are active social networkers in the real world (DiMaggio et al., 2001).

Health and Environment

Communications media affect physical health as well as mental health. We previously noted (page 412) that television viewing is associated with obesity in children, for example. A new category of a television health effect emerged recently: brain seizures. It seems that cartoons with rapidly changing images and extreme colors cause susceptible children to suffer temporary seizures in which they become unconscious and writhe uncontrollably (Smillie, 1997). There is also preliminary evidence that television viewing by young children may cause attention disorders (Christakis et al., 2004).

Very low-frequency (VLF) radiation, the kind that electrical power lines emit, also poses a threat. At one point, EPA scientists concluded that VLF was as dangerous as chemical cancer-inducing agents, although this finding was overruled by EPA administrators. Computer video display terminals (VDTs) emit the same type of radiation, and some scientists suspect that this radiation causes cancer and miscarriages in heavy users. Overall the research is inconclusive on this point (Lim, Sauter, & Schnorr, 1998). Television sets emit the same magnetic fields by the way, but not many people watch with the television in their laps.

Portable telephones have been implicated in brain cancer. Microwave and satellite communication systems are other sources of electromagnetic radiation that may have health effects. However, there is no proven theory about how electromagnetic fields interact with living tissue. Without this "missing link," scientists are unable to blame electromagnetic radiation for health effects or to establish safe exposure levels (Ahlbom & Feychting, 2001).

There is clearer evidence of another public health hazard stemming from mobile phone use. Drivers who use them in their cars have the same degree of impairment as someone who is legally drunk! A growing number of areas are outlawing the use of cell phones while driving as a result. However, there has been no overall increase in traffic fatalities since the inception of cell phones, just the opposite (Curry, 2002), another example of a mismatch between individual-level and societal-level impacts.

Up to a quarter of all computer users suffer repetitive stress injuries, mostly a result of poor posture, bad workstation design, and repetitive tasks, but also a function of work demands and psychological stress (Lim, Sauter, & Schnorr, 1998). Others get them from surfing the web, thwipping video games, or flipping the TV remote control. Extreme cases force sufferers to resort to medication, surgery, and career changes. Computer labs run by high schools and universities combine many of the factors known to increase the risk of injury: nonadjustable work surfaces, chairs with no armrests or footrests, displays perched too high, instructors applying stressful grade pressure.

Media and the Economy

New media technologies in the workplace are having an impact on the economy. They are affecting both the quantity and quality of work.

The Quantity of Work. Information technology improves *productivity* by eliminating employees. For example, nonlinear editing systems are a common productivity-enhancing feature wherever video is edited. Clips are stored and edited from computer disk, eliminating the time-consuming drudgery of moving forward and backward to particular sequences on a long spool of tape. So, more shows are edited per day with fewer editors—that's productivity. Information technology could bring not only the end of a lot of people's jobs but also the end of work itself, as computers take over jobs that people do (Aronowitz & DiFazio, 1994; Rifkin, 1995). A new phenomenon is the "lights out" factory. There are no human workers and thus no need to keep the lights on. This phenomenon is euphemistically called *job displacement* by labor economists. The United States has seen almost complete elimination of a blue-collar middle class in a single generation and nearly a third of U.S. workers are now "contingent employees" without long-term employment agreements. In Chapter 1, we warned you about *offshoring;* that's when advanced communication networks are used to link Americans to customer services agents and loan officers located in developing countries, workers willing to work for a fraction of the salaries paid for comparable jobs in the United States. Many media-related jobs including animation and documentary film production are starting to move offshore.

In the process, the old *corporate pyramid,* in which a few top executives command platoons of middle managers who in turn direct legions of rank-and-file workers, has toppled (Figure 13.3). Information technologies have made it possible for top management to coordinate activities with far fewer middle managers, the *flattened pyramid.* Another model is the *core and ring* in which middle management is eliminated and rank-and-file workers are all contingent employees who are added or subtracted as conditions warrant. Then there is the *virtual corporation* in which even top management is in constant flux, with networks of workers organized for particular tasks and disbanded when no longer needed. Hollywood production companies have long followed this model, but it is spreading to many sectors of the professional service economy populated by artists, writers, web designers, and computer consultants.

However, if information technology reduces costs and increases product quality, then there should be demand for more products and thus *higher* employment (Kilborn, 1993). For example, as computer-generated movies following the *Polar Express* model catch on,

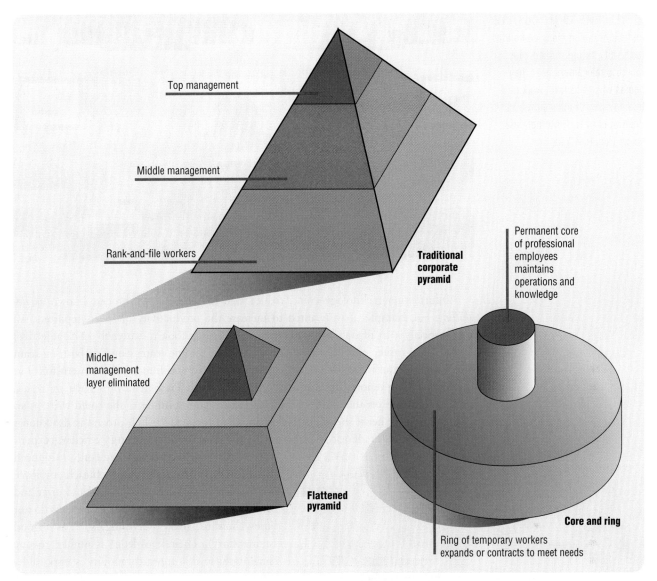

Top management

Middle management

Rank-and-file workers

Traditional corporate pyramid

Permanent core of professional employees maintains operations and knowledge

Middle-management layer eliminated

Flattened pyramid

Core and ring

Ring of temporary workers expands or contracts to meet needs

their costs will drop. Then Hollywood could fill hundreds of new channels with enticing digital entertainment, we would watch TV more and see more ads, creating demand for yet more channels and generating new employment in the television industry. Historically, fears about higher unemployment resulting from automation have proved unfounded, whether the "new technology" was the textile machinery of the 1790s or computers of the 1990s.

But it isn't clear that all the investment in information technology actually improves productivity (Sichel, 1999). A lot of high-tech investments never work quite right or incur hidden costs that sap their profitability. Economists call this the *productivity paradox.* Across the economy it looks like the benefits of information technologies used in businesses (see Chapter 12) have mostly been found in the high-tech industries themselves.

Work Gets Worse. What will work be like for those who still have it? Today's college students will have *several different careers* in their lives, not just several different jobs in the same career path with different employers, which was once the normal pattern. And lifelong employment with one employer is a relic of the past. All of this insecurity could place downward pressure on benefits and wages, except perhaps for the highly skilled elite.

■ **FIGURE 13.3**
Evolving Corporate Structures
The traditional corporate pyramid is being replaced by the flattened pyramid and the core-and-ring structure.

■ WELCOME TO MY CUBICLE
Instead of making long commutes to the city, future workers may report to telecenters near their homes where they will work next to employees of other firms, as illustrated by this Internet café scene from New York City.

Information technology could reduce skill requirements, a process known as *de-skilling*. For example, if we wanted to increase the productivity of sports reporters, we might specify a set of standard lead sentences ("Things looked extremely [pick adjective] for the [city name] nine that day. The score stood [home team score] to [visiting team score] with but an inning left to play"), fire the writer, and hire a college intern to fill in the blanks using reports transmitted on the Associated Press newswire. Then we would hold a stopwatch on the intern to see how many game summaries she could write in an hour and replace her if she fell below the standard for the job. This process is also known as *Taylorism,* after Frederick Winslow Taylor, the early twentieth-century efficiency expert.

Fordism, named after Henry Ford, introduced the assembly-line system, in which each employee performs a single, narrowly defined task over and over again. Taylorized and Fordized workers do not know how to "make" anything (such as a good sports story). Their knowledge is limited to one small task, so that upward mobility is impossible. Only the owners and their white-collar managers (here, the sports editor) know how to organize those tasks to produce goods and services.

De-skilled workers can be paid less and replaced at will, a practice known as *post-Fordism.* Henry Ford was the first to pay rank-and-file factory workers a decent wage so that they could purchase the products that they assembled. Post-Fordism cuts pay to the point that workers can no longer participate in the consumer economy. In our example, the college intern might be paid so little (or perhaps be paid nothing—it's an internship, after all!) that she could not afford an Internet connection to read her own sports stories on the web.

■ FORDISM
Henry Ford built gleaming factories, such as the River Rouge plant shown here, and paid workers a decent wage so that they could buy their own Fords.

Another dismal possibility is that skill requirements will be upgraded to the point that the current workforce does not possess them. This process is known as *up-skilling.* For example, many TV and film production specialists trained on analog technology cannot easily become a part of digital production teams because they lack the necessary computer skills.

Work Gets Better. But there are rays of hope, too, such as work decentralization. Computer networks make it possible to integrate the work of distant suppliers and far-flung backroom (or back lot) operations, moving them farther into the suburbs and rural areas. More employees can work where they want to live and avoid the stress of commuting and relocating at intervals. For example, the global nature of today's TV and film production industry, combined with traffic congestion, air pollution, and sky-high real estate costs in the Los Angeles basin, has prompted substitution of computer networks for travel in the industry. However, telecommuting has been slow to catch on amid concerns about effective supervision (Wells, 2001). Employee motivation is also an issue, and it appears that highly advanced (but highly expensive) systems that convey the sense of actually "being there" in the office through computer simulations may be required (Venkatesh & Johnson, 2002).

Another potential boon is re-skilling: reassigning to current employees tasks that were formerly parceled out to specialized workers. The employee reclaims the role of the preindustrial craftsperson (Zuboff, 1984) as knowledge becomes the cornerstone for business and social relations (Bell, 1973). For example, desktop publishing puts print publication back within the scope of a single person sitting at a personal computer. It hasn't been that way since the days of the medieval manuscript copyists. These changes rock the very foundations of industrial mass media by restoring control to the workers themselves. It is ironic that information technologies, the crowning achievement of industrial capitalism, may yet fulfill Karl Marx's prophecy. It was he, after all, who pointed out that capitalism creates the contradictions that inevitably lead to its own destruction!

STOP & REVIEW

1. What is the difference between individual effects and social effects?
2. What does the knowledge gap hypothesis predict about the effects of new information technologies?
3. What impact do information technologies have on personal relationships?
4. What are the health effects of communications media?
5. How do Taylorism, Fordism, and post-Fordism differ?
6. Give examples of jobs that have been de-skilled, jobs that have been up-skilled, and jobs that have been reskilled.

SUMMARY AND REVIEW

WHY DO PEOPLE USE THE MEDIA?
Through their interactions with the media and their observations of others, people learn expectations about the consequences of media use that shape their media behavior. Positive outcomes include learning new things, diversion, and social interaction. People may also wish to avoid media that they find boring or offensive or that they do not possess the required skills to enjoy. In organizational settings, the social presence of a medium is an important factor in deciding which tasks it is best suited for.

HOW ACTIVE IS THE AUDIENCE?
Audiences read the texts of media in a fairly active way. Some audience members might accept the "preferred" meaning—the reading that the writer or producer intended them to get out of the text. (In this context, a text is not literally printed material. TV programs, films, and web pages are also texts.) Others might use their own experiences and ideas to negotiate their own meaning out of their reading of the material. Others might contest or even oppose the meaning that the author intended.

WHAT IS THE SIGNIFICANCE OF SOCIAL PRESENCE?
Social presence is the degree to which mediated communication possesses the same social cues as live face-to-face communication. Media high in social presence are best suited to complex tasks requiring rich social interaction. Media, like e-mail, that have low social presence are better adapted to routine exchanges of information.

WHY DOESN'T SOMEONE "CLEAN UP" THE MEDIA?
Government control conflicts with the rights of the media to free speech. Media spokespersons question the validity of research that suggests the media's negative effects, and they argue that society's ills have deeper causes than mass media exposure. The media sometimes adopt their own guidelines.

However, these are voluntary standards that are usually eroded by commercial pressures.

WHAT ARE TWO BASIC APPROACHES TO MEDIA EFFECTS?

Media effects are changes in knowledge, attitude, or behavior that result from exposure to the mass media. In the deductive approach, predictions about media effects are derived from theory, and exposure to media content is treated as the causal, or independent, variable that leads to the effects, or the dependent variable. The inductive approach infers the impacts of the media, and theories that explain them are inferred from detailed observations in real-world environments.

WHAT ARE BASIC METHODS OF MEDIA EFFECTS RESEARCH?

Content analysis is used to characterize the content of media systems by enumerating the types of behaviors, themes, and actors that appear in the media, though such analysis cannot be used to make inferences about the actual effects of the media. Experimental research examines the relationship between exposure to media content and audience effects under tightly controlled laboratory conditions that make it possible to rule out competing explanations for the effects that are observed. Survey studies administer questionnaires to large representative samples of subjects to examine relationships between media exposure and media effects; they take into account a wider range of factors than experimental studies. In ethnographic studies, researchers maintain extended contact with subjects so that they can gain insight into social processes involving media systems. Their results, however, may not be generalizable beyond the specific communities they study.

HOW HAVE THEORIES OF MEDIA EFFECTS CHANGED?

Theories of mass media effects have evolved over the years. Early scholars believed the mass media could have immediate and profound effects on their audiences, after the fashion of a speeding bullet or a hypodermic injection. Later, researchers learned that the influence of the mass media is weakened by the intervention of social groups, via a multistep flow process, and by the audience's ability to selectively avoid, misinterpret, or forget content with which they disagree. Social learning theory describes how people can learn behavior from visual media, and cultivation theory shows how people's understanding of the world around them is shaped by media images. Priming theory focuses on the power of media images to activate related thoughts in our own minds.

WHAT IS THE IMPACT OF MEDIA ON ANTISOCIAL BEHAVIOR?

Experimental studies have shown that even relatively short exposure to TV programs featuring violence can provoke violent behavior in viewers, particularly young children. Men exposed to violent pornography harbor more negative feelings toward women. Media also can reinforce sex-role and racial stereotypes that lead to sexism and racism.

WHAT IS THE IMPACT OF MEDIA ON PROSOCIAL BEHAVIOR?

Prosocial behaviors are socially desirable acts such as cooperation, sharing, and racial tolerance. Information campaigns seek to convince mass audiences to adopt socially desirable behaviors. Although such campaigns are sometimes effective, they often suffer from poor planning and execution and from limited audience exposure. Furthermore, they must contend with resistance arising from social influence and selective perception among their audiences. Other varieties of prosocial media combine varying degrees of entertainment and educational content, ranging from distance-learning classes to incidental learning from entertainment programs.

WHAT ARE THE IMPACTS OF ADVERTISING AND POLITICAL CAMPAIGNS?

Despite the huge sums of money spent on commercial and political advertisements, their effects are relatively modest; they directly affect perhaps only a few percent of the audience. Those who are affected by advertisements are likely to be those who are relatively uninformed about or uninterested in the product or candidate to begin with. Interpersonal influence and selective perception act to reduce the impact of advertisements on most audiences. Still, that small percent that is influenced can translate into millions of dollars in a successful advertising campaign, or into crucial deciding votes in a political race.

HOW DO MEDIA IMPACT SOCIAL EQUALITY?

Information technologies do not benefit all groups in society equally. Minorities may be left behind in the transition to the information economy as the digital divide widens. The knowledge gap hypothesis predicts that efforts to improve the plight of the disadvantaged through improved access to communications media will instead result in widening the gap between rich and poor.

HOW DO MEDIA AFFECT SOCIAL RELATIONS?

History shows that new communications technologies augment some forms of interpersonal communication while disrupting others. The advent of the Internet has the potential for bringing about a situation in which everyone is our neighbor in a small, electronically mediated global village. The virtual communities that have formed on the Internet are an initial indication that new types of human relationships may be created. However, there is the danger that the world could evolve into an extremely fragmented postmodern society in which chaos reigns. Information technologies may also degrade the sense of social presence we experience when we talk to people face to face.

DO INFORMATION TECHNOLOGIES CAUSE UNEMPLOYMENT?

Improvements in productivity brought about by applications of information technology have the potential to displace large numbers of jobs. Historically, new waves of industrial technology have increased employment in the long term, and the same is likely to hold true today. In the short term, however, entire categories of workers will be eliminated or see their jobs moved offshore, and workers with useless skills may be forced to seek unstable contingent employment.

DO COMMUNICATIONS MEDIA MAKE WORK LESS SATISFYING?

In some applications, information technologies increase the twin tendencies of Taylorism and Fordism, de-skilling work to meaningless, repetitive, assembly-line tasks. In the extreme, jobs become so degraded that workers no longer command a decent living wage, a condition called post-Fordism. In other instances, information technology up-skills jobs, displacing workers whose skills no longer match job requirements. However, information technologies can also be applied in ways that re-skill jobs, restoring work to a meaningful and dignified pursuit.

MEDIA CONNECTION

For web links, quizzes, and key term flash cards, visit the **Student Companion Website** at http://communication.wadsworth.com/straubhaar5.

 For unlimited easy access to additional and exclusive online study, support, and research tools, log on to **1pass** at http://1pass.thomson.com using the unique access code found on your 1pass passcode card.

 The **Media Now Premium Website** offers *Career Profile* videos, *Critical View* video news clips, and *Media in Motion* concept animations. You'll also find Stop & Review tutorial questions, a sample final exam, and much more.

 InfoTrac College Edition is a fully searchable online database offering anytime, anywhere access to more than 20 years' worth of articles from nearly 5,000 diverse and reliable sources.

vMentor provides live, one-on-one online tutoring to connect you to experts who will assist you in understanding the concepts covered in your course.

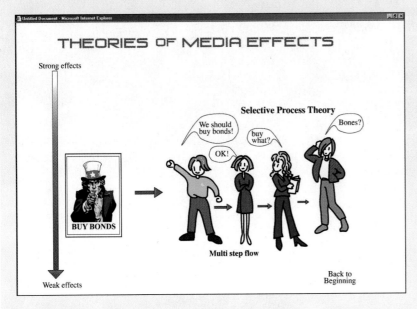

For animated representations of several concepts presented in this chapter, including Theories of Media Effects, watch the Media in Motion animations on the website.

MEDIA POLICY AND LAW

Congress passes laws that shape the media in many ways. Here we recap many of the important social issues covered in previous chapters and put them into context. Government policy and law focus on content issues, such as sex, violence, and libel in the media, as well as technical standards, competition, ownership, equal access, privacy, and copyright.

POLICY AND LAW IN COMMUNICATIONS

The importance of media in public and private life leads to constant concern about what the media are doing and how to guide them. The formation of policy and the passage and enforcement of law involve a collective action of the whole society or its representatives, which requires a good deal of public discussion and the formation of public opinion on what to do. **Policy** reflects government and public consideration of how to structure and regulate social or collective activities, such as those of the media, so that they contribute to the public good. Many groups, such as churches, private companies, industry trade groups, minority groups, and public-interest groups, also monitor media performance and lobby the media and the government to make changes. For example, lobbying by a number of groups led to a crackdown on indecent content on television by the FCC in 2004.

    Laws are binding rules passed by legislatures, enforced by the executive power, and applied or adjudicated by courts. Policies are often turned into laws in order to make them legally binding on people and companies. **Standards** are technical characteristics, such as the number of lines on the television screen, that must be agreed on for a technology to be widely manufactured and used.

Policy is a public framework for how to structure and regulate media so they contribute to the public good.

Laws are binding rules passed by legislatures, enforced by the executive power, and applied or adjudicated by courts.

Standards are agreements about technical characteristics of communication systems.

MEDIA THEN/MEDIA NOW

1733 Peter Zenger trial establishes truth as a defense for press against libel charges

1789 First Amendment to Constitution enshrines freedom of press; Fourth Amendment protects privacy against unwarranted searches and seizures by government

1790 Copyright Act

1865 International Telecommunications Union formed to set telegraph standards

1890 Sherman Antitrust Act limits monopolies' restraint of trade

1934 Communications Act covers broadcasting and telecommunications

1987 Electronic Communications Privacy Act

1996 Telecommunications Act deregulates industries to let them compete; Communications Decency Act declared unconstitutional by Supreme Court

1998 Copyright Term Extension Act; Children's Online Privacy Protection Act

2001 USA Patriot Act widens government surveillance and wiretapping powers in cases of national security

2004 The Congress substantially increases fines for indecency on radio and television after large-scale complaints over the showing of Janet Jackson's breast during the 2004 Super Bowl.

Rather than waiting to be regulated by law or executive branch rules, like those of the FCC, many industries formally regulate themselves. **Self-regulation** pertains to the communication industry's own codes and practices of self-monitoring and controlling the media's performance.

Some issues cut across all these media control mechanisms. For example, sex and violence in the media have been discussed for decades, resulting in government policies, such as the Federal Communication Commission's (FCC) scrutiny of language used on radio, and laws. For example, the 1996 Telecommunications Act required a V-chip system to help people screen out objectionable content in television and cable TV offerings. We have also seen examples of industry self-regulation, such as the Hollywood film rating system. However, public and political pressure can still move federal agencies like the FCC to tighten rules and enforcement. That can lead to changes in behavior, as when a number of stations in 2004 declined to air *Saving Private Ryan,* for fear of FCC actions against violent content, even though the same stations had shown the film previously. In 2005 the FCC ruled that *Saving Private Ryan* was not violent.

KEY COMMUNICATIONS POLICIES

Policies governing free speech, privacy, intellectual property, competition, diversity, and access form the basic framework for guiding communications media in the United States.

Freedom of Speech and the First Amendment

The most fundamental U.S. policy regarding the content and conduct of media is the **First Amendment.** This reflects an underlying agreement, dating from the American Revolution in 1776, that **freedom of speech,** both in person and over media, is a basic requirement for the type of political system and society that the writers of the U.S. Constitution wished to create. Many Americans nowadays take freedom of speech for

Self-regulation pertains to communication industry codes and practices of monitoring and controlling the media's performance.

The **First Amendment** to the U.S. Constitution guarantees freedom of speech and of the press.

Freedom of speech is the idea that speech and media content should be free from government restriction.

■ **STICKS AND STONES!**
Many governments fear criticism
from the press, so they control or
censor it. A cartoon such as this,
criticizing government or a leader,
would not be allowed to run in
many countries.

granted, but those who fought in the Revolution and those who wrote the Constitution,
such as Jefferson, Franklin, and Paine, were well aware of how few places at that time had
freedom of speech and how easily it could be limited.

Development of the First Amendment.   In the early days of printing in Europe, both
church and civil authorities granted licenses to certain guilds or companies to print
books, but they also controlled what could be printed. As people began to be concerned
about the importance of freedom of speech for developing more open societies, such
control by licensing came under increasingly severe criticism from writers and philosophers. For example, in 1644 the essayist and poet John Milton wrote a critique of such
censorship, called *Aeropagitica,* proclaiming the need for religious free speech.

Protecting Political Speech.   Along with economic ideas about the value of a marketplace
competition for goods, the idea developed of a **marketplace of ideas** in which different
voices could compete for attention. In political terms, John Stuart Mill, Edmund Burke,
and other early advocates of democracy promoted the idea of an active, informed citizenry. They pointed to the need for a free press to assist in the wide circulation of ideas
(Altschull, 1995).

Censorship is formal restriction of
media or speech content by
government, political, or religious
authorities.

However, in many times and places, before the American Revolution and since,
governments have directly censored and controlled media. Sometimes governments want
to prohibit, or censor, criticism of themselves. Sometimes they seize control of media to use
them as tools in their own plans for development of a society. At a lower level of control,
many governments have tried to restrain specific kinds of media content that they consider
harmful, such as criticism of rulers. Even Great Britain, the source of many American political traditions, still has laws on the books that permit government to censor media content.

Marketplace of ideas means that the
best ideas will win out in
competition.

Under British rule, the American colonies struggled to protect free speech and criticism of authority in the press. In Peter Zenger's **libel** trial against the British governor in

Libel is a harmful and untruthful
criticism by media that intends to
damage someone.

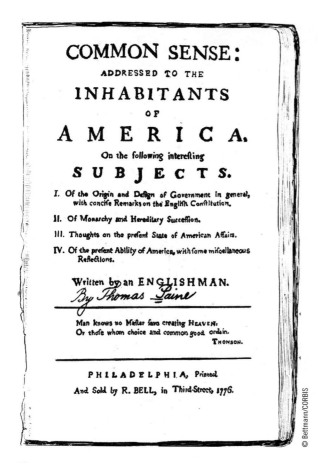

© Bettmann/CORBIS

■ COMMON SENSE AGAINST CENSORSHIP

Publications such as Thomas Paine's challenged British censorship and promoted the American Revolution.

1733 (see Chapter 4), his lawyer successfully urged the jury not to rely on British precedents but to consider that the truth of an article was a sufficient defense against libel. Strong support for protecting freedom of speech and of the press continued to develop during the American Revolution against British colonial rule in 1776–1783. Independent newspapers and pamphlets encouraged the American colonists to resist British rule. Benjamin Franklin published pro-independence newspapers, and Thomas Paine wrote pamphlets, such as *Common Sense,* that were widely read. A free press was so important to the American Revolution that it was firmly enshrined in the Declaration of Independence and in the First Amendment to the U.S. Constitution. The First Amendment says

> Congress shall make no law respecting an establishment of religion, or prohibiting the free exercise thereof, or abridging the freedom of speech, or of the press; or the right of the people peaceably to assemble, and to petition the Government for a redress of grievances.

Limits on the First Amendment

Some kinds of speech are not protected by the First Amendment: defamation, obscenity, plagiarism, invasion of privacy, and inciting insurrection.

Defamation. Defamatory statements (*libel,* if it is written, or *slander,* if it is spoken) are untrue declarations about private citizens that might damage their reputations. Libel means that the information given is false or is intended to damage the reputation of the person being libeled. U.S. legal policy balances libel concerns against the watchdog role of the press, which is to expose corruption or incompetence by officials or public figures. Journalists often have to decide whether a certain kind of story about individuals, or certain treatment of individuals is ethical (see Chapter 15).

Political Speech on the Airwaves and the Fairness Doctrine. Some nations give people who have been criticized a right of reply. That principle has seldom been applied to U.S. print media, because they are numerous and tend to balance each other's excesses. However, the Radio Act of 1927 assumed that the First Amendment goal of promoting a diversity of viewpoints needed regulatory help in the case of radio, where only a few could have direct access to the airwaves. The Act required equal opportunities:

> If any licensee shall permit any person who is a legally qualified candidate for any public office to use a broadcasting station, he shall afford equal opportunities to all other such candidates for that office in the use of such broadcasting station (Sect. 315, Radio Act of 1927).

This principle is still applied to political debates, where all major candidates must be allowed to participate. A far thornier issue has been paid political advertising, where richer candidates' financial resources give them greater access to the airwaves. There, two principles have evolved. First, stations cannot refuse a candidate's advertising. Second, stations have to sell advertising time at their lowest rate to candidates. Congress and the

MEDIA AND CULTURE

George Carlin and "Seven Dirty Words"

The *FCC v. Pacifica Foundation* case (1978) defined a number of key issues relevant to obscenity and indecency. The case centered on whether the Pacifica radio station could play George Carlin's provocative 12-minute monologue about the "seven dirty words you can't say on radio."

The FCC argued that, judged by contemporary community standards, these words are offensive; that broadcasting is an intrusive medium; and that obscenity is separate from indecency. The FCC found that the rules are not overly broad but rather are intended to protect children from "exposure to language that describes, in terms patently offensive as measured by contemporary community standards for the broadcast medium, sexual or excretory activities and organs, at times of the day when there is a reasonable risk that children may be in the audience . . . language which most parents regard as inappropriate for them to hear." The FCC made a later clarification that media can use such words when children are in the audience when they have legitimate artistic, political, or social value (for example, a Shakespeare play). There was considerable criticism, though, in 2003, of an FCC decision to not penalize U2 singer Bono for calling something "f---ing brilliant" during the televised Golden Globe Awards, a decision that the FCC later reversed under pressure.

Pacifica argued that obscenity and indecency are not equal, and that children are in the audience all the time. The

Appeals Court agreed with Pacifica's points. It also noted that what is meant by "children" is not sufficiently defined; that one cannot easily discern the degree of legitimate, artistic, political, or social value; that broadcasters can't protect listeners from everything unpleasant; that there is no empirical evidence that filth would flood the air; and that if the majority of audience members disapprove, market forces will remove the station from competition.

The Supreme Court decided (in *FCC v. Pacifica Foundation,* 98 Supreme Court 326, 1978) that the FCC may sanction licensees who use indecent words because broadcasting is the least protected by the First Amendment because it enters the privacy of people's homes and children have easy access to broadcasting. The FCC can review programming after broadcast and can use that review when considering licensing. It noted that Section 1464 of the U.S. Code lists "obscene, indecent, or profane" but that indecency is different from obscenity. It argued that a nuisance "may be merely a right thing in the wrong place. . . ." While the FCC has not always taken advantage of this power, things changed in 2003–2004. The FCC began to receive more complaints about indecency and reacted to public complaints with more frequent and larger fines (see Chapter 8).

FCC periodically debate whether to require broadcast stations to give free time for political debate and candidates' political commercials, but to no definite conclusion.

The FCC also developed a concept known as the Fairness Doctrine. Its core idea was that the public's right to be informed overrides the right of broadcasters to carry their "own particular views on any matter" (Supreme Court decision in *Red Lion Broadcasting Co. v. FCC,* 395 U.S. 367, 1969). In theory, this concept required stations to schedule time for controversial programming on issues and then to ensure the expression of opposing views. In practice, the FCC did not really require stations to carry issue-oriented programming, so the rule focused on the right of reply to controversial points of view. By the 1980s, some broadcasters were arguing that the right of reply in the Fairness Doctrine actually led stations to avoid controversial programming. Both the FCC and the Supreme Court questioned the original argument that radio and television stations were so scarce that each of them had a unique responsibility to be fair and balanced. The FCC in 1985 therefore stopped enforcing the doctrine and it was finally struck down by the Supreme Court in 2001.

Freedom of Speech: Sex and Obscenity. The First Amendment was originally framed to protect political speech, political criticism, and religious choice. However, the tradition of free speech has gradually been extended to moral issues of sexuality and obscenity. The idea of exercising moral judgment and control on content still has a strong influence in the United States. Although newspapers and newsmagazines have been largely free from censorship on political issues since 1800, books, magazines, radio, film, and television have been subject to content controls on sexuality and language. Novels such as D. H. Lawrence's *Lady Chatterley's Lover* (1928) were widely subjected to censorship in the United States as recently as the 1950s. Congress has created new rules for the Internet on pornography, requiring filtering software for children in schools and libraries in the 2001 Children's Internet Protection Act (see "Indecency and the Internet," page 437).

In a series of decisions, courts have ruled that moral standards for print and other media cannot be decided on a national basis, because those standards vary among communities. Communities are permitted to develop local standards for treatment of sexuality and obscenity. In 1957, in *Roth v. United States,* the U.S. Supreme Court defined **obscenity** in community-based terms: "whether, to the average person, applying contemporary community standards, the dominant theme of the material taken as a whole appeals to prurient interest." In *Miller v. California* (1973), the Court added that states might prohibit the printing or sale of works "which portray sexual conduct in a patently offensive way, and which, taken as a whole, do not have serious literary, artistic, political or scientific value." For example, some communities define certain books, magazines, and videos as pornographic and restrict their sales to adult bookstores or require their covers to be concealed when on public display.

The late twentieth century saw a sharp decline in the limits placed on **indecency,** which is usually defined somewhat more narrowly than obscenity. This was seen as progress for freedom of speech. However, since the 1970s there has been increasing concern about obscenity again. For example, the FCC disciplined the Pacifica radio station in 1973 for broadcasting comedian George Carlin's monologue "The Seven Dirty Words You Can't Say on Radio." It relied on a definition of indecency as "language that describes, in terms patently offensive as measured by contemporary community standards for the broadcast of the medium, sexual or excretory activities or organs," and its action was upheld by the Supreme Court in 1978 (Heins, 1993, p. 26). (See "Media and Culture, George Carlin and 'Seven Dirty Words,'" page 435.) The new FCC chair Martin, in 2005, promised more crackdowns in indecency.

Free-Speech Limits on Broadcasting. The 1934 Communications Act applied the basic idea of protecting freedom of speech to broadcasting:

> Nothing in this Act shall be understood or construed to give the Commission the power of censorship over the radio communications or signals transmitted by any radio station, and no regulation or condition shall be promulgated or fixed by the Commission which shall interfere with the right of free speech by means of radio communication.

These protections of free speech were not changed by the 1996 Telecommunications Act, which notes that FCC authorities or limits not addressed by the 1996 Act are left in place. However, broadcast media have been more regulated than print media. Access to the airwaves is much more limited than access to speaking, writing, or publishing. By the 1980s, as broadcast media became more plentiful, this distinction was diminished for many people.

As we saw in Chapter 8, obscenity and indecency are more limited on broadcasts because they come straight into the home over the airwaves. They are presumed to be more accessible to children, and accessing them does not require the same sort of conscious choice as picking up a book or magazine. Since the 1978 *Pacifica* decision, there has been a tendency to limit indecency on radio and television during hours when children are likely to be listening and to create "safe havens" for absolutely free speech from midnight to 6 A.M. Cable television channels carry a number of programs that contain indecent

Obscenity refers to material where the dominant theme taken as a whole appeals to prurient, or sexually arousing, interest.

Indecency refers to sexual or excretory acts.

material at hours when children are watching, but because cable does not use the public airwaves, it has not been subjected to the same scrutiny by the FCC. The FCC had been gradually allowing more and more nudity and reference to sexuality on cable TV and, to lesser degree, broadcast television as well through the 1990s. However, that changed dramatically in 2004 as the FCC began to respond to complaints about such content by applying pressure on radio and television stations in networks. Major waves of complaint came into the FCC after Janet Jackson's breast was exposed during the 2004 Super Bowl halftime show and then again in November 2004 after *Monday Night Football* featured an ad with a naked Nicolette Sheridan jumping into the arms of Eagles receiver Terrell Owen to promote the show *Desperate Housewives*. More than 500,000 complaints over the Janet Jackson incident led the FCC to take a much harsher view of indecency and increase considerably the number of times it fined offending broadcasters. Congress was considering raising the fines to a maximum of $500,000 in 2005, from a previous maximum of $32,500 per incident. Since indecency is now defined as material "patently offensive as measured by contemporary community standards," and since the levels of complaint over indecency have risen sharply, a key question is whether community standards have changed or whether a vocal minority has figured out how to use the Internet and other tools to make itself more loudly and clearly heard.

The most dramatic result, overall, was the announcement by Howard Stern, one frequent FCC target, of his intention to shift from broadcast radio to satellite radio. Current indecency rules only apply to broadcast radio and television, which enter the home with being explicitly ordered and paid for. For that reason, cable and satellite television, as well as the new satellite radio services, are not subjected to the same rules since ordering them is voluntary on the part of the listener or viewer. So Howard Stern on Sirius satellite radio will not be subject to the same rules (and fines) on broadcast radio, as "Sex and the City" on HBO. Some in Congress have suggested applying the broadcast rules to cable and satellite radio and television.

Indecency and the Internet.   A new challenge is raised by the Internet, which gives both adults and children potential access to indecent materials. The Internet poses some unique problems. The number of "sources" is in the hundreds of millions, and no one is really in charge of network content. The users of the network are also the "publishers," but they do not have to subscribe to any code of ethics or community morality.

The Internet presents new ethical and legal challenges to professionals in news, broadcasting, libraries, and information services about what kinds of materials to permit on interactive services. All schools and most libraries are required to use computer filtering programs that screen sexual content on the Internet since 2003. Civil liberties groups criticize such programs as restricting the free speech of adults. The American Library Association firmly opposed the use of filtering programs, arguing that they could unreasonably limit access to information for adult users (ALA, 1998). Within the Telecommunications Act of 1996, the Communications Decency Act (CDA) created a more inclusive definition of objectionable materials under the term "indecency." Its definition was problematic, however. For example, is the use of the word "breast" indecent in some contexts, like erotica, and not in others, like a discussion of cancer?

The CDA was promptly challenged in court by the American Civil Liberties Union (ACLU), the Electronic Frontier Foundation, and some of the industry actors, such as America Online, that might be held responsible for transmitting indecent material. They argued that the Internet deserves First Amendment protections as broad as those enjoyed by print, rather than the more limited protection given broadcasting. In particular, the restrictions were seen as limiting the free-speech rights of adults too much in an effort to protect children. The Supreme Court agreed and overturned key aspects of the CDA for

overly limiting adults' freedom of speech and relying on a definition of indecency that
was too vague. The 1998 Child On-Line Protection Act narrowed the prohibitions to
cover commercial sites only, targeted only content harmful to children, and required age
verification on adult sites in hopes of passing muster with the First Amendment.

Congress tried again with the Children's Internet Protection Act in 2001. It required
schools and libraries to use filtering software that would block access to material defined
as indecent or lose federal funds. In 2003, the Supreme Court reversed an earlier stand
and found the law constitutional. It has been enforced since on all schools and libraries
which receive federal support under the e-Rule program from the FCC to help connect
public places of access to the Internet.

Regulation vs. Self-Regulation: TV Violence and the V-Chip. Another response to concerns
about controversial content has been proposals for industry self-regulation. In 1993 the
television industry proposed voluntary standards about labeling violent programming,
but critics felt that simple labeling was not effective. This led Congress to add a provision
in the 1996 Telecommunications Act requiring a V-chip to permit television viewers to
block out programs rated as containing sex or violence.

The bill represented an interesting combination of regulation and self-regulation, in
that it required the industry to come up with a system for rating programs for violence,
sex, and language. Film and television industry leaders reluctantly created a rating system
in 1997, modeled on the age-based rating of films (see Chapter 7). Critics had hoped for
a system that would have a separate rating for levels of sex, violence, and indecent
language in each program. Thus the rating represented a compromise between what
industry, Congress, and critics wanted. However, surveys of viewers with V-chip sets have
shown that very few were using this option.

Other examples of industry self-regulation include the Motion Picture Association of
America's film rating system and the National Association of Broadcasters' self-regulation
on the amount of commercial time to be included in broadcasting hours.

Freedom of Commercial Speech.   Commercial speech is that which advertises a product or service for profit or for a business purpose. It is entitled to much less protection than noncommercial speech, since it is not seen as part of the political marketplace of ideas. Misleading commercial speech or commercial speech that proposes unlawful actions has no protection under the law. The Federal Trade Commission monitors **deceptive advertising** in both mass media and online media. However, businesses still have free speech rights as long as their product is legal. That is why we still see cigarette and liquor ads even though those products harm their consumers when used in excess.

Prior to industrialization in the United States, deceptive advertising rarely appeared in regulatory issues. Under the ancient law of caveat emptor ("let the buyer beware"), it was assumed to be the consumer's fault if he or she had been duped by a false advertising claim. With the passage of the Federal Trade Commission Act of 1914, however, the government began cracking down on deceptive practices in advertising. Today, the Federal Trade Commission (FTC) is active in regulating advertisers if (1) the message is likely to mislead the consumer, (2) the consumer is found to be acting reasonably under the circumstances, and (3) the omission, falsehood, or representation is "material" or likely to affect actual purchase decisions. Enforcement procedures by the FTC can include a cease and desist order, prohibiting further communication of the deception, and corrective advertising, requiring public clarification and admission of the falsehood. For example, the FTC is trying to apply these provisions to Internet advertisers that deceive readers into opening their e-mails (CAN-SPAM Act, 2003).

The Fourth Amendment and Protecting Privacy

Although most Americans assume that they have a right to **privacy,** this right is not nearly as clearly established in law as freedom of speech. Some argue that the first 10 amendments to the U.S. Constitution focus on protecting people from invasions of their privacy by government. Supreme Court Justice Harlan in 1965 said that the constitutional right to privacy derives from the First, Third, Fourth, Fifth, Ninth, and Fourteenth Amendments, although it exceeds the sum of its parts (*Griswold v. Connecticut*, 381 U.S. 479, 499–500, 1965). This broad view of privacy remains controversial, however, and groups like the Electronic Privacy Information Center and the Electronic Freedom Forum have called for clearer, more specific laws to specify privacy rights.

The Fourth Amendment guarantees ". . . the right of the people to be secure in their persons, houses, papers, and effects, against unreasonable searches and seizures." It also states that "no (search) Warrants shall issue but upon probable cause . . . particularly describing the place to be searched, and the persons or things to be seized." On the other hand, people are routinely searched without warrants at airports, for tax information, and in other places by governments, and the 2001 Patriot Act makes electronic searches much easier to approve.

The right to privacy includes a generalized "right to be let alone" that includes "the individual interest in avoiding disclosure of personal matters." This line of thought forms the basis for many claims to a right to informational privacy (Chlapowski, 1991). Another strong force now comes from public opinion, which has been sensitized to privacy issues regarding telephones and the Internet. Most surveys now show strong support for protection of privacy online and in computerized databases (Strover and Straubhaar, 2004). Earlier pressure for relief from intrusive telemarketing led to the Federal Trade Commissions 2003 Do Not Call Registry, which permits people to register telephone numbers that telemarketers cannot call.

The current threats to privacy come both from government, as anticipated in the U.S. Bill of Rights, and also from private companies that gather, collate, manipulate, and

Deceptive advertising makes misleading or untruthful claims.

Privacy is the right to avoid unwanted intrusions or disclosure.

Consumer Privacy Tips and Rights

- Periodically review your consumer credit files.
- If you dispute the information in your file, append your own explanation.
- If you want to have your name removed from telemarketing lists, contact the Do Not Call Registry of the FTC.
- Avoid giving out your Social Security number except to your employer or government agencies.
- Do not write your telephone number on credit applications, on subscription forms, or even on the checks you cash.
- Assume that everything you say on a cordless or cellular phone can be overheard.
- Assume that all your e-mail from school or work accounts or computers is monitored by those institutions.
- Ask your phone company about caller ID service.
- Add yourself to the FTC's Do Not Call List

Consumer Privacy Rights

A right to privacy has been articulated in a series of decisions by the federal courts and has been extended to information privacy by several pieces of legislation over the last 25 years. All consumers should be aware of their rights under these laws:

- *The right to inspect.* Under the Fair Credit Reporting Act of 1970, consumers have the right to inspect the information contained in a credit agency's file.
- *The right to challenge.* Consumers have the right to challenge the accuracy of the information and to append their own explanations.
- *The right to updates.* Credit agencies must purge items that are more than seven years old, including records of old arrests and lawsuits.
- *The right of control.* Inquiries for purposes other than hiring, insurance investigations, or credit checks can be made only with the permission of the subject or under a court order. The Privacy Act of 1974 constrains federal agencies—though not state and local government or private companies—from transferring information without consent and from using information for purposes other than that for which it was originally collected.
- *The right to refuse.* The Privacy Act of 1974 stipulates that citizens can refuse to disclose their Social Security number except where required by law. This limits the use of Social Security numbers to match data between sources.
- *The right to notification.* The Right to Financial Privacy Act of 1979 requires that federal law enforcement agencies notify individuals when their financial records are subpoenaed. The Privacy Act of 1974 prohibits secret files and requires government agencies to publish descriptions of the files they keep and the types of information they contain each year.
- The Federal Do Not Call Registry, instituted by the Federal Trade Commission in 2003, gives you the right to register your telephone number to avoid marketing calls at home from commercial sales groups or marketers with whom you are not already doing business.
- *The right to electronic privacy.* A 1967 Supreme Court decision held telephone wiretaps unconstitutional, although Congress later legalized wiretaps conducted under court order. The Electronic Communication Privacy Act of 1986 extended this protection to electronic mail messages. A number of bills to clarify the right to privacy have been introduced in Congress. One of the most closely scrutinized issues is the protection of medical and legal records. New rules under HIPAA (see page 441) permitted greater electronic exchange of medical records with some privacy protection.

even sell information about individuals. Government intrusions on privacy had been carefully limited until recently, but new federal initiatives against terrorism since the attacks of September 11, 2001, have raised many new issues. The private sector intrusion grew with credit bureaus that gather credit information about individuals to sell to banks, loan agencies, and mortgage companies. Companies then began to track sales data about individuals to determine their buying habits and preferences. Magazines, catalogs, and firms that specialized in direct-mail sales also discovered that selling mailing lists of potential customers was a profitable business. Companies gathered and matched different lists or databases to accumulate more information about individuals. The whole process accelerated with the Internet, where many sites gather extensive information from their visitors, which can also be matched with other computer data. Although Congress has considered legislation to limit disclosure and collation of such data. However, political campaigns benefit enormously from the ability to target interest groups that such databases give them, so many politicians are reluctant to regulate them.

The accuracy of computer databases is also becoming a critical issue. Many people already suffer from the consequences of erroneous data in their credit information files. When they apply for a credit card or loan, they may be refused because someone with a similar name or Social Security number has not made payments. Control over the use, release, and sale of information, particularly sensitive items like medical records, is also becoming a major issue for many people (see "Media and Culture, Consumer Privacy Tips and Rights," page 440). This was addressed by the 2001 Data Quality Act, which permits more scrutiny of government data. If successful, this may be extended to cover more private databases.

The United States seems to be moving toward industry self-regulation on the protection of privacy. However, the online and consumer database industries have been slow to provide safeguards against encroachments on privacy. One of the most sensitive areas is privacy of medical records. The Health Insurance Portability and Accountability Act (HIPAA) was passed by Congress in 1996 to set a national standard for electronic transfers of health data, but raised questions of privacy and control over personal medical data. In response, the U.S. Department of Health and Human Services issued the HIPAA Privacy Rule in 2003, which provided some controls but tends to favor medical needs over privacy concerns.

Another source of pressure on American industry to develop standards for protecting privacy is the European Union's Data Protection Directive, which became effective in 1998. These rules require that European citizens be told what their personal data will be used for. They have the right to access data about themselves in companies' files, the ability to correct false information, and the opportunity to opt out before personal data are transferred to a third party. Officials in European countries could impose embargoes against transfers of personal data about European citizens to countries, such as the United States, that have privacy protections they consider inadequate (Kaplan, 1998). This forced the United States to move more quickly on creating a privacy protection system that would satisfy European partners, so that electronic commerce would not be impeded.

Some of the policy movement on privacy issues came from the Federal Trade Commission (FTC), which inspired the passage of the 1998 Child On-Line Protection Act. It requires web publishers to notify visitors about their collection of personal information and restricts the gathering and use of personal information from children 12 and under. The FTC argued that the legislation was necessary because surveys of child-oriented Internet sites indicate that efforts by Internet companies to regulate themselves on privacy matters had not been adequate (Clausing, September 24, 1998). The Federal Trade Commission also enforces rules in the Financial Modernization Act of 1999 to protect financial privacy. The **Fair Credit Reporting Act (FCRA)** is enforced by the Federal Trade Commission to promote accuracy in consumer reports and ensure the privacy of the information in them. The FTC was pursuing new, expanded legislation, but since 2001, has focused on enforcement of existing laws that encourage firms to set and keep privacy standards.

The contents of mail and telephone conversations are legally protected. Government criminal investigators can intercept conversations via wiretap, but only with a court warrant, as specified in the Fourth Amendment. The Electronic Communications Privacy Act of 1987 extended wiretap protections to electronic mail, teleconferences, and other new media. However, although e-mail from home computers and personal accounts is protected, e-mail from office or school computers or accounts may be monitored by employers or school officials. The USA Patriot Act of 2001 loosened rules on all

© Paul Conklin/Photo Edit

■ YEA OR NAY?
Congress makes laws about media issues.

Fair Credit Reporting Act (FCRA)
2002 insures accuracy of credit reports and permits evaluating accuracy.

these areas of wiretap and surveillance if FBI or other officials convince special courts that U.S. national security is threatened by the potential object of surveillance. The old standard of requiring authorities to show **probable cause** has been reduced, so that approval of intercepts was almost automatic in national security cases. However, several court decisions have restored somewhat stricter requirements for probable cause.

The possibility of **encrypting** e-mail messages to ensure their privacy raises new issues. Law enforcement officials would like you to file a copy of your encryption code with a federal agency so that officials would be able to decode your messages—only under court order, of course—to check for criminal or national security violations. Internet users and civil liberties groups are up in arms over this *escrow key encryption* proposal, claiming that it is an unreasonable invasion of privacy by the government and makes all users vulnerable in the quite likely event that someone eventually "cracks" the secret code key. Government efforts to crack such private codes have accelerated considerably in the wake of the September 11 attacks.

Spamming occurs when direct marketers or outright con artists do mass e-mailings to the unwary user, often with names and addresses garnered from chat rooms or newsgroups operating in open cyberspace. Many Internet users do not realize that when they make postings in these public areas they place themselves directly in the crosshairs of direct marketers who employ what are known as "harvesting programs" to automatically extract e-mail addresses. Personal web pages are another fertile hunting ground for spammers. Spam victims can use filtering utilities in their e-mail software to screen some of the junk. Many have resorted to establishing multiple e-mail "identities" so that they can close accounts that attract too much spam while preserving a private e-mail address for close associates that is never exposed in public web spaces. Over two dozen states have now passed laws restricting spam, and Congress passed the **Controlling the Assault of Non-Solicited Pornography and Marketing Act of 2003** (CAN-SPAM Act), which makes commercial e-mail obey a series of rules requiring identification of the e-mailer and his or her intent to make it clearer to the recipients what they are receiving.

Disclosure of personal identities associated with online personae is another controversial topic. Internet users who use the web to gripe about products or people may find themselves the targets of lawsuits when their information service providers expose their identities. Widely available Internet search tools can be used to track down everything you say in Internet newsgroups, and newsgroup archives may mean that your rash statements follow you around for years. In one case, a Navy enlisted man identified himself as "gay" in an America Online profile, only to have this information turned over to the military by AOL for disciplinary purposes. Under the new national security rules, AOL and other providers have new mandates to inspect mail and legal protection from being sued over such disclosures.

Another hotly contested requirement is for ISPs to provide information to the Recording Industry Artists Association on illegal downloaders of music files. The Digital Millennium Copyright Act (DMCA) of 1998 gave strong powers of search via digital media to discover who might be using new digital technologies to illegally reproduce copyrighted materials. Some critics charge that the DMCA gives groups representing copyright holders stronger search powers than those given to the government.

Web users leave tracks. Web servers routinely keep track of the Internet addresses from which requests are received, although these often cannot be traced back to individual users. **Cookies** are a serious privacy threat. Usually, their function is benign: recording information about personal preferences or previous transactions that the site can use to verify our identity or customize its content to our needs. However, the cookies can also store personal information and match it across different websites. (For more on cookies,

Probable cause is a judge's decision that provisional evidence of criminal violation or national security danger justifies a wiretap.

Encryption is translating a message into a secret code.

Spam is unsolicited e-mail with no verifiable return address.

Controlling the Assault of Non-Solicited Pornography and Marketing Act of 2003 restricts Internet spam, especially deceptive spam.

Cookies are small computer programs left behind on your computer when you visit a website.

see Chapter 9.) Congress is considering several bills that would outlaw spyware. Software that collects information from users computers without their knowledge.

The Electronic Communications Privacy Act (1987) supposedly keeps government agencies from snooping without a court order, but that didn't protect the gay sailor. It also did not stop the deployment of Carnivore, the system run by the Federal Bureau of Investigation that can, with a court order, inspect file downloads, chat rooms, and e-mail for illegal activity. Major changes in policy and law toward Internet privacy took place after September 11. In the 2001 USA Patriot Act, officials were given significantly enhanced powers to intercept and eavesdrop on telephone or Internet messages by those suspected of posing a threat to U.S. security. In 2002, Congress passed the Homeland Security Bill. The bill permits federal officials to track and locate Internet users who pose an imminent threat to national security interests or who may perpetrate attacks on protected computers belonging to government or key private interstate commerce or communications companies. It also encourages cooperation from Internet and computer companies by protecting them from being sued for releasing personal information to the government.

Electronic privacy invasions by parties other than government agencies are unrestricted, however, apart from the existing protections regarding the use of consumer credit information. And government agencies, including the IRS, can purchase information from commercial databases.

Further efforts to legislate electronic privacy face the hurdle of opposition from powerful commercial interests, although there is a movement to establish voluntary guidelines that would require websites to inform visitors of their privacy rights. As public concern about privacy increases, there is an increasing demand for clearer legislation to define and protect privacy rights. A number of privacy bills have been introduced in Congress to protect medical information, give individuals the right to fact-check their credit histories in databases, and so on. Furthermore, a number of state legislatures were also considering or passing legislation to define privacy rights at the state level.

STOP & REVIEW

1. What are the distinctions among policy, law, and ethics?

2. What is the First Amendment?

3. What is libel?

4. What is considered indecent in mass media content? Is the standard different for the Internet?

5. What is the right to privacy?

6. What kinds of organizations present the largest current threats to privacy?

Patents and Copyright Law: Protecting Intellectual Property

Intellectual property rights and the more specific area of copyrights present several policy and ethical problems. **Intellectual property** laws protect patents, copyrights, and trademarks.

Patents give inventors the exclusive rights to their inventions for 17 years, during which time they can demand royalties from others who wish to use them. Patents are usually applied to new inventions, like RCA's patent pool to assemble all the new inventions required for broadcasting and receiving radio sounds. The goal is to encourage new technologies and industries through rewarding inventors.

Copyrights grew out of the tradition of kings granting certain authors and printers the right to publish their works. Originally intended for taxation and control, these rights grew to focus on the authors. The Statute of Anne, passed in England in 1710, said that publishers should benefit from their published works. It also established the idea that

Intellectual property is a work of art, writing, film, or software.

Patents secure the rights to an invention for a set number of years.

such rights should have a limited duration, after which works should pass into the public domain, where all could use them.

Article 1, Section 8 of the United States Constitution authorized a national copyright system to "promote the Progress of Science and useful Arts, by securing for limited Times to Authors . . . the exclusive Right to their . . . Writings." The United States (in 1791) and most developed countries established laws to protect authors' work. With the movement of books across borders, a need for international agreement on copyright became apparent, resulting in the Berne Convention in 1886.

The United States expanded the range of works covered by copyright in 1976 to include computer programs, adding to more traditional protection of literature, music, drama, pantomimes, choreography, pictures, graphics, sculptures, motion pictures, audiovisual works, and sound recordings. This list had been earlier expanded in copyright legislation in 1833, 1857, and 1909.

Copyright law is meant to make sure that people who create an intellectual product receive the economic benefit from selling, leasing, renting, or licensing their invention, song, play, book, movie, software program, or other work. The premise of this law is that if people do not benefit from their own intellectual or artistic creations, others will not be motivated to create new material. This issue becomes particularly important as we move further into an information economy in which many people's livelihoods depend directly on creating information.

From the software perspective, patents are superior to a mere copyright in that they protect against *reverse engineering*—making a copy of an invention that performs the same basic functions as the inventor's but uses different underlying computer instructions. Copyright offers protection only against duplication of the underlying computer instructions and of the screen display and command sequences—the general "look and feel" of software, such as a spreadsheet program.

In computer software, television programs, and music, in particular, it is sometimes hard to prove that someone else has copied your idea. Apple was unable to convince courts that Microsoft Windows copied the "look and feel" of the Macintosh graphical user interface, which it in turn had copied from Xerox. As companies try to push copyright into new areas, conflict arises. Producers now copyright the formats for reality television shows and then license the format to others. A British production company created the reality series *Wife Swap* and licensed it to ABC. Fox created a similar series called *Trading Spouses.* The British company filed suit against Fox in 2004, charging that its reality series was a "blatant and wholesale copycat" of the British show.

Until 1990, computer software was considered unpatentable on the grounds that computers merely executed mathematical formulas that were the product of mental processes, rather than patentable devices. But that changed dramatically in the early 1990s. Patents now extend to business processes. For example, Amazon.com holds a patent on the "one click" shopping method that lets return visitors to the site place orders without re-entering their credit card information. Priceline.com holds a patent on the "reverse auction" method in which buyers set the price and sellers bid to meet it. Intellectual property rights are now on a collision course with the freewheeling culture of the Internet. Although copyright is usually discussed in terms of protecting the rights of starving artists and authors, it is also supposed to encourage the creation of new works that build on that which is already published.

Now many believe that the balance is tipping too much in favor of the copyright owners. In 1998 the U.S. Congress passed the Copyright Term Extension Act (CTEA). It extended the period of protection to the life of the author plus 70 years. However, a number of other countries have not extended copyrights in a similar fashion, so some works that are still copyrighted for decades to come in the United States will start losing

Copyright is the legal right to control intellectual property.

copyright protection in some other countries soon. For example, in the United States, under an extension of copyright law, the novel *Gone With the Wind* will not enter the public domain until 2031, 95 years after its original publication. However, in Australia and other places, the book was free of copyright restrictions in 1999, 50 years after author Margaret Mitchell's death. Songs by 1950s and 1960s artists like Elvis Presley and the Beatles are nearing the end of copyright protection in some European countries, so the International Federation for the Phonographic Industry, a trade group for record companies, is urging the European Union to extend copyright protection for them.

© AP/Wide World Photos

The Copyright Term Extension Act also made Internet service providers liable if they knowingly carry sites that violate copyright rules. As mass media conglomerates such as Disney and Time Warner have made a splash on the Internet, they have become very aggressive in closing down sites that use images from copyrighted works they control.

One of the first major music exchange sites on the Internet, Napster, ran afoul of a provision of the CTEA that prohibits actions that circumvent copyright protection. In its defense, Napster cited another part of the law that exempts ISPs, claiming that it had no way of knowing which of those music files were pirated. The company also summoned the Audio Home Recording Act of 1991 to its defense. That law establishes the right of consumers to make copies of their own records and tapes for noncommercial use. The recording industry countered that most of the Napster-ites did not own the recordings they were "sharing" and that the rampant file swapping was undermining the market for copyrighted recordings. And, the Home Recording Act only protects hardware devices (like tape recorders) that make copies, not software that makes copies, which makes software-based programs, like Internet exchange programs or even digital personal video recorders, more open to challenge. Although Napster was driven out of business by lawsuits alleging that it facilitated piracy, other Internet sites or programs have risen to offer similar services. As a sign of the times, Napster returned under new ownership as a pay-to-download music site in 2003 and music rental site in 2005.

Policy makers must devise both legal and policy means to help protect intellectual property as technology and society change. For example, many new digital technologies (from tape recorders, photocopiers, and VCRs to CDs, DVDs, digital video recorders (like TiVo), the Internet, and electronic mail) make it easier for people to copy books, articles, photographs, music, videos, and programs without paying anything to the creators or to those who have bought the distribution rights. One solution has been to make unauthorized copying a crime. Another has been to legally regulate technical aspects of copying technologies to make illegal copying harder. In another area, policy makers must help decide whether owning a copyright to a book automatically gives copyright ownership for electronic publication.

One new approach in the Copyright Term Extension Act of 1998 was to specifically target and make illegal various technical means of circumventing copyright protections. That strengthens lawsuits targeting sites like Napster that facilitate the trading or

■ FREEDOM OR PIRACY?
Although Napster, as it was originally conceived, was driven out of business, other similar services like Morpheus are available to download music for free, while Napster has returned as a pay-to-download music service.

PROFILE

Policy Activist or Scholar?

Name: Professor Robert McChesney

Born: 1952 in Cleveland, Ohio.

Education: Ph.D. in communications at the University of Washington in 1989.

Position: Research Professor in the Institute of Communications Research and the Graduate School of Library and Information Science at the University of Illinois at Urbana-Champaign.

How He Got Started: Prior to entering graduate school in 1983, McChesney was a sports stringer for UPI, published a weekly newspaper, and in 1979 was the founding publisher of *The Rocket, a* Seattle-based rock magazine.

How He Got to the Top: He has written or edited twelve books, including *The Problem of the Media* (Monthly Review Press, 2004), *Telecommunications, Mass Media, and Democracy: The Battle for the Control of U.S. Broadcasting, 1928–1935* (Oxford University Press, 1993), *Rich Media, Poor Democracy: Communication Politics in Dubious Times* (New Press, 2000) and, with Ben Scott, *Our Unfree Press: 100 Years of Radical Media Criticism* (New Press, 2004). He also lectured widely, shifting gradually toward a more activist focus.

His Initiatives: He is one of the founders of Free Press, the Media Reform Network (http://www.freepress.net/). He has campaigned actively against increased concentration of media ownership, in books, in lectures, in magazine articles, and on the Internet.

Greatest Achievement: He and others, such as MoveOn.org, have made particularly strong use of the Internet to mobilize public opinion against new rules that the FCC was considering to permit increased concentration of ownership in cable television, television, radio and increased cross-ownership of newspapers, television and cable television at the local level. Overall, the various efforts in this campaign led to over 2 million e-mails to Congress, which led members of Congress to oppose the FCC's proposed rules. Despite strong support by the Bush administration and industry, the FCC decided in 2004 to abandon the proposed rule changes.

Next Move: The Free Press movement, together with MoveOn.org and others, continues to press for other media reforms. They continue to focus on ownership concentration, particularly in radio, and on corrupt practices, like payola. One of their next focuses seem to be supporting cities which decide to offer free wireless Internet, which has been strongly opposed by the commercial interests that have lobbied state legislatures in Pennsylvania, Texas and other states to prohibit city-run or -subsidized programs as conflicting with the legitimate business interests of commercial Internet providers.

---

exchange of copyrighted music. The first case showing how serious these anticircumvention provisions might be was the 2000 lawsuit of *Universal City Studios Inc. et al. v. Reimerdes.* The defendants had created software (known as DeCSS) that permitted breaking the anticopying technology incorporated in DVDs. Challenges to their conviction were thrown out by the Supreme Court in 2001. The Recording Industry Artists Association had taken over 4000 music exchangers to court by 2005 to make the criminalization of digital music copying more visible and effective.

However, this need to protect copyright holders is only half the story. The other side is that users of creative works need reasonable access to them. This is the concept of **fair use.** This permits academic and other noncommercial users to make copies of parts of copyrighted works for personal use and also for purposes of analyzing them in class-

Fair use permits users limited copying of copyrighted works for academic, artistic, or personal use.

Globalizing Policy Making?

We primarily think of media and telecommunications policy and law as a very national process. Indeed, the United States and many other countries are very jealous of their national control over media, since all governments are concerned about media content. However, communications policy has been increasingly globalized since 1865, when the predecessor of the International Telecommunication Union (ITU) was formed.

In the United States, the main impacts of global regulation have come recently, in new computer-based media. The Internet and computers had developed initially under U.S. government military grants, which is where a great deal of U.S. policy toward research and development of technology is decided. As computers began to become more crucial to all of the world's economies, corporate standards and practices by dominant U.S. firms like Microsoft had major impact on other nations. Both individually, and in groups of nations with multilateral policy making, like the European Union (EU), other countries and regional groups have started reviewing some of Microsoft's and other companies' behavior as potentially anticompetitive. The EU has investigated Microsoft for anti-competitive behavior in bundling Windows with Windows Media Player in 2003–2004 and had also begun to rule on other issues, like corporate mergers, deciding whether music conglomerates could merge, for example. So U.S. firms that operate in Europe are now significantly affected by EU policies.

Similarly, as the Internet began to spread globally out from the United States, a number of key standards, like some of the basic protocols for the World Wide Web, are designed or decided elsewhere. Some of the original U.S.-based mechanisms for deciding standards and allocating resources like domain names, such as ICAHN, have come under challenge. At several recent ITU meetings, other countries have demanded a more multilateral approach to operating such Internet functions. This debate dominated the ITU's World Summit on the Information Society in 2003–2004, although other issues, such as assistance to help developing countries develop Internet service, were originally seen as the dominant issues to be addressed.

rooms, in academic publications, or in artistic works, so long as they do not diminish the market for the works. Guidelines are given for how much of a copyrighted work can be reprinted or redisplayed without incurring the need to pay a license fee. This is being negotiated in the courts. A wholesale challenge to the 1998 DMCA over fair use was dismissed by the Supreme Court in 2001, and the restrictive aspects of the law aimed at copyright protection have been upheld there since.

Information, software, and entertainment products are among America's main exports to the rest of the world. It is particularly difficult to ensure that no one copies these products in international markets without paying for their use. Some countries have permitted practices that the United States considers illegal copying or piracy. Illegal copying and nonpayment of royalties have been a thorny issue between the U.S. and China, for example. (See "World View, Globalizing Policy Making?")

As many countries other than the United States (including China) have their own stake in protecting national revenues from intellectual property sales abroad, international negotiations made much more progress in the late 1990s than in the 1980s. This is true in general trade organizations such as the World Trade Organization, and in more specialized forums, such as the World Intellectual Property Organization (WIPO). Two new WIPO agreements extend copyright protection into digital formats, particularly the Internet and digital storage of music and film. U.S. policy makers are concerned that these two treaties make copyright protection too strong relative to fair-use considerations.

One new approach to re-opening fair use possibilities is the Creative Commons approach. This idea, launched in 2001, by intellectual property experts like Lawrence Lessig, lets artists state how much creative use of their intellectual property they will allow. For example, several musicians released a CD in *Wired Magazine* in 2004 containing songs that could be sampled or remixed.

Ownership Issues

The Sherman Antitrust Act and Monopoly. One of the oldest regulatory traditions affecting current developments in the information society is the extent to which concentration of ownership is permitted. In the 1880s, companies in the oil, banking, and railroad industries formed what were called trusts. These were either a **monopoly,** where a single company controlled an industry, as did the Standard Oil Company, or **oligopolies,** where a few companies dominated an industry or a market, as did the railroads.

Monopoly permitted companies to charge higher prices than would prevail if they had competition. Within oligopolies, potential competitors sometimes colluded to fix prices above what they would be with real competition. Monopolists could also force suppliers and business partners to lower prices for parts and materials, because they were the only market for such suppliers. In addition, they used unfair tactics to drive out or keep out would-be competitors. For example, before 1913 the Bell telephone system would refuse to connect competing local telephone companies to long-distance service for local customers, often forcing those companies either into the Bell system or out of business. More recently, Microsoft has used its control over operating system software, like Windows, to include programs like Windows Media Player to create distinct advantages for its own proprietary standards for playing music on digital media. This kind of activity is an **abuse of market power.**

After widespread realization that monopolistic business practices were hurting public interests, legal and public opinion turned against monopoly and oligopoly. Congress passed the **Sherman Antitrust Act of 1890.** Since then, U.S. courts, charged with enforcing the antitrust laws, and the U.S. Department of Commerce, charged with prohibiting **restraint of trade,** have both been suspicious of any monopoly.

Nevertheless, in some industries it seemed that competition did not make much sense. For many years, telecommunications seemed like a textbook case of a **natural monopoly**— a business that lends itself to domination by a single firm in each service area because of the immense costs of building an infrastructure, like telephone wires and switches, to supply the service. Telephone monopolies had to submit to rate regulation by state-level public utility commissions to prevent the abuse of their monopoly power (see Chapter 12).

Applying antitrust legislation to new communications technology areas has proven to be complicated. The Justice Department and a number of states sued Microsoft for abuse of the market power it holds with its virtual monopoly in computer operating systems. After a multiyear lawsuit, the federal judge found that Microsoft had abused its power over other companies to get them not to use rival Internet browser Netscape. However, the remedies ultimately agreed to by Microsoft were less than what the states had sought. However, the equivalent antimonopoly tribunal of the European Union has threatened to apply more drastic sanctions against Microsoft, showing that controls over such issues are being globalized.

Ownership and Diversity. One of the major goals of the Federal Communications Commission since it was established by the Communications Act of 1934 has been to promote diversity of content among broadcasters. Limited frequencies and high initial costs pose barriers to entry so that relatively few people can actually participate in the "marketplace of

Monopoly is when a single firm dominates a market.

Oligopoly is when a few firms dominate a market.

Abuse of market power is use of dominance within a market to restrict competition.

The Sherman Antitrust Act of 1890 prohibits monopolies.

Restraints of trade limit competition.

A natural monopoly occurs when competition is not feasible.

THE BOSSES OF THE SENATE.

■ **MONOPOLY IS NO GAME**
This nineteenth-century cartoon about industry monopolists shows the kind of problem that antitrust laws were enacted to prevent.

ideas." The FCC decided that it needed to actively promote diversity of content under these conditions.

One continuing issue is whether diversity of ownership is linked to diversity of content. At several points, policy makers have thought that ensuring diversity of ownership might help diversify content. U.S. policy once gave preference to minorities, local owners, and female applicants for broadcast station licenses in the hope that they would increase diversity and better serve their communities. These preferences were gradually eliminated in the 1980s and 1990s, and minority and female ownership of broadcast stations remains very low. Furthermore, recent industry consolidation into a few large ownership groups has resulted in many minority owners selling their stations to larger groups (Irving, 1998). The FCC has renewed policy initiatives on minority ownership, but not much has actually changed.

On another issue of content diversity, whether concentration of ownership restricts content diversity, the evidence is more mixed. With fewer owners, the number of channels of different kinds of music, television, and so forth has actually increased at least on FM radio and cable television. However, if one looks at diversity of ideas and artists within those channels, some critics still complain that ownership concentration limits the number of people making decisions. On one particular, the evidence is clear: concentration of ownership has made for less local ownership, so those decisions are increasingly made by people further away from listeners to radio and viewers of local TV news. In 2004, after heated discussion in public and in Congress over the effects of ownership concentration, the FCC promised to look at how to achieve more localism in ownership and/or content.

■ **MINORITY MEDIA OWNERSHIP FALLING**
Larry Irving, former Assistant Secretary of Commerce for Communications and Information, has pointed out that minority ownership of media outlets is falling behind in the recent wave of mergers.

Concentration of Ownership

The economics of large-scale communications media industries create situations where the need for massive economies of scale tend to favor the dominance of relatively few firms, such as that of CBS, NBC, and ABC during the heyday of network TV in the 1950s–1970s, or the reconcentration of telephone companies since the breakup of AT&T. This creates oligopolies, where business competition is restricted to a few companies. These few media companies have had a much greater influence on society than would a broader, more competitive group of owners (Bagdikian, 2000).

Regulatory Implications of Vertical and Horizontal Integration. The concentration of ownership is reflected in **vertical integration,** which exists when a company owns nearly all aspects of a single industry. For example, the federal government once prohibited the major television networks from producing or owning most of their own programming (see Chapter 8). The policy goal was to ensure that a number of production companies would compete with each other, thereby producing more diversity of content. This policy probably succeeded, but the networks complained that such rules, known as the Financial Interest and Syndication (or Fin-Syn) Rules, weakened them too much, particularly in their competition with cable TV (see Chapter 8), and the rules were relaxed in 1991. That has resulted in a very large increase in the proportion of programming produced in-house by television networks or studios owned by the same groups. This trend has forced the closure or merger of several independent production houses, which reduces the diversity of producers.

Another form of concentration is **horizontal integration,** in which a company owns many outlets of the same kind of medium. Previous U.S. policies had set at seven, then at twelve, the maximum number of radio or television stations that a single company could own. It was assumed that more diverse ownership—and preferably local ownership—would produce more diverse content. The 1996 Telecommunications Act eliminated that limit, raised the proportion of the nation that could be covered by a television network's own stations from 25 percent of homes to 35 percent, and set a cap of 30 percent on what proportion of U.S. households could be covered by a cable system owner. Even these expanded national limits are being challenged in Congress as interfering with free speech of media owners. In 2001, the FCC lifted its ban on one company owning more than one broadcast TV network. For radio, there are no national limits, and local ownership caps increase with market size (see Chapter 6). In 2002, the FCC conducted a major review of its limits with a clear inclination toward increasing the percentage of the U.S. audience that could be covered by a single network or cable operator. However, there was a considerable backlash to concentration of ownership, so that a letter writing campaign to Congress in 2002–2003 produced millions of complaint letters, which moved Congress to prohibit the FCC from increasing the ownership limits on media to allow owning stations covering more than 39 percent of the national television market.

The 1996 act also deregulated telephone ownership structures to permit new combinations of cable TV and phone companies and services, for example. In 2002, the merger of cable systems between AT&T and Comcast took advantage of court challenges to the previous limits on how much of the U.S. market could be covered by a single cable operator. In 2004, the FCC lowered requirements for existing providers, like telephone companies, to facilitate competitors' use of their infrastructure.

Another ownership question has to do with **cross-ownership:** should a company be allowed to own various kinds of media? Traditionally, U.S. regulators did not allow a single entity to own radio, television, and newspapers—and, more recently, cable TV and telephony systems—in the same area to prevent one company from controlling too much content in one locality, thus limiting diversity of ideas. In 2002, federal courts also threw out rules prohibiting cable and television station cross-ownership. In 2005, the FCC gave

Vertical integration concentrates across related businesses.

Horizontal integration concentrates ownership within a single business.

Cross-ownership is when one firm owns different media outlets in the same area.

up on removing other restrictions, such as the ban on newspaper–television station cross-ownership within local markets. Pressure by public anti-monopoly movements pushed Congress to discourage such charges.

The 1996 Telecommunications Act largely deregulates vertical and horizontal integration and voids cross-ownership rules, except those preventing ownership of both local television stations and newspapers. This permits integration of movie studios, broadcast networks, cable providers, and cable channels, for example. Companies have integrated very quickly since 1996, leading a few major firms, such as Disney/ABC, Fox, and AOL Time Warner, to dominate film and television production, film distribution, network and cable TV distribution, and syndication (see Chapters 7 and 8). Some critics now call for policy reassessment of the wisdom of unbridled vertical integration (McChesney, 2000). As Chapters 7 and 8 show, there is a rapid erasure of boundaries between film and television production, for example, which is placing more content decisions in fewer hands. Horizontal integration has also run rampant, particularly in the telecommunications industry, but also in radio, where one company, Clear Channel Communication, owns over 1200 radio stations, including most of the stations in many local markets, including both large and small cities.

In the past there was no apparent need to create policy about who owns newspapers. Competition between newspapers made government regulation unnecessary. Reduction of that competition makes regulation more likely. When the only two competing newspapers in a city, such as Detroit's *Free Press* and *News,* merge and issue combined editions, under what is called a *joint operating agreement,* diversity of content may suffer (see Chapter 4). U.S. policy on joint operating agreements provides that they are subject to the U.S. Attorney General's Office's determination, as to whether they violate antimonopoly laws. Furthermore, horizontal integration is widespread in newspapers, too, with Gannett owning almost 100 newspapers, most of which have no local competitor.

ACCESS TO MEDIA AND UNIVERSAL SERVICE

Modern societies are increasingly built on the promise that everyone has access to basic telecommunications services, such as the ability to call 911 from home in case of emergency. For most of the twentieth century, **universal service** meant trying to get a telephone into every home. Universal telephone service has largely been met—although many people in low-income and minority communities are still without service.

Since the mid-1990s, regulators and researchers have debated whether plain old telephone service is enough or whether telephone companies should be required to make more advanced digital services, such as the Internet, universal. Given the convenience of using the Internet for mail, shopping, information gathering, and business, many assume that it will become virtually necessary to life in modern America. But while three-quarters of Americans have access to the Internet either at home, school, or work, close to half of several minority groups and the poorest Americans do not. That raises questions about whether everyone has equal access to information. Of growing concern to legislators now is how to close the broadband gap to bring broadband services to communities, particularly in rural areas, that do not have them. Overall, the United States now has a lower proportion of homes with broadband than several Asian and European countries, leading to concern about U.S. technological competitiveness (OECD, 2004).

The 1996 Telecommunications Act confirmed that access to basic telephony should be universal, although it is proving difficult to maintain the subsidies even for

Universal service is the goal of providing basic access to telecommunication services for all.

As the United States has fallen
behind other countries by having
a lower proportion of homes with
broadband, several communities,
such as Austin, TX, have tried to
provide universal access.

universal basic phone service in an era of competition. But Congress failed to set a goal of ensuring that all households have access to the Internet. The 1996 Act mandated a commission that made a proposal to subsidize access to the Internet for schools and libraries, so that most people could have at least minimum access through those institutions. To this end, the FCC created a subsidy pool from telecommunications carriers, which could then be given to schools and libraries to make Internet access affordable, particularly in less advantaged areas. This subsidy was termed the "e-rate." A number of telecommunications companies, as well as fiscal conservatives in Congress, have objected to this kind of subsidy, arguing that the social benefits are not worth the cost. Former FCC chairperson Michael Powell called for consolidation and reduction or outright elimination of the e-rate and related federal programs, claiming that the problem of a "digital divide" had been almost completely overcome. Powell suspended the program briefly in 2004 when financial abuses came to light, but was forced by congressional pressure to resume it. The problem is that almost half of African-American, Latino, and Native American minorities still do not have Internet access (Pew, 2004). Thus they depend crucially on school and public access. Schools and libraries depend on the e-rate to afford connections, so political support for the program is widespread. However, even worse, many of those near public access do not have the education or skills to use access. Therefore, now people talk about the *second digital divide,* of preparing people to make effective use of access when they get it (Rojas et al., 2004). Several programs within the Departments of Commerce and Education, as well as in many states, have targeted this need.

Who Gets to Use Radio Frequencies?

One of the main reasons for regulation of broadcasting has been the need to allocate the scarce supply of radio and television frequencies among the many competing companies and groups that would like to use them. The growing crowd of radio stations in the United States in the early 1920s soon required some government intervention to allocate frequencies—that is, to **license** broadcasting on specific channels. In 1927 the Radio Act established the Federal Radio Commission to administer this process. The much more comprehensive Communications Act of 1934 established the Federal Communications Commission. It determined how close stations could be to each other geographically and still use the same or neighboring frequencies (see Chapters 6 and 8).

Because government regulators were now essentially deciding who got to broadcast, they also had to make rules for allocating and renewing licenses. The main criterion was the public interest, but that term was left for the FCC to define, and it has never been given a precise definition. In practice, the FCC tried to promote **localism** by giving licenses to stations to cities of a variety of sizes. The FCC later promoted diversity by giving preferential access to minority owners. After the initial rush of AM licenses in the 1920s and 1930s resulted almost entirely in commercial broadcast stations, which emphasized light entertainment, the FCC also began to reserve some licenses in FM and television specifically for noncommercial stations that emphasized education and culture. The FCC has also used license and frequency allocations to encourage new technology use, such as re-allocating more space for mobile communications like cellular telephones or giving television stations new frequencies to encourage them to move to high-definition and digital television broadcasting.

After 1980, the FCC decided that there was no longer a scarcity of radio stations, given the proliferation of FM stations. They also saw television as inherently competitive because an increasing number of U.S. homes had multichannel cable TV to supplement or replace broadcast television stations (Fowler & Brenner, 1982). Therefore, the **scarcity argument** for regulation was diminished. Furthermore, the probusiness commissioners of the FCC did not think that their predecessors at the FCC had done a particularly good job of picking wireless communication license applicants. They proposed a lottery to pick applicants at random—or an auction, to "sell" frequencies to the highest bidder. Auctions are increasingly used in two-way radio applications, such as cellular, and other uses of radio.

The basic uses of radio spectrum frequencies are defined by the International Telecommunications Union (ITU). This body also allocates radio spectrum frequencies to countries, which their governments then allocate internally. Allocation issues are decided at the World Administrative Radio Congress (WARC), held every four years, and at regional conferences held in each of the ITU regions every two years. It is the WARC that decides, for example, which frequencies will be available for cellular radio service in various countries, which frequencies will be reserved for satellite communication, and how far apart the satellites must be. The regional conferences then deal with communications issues that crop up between neighboring countries.

STOP & REVIEW

1. What kinds of links might exist between forms of ownership and issues of media content?

2. What is the Sherman Antitrust Act?

3. How have ownership rules changed since 1996?

4. What is universal service? Why is it important?

5. Why did the relative scarcity of radio spectrum frequencies require government regulation? Does it still?

License is a legal permission to operate a transmitter.

Localism is ownership and program decision making at the community level.

The scarcity argument says that the small number of stations and cost of entry to broadcasting requires extra regulation of them.

© Robert Wallis/SIPA Press

Defining Technical Standards for Media

Although issues of ownership and content are more dramatic, the main regulatory function of governments is often more technical. Newspapers can function without any technical regulation, but the situation is different for electronic media. Someone has to design the basic equipment standards for how a television image will be broadcast and received. Someone has to establish basic technical standards so that manufacturers, broadcasters, and audiences will know which channel to tune in to receive a particular station. The FCC works with private companies and with engineering-oriented standards organizations to work out the details. Private companies often develop standards for their own equipment, then compete to set the industry-wide standard, such as the 1990s–2000s race to set standards for digital television. Similarly, companies are experimenting with different means and standards to create wireless Internet access for computers, cell phones, and personal digital assistants.

■ HDTV DEBACLE
Standards can determine the success of technology. The analog Japanese version of high-definition TV, shown here, was rendered obsolete by a U.S. decision to adopt a digital standard.

Agreement on basic technological standards is important. Standards signal manufacturers when to mass-produce a new technology. But when a technology continues to improve and evolve, when do we say the moment is right to set standards and make one for everyone to buy? In personal computers, for example, the standards have evolved as technology has changed. That is possible because people buy their own computer equipment and do not have to have strict compatibility with everyone else. However, even in computers, standardization is so desirable to users that Microsoft's Windows has become the de facto standard. Cellular telephony offers a clearer example. Lack of agreement on which system to use and the proliferation of different analog and digital technologies in the United States resulted in a less advanced system with more incompatibilities and less complete coverage than in Europe, which agreed early on a common digital cellular standard, GSM, which has gradually become the dominant world standard. Now there are new efforts to adopt a world standard for the so-called third generation (3G) cell phones (see Chapter 12).

Standards Bodies. In the United States, telecommunications and electronic media standards are set in a variety of ways. Some are set nationally, either by the FCC itself or by committees sponsored by the FCC. Some standards are created by industry associations such as the Institute for Electrical and Electronics Engineers (IEEE) or research groups and are subsequently ratified by the U.S. government. Some standards, like the Windows computer operating system of Microsoft, evolve from a single company. Sometimes the FCC forces industry to create a working group to resolve a conflict over standards. Examples include the National Television System Committee (NTSC), which set the current U.S. television standard in 1941, and the Advanced Television Systems Committee that set the new digital high-definition television (HDTV) standard. In recent years, the United States has tended not to set standards for new technologies, but rather has let industry work them out. In some cases, such as for cellular telephones and digital television, this leads to conflicting technical standards. And this makes choices confusing for both industry and consumers.

International Standards. International bodies have strongly influenced standards in telecommunications because of the clear need for connections between countries in telephony, fax, and data. The International Telecommunications Union (ITU), first formed in 1865 to standardize telegraph traffic between countries, is the oldest international body in the world. Formed to create standards that would permit people to send a telegram from one country to another, it predated the rest of the UN by 80 years, which shows how important international standard-setting is. The ITU standards process involves negotiation and ratification of technical approaches to providing telecommunications services. Representatives from equipment manufacturers, telecommunications carriers, and national regulatory bodies confer within committees to define the standards. (See "World View, Globalizing Policy Making?" page 447.)

THE POLICY-MAKING PROCESS

Government policy is made by representatives elected to Congress or state legislatures, judges appointed to various courts, and those appointed to regulatory agencies in the government. Corporations also make policy through their own decisions, such as what kinds of services to offer and how much to charge, and work through professional lobbyists to influence legislation. Researchers and journalists may help set the agenda for regulation by bringing issues to the attention of government or corporate policy makers: witness the decades of research done on the effects of television violence on children.

Federal Regulation and Policy Making

All three branches of the federal government play an active role in communications regulation (Figure 14.1, page 456). The fundamental bases for regulating media are laws proposed by the executive branch and Congress. The president works with key executive-branch regulatory agencies, such as the National Telecommunications and Information Administration (NTIA), to propose legislation, nearly always in close consultation with Congress. In fact, members of Congress frequently initiate legislation, as well. Congress then considers, alters, and passes the legislation—first in specialized committees, such as the House Subcommittee on Telecommunication and the Internet, and eventually by the full House of Representatives and Senate. Legislation can be modified at all stages. Lobbyists for industries and various public interests also try to affect legislation in favor of their clients at each step of the process. Finally, bills of proposed legislation are either defeated or passed by Congress and then sent to the president, who may either sign or veto them.

The executive branch implements the laws. Cabinet departments monitor industry compliance. For example, the Justice Department examines whether companies are violating the Sherman Antitrust Act. If so, the department then brings a suit against the offender, such as the 1998 suit against Microsoft, in federal courts. Other laws are implemented by executive-branch regulatory agencies, such as the Federal Communications Commission (FCC) and the Federal Trade Commission (FTC). Because actions of the FCC or FTC are taken to federal district courts under the Telecommunications Act of 1996, these courts are often the key media-related element in the judicial branch. Ultimately, though, the Supreme Court often hears cases that are appealed from lower courts, especially if there is a question as to whether the law that is being applied violates any principles of the U.S. Constitution, such as freedom of speech.

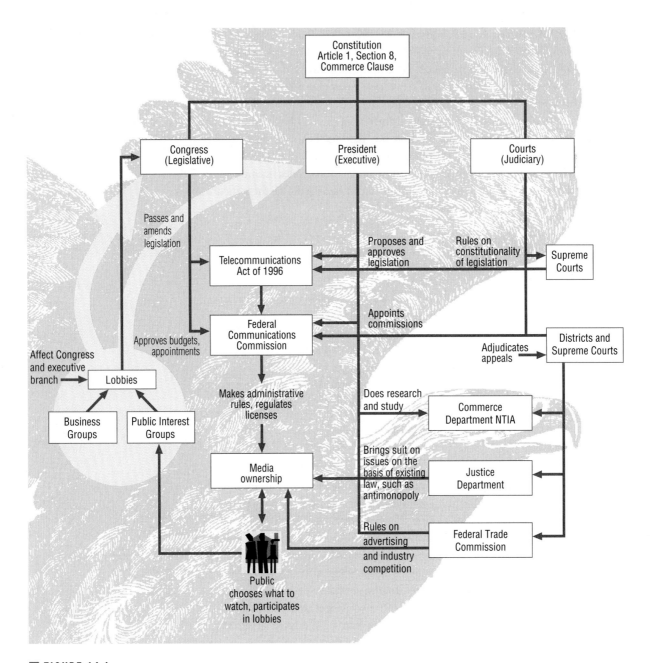

The figure shows a flowchart of the policy process with the following boxes and connections:

- **Constitution Article 1, Section 8, Commerce Clause** (top) connecting to:
  - **Congress (Legislative)**
  - **President (Executive)**
  - **Courts (Judiciary)**

- Congress → "Passes and amends legislation" → **Telecommunications Act of 1996**
- President → "Proposes and approves legislation" → Telecommunications Act of 1996
- Courts → "Rules on constitutionality of legislation" → **Supreme Courts** → Telecommunications Act of 1996
- Telecommunications Act of 1996 → **Federal Communications Commission**
- President "Appoints commissions" → Federal Communications Commission
- "Approves budgets, appointments" (Congress/Lobbies)
- **Lobbies** ← "Affect Congress and executive branch"
  - **Business Groups** → Lobbies
  - **Public Interest Groups** → Lobbies
- Federal Communications Commission → "Makes administrative rules, regulates licenses" → **Media ownership**
- "Does research and study" → **Commerce Department NTIA**
- "Brings suit on issues on the basis of existing law, such as antimonopoly" → **Justice Department** → Media ownership
- "Rules on advertising and industry competition" → **Federal Trade Commission**
- **Districts and Supreme Courts** ← "Adjudicates appeals"
- **Public chooses what to watch, participates in lobbies** (silhouette figures) ↔ Media ownership

■ **FIGURE 14.1**

The Policy Process The executive branch and the legislative branch write and pass media laws such as the Telecommunications Act of 1996. If the laws are challenged, the courts then rule on their constitutionality.

The Federal Communications Commission. The Federal Communications Commission (FCC) regulates broadcasting, satellite/cable TV, and telecommunications. The FCC Mass Media Bureau oversees licensing and operation of broadcast stations and interprets legislation by Congress by making and enforcing regulations, such as those on cable TV. The FCC takes the wording of legislation and goes through a rule-making process. It solicits suggestions from industry, academics, and others; then FCC staff draft rules, which are put up for comment, then implemented.

The FCC's Common Carrier Bureau has primary responsibility for the telecommunications (that is, telephone) industry. With the 1996 Telecommunications Act, the FCC shifted its focus from direct regulation of telecommunications service prices toward less direct oversight of competition among telecommunications companies and market entry rules.

© George Hunter

■ **OPENING NEW MARKETS**
The NTIA is trying to get U.S. telecommunications companies into countries such as Japan, where there is an imbalance in trade with the U.S.

Increasingly, the FCC shares jurisdiction over key issues such as antitrust and monopoly with the Justice Department and Federal Trade Commission. Concerning local telecommunications carriers, such as the **regional Bell operating companies (RBOCs),** or Baby Bells, the FCC shares jurisdiction with their respective state public utility commissions (PUCs). Cable television regulation is also shared between the FCC and local or state level cable commissions.

One problem with the FCC and other regulatory agencies is that they may end up attuned more closely to the interests of the industry than to the interests of the public. Critics say that regulators are often effectively captured by the industry they regulate—a concept referred to as **capture theory.**

Department of Commerce.   The National Telecommunications and Information Administration (NTIA) was established within the Department of Commerce in 1978 to advise on telecommunications policy. The NTIA under Larry Irving in the 1990s helped mobilize concern about the digital divide issue by issuing a series of reports on who was "Falling Through the Net" in 1996–2000. The last report, in 2004, reached a more optimistic conclusion and was titled, "A Nation Online: Entering the Broadband Age." In recent years the NTIA helped represent the United States in international bodies, such as the International Telecommunications Union, that set international telecommunications trade policies and make satellite orbit and communication frequency allocations.

Along with the Office of the United States Trade Representative, NTIA has been active in **multilateral trade negotiations.** These include the North American Free Trade Agreement (NAFTA) and the World Trade Organization (WTO). NTIA also negotiates issues such as the settlements of revenues from international phone calls. They are also working on current issues like trying to limit overseas gambling sites, which has become an issue before the World Trade Organization.

Another branch of the Commerce Department, the U.S. Patent and Trademark Office, and the United States Copyright Office of the U.S. Library of Congress are also involved with the World Intellectual Property Organization in addressing international copyright issues in communications media.

The Federal Trade Commission (FTC).   The FTC is the regulatory agency charged with domestic trade policy. It is responsible for monitoring trade practices such as advertising. It has held hearings on advertising practices aimed at children. It also investigates companies' actions in restraint of trade. In 1989 it began an investigation of possible anticompetitive practices in computer operating systems and programs by Microsoft, Inc. The investigation was picked up by the Justice Department in 1994. The FTC has also scrutinized privacy policies and practices by companies online, as well as advertising violence to children. It is now trying to reduce deceptive spam e-mails with the CAN-SPAM Act of 2003.

The Justice Department.   The Justice Department also plays an important role in the enforcement of general laws that also apply to communications. To enforce the Sherman Antitrust Act, the Justice Department initiated the suit that eventually broke up AT&T, and it investigated and sued Microsoft. In accordance with the 1996 Telecommunications Act, the Justice Department shares jurisdiction on monopoly issues with the FCC. It monitors competitiveness in important sectors of the information economy, such as monopoly practices in the computer industry, and competition in local TV and radio markets. The Bush administration originally wanted to consolidate monopoly enforcement under the Justice Department, but Congress wanted the FTC to stay involved, since it has often been more aggressive in investigating antimonopoly abuses.

Regional Bell operating companies (RBOCs) are the local telephone companies created by the breakup of AT&T in 1984.

Capture theory explains that regulators are unduly influenced by the industry they regulate.

Multilateral trade negotiations are among a number of countries at the same time.

The Courts. The judiciary interprets challenges made to laws made by Congress and rules made by the FCC and other federal agencies to see whether they are consistent with the U.S. Constitution. The Supreme Court and federal district courts are both important in decisions such as freedom-of-speech issues based on the First Amendment, privacy issues based on several amendments, and monopoly issues based on the Sherman Antitrust Act. The Supreme Court is also the ultimate court of appeal for decisions by lower courts, so it usually ends up reviewing decisions made in major cases involving the Communications Decency Act or recent decisions about FCC indecency penalties and local telephone competition. Courts also often interpret and enforce legal decisions. For example, the Third District Court of the District of Columbia supervised the breakup of the old Bell system in 1984, one of the most powerful government interventions in a communications industry.

The Congress. It is the U.S. Congress that ultimately writes and rewrites the communications laws of the land. After years of debate, Congress finally updated the 1934 Communications Act in 1996 because so many crucial issues required substantial definition or redefinition in law, not just regulatory decree or judicial interpretation. In 1996, those issues included competition within and across media and telecommunications industries, ownership restrictions, and regulation of violent and sexual content on TV. Congress is now working on potentially contradictory directions: the need to deal with national security and with citizen privacy concerns.

Many congressional committees are involved in communications issues. For the 1996 Telecommunications Act, for example, much of the crucial debate and lobbying took place in the House Telecommunications Subcommittee since renamed the Subcommittee on Telecommunications and the Internet, which shaped the basic provisions that went before the full House of Representatives.

State and Local Regulation

States and municipalities are increasingly involved in the regulation of telecommunications. They have been less involved in mass media, except in cable TV.

For many years, state-level **public utility** commissions regulated local and regional telephone companies' rates. The state regulators promoted the widest possible availability of telephone service at the lowest possible cost. The phone companies they regulate, such as Southwestern Bell, are entering into cable TV, which municipalities usually regulate, and cable TV companies and others are offering local telephone services, which the states regulate. Some state legislatures have also tried to intervene to set rules on telephone service or in a number of states, to prohibit cities, such as Philadelphia, that were building municipal wi-fi networks that private telecommunications companies felt interfered with their areas of business.

However, a number of states have drastically reduced their levels of regulatory oversight, becoming laboratories for experiments in deregulation. Some have **deregulated** telecommunications almost entirely by removing most of the restrictions on the nature and scope of activities that such companies engage in and the prices they charge. One area that states and localities are not involved in is regulation of the Internet. Congress has placed a moratorium on local regulation—and taxation—of the Internet in hopes of fostering the growth of the new medium. However, some states are beginning to impose their own regulations on privacy and consumer issues, as well as financial issues like applying state sales taxes to Internet purchases.

Public utilities are regulated monopolies.

Deregulation removes restrictions on the nature and scope of activities that companies engage in and the prices they charge.

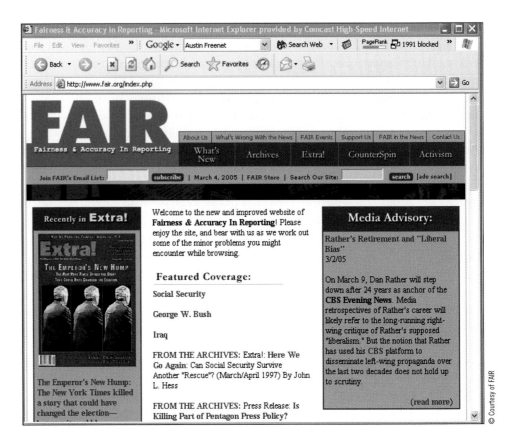

Lobbies

Industry and public-interest groups lobby to influence proposed legislation in the executive branch and in Congress. Lobbies also try to affect how laws and rules are interpreted and enforced once they are made. For example, since passage of the 1996 Act, broadcasters and cable companies have lobbied Congress and the president to get the FCC to permit more concentration of ownership and more cross-ownership between local media.

Increasingly, telecommunications policy issues cut across industry boundaries, so the powerful lobbies of the publishing and motion picture industries also get involved. These groups not only lobby directly about the substance of legislation and enforcement of laws; they also reinforce their arguments with campaign contributions, and form political action committees (PACs) to lobby and to run advertisements for candidates. Sometimes they even give favorable publicity, travel junkets, or financial deals to politicians in exchange for preferential treatment. For example, during the 2004 election, the Sinclair ownership group was going to have all its stations carry a documentary critical of Democratic candidate John Kerry, reportedly to help gain points for looser ownership rules in a second Bush administration. Such strategies can also backfire. Sinclair not only had to back down after a publicity campaign mobilized some advertisers against it, the controversy also highlighted a negative view of its issue, since the episode struck many as an abuse of concentrated broadcast ownership power.

Other lobby groups serve the public interest. The American Association of Retired Persons (AARP) and the Benton Foundation lobbied for years to preserve universal, low-cost "lifeline" local telephone service for older and poverty-stricken Americans. Meanwhile, telecommunications companies lobbied to reduce or lower their obligation to subsidize universal service. Competing special interests and public interests make it difficult to pass legislation. For example, some public-interest groups continue to press for restrictions on television indecency, which are resisted strenuously by the National Association of Broadcasters (NAB) and the television networks, whose members produce most television programming and who fear being fined for indecency by stepped-up FCC enforcement after 2004. Content restrictions are ordinarily considered unconstitutional, but the public interest groups have persuaded the FCC to threaten fines on stations showing or airing too much violence, along with indecency, which led to Clear Channel taking Howard Stern's radio show off their stations in 2004.

The Fourth Estate

The mass media act as lobbyists for their own interests, either directly in their own channels or through associations such as the NAB and the MPAA. However, media also have a much broader role as the forum in which much of the policy debate takes place.

The news media pursue the goal of reporting such controversies and issues objectively, but they sometimes have a position or agenda of their own. For example, do news media tend to have a generally liberal or generally conservative bias, and are they biased for or against specific groups, such as business or the military? Observers disagree. For example, the group Fairness and Accuracy in Reporting (http://www.fair.org/) tracks what it considers conservative bias in media coverage, whereas Accuracy in Media (http://www.aim.org/) tracks perceived liberal bias.

SUMMARY AND REVIEW

WHAT ARE THE DISTINCTIONS, IN THE CONTEXT OF THE COMMUNICATIONS MEDIA, BETWEEN POLICY AND LAW?
Policy is government and public consideration of how to structure and regulate media so that they contribute to the public good. Public policy involves a collective action of the whole society or its representatives. Laws passed by Congress and enforced by the executives cover some, but not all, of the policy and ethical issues in media, which tend to focus on individual decisions where formal legal guidance is not clear.

WHAT IS THE RELATIONSHIP BETWEEN THE MARKETPLACE OF IDEAS AND FREEDOM OF SPEECH?
The marketplace of ideas reflects the concept that, with free speech, the best ideas will win out in any competition with others. The concept of a free press is the extension of freedom of speech to media.

WHAT IS THE FIRST AMENDMENT?
The First Amendment to the U.S. Constitution says, "Congress shall make no law respecting an establishment of religion, or prohibiting the free exercise thereof, or abridging the freedom of speech, or of the press. . . ." The kinds of speech not protected by the First Amendment are libel, defamation, indecency, plagiarism, invasion of privacy, and inciting violence.

WHAT IS LIBEL?
Libel is harmful and untruthful written remarks that damage someone's reputation or good name. To be legally liable, the person or organization accused of libel must be shown to have known that the information was false, and its use must have been intended to damage the reputation of the person being libeled.

HOW ARE MEDIA AND TELECOMMUNICATIONS STANDARDS SET?

Companies often develop standards for their own equipment and compete to set the industry-wide standard. Industry committees sometimes set collective standards, often when spurred or required by government bodies such as the FCC. Internationally, most standards are set or endorsed by the International Telecommunications Union (ITU).

WHAT IS THE PRIMARY LAW REGULATING ELECTRONIC MEDIA?

The Communications Act of 1934 established the FCC, regulated broadcasting by regulating scarce frequencies, and regulated the monopolies of AT&T and, later, the regional Baby Bells. The 1996 Telecommunications Act encouraged competition between industries such as cable TV and telephony. It relaxed rules on how many stations a group could own and on cross-ownership of broadcasting, cable TV, telephone companies, and movie studios. It deregulated telephony ownership structures, areas of activity, and prices but tried to maintain universal service. The Act also proposed restrictions on Internet pornography, since struck down by the Supreme Court.

WHAT ASPECTS OF PRIVACY ARE IMPORTANT TO MEDIA?

Many people are concerned about privacy or control of personal individual information held in consumer credit databases and gathered on the Internet. No overall laws have yet been written on privacy rights, although use of data by government and the interception of messages are controlled by law.

WHO REGULATES PRIVACY?

A right to privacy has been judicially interpreted from the Fourth Amendment. Congress has written laws both extending and limiting information privacy rights, which have been interpreted and reviewed by the courts.

WHAT KINDS OF LINKS MIGHT EXIST BETWEEN FORMS OF OWNERSHIP AND MEDIA CONTENT ISSUES?

Some owners may try to influence content to promote their own ideas and interests. If owners are too much alike, they may not produce diverse content, whereas a greater diversity of ownership may produce more diverse content.

WHAT MAKES FOR A NATURAL MONOPOLY IN MEDIA OR TELECOMMUNICATIONS?

An industry is considered a natural monopoly when competition would not be economically feasible. This is particularly true when the infrastructure for supplying the service is extensive and costly, such as local telephone networks.

WHAT IS THE CAPTURE THEORY OF REGULATION?

Capture theory implies that regulators are often effectively captured by the interests of the industry they regulate. They become dependent on the industry for information, they sometimes work in it before or after government service, and they frequently come to identify with industry players and their goals.

WHY DOES THE RELATIVE SCARCITY OF RADIO SPECTRUM FREQUENCIES NECESSITATE GOVERNMENT REGULATION?

The fact that there are far fewer frequencies than there are people who want to use them, both for broadcasting and for two-way services such as cellular telephony, requires that someone or some agency track who is using what and allocate frequencies in such a way that radio spectrum users do not interfere with each other. Because the scarcity of frequencies requires that some people be given frequencies and others not, rules imposed by governments for allocating and renewing licenses were necessary.

WHAT ARE THE MAIN INSTITUTIONS IN THE MEDIA POLICY-MAKING PROCESS?

The main institutions in the executive branch are the Federal Communications Commission (FCC), which regulates most aspects of communication; the National Telecommunications and Information Administration (NTIA), which covers some aspects of policy research and international policy; and the Federal Trade Commission (FTC), which monitors trade and business practices. Congress passes laws about communication. The Justice Department and the court system, particularly the federal district courts, enforce and interpret the existing laws.

WHAT IS A LOBBY GROUP? WHAT ARE THE MAIN LOBBIES THAT ADDRESS COMMUNICATIONS MEDIA ISSUES?

Lobbies are interest or business groups that try to influence lawmaking or enforcement. Some of the main business lobbies are the Baby Bells, the National Association of Broadcasters, the National Cable Television Association, and the Motion Picture Association of America.

MEDIA CONNECTION

For web links, quizzes, and key term flash cards, visit the **Student Companion Website** at http://communication.wadsworth.com/straubhaar5.

 For unlimited easy access to additional and exclusive online study, support, and research tools, log on to **1pass** at http://1pass.thomson.com using the unique access code found on your 1pass passcode card.

 The **Media Now Premium Website** offers *Career Profile* videos, *Critical View* video news clips, and *Media in Motion* concept animations. You'll also find Stop & Review tutorial questions, a sample final exam, and much more.

 InfoTrac College Edition is a fully searchable online database offering anytime, anywhere access to more than 20 years' worth of articles from nearly 5,000 diverse and reliable sources.

vMentor **vMentor** provides live, one-on-one online tutoring to connect you to experts who will assist you in understanding the concepts covered in your course.

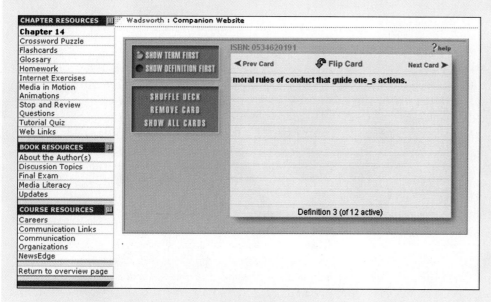

To reinforce your understanding of this chapter's Key Terms, work with its corresponding interactive Key Term Flash Cards on the Student Companion Website. You'll find them under Chapter Resources.

15

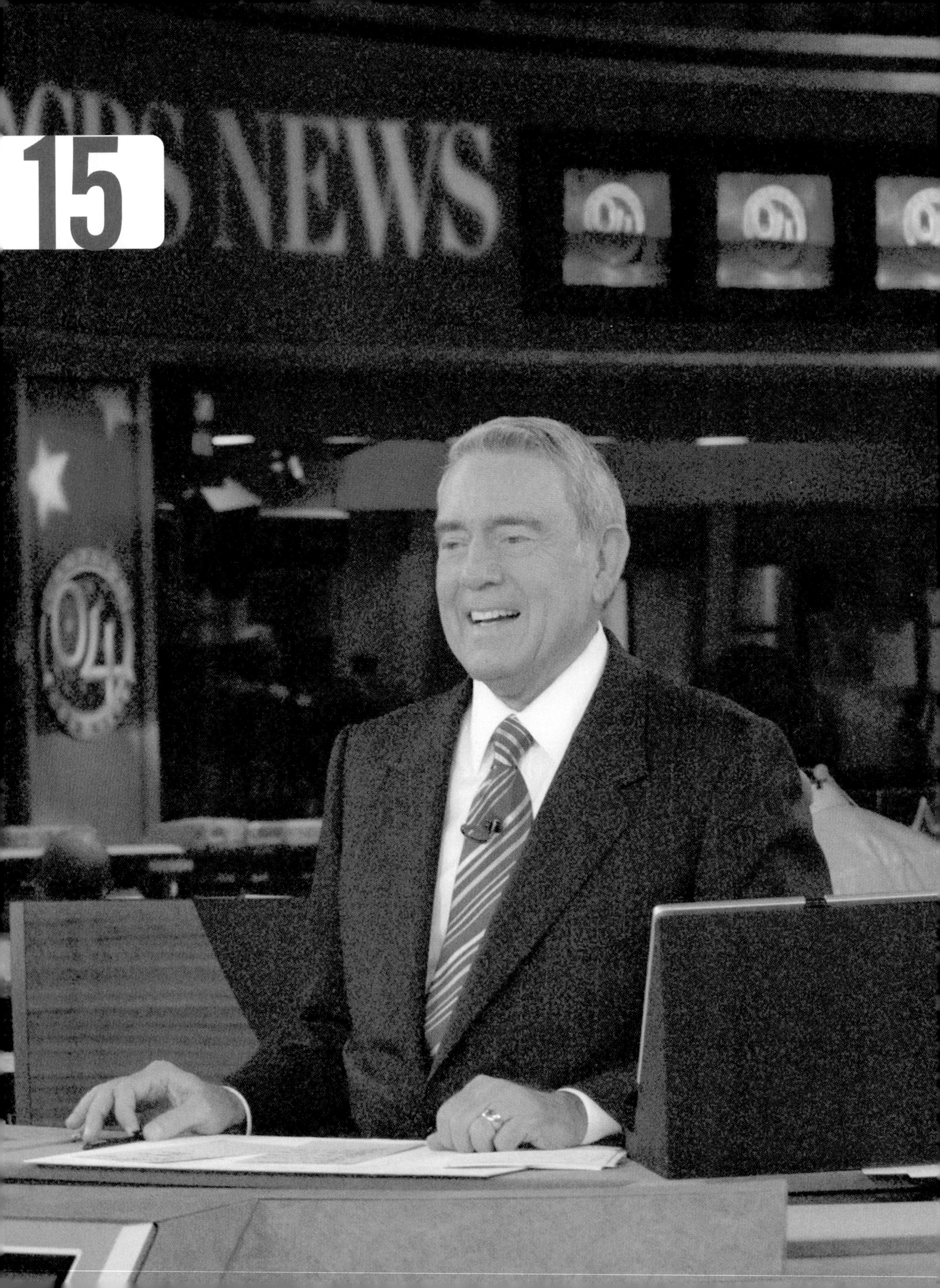

Should Dan Rather have checked his stories more carefully? Should *Newsweek* have retracted its Koran defilement report? These and many other ethical issues face media professionals every day. This chapter covers ethics for media. Ethics and values guide individuals and professional groups as they make choices on such matters as accuracy, respect for sources' or clients' privacy, and controversial content.

ETHICAL THINKING

The First Amendment gives media professionals a great deal of freedom, but media professionals and others are always guided in their choices by community standards, professional ethics, and personal values. Still, many wonder at the quantity of inaccurate stories, character assassination, violence, sex, racial stereotypes, and other questionable content that results from many of these media choices. In this chapter we ask, how do media professionals make these choices and how can we in the audience judge them?

Ethics are guidelines or moral rules for situations in which the media may have negative effects and laws do not dictate behavior. Some of these guidelines are codified by professional organizations, whereas others represent broad systems of ethics. Churches, private companies, industry trade groups, minority groups, and public-interest groups also monitor media performance. But individual media professionals themselves must also act as their own ethical watchdogs. When society cannot find a consensus on which to make laws governing the conduct of the media, we hope that individual ethics will prevail.

Ethics are moral rules of conduct that guide one's actions.

384–322 B.C.E.	Aristotle discusses the golden mean in *Nicomachean Ethics*	**1947**	Hutchins Commission promotes social responsibility of the press
1787	First Amendment to the U.S. Constitution	**1950**	Public Relations Society of America established
1790	Kant introduces the categorical imperative in his *Critique of Practical Reason*	**1974**	Deep Throat becomes source for Watergate reporters
1863	John Stuart Mill publishes *Utilitarianism*	**2005**	Government-sponsored public relations scandal

The ethics of journalists receive a lot of coverage and debate, but professionals involved in all aspects of the media face moral dilemmas every day. Increasingly, media audiences face ethical dilemmas of their own. Imagine what you might do in the following situations:

- You are a student reporter for a campus newspaper. One of your professors is on a confidential committee investigating off-campus sex parties for football recruits. The professor has "leaked" some incriminating information to you, which you can't corroborate, on condition that you won't identify the source. Do you print the information? What do you say about your source?

- You are an aspiring young disk jockey. An independent programming consultant who works for a record company offers you concert tickets if you will just listen to some new recordings from the company label—no strings attached! Do you accept?

- You are making a student video that you hope will land you a job in Hollywood. Violence isn't really integral to the plot, but a couple of your actor friends have some fake blood and say it would be "more dramatic" to stage a fistfight. Do you take them up on the offer?

- Someone online gives you a link to download a movie that is not in the theaters yet. Do you use it or pay to see the movie?

So what are our guidelines, and where do they come from? We will look first at some general systems of ethics that are prevalent now. Then we will look specifically at some of the current ethical issues and how individual media professionals have struggled to resolve them.

ETHICAL PRINCIPLES

Many ethical decisions are based on people's underlying religious, philosophical, and cultural ideals. Let us begin by considering several ideals that have been especially useful in evaluating media ethics.

Aristotle's golden mean holds that "moral virtue is appropriate location between two extremes." Moderation and balance are the key points (Merrill, 1997). That entails giving balanced points of view or including various points of view to provide balance. Similarly, in making decisions, media organizations may balance the interests of getting a good story against withholding details in order to safeguard the public interest. For example, war correspondents may voluntarily omit details that might reveal secrets to the other side.

"Sexing Up" *Cosmo*

Bonnie Fuller is a sensation in the magazine world. After "sexing up" *Cosmopolitan* magazine, she moved to *Glamour* to do a makeover on it. She had previously changed *Young Miss* into *YM: Young and Modern* and had reworked *Marie Claire,* all with substantial circulation increases. She left *Cosmo* with a very healthy circulation of 2.6 million (as of 2000). Something Fuller does is clearly working with the readers.

Part of *Cosmo*'s appeal on the newsstand is a sexy cover, a model with perfect cleavage, and cover lines like "His secret moan zones . . . ." But another part is dramatic writing that offers, or seems to offer, real stories about real people. There is something intriguing to readers about tantalizing bits of the sex lives of real people. This raises questions about how far a magazine ought to go in using sex to draw in an audience. In particular, should a magazine pander to a sort of voyeurism that leads people to want to know real details about real people?

Another problem is that the people featured in the magazine aren't always real. And sometimes the quotes are "sexed up" to make them more dramatic or more explicit. This alteration of quotes has some writers worried. What should a writer do when an editor changes a quote? What should the fact-checking department do when the editor wants to make a story more dramatic by fictionalizing it slightly?

The editors of *Cosmo* note that most of the stories are very personal accounts, often submitted by readers. Fact checkers aren't going to call and ask such a contributor if he really "touched her there." Editors note that sometimes both people and experiences are composites, created by blending several real people and their quotes. That is different from

© AP/Wide World Photos

■ **IS THERE A RESPONSIBILITY TO LIMIT SEX APPEALS?** Magazine covers, along with many other media, routinely use sex to grab attention. It's pervasive, but is it ethical?

complete fabrication. Or is it? A related point is that *Cosmo* may well be entitled to have different standards for talking about sex lives than the *New York Times* should adhere to when talking about weapons of mass destruction. People probably don't have quite the same expectations about *Cosmo*'s ethics on the use of quotes and fact checking, but exactly what standards do apply to a magazine like *Cosmo* is still an interesting question.

The golden rule, "Do unto others as you would have them do unto you," comes from the Bible but can be found in many other cultural traditions as well. Translated into media terms it might read, "create the kind of media that you would like others to create for you." If it is not good enough for you, it probably won't be good enough for others. If you would not like to be photographed crying as you emerge from a funeral, don't take pictures of others leaving a funeral home in tears.

Immanuel *Kant's categorical imperative* holds that you should "act on that maxim which you will [wish] to become a universal law." That is, act according to rules that you would like to see universally applied (Day, 1991). What is good for one person or situation should be good for all, but the categorical imperative also stresses that individuals act according to their own conscience. For example, reporters who would like all other reporters to avoid deception about news sources should avoid deception themselves.

Situation ethics considers moral principles to be relative to the situation at hand, not absolute. Individuals may trust their intuitive sense of what is right and rules may be

■ **FIGURE 15.1**
Potter's Box Potter's Box gives
a four-step model for thinking
through ethical decisions.

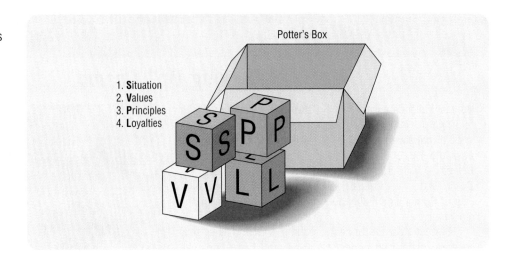

Potter's Box

1. **S**ituation
2. **V**alues
3. **P**rinciples
4. **L**oyalties

broken if the overall purpose is good (Day, 1991). For instance, using hidden recording devices to document lawbreaking might be acceptable if revealing the story will serve the public interest, even though principles and law may both be violated.

John Stuart *Mill's principle of utility* holds that we should "seek the greatest happiness for the greatest number." Mill was concerned about what would bring the greatest good for society, which he defined as benefiting the largest number of people (Christians et al., 1991). Here, we consider potential benefits and harm, determine which action would benefit the most people (or harm the fewest), and choose that. As with situation ethics, a reporter could conclude that illegally gathering important information would benefit more people than it would harm.

Pragmatic ethics were postulated by John Dewey, an early twentieth-century American social philosopher and educator. He argued that actions had to be judged by their results, not whether they adhered to a particular philosophy or guideline. This directs us to think ahead about the consequences of our actions. For example, will publishing a lurid photo of a beheading upset our audience?

Thinking through Ethical Problems: Potter's Box

Potter's Box is a process approach to deciding on ethical actions, developed by Harvard divinity professor Ralph Potter (see Figure 15.1). It is a four-stage model in which each stage helps clarify one aspect of the ethical problem at hand. Potter represented the stages as four quadrants of a box, hence the name.

In quadrant one of the box, we define or clarify the facts of the situation. For example, in designing a public campaign against drunken driving, the media planners want to address a serious public safety problem by making the consequences of drunken driving visible. They consider featuring a young woman who was disfigured in an accident caused by a drunken driver. She is perfectly willing to have her image used and signs a release form.

In the second quadrant, we identify our choices and the values or ethical issues that underlie the options. Will the shock value of the images deter potential drunk drivers? Or, will the images be in bad taste, violating community sensibilities, going beyond moderation? Could the publicity harm the young woman despite her willingness to participate?

Next, we look for general principles that underlie our options. Based on Mill or situation ethics, one could argue that the greater good of public safety outweighs the lesser evil of bad taste. Aristotle's golden mean might argue against using an extreme image, going beyond past practices. The golden rule might make us hesitate to put the young woman through an ordeal that we would not wish to suffer ourselves. This helps link concrete options to overarching principles, getting us to think about our own basic values.

In the fourth quadrant, we clarify our loyalties. Are we more concerned about being true to our own values or about the effectiveness of the campaign? Are we more excited about being connected to something edgy or new? Is the greater good more important than the golden mean?

Clearly Potter's Box is not a solution for any dilemma—it just helps us think about them more clearly. It focuses on ethical or moral issues, not pragmatic or legal ones, like whether you will get fired or sued. However, everyone will run into ethical dilemmas where laws, professional training, or organizational rules are not always clear. Potter's Box can help us think through what to do.

CODES OF ETHICS

To assist their members in ethical decision making, various organizations of media professionals have adopted more concrete guidelines to ethical decisions. The recommendations of the 1947 Hutchins Commission on social responsibility in journalism have been quite influential among both newspaper journalists and broadcasters and serve as a model for other media professions, so we will use them as an illustration.

The guidelines were based on two fundamental ideas: One, whoever enjoys a special measure of freedom, like that of professional journalist, has an obligation to society to use their freedoms and powers responsibly. Second, society's welfare is paramount, more important than individual careers or even individual rights. The Commission went further to list five guidelines for the press. The first was to present meaningful news, accurate and separated from opinion. The second was to serve as a forum for the exchange of comment and criticism and to expand access to diverse points of view. The third was to project "a representative picture of the constituent groups in society," by avoiding stereotypes and including minority groups. The fourth requirement was to clarify the goals and values of the society; implicit was an appeal to avoid pandering to the lowest common denominator. The fifth was to give broad coverage of what was known about society. That has been interpreted as prying open government secrets and presenting scientific discoveries.

These principles inspired the Society of Professional Journalists' Code of Ethics, the current version of which was adopted in 1996. It attempts to anticipate far more specific situations and to offer journalists guidance on how to deal with them (see "Media and Culture: Society of Professional Journalists' Code of Ethics," page 470). If all journalists followed the Society's guidelines, recent ethical missteps would have been avoided. For example, the Code says, "Test the accuracy of information from all sources and exercise care to avoid inadvertent error." If producers at CBS News had followed that maxim, perhaps they would not have broadcast phony documents about President Bush's National Guard service during the 2004 election. This ethical breach led to the dismissal of CBS news staff and perhaps hastened the retirement of long-time CBS news anchor Dan Rather who first reported the story.

Corporate Ethics

Our discussion thus far has emphasized individual ethical choices. However, most media professionals work within large corporations that present a fundamental moral conflict on a daily basis: my ethics or my job? In the wake of the Enron scandal of the late 1990s, there is a growing awareness of a general breakdown in corporate ethics. Indeed, many of

Society of Professional Journalists' Code of Ethics

Seek Truth and Report It

Journalists should be honest, fair, and courageous in gathering, reporting, and interpreting information. Journalists should:

- Test the accuracy of information from all sources and exercise care to avoid inadvertent error. Deliberate distortion is never permissible.
- Diligently seek out subjects of news stories to give them the opportunity to respond to allegations of wrongdoing.
- Identify sources whenever feasible. The public is entitled to as much information as possible on sources' reliability.
- Always question sources' motives before promising anonymity. Clarify conditions attached to any promise made in exchange for information. Keep promises.
- Make certain that headlines, news teases, and promotional material, photos, video, audio, graphics, sound bites, and quotations do not misrepresent. They should not oversimplify or highlight incidents out of context.
- Never distort the content of news photos or video. Image enhancement for technical clarity is always permissible. Label montages and photo illustrations.
- Avoid misleading reenactments or staged news events. If reenactment is necessary to tell a story, label it.
- Avoid undercover or other surreptitious methods of gathering information except when traditional open methods will not yield information vital to the public. Use of such methods should be explained as part of the story.
- Never plagiarize.
- Tell the story of the diversity and magnitude of the human experience boldly, even when it is unpopular to do so.
- Examine their own cultural values and avoid imposing those values on others.
- Avoid stereotyping by race, gender, age, religion, ethnicity, geography, sexual orientation, disability, physical appearance, or social status.
- Support the open exchange of views, even views they find repugnant.
- Give voice to the voiceless; official and unofficial sources of information can be equally valid.
- Distinguish between advocacy and news reporting. Analysis and commentary should be labeled and not misrepresent fact or context.
- Distinguish news from advertising, and shun hybrids that blur the lines between the two.
- Recognize a special obligation to ensure that the public's business is conducted in the open and that government records are open to inspection.

Minimize Harm

Ethical journalists treat sources, subjects, and colleagues as human beings deserving of respect. Journalists should:

- Show compassion for those who may be affected adversely by news coverage. Use special sensitivity when dealing with children and inexperienced sources or subjects.
- Be sensitive when seeking or using interviews or photographs of those affected by tragedy or grief.
- Recognize that gathering and reporting information may cause harm or discomfort. Pursuit of the news is not a license for arrogance.
- Recognize that private people have a greater right to control information about themselves than do public officials and others who seek power, influence, or attention. Only an overriding public need can justify intrusion into anyone's privacy.
- Show good taste. Avoid pandering to lurid curiosity.
- Be cautious about identifying juvenile suspects or victims of sex crimes.
- Be judicious about naming criminal suspects before the formal filing of charges.
- Balance a criminal suspect's fair trial rights with the public's right to be informed.

Act Independently

Journalists should be free of obligation to any interest other than the public's right to know. Journalists should:

- Avoid conflicts of interest, real or perceived.
- Remain free of associations and activities that may compromise integrity or damage credibility.
- Refuse gifts, favors, fees, free travel, and special treatment, and shun secondary employment, political involvement, public office, and service in community organizations if they compromise journalistic integrity.
- Disclose unavoidable conflicts.
- Be vigilant and courageous about holding those with power accountable.
- Deny favored treatment to advertisers and special interests and resist their pressure to influence news coverage.
- Be wary of sources offering information for favors or money; avoid bidding for news.

Be Accountable

Journalists are accountable to their readers, listeners, viewers, and each other. Journalists should:

- Clarify and explain news coverage and invite dialogue with the public over journalistic conduct.
- Encourage the public to voice grievances against the news media.
- Admit mistakes and correct them promptly.
- Expose unethical practices of journalists and the news media.
- Abide by the same high standards to which they hold others.

Source: http://sss.spj.org/ethics/code, revised and adopted 1996. Used by permission.

the corporate names we have run across in this book have been tarnished by ethical breaches: Time Warner, MCI, Adelphia Cable, and Qwest.

Large media firms share some basic ethical dilemmas with other large corporations. Many believe that the ethical crisis is the result of a fundamental shift in the values of large corporations and their top managers over the last two decades. Their mantra has become improving their "bottom line" and providing "value to the shareholder." In other words, the sole focus has become maximizing profits. That may sound perfectly sensible, but the goal has shifted a bit to providing the *appearance* of profits and to improving that appearance every three months when corporations report their earnings to Wall Street investors. The temptation to improve the numbers by hiding losses (alleged in Enron's case), recording phony profits (in the case of Qwest and Time Warner), or shortchanging public service obligations (endemic throughout the electronic media) has proven irresistible to some ethically challenged executives.

Another source of ethical corruption has been the practice of compensating senior executives with lucrative options to buy stock in their own companies. This also seems to make sense: the options are worth more if the company succeeds and everyone wins, including the chief executives and the investors. But that supplies further pressure to make the numbers look good and to manipulate stock prices for the sake of insider trading (that's what fine-living media maven Martha Stewart was convicted of in 2004) without really increasing the value of the company.

Perhaps it is time to return to the *corporate responsibility model* that preceded the obsession with the bottom line. That parallels the social responsibility model that guides individual journalists. Ethical corporations are expected to "give back" to the communities in which they do business by making charitable contributions and performing public service. Their executives have an obligation to serve with community organizations and, individually and collectively, make their communities a better place to live. Furthermore, corporations do have a responsibility to foster ethical behavior among their own employees. By emphasizing fair play and a respect for law, they aim to develop a corporate culture that rewards ethical behavior, not just the blind pursuit of the bottom line.

Making Ethics Work

In some professions, notably medicine and law, ethical codes are tied to licensing requirements. The penalty for ethical violations can be revocation of one's license to practice. There is no licensing in media professions, although the CBS news scandal illustrates how serious ethical lapses can be career-ending. This brings us to the question of how codes of ethics have any impact if they do not have the force of law or carry threats to one's livelihood.

Perhaps the most important impact of professional codes is to popularize the idea that media professionals do have a responsibility to society. Since relatively few people get to create professional media content, those who do need to consider the impact of their actions on society. In the United States, this sense of social responsibility is the prevailing ethic for media.

Although compliance with professional media codes is purely voluntary, there are nonetheless severe consequences for violating them. That is because media managers hold them up as norms for employee conduct. In several well-publicized cases, reporters who fabricated stories or plagiarized material for their columns were not only fired from their jobs, but were unable to find work at any other newspaper in the country. Even editors may lose their jobs if their oversight is too lax. But who oversees the boss's boss in a large media organization, especially if the "higher ups" have no background as journalists themselves?

The Watchdog's Watchdog

Name: Michael Getler

Born: 1935 in New York City

Education: Graduated from City College of New York and worked at the *Riverdale* (N.Y.) *Press* while in college.

Position: Ombudsman for the *Washington Post*

Style: Every Friday he issues an "Omb Memo," a pointed, one- or two-page assessment of the staff's recent failings and accomplishments. These are apparently widely anticipated in the newsroom to see who is praised and who is critiqued. He also writes a Sunday column on the editorial page in the *Post* that addresses readers' concerns, and some of his own, about pieces felt by some to be politically biased, mean-spirited, unfair, or inaccurate. He also addresses questions of how some stories are covered and why some stories are missed.

How He Got to the Top: Before taking on this position in November 2000, he served as executive editor of the *International Herald Tribune* from 1996 until 2000. Before that, Getler worked for the *Washington Post* for 26 years.

Biggest Impact as Ombudsman: He has taken on very controversial topics that obviously upset some readers and generally achieved a balance between understanding what a *Post* writer was trying to get across, critiquing errors of judgment and writing, and being respectful of readers' concerns. For example, a *Post* reporter conveyed (and sympathized) with concerns by African-American residents that they had to resist gentrification by whites. The reporter was accused of being racist by a number of readers. Getler tried to understand the story, but was critical of it at the same time.

Most Dubious Achievement: Some *Washington Post* reporters definitely fear his Friday memos as well as his columns. But even most targets of his critiques feel he is fair, according to an article in *American Journalism Review* by David A. Markiewicz, called "Mike'll Get Ya" (November 2001).

Inspiration: To seriously address reader concerns in a way that will improve journalism. He says, "Even a first-rate newspaper like the *Washington Post* has to be challenged. It has to fix what it's doing wrong, improve around the edges."

Entry Level: From 1956 to 1960, Getler served as a U.S. Navy officer. He started in 1961 as a reporter on specialized magazines in the defense, aviation, and space fields published by *American Aviation Publications*. He joined the *Post* in 1970 as a military affairs correspondent.

■ MICHAEL GETLER

© Michael Lutzky/The Washington Post

One approach to safeguarding corporate ethics is to appoint an in-house ombudsman to oversee ethical issues. A newspaper ombudsman is usually an experienced reporter or editor who serves the newspaper as an internal critic and spokesperson for the public's interests (see "Profile: Michael Getler: The Watchdog's Watchdog"). According to the Organization of Newspaper Ombudsmen (ONO), the ombudsman represents the reader, alerts the newspaper to public complaints, investigates them, and recommends action when warranted. Ombudspeople also serve as in-house critics, writing critical columns to the public about the newspaper's policies, but also defend the newspaper when warranted. For example in 2004, the *New York Times'* ombudsman took his own paper to task for failing to question reports about weapons of mass destruction in Iraq that were offered as a justification for war. Unfortunately, fewer than 40 American newspapers have an ombudsman (Organization of Newspaper Ombudsmen, 2003).

Finally, educators play a vital role in making ethics work, in courses like the one you are taking now. Ethics are an important component of the education of journalists, and they are a required part of the curriculum in accredited journalism programs everywhere. So, if you plan a career in journalism it is not too soon to start thinking about the choices you will face and the personal values you will bring to those decisions.

ETHICAL ISSUES

Now that we understand some of the principles, challenges, and procedures involved in media ethics, we turn to consider some recurring ethical issues. These are organized around the various media professions. Among them we include ourselves, the audience, because there are ethical standards for us now, too.

Journalism Ethics

We begin with journalism ethics since these were among the first and most highly developed ethical issues in the media.

Ethical Limits on Free Speech.   The First Amendment was originally framed to assure freedom of the press, but that is not an absolute freedom, and is still not enjoyed in many parts of the world today (see World View, page 475). In the last chapter we saw that there are legal limits on freedom of the press having to do with libel, public safety, indecency, and obscenity. But even perfectly legal stories are still subject to ethical restraints.

Indecency is a particularly sensitive issue since the courts have ruled that moral standards vary among communities, which are permitted to develop local standards for treatment of sexuality. Media professionals need to think about the ethics of indecency in individual terms ("do I really think this is a good idea?"), in institutional terms ("what do we as a company want to say to the public?"), and in terms of community standards and values ("is this an appropriate thing to say to this community?"). For example, in reporting the infamous Super Bowl halftime incident in which Janet Jackson's breast was exposed, the media might have shown the offending naked breast, if preceded with warnings for parents. Following situation ethics, they could have argued that the public's need to see just how offensive (or innocuous) the display was outweighed the offense it may have given to those with strict moral values. Indeed, pictures of the exposed breast were available on Internet news sites, but the mainstream media opted to show a digitally blurred image. In the wake of the incident, the electronic media adopted further ethical guidelines covering indecency in all programming, at least temporarily. However, even the blurred picture was no doubt offensive to some, and the very discussion of the incident may have been in bad taste. So in some communities, the proper ethical choice could have been to show no picture at all.

Accuracy.   In conventional news media, prevailing journalistic ethical principles about the accuracy of information are quite strict. Journalists are not to fabricate evidence, make up quotes, create hypothetical individuals to focus stories around, or create or manipulate misleading photographs, any of which might deceive the public. In 2003, a *New York Times* columnist, Jayson Blair, was discovered to have copied some of his stories from other newspapers and to have completely fabricated interviews and field trips in others. Not only was Blair fired, but the editors who were supposedly managing him at the *Times* were forced to step down as well.

© CBS /Landov

■ **WATCHING THE WATCHDOG?**
Ethical lapses like CBS's reporting of false documents during the 2004 presidential election erode public confidence in the media.

© Neville Elder/Corbis

■ **A SIGN OF THE TIMES?**
New York Times columnist Jayson Blair was accused of fabricating stories. Both Blair and his editor were fired for these violations of journalistic ethics.

Accuracy also means jeopardizing a scoop by checking facts and waiting to have at least two sources who can confirm a story before running it. Facts were at issue during the 2004 presidential election campaign, when CBS was accused of being overeager in reporting a story about President Bush's National Guard service. The story was based on documents that proved to be forged. At press time, improper sourcing seems to be at the center of the controversy and tragedy surrounding a retracted Newsweek report that American interrogators defiled a copy of the Koran.

Standards are far less strict on Internet news sites. Internet columnist Matt Drudge, for example, routinely violates the norms of professional journalism by publishing unconfirmed reports that may turn out to be only rumors. He considers journalism not as a profession but as a simple reporting function that can be performed by anyone who is determined to seek the truth and has a means to publish it, such as the Internet (McClintick, 1998). In his defense, Drudge might note that without him the press might still be sitting on the Monica Lewinsky scandal, a story he "broke" when it was still an unconfirmed rumor. And, in the CBS news incident, Internet bloggers were the first to uncover problems with the forged documents, which traditional press outlets were slow to discover.

Fairness.   Journalists and editors constantly make choices about what to cover. They can advance certain companies, people, and causes over others by the decisions they make on whom and what to cover. So, it is important to be fair.

To what degree can reporters be unfairly critical of the subject of a story? And if they are, to what degree are they responsible for consequences to that person? For example, was it ethical for the *New York Times* newspaper to run early stories about possible espionage by scientist Wen Ho Lee at the Los Alamos nuclear lab before the facts and context were complete? The *Times* itself later apologized in print, saying an internal review "found some things we wish we had done differently in the course of the coverage to give Dr. Lee the full benefit of the doubt" (the *New York Times,* September 26, 2000).

On the other hand, should reporters publicize someone they know, a cause they agree with, or a company they are employed by at the expense of others? For example, should ABC News run stories about Disneyland theme parks owned by its parent company, Disney Corporation? Should a reporter who accepts a trip to see a company's new product feel obliged to write about it or write favorably about it (Black, Steele, & Barney, 1998)? Should financial reporters be allowed to tout stocks of companies that they own interests in? Here, the accepted practice is to disclose the relationship that raises a conflict of interest so that the audience can be alerted to the potential bias.

Confidentiality.   News reporters need to protect the confidentiality of their sources so that they can win the trust of citizens who may have inside information about important stories (Meyer, 1987). For example, if a reporter is doing a story on the drug trade, she will end up talking to drug dealers. Because the knowledge the reporter gains from her

Reporters Without Borders

In much of the world, press ethics have as much to do with treatment *of* the press as treatment *by* the press. Reporters Without Borders is a multinational volunteer organization that documents abuses of the free press worldwide. Halfway through 2004, they counted 20 journalists killed and 136 imprisoned. In a typical week they cited the following incidents:

Politically motivated charges were brought against two journalists in Algeria.

A newspaper editor in Iraq was killed in a grenade attack.

Another editor was beaten up in Ukraine.

In Belarus, their Supreme Court threatened to close a newspaper.

China, Cuba, Saudi Arabia, Libya, and Zimbabwe are among the worst offenders. In Zimbabwe, for example, the only remaining independent newspaper was shut down and foreign reporters were forced to leave. The group petitioned the European Commission to pressure Cuba to release three dozen dissident reporters imprisoned by the Castro dictatorship.

Overall, the United States wins only a satisfactory rating, as its record is far from spotless. Reporters Without Borders criticizes the U.S. government for arresting 20 reporters and deporting correspondents from several countries, including Denmark, France, and Sweden as well as Islamic countries. Restrictions on photos of the coffins of soldiers killed in the Iraq war and access to detainees at the Guantanamo Naval base in Cuba are among the obstructions to a free press cited. The group also observes that the United States seems more dedicated to the ideals of a free press within its borders than without.

The group has its own code of ethics with many of the same provisions, such as a dedication to the truth, found in the Society of Professional Journalists' Code. One significant addition is to avoid situations in which reporting might be used for propaganda purposes.

Source: http://www.rsf.org/rubrique.php3?id_rubrique=20

sources could help convict them, law enforcement officials sometimes try to get reporters to reveal the identity of the sources. However, this is one ethical issue on which there is fairly widespread agreement: the reporter has promised either implicitly or explicitly to keep secret the source's identity and any of the details that could incriminate the source.

A related question is **source attribution**—how to cite sources without revealing their identity. The reporter wants to reveal as much as possible about the competence and position of her source in order to bolster the credibility of the story. On the other hand, many sources will talk only if they cannot be identified from what is said about them in the story. This issue becomes more complex when the source is a well-known public figure who wants to "leak" a story on which he or she is not yet ready to be quoted. Presidential advisors are continually leaking ideas about what the president might do about a certain problem; such leaks have become a means of trying out tentative ideas—trial balloons (Merrill, 1997). For example, in 2003, material about Iraq's alleged noncompliance with U.N. resolutions on weapons of mass destruction was leaked to the press because intelligence sources were worried that if they "went on the record;" that is, allowed themselves to be quoted directly, it would compromise their own sources in Iraq. That's why we often see stories attributed to a "highly placed official," or perhaps a "cabinet-level source." The most famous example was the Watergate scandal of the 1970s, wherein key inside information was supplied by a confidential source known only as "Deep Throat" even unto this day.

Source attribution means citing sources to reflect their credibility without revealing their identity.

■ **CULTIVATING YOUR SOURCES**
Robert Woodward, left, and his partner, Carl Bernstein, right, became famous in part for the revelations about Watergate given them by an unnamed inside source referred to as "Deep Throat."

Sensationalism. Sensationalism has characterized newspapers since at least the days of yellow journalism, when Hearst and Pulitzer relied on sensational stories to compete with each other for readers (see Chapter 4). Some consider sensationalism simply a matter of pandering to bad taste, so that highlighting stories about the bad behavior of celebrities, Kobe Bryant for example, is just a question of giving the audiences what they want. If audiences want higher-minded material, they should turn to other media or at least turn the page.

However, sensationalism crosses the line when it affects the legal process. During the highly publicized trial of Tyco Corporation CEO William Koslowski, newspapers ran sketches of a juror who allegedly flashed an "OK" sign to the defendant's lawyers and later identified her by name, forcing a mistrial. Sensational media coverage also makes it difficult to find jurors who have not been influenced by the media to form a biased opinion. Where in the United States, if not in the world, could we find a juror who could honestly say they had heard nothing of the Michael Jackson child molestation case, for example?

Sometimes to get sensational headlines, reporters are even tempted to break the law to get information, or to dramatize some issue. In October 2001, only a month after 9/11, two *New York Daily News* reporters attempted to smuggle weapons through the security systems in Boston's Logan airport. Although the reporters dramatized the continuing problems with airport security, they still broke the law. And, in so doing, did they publicize a security breach that may have provided useful information for a future hijacking?

Sensationalism also runs the risk of offending both readers and those connected with the subjects of the coverage. In one recent example, the *Boston Phoenix* published a photograph of the severed head of Daniel Pearl, the *Wall Street Journal* reporter who was killed by Islamic militants in Pakistan. That was denounced by the *New York Times* and other media as overly sensational and offensive to Pearl's family.

■ **RESPONSIBLE REPORTING**
Most embedded reporters in the Iraq War, like Jim Axelrod of CBS, followed the rules to maintain operational secrecy. But the military asked Geraldo Rivera to leave Iraq for breaking those rules.

Bribery. Many news organizations have a hard time paying expenses for reporters and reporting itself is a somewhat lowly paid occupation, so it is tempting to let someone else pay for the reporter's travel to exotic locations. The **junket** is an expense-paid trip that the sponsor hopes will attract the attention of reporters or influence how a subject is portrayed. For example, a resort operator might pay for travel writers to visit in hopes of getting a favorable story into a newspaper or magazine that might entice visitors. Or, a company might fund a trip that is only vaguely related to a particular topic but that might make the writer feel more positive toward the sponsoring organization in the future. If you liked their luxury resort (and want to be invited back), you should also like their parent company's stock, right?

Another form of bribery is freebies. Small media outlets don't always have the money to pay for books, theater tickets, and so on for reviewers, so it is tempting for reviewers to accept free copies and passes, even though that might bias what gets covered in favor of who provides free access versus who does not. Would you write a scathing review of a restaurant that just provided you a free meal? Perhaps you would not if you wanted to eat for free again in that establishment. But not all freebies are small time. The automobile industry is in the habit of providing, and many automotive reporters are in the habit of accepting, the "loan" of automobiles for extended test drives that can last for weeks.

Commercialism. Is there a conflict between news value and shareholder value? Hundreds of news jobs were eliminated in the corporate takeovers of the 1980s (Auletta, 1990), and news operations were forced to become more ratings-minded to reverse the financial losses of network news divisions. The latest round of acquisitions and mergers has created the additional burden of pleasing corporate masters who are unschooled in journalistic standards.

Increasingly, broadcast news focuses on stories that have a dramatic visual element that makes for good ratings. There is an inclination to lead newscasts with footage of car wrecks, wars, or airplane crashes. "If it bleeds, it leads," as the saying goes. There is also a temptation to ignore or downplay an important story because it doesn't have eye-catching footage to go with it.

It is also tempting to stage visuals. In an infamous incident NBC News staged a fiery truck crash. The producers failed to inform the audience that they used an incendiary device to ignite the vehicle's gas tank. On this point, the Society of Professional Journalists' Code (see "Media and Culture: Society of Professional Journalists' Code of Ethics," page 470) urges journalists to "Avoid misleading reenactments or staged news events. If reenactment is necessary to tell a story, label it." (http://spj.org/ethics/, 1998).

Pressure to improve ratings can also compromise news values. Many stations run sensationalized stories about crime and prostitution during ratings sweep periods, even though there is not really anything new to report about these problems. ABC News once hired movie star Leonardo DiCaprio to interview then-President Bill Clinton. DiCaprio never went to journalism school, so critics saw this as a serious breach of journalistic standards.

Vertical integration creates the potential for interference with news coverage by media owners. When journalists in a company's media holdings cover other parts of the

© Reuters/Landov

■ SOCIALLY IRRESPONSIBLE?
Correspondent Peter Arnett was fired for giving an interview to state-controlled Iraqi TV during the second Gulf War that was used for propaganda purposes.

A **junket** is an expense-paid trip intended to influence media coverage.

company's operations, there is a natural tendency to mute any criticism. For example, ABC News canceled a story about child molesters employed by Disneyland to please its corporate parent, Disney Corporation. The news editor protested, but the story did not air. This creates a climate of self-censorship in which reporters come to know that it isn't a good idea to prepare critical stories about their corporate cousins.

Press Release Journalism.   Press releases can become an unethical crutch if an over-worked journalist simply uses all or almost all of a press release or a video news release as the news story. Press releases are by definition prepared by advocacy groups, pushing for one point of view or another. They are often paid advocates, working for public relations firms. They are not journalists. They are promoting or advocating the interests of their client or their own organization, not necessarily pursuing a balanced account that is intended to serve the public interest.

Privacy.   A complex ethical dilemma for reporters is respecting the privacy of people who are subjects of news reports. Many reporters are little concerned about the privacy of those they are covering since they have a natural desire to expose and describe the topic of the story. It adds legitimacy and human interest to a story to provide personal details about the people involved. Some kinds of details may cause harm to those covered or their families. In the Iraq war, for example, most media refrained from revealing the names of military casualties until their families could be contacted.

Increasingly, electronically intercepted information might provide input to news stories. Gossip reporters could certainly learn a lot by listening to celebrities phone conversations or reading their e-mail. During the investigation of President Clinton's affair with Monica Lewinsky, her supposed confidante Linda Tripp began recording telephone conversations with Lewinsky, first on her own and then at the request of FBI investigators. Tripp's initial recordings of their phone conversations probably violated Lewinsky's right to privacy, but federal investigators with a warrant could then legitimately ask Tripp to keep taping the phone calls.

STOP & REVIEW

1. What distinguishes ethics from policy and law as guides to communicators?

2. What are the main areas of concern in media ethics?

3. What are some of the classic ethical principles that people apply to issues that arise in media ethics?

4. What is the concept of social responsibility, and how does it affect media ethics?

5. What is the Society of Professional Journalists' Code of Ethics, and how might it be useful?

Ethical Entertainment

Do filmmakers need to think about the social impacts of their films? Should viewers have the right to edit filmmakers' movies to meet their own moral standards?

Who's Responsible for Media Effects?   In a movie about Hollywood, *Grand Canyon* (1991), one of the main characters is a filmmaker who makes very violent movies. One day he is shot in a mugging attempt and is suddenly caught up in remorse. Has he contributed to the wave of violence that just engulfed him, too? As he recovers—and realizes that violent films are his livelihood—he is suddenly struck again by the need for artistic freedom, which includes expressing the violence in our culture.

While this character is a satire, the movie raises a real issue. Should producers take responsibility for the social effects of their creations? Or is their role to create art and let the chips fall where they may? Most filmmakers, musicians, and television entertainment producers, for example, say that they are not responsible for the social impacts of their

© AP/Wide World Photos

■ **LOST YOUR ETHICS?**
When it came to unscrupulous accounting and other dubious business practices, a number of communications firms, like MCI WorldCom, became notorious and sometimes went bankrupt.

creations. If someone gets hurt imitating the latest humiliating stunt on *Fear Factor,* that is their problem, not the producers'.

As Chapter 13 discusses, even the researchers do not always agree on how deep or pervasive the effects of violence or sex in the media really are. Yet headlines constantly remind us that some people seem to imitate specific acts of violence or reckless behavior that they have seen on screen or heard about on a disc. If even a few mimic an unusual act of violence, should its producer feel any responsibility? What if larger numbers of people don't directly imitate the act but come to see it as more normal or acceptable?

Industry spokespeople usually make two counterarguments: first, that individuals are not as vulnerable as is commonly supposed; and second, that individuals and families have a responsibility to make their own decisions about what to watch and what to make of it. For the mainstream of society, making responsible choices is probably the right answer. But how far should they go? People always make choices about what to see. One current response within public schools is to teach *media literacy* so that children and adolescents can make more informed choices. A number of churches and other groups are also doing this to supplement what children do or don't learn at home about making such choices.

However, there is a certain degree of hypocrisy attached to the latter argument since the industry also opposes a potentially effective new form of parental regulation. Now some companies offer software that skips indecent scenes or words in DVDs, and real-time editing of TV shows and music CDs may be technically feasible soon. The industry wants to outlaw the product on the grounds that it violates the sanctity of the movie studio's copyright.

Until recently, the prevailing trend in America was toward unrestricted artistic freedom divorced from social considerations. But religious critics and social philosophers, present and past, such as Walter Benjamin (1966), have argued that the artist is not absolved from responsibility to contribute positively to society. These critics argue that artists should either raise people's consciousness about issues or, at the very least, refrain from contributing to social harm. We would like to think that in the wake of the infamous Super Bowl halftime incident involving Janet Jackson, the entertainment media have begun to rise to a higher ethical ground. Unfortunately, if indecency is taboo, producers may turn up the heat on the other form of media content that raises ethical issues—violence.

Payola. The music and radio industries also face questions about the antisocial effects of their products, but they also face unique ethical challenges all their own. Record company representatives and, more recently, independent promoters dispense trips, contacts with artists, concert tickets, gifts, free music, and even sometimes drugs, sex, and bribes to get their records played on the air by DJs or placed into rotation by music directors. This practice, called **payola,** caused a scandal in the 1950s and was repressed by an amendment to the Communications Act of 1934 but still persists today. While illegal, it is common enough that it also presents a routine ethical choice to the DJs and music directors who are targeted with such favors. **Plugola** implies providing consideration to get one's product mentioned or "plugged" on the air. Overt bribery to obtain this kind of visibility seems unethical, but a number of variations are quite widespread today including **product placement fees** paid to movie producers in exchange for showing brand name products in movies. Oprah Winfrey was criticized for plugola by giving new Pontiac automobiles to all members of her studio audience one day in 2004.

Public Relations Ethics

Public relations can be a two-edged sword. It can be used for the public good even as it advances private advantage. Or it can be used to gain private advantage without regard for—

Payola occurred when record companies gave gifts or even bribes to key DJs to get their records played.

Plugola is when companies give products or gifts to get a product promoted within a broadcast.

Product placement is when companies give products or simply pay a fee to get a product promoted within a film.

© The New York Times

■ **UNETHICAL VNR?**
An ethics controversy flared around the broadcast of this video news release, which the U.S. Department of Health and Human Services (DHHS) created to promote the Medicare drug bill that was enacted in 2004. The spot's narrator gave the impression that she was a news reporter rather than a public relations professional paid by the DHHS, making the spot covert governmental propaganda in the eyes of many critics.

and occasionally at the expense of—the public good by manipulating the public interest or sugarcoating an otherwise commercial objective. At the macro level, critics such as Marvin Olasky (1967) say that professional public relations works to restrict economic competition. At the micro level, it has been accused of being frivolous, inaccurate, or superficial.

One such critic is the Center for Media & Democracy, whose website (http://www.prwatch.org) and e-mail newsletter ("The Weekly Spin") criticize assaults against the public interest. For example, the Center criticized think tanks, airline industry lobbyists, and the Bush Administration for using the 9/11 attacks to further their own agendas. Historically, there are innocuous incidents such as the Hollywood publicist who fabricated a story about a fictitious "best-dressed" contest to promote the career of an unknown actress named Rita Hayworth, who later became a famous movie star of the 1940s and 1950s. In the early 1900s, in a case that wound up before the Supreme Court, railroad publicists created phony organizations to criticize the rival trucking industry. The Court ruled that such a tactic was illegal. Even the routine task of planting stories through press releases poses an ethical concern. There is a tendency for PR professionals to feel a pride of victory if their press release is used almost in its entirety. However, in so doing does the PR professional cross the line from informing the public debate on behalf of his or her client to controlling the press output in a way that is invisible or transparent to the audience?

The key to ethical behavior for both individual practitioners and the institutions they serve is organizational performance. If a company, for example, acts in a manner that harms rather than helps the people it depends on for success, no amount of public relations can save the day, no matter how well the effort is designed or executed. Temporarily, the strategies and tactics used may dampen criticism among those most directly affected (for example, employees or investors), but the only real solution for the guilty party is management action that corrects the problem.

Down the years, ethical and legal breaches of conduct led to the formation of the Public Relations Society of America (PRSA) in 1948 and to the promulgation by that organization in 1950 of a Code of Professional Standards (see "Media and Culture: PR Ethics"). However, enforcement is rather lax. In 2000, PRSA completely revised its Code so that its power to expel a member applies only if he or she has been "sanctioned by a government agency or convicted in a court of law." Now, the Code is framed as a self-directed teaching tool that expresses the "universal values that inspire ethical behavior and performance." Other public relations membership organizations, such as the International Public Relations Association (IPRA) and the International Association of Business Communicators (IABC), have continued to promulgate codes of conduct with specific examples of what they consider unprofessional and/or unethical behaviors, but as with PRSA, neither organization has an enforcement program in place that can realistically punish breaches of its code.

Still, professional organizations can be effective even without enforcement power, as a 2005 incident involving columnist and talk show host Armstrong Williams illustrated. Williams was paid through a major PR firm, Ketchum, to advocate the Bush Administration's No Child Left Behind educational policy, a relationship that Williams—and Ketchum—failed to disclose, and which therefore violated public relations ethics. Under pressure from PRSA and other PR organizations, Ketchum management admitted their mistake and promised a review of their government contacts to prevent a recurrence.

Advertising Ethics

In advertising, ethical decisions revolve around selecting one moral value over another when writing, designing, or placing advertisements.

Harmful Products. The promotion of harmful products creates obvious ethical dilemmas for advertising professionals. Emerson Foote resigned as chairman of McCann-Erickson, one of the world's largest and most prestigious ad agencies, in protest over its willingness to create cigarette advertising (Fox, 1984). He was making a choice between the value of free expression on the one hand (tobacco companies produce legal products and have a right to advertise) and the value of health concerns (mounting evidence of the link between smoking and cancer) on the other.

Other advertising professionals have not been so scrupulous. It is now evident that some knowingly participated in the infamous Joe Camel cigarette advertising campaign that was secretly targeted to children in an effort to get youngsters to develop a life-shortening tobacco habit. Perhaps their sense of professional responsibility to the advertising client, or perhaps the desire to continue their own employment, outweighed their ethical responsibility to the children of America. Recently, though, after a series of legal battles, tobacco advertisers have become more sensitive to their responsibilities toward children. For example, they pulled cigarette advertising from magazines with substantial numbers of young readers, and outdoor billboard advertising is banned.

© The Kobal Collection/MGM/EON/Hamshere, Keith

■ **LICENSE TO PLUG**
Now James Bond movies sell BMWs. Some ad agencies specialize in this kind of "product placement," but is it ethical?

Product placement. This practice is common in films and is becoming more acceptable on television as advertisers grapple with the problem of "commercial skipping" DVRs. The pivotal event may have been the phenomenal promotion given by the film *E.T.* to the candy Reese's Pieces. Sales increased enormously after the film's alien developed a fondness for them on camera. Such placement now commands fees, which have grown dramatically in recent years. More recently, sales of Dr. Pepper receiving a boost from a product placement in *Spider Man 2* (on the refrigerator, in the pizza shop where Peter Parker works). Advertising professionals now see this as one of the more effective forms of advertising, since it is not obvious to many viewers that this is, in fact, commercial advertising bought and paid for. But it is precisely that lack of transparency that poses the ethical dilemma: should advertisers be "hidden persuaders" who do their work in secret? Television game shows are another frequent form of product exposure through the choice of what prizes are given away. Although these forms of promotion seem to have become common, media professionals still need to think about whether they are ethical.

Stereotyping. There are also questions about the ethics of using ethnic and sex-role stereotypes in advertising. Did you ever notice how almost all the women who appear in ads are beautiful and thin, while the African-American males tend to be professional athletes? Are such portrayals harmless appeals to advertising target markets, or do they perpetuate harmful racial stereotypes that foster racism and sexism?

Images of groups portrayed in advertising may have negative effects even when they do not include blatant stereotypes. Numerous studies (for example, Mastro, 2003) have shown that the models appearing in ads do not reflect the racial and gender balance of the American population. Indeed, some groups, including Asians, Native Americans, and female business executives, are nearly invisible in ads. Perhaps that sends the message that minorities and females have inferior positions in society. There are also valid concerns about targeting vulnerable groups with potentially harmful products, like selling high-alcohol malt liquor or cheap wine in low income areas or potentially unhealthful diet aids to females.

Guidelines for Internet Advertising and Marketing

Article 1   Rules

All advertising and marketing should be legal, decent, honest, and truthful. "Legal," in the context of these guidelines, is presumed to mean that advertising and marketing messages should be legal in their country of origin.

Advertising and marketing messages should be sensitive to issues of social responsibility and should in addition conform to generally accepted principles as regards ethical marketing.

Advertising and marketing messages should not be designed or transmitted in such a way as to impair overall public confidence in the Internet as a medium and marketplace.

Article 2   Disclosure of identity

Advertisers and marketers of goods and services who post commercial messages via the Internet should always disclose their own identity and that of the relevant subsidiary, if applicable, in such a way that the user can contact the advertiser or marketer without difficulty.

Article 3   Costs and responsibilities associated with electronic sales and marketing

Advertisers and marketers should clearly inform users of the cost of accessing a message or a service where the cost is higher than the basic telecommunications rate. Users should be provided with such notice of cost at the time they are about to access the message or service. This notice mecha-

nism should allow users a reasonable amount of time, as set by the marketer or mandated by applicable law, to disconnect from the service without incurring the charge.

Article 4   Respect for public groups

Advertisers and marketers should respect the role of particular electronic news groups, forums, or bulletin boards as public meeting places which may have rules and standards as to acceptable commercial behavior. Advertising and marketing messages posted to public sites are appropriate:

* when the forum or site receiving the message has a fundamentally commercial nature or activity; or
* when the subject or theme of the bulletin board or news group is pertinent to the content of the advertising or marketing message; or
* when the forum or site has otherwise implicitly or explicitly indicated consent to the receipt of advertising and marketing messages.

Article 5   Users' rights

1. *Collection and use of data* Advertisers and marketers should disclose the purpose(s) for collecting and using personal data to users and should not use the data in a way incompatible with those purposes. Data files should be accurate, complete, and kept up to date.
2. *Data privacy* Advertisers and marketers should take reasonable precautions to safeguard the security of their data files.

Consumer Privacy.   The ability to compile massive individual files of consumer and media behavior data takes *market segmentation* to its logical extreme, making it possible to address consumers as individuals, the practice of relationship marketing. However, this type of research is also important in *data mining*, which allows advertisers to sift through massive databases to come up with unique market segments, such as hair-care product users who enjoy hair care and like to talk about it with their friends.

These new capabilities raise concerns about the misuse of personal information being collected and stored through databases and websites. Many websites require the disclosure of personal information including name, address, telephone number, and credit card numbers. They can also track the media behavior of users while at their own websites, collate that information with information obtained from other websites and from the visitor's own computer, merge it with consumer credit information from the off-line world, and sell the information to third parties.

Industry self-regulation has thus far been the preferred method of dealing with privacy issues (see "Media and Culture: Guidelines for Internet Advertising and Marketing"). The Federal Trade Commission has issued guidelines that require websites to disclose their privacy policies, and privacy seal authorities have been established to monitor compliance. However, those disclosures may only give the appearance of trustworthiness whereas in fact

Guidelines for Internet Advertising and Marketing, *continued*

3. *Disclosure of data*   The user should be given the opportunity to refuse the transfer of data to another advertiser or marketer. Personal data should not be disclosed when the user has objected except by authority of law. Online mechanisms should be put in place to allow users to exercise their right to opt out by electronic means.

4. *Correction and blocking of data*   Advertisers and marketers should give the user the right to obtain data related to him and, where appropriate, to have such data corrected, completed, or blocked.

5. *Privacy policy statements*   Advertisers and marketers are encouraged to post their privacy policy statement on their online site. When such privacy policy statements exist, they should be easy to find, easy to use, and comprehensible.

6. *Unsolicited* commercial messages Advertisers and marketers should not send unsolicited commercial messages online to users who have indicated that they do not wish to receive such messages. Advertisers and marketers should make an online mechanism available to users by which the users can make known to the advertisers and marketers that they do not wish to receive future online solicitations. Unsolicited online advertising or marketing commercial messages should be clearly identified as such and should identify the advertiser or marketer.

Article 6   Advertising to children

Advertisers and marketers offering goods or services to children online should:

- not exploit the natural credulity of children or the lack of experience of young people and should not strain their sense of loyalty;
- make sure the goods or services do not contain any content which might result in harm to children;
- identify material intended only for adults;
- encourage parents and/or guardians to participate in and/or supervise their children's online activities;
- encourage young children to obtain their parent's and/or guardian's permission before the children provide information online, and make reasonable efforts to ensure that parental consent is given;
- provide information to parents and/or guardians about ways to protect their children's privacy online.

Article 7   Respect for the potential sensitivities of a global audience

Given the global reach of electronic networks, and the variety and diversity of possible recipients of electronic messages, advertisers and marketers should be especially sensitive regarding the possibility that a particular message might be perceived as pornographic, violent, racist, or sexist.

Source: International Chamber of Commerce, April 2, 1998.

---

they assure the website visitor that their privacy *will* be invaded (LaRose & Rifon, 2005). Thus, consumer privacy protection is still largely a matter of the ethical choices made by website proprietors.

Intrusiveness.   The ubiquitous nature of advertising has raised another type of privacy question: are there places that should be protected from advertising? In recent years, advertising has appeared on eggs, on parking meters, and in public bathroom stalls; proposals have been made to put commercial messages on postage stamps. Now marketers send attractive young shills to cybercafés and bars to plant plugs for computers and liquor products in casual conversations. Consumers are often annoyed when they are powerless to separate themselves from commercialism. Telemarketers interrupt family meals, advertisers tie up fax machines and e-mail in-boxes, and through satellite channels such as Channel One, commercials are now shown in public schools, a domain that was previously commercial free.

With the exception of the "do not call" lists for telemarketers, recent antispam legislation, and restrictions on cigarette advertising, there is little legal protection from the advertising barrage. Advertising on broadcast network television is limited by a voluntary agreement among broadcasters, and most media organizations have standards that prohibit ads for certain products, such as condoms. Other than that, advertisers enjoy broad free-speech protections, so incessant advertising bombardment comes down to a choice between ethics and commerce for the advertiser.

Subliminal Advertising. Another concern is with advertising messages that are so unintrusive that you don't even notice them. *Subliminal ads* are words and messages that are presented below the audience's level of awareness. For example, in magazine ads with attractive female models, look carefully at their hair. Can you see "sex" spelled out in the strands of hair? Ice cubes in liquor ads are another good place to look, for images of skulls and naked women (Key, 1992). Subliminal ads have been discouraged since a scandal in the late 1950s, but they are by definition impossible to "prove" and no one in the industry will admit they are there, if in fact they are! So, once again, their usage is an ethical choice: is it ethical to use surreptitious advertising?

Deceptive Advertising. In order to preserve their good name, most advertisers go to great lengths to avoid deceptive advertising. However, blunders can happen, particularly when the advertising message is prepared by a third party—the advertising agency. In 2005 a judge ordered the makers of Listerine to withdraw ads that falsely claimed the product worked as well as dental floss.

The government, however, does not usually regulate what is called *puffery,* or exaggerated assertions in advertising that can't be proved. Puffery ranges from small-business claims such as "Best pizza in the world" to national slogans such as Gillette's "The best a man can get." These statements, though seemingly harmless on the surface, raise a number of questions about truth in advertising. At which point should advertisers be required to substantiate their claims? Are particular audiences such as children more vulnerable to puffery? Is it up to the government to monitor the total range of deception in the advertising industry? Is puffery "deceptive" in the same way as falsehood?

Research Ethics

Communications research is a vital component of many media professions. It is everywhere, it seems: from questionnaires in the mail, to phone calls at home, to the questionnaires your professor asks you to fill out in class. Sometimes you just might try to make it stop, but that only triggers more mailings, phone calls, and urgings to "please take the survey if you want extra credit" as the researchers make further attempts to get you to complete their study.

What gives the researchers the right to intrude? It is important to remember that both you and society can benefit from your cooperation in research studies. Ratings, reader surveys, and cable subscriber surveys provide the feedback that the media industry needs to serve you better. The studies that social scientists conduct help increase our knowledge of the role that communications media play in society (see Chapter 13), or they help to inform public policy debates. Your opinions truly do count in communications research studies, so you should provide them willingly and honestly when you can.

However, not all surveys are legitimate, and not all researchers adhere to accepted ethical guidelines. This is a special problem with phone surveys. Too many times, what starts out as a survey winds up being a sales pitch. If you don't go along, the so-called "interviewer" may resort to abuse, begging, or intimidation to keep you on the line. The information you give, along with your name, address, and phone number, may be turned over to direct marketers who put you at the top of their "sucker lists." In the most blatant cases, the interviewer will suddenly turn salesperson on you while you are still on the phone. The new "do not call" lists offer little protection, except in the last case, since researchers are exempt.

Such "researchers" are acting unethically. According to the ethical guidelines of the American Association for Public Opinion Research, professional researchers may not lie to you or coerce you in any way. All information that can be used to identify you through your responses must be kept confidential and your name may not be disclosed for nonresearch purposes (marketing, for instance).

Academic researchers must adhere to even stricter standards. The American Psychological Association (APA), for example, expects ethical researchers to stress that your participation is voluntary and that you may withdraw at any time. They should seek your informed consent to participate, after informing you of the nature of the study and the amount of time—or other commitment—that is expected of you. And, if you are participating in the study for extra credit in a class, an alternative activity should be available by which you could earn the same credit.

Experimental and ethnographic studies raise their own issues. Experimental manipulations (such as those that administer simulated electrical shocks) can have harmful psychological effects on participants. Ethnographic studies that observe people in Internet discussion groups may violate the privacy of participants if they have an expectation that they are "speaking" to a closed group of associates. Only content analysis studies are completely free of human subjects ethics concerns.

Many colleges and universities also have a human subjects committee that is mandated by the federal government to safeguard your rights as a research subject. Such committees review and approve research studies prior to their implementation, especially if an experimental design is used or if sensitive information (such as information about your sexual behavior) is collected. Some human subjects committees also uphold the APA guidelines and have special provisions of their own. Other human subjects committees may require that all projects, including interviews and surveys, be approved by them.

Consumer Ethics

In the transition from "old media" to "new media," one important change is that the receiver, or audience, for the media is also the source of media content (see Chapter 1). That raises ethical issues for you, the audience.

Web Surfing. Sometimes it may seem that the Internet has no rules, but that is not true. Most Internet providers have a code of ethics on their home page under "Acceptable Uses" or "User Policy." These are guidelines, not laws, but the penalty for disobeying them can be the heavy Internet users' equivalent of "death": termination of your account. Some general rules to follow:

No harassment. Don't use the Internet to harass other users such as by sending them abusive e-mail, spam, or "mail bombs" of repetitive, unwanted messages. "Trolling"—making provocative statements in newsgroups to get people to visit your website, for example—is also to be avoided. If your account is at a university, school authorities will take an especially dim view of sexual or racial harassment, and it may have legal or disciplinary consequences far beyond cancellation of your e-mail privileges.

No misrepresentation. Middle-aged men posing as teenagers in hopes of luring young sex partners obviously violate this guideline. But it also precludes using someone else's name to sign up for services or listservs. Of course, if you are in a multiuser game or another Internet environment where everyone has a false identity and everyone knows and agrees on the rules, this "misrepresentation" is acceptable. However, "stealing" someone's identity online is a serious issue that could create real damage to the person you are pretending to be.

No hacking. That means don't use the Internet to gain unauthorized access to other people's accounts or to computers run by organizations. Also, don't steal passwords or credit card numbers. And don't sabotage other people's computers or web pages or the Internet itself.

No lawbreaking. If you use the Internet to commit an act that would be illegal in the "real world" you may make yourself liable to prosecution under the laws that cover the real-world behavior. Thus, to make explicit what should go without saying, don't use the Internet to deal drugs, distribute child pornography, defraud others, violate copyright protection, or publish lies (libel) about others.

Your own provider may have additional guidelines. Universities, for example, generally have a policy that prohibits the commercial use of the Internet. Using your web page to promote your rock band might get you into trouble, and using it to sell pirated recordings of an Aerosmith concert almost certainly will.

Providers also vary in how they check for violations. Some respond only to complaints, whereas others take it upon themselves to seek out abusers by monitoring chat rooms and discussion areas. Also, be advised that if your e-mail is an organizational account (and that *does* include student accounts) you have *no right to privacy.* Employers (and university administrators) have the legal right to inspect your e-mail for violations of their acceptable uses policies. Now the FBI is working with a trade group, the Information Technology Association of America, to promulgate ethical guidelines to young Internet users, their schools, and their parents. These are phrased as Biblical commandments, examples of what Kant called "categorical imperatives":

Thou shalt not vandalize web pages.

Thou shalt not shut down websites.

Sharing or Stealing? Intellectual property rights are now on a collision course with the freewheeling culture of the Internet. Let there be no doubt, it is unlawful to share copyrighted music and video files over the Internet without permission from (and also payment to) the copyright owner (see Chapter 14). You may call it "sharing" or "downloading," but in fact it is stealing and if the Recording Industry Association or Motion Picture Association of America targets you with one of their lawsuits, you will pay the penalty. Individual violations have reached such volumes as to make prosecution of all the violators unlikely, so the ethics issue remains important. Like speeding and underage drinking, file sharing is illegal but the odds of getting caught seem small. So what ethical justification can you produce? I won't get caught? Everyone else is doing it? The Big Media are ripping us all off? I can't afford the CD anyway?

Some forms of copying are both ethical and legal. Consumers may make, for their own use, a videotape copy of a film that is being broadcast. However, they may not sell or rent that copy to anyone else. A consumer may not make a copy of a videotape playing from one VCR or DVD onto another. That deprives the film copyright holder of possible future revenue if the consumer should want to see the movie again. This is why all videotaped films have an FBI warning against illegal copying at the beginning of the tape. Increasingly, too, both music CDs and DVDs of films have technological safeguards against copying, and "cracking" the encoding technology they use, even for the purposes of making a personal back-up copy, is an unlawful act.

New technologies continue to pose new ethical issues. For example, what about using your DVR to skip obnoxious commercials? The television networks that provide the programs consider that a form of stealing as well, because the lost ad exposure translates into lost advertising revenue for them. There is no law against skipping (although the networks are trying to get one), so it is up to you and your ethical standards.

Plagiarism.   Another ethical dilemma for students is downloading material from the Internet into term papers or downloading (or even buying) entire papers. There are sites that offer term papers for sale (we won't tell you where), but many students just use Google to find relevant snippets of documents and cut and paste them into their own papers. Both are plagiarism.

Or would you like some nice graphics to spice up your paper (and fill out the minimum page requirement)? Just about anything you copy off a website or out of a print publication is probably a copyright violation unless you obtain permission from the author. Sometimes the site explicitly says that you are free to use the images there as long as you credit the source, but you have to be sure that the site you copy from owns the rights to the work in the first place. There are many online sources of "free" graphics, called *clip art* (for example, http://www.clipart.com), but be careful to read the fine print at the bottom of the page. Some demand citation or permission, and others limit use to off-line applications. However, even if citation is not required, copying someone else's diagram, photo, or artwork into your paper is as much an act of plagiarism as copying their words.

Most colleges and universities have honor codes that specifically prohibit that, with penalties ranging from flunking the assignment to expulsion. Just so we are clear, that is not only a copyright violation but a breach of your school's honor code, even when you take the trouble to look up synonyms for a few words and rewrite the lead sentences. Even copying the order in which the arguments are made in someone else's work is plagiarism. You need to quote and cite what you copy exactly and paraphrase and cite ideas that you borrow. And, having a reference to work containing the paragraph you are stealing somewhere else in your paper does not cover you; every quote you copy or paraphrase must be properly cited at the point it is found in the text.

Beware, professors can Google, too, and can turn up the works you steal from. And, they have tools like http://www.turnitin.com that can pick out passages that were edited to replace keywords. So how many words is it ethically acceptable to copy? *None!* You need to reinterpret everything, process it in your own words and thoughts, and cite the sources you have used for inspiration.

STOP & REVIEW

1. What is wrong with payola?
2. What are the ethical implications of data mining?
3. What are your rights as a research subject?
4. What is unethical about file sharing?
5. What is plagiarism and how can you avoid it?

SUMMARY AND REVIEW

WHAT ARE MEDIA ETHICS?

Laws cover some, but not all, of the ethical issues in media, so ethics are particularly important in situations not defined by law but left up to individual or organizational judgments. Ethics guide communicators in how to behave in situations in which their activities may have a negative impact on others.

WHAT ARE THE MAIN AREAS OF CONCERN IN MEDIA ETHICS?

The main ethical issues that arise in communications media are accuracy or truthfulness, fairness and responsibility of treatment, privacy for media subjects and people in information services, and respect for the intellectual property or ideas of others.

WHAT ARE SOME OF THE CLASSIC ETHICAL PRINCIPLES THAT PEOPLE APPLY TO ISSUES THAT ARISE IN MEDIA ETHICS?

Some are absolute standards. Kant's categorical imperative directs us to act according to rules that we would like to see universally applied. Other principles make judgments more relative to situations. With situation ethics, for example, moral ideas and judgments must be made in the context of the situation at hand. According to Aristotle's golden mean, "moral virtue is appropriate location between two extremes." Mill's principle of utility states that we should "seek the greatest happiness for the greatest number."

WHAT ARE THE ETHICAL IMPLICATIONS OF SOCIAL RESPONSIBILITY FOR JOURNALISTS?

Whoever enjoys a freedom or a position like that of professional journalist has an obligation to society to use their freedoms and powers responsibly.

WHAT ARE THE MAJOR CODES OF ETHICS FOR COMMUNICATORS?

The Society of Professional Journalists' Code of Ethics and the Public Relations Society of America's Code of Professional Standards

WHAT IS POTTER'S BOX?

Potter's Box is a process approach to deciding on ethical actions, developed by Harvard divinity professor Ralph Potter. In four stages, one defines the facts of the issue, identifies the different values for choices that can be made, looks for general principles that underlie the options identified, and clarifies where his or her main loyalties in the situation lie.

WHAT IS AN OMBUDSMAN?

A newspaper ombudsman is usually an experienced reporter or editor who serves the newspaper as an internal critic and spokesperson for the public's interests.

WHAT ARE THE PREVAILING JOURNALISTIC ETHICAL PRINCIPLES ABOUT THE ACCURACY OF INFORMATION?

Journalists are not to fabricate evidence, make up quotes, create hypothetical individuals to focus stories around, or create or manipulate misleading photographs, any of which might deceive the public.

WHAT ARE THE JOURNALISTIC ETHICAL ISSUES ABOUT FAIRNESS AND RESPONSIBILITY?

They include avoiding favoritism or partisanship in coverage; protecting sources; and avoiding corruption, bribery, or accepting favors.

WHAT ASPECTS OF SENSATIONALISM CONCERN ETHICS?

Sensationalism in news coverage can affect the process of legal trials. It can affect perceptions of violence, fear, and racial tensions. It can lead to bad decisions about journalistic methods.

WHAT ASPECTS OF MEDIA COMMERCIALISM THREATEN ETHICAL BEHAVIOR?

Pressure to improve ratings or sales can lead to overdramatizing sensational elements and compromising news values. Corporate strategies and vertical integration can lead to unfairly favoring in-house interests.

WHAT ARE THE ETHICAL IMPLICATIONS OF RELYING ON PRESS RELEASES?

They can become an unethical crutch if an overworked journalist simply uses all or almost all of a press release as his or her news story.

WHAT ARE A REPORTER'S ETHICAL RESPONSIBILITIES TO HIS OR HER SOURCES?

Reporters are usually concerned about protecting their sources, but they also need to refer to them as explicitly as possible to increase the credibility of what they write. Confidentiality of sources is crucial to reporters, both to protect those sources and to gain and maintain access to them.

WHAT ASPECTS OF PRIVACY ARE IMPORTANT TO MEDIA ETHICS?

Reporters must make decisions about when to disturb the privacy of individuals.

DO FILMMAKERS, MUSICIANS, AND TELEVISION PRODUCERS HAVE AN ETHICAL RESPONSIBILITY FOR THE ENTERTAINMENT THEY CREATE?

Those who hold the idea of social responsibility for media professionals would say yes, but most entertainment creators say no. Research shows that entertainment may have considerable impact, but industry groups minimize social effects and say that people should make more responsible choices about what they consume.

WHAT ARE RADIO ETHICS ISSUES?

DJs and programmers need to avoid plugola and payola, favors in exchange for giving music exposure, even when they seem innocuous.

WHAT ARE THE MAIN PUBLIC RELATIONS ETHICS ISSUES?

The main issues are dealing fairly and responsibly with both clients and the public, not harming the public interest.

WHAT ARE THE ETHICS ISSUES FOR ADVERTISING?

In advertising, ethics is about the process of selecting and balancing moral values over another when writing, designing, or placing advertisements; avoidance of promoting harmful products; avoiding deceptive advertising; and protecting privacy in direct marketing.

WHAT ETHICAL BEHAVIOR SHOULD INTERNET USERS FOLLOW?

Internet users should avoid harassment of other users, not misrepresent themselves or others, not hack or vandalize others' sites, not violate others' privacy, not use web sources for plagiarism, and get permission for things they copy onto their websites.

WHAT ARE THE MAIN ETHICAL ISSUES FOR MEDIA CONSUMERS?

Consumers owe reasonable compensation to people who produce intellectual property—the things you read, watch, and listen to, so don't illegally download copyrighted music or video.

MEDIA CONNECTION

For web links, quizzes, and key term flash cards, visit the **Student Companion Website** at http://communication.wadsworth.com/straubhaar5.

 For unlimited easy access to additional and exclusive online study, support, and research tools, log on to **1pass** at http://1pass.thomson.com using the unique access code found on your 1pass passcode card.

 The **Media Now Premium Website** offers *Career Profile* videos, *Critical View* video news clips, and *Media in Motion* concept animations. You'll also find Stop & Review tutorial questions, a sample final exam, and much more.

 InfoTrac College Edition is a fully searchable online database offering anytime, anywhere access to more than 20 years' worth of articles from nearly 5,000 diverse and reliable sources.

vMentor **vMentor** provides live, one-on-one online tutoring to connect you to experts who will assist you in understanding the concepts covered in your course.

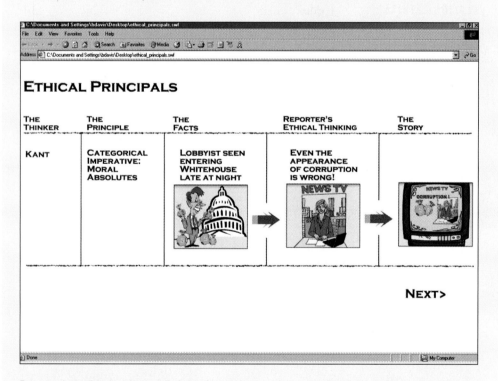

For an animated look at how ethical theories relate to media, watch the Media in Motion animation for this chapter on the website.

16

GLOBAL COMMUNICATIONS MEDIA

What's on in Afghanistan is sometimes the same as what's on where you live. Hollywood seems to be everywhere. However, a growing number of countries not only are taking in imports, but are also creating their own media and even exporting to other countries. Some American media companies, including Time Warner, Disney/ABC, and Microsoft, moved into the global arena very quickly. For a number of foreign firms, like Sony, going global means buying up major American media companies. This chapter examines these global trends and their implications.

ACTING GLOBALLY, REGIONALLY, AND NATIONALLY

The global aspect of media is very striking. *The Simpsons* was on television in over 60 countries in 2004, while *Spiderman II* covered many movie and video screens worldwide, making more money outside the United States than inside it. Australian media magnate Rupert Murdoch's various companies reach about three-fourths of the globe with satellite TV signals and even more countries with movies and TV programs. Global media are not just a Hollywood monopoly anymore. In fact, some major U.S. media companies are or have recently been owned by Japanese (Sony), Canadian (Warner Records) and French (Vivendi-Universal) companies. Mexican and Brazilian soap operas (telenovelas) reach as many countries as *Friends* and are far more popular in some places, such as Latin America and, interestingly, Eastern Europe and Central Asia (see Figure 16.1 on page 496). When SBC (Southwest Bell Communications) invests in or starts foreign telecommunications companies, it has to compete closely with British Telecom (Great Britain), France Telecom (France), and Telephonica (Spain), both abroad and in the United States.

Although American-made programs remain attractive to world audiences, we are seeing the emergence of global, regional, national, and local communication industries, audiences, and regulatory bodies, with a wide variety of ideas, genres, and agendas. More countries are competing to sell or broadcast media to others. Some, such as Mexico, Brazil, India, and Hong Kong, compete worldwide. Egypt dominates a regional market in the Middle East characterized by shared geography, language, and culture, similar to the regional market of Mexico that includes U.S. Hispanics.

Globalization of media is probably most pervasive at the level of media industry models—ways of organizing and creating media. The world is becoming a much more integrated market based in capitalist, that is, marketplace economics. This exerts pressures on nations to make media more commercial, supported by advertising, aimed at consumers, and to privatize telecommunications companies that formerly were government owned. The resulting rapid changes have had a profound impact well beyond the immediate ratings of *Big Brother* or *The Simpsons*. As we shall see, most countries produce increasing amounts of their own television, music, and magazines. But if they produce them by drawing on

Globalization is reducing differences that existed between nations in time, space, and culture.

■ **FIGURE 16.1**

International Media Flows
Although the United States has initially dominated international flows in most media, other countries are beginning to sell more media and information to each other. (In the figure, wider arrows indicate heavier flows.)

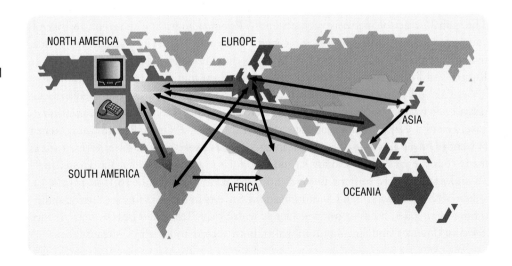

U.S., British, or Japanese models and genre ideas, then those "national" media products are still at least somewhat globalized. And even if a national soap opera reflects largely local culture in its plot and characters, it still helps Colgate-Palmolive and other firms sell soap in yet another part of the global market. Roland Robertson (1995) calls such combinations **glocal**—local productions done with global forms and ideas.

Global institutions and companies also have major impact. Global standards bodies such as the International Telecommunications Union allocate satellite orbits, determine broadcast frequencies, and define the standards for telephones, mobile phones, faxes, and Internet connections. Global telecom companies, like Cable & Wireless, run much of the world's communications infrastructure of optical fiber cables, satellites, and high-speed lines. Global media companies, like Rupert Murdoch's News Corporation, not only reach people directly with media but also force competitors to react to them. When Murdoch's Star TV started broadcasting in India, the state television broadcaster had to respond with more competitive entertainment or lose its audience.

The other major aspect of globalization is the increasingly worldwide penetration of media technology. Almost all nations now have at least a few people using the Internet and satellite television. Whereas the world's richest and best educated now use such new media, most of the people in the world are just now for the first time seeing television, a new medium with high impact for many of them.

Regionalization

Regionalization of media is growing as well. In several regions of the world (such as Europe, North America, and the Middle East), magazines, newspapers, and books have been transported easily across borders for centuries. Today, radio, television, and satellite television signals also spill directly from one country to its neighbor. Well over half of the Canadian population can directly receive U.S. radio and television signals, for example.

In the European Union (EU) and the North American Free Trade Agreement (NAFTA—Canada, the United States, Mexico) regions, governments have negotiated agreements on how to handle such media border crossings. The EU went further in 1989 to try to have "television without frontiers" within the EU. However, the attempt to produce programming for a Europe-wide television market is proving difficult, despite being promoted heavily by the European Union. Europeans are still divided by language and culture. Many still don't want to watch, read, or listen in another language (Schlesinger, 1991). The French still prefer French television to German or British television. However, Europeans are more willing to listen to other nations' music, with U2 topping the charts in several European countries in 2004. So the music industry has regionalized somewhat further in Europe than television, even as some countries, particularly France, still tend to protect their national film industries.

Cultural Proximity

Although geographical closeness or proximity helps media cross borders, language and culture seem more important than geography, as the example of Europe shows. It seems that people there and elsewhere tend to look for television programming, Internet sites, and music that are more culturally proximate.

Cultural proximity is the desire for cultural products as similar as possible to one's own language, culture, history, and values. Thus, even though people often like the cosmopolitan appeal of European or American television, movies, and music, they tend to choose media from their own culture or one very similar. When AOL enters a market like Brazil to sell Internet access and content, it has a hard time competing with the

Glocal is combining global ideas or forces with local ones.

Regionalization links nations together based on geographic, cultural, linguistic, and historical commonalities.

Cultural proximity is the preference of audiences for media in their own language and culture.

■ SEX SELLS GLOBALLY
Although most countries produce an increasing amount of their own TV shows, highly produced U.S. shows that emphasize sex or action adventure can still sell to many countries as has *Sex and the City.*

culturally relevant content provided by UOL (Universe On-line), operated by a major Brazilian newspaper and magazine publisher.

Language is a crucial divider of media markets. Increasingly, trade in television between countries is shaped by language (Wildman & Siwek, 1988), and language seems to be shaping music and Internet patterns as well. Language provides a strong natural barrier to media imports. The United States is a prime example. Most of what little imported television and film Americans watch comes from Great Britain, New Zealand, or Australia, culturally similar English-speaking countries. Likewise, British pop music is widely accepted, other musicians such as Icelander Bjork have to sing in English to break into the U.S. market.

Economics also shapes what can be done in cultural markets. Larger and richer countries tend to produce more of their own media products. Smaller countries usually have to import much more media from outside.

Besides language, other aspects of culture are important in defining audiences: jokes, slang, historical references, political references, gossip about stars, and remarks about current people and events are often culture- and even nation-specific. Such cues, where they are shared across borders, can help build cross-national markets. For instance, Latin American countries used to import American situation comedies. Now they tend to import comedy shows from each other, because the cultural proximity of Spanish-speaking Latin American nations makes slang, jokes, and references to current events easier to understand. That is also true for U.S. Spanish-speaking audiences, who often prefer Mexican shows to Hollywood, since Mexican (or Colombian or Venezuelan) shows feel more familiar to many of them.

However, many producers have discovered that when they make too many references to current politics, use too much slang, or otherwise focus too narrowly on current local issues, their programs are less well received in other parts of the world. Hollywood has long experienced this dilemma. Sometimes a very popular sitcom, such as *Seinfeld,* is too United States-specific to export broadly in the global market, whereas a show such as *Sex and the City,* featuring sex appeal, does better abroad, even after the U.S. market tires of it. While cultural proximity is a strong factor, audiences in many countries still respond very well to some kinds of imported programs. Those who prefer an imported program like *Sex and the City* are also more likely to be well off, better educated and urban, not the general audience. Those whose emphasis is on action, sex, and violence cross cultural boundaries fairly easily. Among the few foreign, non-English-speaking film and television genres to be hits in the United States are stylish but violent action films from Hong Kong and China, and cartoons from Japan, which are often sexy and violent. Sports are another genre with nearly universal appeal. We will also see that some elements of pop music are globalized, whereas others are localized, another example that complicates the logic of cultural proximity.

In many cases, *cultural-linguistic markets* are emerging at a level smaller than global but larger than national. These markets build on common languages and common cultures that span borders. Just as the United States grew beyond its own market to export globally, a number of companies have grown beyond their original national markets to serve these cultural-linguistic markets.

National Production

However, although global and cultural linguistic markets for media are all increasingly important, the main point at which media are created, regulated, and consumed remains the nation state. The vast majority of media companies are structured to serve national markets. National governments have far more effective control over media through station licensing, economic controls, technology controls, and subsidies than regional or global institutions or treaties. And ratings and audience research over the years tend to show that, given a choice, people tend to prefer to see national content in media (de Sola Pool, 1983; Tracey, 1988; Straubhaar, 2004).

However, nations vary considerably in what they can or will do to create media. Larger, more prosperous nations can create more media content than small, poorer nations. The United States, United Kingdom, Japan, and other industrialized countries can afford lavish production values that can overwhelm the modest productions of local media. This has been especially notable in film. There can be a contradictory tug-of-war between cultural proximity and imported production values. Nations that share a large cultural-linguistic community can create more for home and export than can smaller, linguistically isolated nations, such as Albania or Serbia. National governments can help media grow or can hinder them. National goals for media, reflected in government policies, are often very different, and they significantly affect how media are structured and what they create.

© Getty Images

■ OSAMA BIN LADEN, SUPERSTAR

Since the Sept. 11, 2001 attacks on the U.S. by Osama Bin Laden's Al Qaeda organization, he has used television to mobilize people to support him and his idea of an Islamic revolution. He is seen by many as a charismatic speaker. His videotapes on Arabic TV stations like Al-Jazeera draw huge audiences, perhaps in part because people admire him for succeeding in striking a powerful enemy. Fearing his propaganda impact, the U.S. government has tried hard to persuade Arabic media to not play his tapes.

THE GLOBAL MEDIA

Twenty years ago people talked about Americanization of media in the world. Today people talk more about globalization because it is apparent that although American media still play a prominent role in the global scene, media industries from a number of other countries are also heavily involved across the world.

A handful of firms dominate the globalized part of the media system. The six largest are Time Warner (U.S.), Disney (U.S.), Bertelsmann (German), Viacom (U.S.), Rupert Murdoch's News Corporation (Australian) and Sony/Columbia/TriStar (Japanese). The other five main global firms are Comcast (U.S.), Microsoft (U.S.), and two media groups that are part of larger industrial corporations: General Electric/NBC/Universal (U.S.) and Seagram-Universal (Canadian) (*Variety*, 2004). Of the top 10 global media firms, then, six are American. These types of companies are growing and globalizing quickly. Time Warner and Disney generated around 15 percent of their income outside of the United States in 1990, a figure that rose to 30–35 percent by 2004.

Behind the top global firms is a second tier of three or four dozen media firms that do between $1 billion and $8 billion yearly in media-related business. These firms tend to have national or cultural-linguistic strongholds or to specialize in specific global niches, as the BBC specializes in news. Some are American (including Gannett, Advanced, and Cox). Most of the rest come from Europe (Hachette, Havas, EMI, Reuters, TF1, Mediaset, NTL, RTL, BBC) or Canada (Rogers, Shaw), and a handful are based in East Asia (NHK, TVB, Fuji, Nippon TV, Asahi, Chinese Central TV) and Latin America (TV Globo, Televisa, Clarin/Argentina). It is no stretch to add computer media, and telecommunications so we should add Google, Yahoo, game companies Nintendo and Electronic Arts, and SBC, Verizon, Deutsche Telecom, France Telecom, and Telefonica to the list.

■ JOSH RUSHING

© Courtesy of Magnolia Pictures

PROFILE

One of the United States Ambassadors to the Arab World

Name: Former Marine Captain Joshua Rushing

Born: 1972 in Lewisville, Texas

Education: He graduated from Lewisville (Texas) High School in 1990 and was vice president of his class. He attended university while in the Marines, as part of his training.

Position: He joined the Marines at 18, went through officer candidate training, and ended up in military public affairs.

How He Got to the Top: He was assigned to talk to Arab television news network Al Jazeera as one of U.S. Central Command (CentCom)'s liaisons to the Arab media at the beginning of the Iraq war. He said later that he learned what he knew of Iraq from a couple of Bernard Lewis (an authority on Arab history) books and a copy of *Iraq for Dummies* that he bought before going to Central Command to work on public affairs regarding the Iraq War. He was surprised that he, instead of someone more senior or more knowledgeable about the Arab World, was assigned to talk to up to 45 million viewers of Al-Jazeera. He felt that relations with Al Jazeera should have been much higher in the administration's planning and priorities.

His Initiatives: Besides talking to Arab media, he started going into a variety of chat rooms on the Internet and offering, as a spokesperson for CentCom, to explain why the United States was going to war in Iraq.

Greatest Achievement: He became well known after he was featured as a central figure in the documentary *The Control Room* by Jehane Noujaim (2003), about CentCom and Al Jazeera, which became a hit at the Sundance Film Festival. When he was assigned as liaison to the film, people thought it was just a student film, but he treated the film fairly and seriously. He did not know what had become of it until someone left him a phone message after its success at Sundance.

Most Controversial Achievement: He argued in scenes captured in the film that the U.S. needed to engage with Al Jazeera: "The fodder that feeds the fires of 9/11 is the Arab perspective. There's no great shaper that we have access to than Al Jazeera. It is too important to ignore." At the same time, Al Jazeera was being heavily critiqued by U.S. leaders like Secretary of Defense Donald Rumsfeld. Even when Al Jazeera depicted the United States in a negative way, Rushing felt that Al Jazeera should be held accountable, but that the United States could not cut it off as some wished to.

Style: He is very analytical and fair. For example, in *The Control Room,* he says "It benefits Al Jazeera to play to Arab nationalism because that's their audience, just like Fox plays to American patriotism, for the exact same reason . . . because that's their audience. The big thing for my generation is for these two perspectives—my perspective, the Western perspective, and the Arab perspective—to understand each other better . . . because, truly, the two worlds are colliding at a rapid rate."

What Tripped Him Up: After the movie came out, many reviews portrayed him as someone within the military who opposed, or at least held a complex view of, the Iraq War, particularly for one statement in the film in which he said, "It made me hate war, but it doesn't make me think we're in a world yet where we don't need war." That made him very controversial for his military supervisors in media relations in Los Angeles.

Reason for Leaving His Position: He was frustrated with the military decision that refused to let him talk to the media after the film came out. Since he believed strongly in what he had been telling the news media about U.S. reasons for going to war in Iraq, he also began to feel more ambivalent about his earlier statements when some of the reasons he had been giving for the war, such as the threat of weapons of mass destruction held by the Saddam Hussein regime, proved unfounded.

Next Move: He left the Marine Corps in 2004 after 14 years. He was last working in the military liaison office with Hollywood in Los Angeles. In 2005, he was on a speaking tour of universities and other groups.

Some media industries, such as the Hollywood film and TV studios represented by the Motion Picture Association of America, have long been global in their operation and scope. They have controlled a number of the companies in other countries that distributed and exhibited (in theaters) the films produced in the United States. More recently, the ownership of Hollywood itself has become globalized, as we have seen. The resulting operation has been scrutinized by critics to see whether the kinds of films produced by Sony will now reflect Japanese rather than American sensibilities. No real changes have been found (Griffin & Masters, 1997). In 2005, Howard Stringer, who has both British and U.S. citizenship, was named Chief Executive Officer of Sony after working at Sony and CBS, so Sony is itself becoming globalized.

Record companies are similarly structured except that they have a more diverse set of origins and an even more international ownership. More of the big five are officially based in the United States; the main firms are: Warner-EMI (Canada), Sony Music Group (Japan), Vivendi-Universal (France), and Bertelsmann's BMG Entertainment (Germany). Major recording companies are also based in Great Britain (Thorn), and the Netherlands (Philips). These companies have consolidated across borders. Philips now owns Polygram (formerly of the United Kingdom), Bertelsmann now owns RCA (formerly of the United States), Seagram Universal now owns Warner-EMI and MCA (formerly of Matsushita-Japan, originally United States). Most of these companies also have large foreign branches that often produce and distribute records within other markets as well as distribute American and European music. As record companies have also been acquired by multinational companies, these firms have become more global and less national in character.

Still, there are some important distinctions in the ways that various media are organized around the world. In the following sections we will consider those differences and analyze the flow of media between them.

News Agencies

News has been flowing across borders in one medium or another for a long time. Many early newspapers and newsletters installed correspondents in other countries so that they could publish foreign news for their readers.

International news flow took a significant step forward in speed and volume with the development, in the 1840s, of newswire services based on the then-new technology of the telegraph. The Associated Press (AP) developed as a cooperative of American newspapers. Reuters grew to cover international news for the British Empire. Agence France Presse (AFP) was a joint government-private agency that served primarily France and its former colonies but also grew into a third primary international news source. These wire services were the first electronic news service, anticipating in many ways the increase in speed and volume of information that the Internet would amplify much further in the 1990s and later.

By the 1970s, a number of critics asserted that the major newswire services had too much control over international news flow. Such services followed standard American and European definitions of what was news: disasters, sensational or unusual events, political upheaval, wars or conflicts, famous personalities, and current (versus long-term) events. Although this approach fits the

STOP & REVIEW

1. What is globalization?

2. What is cultural proximity?

3. What are some of the bases that define cultural-linguistic markets for media?

4. What are the main reasons why companies buy or start up media in other countries?

5. Which companies are the main global owners of media?

6. How does news flow between countries?

Newspaper Circulation and Access Newspaper circulation and access are uneven and unequal in different regions of the world, mostly depending on wealth and economic resources.

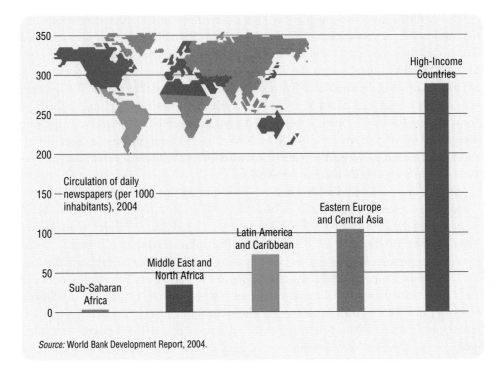

Source: World Bank Development Report, 2004.

Western ideal of the press as a critic and watchdog, it often produces negative coverage and images of other countries.

As radio and television became the dominant news media in many countries, the wire services developed material for them, and, later, so did satellite news channels like CNN. Now, news agencies, particularly Reuters, are beginning to bypass the middleman, like newspapers and TV networks, and reach readers directly via the Internet.

Radio Broadcasting

Because the print media's reach is limited in many countries by low literacy and income levels (Figure 16.2), broadcast media take on increased importance. In the poorest countries, radio is the main mass medium. However, in Africa and South Asia, many people do not even have access to radio, either because the signal doesn't reach them, they can't afford a receiver, or they don't have electricity. Many are covered only by short-wave radio, since they live too far from cities to get AM or FM.

International Radio. In some of the poorest countries, where domestic radio stations don't cover all the country, people in remote areas listen to international broadcasters. Such international radio is usually on **shortwave** frequencies that can carry across thousands of miles, compared to the limited range of FM and AM radio. In Africa, people in remote areas listen on shortwave to continent-spanning commercial radio stations such as Africa One, as well as to foreign government stations such as the Voice of America (VOA), Radio France, and the BBC (Bourgault, 1994). Digital shortwave is beginning to make music-oriented stations possible too. Plus VOA, and other international stations are now streamed over the Internet. There, however, they have to compete with thousands of stations streamed in dozens of languages from many countries.

Most international radio has been broadcast by governments over shortwave for largely political and public relations purposes—what has sometimes been called *public diplomacy*—trying to reach and influence public opinion in other countries (see "Media and Culture: The Cuban-American Radio War," on page 503). The main examples histor-

Shortwave radio broadcasts carry across oceans by bouncing off the earth's atmosphere.

The Cuban-American Radio War

One of the more fiercely fought international radio wars of the twentieth century was waged just off the Florida coast. After Fidel Castro led the Cuban Revolution to power in 1959, Cuba and the United States sank into a "cold war" in which radio broadcasting of propaganda seemed to substitute for more active military hostilities following the failure of the Bay of Pigs attack on Cuba. Cuba broadcast its own programs in Spanish and English at the United States. Cuba also provided a base for Soviet radio transmitters for Radio Moscow and Radio Peace and Progress. The United States broadcast at Cuba not only its Spanish Service from the Voice of America but also Radio Swan in the 1960s and a specific anti-Castro service called *Radio Marti,* starting in 1984, and a television version called *TV Marti,* starting in 1990. *Radio Marti* and *TV Marti* represented an escalation of the radio war by the Reagan administration, which was much more anti-Castro than its predecessors. *Radio Marti* had a very strong 50,000-watt AM signal, and the Cubans demonstrated an ability to jam it, interfering with several U.S. AM radio stations on the same frequency. *TV Marti* followed but never functioned well technically.

In 1995, the U.S. government reviewed its whole strategy of international radio and television, in an effort to determine how much to change its propaganda strategy now that the cold war with the former Soviet Union was over. *Radio Marti* survived, thanks to intense lobbying by Cuban exiles in the United States, but many other American international radio broadcasts to various countries were shut down. Want to see what the United States is broadcasting to Cuba on *TV Marti* or listen to what *Radio Marti* has to tell people in Cuba? Look at its site, http://www.ibb.gov/marti/.

ically were Voice of America, Radio Moscow, and Radio Havana. Some international radio has also been broadcast for religious reasons (by Vatican Radio and several American Protestant groups, for instance) and for commercial entertainment, news, and advertising (such as Radio Monte Carlo, run in the Middle East by the French company Sofirad).

National Radio. In more developed countries, national and local radio becomes much more important than international radio. Many countries have important national radio networks, which are widely listened to. However, radio in most places is tending to become more local. Radio is a good local medium because its production costs are only a fraction of those for television.

Radio can cater to the apparently widespread audience desire for local news, local weather and information, local talk shows, and local music. In radio, the urge for cultural proximity by audiences and market segmentation by advertisers favors the very local, although people still want to hear national and global music and news. Local music can reflect local preferences, and local news and talk tend to cover the things that most concern people's daily lives. In Wales, some radio stations try to attract people to listening in Welsh in order to help keep the language alive, and sell ads to the locals.

Music

The strength of national and local radio has a great deal to do with a revival in national and local music around the globe. U2 can be heard around the globe on many stations that appeal to affluent and globalized young people, but other stations are playing music by local artists as well, which tend to appeal to more middle-class, working—class, and poor people (Straubhaar et al., 2005).

Music around the world seems to be both the most globalized and the most localized of media. Travelers to almost any country will hear a great deal of American and European music, but they will also hear an astonishing variety of local music—nearly all cultures (and economies) have a musical tradition (and market niche). Such traditional music usually adapts well to being recorded, played on the radio, and sold on CDs and cassettes.

■ POP GOES THE WORLD
The success of Colombian rock/pop singer Shakira in English in the United States shows an ongoing crossover and blurring of musical categories like world, pop, and Latin music.

© AP/Wide World Photos

There is a truly global music industry, based primarily in the United States, that speaks to a globalized youth culture. But there are also thriving national and regional music industries, with a wide variety of genres and audiences, that also remain popular in most countries. Distinct music genres and variations on genres have emerged, such as reggae in Jamaica and ska in Great Britain. Audience tastes tend to be multilayered, with many people listening to global music, regional or national music, and local music to suit different needs and interests, including local advertisers (Colista & Leshner, 1998).

Governments sometimes require that a certain proportion of nationally produced music be played on radio stations. For example, Canada requires satellite radio Sirius to include Canadian content. Some also subsidize national music industries to make sure that local music, or at least some of the rarer forms of it, is produced. Most often, though, music development has been left to musicians' initiative, market forces, and audience demand. That works fairly well in many countries, because audience members are willing to pay for local and national music, although they also listen to and purchase global music. Music, too, is much cheaper to produce than film or television—so much so that it serves a wide variety of subcultures and market niches within and across nations, such as Turkish music among Turkish residents in Germany.

One threat to both global and local music industries is piracy of CDs and cassettes. In some countries, like Russia, local and national musicians simply cannot make any money at all by selling recordings, since nearly all copies sold are pirated illegally. The only way such artists support themselves is by touring and giving concerts, which deters many from being musicians. In 2004, worldwide music sales dropped 7 percent to $32 billion, according to the International Federation of the Phonographic Industry (IFPI), a record industry lobbying group. While the evidence is complex, the industry claims that much of the drop is due to music piracy, both local pirated copies and global exchanges of MP3s.

The international music trade is dominated by several major international companies. These are Seagram-Warner, Universal, Sony, EMI, and Philips. They import and sell the dominant American and European pop music around the world. In many countries and regions, however, they also record and sell works by national or cultural-linguistic market artists. That gives them something of a stake in promoting those artists, both at home and abroad, when they perceive that there might be an export market. For example, multinational firms record Jamaican reggae as well as Caribbean salsa and merengue, sell them at home, and also export them to the United States. Furthermore, those international companies are more willing to risk distributing national music recordings than national television programs, because musical tastes are more diverse and the costs (and financial risks) of recording, distributing, and promoting music recordings are much lower. So global firms end up selling both global and local music.

Film

Of all the international media examined here, films are perhaps the most globalized and the most difficult to produce on a sustained national basis. First, film is a relatively expensive medium to produce. Even cheap feature films, paying almost nothing to actors and technicians, cost hundreds of thousands of dollars, and an average Hollywood film costs over $60 million. (Cheaper digital production equipment may change this soon but has not had a clear effect so far, and promotion costs continue to rise sharply.) Second, the economic success of a film is never guaranteed, so it represents an expensive, risky investment to the producer, investors, and other funding sources. Third, the distribution channels that enable a film to make money have been globalized to a degree unlike that of any other medium. Films from independent producers or from outside the English-speaking world have a hard time breaking into the international distribution system, which is largely controlled by companies associated with the Motion Picture Association of America. However, an increasing number of firms, like Miramax and Lion's Gate, do actively look for international films to distribute in the United States and abroad, as well as for opportunities to coproduce films with foreign companies. Even Disney has begun to look for international cartoons to distribute, like those of Japanese Hayao Miyazaki's *Howl's Floating Castle* (2004). Some foreign films, like *Hero* (2004) or *City of God* (2003), are internationally distributed and do well, but most films produced in other countries never get distributed outside their home countries.

Films of significant quality and interest have been produced in many countries, but few countries are currently producing many feature films. A number of poor nations, such as the Dominican Republic, have produced only a few feature-length films in their histories—and some have made none at all. Furthermore, film production has slowed down in many countries, such as most of Latin America and Africa, as many companies have fallen into debt or suffered other economic crises. In a number of countries where film production had been heavily subsidized, governments have found themselves unable to continue to support it. Some countries, including France and Spain, still continue to subsidize their film industries, but this led to conflicts in trade talks (such as the World Trade Agreement) with the United States, which considers these subsidies an unfair form of protectionism (U.S. Dept. of Commerce, 2004). The big problem is that international films, even when produced at national expense, do not break through the largely Hollywood-based control of international distribution, and most national markets, with the exception of India and China, perhaps, are not big enough to make money with films that have little chance of international distribution.

The United States has dominated international film production and distribution since World War I (1914–1918). Both world wars disrupted a number of the other major international film producers (Italy, Germany, Japan, France, and Great Britain) and cut off their industries from world trade in films.

American films have succeeded in a variety of markets around the world for several reasons. One is the enormous size of the U.S. market for movies, which permits Hollywood to recover most of the costs of films in their domestic release. No other country has such a large and affluent national film audience. Second is the heterogeneous nature of the U.S. audience, which includes diverse groups that demand simple, more entertainment-oriented, and more universal films. Because of these elements, Hollywood has been the world's film production center, drawing money and talent from around the world and away from competing film industries abroad. Since the 1920s, Hollywood has drawn actors, directors, writers, and musicians from Europe, Latin America, and Asia (Guback & Varis, 1982).

Furthermore, Hollywood studios, organized under the Motion Picture Association of America, have worked together to promote exports and control overseas distribution networks. They have done so with a degree of cooperation or collusion that might be considered anticompetitive and a violation of antitrust laws if it were done domestically but that has been specifically permitted overseas by the U.S. Congress under the Webb-Pomerene Act (Guback & Varis, 1986).

Today the United States clearly dominates world film. American films filled over 80 percent of the theater seats in Europe in 2004. Overseas sales can more than double those in the United States for films like *The Matrix Reloaded* and *Spiderman II*, so Hollywood studios come to depend on overseas markets (*Variety,* 2004). Government protection of film industries in other countries is not surprising: they simply want to ensure that national film industries survive. Quite a few films are produced in Asia, primarily in Hong Kong and India (which has produced more films than the United States in some years). Egypt is the film center of the Arab world and Nigeria of West Africa. Brazil and Mexico produce far more than other Latin American countries. These countries do show that film industries can be maintained, even in some developing countries, if the domestic market is large or if the film companies produce for a multicountry audience and market. Some countries are also getting creative with financial incentives to promote national film production. Since Brazil, for example, began letting national companies deduct any losses on film investment from their taxes, film investment and production has shot up.

Many international producers have also started working with Hollywood in financing, distribution or even broader coproduction. Other countries, like Canada, offer sizeable production incentives which have moved Hollywood companies to shoot there. It is becoming common to shoot exteriors in one country, sound stage scenes in another, edit sound in another, and add special effects in yet another.

Video

In many countries, films are now most commonly seen on video or on television, rather than in cinema houses. In the more affluent parts of most countries, increasing numbers of the middle class and economic elite have VCRs, DVDs, and satellite or cable TV (Boyd, 1999; McDaniel, 2002). U.S. productions largely dominate video rental stocks, as well, since they are supplied by the same Hollywood firms that dominate theatrical distribution. However, video rentals are somewhat more diverse, since there are parallel circuits for distributing films and even television programs from local producers in China, Korea, Turkey, and India, to immigrant populations around the world who miss media from home. For example, almost any medium-size city in the United States has a number of ethnic stores that also rent videos, movies, and television programs from "home." Plus a number of countries are creating cable channels that show nationally produced movies almost exclusively, which provides a notable distribution vehicle for national films that many viewers would not otherwise see.

Television

Compared to print media, television broadcasting in many countries is far more divided among public, governmental, and private ownership. Because most broadcasters use the scarce VHF frequencies of the radio spectrum, relatively few channels are available and fewer people or groups can be involved. Television is also very expensive, too expensive for private media to make it profitable in some small, poor countries. Almost all governments get involved in planning who gets to own or operate radio or television stations, which also leads them to get involved in controlling content.

In Africa, Asia, and Eastern Europe, governments often have owned-and-operated broadcasting systems in order to control radio and TV. Their stated intention has usually been to use radio and television as powerful tools to develop their societies, but controlling politics is often the hidden agenda. India's state television, Doordarshan, initially tried to use television to teach better health and agricultural practices to villagers, but then-President Indira Gandhi also discovered it to be a very powerful political tool. But urban and middle-class viewers of the single national channel rebelled, demanding more entertainment. Now Doordarshan also faces private satellite competition and must be content to insinuate subtle prodevelopment themes, such as child health care and family planning into soap operas that both urban and rural people like to watch (Singhal, Rogers, 2001). Satellite television also brought in new forms of competition, which has also forced broadcast television to change. This has been true in India, Turkey, several Arab nations, and several parts of Asia.

Access to television is still very unequal around the globe. In many parts of the world, including much of Africa, most of the population doesn't see television much, if at all,

■ **DRAWING POWER**
In many places, people see TV as so important that it comes before almost all other purchases. Even temporary shelters like this one may have a dish to receive satellite TV.

particularly outside the main cities. In Mozambique, one of the poorest countries, only around 25–30 percent of the population has a television, roughly the same 30–35 percent who speak Portuguese, the language used on television. In contrast, most people, even among the poor, in Latin America and East Asia (Taiwan, Hong Kong, and so on) have television. Most people in the world work very hard now to gain access to television, perhaps more than any other medium. One of the authors has visited Brazilian, Peruvian, and South African homes where auto batteries power the TV sets in homes with no other electricity.

In many countries, including most of Western Europe, either governments or not-for-profit *public corporations* have tended to operate television broadcasting, with little or no private competition. Since the 1990s, a number of these countries have also introduced commercial television, which is becoming economically and culturally powerful. The goal of public broadcasters has been to use broadcasting to promote education and culture. An example is the BBC in Great Britain. To a large extent, the public broadcasters in Europe and Japan have outpaced the U.S. Public Broadcasting System (PBS) and National Public Radio in creating more educational, informational, and cultural programming. However, in some countries, such as Italy, public broadcasters sometimes have let political parties control their news and information programs.

State broadcasters are usually supported from government funds. Public radio and television networks are often supported by audience license fees. This is in order to maintain independence from both government budget control and commercial pressures by advertisers. In Britain and Japan, everyone who owns a radio or a television set pays an annual license fee. That fee goes directly to the public broadcasters (BBC in Britain and NHK in Japan), who use it to finance program production and development. Some audiences in Great Britain have complained that programming tended to be elitist and stiff, while others support its emphasis on news and education.

Broadcasting has mostly been privately owned in Canada, Central America, and South America, in part because of the strong influence of U.S. media corporations and advertisers, who promoted commercial approaches in the 1930s and 1940s (Schwoch,

1990). However, government controls over private broadcasters have varied among these countries. In contrast to the minimal controls in the United States, there are strict controls in Canada, where the government has tried to restrict the importation of programs from the United States. Many Latin American and Eastern European governments have exerted strong control over private broadcasters to obtain political support, mostly through economic pressures such as selectively awarding government advertising to supportive broadcasters. In most of the private broadcasting systems, entertainment programming has dominated, although some privately run, nonprofit radio education programs, run by the Catholic Church, have been effective in teaching basic education in Latin America.

There is a general recent tendency in European, Asian, and other countries to increase private commercial broadcasting and reduce government and public ownership. Publics often push for more broadcast choices, whereas advertisers, both foreign and local, push to be able to put advertising on commercial stations. Most countries are liberalizing competition in broadcasting by permitting new private companies to enter the market. Many individuals and companies would like to own broadcast stations. Such individuals often come from print publishing, such as Silvio Berlusconi, now prime minister of Italy, who currently controls the three major private Italian television networks. Many countries are also **privatizing** some public or government broadcast stations and networks. Sometimes this is to reduce government political control over state stations, such as when France privatized some of the state television networks. Sometimes, too, privatizing is done to take broadcasting out of the public budget and make it privately supported through advertising.

Some public broadcasters are feeling budget pressures, which also tends to make them turn to advertising as an alternative source of funding. Changing public media to a commercial basis to be supported by advertising is often referred to as *corporatization.* British study commissions have even considered putting ads on the BBC, which has been the very prototype of a public station supported by receiver license fees. With an increasing number of commercial choices, British viewers are less willing to pay directly for public television, and this puts the BBC under pressure to change its orientation and corporatize, perhaps moving to allow advertising. The BBC also went through crises in 2003–04 for being too aggressive and overly critical in its coverage of the Blair government.

Television Flows. Television exhibits a much more complicated flow between countries than does film. American television programs are very common and visible globally, but many other producers now sell programs to national and cultural linguistic markets, as well. At first, U.S. film studios and independent producers sold television programs worldwide with the same economic and cultural advantages that American film producers had enjoyed. In the 1960s–1970s, American films, sitcoms, action adventures, and cartoons flooded into many other countries. A 1972 study for the United Nations Educational, Scientific, and Cultural Organization (UNESCO) found that over half of the countries studied imported over half of their TV programs—mostly entertainment and mostly from the United States. Because television production was expensive and new, not many countries had the equipment, people, or money to produce enough programming to meet their own needs. A few countries decided to limit broadcast hours to what they could fill themselves, but most responded to audience demands for more television by drawing on external sources.

A number of countries, from Great Britain to Taiwan to Canada, have established quotas limiting the amount of imported television programming that can be shown. In

Privatizing government assets refers to selling them to private owners.

© Vallon Fabrice/Corbis Sygma

1989, the European Economic Community required member nations to carry at least 50 percent of television programming produced within Europe, which was challenged in 2004 by European states working to reduce this quota. Hollywood and U.S. government officials protested these rules at trade talks in the World Trade Organization and in regional treaties like the North American Free Trade Agreement (NAFTA).

American television exports represent a steadily increasing share of television producers' profits. Because many shows now make more money overseas than in the United States, a number of American producers are beginning to shape their programs to anticipate and maximize overseas sales (Waxman, 1998). However, now the high cost of U.S. TV programs also limits their distribution. The fees charged to foreign stations are set in relation to ratings. That makes U.S. shows more expensive than domestic ones; plus lower local ratings often relegates them to late-night hours when few are watching.

American television programs are also facing increased competition in a number of areas. More nations at virtually all levels of wealth are creating more of their own programming. Production technology costs are going down, groups of experienced technicians and artists have been trained in most countries, and a number of low-cost program forms or genres have been developed, including talk, variety, live music, reality shows, and game shows. More expensive shows, like soap operas are also being produced nationally (see "World View: Soap Operas Around the World," on page 510). As ratings and program schedules in many countries reflect, audiences usually tend to prefer local programming when they can get it (Straubhaar et al., 2005). And now, foreign format shows are invading television in the U.S. and elsewhere in a big way. *Big Brother* is a ratings hit based on a format developed in Europe, for example, with productions in over 20 countries and unlicensed copies in another half dozen. Licensing formats like *Big Brother* or *Survivor* is now a rapidly increasing global business. A great deal of "local" programming is now based on such international formats and models.

A significant exception to the localization of television in many places is TV news. Since the 1970s, television news flow began to increase steadily from wire services, such as Associated Press and news film sources from Great Britain. They offered filmed (and later video) footage for various national television news operations to use in their newscasts. Television news flow increased dramatically as CNN, the BBC, and other satellite-based news operations began to offer entire newscasts and even all-day news coverage across borders, primarily to satellite television receivers and cable television operations.

■ BIG BROTHER, PARLEZ-VOUS FRANÇAIS?

In 2001, the French adaptation of *Big Brother*, called *Loft Story*, was a smash hit. It propelled M6, a niche TV company that specialized in U.S. programs and other imports, to prime-time market leadership. Local versions of imported reality show formats like *Big Brother* permit new networks to break into local production, but critics wonder just how local the content really is.

STOP & REVIEW

1. What role has radio played in communication between countries?

2. Why is music more likely to be produced in a wide variety of countries than film or TV?

3. Why did American films come to dominate world film markets?

4. What competes with American media products, such as *The Simpsons*, around the world?

5. Why is television more locally produced around the world than film?

6. How do changes like privatization affect TV production and flow?

Soap Operas Around the World

Although American soap shows are still popular in many other countries, now they have to compete with soaps from Mexico and Hong Kong. More important, most people prefer soap operas or serial dramas set in their home countries or regions.

In Latin America, *telenovelas* run in prime time and usually depict romance, family drama, and upward mobility. The archetypal telenovela for many was *Simplemente Maria,* about a Peruvian peasant girl who moves to the city, works as a maid, saves money, buys a sewing machine, and becomes a successful seamstress. All sewing machines in Lima sold out after that plot development. Mexico, India, and South Africa have all used soap operas to convey themes that development planners want to communicate, such as family planning in Mexico and India, and working against domestic violence in South Africa. On the commercial side, Brazilian telenovelas' product placement often represents close to 50 percent of the advertising money spent on the program. Telenovelas are also hot exports, still playing to large audiences in Romania, Russia, and even China.

Martial arts dramas from Hong Kong and China follow some soap opera themes—romance, love, family intrigues, and rivalries—but add martial arts action, dramatic battles, historical plots, and period costumes. These are popular throughout Asia. Japan makes its own versions, focused on the Samurai era and featuring a similar mix of rugged heroes, beautiful heroines, and battles. These programs are also becoming popular worldwide.

Indian soap operas tend to be more epic, mythological, and even religious. A popular soap opera retold the national Hindu religious epic *The Ramayana,* the story of the Hindu gods. It had a powerful effect according to critics, who saw it as reinforcing nationalist Hindu political parties and standardizing throughout India a previously diverse set of versions of *The Ramayana.*

Many of these series are also popular in other markets, especially those that share languages and cultures. Telenovelas now sell to all of Latin America; Hong Kong soaps sell in southern China and feature on satellite Star TV; and Indian soaps are popular even in neighboring (and rival) Pakistan. Some of these exporters are also breaking into the global market. Mexican soap operas are popular now in Eastern Europe, and Hong Kong martial arts serials can be seen in Los Angeles dubbed into Spanish. If the theme is interesting enough, like in a recent Colombian telenovela, *Betty la fea* (Betty the Ugly Girl), about a spunky girl and her friends who were all considered ugly, or at least unfashionable, then people watch who don't even speak the language, but get the emotional impact, as did many English-language viewers when it played on Spanish-language television in the United States.

What do people find most interesting about international soap operas, like telenovelas? Colombian professor Jesus Martín-Barbero thinks that melodrama speaks very deeply to key issues for almost everyone: the need to get ahead; the need to keep your family together while you do that; and the complex emotions that family life stirs up. (Martín-Barbero, 1993).

Cable and Satellite TV

Cable TV, which has been familiar to most Americans, Canadians, and some Europeans for years, is now expanding in most other countries of the world. **Direct satellite broadcasting** (DBS) or Direct-to-Home (DTH) started in Japan and Britain and has rapidly spread to many other countries, often spanning the borders of neighboring countries.

By the 1990s, cable systems and private satellite TV channels to feed them were blossoming in Europe, Latin America, and Asia. These cable systems delivered what is for the most part a one-way expansion of new video channels, especially U.S. cable channels, into these new markets. A number of channels quickly became global in reach: CNN, MTV, HBO, ESPN, TNT, Nickelodeon, the Cartoon Network, Discovery, Disney, and others began to sell their existing channels in these countries or even to translate and adapt their U.S. channels to the languages and cultures of the new audiences.

A number of cable channels and DBS services started with a more specific language or regional target. Some European channels focused on news, music, sports, films, children's shows, and other targeted programming. One satellite television service in Asia, Star TV, owned by Rupert Murdoch, originally targeted the whole of Asia with American (MTV, film), European (BBC, sports), and Chinese-language channels. It has since

Direct satellite broadcasting is a television or radio satellite service that is marketed directly to home receivers.

begun to target more specific markets, such as India, Taiwan, China, South Asia, Indonesia, and Japan, with more **localized** programming, such as its own adaptations of the music video format and more language-specific programs.

Satellite TV and cable television are also beginning to expand in Latin America and the Middle East. Again, channels exported from industrialized nations (CNN, BBC, MTV, and so on) are popular, but several nations (China, Hong Kong, Mexico, Egypt, Saudi Arabia) are developing their own satellite television channels aimed both at national audiences and neighbors within the same cultural-linguistic markets. For example, the Qatar channel Al Jazeera has aimed to provide regional news to the Middle Eastern regional market of Arabic speakers. By covering the U.S. war against Iraq in a way that gave considerable coverage to Iraqi civilian casualties as well as providing pro-Palestinian coverage of the Israeli-Palestinian conflict, Al Jazeera has won many viewers in the region, as well as major conflict with Western governments, who found they had little leverage over it. Other countries began to use Al Jazeera footage as a news source.

© AP/Wide World Photos

Some other countries moved into fully digital television and cable TV before the United States. Japan and some European countries were operating broadcast digital TV early in 1998, and British Sky Broadcasting in Great Britain, owned by Murdoch, initiated 140 channels of fully digital cable TV in 1998. And has moved to provide interactive digital television (see Chapter 8). Like the latest cable systems in the United States, some systems in both developed and developing countries are beginning to offer two-way information services. For instance, the government of Singapore has offered broadband information services to almost all residents for several years.

Telecommunications Systems

The infrastructure for international media and information services has also become increasingly globalized. For transoceanic transmission there are several worldwide public satellite networks, such as INTELSAT, a global consortium of telephone companies that handles much of the world's international telephone and data traffic, and INMARSAT, which handles much of the world's maritime and other mobile communications (see Chapter 12). There are also a number of regional satellite systems, including the Arab League's ArabSat and the European Union's Eutelsat. Quite a few national satellite systems also offer telephone and television transmission services to neighboring countries. Privately owned satellite systems, such as PanAmSat, are also increasing in numbers.

Satellites are being at least partially displaced by an extensive set of world and regional fiber-optic networks owned by SBC, Cable & Wireless of Great Britain, and others. Fiber-optic cables can carry the same kinds of signals carried by satellites across transoceanic distances, with greater speed and less distortion. Increasingly, for the

■ **NEWS WITH AN ARAB SPIN?**
Since 1996, Al Jazeera, based in Qatar, has become "the CNN of the Arab World." By taking a very independent line on covering the Israeli-Palestinian conflict and on the wars in Afghanistan and Iraq, it has also become very controversial outside the Arabic-speaking world.

Localized media productions are those adapted to local tastes and interests.

Telephones and Cell Phones Around the World Telephone lines are unequally available around the world, which keeps much of the world's population cut off from telephones, electronic mail, faxes, and other services that use telephone lines. This graph shows regular telephone lines and cell phone subscribers combined, since many countries now have more cell phones than regular phone lines.

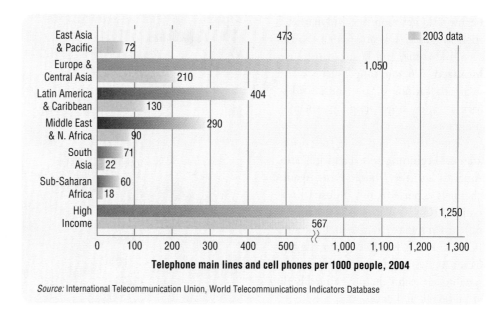

Source: International Telecommunication Union, World Telecommunications Indicators Database

frequently-used routes linking Europe, North America, and Asia, the fiber-optic cables are also more cost efficient. Costs fell further when the technology bubble burst in 2000 at the realization that much more optical fiber had been laid around the world than had likely markets or customers in the foreseeable future.

In another globalizing development, a number of national telecommunications companies are going international. The Baby Bells, France Telecom, Telefonica of Spain, and others bought telephone, cellular telephone, and data communications companies in Latin America, Africa, and Asia in the 1990s. These firms invested in a number of the telephone companies that have been privatized in various nations. They also eagerly sought to supply new services, such as cellular mobile telephony, in countries where foreign investments have been allowed under newly liberalized rules (Mody, Bauer, & Straubhaar, 1995). However, after the current global telecommunications capacity glut and bust, as well as the decline in profitability of many telecommunications operating companies, some of these firms have sold off some of their international interests. One pattern that emerged was of companies refocusing on markets where they traditionally had influence, like Telefonica in Latin America and Cable & Wireless in the Caribbean. Major companies have also suffered set-backs speculating in licenses for emerging wireless technologies like third generation (3G) wireless.

At the national level, telephone, telegraph, and other telecommunications systems have also developed at different rates in various countries. The United States, Japan, and a few other countries have more than 60 telephones per 100 people and are speeding toward the construction of an Internet (e-mail and World Wide Web) built on the telephone and cable television infrastructures. But some African and South Asian nations have less than 1 telephone per 100 people (Figure 16.3).

Until the 1990s, most telephone systems were operated by postal, telephone, and telegraph administrations (PTTs), state-owned telecommunications monopolies. Governments tended to see telephones as essential to their social and economic development. In many countries, governments have been willing to invest in telephones even when the services are not profitable, such as those to rural areas.

More recently, though, a number of governments have decided to privatize their phone companies, or sell them off to private operators. The reasons are usually financial—

■ **CAN YOU HEAR ME NOW?**
In many countries, where telephone lines are limited, the first phone for many people is now a cell phone.

to reduce debt or gain new resources to expand the phone or information systems. Other reasons for privatization can include trimming the size of government and making telephone operation more efficient by cutting inefficiencies arising from overgrown, bureaucratic PTTs.

Some countries keep the telephone company within the government but still open up some of the newer services, such as cellular telephony, data services, and electronic mail, to competition—a process called *liberalization of competition.* However, some privatizations have been derailed by debt and, in the current telecom downturn, attracting new private companies into many countries has become much harder.

For many of those countries in which the regular wired telephone system never reached most of the population, there has been a very rapid movement into cellular or mobile telephony as the standard telephone service. It has proved faster and cheaper to cover large numbers of new telephone subscribers with wireless service. In many cases, it costs no more than regular service, avoids long waits for delivery of service, and offers the advantage of mobility. In many countries in Africa, Eastern Europe, Latin America, and South Asia, more people have cell service as their primary telephone than have regular fixed lines. Starting in Japan and Finland, and spreading quickly, text messaging and some Internet access is becoming widespread over wireless, more so than over the wired Internet. This trend is spreading rapidly, as is the growth of cell phones and personal digital assistants capable of wireless access to the Internet. Also spreading fast is wireless (WiFi) access to laptops and other computers in both rich and poor countries.

Wireless service is also growing rapidly in the industrialized nations of Europe and the Far East, much more rapidly than in the United States. Part of the reason is near-universal (excepting the United States) acceptance of a worldwide standard for digital cellular telephone systems, GSM (Global System for Mobile communications). (See Chapter 12.) Other reasons are new services, like text messaging and the spread of new third-generation wireless services for high-speed Internet access, and billing systems where the calling party pays the costs. Wireless service is growing even faster in many developing countries where most new telephone users have a cell phone, because it is much faster and cheaper than a fixed line.

Telephone service has become a major international trade issue as well. The rates, or tariffs, that are charged for international calls are split between the country that originates them and the receiving country, and many nations outside of the United States have looked upon this as a significant source of revenue—and a way of protecting the revenues of their national communication carriers. However, under pressure from the World Trade Organization and the threat of competition from low-cost (and unregulated) Internet telephone services (see Chapter 12), international telephone tariffs are beginning to edge downward.

The production of computers has been limited to a few countries in North America, Europe, Latin America, and East Asia. Although China, Korea, and Taiwan have developed successful computer hardware industries, the efforts of most other less industrialized countries, such as Brazil and India, to develop computer hardware industries have often been frustrating and expensive, although India and others have developed successful software industries. The use of computers is still concentrated in the most industrialized countries because of the relatively high cost of hardware and software and the unequal distribution of income that makes relatively few in the developing world able to afford computers. Even though personal computers can cost less than $400 in the United States, they tend to be considerably more expensive in many other countries. Furthermore, many countries have average monthly incomes well under $200, which makes acquiring even a $400 computer difficult for most of the world's population. Figure 16.4

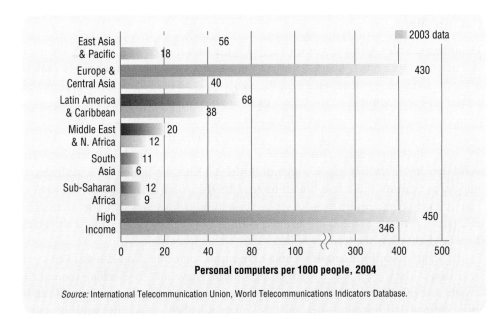

FIGURE 16.4
Computer Access   Most people in the world lack access to computers, which also cuts them off from the Internet.

East Asia & Pacific — 56 / 18
Europe & Central Asia — 430 / 40
Latin America & Caribbean — 68 / 38
Middle East & N. Africa — 20 / 12
South Asia — 11 / 6
Sub-Saharan Africa — 12 / 9
High Income — 450 / 346

2003 data

Personal computers per 1000 people, 2004

0   20   40   60   80   100   300   400   500

Source: International Telecommunication Union, World Telecommunications Indicators Database.

shows how computers are still concentrated in the industrialized countries, although their use is beginning to spread.

Thus the purchase and use of computers have been spreading worldwide, but unequally. In some countries, only government bureaucrats and a few of the wealthiest professionals and business owners can afford access to computers. In fact, many experts fear that relatively limited access to computers will keep businesses and professionals in the poorest developing countries from competing in a globalized market where others have a sophisticated computer infrastructure to work with, particularly those in Europe, North America, and East Asia.

However, computers are entering globally into business at a considerable rate, as is Internet use. The most significant initial global impact of information services and data communications worldwide was the interconnection of far-flung operations of multinational corporations via data networks. In the 1970s and 1980s, well before the Internet brought these kinds of services to ordinary consumers, companies were learning the economic value of sharing data among branches in Japan, the United States, and Europe. Even though they had to pay enormous costs to rent special telephone lines to connect computers, the payoff in terms of faster, more accurate internal communications was worth it. In the 1980s and 1990s, companies began to press to connect more and more of their own branches, suppliers, and customers throughout the global economy to their networks, mostly for the sake of United States-based multinationals.

U.S. dominance of **transborder data flow** is no longer pronounced, and the corporations and governments of a number of developing countries are beginning to participate. In India, for example, telecommunications networks and the Internet permit outsourcing of work from the U.S. ranging from computer programming to telephone call centers. The arrival of the Internet standardized many of these technologies into a single network that was much cheaper to use, so small business and individual users outside of big business and government can now afford access to rapid, high-capacity international data, text, and graphics communications. However, lack of access to information communication technology still hampers many poorer countries (World Bank, 2004). There is a global digital divide between rich and poor countries that is much more severe than the U.S. domestic one between rich and poor people.

Transborder data flow is the transfer of computer data across national borders.

The Internet

The Internet has exploded out of the United States into the rest of the world. The idea of sending text, graphics, images, and even music and video via computer has proved attractive almost everywhere. However, the computers and telephone lines that form the backbone of the Internet are in much shorter supply in most other countries. Therefore, the spread of the Internet was initially slower outside Japan, Australia, North America, and Northern Europe, although it is now growing rapidly almost everywhere.

As in the United States, the earliest adopters or users of the Internet around the world were in universities or governments. Businesses have also moved onto the Internet quickly, particularly those that are affiliated with the major multinational companies. The Internet often permits them to replace expensive private data networks with standard public network connections that give them access to more people, but it also gives them headaches over the security of their data and communications.

In Scandinavia, for example, people have rushed onto the World Wide Web even faster than in the United States. Many college students have web pages telling about their favorite movies and giving lyrics to the songs they sing at parties. There are a wide variety of cultural and historical sites, such as Project Runeberg, which has pages on most Scandinavian authors, with selections from their texts. The proportion of small businesses with web pages is perhaps even larger in Scandinavia than in the United States. Singapore and South Korea are pushing hard to get all their citizens on the Internet, with a high-capacity multimedia broadband network. However, it is not surprising that in fairly prosperous countries, well-educated people, many of whom speak English, would start using the Internet. What is more surprising is how many other people around the world are using it. For example, relatively few people in Korea speak English, but many use the Internet. In fact, Korea has a much higher proportion of broadband users than does the United States, in part due to the considerable popularity of online gaming in Korea, but also due to government programs to push this infrastructure (OECD, 2004).

The Internet has attracted a wide variety of unexpected new users in a variety of countries. Nonprofit and nongovernmental organizations (NGOs), such as human rights groups, environmental activists, churches, labor unions, and political party networks, have found the Internet a useful communications tool (see "Media and Culture: The Zapatista Revolution on the Internet," page 517). There is a worldwide network of activist groups coordinated by the Association for Progressive Communications (APC), which has pioneered opening the Internet to nongovernmental organizations, setting up Internet service providers, and showing groups how to use the Internet to promote social causes—all on a global scale (Frederick, 1993). In fact, in Latin America, Asia, and the Middle East, many NGOs are using the Internet to get access to information, network with each other, and get their message out to the world. The most dramatic example was the Zapatista Liberation Front in southern Mexico using the Internet in 1991 to get a worldwide constituency to protest to the Mexican government about its treatment of indigenous people in the Zapatista area (Cleaver, 1995). However, most uses are less dramatic, in which NGOs play an intermediary role between their constituencies and the Internet, looking for information, ideas, and resources that they can pass on to those who rely on them.

The Internet raises a number of new prospects for communication across borders. The structure of the Internet permits anyone with access to a computer and telephone to send or receive electronic mail to or from anyone else on the planet who has an Internet connection. Use of the World Wide Web, with its rich graphics, is much more problematic for

The Zapatista Revolution on the Internet

The use of the Internet by the Zapatista Liberation Front in the southern Mexico state of Chiapas has become "one of the most successful examples of the use of computer communications by grassroots social movements" (Zapatistas in Cyberspace, 1998).

This revolutionary group issued a Declaration of War against the Mexican government from the Lacandona Jungle on December 31, 1993, by fax and the Internet. The Zapatistas have explained that their struggle is for work, land, housing, food, health care, education, independence, liberty, democracy, justice, peace, culture, information, security, combating corruption, and protection of the environment.

The Zapatistas don't propose the usual form of revolution: capturing the capital and proclaiming a government. They see a more gradual process: "We think that revolutionary change in Mexico will not be a product of action in just one direction. In other words, it will not be, in the strict sense, an armed revolution or a peaceful revolution . . . the result will be, not one of a party, organization, or coalition of organizations with its triumphant specific social proposals, but a sort of democratic space for the resolution of confrontation between diverse political proposals" (Zapatista declaration, January 20, 1994). Their main method seems to be using modern media, such as the Internet, to create sympathy abroad and exert pressure on the Mexican government to enact reforms and make concessions (Arquilla & Ronfeldt, 1993).

For example, shortly after the Zapatista declaration in January 1994, the Mexican Army moved into the rebel areas to put down the revolt. Impassioned pleas from the Zapatista leaders, foreign anthropologists in the region, and others went out over the Internet asking people to urge the Mexican government to stop the bombardment. One of the authors of this book got seven versions of one of these messages, forwarded by different e-mail groups and lists, within 48 hours of the Mexican government attack. A large number of people did then fax, e-mail, and call Mexican government

An Accion Zapatista Report:

ZAPATISTAS IN CYBERSPACE

A GUIDE TO ANALYSIS & RESOURCES

© Courtesy of ZFLN

The international circulation through the Net of the struggles of the Zapatistas in Chiapas, Mexico has become one of the most successful examples of the use of computer communications by grassroots social movements. That circulation has not only brought support to the Zapatistas from throughout Mexico and the rest of the World, but it has sparked a world wide discussion of the meaning and implications of the Zapatista rebellion for many other confrontations with contemporary capitalist economic and political policies.

The indigenous character of the Zapatista rebellion has also provoked new awareness, respect and study of the much broader phenomenon of indigenous revival and struggle in this period.

The Zapatista analysis of neoliberalism (the Latin American term for pro-market, pro-business and anti-worker/peasant policies) has led to discussions and analyses of the similarities with Thatcherism in England, EU-Maastricht policies in Europe, IMF adjustment programs in Africa and Asia, Reagan-Bush-Clinton supply-side policies in the US and so on. The enormous response to the 1996 Zapatista call for a series of continental and intercontinental Encounters led to an historic gathering in Chiapas at the end of July 1996 where over 3,000 grassroots activists and intellectuals from 42 countries on 5 continents came together to discuss the struggle against neoliberalism on a global scale.

As a result of the summer meeting there are spreading and deepening efforts to knit together an Intercontinental Network of Alternative Communication (Spanish acronym = RICA) to accelerate the intercontinental circulation of struggle by providing a vehicle for the sharing of experience and the discussion of strategies for fighting for the overthrow of neoliberalism, of capitalism more generally and for the development and spread of a wide variety of alternative ways of organizing social life. These efforts are proceeding in many areas of communication including cyberspace, radio & television, music and film.

Against this backdrop, this guide has been compiled to provide not only an introduction to the variety of efforts that have developed in cyberspace, but also one point of departure for further developments. The number of activities associated with the Zapatistas continues to grow and as that energy circulates into the building of an Intercontinental Network linking a much broader array of struggles, achieving an overview of the structure and content of the Network will be increasingly difficult.

■ THE REVOLUTION WILL NOT BE TELEVISED

But it will be on the web, apparently. Revolutionary organizations, such as the Zapatista Front of National Liberation, use the web to publish their communiqués and seek supporters both at home and abroad.

offices. Concerned about international public opinion, the Mexican government called off the attack and opened negotiations. Hostilities and negotiations alternated for years subsequently. But the new government of President Vicente Fox in 2001 decided to welcome the Zapatistas to come to Mexico City to negotiate, which they did in a festive caravan in March 2001. Mexican government behavior over the years has been constrained and ultimately pushed to compromise over the years by Zapatista communications with the outside via Internet, fax, and telephone, which can still mobilize international support or protests.

ACCION ZAPATISTA
http://www.utexas.edu/students/nave/zaps.html

Zapatistas in Cyberspace
http://www.eco.utexas.edu/faculty/Cleaver/zapsincyber.html

TECHNOLOGY DEMYSTIFIED ■■■■■■

A Closed or an Open Internet—The Great Firewall of China

For a number of years, PRC (People's Republic of China) Public Security Bureau has blocked thousands of foreign websites that carry objectionable material by preventing IP addresses from being routed through its servers. It does this using standard firewalls and proxyservers at Internet gateways. Public security uses keyword filtering technology to identify sites and sends the current list of objectionable sites to the entry points periodically. In November 2004 Amnesty International identified 33 multinational companies such as Microsoft, Sun Microsystems and Cisco Systems that were providing the Chinese Government with technology to achieve its censorship objectives.

A 2004 crackdown, a 'People's war' on pornography has accentuated the Chinese attempts at control. Government regulations requiring Internet service providers to implement registration systems forbidding the collection of service charges from pornographic websites. Those caught violating the rules will be blacklisted by supervisory officials. They have requested that Internet cafés install software to monitor their customers. Internet cafés are not allowed to permit people under 18 to use their services.

Current reviews indicate that the Chinese firewall is largely ineffective and can be avoided by using proxy servers outside of China. The U.S. government commissioned software to let Chinese websurfers circumvent the firewall. The software enables PC's using Microsoft Windows XP or 2000 operating systems to circumvent or essentially dig a tunnel under the firewall, so they can gain access to uncensored news. Unsurprisingly this technology can also be used by people seeking access to pornographic and other illicit censored material. However, the government also relies on the fact that most people will not actively seek out objectionable material against government wishes. That has been reinforced by prosecution and severe punishment of those who use the Internet in forbidden ways.

E-mail is generally unaffected by blocking. Chinese-language e-mail magazines such as the Huaxia Digest distributed by *China News Digest* (http://www.cnd.org) and other organizations are received by thousands of Chinese. News items e-mailed by the Voice of America since early 1998 are similarly unaffected by net blocks. Dissident organizations outside China collect thousands of e-mail addresses and send them to Chinese netters, although several people have been prosecuted over the years for providing such email lists to outsiders. One academic said that Chinese are not held responsible for undesirable material that shows up in their e-mail mailbox but might incur a penalty for sending it along to other people. Since blocking access to sites has been technologically difficult, the Chinese government is more recently working on controlling access, particularly at public cybercafes, by making people register and making cybercafe owners responsible for what is accessed. In 2002, the government temporarily shut down most Beijing cybercafes as a warning.

Source: This was originally based on "PRC Internet: Cheaper, More Popular and More Chinese," an October 1998 report from U.S. Embassy Beijing, but has been updated from several sources, including Chongxiang Wang, "Online discussion of SARS in China : a content analysis." Unpublished M.A. Thesis, University of Texas at Austin, 2004, and "Internet Censorship – China" in M/Cyclopedia of New Media <http://wiki.media-culture.org.au/index.php/Main_Page>.

---

many global users, because Internet connections in developing countries may rely on unreliable telephone lines that permit only the slowest connections, making the transmission of graphics, let alone music and video, impractical.

Although Internet users in developing countries may not yet be able to see photos or watch music videos over the Internet, they can get access to literally a world of text information. A student in Lebanon can read news about his country not only from official sources, but from foreign newspapers, international newswire services, political dissidents and insurgents (such as the Al Qaeda), and other sources not approved by his government. Before the Internet and satellite television, a government such as the United States would have been able to manipulate press coverage to keep a small group like the Al Qaeda largely unknown. This makes the Internet a revolutionary force in global information flow, as we shall see in the next section. It also makes the Internet the main current challenge for many governments, such as China and Singapore, that are concerned about controlling information flows into their country (see "Technology Demystified: A Closed or an Open Internet"). China and other nations that wish to control political content on the Internet are working hard on ways to give access to the information people need to participate in a global Information Age economy—while controlling access to politically threatening information and news from the rest of the world. Access to the Internet has grown rapidly, but the government continues to use various controls to limit access to critical political commentary, particularly from outside China. This effort continues to cast some doubt on the idea that the Internet would tend to eliminate political control over information.

INTERNATIONAL REGULATION

International media and telecommunications systems are regulated differently from national media systems. As with most aspects of **international law,** there is no direct enforcement power, and regulation requires a consensus among nations that the proposed regulations or changes serve their various interests. Failing that, nations tend to assert their self-interest, and the larger, more powerful nations tend to get their way (McPhail, 1989).

One of the few international organizations that has achieved real compromises and real changes is the International Telecommunications Union (ITU). Technical standards have to be established so that users of telegraph, telephone, fax, and electronic mail equipment in various countries can communicate with each other across borders. For instance, the ITU has had to create systems for URLs in all languages to enable truly global use of the Internet. One of the main ITU divisions, ITU-T (telecommunications), is primarily involved with technical standards for telecommunications.

The ITU faces some of the same crucial regulatory problems that individual nations must solve within their borders. For example, radio spectrum frequencies have to be allocated to different uses in various nations to avoid interference between users. Even more important, the ITU allocates the space orbits for satellites. This is because satellites occupy orbits that lie above and across national boundaries. Also, **satellite footprint** areas almost automatically cover multiple countries, requiring international agreements on coverage and standards. Frequency and orbit allocations are routinely recorded by the ITU's B (broadcasting) division and are overseen by periodic World Administrative Radio Conferences that decide ultimately which country gets which orbits and frequencies. Poorer countries have complained since the 1970s that this process favors the larger, more industrialized countries. The ITU has responded by creating a third major division, Development, to work with developing countries to accelerate their adoption of new telecommunications and broadcast-related technologies. That group organized the World Summit on the Information Society (WSIS) in 2003–2004, which focused a great deal of attention on the need to promote greater Internet access in developing countries.

The Internet has posed interesting challenges to international regulation. It has required some new regulatory mechanisms for basic tasks like setting standards and assigning domain names, such as ICANN, ISOC, and IETF (see Chapter 9 for details). Much of the discussion in the 2003 WSIS ended up focusing on the need to globalize the functions of ICANN in assigning domain names, for example. Privacy laws are an area that has already required intense negotiation between European Community standards, which are very protective of privacy, and American standards, which have been much looser and less defined. In order for American firms to do Internet business in Europe, they have to negotiate an adjustment to those European rules. In fact this is an area in which European standards may well push the United States toward stricter rules on privacy than would otherwise have been the case. However, the U.S. desire to open Internet communications to scrutiny against terrorism will lead in the other direction.

There are other tough regulatory issues on the near horizon for the global Internet, like setting and collecting taxes on Internet commerce. Even more than with American states, many European and other countries get much of their revenue from sales taxes that

© AP/Wide World Photos

■ THE MAIN SOURCE
Most people in the world now have access to TV, which brings images from around the world.

International law includes treaties between countries, multi-country agreements, and rules established by international organizations.

A satellite footprint is the surface area covered by the satellite's signal.

are evaded by Internet commerce. Countries around the world also have very different positions on things like pornography or hate speech. Some of the more controversial attempts at Internet regulation so far have been German attempts to regulate cross-border anti-Semitic hate speech, which violates strict laws put in place in Germany after the nightmare of Hitler's Holocaust against the Jews in World War II.

The Internet is challenging not only global rules but regional ones like the privacy rules of the European Union. It is perhaps even more challenging to the internal rules of a number of countries. Nations as varied as Saudi Arabia, China, and Malaysia have tried to create restrictions on access to and use of the Internet in order to protect political control, national cultures, and religions. China has been a much-observed and commented-on example of a country that has tried to embrace the Internet for electronic commerce, while restricting its use for the flow of political information into China. In contrast, Saudi Arabia has been more concerned with the affront to Islamic values created by easy access to pornography over the Internet—an issue that also vexes many in the U.S. Congress.

MEDIA LITERACY: WHOSE WORLD IS IT?

Among the main issues in globalization of communications media are transborder data flow, **cultural imperialism,** media and information flows, the free flow of information, media trade, and the effects of media on national development.

Political Economy of Transborder Data Flows

Critics such as Herbert Schiller, in his book *Information in the Age of the Fortune 500* (1981), expressed the fear that transborder data flows would be a tool for increasing U.S. corporate power throughout the world, to the detriment of developing economies, political systems, and cultures. One example of how technologies permitted an increase in U.S. control came with the use of satellites to observe resources on the earth. Satellite **remote sensing** could observe the health of the Kenyan coffee crop or even locate copper deposits in Africa. Both the access to satellite signals and the computers required to interpret them were initially very expensive and for a number of years gave corporations an advantage over poor governments (Schiller, 1981). More recently, access has become cheaper, but corporate and military technologies for remote sensing remain more sophisticated than those available to smaller, poorer users.

Transborder data flows also permitted some corporations to centralize control over worldwide operations, sometimes causing branches to be downsized, jobs to be moved, and governments to lose tax revenues. However, other observers (Reich, 1991) note that although computers can promote U.S. corporate centralization of global operations, computer networks and data transfers also permit high-level jobs such as computer programming to be transferred to low-wage nations such as India, which has become an offshore outsourcing center for many corporations. This situation represents an economic opportunity for millions of Indians but a loss of jobs for many Americans who had previously done the work. And high-level programming and systems analyst jobs are also being increasingly exported to countries such as India, reversing the pattern of dominance that Schiller alerted us to. In fact, an increasingly dense and complex integration of companies' operations between the United States, India, and lots of other places via the Internet is now one of the most crucial defining characteristics of globalization for many people. This enables *outsourcing* of jobs, in areas like telephone call centers, database

Cultural imperialism occurs when some countries dominate others through the media.

Remote sensing is satellite observation of objects, vegetation, and weather patterns.

entry, and even software development, from the United States to India and other countries where labor costs are low. (See Chapter One.) Workers there can easily and cheaply be connected to companies in the Untied States, given the relatively low cost of telecommunications between the two countries. This has become common enough to become an issue in the 2004 presidential election.

Political Economy of Cultural Imperialism

Perhaps the biggest international issue in communications media has been what many nations call *cultural imperialism,* particularly the unequal flows of film, television, music, news, and information. This *unbalanced flow* bothers many nations on several levels. First, it is seen as a cause of cultural erosion and change. So many media products and cultural influences flow into some countries from the United States that traditionalists fear American ideas, images, and values will replace their own. Some of the fears seem trivial to U.S. observers, as when French authorities fought to keep American words such as "drugstore" and "weekend" from creeping into common use by French people. However, some consequences of media flows can be deadly serious. Some poor countries in Africa saw epidemics of infant diarrhea and death when mothers gave up breast-feeding for bottle-feeding, which they had seen in European and American television programs and advertising. (The problem was caused by mixing infant formula with unsanitary water.)

Other critics of cultural imperialism have been more concerned about the increasingly global economics underlying the flows of media. Underlying the fear of commercial media, in particular, is the idea that they tend to tie countries into a global economy based on advertising and consumption, which offers the poorer countries little and may alienate those in the population who are frustrated by exposure to goods they cannot have.

The cultural imperialism argument has lost some of its force as many countries increase the amount and kinds of media contents they produce. Some governments, such as Japan and Taiwan, have pressured national television broadcasters to produce more programming. Others, such as France, subsidize their national film industries to keep them strong. Another solution is to limit media imports, such as the amount of foreign television and film. However, such limits have been strongly opposed by the United States in the World Trade Organization. Many countries have discovered that national and regional television and music production tend to increase more or less naturally, because they are feasible economically and because audiences want them. However, for many critics, the global transformation of the economics of media into steadily more capitalist, commercial forms of operation in most countries reflects the continuation of many of the economic issues of cultural imperialism into the new framework of globalization.

Cultural Impact of Media and Information Flows

Even though nations differ culturally and politically, they are not isolated. As we look at the globalization of media, we see that one of its most obvious aspects is an extensive flow of a variety of kinds of media contents between countries. Elements of media, such as books, songs, stories, and news, have always flowed across borders; cultures have never been truly isolated. Even before Gutenberg's printing press, the Christian Bible and the Islamic Koran had both moved powerfully across a number of countries and cultures, as handwritten copies motivated leaders who led millions into massive religious and cultural change.

However, many people worry that modern media move new ideas and values across borders in such quantities, and at such speed, that we have entered a new age of much more pervasive and rapid change in the world's cultures. Marshall McLuhan (1964) looked at the electronic media and anticipated a "global village." What kind of global village might the media construct? Much of what flows across borders originates in Hollywood, so some fear that the "village" will be as Americanized as a San Fernando Valley mall multiplex theater.

A major issue is the impact of Hollywood-style material on other cultures. Because Hollywood films, television, and Anglo-American pop music often include sex, violence, drugs, and gender roles and racial images that clash strongly with local values around the world, many people fear its influence, particularly on the young. After September 11, 2001, some in the Arab nations cited such clashing images as part of what made a number of religious Muslims fear U.S. cultural influence on their national values. Many worry that new media like satellite television and the Internet simply amplify the availability of these messages. However, after September 11, 2001, satellite television in the Arab nations also became notable for carrying Al Jazeera's Arab version of the news, which competed very strongly with both commercial American media and official U.S. efforts by the State Department's Office of Public Affairs.

A more optimistic vision of the global future is that media and information technologies will decentralize the global village, so that information and culture will flow in many directions, from a variety of sources, with many different messages. This scenario sees a variety of different kinds of companies and groups, such as environment or human rights groups, reaching broader audiences across borders. An example might be the Association for Progressive Communications, which provides Internet access and international coordination for groups like PeaceNet and EcoNet. Another example is U.S. human rights groups that work with developing country movements like Mexico's Zapatistas to try to influence both U.S. and Mexican policies (Cleaver, 1995).

Free Flow of Information

One of the fears in many countries is that unbalanced media flows will diminish **national sovereignty,** reducing countries' cultural autonomy and governments' abilities to support and protect their cultures. In contrast, the idea of a **free flow of information** reflects the basic concept of freedom of speech, whereby all people ought to be as free as possible to both send and receive information across borders. But according to the idea of national sovereignty, governments or other domestic forces are entitled to assert national control over natural resources, culture, politics, and so on. Both approaches are established as basic principles in the UNESCO charter and the 1948 U.N. Declaration on Human Rights. In 2005, a new draft convention on protection of endangered cultures in UNESCO will raise these issues again.

Those who consider the current international flows of information and culture unequal tend to emphasize national sovereignty as a justification for a country's asserting control over media flows. The United States has opposed many such proposals. It does so in part because American commercial media interests are threatened by proposed restrictions on media sales and flows. But the United States has also opposed certain proposed restrictions on principle. The United States and a number of other nations believe it is important to keep as free a flow of information as possible to promote freedom of speech globally.

Debate raged in UNESCO over these issues in 1976–1983 until the United States decided to withdraw in protest of proposed policies that it thought violated the values of the free flow of information and journalistic freedom. UNESCO proposed that countries

National sovereignty is the policy of keeping domestic forces in control of a nation's economy, politics, and culture.

Free flow of information occurs when information flows as freely as possible between countries.

create national policies to balance the flow of information. The United States feared that UNESCO's policies would give too much power to governments, which would be likely to restrict free speech and the free flow of information. The compromise proposal in 1979 in UNESCO (subsequently rejected by the United States in 1982) was to promote a *free and balanced flow* by helping developing countries build up their own abilities to produce and export media and cultural products.

Although this idea received little financial support, a number of developing nations succeeded in producing more media anyway. The most notable regional news agency launched in the Middle East, the Caribbean, and Africa has been Al Jazeera. More recently, the Internet has permitted a much more diverse flow of news, although most major news media continue to use the same old commercial news agencies. As described earlier in this chapter, a number of national media ventures have been started to try to balance the flow of television, film, and music among nations.

Trade in Media

Media flow and trade issues have been raised in regional treaty organizations, such as the European Union (EU) and the North American Free Trade Agreement (NAFTA), as well as in the World Trade Organization (WTO). The United States tends to see cultural industries as a trade policy issue, because such exports are a significant part of the American balance of trade, compensating for American purchases of Japanese DVDs, radios, and other consumer electronics, for example. European and Canadian governments, desiring to boost their own producers, see these matters partially as a trade issue, but they also see a cultural policy issue and believe the distinctness of national cultures ought to be preserved on television, music, and film.

The same issue has come up in the General Agreement on Trade and Tariffs (GATT), which was dedicated to lower **tariffs** on trade, and its successor, the World Trade Organization (WTO). In the last round of GATT negotiations, in the early 1990s, the United States pushed hard to impose new international trade rules on audiovisual materials (television and film) that would keep countries from protecting their own national film and television industries or setting *quotas* to keep out imported films and programs. The European Union rallied around the French, who opposed such a change (existing GATT rules permitted protection and subsidy of film industries), but audiovisual materials will still be included in more liberal trade rules under the WTO. At the same time, the European Union has been opening up Europe for greater competition, trade, and non-European investment in telecommunications, since telecommunications is not seen as having the same cultural impact as film and television. International trade in computer and telecommunications products and services is also an important topic.

In the late 1990s, the WTO moved into another crucial area for new digital media: copyright and intellectual property protection. It created significantly stronger copyright protection in digital media, such as the Internet and digital recordings (CDs, CD-ROMs, digital audiotape), in 1998. A specific organization, the World Intellectual Property Organization (WIPO), was created in 1974 to safeguard copyright and related interests. It has become an increasingly central part of world trade in information, media, and cultural products, as those products assume a larger role in world trade now.

Tariffs are taxes imposed by governments on goods imported from other countries.

Media and National Development

Another main issue is whether media, information technologies, and telecommunications can be made to serve national development better. As we noted earlier, part of the fear expressed in international debates is that media are primarily serving global commercial interests, not the needs of the populations of the various countries, whether rich or poor. Many government planners and social critics feel that most people in developing nations need media that offer more than slick American entertainment and advertising.

Many governments and international organizations, such as UNESCO, have worked hard to create models using media to promote education, health, agriculture, local religious and cultural values, and so on. Some of these programs have succeeded, particularly radio programs based in rural areas (McAnany, 1980).

The International Telecommunications Union and the World Bank are encouraging national governments and foreign investors to invest more funds in the expansion of developing world telephone and telecommunications systems, such as rebuilding Afghanistan's telecommunications system. World Bank and other research shows that such investment contributes to economic growth. This issue is currently discussed primarily in terms of poor countries' access to the Internet. Debate at the 2003 World Summit on the Information Society showed countries feared falling behind in their abilities to compete in economic areas where widespread and fast Internet connection was crucial. Furthermore, these countries fear the impact on their citizens as well as their economies. Since many people in most countries do not have access to the Internet, one of the main immediate impacts is increased economic and social differences between those who can e-mail and surf the Net, and those who do not.

SUMMARY AND REVIEW

WHY DO GOVERNMENTS OWN MORE BROADCASTING THAN PRINT MEDIA IN MANY COUNTRIES?
Broadcast media always require frequency regulations or standards by governments, which leads governments to take control of radio and television as they regulate. In some poor countries, governments are the only institution with enough money to support television. Electronic media also have the potential to affect more people. Some governments see electronic media as valuable tools for either development or political control. In some of the poorest countries, governments may be among only a few bodies that have enough money to run broadcasting or telecommunications.

WHAT IS THE PURPOSE OF PUBLIC BROADCASTING?
Public broadcasting is oriented toward providing the public with education and information, balanced with entertainment. Public broadcasting corporations are usually not-for-profit companies financed by government or by license fees paid by everyone who owns a radio or television set.

WHY DID MOST COUNTRIES ONCE HAVE GOVERNMENT TELEPHONE COMPANIES?
Government-owned and -operated PTTs (post, telephone, and telegraph administrations) were the telephone companies in nearly all countries. Government monopolies were seen as capable of unifying national services, investing in expansion, and extending services to those not served.

WHY DID COUNTRIES PRIVATIZE TELEPHONE COMPANIES?
Government PTTs came to be seen as inefficient, overstaffed, and incapable of generating the necessary resources for investment. Private companies, both domestic and foreign, were seen as bringing in financial resources and as a more efficient approach to management.

WHY DO AMERICAN FILMS DOMINATE WORLD FILM MARKETS?

American films were made to appeal to a large immigrant audience through a universal and entertainment-oriented style, which made it easy for diverse international audiences to accept its films. The United States also benefited from the destruction or blockage of foreign film industries during World War I and World War II. U.S. producers developed an efficient export cartel, the Motion Picture Association of America (MPAA), which owned much of the world distribution and exhibition structure.

WHY DID AMERICAN TELEVISION ALSO DOMINATE?

U.S. television programs were produced primarily by the MPAA film studio companies, which gave them the benefit of an existing international distribution structure. American television also used many of the popular techniques and formulas of Hollywood film producers, which gave its productions much of the same universal entertainment appeal. Many other countries found that showing American television programs was cheaper than the cost of local production and provided an easy solution to filling schedules, although U.S. programs are increasingly expensive, so they are sometimes not cheaper than local productions in some countries.

WHAT IS THE IMPACT OF AMERICAN MEDIA PRODUCTS?

American television programs, films, and music are very popular, particularly among young people, but some people in other nations fear that American ideas, images, and values will replace those of their own cultures. Actual effects seem to have been less than was anticipated, because many people have increasingly begun to watch local programs and do not watch American programs as much, and they tend to interpret them in their own way.

WHY IS AMERICAN DOMINANCE IN TELEVISION SLIPPING?

As technology costs for television production decline and experience in producing shows increases, people in many countries are finding it easier to make their own shows. Furthermore, once countries develop television genres that are popular at home and in nearby cultural-linguistic markets, audiences tend to prefer the local programs, and companies now export formats to the United States, reversing the conventional flow of entertainment programs.

WHAT ARE THE MAIN CULTURAL DIFFERENCES IN TELEVISION PROGRAMS?

Soap operas, variety shows, and music and talk shows tend to be more prominent in programming abroad than in the United States. Some countries are too small to produce certain kinds of programming. Smaller countries tend to focus on these lower-cost genres.

WHY DO MORE COUNTRIES PRODUCE MUSIC THAN TELEVISION?

Recorded music is cheaper to produce than television shows. Musical preferences are often more localized to regions within countries and to subcultures defined by age, ethnicity, and religion. Thus there is demand for a large, diverse set of artists and recording companies.

WHAT ARE THE MAIN GLOBAL IMPACTS OF THE INTERNET?

Since many people in most countries do not have access to the Internet, one of the main immediate impacts is increased economic and social differences between those who can e-mail and surf the Net, and those who do not. For those with access, the Internet helps globalize economic activity, making it easier to sell things and outsource jobs across borders. It also challenged attempts at news control and censorship. It enables nontraditional groups, from EcoNet to Al Qaeda to network and coordinate across the world.

WHICH COMPANIES ARE THE MAIN GLOBAL OWNERS OF MASS MEDIA?

The main companies are Time Warner (U.S.), Disney/ABC (U.S.), Rupert Murdoch's News Corporation (Australia), Seagram-Universal (Canada), Bertelsmann (Germany), Comcast (U.S.), and General Electric/NBC (U.S.). Companies beyond traditional mass media, such as Microsoft and Telefonica (Spain), should be considered, too.

WHAT ARE THE LIMITS ON INTERNATIONAL LAW?

International law is a collection of treaties between countries, multilateral agreements or treaties among groups of countries, and rules set by international organizations. The problem is that they all rely on voluntary compliance and consensual behavior by individual governments.

WHAT ORGANIZATIONS MOST AFFECT INTERNATIONAL MEDIA?

The main international organization is the ITU (International Telecommunications Union), which has telecommunication, broadcasting, and development divisions. It allocates frequencies and satellite orbits (through the World Administrative Radio Conferences) to countries and, together with the International Standards Organization, sets international standards for telecommunications. UNESCO (United Nations Educational, Scientific, and Cultural Organization) debates the unbalanced flows of media and news between countries, and whether countries have a right to protect their cultures from outside influence. The EC (European Commission) sets standards, establishes rules about media flow, and creates regional markets. The World Trade Organization (WTO) has also become important in debates about trade in media products and information services.

WHAT IS CULTURAL IMPERIALISM?

Cultural imperialism is an unbalanced relationship in culture and media between countries. The main specific issue is unequal flows of film, news, television programs, cable channels, and music from the United States to other countries. Other aspects include the globalization of media ownership, foreign investment in national media, and the use of foreign media models. International media flows seem to become more balanced as other countries produce and export more. This tendency toward balance is more notable in music and television than in film or news.

WHAT IS THE TRADE-OFF BETWEEN NATIONAL SOVEREIGNTY AND THE FREE FLOW OF INFORMATION?

The United States promotes the free flow of information as an international extension of its national values about freedom of expression. Other countries complain that the free flow of ideas permits the United States to dominate international flows of media. These countries wish to exercise their national sovereignty. However, giving such power to government raises the prospects of censorship and control of information.

MEDIA CONNECTION

For web links, quizzes, and key term flash cards, visit the **Student Companion Website** at http://communication.wadsworth.com/straubhaar5.

 1pass™ For unlimited easy access to additional and exclusive online study, support, and research tools, log on to **1pass** at http://1pass.thomson.com using the unique access code found on your 1pass passcode card.

The **Media Now Premium Website** offers *Career Profile* videos, *Critical View* video news clips, and *Media in Motion* concept animations. You'll also find Stop & Review tutorial questions, a sample final exam, and much more.

InfoTrac College Edition is a fully searchable online database offering anytime, anywhere access to more than 20 years' worth of articles from nearly 5,000 diverse and reliable sources.

 vMentor provides live, one-on-one online tutoring to connect you to experts who will assist you in understanding the concepts covered in your course.

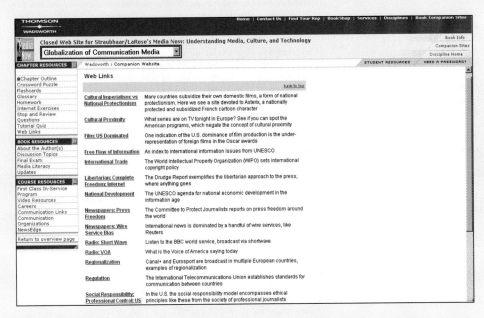

The Student Companion Website provides live, maintained and updated links for all web resources mentioned in the chapter. You'll find them under Chapter Resources.

GLOSSARY

Abuse of market power is exploitation of a dominant market position to keep potential competitors out.

Account executives are the liaisons between the agency and the client.

Accuracy is the responsibility to ensure that information content is truthful.

Acoustic is a sound that is not electronically amplified.

Advertising is communication that is paid for and is usually persuasive in nature.

Advertising managers coordinate the advertiser's efforts across all of its products.

Advertising media are the communication channels that carry messages to consumers.

The **advertising plan** is a written document outlining the objectives and strategies for a product's advertising.

Advertorial is a type of printed advertisement that blends the formatting styles of advertising and news.

Affiliate fees are monthly per-subscriber fees that cable programming services charge local cable operators for their programs.

Affiliates contract with networks to distribute their programming.

Almanacs are book length collections of useful facts, calendars and advice.

AM or amplitude modulation carries information in the height, or amplitude, of the radio wave.

Analog communication uses continuously varying signals corresponding to the light or sounds originated by the source.

Anticompetitive practices are those that unfairly use market power to damage potential competitors.

Antisocial behavior is behavior contrary to prevailing social norms.

Asynchronous media are not consumed simultaneously by all members of the audience.

Audience segment is a subgroup of consumers with specialized tastes and media habits.

Audiophiles are those who seek the highest audio reproduction quality.

Backlist books are not actively promoted but are still in print.

Barriers to entry are obstacles companies must overcome to enter a market.

B-movies are cheaply and quickly made genre films.

Blog, short for web log, is a personl home page with commentary addressed to the web audience.

Brand identification is a product's name, design, and symbols, which distinguish it from other products.

Brand loyalty is the consumer's propensity to make repeat purchases of a specific brand of product.

Brand managers are in charge of one specific product.

Broadband systems carry multiple channels of video, audio, and computer data simultaneously.

Browsers are the computer programs that display information found on the web.

The **bullet model,** or hypodermic model, posits powerful, direct effects of the mass media.

A **byte** is (usually) eight computer bits. Each byte can represent a single numerical digit or letter.

The **buying motive** explains the consumer's desire to purchase particular products.

Cable modems connect computers to cable television systems.

Cable television transmits television programs via coaxial cable or fiber.

Capture theory explains that regulators are unduly influenced by the industry they regulate.

Censorship is prohibition of certain media contents by government, religious or other societal authorities.

Chain broadcasting is synonymous with a broadcasting network.

A **channel** is an electronic or mechanical system that links the source to the receiver.

Chapbooks were cheaply made publications aimed at a broad audience.

Click through rate is the percentage of readers who click on the ad to visit the advertiser's page.

Coaxial cable is the high-capacity wire used for cable television transmission.

Common carriers provide service to all on an equal basis.

Communication is an exchange of meaning.

The **communications spectrum** includes the range of electromagnetic radiation frequencies that are used in wireless communication systems.

Community access means created by community residents without the involvement of the cable operator.

Compositing is merging several layers of images that were shot separately.

Computer-to-plate technology transfers page images composed inside a computer directly to printing plates.

Concentration of ownership occurs when media are owned by a small number of individuals, government agencies, or corporations.

Concentration of power by integration of many aspects of media into one company creates concerns about political control and loss of diversity.

Confidentiality protects the identity of news sources.

Conglomerates are made up of diverse parts from across several media industries.

Content analysis is a quantitative description of the content of the media.

Controlling the Assault of Non-Solicited Pornography and Marketing Act of 2003 restricts Internet spam, especially deceptive spam.

Convergence is the integration of mass media, computers, and telecommunications.

Cookies are small files that websites leave on their visitors' computers.

Copy testing evaluates the effectiveness of advertisements.

A **copyright** is a legal privilege to use, sell, or license creative works and to control intellectual property.

Corantos were irregular newssheets that appeared around 1600.

Correlated means that there is a statistical measure of association between two variables.

Cost per thousand is how much a commercial costs in relation to the number of viewers that see it, in thousands.

Cover are artists' performances of others songs.

Critical studies examine the overall impact of media.

Cross-ownership is ownership of different kinds of media.

Cultivation theory argues that mass media exposure cultivates a view of the world that is consistent with mediated "reality."

Cultural imperialism occurs when some countries dominate others through the media.

Cultural proximity is the preference of auciences for media in their own language and culture.

Cultural studies explains interrelationships among audiences, media, and culture.

Data mining is the compiling of personal, pertinent, actionable information about purchasing habits of an organization's customers.

Database marketing is used when advertisers store information about consumers so that they can personalize messages.

Deceptive advertising makes misleading or untruthful claims.

Demographic segmentation is based on social or personal characteristics, such as age, sex, education, or income.

Dependent variables are the consequences, or effects, of media exposure.

Deregulated removes restrictions on the nature and scope of activities that companies engage in and the prices they charge.

Desktop publishing is editing, laying out, and inserting photos on a desktop computer.

Diffusion is the spread of innovations.

Digital audio broadcasting (DAB) is the transmission of radio signals in digital format.

Digital compression reduces the number of computer bits.

The **digital divide** is the gap in Internet usage between rich and poor, anglos and minorities.

Digital means computer-readable formatted in 1's and 0's.

Digital subscriber line (DSL) is a high-speed digital phone service that can transmit audio, video, and computer data over conventional phone lines.

Digital television is television that is transmitted in a digital format.

Digital video is recorded, edited and often transmitted in digital form as used by computers.

Dime novels were inexpensive paperback novels of the nineteenth century.

Direct broadcast satellites (DBS) transmit television signals from satellites to compact home receivers.

Direct marketing is a form of advertising that requests an immediate consumer response.

Direct satellite broadcasting is a television or radio satellite service that is marketed directly to home receivers.

A **Disc jockey** (DJ) is a radio station announcer who plays records and often emphasizes delivery and personality.

Distant signals are cable channels imported from major television markets.

Diurnos were seventeenth century ancestors of the daily newspapers.

Diversity of content implies a variety of ideas in media.

Diversity of ownership implies that media owners are a diverse ethnicity and gender.

A **duopoly** exists when two companies dominate.

E-commerce (electronic commerce) completes on-line purchases and financial transactions on the web.

Economics studies the forces that allocate resources to satisfy competing needs.

Economies of scale are when unit costs go down as production quantities increase.

Electromagnetic recording is a method of storing information as magnetized area on a tape or disk.

Electronic marketing theory explains that people use e-commerce to minimize their search and transaction costs.

Encryption means writing a message in a secret code.

In the **era of creativity** advertisers emphasized entertainment as well as information.

Encrypting is translating a message into a secret code.

Ethics are moral rules of conduct that guide one's actions.

Ethnography is a naturalistic research method in which the observer obtains detailed information from personal observation or interviews over extended periods of time.

Experimental research studies the effects of media in carefully controlled situations that manipulate media exposure and content.

Fair Credit Reporting Act (FCRA) 2002 insures accuracy of credit reports and permits evaluating accuracy.

Fair use permits users limited copying of copyrighted works for academic, artistic, or personal use.

Fairness is the responsibility to present all sides of a story equally.

Feature films are longer story films, usually over 1½ hours.

The **Federal Communications Commission (FCC)** regulates communication in the United States.

Fiber optic systems use light instead of electricity to communicate.

Film noir were "dark" moody America films of the 1940s often focused on detectives or similar themes.

Filtering software automatically blocks access to websites containing offensive material.

Fin-Syn or Financial Interest in Syndication rules kept TV networks from producing or owning entertainment programming.

The **First Amendment** to the U.S. Constitution guarantees freedom of speech and of the press.

First-run distribution for films is to movie theaters.

FM or frequency modulation carries information in variations in the frequency of the radio wave.

Format for radio groups.

Format clock is an hourly radio programming schedule.

45's are smaller, one song records that turn at 45 revolutions per second.

Free flow of information occurs when information flows as freely as possible between countries.

Freedom of speech is the idea that speech and media content should be free from government restriction.

Free press is the extension of freedom of speech to media.

Frequency is the number of cycles that radio waves complete in a second.

A **front group** works on behalf of another organization whose direct involvement might be controversial.

Front projection lets actors be photographed in front of an image so that they appear part of it.

Full-service agencies offer research, strategy development, and media placement.

Functionalism examines the social functions media fulfill.

Gatekeepers decide what will appear in the media.

Gatekeeping is deciding what will appear in the media.

Generalizability is the degree to which research procedures and samples may be generalized to the real world.

Genres are types or formats of media content.

Geosynchronous satellites are satellites whose rotation matches that of the earth so they stay in a fixed position relative to the earth's surface.

Globalization is reducing differences existing between nations in time, space, and culture.

Glocal is combining global ideas or forces with local ones.

Gross is the total box office revenue before expenses are deducted.

Group owners own a number of broadcast stations.

Headends are where signals are fed into the local cable network.

Hegemony is an underlying consensus of ideology that serves the dominant groups in society.

Hertz (Hz) is a measure of the frequency of a radio wave in cycles per second.

High-definition television (HDTV) is digital television that provides a wider and clearer picture.

High fidelity is accurate reproduction of natural sound.

Horizontal integration is concentrating ownership by acquiring companies that are all in the same business.

Hypertext markup language (HTML) is used to format pages on the web.

Hypertext transfer protocol (http) is the Internet protocol used to transfer files over the web.

Indecency refers to sexual or excretory acts.

Indecent speech is graphic language that pertains to sexual or excretory functions.

Independent film is made by a wide variety of people but outside the complete control of the major studios.

Independent variables are the causes of media effects.

Information campaigns use the techniques of advertising in an attempt to convince people to adopt prosocial behaviors.

The **information sector** of the economy includes broadcasting, publishing, telecommunications, Internet, and computer software industries.

In an **information society,** the exchange of information is the predominant economic activity.

Infomercials are ads that appear before the ISP connects to the Internet.

The **infrastructure** is the underlying physical structure of communication networks.

Integrated marketing communications (IMC) assures that the use of all commercial media and messages is clear, consistent, and achieves impact.

Intellectual property is a creative work.

Interactive communication uses feedback to modify a message as it is presented.

Interactive TV combines conventional television programming with Internet content.

International law includes treaties between countries, multi-country agreements, and rules established by international organizations.

Internet 2 is a new, faster version of the internet.

Internet service providers (ISPs) are the companies that provide connections to the Internet.

Joint operation agreements allow competing newspapers to share resources while maintaining editorial independence.

Junket is an expense-paid trip intended to influence media coverage.

The **law of supply and demand** describes the relationship among the supply of products, prices, and consumer demand.

Laws are binding rules passed by legislatures, enforced by the executive power, and applied or adjudicated by courts.

Libel is a harmful and untruthful criticism that damages someone.

Licenses grant legal permission to operate a transmitter.

Limited effects holds that the effects of the mass media on individuals are slight.

Literacy is the ability to read and understand a variety of information.

Local area networks (LANs) link computers within a department, building, or campus.

Local market monopoly is dominating at one or more local markets by a firm.

Local origination means created within the community by the cable operator.

Localism is the granting of broadcast licenses to local owners to manage local content.

Localized media productions are those adapted to local tastes and interests.

Lower-power stations have more limited transmission power and cover smaller areas than regular FM stations.

Major film studios like Fox or Disney integrate all aspects of production and distribution.

Marginal costs are the incremental costs of each additional copy.

Marketing managers are in charge of a family of products for an advertiser.

Marketplace of ideas is the concept that the best ideas will win out in competition.

Mass communication is one-to-many, with limited audience feedback.

Mass media is one-to-many communication delivered through an electronic or mechanical channel.

Mattes are background paintings or photographs that are combined with performers in the foreground.

Media departments negotiate on behalf of the advertiser to buy space from media companies.

Media effects are changes in knowledge, attitudes, or behaviors resulting from media exposure.

Media literacy means learning to think critically about the role of media in society.

Media relations focus on establishing and maintaining good relations with the media.

Mediated is communication transmitted through an electronic or mechanical channel.

Microwave transmits information between relay towers on beams of high-frequency radio waves.

Miscellanies were magazines with a wide variety of contents.

Modems convert digital data to analog signals.

Monopoly exists when one company dominates a market.

Motion Picture Code of 1930 (Hayes code) was self-regulation of sex on screen by the motion picture industry.

Motivational research examines why people purchase or do things.

MP3 is a sound digitization and compression standard, short for MPEG-2 Layer 3.

MPAA (Motion Picture Association of America) is a trade organization that represents the major film studios.

MPAA ratings is a movie rating system instituted in 1968.

Muckraking is journalism that "rakes up the muck" of corruption and scandal.

Multilateral trade negotiations take place among a number of countries at the same time.

Multimedia systems integrate text, audio, and video.

Multiple system operators (MSOs) are cable companies that operate systems in two or more communities.

The **multistep flow** model assumes that media effects are indirect and are mediated by opinion leaders.

Must carry is the policy that requires cable companies to carry local broadcast signals.

Narrowcasting targets media to specific segments of the audience.

National sovereignty is the policy of keeping domestic forces in control of a nation's economy, politics, and culture.

A **natural monopoly** occurs when competition is not feasible.

New journalism was the investigative reporting of the nineteenth century.

Newsmagazine a weekly magazine focused on news and analysis.

A **news release** summarizes news and information in a form and style that is preferred by the media.

Nickelodeon is a phonograph or player piano operated by inserting a coin, originally a nickel.

Nonlinear editing uses digital equipment to rearrange scenes to make the master copy.

Novels are extended fictional works usually of book length.

Obscene speech depicts sexual conduct in a way that appeals to sexual interests in a manner that is "patently offensive" to community standards, and lacks serious artistic, political, or scientific value.

Obscenity refers to material where the dominant theme taken as a whole appeals to prurient, or sexually arousing interest.

Offshoring is the export of jobs to other countries.

Oligopoly is when a few firms dominate.

Overhead is the institutional cost of running a film company.

Owned-and-Operated Stations (O&O's) are stations owned and operated by networks.

Packet network, Packet switching breaks up digital information into individually addressed chunks, or packets.

Patents give an inventor the exclusive right to an invention.

Pay TV charges cable customers an extra monthly fee to receive a specific channel.

Payola occurs when record companies give bribes to DJs to get their records played.

Pay-per-view charges viewers for each showing of a program.

Penny Press were daily newspapers that sold for one cent.

Permission marketing is when the consumer authorizes and welcomes contact from advertisers on the Internet.

Persuasion is the use of convincing arguments to change people's beliefs, attitudes, or behaviors.

Pitch letters are designed to interest editors and reporters in covering a topic from a given perspective or "angle."

Plagiarism is using the ideas of another without citation..

Playlists are the songs picked for air play.

Plugola is when companies give products or gifts to get a product promoted within a broadcast.

Policy is a public framework for how to structure and regulate media so they contribute to the public good.

Political economy analyzes patterns of class domination.

Popular culture includes art and entertainment that is widely shared by a population.

Postproduction includes editing, sound effects, and visual effects that are added after shooting the original footage.

Press kit is a collection of promotional materials.

Priming theory states that media images stimulate related thoughts in the minds of audience members.

Print on demand technology prints books only when they are ordered by customers.

Privacy is the right to be protected from unwanted intrusions or disclosure.

Privatizing government assets refers to selling them to private owners.

Probable cause is a judge's decision that provisional evidence of criminal violation or national security danger justifies a wiretap.

Product placement is when companies give products or simply pay a fee to get a product promoted within a film.

Profits are what is left after operating costs, taxes, and paybacks to investors.

Propaganda is the intentional influence of attitudes and opinions.

Prosocial behaviors are those that a society values and encourages.

Protocols are rules for data communication.

Public broadcasters aim to serve public interests with information, culture, and news.

Public opinion is the aggregate view of the general population.

Public relations are organized activities intended to favorably influence the public.

Public service or public utilities commissions regulate telecommunications at the state level.

Public utilities are regulated monopolies.

Radio Act of 1912 first licensed radio transmitters.

Radio Act of 1927 created a Federal Radio Commission.

Radio waves are composed of electromagnetic energy and rise and fall in regular cycles.

Ragtime is an early form of jazz.

Ratings measure the proportion of television households that watch a specific show.

Rear projection effects have images projected behind performers who are in the foreground.

Regional Bell operating companies (RBOCs) are the local telephone operating companies of which AT&T divested itself in 1984.

Relationship marketing is when consumers develop a strong preference for brand through one-to-one communication.

Reliability is the extent to which a result is stable and consistent.

Remote sensing is satellite observation of objects, vegetation, and weather patterns.

Research organizations compile statistics about consumers and their media habits and evaluate advertising messages.

Restraints of trade limit competition.

A **royalty fee** is a payment for use of a creative work.

Satellite systems send information back and forth to relays in orbit around the earth.

Sales promotion are specific features like coupons to directly spur sales.

A **satellite footprint** is the surface area covered by the satellite's signal.

Scanning means making TV pictures out of a series of separate picture lines.

The **scarcity argument** maintains that regulation is necessary to allocate limited frequencies.

Scoop is an exclusive story published ahead of the competition.

Seditious speech undermines the government.

Segmentation occurs when media focus on more specific target audiences.

Self-regulation refers to industry codes and practices for oversight of its own performance.

Semiotic analysis describes how meaning is generated through the "signs" used in media "texts."

78 rpm records are records that turn at 78 revolutions per minute.

The **Sherman Antitrust Act** (1890) prohibits monopolies and the restraint of free trade.

Shortwave radio broadcasts carry across oceans by bouncing off the earth's atmosphere.

Social learning theory explains media effects in terms of imitating behavior seen in the media.

The **social responsibility model** calls on journalists to monitor the ethics of their own writing.

Source attribution means citing sources to reflect their credibility without revealing their identity.

The **Source-Message-Channel-Receiver (SMCR)** model of mass communication describes the exchange of information as the message passes from the source to the channel to the receiver, with feedback to the source.

Spamming is unsolicited commercial e-mailing.

Standards are agreements about technical characteristics of communication systems.

The **star system** was the film studios' use of stars' popularity to promote their movies.

Stereotyping is the making of generalizations about groups of people on the basis of limited information.

Stereo is splitting recorded sound into two separate channels.

Stop-action animation is made by slightly moving clay or other figures for each frame to gradually create an image of motion.

The **studio system** in Hollywood put all aspects of a film into one production and distribution company.

Subscription libraries lent books to the public for a fee.

A **superstation** is a distant signal that is distributed nationally via satellite.

Survey studies make generalizations about a population of people by addressing questions to a sample of that population.

Syndication is rental or licensing of media products.

Tabloids are sensationist, feature bold headlines and shocking photos, and focus on divorce, murder, and crime.

Talkies are motion pictures with synchronized sound for dialogue.

Tariffs are taxes imposed by governments on goods imported from other countries.

TCP/IP (transmission control protocol/Internetworking protocol) is the basic protocol used by the Internet.

Technological determinism explains that the media cause changes in society and culture.

1996 Telecommunications Act is federal legislation that deregulated the communications media.

Television receive-only (TVRO) was a backyard satellite system that let individual homes receive the same channels intended for cable systems.

Theatrical films are those released for distribution in movie theaters.

Theories are general principles that explain and predict behavior.

33⅓ long playing (LP) albums contain up to 70 minutes of music, and turns at 33⅓ revolutions per minute.

Top 40 is a radio format that replays the top 40 songs heavily.

Transborder data flow is the communication of data across political borders.

UHF stands for Ultra High Frequency, channels 14 to 69.

Underwriting is corporate financial support of public television programs in return for a mention of the donor on the air.

Uniform resource locators (URLs) are the addresses of web pages.

Universal service is the principle that everyone should have access to infrastructure networks.

Uses and gratifications explains media selections in terms of the needs they satisfy.

Vacuum tubes amplify and modulate signals by controlling the flow of electrical charges inside a glass tube.

Validity is the degree to which we are actually measuring what we intend to measure.

The **V-chip** is a computer chip that automatically filters out objectionable TV programs.

Vertical integration: 1. When companies with the same owner handle different aspects of a business, such as film production and distribution. 2. Concentrating ownership by acquiring companies that are in related businesses.

VHF is the Very High Frequency television band, channels 2 to 13.

Victrola was the trade name for an early phonograph.

Videotex is the delivery of textual information to consumers over telephone networks.

Viral marketing is from specific people spreading ideas about products in chat rooms or similar fora.

Virtual reality gives users the sense that they are "inside" a computer-generated reality.

webcast is a real-time event broadcast over the Internet.

Wide area networks (WANs) connect computers that are many miles apart.

Windows are times in the sequence for releasing films to different outlets. Films are now released in a series of "windows" to a variety of media.

Wire services supply news to multiple publications; they were named originally for their use of telegraph wires.

Yellow journalism was the sensationalistic reporting of the nineteenth century.

REFERENCES

AAUW Educational Foundation (2000). *Tech-savvy: Educating girls in the new computer age.* Washington, DC.

Abramson, A. (1987). *The History of Television, 1880 to 1941.* Jefferson, NC: McFarland.

Adbusters (1999). Buy nothing day. Available online: http://www.adbusters.org/uncommercials/bnd/index.html

Adorno, T., & Horkheimer, M. (1972). The culture industry: Enlightenment as mass deception. In *The dialectics of enlightenment.* New York: Herder and Herder.

Ahlbom, A., & Feychting, M. (2001, April 14). Current thinking about risks from currents. *The Lancet,* 357(9263), 1143–1144.

ALA (1998). Statement of the American Library Association to the Senate Commerce, Science and Transportation Committee on indecency on the Internet for the Hearing Record. Washington, DC: American Library Association. Available online: http://www.ala.org/washoff/mccain.html

Allen, M., D'Alessio, D., & Brezgel, K. (1995). A meta-analysis summarizing the effects of pornography. Aggression after exposure. *Human Communication Research,* 22(2), 258–283.

Allen, M., D'Allessio, D., & Emmers-Sommer, T. (1999). Reaction of criminal sexual offenders to pornography: A meta-analytic summary. In Roloff, M. E. (ed). *Communication Yearbook 22.* Thousand Oaks, CA: Sage: 139–170.

Allen, R. (1992). *Channels of discourse, reassembled.* Chapel Hill, NC: University of North Carolina Press.

Alsop, R., (ed.) (1997). *The Wall Street Journal almanac, 1998.* New York: Ballantine Books.

Altheide, D. (1974). *Creating reality.* Beverly Hills, CA: Sage.

Altschull, H. (1995). *Agents of power,* 2nd ed. New York: Longman.

American Film Institute, http://www.afi.org

Anderson, B. (1983). *Imagined communities: Reflections on the origin and spread of nationalism.* London: Verso.

Anderson, C., & Bushman, B. (2001). Effects of violent video games on aggressive behavior, aggressive cognition, aggressive affect, physiological arousal, and prosocial behavior: A meta-analytic review of the scientific literature. *Psychological Science,* 12(5), 353–359.

Anderson, J., & Meyer, T. (1988). *Mediated communication.* Newbury Park, CA: Sage.

Ang, I. (1985). *Watching Dallas.* New York: Methuen.

Aoyama, Y., & Castells, M. (2002). An empirical assessment of the informational society: Employment and occupational structures of G-7 countries, 1920–2000. *International Labour Review,* 141(1/2), 123–160.

AP (Associated Press). (1998). China maintains tight control of Internet. November 15.

Applegate, E. (1993). The development of advertising, 1700–1900. In Sloan, W., Stovall, J., & Startt, J. (eds.), *The media in America,* 2nd ed. Scottsdale, AZ: Publishing Horizons.

Arfin, F. (1994). *Financial public relations.* Philadelphia: Trans-Atlantic.

Aronowitz, S., & DiFazio, W. (1994). *The jobless future: Sci-tech and the dogma of work.* Minneapolis: University of Minnesota Press.

Arquilla, J., & Ronfeldt, D. (1993). Cyberwar is coming! *Comparative Strategy,* 12(2), 141–165.

Association of American Publishers (2004). Available at: http://www.publishers.org/ http://www.publishers.org/industry/index.cfm

Atkin, C. (1985). *The effects of mass media: Readings in mass communication and society.* East Lansing: Department of Communication, Michigan State University.

Attewell, P. (1994). Information technology and the productivity paradox. In Harris, D. (ed.)., *Organizational linkages: Understanding the productivity paradox.* Washington, DC: National Academy Press.

Attorney General of the United States. (1986). *Final report of the Attorney General's Commission on Pornography.* Washington, DC: U.S. Government Printing Office.

Aufderheide, P. (1999). *Communications Policy and the Public Interest: The Telecommunications Act of 1996.* New York: Guilford Press.

Auletta, K. (1991). *Three blind mice: How the TV networks lost their way.* New York: Random House.

———. (1997, Nov. 17). Demolition man. *New Yorker,* 17(35), 40–45.

Baar, A. (2004, July 26). Indiana Governor's race offers a touch of reality TV. *AD Week,* 14.

Bacard, A. (1995). *The computer privacy handbook.* Berkeley, CA: Peachpit Press.

Bagdikian, B. (2000). *The media monopoly,* 4th ed. Boston: Beacon Press.

Baldwin, T., & McVoy, D. (1983). *Cable communications.* Englewood Cliffs, NJ: Prentice-Hall.

Baldwin, T., McVoy, D., & Steinfield, C. (1996). *Convergence: Integrating media, information & communication.* Thousand Oaks, CA: Sage.

Bandura, A. (1965). Influence of models' reinforcement contingencies on the acquisition of imitative responses. *Journal of Personality and Social Psychology,* 1, 589–595.

———. (1983). Psychological mechanisms of aggression. In Geen, R., & Connerstien, E. (eds), *Aggression: Theoretical and empirical reviews.* New York: Academic Press.

———. (1986). *Social foundations of thought and action.* Englewood Cliffs, NJ: Prentice-Hall.

Bank, D. (1997, September 11). Changing picture: The advent of digital broadcasting makes the convergence of television and PCs a real possibility. *Wall Street Journal,* R15.

———. (1997, September 15). Microsoft's webTV unit to introduce process that uses web to enhance TV. *Wall Street Journal,* Ae.

Bannon, L. (1998, March 19). Turning points: Great moments in technology and film. *Wall Street Journal,* R4–6.

Barak, A., & Fisher, W. (1997). Effects of interactive computer erotica on men's attitudes and behavior toward women: An experimental study. *Computers in Human Behavior,* 13(3), 353–369.

Bar-on, M., Broughton, D., Buttross, S., Corrigan, S., et al. (2001). Media violence. *Pediatrics,* 108(5), 1222–1226.

Barner, M. R. (1999). Sex-role stereotyping in FCC-mandated children's educational television. *Journal of Broadcasting & Electronic Media,* 43: 551–564.

Barnouw, E. (1966). *A history of broadcasting in the United States.* New York: Oxford University Press.

———. (1990). *Tube of plenty: The evolution of American television,* 2nd rev. ed. New York: Oxford University Press.

Baudrillard, J. (1983). *Simulations.* New York: Semiotext.

Bauserman, R. (1996). Sexual aggression and pornography: A review of correlational research. *Basic and Applied Social Psychology,* 18(4), 405–427.

———. (1998). Egalitarian, sexist and aggressive sexual materials: Attitude effects and viewer responses. *Journal of Sex Research* 35(3): 244–253.

Beatty, S. (1998, August 20). Companies push for much bigger, more-complicated online ads. *Wall Street Journal,* B10.

Bell, D. (1973). *The coming of post-industrial society.* New York: Basic Books.

Bell, G., & Gray, N. (1997). The revolution yet to happen. In Denning, P., & Metcalfe, R. *Beyond calculation: The next fifty years of computing.* New York: Springer-Verlag.

Bellis, M. (2002). Walkie talkies: Al Gross. Available online: http://web.mit.edu/invent/iow/gross.html

Belz, C. (1972). *The story of rock.* New York: Harper & Row.

Benjamin, W. *Illuminations.* Edited and intro by Hannah Avendy. New York: Shochen Books, 1966.

Bensley, L., & van Eenwyk, J. (2001). Video games and real-life aggression: Review of the literature. *Journal of Adolescent Health,* 29, 244–257.

Benson, K., & Whitaker, J. (1990). *Television and audio handbook.* New York: McGraw-Hill.

Benton Foundation (1996). Public Interest advocates, universal service, and the Telecommunications Act of 1996. Available online: http://www.benton.org /Library/ Advocates /advocates.html

Berger, A. (1992a). *Media analysis techniques.* Newbury Park, CA: Sage.

———. (1992b). *Popular culture genres.* Newbury Park, CA: Sage.

Berkowitz, L. (1984). Some effects of thought on anti- and pro-social influences of media effects. *Psychological Bulletin,* 95, 410–427.

Bernays, E. (1961). *Crystallizing public opinion.* Norman: University of Oklahoma Press.

Bernstein, C., & Woodward, B. (1974). *All the president's men.* New York: Simon & Schuster.

Bertrand, K. (1998, March/April). An unqualified success: Inside & out. *Integrated Marketing & Promotion,* 22–27.

Beuf, A. (1974). Doctor, lawyer, household drudge. *Journal of Communication,* 24(2), 142–145.

Biagi, S. (1998). *Media impact.* Belmont, CA: Wadsworth.

Bikson, T., & Panis, C. (1997). Computers and connectivity: Current trends. In Kiesler, S. (ed.) *Culture of the Internet.* Mahwah, NJ: Lawrence Erlbaum.

Biocca, F. (1997). The cyborg's dilemma: Progressive embodiment in virtual environments. *Journal of Computer-Mediated Communication,* 3(2). Available at: http://www.ascusc.org/jcmc/vol3/issue2 /biocca2.html

Biocca, F., Lauria, R., & McCarthy, M. (1996). Virtual reality. In Grant, A. (ed.), *Communication technology update,* 5th ed. Boston: Focal Press, 176–195.

Bittner, J. (1982). *Broadcast law and regulation.* Englewood Cliffs, NJ: Prentice-Hall.

Black, J., Steele, B., & Barney, R. (1998). *Doing ethics in journalism.* Greencastle, IN: Society for Professional Journalists.

Blanchard, M. (1977). The Hutchins Commission, the press and the responsibility concept. *Journalism monographs; no. 49.* Minneapolis: Association for Education in Journalism.

———. (1993). Freedom of the press. In Sloan, W., Stovall, J., & Startt, J. (eds.), *The media in America.* Scottsdale, AZ: Publishing Horizons.

Blanton, J. (1996, March 26). A novel medium: Hypertext fiction. *Wall Street Journal,* RIO.

Bleifuss, J. (1994, March 20). New angles from the spin doctors. *New York Times,* F13.

BLS, Bureau of Labor Statistics (1999). Employed persons by detailed occupation, sex, race, and Hispanic origin. Available at: ftp://ftp.bls.gov/pub/special.requests/lf/aaat11.txt

———. (2003). Tomorrow's jobs. Available online: http://www.bls.gov/oco/oco2003.htm

Borgida, E., Sullivan, J., Oxendine, A., Jackson, M., et al. (2002). Civic culture meets the digital divide: The role of community electronic networks. *The Journal of Social Issues,* 58(10), 125–141.

Bowman, H., & Christofferson, M. (eds.). (1992). *Relaunching videotext.* Boston, MA: Kluwer Academic Publishers.

Bourdieu, P. (1984). *Distinction: A social critique of the judgement of taste.* Cambridge, MA: Harvard University Press.

———. (1998). *On television.* New York: New Press.

Bourgault, L. (1994). *Mass media in sub-Saharan Africa.* Bloomington, IN: Indiana University Press.

Bowen, B. (1999). Four puzzles in adult literacy: Reflections on the National Adult Literacy Survey. *Journal of Adolescent & Adult Literacy* 42(4), 314–324.

Boyd, D. (1999). *Broadcasting in the Arab world: A survey of the electronic media in the Middle East,* 3rd ed. Ames, Iowa: Iowa State University Press.

Boyd, D., Straubhaar, J., & Lent. J. (1989). *The videocassette recorder in the third world.* New York: Longman.

Braestrup, P. (1977). *Big story: How the American press and television reported and interpreted the crisis of Tet 1968 in Vietnam and Washington.* Boulder, CO: Westview Press.

Braudel, F. (1994). *A history of civilizations.* New York: Penguin.

Braunstein, Y. (2000). The FCC's financial qualification requirements: Economic evaluation of a barrier to entry for minority broadcasters. *Federal Communications Law Journal,* 53(1), 69–90.

Braverman, A. (1996, December 3). The roadmaps of the Internet. *CS First Boston Industry Report.*

Braverman, H. (1974). *Labor and monopoly capitalism.* New York: Monthly Review Press.

Brenner, V. (1997). Psychology of computer use. XLVII. Parameters of Internet use, abuse and addiction: The first 90 days of the Internet usage survey. *Psychological Reports,* 80, 879–882.

Briere, D. (1993). Communications services: An overview. In *Managing voice networks.* Delran, NJ: McGraw-Hill Information Services.

Briggs, R., & Hollis, N. (1997). Advertising on the web: Is there response before click-through? *Journal of Advertising Research,* 37(2), 33–45.

Brinkley, J. (1997, July 21). Companies' quest: Lend them your ears. *New York Times,* Cg.

Britt, S., Adams, S., & Miller, A. (1972). How many advertising exposures per day? *Journal of Advertising Research,* 12, 3–9.

Brockway, A., Chadwick, T., & Hall, D. (1997). Persistence of vision: Moving images through the ages. Available at: http://www.iup.edu/~gcfg/vision/frames.html

Brody, G. (1990). Effects of television viewing on family interactions: An observational study. *Family Relations,* 29, 216–220.

Bromberg, H., Campana, M. Deisman, W., Lee, R., McLeod, R., Pardoe, T., & Tyrell, M. (1996). Contradictions in cyberspace: Collective response. In Shields, R. (ed.), *Cultures of the Internet.* Thousand Oaks, CA: Sage.

Brooks, J. (1976). *Telephone: The first hundred years.* New York: Harper & Row.

Broom, G., & Dozier, D. (1991). *Using research: Methodological foundations.* New York: Dryden Press.

———. (1989). *Using research in public relations: Applications to program management.* Englewood Cliffs, NJ: Prentice-Hall.

Brosnon, J. (1974). *Movie magic.* Scranton, PA: The Haddon Craftnien.

Brunsdon, C. (2000). *The feminist, the housewife, and the soap opera.* Oxford University Press.

Brynjolfsson, E., & Hitt, L. (1996). Paradox lost? Firm-level evidence on the returns to information systems spending. *Management Science,* 42(4), 541–558.

Bucy, E. P., & D'Angelo, P. (1999). The crisis of political communication: Normative critiques of news and democratic processes. In Roloff, M. E. (ed.), *Communication Yearbook 22.* Thousand Oaks, CA: Sage: 301–340.

Buijzen, M., & Valkenburg, P. (2000). The impact of television advertising on children's Christmas wishes. *Journal of Broadcasting & Electronic Media,* 44(3), 456–470.

Bulkeley, W. (1997, November 11). Hard lessons. *Wall Street Journal,* R1.

Burnett, J., & Moriarty, S. (1998). *Marketing communications: An integrated approach.* Upper Saddle River, NJ: Prentice-Hall.

Bushman, B., & Stack, A. (1996). Forbidden fruit versus tainted fruit: Effects of warning labels on attraction to television violence. *Journal of Experimental Psychology—Applied,* 2(3), 207–226.

Cable Television Advertising Bureau (1997). 1997 Cable TV facts. Available at: http://www.mabinternational.com /infofact.htm

———. (1998). 1997 cable TV facts on access CAB. Available at: http://www.cabletvadbureau.com/infofact.html

CableLabs (1997). Available at: http//www.cablelabs.org

Cairncross, F. (1997). *The death of distance: How the communcations revolution will change our lives.* Cambridge, MA: Harvard Business School Press.

Calica, B., & Newson, G. (1996, January 2). When did you get multimedia? *NewMedia,* 48–52.

Campbell, J., & Carlson, M. (2002). Panopticon.com: Online surveillance and the commodification of privacy. *Journal of Broadcasting & Electronic Media,* 46(4), 586–606.

Canclini, N. Garcia. (1995). *Hybrid cultures: strategies for entering and leaving modernity.* Minneapolis: University of Minnesota Press.

Carey, James W. *Communication as culture: essays on media and society:* Boston: Unwin Hyman, 1989.

Carey, J. (1972). Politics of the Electronic Revolution or 1989 Commas Culture? Urbana, IL: University of Illinois.

Carlebach, M. (1997). *American photojournalism comes of age.* Washington, D.C.: Smithsonian Institution Press.

Carter, T. (1991). Paper and block printing—From China to Europe. In Crowley, D., & Heyer, P. (eds.), *Communication in history.* New York: Longman.

Carvajal, D. (1996, April 28). Do it-yourselfers carve out a piece of the publishing pie. *New York Times,* Al.

———. (1998, March 9). There's room for every book in a virtual bookstore. *New York Times,* Cybertimes edition.

Cassell, J., & Jenkins, H. (1998). From Barbie to Mortal Kombat: Gender and computer games. Cambridge, MA: MIT Press.

Cauley, L. (1996, September 16). In the loop. *Wall Street Journal,* R21.

Cavazos, E. (1994). *Cyberspace and the law: Your rights and duties in the on-line world.* Cambridge, MA: MIT Press.

Caywood, C. (ed.) (1997). *The handbook of strategic public relations and integrated communications.* New York: McGraw-Hill.

Center, A. (1983). The truth is in the consequence. Address to the Arthur W. Page Society, April 15, University of Texas at Austin.

Center, A., & Jackson, P. (1995). *Public relations practices: Managerial case studies and problems.* Upper Saddle River, NJ: Prentice-Hall.

Centerwall, B. (1989). Exposure to television as a cause of violence. In Comstock, G. (ed.), *Public communication and behavior.* Orlando, FL: Academic Press.

CERN (1998). Available at: http://www.cn.cern.ch/pdp/ns/ben/TCPHIST.html

Chapman, S. (1998, September 3). Don't unleash the cyber-censors on libraries. *Chicago Tribune Internet Edition.* Available at: http://chicagotribune.com

Chartrand, S. (1998, October 19). Congress extends protection for Goofy and Gershwin. *New York Times,* Cybertimes edition.

Children Now. (2002). Fall colors 2001–2002. Prime time diversity report. Retrieved from the web, June 1, 2002: http://www.childrennow.org/media/fc2002/fc-2002-report.pdf

Chlapowski, F. (1991). The constitutional protection of informational privacy. *Boston University Law Review,* 71, 133.

Chomsky, N., & Herman, E. (1988). *Manufacturing consent: The political economy of the mass media.* New York: Pantheon Books.

Christians, C., Rotzoll, K., & Fackler, M. (1991). *Media ethics: Cases and moral reasoning,* 3rd ed. New York: Longman.

Ciotta, R. (1998). Baby you should drive this car. In Wickham, K. (ed.), *OnLine Journalism.* Boulder, CO: Coursewise Publishing.

Clark, C. (1972). Race, identification and television violence. In Comstock, G., Rubenstein, E., & Murray, J. (eds.), *Television and social behavior,* vol. 5. Washington, DC: U.S. Government Printing Office.

Clausing, J. (1998, April 9). In rejecting dismissal of filtering case, judge sets high standard for libraries. *New York Times,* Cybertimes edition.

———. (1998, September 24). Senate panel debates children's online privacy. *New York Times,* Cybertimes edition.

Cleaver, H. (1995). The Zapatistas & the electronic fabric of struggle, November 1995. Available at: http://www.eco.utexas.edu/faculty/Cleaver/ zaps.html

Cohill, A., & Kavanaugh, K. (1997). *Community networks: Lessons from Blacksburg, Virginia.* Boston: Artech House.

Cole, B. (1991). *After the breakup.* New York: Columbia University Press.

Cole, J. (1997, March 18). New satellite era looms just over the horizon. *Wall Street Journal,* B1.

Colista, C., & Leshner, G. (1998). Traveling music: Following the path of music through the global market. *Critical Studies in Mass Communication,* (15), 181–194.

Columbia Journalism Review, *State of the Media* (2004). Available at: http://www.stateofthenewsmedia.org/narrative_newspapers_ownership.asp?cat=5 & mdia=2[BL78].

Compaigne, B. (1982). *Who owns the media? Concentration of ownership in the mass communication industry.* New York: Crown.

Confessore, N. (1999). The virtual university. *The New Republic;* Washington; Oct. 4, 221(14), 26–28.

Cook, T., Appleton, H., Conner, R., Shaffer, A., Tamkin, G., & weber, S. (1975). *Sesame Street revisited: A case study in evaluation research.* New York: Russell Sage Foundation.

Cringely, R. (1998). Nerds 2.0.1. Retrieved from the web, September 17, 2002: http://www.pbs.org/opb/nerds2.0.1/

Cuneo, A., & Petrecca, L. (1998, March 30). The best agencies. *Advertising Age,* S1–11.

Curran, James. The New Revisionism in Mass Communication Research: A Reappraisal. *European Journal of Communication* (5) 2–3: 135–164.

Cutlip, S. (1995). *Public relations history: From the seventeenth to the twentieth century.* Hillsdale, NJ: Erlbaum.

———. (1994). *The unseen power: Public relations, a history.* Hillsdale, NJ: Erlbaum.

Cutlip, S., Center, A., & Broom, G. (1999). *Effective public relations,* 6th ed. Englewood Cliffs, NJ: Prentice-Hall.

Cyberatlas (1998). Available at: http://www.cyberatlas.com

Czitrom, D. (1982). *Media and the American mind.* Chapel Hill, NC: University of North Carolina Press.

Dates, J., & Barlow, W. (1997). Does mass media realistically portray African American culture? No. In Alexander, A. & Hanson, J. (eds.), *Taking sides: Clashing views on controversial issues in mass media and society.* Guilford, CT: Dushkin/Brown & Benchmark.

Davidson, M., & Cooper, C. (1987). *Women and information technology.* New York: Wiley.

Davis, B. (1994, March 22). Clipper Chip is your friend, NSA contends. *Wall Street Journal,* B1.

Davis, K. (1985). *Two-bit culture.* Boston: Houghton Mifflin.

Day, L. (1991). *Ethics in media communications: Cases and controversies.* Belmont, CA: Wadsworth.

de Sola Pool, I. (1983). *Forecasting the telephone: A retrospective technology assessment of the telephone.* Norwood, NJ: Ablex.

DeBarros, A. (1998, June 7). Radio's historic change: Amid consolidation, fear of less diversity, choice. *USA Today,* A1-2.

December, J. (1996). Units of analysis for Internet communication. *Journal of Communication,* 46(1), 14–38.

Dery, M. (1996). *Escape velocity: Cyberculture at the end of the century.* New York: Grove Press.

Dessauer, J. (1981). *Book publishing—What it is, what it does,* 2nd ed. New York: R. R. Bowker.

Dietrich, D. (1997). (Re)-Fashioning the techno-erotic woman: Gender and textuality in the cybercultural matrix. In Jones, S. (ed.), *Virtual culture.* Thousand Oaks, CA: Sage.

Difranza, Jr., Richards, J., Paulman, P., Wolfgillespie, N., Fletcher, C., Jaffe, R., & Murray, D. (1991). RJR Nabisco's cartoon camel promotes Camel cigarettes to children. *Journal of the American Medical Association,* 266(22), 3149–3153.

Dill, K., & Dill, J. (1999). Video game violence: A review of the empirical literature. *Aggression and Violent Behavior,* 3(4), 407–428.

DiMaggio, P., Hargittai, E., Neuman, W., & Robinson, J. (2001). Social implications of the Internet. *Annual Review of Sociology,* 27, 307–336.

DiOrio, C. (1996, April 16). PacBell direct dials H'wood. *Hollywood Reporter,* 1.

Dizard, W. (1993). *The coming information age.* New York: Longman.

———. (1997). *Old media, new media.* New York: Longman.

Dobrow, J. (1989). Away from the mainstream? VCRs and ethnic identity. In Levy, M., (ed.), *The VCR age.* Thousand Oaks, CA: Sage.

Dominick, J. (1993). *The dynamics of mass communication,* 4th ed. New York: McGraw-Hill.

Dordick, H., & LaRose, R. (1992). *The telephone in daily life: A study of personal telephone use.* East Lansing, MI: Department of Telecommunication.

Dordick, H., & Wang, G. (1993). *The information society: A retrospective view.* Newbury Park, CA: Sage.

Dortch, S. (1996). Going to the Movies. *American Demographics,* 18(12), A–7.

Downing, J., Mohammadi, A., & Sreberny-Mohammadi, A. (1990). *Questioning the media: A critical introduction.* Newbury Park, CA: Sage.

Duffy, J. (1997). *College On-line: How to take college courses without leaving home.* New York: Wiley.

Duncan, T., & Moriarty, S. (1997). *Driving brand value: Using integrated marketing to manage profitable stakeholder relationships.* New York: McGraw-Hill.

Durry, D. (2002). In-vehicle cell phones: Fatal distraction? *Professional Safety,* 47(3), 28–33.

Dutton, W., Rogers, E., & Jun, S. (1987). The diffusion and impacts of information technology in households. In Zorkoczy, P. (ed.), *Oxford surveys in information technology* (vol. 4). New York: Oxford University Press.

Dyson, E. (1997). *Release 2.0: A design for living in the digital age.* New York: Broadway Books.

Eastman, L. (1993). *Broadcast/cable programming.* Belmont, CA: Wadsworth.

Eastman, S., Head, S., & Klein, L. (1989). *Broadcast/cable programming: Strategies and practices,* 3rd ed. Belmont, CA: Wadsworth.

Editor and Publisher website. (1998). Available at: http: //www.naa.org.info.facts.html

EFF. (2001). EFF analysis of the provisions of the USA Patriot Act. Available at: http://www.eff.org/Privacy/Surveillance/Terrorism_militias/20011031_eff_usa_patriot_analysis.html

Eighmey, J., & McCord, L. (1998). Adding value in the information age: Uses and gratifications of sites on the World Wide Web. *Journal of Business Research,* 41(3), 187–195.

Elasmar, M., & J. Hunter. (1996). The impact of foreign TV on a domestic audience: a meta-analysis. *Communication Yearbook* 20, 47–69.

Elliott, S. (2001, February 26). Advertising: Agencies seek strength through media diversity. the *New York Times:* www:nytimes.com/2001/02/26/business/26ADCO.html

Ellis, J. (1990). *A history of film,* 3rd ed. Englewood Cliffs, NJ: Prentice-Hall.

Ellul, J. (1990). *The technological bluff.* Grand Rapids, MI: Eerdmans.

Emes, C. (1997). Is Mr. Pac Man eating our children? A review of the effect of video games on children. *Canadian Journal of Psychiatry,* 42(4), 409–414.

Endicott, R. (2000, Sept. 25). 100 leading national advertisers. *Advertising Age,* S4.

Engelman, R. (1996). *Public radio and television in America: A political history.* Thousand Oaks, CA: Sage Publications.

Engleberg, S. (1993, March 17). A new breed of hired hands cultivates grass-roots anger. *New York Times,* A1.

Evans, C. (1981). *The making of the micro: A history of the computer.* New York: Van Nostrand Reinhold.

Everett, G. (1993). The age of new journalism, 1883–1900. In Sloan, W., Stovall, J., & Startt, J. (eds.), *Media in America: A history,* 2nd ed. Scottsdale, AZ: Publishing Horizons.

Ewen, S. (1976). *Captains of consciousness.* New York: McGraw-Hill.

———. (1996). *PR! A social history of spin.* New York: Basic Books.

Ewen, S., & Ewen, E. (1992). *Channels of desire—Mass images and the shaping of American consciousness.* Minneapolis: University of Minnesota Press.

Fagen, M. (ed.). (1975). *A history of engineering and science in the Bell System: The early years, 1875–1925.* Murray Hill, NJ: Bell Telephone Laboratories.

Farrelly, M. (2002). Getting to the truth: Evaluating national tobacco countermarketing campaigns. *American Journal of Public Health,* 92(6), 901–907.

Feather, F. (2000). *Future Consumer.com: The webolution of Shopping to 2010.* Toronto: Warwick.

Featherstone, M. (1990). Perspectives on consumer culture. *Sociology,* 24.

———. (1991). *Consumer culture and post-modernism.* Newbury Park: Sago.

Federal Communications Commission (1997). 1997 *monitoring report,* Section I. Available at: http://www.fcc.gov/Bureaus/Common_Carrier/Reports/FCC-State_Link/monitor.html

Federal Trade Commission (1998). Privacy online: A report to Congress. Available at: http://www.ftc.gov/reports/privacy3/toc.htm

Federman, J. (1998). *National television violence study,* vol. 3, *Executive summary.* Santa Barbara, CA: University of California Santa Barbara, Center for Communication and Social Policy.

Felson, R. (1996). Mass media effects on violent behavior. *Annual Review of Sociology,* 22, 103–128.

Feshbach, S., & Singer, R. (1971). *Television and aggression.* San Francisco: Jossey-Bass.

Feurey, J. (1986). Video news releases. In *New technology and public relations.* New York: Institute for Public Relations.

Fife, M. (1984). Minority ownership and multiple ownership in the deregulated broadcast marketplace. Paper presented at the Telecommunications Policy Research Conference, Airlie, Virginia.

Fine (2000, August 7). Publishing executives downplay ad turndown. *Advertising Age,* s42.

Fisch, S., & Truglio, R. (eds.) (2001). *"G" is for growing: Thirty years of research on children and Sesame Street.* Mahwah, NJ: Erlbaum.

Fischer, C. (1992). *America calling.* Berkeley: University of California Press.

Fitzgerald, (1998, August 3). Beyond advertising. *Advertising Age,* 1,14.

Fleming, S., & McLaughlin, M. (1993, July 12). ADSL: The on-ramp to the information highway. *Telephony,* 111–114.

Folkerts, J., & Teeter, D. (1994). *Voices of a nation: A history of mass media in the United States.* New York: Macmillan.

Ford, T. (1997). Effects of stereotypical television portrayals of African-Americans on person perception. *Social Psychology Quarterly,* 60(3), 266–275.

Fortini-Campbell, L. (1992). *Hitting the sweet spot: How consumer insights can inspire better marketing and advertising.* Chicago: The Copy Workshop.

Fowler, M., & Brenner, D. (1982). A marketplace approach to broadcast regulation. *Texas Law Review,* 60, 207–257.

Fowles, J. (1999). The case for television violence. Thousand Oaks, CA: Sage Publications.

Fox, S. (1984). *The mirror makers: A history of American advertising.* London: Heinemann.

Frederick, H. (1993). *North American NGO networking on trade and immigration: Computer communications in cross border coalition building.* Unpublished paper, Benson Latin American Collection, University of Texas, Austin.

Freedman, J. (1984). Effect of television violence on aggressiveness. *Psychological Bulletin,* 96(2), 227–246.

Freeman, S. (2004, September 14). Oprah's GM Giveaway was stroke of luck for agency and audience. The *Wall Street Journal,* B1.

Freiberger, P., & Swaine, M. (1984). *Fire in the valley: The making of the personal computer.* Berkeley, CA: Osborne/McGraw-Hill.

Freud, S. (1949). An outline of psychoanalysis. Authorized translation by James Strachey. (1st ed.) New York, W. W. Norton.

Freuh, T., & McGhee, P. (1975). Traditional sex role development and the amount of time spent watching television. *Developmental Psychology*, 11(1), 109.

Friedland, L. (1996). Electronic democracy and the new citizenship. *Media, Culture, and Society*, 18, 185–212.

Friedlander, B. (1993). Community violence, children's development and mass media, *Psychiatry*, 56(1), 66–81.

Frost, R. (1996). The electronic Gutenberg fails to win mass appeal. *Wall Street Journal*.

Fulk, J., Schmitz, J., & Steinfield, C. (1990). A social influence model of technology use. In Fulk, J., & Steinfield, C. (eds.), *Organizations and communication technology*. Thousand Oaks, CA: Sage.

Galbraith, John Kenneth. (1967) *The Affluent Society*. Boston: Houghton-Mifflin.

Gandy, O. (1982). *Beyond agenda setting: Information subsidies and public policy*. Norwood, NJ: Ablex.

———. (1993). *The panoptic sort*. Boulder, CO: Westview.

Gartner Group (2000). Gartner says North American Internet retailing market to grow 75 percent in 2000. Downloaded from the web, July 13, 2000: http://gartner3.gartnerweb.com/public/static/aboutgg/pressrel/pr20000627a.html

Gaziano, C. (1997). Forecast 2000: Widening knowledge gaps. *Journalism and Mass Communication Quarterly*, 74(2), 237–264.

Gentry, C. (1991). Pornography and rape: An empirical analysis. *Deviant Behavior*, 12, 277–288.

George, R. (1998, July 5). Would Jesus sue? the *Houston Chronicle*, 4.

Gerbner, G., Gross, L., Morgan, M., & Signorelli, N. (1994). Growing up with television: The cultivation perspective. In Bryant, J., & Zillmann, D. (eds.), *Media effects: Advances in theory and research*. Hillsdale, NJ: Lawrence Erlbaum.

Ghareeb, E. (1983). *Split vision: The portrayal of Arabs in the media*. Washington, DC American-Arab Affairs Council.

Giddens, A. (1984). The constitution of society: outline of the theory of structuration. *University of California Press*, Berkeley.

Gilder, G. (2000). Telecosm: How infinite bandwidth will revolutionize our world. New York: Free Press.

Gitlin, T. (1983). *Inside prime time*. New York: Pantheon Books.

———. (1995). *The twilight of common dreams: why America is wracked by culture wars*. New York: Metropolitan Books. Henry Hold.

Gladwell, M. (1998, July 6). The spin myth. the *New Yorker*, 66–73.

Glascock, J. (2001). Gender roles on prime-time network television: Demographics and behaviors. *Journal of Broadcasting & Electronic Media*, 45(4), 656–669.

———. (2003). Gender, race, and aggression in newer TV networks' primetime programming. *Communication Quarterly*, 51(1), 90–100.

Glascock, J., & LaRose R. (1993). Dial-a-porn recordings: The role of the female participant in male sexual fantasies, *Journal of Broadcasting and Electronic Media*, 37(3), 313–324.

Gomery, D. (1991). *Movie history: A survey*. Belmont, CA: Wadsworth.

Gortmaker, S., Must, A., Sobol, A., Peterson, K., Colditz, G., & Dietz, W. (1996). Television viewing as a cause of increasing obesity among children in the United States, 1986–1990. *Archive of Pediatric and Adolescent Medicine*, 150, 356–362.

Graber, D. (1996). The "new" media and politics: What does the future hold? *PS: Political Science and Politics*, 29: 33–36.

Gramsci, A. (1971). *Selections from the prison notebooks*. New York: International Publishers.

Gray, H. Watching race: television and the struggle for "Blackness." Minneapolis: University of Minnesota Press, 1995.

Graybow, M. (Fri Jan 7, 2005). *New York Times Mulls Charging web Readers*. New York: Reuters.

Greenberg, B., et al. (1980). Antisocial and prosocial behaviors on television. In Greenberg, B. (ed.), *Life on television: Content analysis of U.S. TV drama*. Norwood, NJ: Ablex.

Greenberg, B., & Brand, J. (1994). Minorities and the mass media: 1970s to 1990s. In Bryant, J., & Zillmann, D. (eds.), *Media effects: Advances in theory and research* (pp. 273–314). Hillsdale, NJ: Erlbaum Associates, Inc.

Greenfield, P. (1994). Video games as cultural artifacts. *Journal of Applied Developmental Psychology*, 15(1), 3–12.

Grefe, E. (1986). Relational data base management. In *New technology and public relations*. New York: Institute for Public Relations.

Grier, S. (2001). The Federal Trade Commission's report on the marketing of violent entertainment to youths: Developing policy-tuned research. *Journal of Public Policy & Marketing*, 20(1), 123–133.

Griffin, N., & Masters, K. (1997). *Hit and run: How Jon Peters and Peter Guber took Sony for a ride in Hollywood*. New York: Touchstone Books.

Griffiths, M. (1998). Violent video games and aggression: A review of the literature. *Aggression and Violent Behavior*, 4(2), 203–212.

——— (2000). Does Internet and computer "addiction" exist? Some case study evidence. *CyberPsychology and Behavior*, 3, 211–218.

Grohol, J. (1996). Psychology of the Internet research and theory: Internet additions. Available at: http://www.cmhc.com/mlists/research

Grossberg, L. (1993). Can cultural studies find true happiness in communication? *Journal of Communication*, 43, 89–97.

Grossnickle, J., & Raskin, O. (2001). *Handbook of online marketing research*. New York: McGraw-Hill.

Gruley, B. (1997, March 11). TV stations, satellite firms reach pact. *Wall Street Journal*, A2.

———. (1997, April 3). FCC prepares for rollout of digital TV. *Wall Street Journal*, B2.

Gruley, B., & Robichaux, M. (1997, April 1). Justices uphold "must carry" broadcast rules. *Wall Street Journal*, B1.

Grunig, L. A., Toth, E. L., & Hon, L. C. (2001). Women in public relations: How gender influences practice. New York: Guilford Press.

Guback T., & Varis T. (1982). Transnational communication and cultural industries. *Reports and Papers on Mass Communication*. UNESCO, Paris, No. 92.

Guernsey. L. (2001, September 20). An unimaginable emergency put communications to the test. *New York Times*, online edition: http://www.nytimes.com/2001/09/20/technology/circuits/201NFR.html

Gunter, G. (1998). Ethnicity and involvement in violence on television: Nature and context of on-screen portrayals. *Journal of Black Studies*, 28, 683–703.

Haley, E., White, C., & Cunningham, A. (2001). Branding religion: Christian consumers' understandings of Christian products. In Stout, D., & Buddenbaum, J. (eds), *Religion and popular culture: Studies on the interaction of worldviews*. Ames, IA: Iowa State University Press, 269–288.

Hall, S. (1980). "Encoding/Decoding." In Hall, S., Hobson, D., Lowe, A., & Willis, P. (eds.) *Culture, media language*. London: Hutchinson.

Hamlin, S. (1995, September 6). Time flies, but where does it go? *New York Times*, B1.

Hansell, S. (1998, August 16). Big web sites to track steps of users. *New York Times*, Cybertimes edition.

Hardy, Q. (1996, September 16). Wireless wagers. *Wall Street Journal*, R18.

Harmon, A. (1997, December 7). The self-appointed cops of the Information Age. *New York Times*, A-1.

———. (1998, April 17). Blacks less likely to have access to Internet, study shows. *New York Times*, A1.

Harris, T. (1993). *Marketer's guide to public relations: How today's top companies are using the new PR to gain a competitive edge*. New York: John Wiley.

Harris Interactive (1999, November 18). Six types of women who use the net. Downloaded from the web May 24, 2000: http://www.nua.ie/surveys/index.cgi?f=VS & art_id= 905355414 & rel=true

Harrison, E. (1993). *Going green: How to communicate your company's environmental commitment*. Homewood, IL: Irwin.

Harrison, S. (1990). Pedagogical ethics for public relations and advertising. *Journal of Mass Media Ethics*, 5, 256–262.

Hart, M. (1990). *Drumming at the edge of magic*. New York: HarperCollins.

Harte, L., Levine, R., & Prokup, S. (1997). *Cellular and PCS: The big picture*. New York: McGraw-Hill.

Harwood, J., & Anderson, K. (2002). The presence and portrayal of social groups on prime-time television. *Communication Reports*, 15(2), 81–97.

Haywood, T. (1995). *Info-rich/info-poor: Access and exchange in the global information society*. West Sussex, England: Bowker/Saur.

Head, S., Sterling, C., & Schofield, L. (1994). *Broadcasting in America*, 7th ed. Boston: Houghton Mifflin.

Hearold, S. (1986). A synthesis of effects of television on social behavior. In Comstock, G. (ed.), *Public communication and behavior*, vol. I. New York: Academic Press.

Heins, M. (1993). *Sex, sin and blasphemy*. New York: New Press.

Hendrix, J. (2001). *Public relations cases*, 5th ed. Belmont, CA: Wadsworth.

Hennigan, K., Del Rosario, M., Heath, L., Cook, T., Wharton, J., & Calder, B. (1982). The impact of the introduction of television on crime in the United States. *Journal of Personality and Social Psychology*, 42, 461–477.

Herman, E., & McChesney, R. (1997). *The global media: the new missionaries of global capitalism*. Washington: Cassell.

Hicks, T. (2000, August 23). Data mining offers mother lode of information. *Sporting Goods Business*, 16.

Hiebert, R. (1966). *Courtier to the crowd: The story of Ivy L. Lee and the development of public relations*. Iowa City, IA: Iowa State University Press.

Hiltz, S. (1994). *The virtual classroom: Learning without limits via computer networks*. Norwood, NJ: Ablex.

Hirsch, P. (1980). The "scary world" of the nonviewer and other anomalies: A reanalysis of Gerbner et al.'s findings on cultivation analysis. *Communication research*, 7, 403–456.

Ho, A. (2002). Reinventing local governments and the e-government initiative. *Public Administration Review*, 62(4), 434–444.

Holzmann, G., & Pherson, B. (1994). The early history of data networks. Available at: http://www.it.kth.se/docs /early_net/toc.html

Horkheimer, M., & Adorno, T. W. (1972). *Dialectic of Enlightenment*, translated by John Cumming. New York: Herder and Herder.

Horvitz, L. (2002). *Eureka!: Scientific breakthroughs that changed the world*. New York: J. Wiley.

Houston, P. (1993, March 16). Phone frenzy in the Capitol. *Los Angeles Times*, A1.

Hovland, C., Lumsdane, A., & Sheffield, F. (1949). *Experiments on mass communications*. Princeton, NJ: Princeton University Press.

Howard, C., & Mathews, W. (1997). *On deadline: Managing media relations*, 3rd ed. Prospect Heights, IL: Waveland.

Hudson, H. (1990). *Communication satellites: Their development and impact*. New York: Free Press.

Huesmann, L., (1982). Television violence and aggressive behavior. In Pearl, D., Bouthliet, L., & Lazar, J. (eds.), *Television and behavior: Ten years of scientific progress and implications for the eighties*. Washington, DC: National Institute for Mental Health.

Huesmann, L., & Eron, L. (1986). The development of aggression in American children as a consequence of television violence viewing. In authors (eds.), *Television and the aggressive child*. Hillsdale, NJ: Lawrence Erlbaum.

Huntzicker, W. (1993). The frontier press 1800–1900. In Sloan, W., Stovall, J., & Startt, J. (eds.), *Media in America: A history*, 2nd ed. Scottsdale, AZ: Publishing Horizons.

Huston, A., et al. (1992). *Big world, small screen: The role of television in American society*. Omaha: University of Nebraska Press.

Hynds, E. (1980). *American newspapers in the 1980s*. New York: Hastings House.

InterMedia. (1989). There Never Was a Mass Audience . . . *Intermedia*, (17)2.

Internet sapping broadcast news audience. Downloaded from the web: http://www.people-press.org/media00rpt.htm

Institute for Alternative Journalism (October 1997). *The synergy report (25 select case studies)*. Available at: http://www.fourthestate.com/synergy.html

Irving, L. (1998, September 18). *Minority commercial broadcast ownership report*. National Telecommunications and Information Administration. Washington, DC.

ITV (2003). News report. Available at: http://www.itv.com/news/

Iyengar, S., & Reeves, R. (eds.) (1997). *Does the media govern? Politicians, voters and reporters in America*. Thousand Oaks, CA: Sage.

Janal, D. (1999). *Guide to marketing on the Internet*. New York: Wiley.

Jeffres, L. (1986). *Mass media processes and effects*. Prospect Heights, IL: Waveland Press.

Jensen, E., & Graham, E. (1993, October 26). Stamping out TV violence: A losing fight. *Wall Street Journal*, B1.

Jerram, P. (1997, June 2). Energize your brand. *New Media*, 35–42.

Jodges, J. (2000, November 14). Commerce in context. *Business 2.0*, 126–131.

Johnson, J. G., Cohen, P., Smailes, E. M., Kasen, S., & Brook, J. S. (2002). Television viewing and aggressive behavior during adolescence and adulthood, *Science*, Mar 29: 2468–2471.

Johnston, C. (1995, November 24). Anonymity on line? It depends who's asking. *Wall Street Journal*, B1.

Johnston, J. (1987). *Electronic learning*. Hillsdale, NJ: Lawrence Erlbaum.

Jones, C. (1996). *Winning with the news media*. Tampa, FL: Video Consultants, Inc.

Jones, S. (1992). *Rock formation: Music, technology and mass communication*. Newbury Park, CA: Sage.

Jung, C. G. *Analytical psychology: its theory and practice; the Travistock lectures*. Forward by E. A. Bennet. New York: Vintage Books, 1970.

Kahin, B., & Varian, H., (ed.) (2000). *Internet publishing and beyond: The economics of digital information and intellectual property*. Cambridge, MA: MIT Press.

Kaiser Family Foundation. (2001). Parents and the v-chip 2000. Downloaded from the web, June 1, 2002: http://www.kff.org/content/2001/3158/summary.pdf

———. (2004, August). Digital divide. Retrieved October 2, 2004, from http://www.kff.org/entmedia/loader.dfm?url=/commonspot/security/getfile.cfm & PageID=46366

Kaplan, C. (1998, October 9). Strict European privacy law puts pressure on U.S. *New York Times*, Cybertimes edition.

———. (2001). Legal victory for Internet advertising industry. The *New York Times*: http://www.nytimes. com/2001/04/06/technology/06CYBERLAW.html

Kateb, G. (1989). *Walt Whitman and the cultural democracy*. New Brunswick, NJ: Rutgers Unviersity.

Katz, E., & Lazarsfeld, P. (1955). *Personal influence*. New York: Free Press.

Katz, E., & Wedell, G. (1976). *Broadcasting in the third world*. Cambridge, MA: Harvard University Press.

Katz, J. E., & Aspden, P. (1996). Motivations for and barriers to Internet usage: Results of a national public opinion survey. Paper presented to the 24th Annual Telecommunications Policy Research Conference, Solomons, MD, October 6.

Kaye, B., & Medoff, N. (2001). *Just a Click Away: Advertising on the Internet*. MA: Allyn and Bacon.

Kaye, B., & Johnson, T. (2003). From here to obscurity?: Media substitution theory and traditional media in an online world. *Journal of the American Society for Information Science and Technology*, 54(3), 260–273.

Keen, P. (1988). *Competing in time*. New York: Harper.

Keller, J. (1996, September 19). The "new" AT & T faces daunting challenges. *Wall Street Journal*, B1.

Kernan, M., & Howard, G. (1990). Computer anxiety and computer attitudes: An investigation of construct and predictive validity issues. *Educational and Psychological Measurement*, 50, 681–690.

Kerwin, B., & Cappuccio, D. (1998). Technology migrations toting up the hidden costs. *Data Communications*, 27(7), 31–33.

Kiesler, S., Siegal, J., & McGuire, T. (1984). Social psychological aspects of computer-mediated communication. *American Psychologist*, 39(10), 1123–1134.

Kilborn, P. (1993, March 15). New jobs lack the old security in time of "disposable workers." *New York Times*, A1.

Kim, J. (1996, October 30). Net use strains phone lines. *USA Today*, A1.

———. (1997). Teaching over the 'net. *Computerworld*, 31(20), 59–61.

Klapper, J. (1960). *The effects of mass communication*. New York: Free Press.

Kling, R. (1980). Social analyses of computing: Theoretical perspectives in recent empirical research. *Computing Surveys*, 12(1), 61–110.

Knight, A. (1979). *The liveliest art*. New York: New American Library.

Kottak, C. (1990). *Prime time society*. Belmont, CA: Wadsworth.

Kounalakis, M., Banks, D., & Daus, K. (1999). *Beyond spin: The power of strategic corporate journalism*. New York: Jossey-Bass.

Kraut, R., Kiesler, S., Boneva, B., Cummings J., Helgeson, V., & Crawford, A. (2002) The Internet paradox revisited. *Journal of Social Issues*, 58, 49–74.

Kraut, R., Patterson, M., Lundmark, V., Kiesler, S., Mukophadhyay, T., & Scherlig, W. (1998). Internet paradox: A social technology that reduces social involvement and psychological well-being? *American Psychologist*, 53(9), 1017–1031.

Kroker, A., & Weinstein, M. (1994). *Data trash: The theory of the virtual class*. New York: St. Martin's.

Kubey, R. (1991, March 6). The case for media education. *Education Week* (24), 1.

Kuchinskas, S. (2000, November 14). The end of marketing. *Business 2.0*, 134–139.

Kunkel, D. (1998, May). Policy battles over defining children's educational television. (Children and Television). *The Annals of the American Academy of Political and Social Science*, 57(15), 37.

Kunkel, D., Cope-Farrar, K., Biely, E. Maynard-Farinola, W., & Donnerstein, E. (2001). *Sex on TV*. Menlo Park, CA: Kaiser Family Foundation. Retrieved from the World Wide Web on March 7, 2001: http//www.kff.org/content/2001/3087/sexontv.pdf

Kutchinsky, B. (1991). Pornography and rape: Theory and practice? Evidence from crime data in four countries where pornography is easily available. *International Journal of Law and Psychiatry*, 14(1–2), 47–64.

Kwak, N. (1999). Revisiting the knowledge gap hypothesis. *Communication Research*, 26(4), 385–413.

Landler, M. (1995, December 26). Multiple family phone lines, a post-postwar U.S. trend. *New York Times*, A1.

Langdale, J. (1991). *Internationalization of Australia's service industries*. Canberra: Australian Government Publishing Service.

LaRose, R. (1999). *Understanding personal telephone behavior*. In Sawhney, H., & Barnett, G. (eds.), *Progress in communication science*, vol. XV: *Advances in telecommunication theory and research*. Norwood, NJ: Ablex.

LaRose, R., & Atkin, D. (1988). Satisfaction, demographic and media environment predictors of cable subscription. *Journal of Broadcasting and Electronic Media*, 32(4), 403–413.

LaRose, R., & David, A. (1992). Audiotext and the Re-Invention of the Telephone as a Mass Medium, *Journalism Quarterly*, 69 (2), Summer, 1992, 413–421.

LaRose, R., Gregg, J., & Eastin, M. (1999). Audiographic telecourses for the web. An experiment. *Journal of Computer Mediated Communication*. 4(2). Available at: http://www.ascusc.org/jcmc/vol4/issue2/larose.htm

LaRose, R., Lin, C., & Eastin, M. S. (2002). Media addiction, media habits and deficient self-regulation in the case of the Internet. Paper presented to the International Communication Association, Communication and Technology Division, Seoul, Korea, July, 2002.

LaRose, R., Mastro, D., & Eastin, M. (2001). Understanding Internet usage: A social cognitive approach to uses and gratifications. *Social Science Computer Review*.

Lau, R., Sigelman, L., Heldman, C., & Babbitt, P. (1999). The effects of negative political advertisements: A meta-analytic assessment. *The American Political Science Review*, 93(4), 851–875.

Lavine, H., Sweeney, D., & Wagner, S. (1999) Depicting women as sex object in television advertising: Effects on body dissatisfaction. *Personality and Social Psychology Bulletin*, 25(8), 1049–1058.

Lazarsfeld, P. (1941). Remarks on adminstrative and critical communication research. *Studies in Philosophy and Social Science*, 9, 2–16.

Lazarus, W., & Mora, F. (2000). *On-line content for low-income and underserved Americans: The Digital Divide's new frontier*. Santa Monica, CA: The Children's Partnership.

Ledbetter, J. (1997). *Made Possible by: The death of public broadcasting in the United States*. New York: Verso.

Lee, K. (2004). Presence, explicated. *Communication Theory*, 14(1), 27–50.

Lefkowitz, M., Eron, L., Walder, L., & Huesmann, L. (1972). Television violence and child aggression: A follow-up study. In Comstock, G., & Rubenstein, E. (eds.), *Television and social behavior*, vol. 3. Washington, DC: U.S. Government Printing Office.

Leiner, B., Cerf, V., Clark, D., Kahn, R., Kleinrock , L., Lynch, D., Postel, J., Roberts, L., & Wolf, S. (2000). A brief history of the Internet. Retrieved from the web, September 16, 2002: http://www.isoc.org/internet/history/brief.shtml

Leiss, W., Kline, S., & Jhally, S. (1990). *Social communication in advertising*. Ontario: Nelson Canada.

Leland, J. (1995, December 11). Violence, reel to real. *Newsweek*, 46–48.

Lemos, A. (1996). The labyrinth of Minitel. In Shields, R. (ed.), *Cultures of the Internet*. Thousand Oaks, CA: Sage.

Letter to Congress explaining FTC's new deception policy. (1983). *Advertising Compliance Service*. Westport, CT: Meckler Publishing.

Levy, P. (2001). *Cyberculture*. Bononno, R. Minneapolis, MN: University of Minnesota Press.

Levy, S. (1994). E-money. *Wired*, 2(12), 124–129.

———. (1996, September 16). The Internet crash scare. *Newsweek*, 96.

Lewis, M. (2000, August 13). Boom box. The *New York Times Magazine*, Section 6, 36–41, 51, 65–67.

Lewis, P. (1990, July 8). Worries about radiation continue, as do studies. *New York Times*, F8.

Lewis, T. (1991). *Empire of the air*. New York: Harper.

Liebert, R., & Sprafkin, J. (1988). *The early window*. New York: Pergamon Press.

Liebes, T., & Katz, E. (1989). *The export of meaning: Cross-cultural readings of Dallas.* New York: Oxford University Press.

Lim, S., Sauter, S., & Schnorr, T. (1998) Occupational health aspects of work with video display terminals. In Rom, W. (ed)., *Environmental and occupational medicine,* 3rd ed. Philadelphia: Lippincott-Raven.

Limmer, J. (ed.). (1981). *The Rolling Stone illustrated history of rock and roll.* New York: Random House.

Lin, C. (2003). An interactive communication technology adoption model. *Communication Theory,* 13(4), 345–365.

Lindlof, T. (1995). *Qualitative communications research methods.* Thousand Oaks, CA: Sage.

Linnett, R. (2000, July 31). Generation media a hit. *Advertising Age,* s2–s3.

Lippmann, W. (1922). *Public opinion.* New York: Macmillan.

Livingstone, S. (1998). *Making sense of television: The pyschology of audience interpretation,* 2nd ed. New York: Routledge.

Lodish, L., Abraham, M., Livelsberger, J., Lubetkin, B., Richardson, B., & Stevens, M. (1995). A summary of 55 in-market experimental estimates of the long-term effect of TV advertising. *Marketing Science,* 14(3), G133–140.

Loeffler, R. (1993). *A guide to preparing cost-effective press releases.* Binghamton, NY: Haworth Press.

Lohr, S. (1993, April 14). Recycling answer sought for computer junk. *New York Times,* A1.

Lyotard, J. (1984). *The postmodern condition.* Manchester, England: Manchester University Press.

———. (1984). *The postmodern condition: a report on knowledge.* Translation from the French by Geoff Bennington and Brian Massumi. Minneapolis: University of Minnesota Press.

Lynam, D., Milich, R., Zimmerman, R., Novak, S., et al. (1999). Project DARE: No effects at 10-year follow-up. *Journal of Consulting and Clinical Psychology,* 67(4), 590–593.

MacDonald, J. (1979). *Don't touch that dial! Radio programming in American life from 1920 to 1960.* Chicago: Nelson-Hall.

Magazine Publishers of America (2004). Publisher's Information Bureau. Available at: http://www.magazine.org

——— (2004). Audit Bureau of Circulations Statement. Available at: http://www.magazine.org

——— (2004). Circulation trends and magazine handbook. Available at: http://www.magazine.org/Circulation/circulation_trends_and_magazine_handbook/1318.cfm

Mahoney, M. Report: Women top men as net buyers. *E-Commerce Times,* December 8, 2000: http://www.ecommercetimes.com/perl/story/5929.html

Maibach, E., & Holtgrave, D. (1995). Advances in public health communication. *Annual Review of Public Health,* 16, 219–238.

Malamuth, N., Addison. T., & Koss, M. (2000). Pornography and sexual aggression: Are there reliable effects and can we understand them? *Annual Review of Sex Research,* 11, 26–91.

Mandell, S. (1990). Computer crime. In Ermann, M., Williams, M., & Gutierrez, C. (eds.), *Computers, ethics and society.* New York: Oxford University Press.

Manheim, J. (1991). *All of the people, all of the time: Strategic communications & American politics.* Armonk, NY: M. E. Sharpe.

Mannes, G. (1996).The birth of cable TV. *Invention and Technology,* 12(2), 42–50.

Marcuse, H. (1964). *One-dimensional man.* Boston: Beacon Press.

Marien, M. (1996). New communications technology: A survey of impacts and issues. *Telecommunications Policy,* 20(5), 375–387.

Marketing Translation Mistakes. Retrieved September 21, 2004, from the World Wide Web: http://www.il8nguy.com/translations.html

Marketing violent entertainment to children: A review of self-regulation and industry practices in the motion picture, music recording & electronic game industries. (2000). Report of the Federal Trade Commission. Washington, DC: FTC.

Markus, L. (1990). Toward a "critical mass" theory of interactive media. In Fulk, J., & Steinfield, C. (eds.), *Organizations and communication technology.* Thousand Oaks, CA: Sage.

Marriott, M. (1999, January 7). "If only DeMille had owned a desktop." *New York Times,* Circuits.

Marsh, H. (1993). The contemporary press. In Sloan, W., Stovall, J., & Startt, J. (eds.), *Media in America: A history,* 2nd ed. Scottsdale, AZ: Publishing Horizons.

Martin, D., & Coons, D. (1998). *Media flight plan.* Provo, UT: Deer Creek Publishing.

———. (1998a, April 20). Court KO's EEO. *Broadcasting & Cable,* 6.

Martin, M. (1991). *"Hello, central?" Gender, technology and culture in the formation of telephone systems.* Montreal, Canada: McGill-Queen's University Press.

Martin-Barbero, J. (1993). *Communication, culture, and hegemony: From the media to the mediations.* Thousand Oaks, CA: Sage.

Martinez, B. (1997, September 11). The holy grail: Cellular Visions' grasp may exceed its reach, but it's a quest worth watching. *Wall Street Journal,* R26.

Marvin, C. (1988). When old technologies were new: Thinking about electric communication in the late nineteenth century. NY: Oxford University Press.

Marx, K. (1967). *Capital, a critique of political economy,* vol. 1. New York: International Publishers.

Mast, G., & Kawin, B. (1996). *The movies: A short history.* Needham Heights, MA: Simon & Schuster.

Mastro, D., & Greenberg, B. (2000). The portrayal of minorities on prime time television. *Journal of Broadcasting and Electronic Media,* 44, 690–703.

McAnany, E. (1980). *Communication in the rural third world: The role of information in development.* New York: Praeger.

McChesney, R. (1993). Critical communication research at the crossroads. In Levy, M., & Gurevitch, M. (eds.), *Defining media studies.* New York: Oxford University Press.

———. (1996). The Internet and U.S. communication policy making in historical and critical context. *Journal of Communication,* 46(1), 98–124.

———. (1997). *Corporate Media and the Threat to Democracy.* New York: Seven Stories Press.

———. (November 1997). The global media giants: The nine firms that dominate the world. *EXTRA! The magazine of Fairness and Accuracy in Media:* http://www.fair.org/extra/index

———. (1999). *Rich media, poor democracy: communication politics in dubious times.* Urbana: University of Illinois Press.

———. (2002). *Rich media, poor democracy.* New York: New Press.

McClintick, D. (1998, November). Town crier for the new age. *Brill's Content,* 113–127.

———. (1998b, July 20). Minority ownership: A not-much-progress report. (Department of Commerce report on minority ownership of media) *Broadcasting & Cable,* 7.

McConnell, B. (2002). Another go on EEO rules, *Broadcasting & Cable,* Nov 11, vol. 132, Iss. 46, pg. 20.

McConnell, C. (1998b). Minority ownership: A not-much-progress report, *Broadcasting & Cable,* Jul 20, vol. 128, Iss. 30, pg. 7.

McCourt, J. (1998). Satisfaction guaranteed. *Video Store,* 20(46), 12–17.

McCracken, H. (1997, November). The new set-top boxes. *PC World,* 169–174.

McDaniel, D. (1994). *Broadcasting in the Malay world.* Norwood, NJ.: Ablex.

McDaniel, (2002).Electronic Tigers of Southeast Asia. Iowa State University, 2002.

McDaniel, D. (2002). Southeast Asia's electronically charged media revolution. *Nieman Reports,* 56(2), 63-65. Available at: http://www.nieman.harvard.edu/reports/02-2NRsummer/63-65.pdf

McGovern, P. (1993, August 6). Plug in for productivity. *New York Times,* F7.

McGuire, W. (1986). The myth of massive media impact: Savagings and salvagings. In Comstock, G. (ed), *Public communication and behavior.* New York: Academic Press.

McKearns, J. (1993). The emergence of modern media, 1900–1945. In Sloan, W., Stovall, J., & Startt, J. (eds.), *Media in America: A history,* 2nd ed. Scottsdale, AZ: Publishing Horizons.

McLaughlin, M., Osborne, K., & Ellison, N. (1997). Virtual community in a telepresence environment. In Jones, S. (ed.), *Virtual community.* Thousand Oaks, CA: Sage.

McLeod, J., Kosicki, G., & McLeod, D. (1994). The expanding boundaries of political communication effects. In Bryant, J., & Zillman, D. (eds.), *Media effects.* Hillsdale, NJ: Lawrence Erlbaum.

McLuhan, M. (1962). *The Gutenberg galaxy: the making of a typographic man.* Toronto: University of Toronto Press.

——— (1964). *Understanding media: the extensions of man.* New York: McGraw-Hill.

McLuhan, M., & Powers, B. (1989). *The global village: Transformations in world life and media in the 21st century.* New York: Oxford University Press, 1989.

McPhail, T. (1989). *Electronic colonialism.* Newbury Park, CA: Sage.

McQuail, D. (1987). *Mass communications theory—An introduction,* 2nd ed. Beverly Hills, CA: Sage.

Media Brief—CurtCo Media Group: Worth Magazine to be Acquired For $2.4 Million, Plus Liabilities. *Wall Street Journal.* (Eastern edition). New York, N.Y.: Jun 23, 2003. pg. A.7

Mediamark Research Inc. (2004, Fall). MRIPlus Database. Available at: http://www.mriplus.com/

MediaMetrix (1997, December). New Media Watch. Available at: http://www.mediametrix.com/

MediaPost Communications. (1998). Synopsis of tech, p. 1; http//www.medipost.com

Media Studies Journal (1996, Spring/Summer). "Media Mergers." Media Studies Center. Available at: http://www.mediastudies. org/nymeger.html

Mendelsohn, H. (1973). Some reasons why information campaigns can succeed. *Public Opinion Quarterly,* 37, 50–61.

Merli, J. (1998, January 5). Listening while driving most popular. *Broadcasting & Cable,* 128(1) 40.

Merrill, J. (1997). *Journalism ethics: Philosophical foundations for news media.* New York: St. Martin's Press.

Messner, S., & Blau, J. (1987). Routine leisure activity and rates of crime: A macro-level analysis. *Social Forces,* 65, 1035–1052.

Meyer, P. (1987). *Ethical journalism.* New York: Longman.

Mickelson, K. (1997). Seeking social support: Parents in electronic support groups. In Kiesler, S. (ed.), *Culture of the Internet.* Mahwah, NJ: Lawrence Erlbaum.

Middleton, K., & Chamberlin, B. (1994). *Law of public communication,* 3rd ed. London: Longman.

Milavsky, J., Kessler, R., Stipp, H., & Rubens, W. (1982). Television and aggression: Results of a panel study. In Perarl, D., Bouthliet, L., & Lazar, J. (eds.), *Television and behavior: Ten years of scientific progress and implications for the eighties,* vol. 2. Washington, DC: National Institute for Mental Health.

Miller, G. (1987). A neglected connection: Mass media exposure and interpersonal communication process. In Gumpert, G., & Cathcart, R. (eds.), *Intermedia: Interpersonal communication in a media world,* 3rd ed. New York: Oxford University Press.

Miller, J. (2000). *A.U.S. Television Chronology, 1875–1970.* Available online: http://members.aol.com/jeff560/chronotv.html

Miller, T., & Clemente, P. (1997). 1997 American Internet User Survey. New York: FIND/SVP Emerging Technologies Research Group. Available at: http://etrg.findsvp.com/internet/findf.html

Millman, S. (1984). *A history of engineering & science in the Bell System: Communications sciences, 1925–1980.* Murray Hill, NJ: AT&T Bell Laboratories.

Mody, B., Bauer, J., & Straubhaar, J. (1995). *Telecommunications politics: Ownership and control of the information highway in developing countries.* Hillsdale, NJ: Lawrence Earlbaum.

Moore, G. (1996). Nanometers and gigabucks—Moore on Moore's Law. University Video Corporation Distinguished Lecture. Available at: http://www.uvc.com/

Morgan, M., & Shanahan, J. (1997). Two decades of cultivation research. In B. R. Burelson (ed.), Communication yearbook 20 (pp. 1–47). Thousand Oaks, CA: Sage.

Morley, D. (1980). *The Nationwide audience: structure and decoding.* London: British Film Institute.

———— (1992). *Television, audiences and cultural studies.* New York: Routledge.

Morley, N. (1986). *Family television: Cultural power and domestic leisure.* London: Routledge.

Morse, R. (1985). Videotex USA. In Zarkoczy, *Oxford surveys in information technology,* vol. 2. New York: Oxford University Press.

Mosco, V. (1982). *Pushbutton fantasies: Critical perspectives on videotex and information technology.* Norwood, NJ: Ablex.

————. (1989). *The pay-per society: Computers and communication in the information age.* Norwood, NJ: Ablex.

————. (1996). *The political economy of communication.* Thousand Oaks, CA: Sage.

Motion Picture Association of America, http://www.mpaa.org/useconomicreview

———— "U.S. Entertainment Industry: 2004 MPA Market Statistics" report. Available at: http://www.mpaa.org/home/htm

Moyal, A. (1988). *Women and the telephone in Australia: Study of a national culture.* Paper presented to the International Communication Association, Dublin, Ireland.

Mueller, M., & Schement, J. (1995). *Universal service from the bottom up: A profile of telecommunications access in Camden, New Jersey.* New Brunswick, NJ: Rutgers University School of Communication, Information and Library Studies.

Murphy, J., & Hofacker, C. (1997, June 21). Move over '.com'! There's a whole world of good domain names. *New York Times,* Cybertimes edition.

Muto, S. (1995, September 15). From here to immodesty: Milestones in the toppling of TV's taboos. *Wall Street Journal,* B1.

Naisbitt, J. (1999). *High tech, high touch: Technology and our search for meaning.* New York: Broadway Books.

Napoli, P. (2002). Audience valuation and minority media: An analysis of the determinants of the value of radio audiences. *Journal of Broadcasting & Electronic Media,* 46(2), 169–184.

Nash, E. (1992). *The direct marketing handbook,* 2nd ed. New York: McGraw-Hill.

National Cable Television Association (1998). Available at: http://www.ncta.com/directory.html

National Commission for Employment Policy. (1986). *Computers in the workplace: Selected issues.* Washington, DC: U.S. Government Printing Office.

National Endowment for the Arts (2004). *Reading at Risk: A Survey of Literary Reading in America.* Available at: http://www.nea.gov/pub/ResearchReports_chrono.html

Neff, J. (2000, July 31). P & G, Unilever ads get grip on reality with home videos. *Advertising Age.* p. 4.

Negroponte, N. (1995). *Being digital.* New York: Knopf.

Nelson, E. (2002, December 9). Can "Kingpin" settle score with HBO's Tony Soprano? NBC hopes a dark drug-cartel pilot can lure back fans of "The Sopranos." *Wall Street Journal,* online edition.

NetRatings. (1999). Current reports. Available at: http://www.netratings.com/sample.htm

————. (2002). Hot off the net: Retrieved December 8, 2002 from the web: http://www.neilsen-netratings.com/hot_off_ net_i.jsp

Network Solutions, Inc. (1998). The history of the Internet. Available at: http://csis.swac.edu/~thomas/CSIS105/Internic.guide/Internet.History/history/sld01.html

Newcomb, H. (1992). *Television: A critical view,* 5th ed. New York: Oxford University Press.

Newcomb, H., & Hirsch, P., (2000). Television as a cultural forum in Horace Newcomb, ed., *Television: The Critical View, Sixth Edition.* Oxford University Press.

Newman, R., & Johnson, F. (1999). Sites for power and knowledge? Towards a critique of the virtual university. *British Journal of Sociology of Education,* 20(1): 79–88.

Newsom, D., & Carrell, B. (2000). Public relations writing: Forms and style. Thomson Learning.

Newsom, D. et al. (2000). This is PR: The realities of public relations. Belmont, CA: Wadsworth.

Newspaper Association of America. (2004). Available online at http://www.naa.org

————. (2004). Available online at http://www.naa.org/info/facts04/readership-sections.html

Noam, E. (1983). *Telecommunications regulation today and tomorrow.* New York: Law and Business.

————. (1996). Going beyond spectrum auctions. Available at: http://www.columbia.edu/dlc/wp/citi/citinoam22.html

Noelle-Neumann, E. (1984). *The spiral of silence: Public opinion—our social skin.* Chicago: University of Chicago Press.

Nora, S., & Minc, N. (1980). *The computerization of society.* Cambridge, MA: MIT Press.

Norwood, S. (1990). *Labor's flaming youth.* Urbana: University of Illinois Press.

Novak, T., & Hoffman, D. (1998). Bridging the digital divide. Available at: http://www.2000.ogsm.vanderbilt.edu/papers/ race/science.html

NPD (1997, December). Softrends topsellers ranked on unit sales. Available at: http://www.npd.com/corp/products/product_indsoft97.htm

NTIA (National Telecommunications and Information Administration) (1998). *Falling Through the Net II.* Washington, DC: NTIA. Available at: http:// www.ntia.doc.gov/ntiahome/ net2/falling.html

————. (1999). Falling through the net: Defining the Digital Divide. Downloaded from the World Wide Web, September 8, 2000: http://www.ntia.doc.gov/ ntiahome/fttn99/contents.html

————. (2000). Falling through the net: Toward digital inclusion. Retrieved from the World Wide Web, January 20, 2001: http://www.ntia.doc.gov/ntiahome/digitaldivide/execsumfttn00.htm

————. (2002). A Nation Online. Downloaded from the web November 5, 2002: http://www.ntia.doc.gov/ntiahome/dn/hfm/toc.htm

————. (2002). A Nation Online: How Americans are expanding their use of the Internet. Washington, DC. Downloaded from the World Wide Web, February 2002: http://ntia.doc./gov/ntiahome/dn/index.html

————. (2004). A Nation Online: Entering the Broadband Age. Downloaded from the web November 25, 2004: http://www.ntia.doc.gov/reports/anol/index.html

Nussenbaum, E., (2004, September 6). Products slide into more TV shows, with help from new middlemen. *New York Times.* Available at: http://www.nytimes.com/ref/membercenter/nytarchive.html

OECD. (2004). The development of broadband access in rural and remote areas. Organization for Economic Cooperation and Development. May 10, 2004.

Odlyzko, A. (2001). Content is not king. Available online: http://firstmonday.org/issues/issue6_2/odlyzko/index.html

O'Keefe, S. (1996). *Publicity on the Internet.* New York: Wiley.

O'Neill, E. (ed.). (1985). *A history of engineering and science in the Bell System: Transmission technology, 1925–1975.* Murray Hill, NJ: Bell Telephone Laboratories.

Olasky, M. (1987). *Corporate public relations & American private enterprise.* Hillsdale, NJ: Erlbaum.

Orwall, B. (1997, April 29). Ticketmaster sues Microsoft Corp. over Internet link. *New York Times,* B8.

Opensecrets.org (2001). Communications/electronics long-term contribution trends. Retrieved from the World Wide Web, March 10, 2001: http://www.opensecrets.org/industries/contrib.asp?Ind=B

Overbeck, W. (1998). *Major principles of media law,* 1997–1998 ed. Fort Worth, TX: Harcourt Brace College Publishers.

Owen, B., & Wildman, S. (1992). *Video economics.* Cambridge, MA: Harvard University Press.

Packard, V. (1956). *The hidden persuaders.* New York: D. McKay Co.

Paik, H., & Comstock, G. (1994). The effects of television violence on social behavior: A meta-analysis. *Communication Research* 21, 516–545.

Palmgreen, P., & Rayburn, J. (1985). An expectancy-value approach to media gratifications. In Rosengren, K., Wenner, L., & Palmgreen, P. (eds.), *Media gratifications research: Current perspectives.* Thousand Oaks, CA: Sage.

Papacharissi, Z., & Rubin, A. M. (2000). Predictors of Internet usage. *Journal of Broadcasting and Electronic Media,* 44, 175–196.

Pappas, C. (2000, July 10). Ad nauseam. *Advertising Age,* 16–18.

Parks, M., & Floyd, K. (1996). Making friends in cyberspace. *Journal of Communication,* 46(1), 80–97.

Parsons, P., & Frieden, R. (1998). *The cable and satellite television industries.* Needham Heights, MA: Allyn and Bacon.

Pavlik, J. (1987). *Public relations: What research tells us.* Newbury Park, CA: Sage.

————. (1998). *New media technology: Cultural and commercial perspectives,* 2nd ed. Boston: Allyn and Bacon.

Payne, D. (1993). The age of mass magazines, 1900–present. In Sloan, Stovall, & Startt (eds.), *Media in America: A history,* 2nd ed. Scottsdale, AZ: Publishing Horizons.

Peal, D., & Savitz, K. (1997). *Official America Online Internet guide.* New York: McGraw-Hill.

Pechmann, C., & Shih, C. (1999) Smoking scenes in movies and antismoking advertising before movies: Effects on youth. *Journal of Marketing,* 63(3): 1–13.

Perrolle, J. (1987). *Computers and social change: Information, property and power.* Belmont, CA: Wadsworth.

Perry, S. D., & Wolfe, A. S. (2001). *Testifications.* In Stout, D., & Buddenbaum, J. (eds.) *Religion and popular culture: Studies on the interaction of worldviews.* Ames, IA: Iowa State Press.

Pew Research Center (1999). *The Internet News Audience Goes Ordinary.* Available at: http://www.people-press.org/tech98sum.htm

————. (2000). Tracking online life: How women use the Internet to cultivate relationships with family and friends. Retrieved May 10, 2000, from the World Wide Web: http://www.pewinternet.org/reports/toc.asp?Report=11

————. (2002). Getting serious online: As Americans gain experience, they use the web more at work, write e-mails with more significant content, perform more online transactions, and pursue more serious activities. Retrieved March 3, 2002, from the World Wide Web: http://www.pewinternet.org/reports/toc.asp?Report=55

————. (2003). America's online pursuits: The changing picture of who's online and what they do. Retrieved December 22, 2003, from the World Wide Web: http://www.pewinternet.org/reports/toc.asp?Report=106

————. (2004). Cable and Internet loom large in fragmented political news universe: Perceptions of partisan bias seen as growing—especially by Democrats. Retrieved January 11, 2004, from the World Wide Web: http://www.pewinternet.org/reports/toc.asp?Report=110

————. (2004). Rural Areas and the Internet. Pew Internet and American Life Project. Feb. 17, 2004.

Pew Research Center (2004). Available at: pewresearch.org

———— (2004). Pew Studies on Internet Life. Available at pewresearch.org

Phillips, D. (1999, July). Now hear this. *Entrepreneur*, p. 32.

Picard, R. (1989). *Media economics: Concepts and issues.* Thousand Oaks, CA: Sage.

————. (2002). The economics and financing of media companies. New York: Fordham University Press.

Pieterse, Jan Nederveen. (2004). Globalization and Culture: Global Melange, Rowan & Littlefield.

Pinsdorf, M. (1986). *Communicating when your company is under siege: Surviving public crisis.* New York: Free Press.

Pipher, M. (1994). *Reviving Ophelia: Saving the selves of adolescent girls.* New York: Ballantine Books.

Pope, K. (1998, April 3). TV plans to use new digital capacity to improve picture, not add channels. *Wall Street Journal*, A4.

Postman, N. (1986). *Amusing ourselves to death: Public discourse in the age of show business.* New York: Penguin Books.

————. (1992). *Technopoly.* New York: Knopf.

Powell, K., & Abels., L. (2002). Sex-roles stereotypes in TV programs aimed at the preschool audience: An analysis of Teletubbies and Barney & Friends. *Women and Language*, 25(1), 14–22.

Pricewaterhouse Coopers Global Media and Entrtainment Outlook 2004–2008.

Presstime (December 1999, p. 29)

Public Broadcasting Service (PBS). (2004). Public broadcasting's history. Available online: http://www.current.org/history/

Public Relations Society for America (2002). PRSA Member Code of Ethics. Available online. http://prsa.org/_About/ethics/preamble.asp?ident=eth3

Publishers Information Bureau (2002). Measuring the mix. http//www.magazine.org. Audit Bureau of circulation. http//www.abcinteractive/audits.com

Pulley, B. (1998, January 31). On Antigua it's sun, sand and 1-800 betting. *New York Times*, Cybertimes edition.

Putnam, R. (2002). Bowling Alone: The Collapse and Revival of American Community. New York: Simon & Schuster.

Quick, R. (1997, January 22). "Framing" muddies issue of content ownership. *Wall Street Journal*, B6.

————. (1997, September 12). Is the Internet outgrowing its volunteer traffic cops? *Wall Street Journal*, B5.

————. (1998, February 5). Internet incident raises concern over control. *Wall Street Journal*, B6.

————. (1998, February 6). Don't expect your secrets to get kept on the Internet. *Wall Street Journal*, B6.

Rafaeli, S. (1988). Interactivity: From new media to communication. In Hawkins, Pingree, & Weimann (eds.), *Advancing communication sciences*, vol. 16. Beverly Hills, CA: Sage.

Rafaeli, S., & LaRose, R. (1993). Electronic Bulletin Boards and "Public Goods" Explanations of Collaborative Mass Media, *Communication Research*, 28(2), 277–297.

Raleigh, I. (1957). *Matthew Arnold and American culture.* Berkeley: University of California Press.

Rainey, R. (1998, September 8). Santa Monica seeking a return to on-line civic forum of yore. *New York Times*, 16.

————. (1999, November 23). Cheap online fundraising is a boon to political groups. *New York Times*.

Rajeev, P., & Lonial, S. (1990). Advertising to children: Findings and implications. *Current Research and Issues in Advertising*, 12, 231–274.

Rakow, L. (1992). *Gender on the line.* Urbana: University of Illinois Press.

Ramstad, E. (1998, February 26). Audionet scores by tapping a mundane medium. *Wall Street Journal*, B8.

Raney, R. (1998, Feburary 11). E-Mail sender convicted of civil rights violation. *New York Times*, Cybertimes edition.

Real, M. (1989). *Super media: A cultural studies approach.* Thousand Oaks: Sage.

Reeves, B., & Nass, C. (1996). *The media equation.* New York: Cambridge University Press.

Reich, R. (1991). *The work of nations.* New York: Knopf.

Research on the effects of television on children (1977). National Science Foundation, 45.

Reuters, (2005, Jan. 7) Italian DJ Fined 1.4 Mln Euros for Music.

Rheingold, H. (1993). *The virtual community: Homesteading on the electronic frontier.* Reading, MA: Addison-Wesley.

Rice, R., & Bair, J. (1984). New organizational media and productivity. In R. Rice, & Associates (eds.), *The new media.* Beverly Hills, CA: Sage.

Rice, R., & Atkin, C. (2000). *Public Communication Campaigns*, 3rd ed. Thousand Oaks, CA: Sage.

Richtel, M. (1998, March 5). Usenet death penalties: The long arm of the self-appointed law. *New York Times*, Cybertimes edition.

Ricks, D. (1999). Blunders in international business. 3rd ed. Malden, MA: Blackwell. Marketing Translation Mistakes. Retrieved September 21, 2004, from the World Wide Web: http://www.il8nguy.com/translatins.html

Rifkin, J. (1995). *The end of work: The decline of the global labor force and the dawn of the post-market era.* New York: Tarcher & Putnam.

Rigdon, J. (1997, February 28). The letter P in your home PC just might mean potted plant. *Wall Street Journal*, B1.

Riley, S. (1993). American magazines, 1740–1900. In Sloan, W., Stovall, J., & Startt, J. (eds.), *Media in America: A history*, 2nd ed. Scottsdale, AZ: Publishing Horizons.

Rivers, W., & Schramm, W. (1980). *Responsibility in mass communication.* New York: Harper & Row.

Roberts, M., Wanta, W., & Dzwo, T. (2002) Agenda setting and issue salience online. *Communication Research*, 29(4), 452–465.

Robertson, R. (1995). Globalization: Time-Space and Homogeneity-Heterogeneity. In Featherstone, M., Lash, S., & Robertson, R., (eds.), *Global modernities.* Thousand Oaks, CA: Sage.

Robins, K. (1996). Cyberspace and the world we live in. In Dovey, J. (ed.), *Fractal dreams.* London: Lawrence & Wishart.

Robinson, J., Levy, M., & Davis, D. (1986). *The main source: Learning from television news.* Beverly Hills: Sage Publications.

Roche, B. (1993). The development of modern advertising, 1900-present. In Sloan, W., Stovall, J., & Startt, J. (eds.), *The media in America*, 2nd ed. Scottsdale, AZ: Publishing Horizons.

Rogers, E. (1986). *Communication technology—The new media in society.* New York: Free Press.

————. (1995). *Diffusion of innovations*, 4th ed. New York: Free Press.

Rojas, V., Straubhaar, J., Fuentes, M., & Pinon, J. (2005). Still Divided: Ethnicity, Generation, Cultural Capital and New Technologies. In O. Janiero and J. Straubhaar. Politics de informaggao e comunicacao jornalismo e inclusoo digital: o local e global em Austine Salvador. Salvador, Brazil, Edufba.

Rose, B. (1998, March 19). Digital distortions. *Wall Street Journal*, R6.

Rosenbaum, M. (1994). *Selling your story to Wall Street: The art & science of investor relations.* Chicago, IL: Probus.

Roszak, T. (1994). *The cult of information*, 2nd ed. Berkeley, CA: University of California Press.

Rotheberg, R. (1996, December). The age of spin. *Esquire*, 73.

————. (1996, February). Life in cyburbia. *Esquire*, 56–64.

Sadler, R. (1995, February 20). "Big Bird and Barney." Posted on cyber-rights http://www.cpsr.org/:cpsr/lists/listserv_archives/cyber-rights/950224

Sandage, C., Fryburder, V., & Rotzoll, K. (1989). *Advertising theory and practice.* New York: Longman.

Sandberg, J. (1999, September 20). Losing your good name online. *Newsweek*, 56.

————. (2000, November 3) Reveille for couch potatoes? AOL rolls out interactive TV with Time Warner links; Rivals complain of bias. *The Wall Street Journal*, Marketplace, B1.

Scarborough Research Corporation. (1998). Available at: http://www.scarborough.com

Schement, J., & Curtis, T. (1995). *Tendencies and tensions of the information age.* New Brunswick, NJ: Transaction Publishers.

Schement, J., & Lievrouw, L. (eds.). (1987). *Competing visions, complex realities: Social aspects of the information society.* Norwood, NJ: Ablex.

Scheufele, D., Shanahan, J., & Kim. S. (2002). Who cares about local politics? Media influences on local political involvement, issue awareness, and attitude strength. *Journalism and Mass Communication Quarterly*, 79(2), 427–444.

Schiller, D. (1996). Theorizing communication: a history. New York: Oxford University Press.

Schiller, H. (1969). *Mass communications and American empire.* New York: A. M. Kelley.

————. (1976). *Communication and cultural domination.* Armonk, NY: Sharpe.

————. (1981). *Information in the age of the Fortune 500.* Norwood, NJ: Ablex.

————. (1989). *Culture, Inc.: The corporate takeover of public expression.* New York: Oxford University Press.

Schindler, G. (ed.). (1982). *A history of engineering and science in the Bell System: Switching technology, 1925–1975.* Murray Hill, NJ: Bell Telephone Laboratories.

Schlesinger, P. (1991). *Media, state and nation.* Newbury Park, CA: Sage.

Schmitz, J. (1997). Structural relations, electronic media, and social change: The public electronic network and the homeless. In Jones, S. (ed.), *Virtual Culture.* Thousand Oaks, CA: Sage.

Schon, D., Sanyal, B., & Mitchell, W. (eds.) *High technology and low-income communities.* (pp. 349–369). Cambridge, MA: MIT Press.

Schramm, W. (1982). *Men, women, messages and media.* New York: Harper & Row.

————. (1988). *The story of human communication: Cave paintings to micro-chip.* New York: HarperCollins.

Schudson, M. (1984). *Advertising, the uneasy persuasion.* New York: Basic Books.

Schutte, J. (1997). Virtual teaching in higher education: The new intellectual superhighway or just another traffic jam? Available at: http://www.csun.edu/sociology/virexp.htm

Schwartz, J. (1990). The American radio industry and its Latin American activities, 1900–1939. University of Illinois Press.

————. (1999). Study: Cell phones may have cancer link. *Washington Post*, May 22, E1.

Schwoch, J. (1990). *The American Radio Industry and Its Latin American Activities, 1900-1939.* Champaign: University of Illinois Press.

Sears, D., & Freedman, J. (1972). Selective exposure to information: A critical review. In Schramm, W., & Roberts, D. (eds.), *The process and effects of mass communication.* Chicago: University of Illinois Press.

Seitel, Fraser P. (2000). *The practice of public relations.* Upper Saddle River, NJ: Prentice Hall.

Seiter, E. (1992). Semiotics, structuralism, and television. In Allen, R. (ed.), *Channels of discourse, reassembled.* Chapel Hill, NC: University of North Carolina Press.

Shaheen, Jack G. (1984) The TV Arab. Bowling Green, Ohio: Bowling Green State University: Popular Press.

———. (2001). *Reel bad Arabs: How Hollywood Vilifies a People.* New York: Olive Branch Press.

Sharpe, M., *Communications & American politics,* 3rd ed. New York: Macmillan.

Shaw, D. (1998, March 30). Cooperation within *Times* Viewed with Trepidation. *Los Angeles Times* Special Reports. Available at: http://www.timesoc.com/HOME/NEWS/REPORTS/THEWALL/t000030398.1.html

Shefrin, D. (1993). Rediscovering an olde technology: Facsimile newspaper lessons of invention and failure. In Pavlik, J., & Dennis, E. (eds.), *Demystifying media technology.* Mountain View, CA: Mayfield Publishing.

Sherry, J. (2001). The effects of violent video games on aggression: A meta-analysis. *Human Communication Research,* 27(3), 409–431.

Shoemaker, P. (1991). *Gatekeeping.* Newbury Park, CA: Sage.

Short, J., Williams, E., & Christie, B. (1976). *The social psychology of telecommunications.* New York: Wiley.

Sichel, D. (1999, April). Computers and aggregate economic growth: An update. *Business Economics,* 34(2), 18–24.

Sieber, U. (1986). *The international handbook of computer crime.* New York: Wiley.

Siebert, F., Peterson, T., & Schramm, W. (1956). *The four theories of the press.* Urbana, IL: University of Illinois Press.

Signorelli, N. (1989). Television and conceptions about sex roles: Maintaining conventionality and the status quo. *Sex Roles,* 21(5–6), 341–360.

Signorelli, N., & Bacue, A. (1999). Recognition and respect: A content analysis of prime-time television characters across three decades. *Sex Roles,* 40, 527–544.

Silva, C. E. Lins da. (1990). O adiantado da hora: a influencia americana sobre o jornalismo brasileiro. (The Avant-Guard: American Influence on Brazilian Journalism.) Sao Paulo: Summus.

Simon, R., & Wylie, F. (1994). *Cases in public relations management.* Lincolnwood, IL: NTC Business.

Singhal, A., & Rogers, E.M. (2001), *India's Communication Revolution: From Bullock Carts to Cyber Marts,* Delhi: Sage/India.

Sirgy, M. (1998). *Integrated marketing communication: A systems approach.* Upper Saddle River. NJ: Prentice-Hall.

Sloan, W., Stovall, J., & Startt, J. (eds.). (1993). *Media in America: A history,* 2nd ed. Scottsdale, AZ: Publishing Horizons.

Smillie, B. (1997, December 18). Japanese TV cartoon show stuns hundreds. *Lansing State Journal,* 15A.

Smith, A. (1980). *Good-bye, Gutenberg.* New York: Oxford University Press.

Smith, S., Nathanson, A., & Wilson, B. (2002). Prime-time television: Assessing violence during the most popular viewing hours. *Journal of Communications,* 5(10), 84–111.

Smythe, T. (1993). The press in industrial America. In Sloan, W., Stovall, J., & Startt, J. (eds.), *Media in America: A history,* 2nd ed. Scottsdale, AZ: Publishing Horizons.

Software Publisher's Association (1997). 1996 personal computer application software sales pass $10 billion for the first time. Available at: http://www.spa.org/research/releases/1996NA.html

Spohn, D. (1997). *Data network design.* New York: McGraw-Hill.

Spretnak, C. (1997, July). Resurgence of the real. *UTNE Reader,* 59–63, 106.

Sproull, L., & Faraj, S. (1997). Atheism, sex, and databases: The net as a social technology. In Kiesler, S. (ed.), *Culture of the Internet.* Mahwah, NJ: Lawrence Erlbaum.

Standage, T. (1998). The Victorian Internet. NY: Berkley Books.

Stanley, T. (2004, June 28). Marketers step up in-cinema efforts. *Advertising Age,* 49.

Stauber, J., & Rampton, S. (1995). *Toxic sludge is good for you! Lies, damn lies and the public relations industry.* Monroe: Courage Press.

Steeves, H. (1993). Creating imagined communities: Development communication and the challenge of feminism. In Levy, M., & Gurevitch, M. (eds.), *Defining media studies.* New York: Oxford University Press.

Steinfield, C., & Whitten, P. (2000). Community level socio-economic impacts of electronic commerce. *Journal of Computer Mediated Communication,* 5(2). Downloaded from the World Wide Web, May 23, 2000: http://www.ascusc.org/jcmc/vol5/issue2/steinfield.html

Stephens, M. (1989). *A history of news.* New York: Penguin.

Sterling, C., & Kittross, J. (1990). *Stay tuned—A concise history of American broadcasting,* 2nd ed. Belmont, CA: Wadsworth.

Sterngold, J. (1998, December 29). Prime-time TV's growing racial divide frustrates industry's blacks. *New York Times.* Arts section.

Stevens, E. (1998, December). Mouse•ke•fear. *Brill's Content,* 1(5), 94.

Stevens, J. (2002). *Backpack Journalism Is Here to Stay.* Available online: http://ojr.org/ojr/workplace/1017771575.php

Stoll, C. (1995). *Silicon snake oil: Second thoughts on the information superhighway.* New York: Doubleday.

Storey, J. (1993). *An introductory guide to cultural theory and popular culture.* Athens, GA: University of Georgia Press.

Stout, D., & Adams, E. (2003, in press). *The meta-industry of advertising.* New York: Fordham University Press.

Stout, D., & Mouritsen, R. (1987). Prosocial behavior in advertising aimed at children. *Southern Speech Communication Journal,* 53, 159–174.

Straubhaar, J. et al. (1992). The emergence of a Latin American market for television programs. Paper presented at International Communications Association Conference, Miami.

Straubhaar, J., Fuentes, M., Abram, D., McCormick, P., & Campbell, C. "National and Regional TV Markets and TV Program Flows," KEIO Communication Review.

Streeter, Thomas. (1996). *Selling the Air: A critque of the policy of commercial broadcasting in the United States.* University of Chicago Press.

Stump, M., & Jessell, H. (1988, November 21). Cable: The first forty years. *Broadcasting,* 37–49.

Sussman, G. (1997). *Communication, technology and politics in the information age.* Thousand Oaks, CA: Sage.

Tankard, James W. Jr., & Lasorsa, Dominic L. Journalism & Mass Communication Educator. Columbia: Autumn 2000. Vol. 55, Iss. 3; p. 14.

Tapscott, D. (1998). *Growing up digital.* New York: McGraw-Hill.

Tebbel, J. (1969a). *The compact history of the American newspaper.* New York: Hawthorne Books.

———. (1969b). *The American magazine: A compact history.* New York: Hawthorne Books.

Tech Law Journal (1998). Judge denies motion to dismiss Loudoun blocking software case. Available at: http: //www.techlawjournal.com/censor/80408.htm

Tedeschi, B. (2001, February 26). E-commerce report: New alternative to banner ads. the *New York Times:* http//www.nytimes.com/ 202/02/26/technology/ 26ecommerce.html

Temin, P. (1987). *The fall of the Bell System.* New York: Cambridge University Press.

Thelist (1998). Thelist of Internet access providers. Available at: http:// www.thedirectory.org/

Tiffin, J., & Rajasingham, L. (1995). *In search of the virtual class.* New York: Routledge.

Toffler, A. (1990). *Powershift.* New York: Bantam Books.

The top 25 worldwide. *Variety,* 2002. http//www.variety.com

———. *Variety,* 24 January 2000, p. 22.

Tracey, M. (1988). Popular culture and the economics of global television. *Intermedia,* (2), 9–25.

Trade Point (1995). U.S. global trade outlook. Available at: http://www.itrade .com/dir03/mrktinfo/usglobal/

Tucker, E., & Stout, D. (1998, August). *Advertising ethics and pedagogy: Findings from the 1995 Advertising Division membership survey.* Paper presented at the annual meeting of the Association of Journalism and Mass Communication (AEJMC), Baltimore, MD.

Tucker, K. (1996). *Public relations writing: An issue-driven behavioral approach.* Englewood Cliffs, NJ: Prentice-Hall.

Turkle, S. (1995). *Life on the screen: Identity in the age of the Internet.* New York: Simon & Schuster.

Turner, R. (1993, March 26). Hollyworld. *Wall Street Journal Reports,* R1.

Tyack, D., & Cuban, L. (1995). *Tinkering toward utopia: A century of public school reform.* Cambridge, MA: Harvard University Press.

Tye, L. (1997). *The father of spin: Edward L. Bernays and the birth of public relations.* New York: Crown.

Udelson, Joseph H. (1982). *The great television race: a history of the American television industry, 1925–1941.* University, Ala.: University of Alabama Press.

(U.S.H.H.S.) U.S. Department of Health and Human Services (2001). Youth violence: A report of the surgeon general, Rockville, MD.

U.S. Census (1993). Level of access and use of computers. Available at: http://www.census.gov/population/socdemo/computer/compusea.txt

U.S. Dept. of Commerce. (1998). *France—Economy—Trade Barriers.*

U.S. Dept. of Education. (1999). *Indicators of school crime and safety.* Washington, DC: U.S. Department of Education. Available online: http://nces.ed.gov/pubs99/1999057.pdf

University Consortium for Advanced Internet Design. (1998). Internet 2 home page. Available at: http://www.internet2 .edu/

University of Texas (2000). The Internet economy indicators. Austin, TX: Center for Research in Mass Commerce, University of Texas. Downloaded from the web, September 8, 2000: http://www.internetindicators.com/the_indicators_june_00.htm

Vakratsas, D., & Ambler, T. (1999). How advertising works: What do we really know? *Journal of Marketing,* 63(1): 26–43.

Van Erva, J. (1990). Television and child development. Hillsdale, NJ: Lawrence Erlbaum.

Variety. (2004). *Variety's Global 50.* http://www.variety.com

Veloso, Caetano. (2000, August 20). Orpheus, Rising From Caricature. *New York Times,* Arts and Leisure.

Venkatesh, V., & Johnson, P. (2002). Telecommuting technology implementations: A within-and-between-subjects longitudinal field study. *Personnel Psychology,* 55(3), 661.

Venkatraman, N., & Henderson, J. (1998). Real strategies for virtual organizing. *Sloan Management Review,* 40(1), 33–49.

Veronis, Suhler & Associates. (2002). *VS&A communications industry forecast.* New York: Veronis, Suhler & Associates.

Veronis, Suhler, & Stevenson, Media Merchant Bank (2004). *2004 Communications Industry Forecast & Report.* Available at: http://www.veronissuhler.com/pubs/pubs_cif.html

Virnoche, M. (1998). The seamless web and communications equity: The shaping of a community network. *Science, Technology & Human Values,* 23(2):199–218.

Viviana Rojas, V. et al. (2004). Communities, cultural capital and the digital divide. In Bucy, E. & Newhagen, J.E. (eds.) *Media Access: Social and Psychological Dimensions of New Technology Use.* NJ: Lawrence Erlbaum.

Volgelstein, F. (1998, February 2). A really big disconnect. You call this reform? Try getting a phone line in the sticks. *U.S. News & World Report, 39.*

Walter, J. (1996). Computer mediated communication: Impersonal, interpersonal and hypersonal. *Communication Research* 23(1), 3–41.

Warlaumount, H. (1996). Advertising: Social institution in the American marketplace. In Sloan, W., Staples C., Gonsenbach, W., & Stovall, J. (eds.), *Mass communication in the information age.* Northport, AL: Vision Press.

Wanta, W. (1997). The public and the national agenda. Mahawh, NJ: Lawrence Erlbaum.

Waxman, S. (1998, November 29). As Hollywood looks afar, minorities often lose out. *Washington Post News Service* in *Austin American-Statesman,* November 29, G-1.

weber, T. (1996, December 9). Who uses the Internet? *Wall Street Journal,* R6.

Weiner, R. (1996). *webster's new world dictionary of media and communications,* 3rd ed. New York: Macmillan.

Weiss, M. (1988). *The clustering of America.* New York: Harper.

Wellman, B., & Gulia, M. (1999). Virtual communities as communities: Net surfers don't ride alone. In Smith, M. A., & Kollock, P., *Communities in Cyberspace.* NY: Routledge.

Wellner, A. (2002). Our true colors. Supplement to *American Demographics,* S2–S3.

Wells, S. (2001). Making telecommuting work. *HRMagazine,* 46(10), 34–45.

Wells, W., Burnett, J., & Moriarty, S. (1995). *Advertising principles and practice.* Engelwood Cliffs, NJ: Prentice-Hall.

Werneke, D. (1985). Women: The vulnerable group. In Forester, T. (ed.), *The information technology revolution.* Cambridge, MA: MIT Press.

Westen, T. (1998). Can technology save democracy? *National Civic Review,* New York, 87(1): 47–56.

Whetmore, E. (1981). *The magic medium: An introduction to radio in America.* Belmont, CA: Wadsworth.

White, C., & Kinnick, K. (2000). One click forward and two clicks back: Portrayal of women using computers in television commercials. *Women's Studies in Communication,* 23: 392–412.

White, D. (1949). The gate-keeper: A case study in the selection of news. *Journalism Quarterly,* 27.

Wiggins, R. (1997, October 13). Corralling your content. *NewMedia,* 40–45.

Wilcox, D., & Nolte, L. (1994). *Public relations writing and media techniques,* 2nd ed. New York: HarperCollins.

———. (1996). *Public relations writing and media techniques.* New York: Addison Wesley Longman.

Wildman, S., & Siwek, S. (1988). *International trade in films and television programs.* Cambridge, MA: Ballinger.

Wilkinson, K. (1995). *Where culture, language and communication converge: The Latin-American cultural linguistic market. University of Texas–Austin.* Ph.D. thesis.

Williams, B., & Carpini D. (2004). Monica and Bill all the time and everywhere: The collapse of gatekeeping and agenda setting in the new media environment. *American Behavioral Scientist,* 47(9), 1208–1230.

Wilson, B., Smith, S., Potter, W., Kunkel, D. et al. (2002). Violence in children's television programming: Assessing the risks. *Journal of Communications,* 52(1), 5–35.

Williams, G., Brown, K., & Alexander, P. *Radio Market Structure and Music Diversity.* FCC Report, September 2002.

Williams, R. on television: selected writings. Edited by Alan O'Connor. New York: Routledge, 1989.

Wimmer, R., & Dominick, J. (1997). *Mass media research,* 5th ed. Belmont, CA: Wadsworth.

Winkler, A. (1999). *Warp-speed branding: The impact of technology on branding.* New York: John Wiley & Sons.

Wittenberg, E., & Wittenberg, E. (1994). *How to win in Washington.* Oxford, England: Blackwell.

Wolf, M. (1999). *The entertainment industry: How mega-media forces are transforming our lives.* New York: Times Books/Random House.

Wood, J. (1994). *Gendered lives: Communication, gender, and culture.* Belmont, CA: Wadsworth.

———. (2001). *Gendered lives: Communication, gender, and culture,* 4th ed. Belmont, CA: Wadsworth.

World Bank, The (2004). World Development Report 2004. Available at: http://econ.worldbank.org

World Bank. (1998). *Knowledge for development.* Washington, DC.

———. (2000). World development indicators 2000. Washington, DC: The World Bank Group. http://www.worldbank.org/html/extpb/wdi2000.htm

Wright, C. (1974). Functional analysis and mass communications revisited. In Blumler, J., & Katz, E. (eds.), *The uses of mass communications.* Beverly Hills: Sage.

Wulforst, H. (1982). *Breakthrough to the computer age.* New York: Scribner's.

Wynter, L. (1998, December 24). Business & Race. *Wall Street Journal.*

Yale, D. (1991). *The publicity handbook.* Lincolnwood, IL: NTC Business.

———. (1992). *The publicity handbook.* Lincolnwood, IL: NTC Publishing Group.

Yaverbaum, G., & Nadarajan, U. (1996). Learning basic concepts of telecommunications: An experiment in multimedia learning. *Computers in education,* 26(4), 215–224.

Yioutas, J., & Segvic, I. (2003). Revisiting the Clinton/Lewinsky Scandal: the convergence of agenda setting and framing. *Journalism and Mass Communication Quarterly,* 80(3), 567.

Young, J. (1988). Steve Jobs: *The journey is the reward.* Glenview, IL: Scott, Foresman.

Zapatistas in Cyberspace, (1998). Available at: http://www.actlab.utexas.edu/-zapatistas/guide.html.

ZapNet, "Zapatistas in Cyberspace," (1998). Available at: http://www.eco.utexas.edu/faculty/Cleaver/zapsincyber.html

Zelezny, J. (1993). *Communications law.* Belmont, CA: Wadsworth.

Zickmund, S. (1997). Approaching the radical other: The discursive culture of cyberhate. In Jones, S. (ed.), *Virtual culture.* Thousand Oaks, CA: Sage.

Zientara, M. (1987). *Women, technology and power.* New York: American Management Association.

Zimmerman, J. (1990). Some effects of the new technology on women. In Ermann, M., Williams, M., & Gutierrez, C. (eds.), *Computers, ethics and society.* New York: Oxford University Press.

Zuboff, S. (1984). *In the age of the smart machine.* New York: Basic Books.

Zuckman, H., & Gaynes, M. (1983). *Mass communications law,* 2nd ed. St. Paul, MN: West Publishing.

Twain, Mark, 83, 91
Tweed Ring, 92
Twentieth Century-Fox, 187, 188, 198, 220
Twilight of Common Dreams, The (Gitlin), 281
2.5G phones, 373, 377
Two-way communication, 20
Two-way radio, 360
Tyco Corporation, 476
Typesetting, 68
Typographical logic, 60

U

UHF (ultra-high frequency) bands, 226
UHF (ultra-high frequency) television, 164, 214, 218, 219, 220
Unbalanced media flow, 521
Uncle Tom's Cabin (Stowe), 62, 63
Underground films 190
Unequal access, 43
Underwriting, 235
UNESCO, 508, 522–523, 524
Uniform Resource Locator (URL), 266, 275
United Artists, 185, 187, 188, 189, 190
United Nations, 287
United Press, 94
U.S.A. Patriot Act of 2001, 288, 386, 441–442, 443
U.S. Congress, policy-making process and, 458, 459
U.S. Copyright Office, 458
U.S. Library of Congress, 458
U.S. Patent and Trademark Office, 458
UNIVAC, 256
Universal Pictures, 187, 189, 198
Universal Serial Bus (USB), 195, 263
Universal service, 287, 359, 384–385, 451–455, 461
University presses, 80
Up-front season, 240
Uplink, 366
Up-skilling, 426
Usage fees, 36
USA Today (newspaper), 97, 104, 109
Usenet, 259, 266
User Datagram Protocol (UDP), 269
Uses and gratifications perspective, 400, 402
Utility principle, Mill's, 468

V

Vacuum tubes, 152, 163, 262
Validity, 396–397, 400
Values transmission/socialization, 46
Vanderbilt, William, 296
Variable resistance transmitter, 364
Variety magazine, 204
V-chip, 247, 438
VCRs. *See* Videocassette recorders
Velvet ghetto, 315
Verizon, 362
Vertical blanking interval (VBI), 226
Vertical integration, 166, 187, 245, 285, 358, 450–451, 477–478
Very high-speed Backbone Network Service (vBNS), 275
Very large-scale integrated (VLSI) chips, 262
Very low-frequency (VLF) radiation, 423
VHF (very high frequency) bands, 226
VHF (very high frequency) television, 164, 214, 506
VH-1, 142
Viacom, 143, 199, 221, 222, 231, 499
Victrola, 122, 123, 130, 131–132
Video
    cell phone access, 16
    globalization of, 506
Video camera, 228
    reporters', 98
Videocassette recorders (VCRs), 24, 48, 49, 191, 198, 204, 206, 220, 227, 489, 506
Video compression, digital, 366
Videoconferencing, 301
Video game advertising, 334

Video Home System (VHS) players, 227
Video news releases (VNRs), 300–301, 478
Video on demand, 371
Video production trends, 228
Video recording, 226–228
Video rentals, 191, 192, 220, 506
Videotapes, 80
Videotape technology, piracy and, 206
Videotex, 99, 258
Vietnam War, 96, 112, 218
Violence
    film ratings and, 205–206
    in media, 9, 407–407
    television, 247–248, 394–396, 398, 407–408, 438
Vioxx scandal, 310
Viral marketing, 329
Virtual ads, 333
Virtual bookstores, 70, 77
Virtual communities, 46
Virtual corporation, 424
Virtual private network (VPN), 382
Virtual reality, 266
Virtual university, 417
Vision, persistence of, 181, 224
Voice mail, 376
Voice-over IP (VOIP) providers, 368, 377, 378
Voter participation, media coverage and, 419-420

W

Walkie talkie, 360
Wall Street Journal, The, 96, 97, 99, 102, 110, 115
Wal-Mart, 134, 138, 139, 144, 145, 146, 200
Warner Bros., 185, 187, 188, 189, 198
Washington Monthly, 64
Washington Post, 96, 107, 111
Watergate scandal, 96, 111, 112–113. 476
.WAV format, 134
WEAF radio station, 153, 154
Weaver, Sylvester "Pat," 215
web. *See* World Wide Web
webb-Pomerene Act, 505
web bugs, 270
webcams, 268
webcast, 162, 165–166, 302–303
web courses, 280
weber, Max, 60
web logs (blogs). *See* Blogs
web pages, 267, 274–275, 283–284, 442
web rings, 280
web servers, 266
web sites
    blocking by China, 518
    copying material from, 489
    corporate, 276, 307
    covering public relations, 314
    e-commerce, 280–283
Weeklies, 103–104, 109
Welles, Orson, 188
Westinghouse, 152, 153
Whitman, Meg, 282
Whitman, Walt, 41
Wide area network (WAN), 256
Wide-screen film, 189, 194
WiFi (IEEE802. 11), 268, 374–375, 377, 385, 514
Williams, Armstrong, 482
Williams, Raymond, 249
WiMax, 375
Winamp, 165
Windows, films distributed to series of, 200
Windows browser, 270
Windows Media Audio (WMA), 134
Winfrey, Oprah, 66, 334
Wireless communication, 361, 371, 373–375
Wireless Internet access, 16, 101, 165, 268, 332, 374–375
Wireless Mark-Up Language (WML), 269
Wireless music downloads, 135
Wireless service, 360, 376–377, 514

Wireless telegraphy, 151–152
Wire-line services, 375–376
Wire services, 91, 105–106
Wiretaps, 386, 442
WMA. *See* Windows Media Audio
Wolfman Jack, 157
Women. *See also* Diversity
    discrimination against, 315
    in information society, 13
    in media, feminist studies of, 43–44
    media ownership by, 449
    pornography and attitudes toward, 410–412
    in public relations, 315
    stereotyping of, 348, 353, 408–409, 483
    in television industry, 246
Women Executives in Public Relations (WEPR), 314
Women in Communications Incorporated (WICI), 314
Women's magazines, 62, 64, 66
Wonkette.com, 105, 106, 107, 280
Woodward, Robert, 96, 111, 476
Workplace media technologies, impact on economy, 424–427
    quality of work, 425–427
    quantity of work, 424–425
World Administrative Radio Congress (WARC), 453
World Bank, 524
WorldCom, 299, 363
World Intellectual Property Organization (WIPO), 447, 458, 523
World Music, 141
World Summit on the Information Society, 287, 519, 524
World Trade Center attacks. *See* September 11, 2001 terrorist attacks, changes after
World Trade Organization (WTO), 288, 447, 458, 509, 514, 521, 523
World Wars
    books during, 67
    film production after, 187–188
    music during, 123
    newspapers during, 94
    radio during, 155–156
    television and, 213–214
World Wide Web
    birth of, 259–261
    and censorship issues, 83
    content of, 275–284
    education on, 280
    globalization of, 516, 518
    global policy, 447
    interactivity of, 21–22
    journalism and, 98, 113
    magazines on, 64, 66, 70, 73
    newspapers on, 97, 99–100, 112
    personalization and, 38–40
    publishing on, 66, 81
    radio on, 162
    surfing, 266–268
    top 10 properties, 276
    tracking on, 270–271
    virtual university on, 417

X

Xbox, 230, 264, 278
XHTML, 267, 269
XML, 267, 269
XM satellite radio, 160, 165

Y

Yahoo!, 7, 38, 100, 101, 105, 162, 165, 260, 279
Yang, Jerry, 260
Yellow journalism, 92–93

Z

Zapatista Liberation Front, use of Internet by, 516, 517
Zenger, Peter, 88–89, 433–434
Zip drive, 262
Zworykin, Vladimir, 224, 226